THE

TH3 17V1518L35: **THE INVISIBLES:**
>> 6027T176 T0 76 >> **COUNTING TO NONE**

>> WR1T3R   >> **WRITER**
6R47T M0RR1507   GRANT MORRISON

>> P3761113R5   >> **PENCILLERS**
PH11 J1M3732   PHIL JIMENEZ
M16H431 14RK   MICHAEL LARK
6HR15 W35T07   CHRIS WESTON
PH111P 807D   PHILIP BOND

>> 17K3R5   >> **INKERS**
J0H7 5T0K35   JOHN STOKES
K31TH 41K37   KEITH AIKEN
M4R6 H3MP31   MARC HEMPEL
R4Y KRY55176   RAY KRYSSING
61Y7 D11107   GLYN DILLON

>> 6010R15T5   >> **COLORISTS**
D47131 V0220   DANIEL VOZZO
R16K T4Y10R   RICK TAYLOR
K3V17 50M3R5   KEVIN SOMERS

>> 13TT3R3R   >> **LETTERER**
T0DD K1317   TODD KLEIN

>> TH3 17V1518135 >> **THE INVISIBLES CREATED BY**
6R47T M0RR1507   GRANT MORRISON

V3RT160/D6 60M16 VERTIGO/DC COMICS

THE

INVISIBLES

R4663D R081N

>> JACK FROST

BOY

LORD FANNY

RAGGED ROBIN

KING MOB

6H4R46T3R 8186R **CHARACTER BIOGRAPHIES**

>> J46K 7R05T.
W021D Y02 8311302 **>> JACK FROST**
70RM3R 8R1T P27K WOULD YOU BELIEVE THE FUTURE BUDDHA IS ACTUALLY A
D8. J46K'5 J25T H4 FORMER BRIT PUNK ONCE CALLED DANE? **THE INVISIBLES** DO.
JACK'S JUST HAVING A GOOD TIME.

>> 88Y
8370R3.TH3 6075P1 **>> BOY**
834T. 70W 5H3 8PP0 BEFORE THE CONSPIRACY, BOY WAS A COP ON THE HARLEM
7R07I173S W1TH 5 BEAT. NOW SHE OPPOSES TYRANNY AND IGNORANCE ON THE
4RT5 3XP3RT153. FRONTLINES WITH SOME STREETWISE SAVVY AND MARTIAL
ARTS EXPERTISE.

>> 16RD 7477Y
TH3 17V1518135' **>> LORD FANNY**
5H4M47 7R8M R18 1 **THE INVISIBLES'** RESIDENT GLAM-GIRL TRANSVESTITE
M47. 78T TH4T Y82 SHAMAN FROM RIO LOOKS LIKE A GIRL BUT IS BUILT LIKE A
MAN. NOT THAT YOU'D NOTICE.

>> R4663D R0817 **>> RAGGED ROBIN**
TH3 T313P4TH16 W1 THE TELEPATHIC WITCH RAGGED ROBIN RETURNED FROM
Y34R 2012 87 4 M15 THE YEAR 2012 ON A MISSION UNKNOWN TO HER FELLOW
17V1518135. WH8M **INVISIBLES**, WHOM SHE'S LED SINCE THE BLOODY ASSAULT
TH3 536R3T D2163 ON THE SECRET DULCE INSTALLATION. SHE'S ALSO SLEEPING
W1TH K176 M88. WITH KING MOB.

>> K176 M88 **>> KING MOB**
56H8813D 17 PHY51 SCHOOLED IN PHYSICAL AND PSYCHIC COMBAT AT THE
17V1518813 681136 **INVISIBLE** COLLEGE, KING MOB KNOWS ALL THE
68.75P1R46135 4R3 CONSPIRACIES ARE TRUE AND WILL DO HIS PART TO LIBERATE
M47K17D. 14T31Y H MANKIND. LATELY HE'S BEGUN TO WONDER IF HE'S TRULY A
7R33D8M 716HT3R... FREEDOM FIGHTER...OR JUST A MURDERER.

>> M4S07 1476 **>> MASON LANG**
1MP055181Y R16H. IMPOSSIBLY RICH, MASON BELIEVES HE WAS ABDUCTED BY
411375 45 4 6H11D ALIENS AS A CHILD AND ALLOWED TO DRINK FROM THE HOLY
6R411. H3'5 4 787T GRAIL. HE'S A FONT OF KNOWLEDGE, FUNDING RESEARCH INTO
3V3RYTH176 TH3 17 EVERYTHING **THE INVISIBLES** HOLD TRUE.

THE INVISIBLES

COUNTING TO NONE

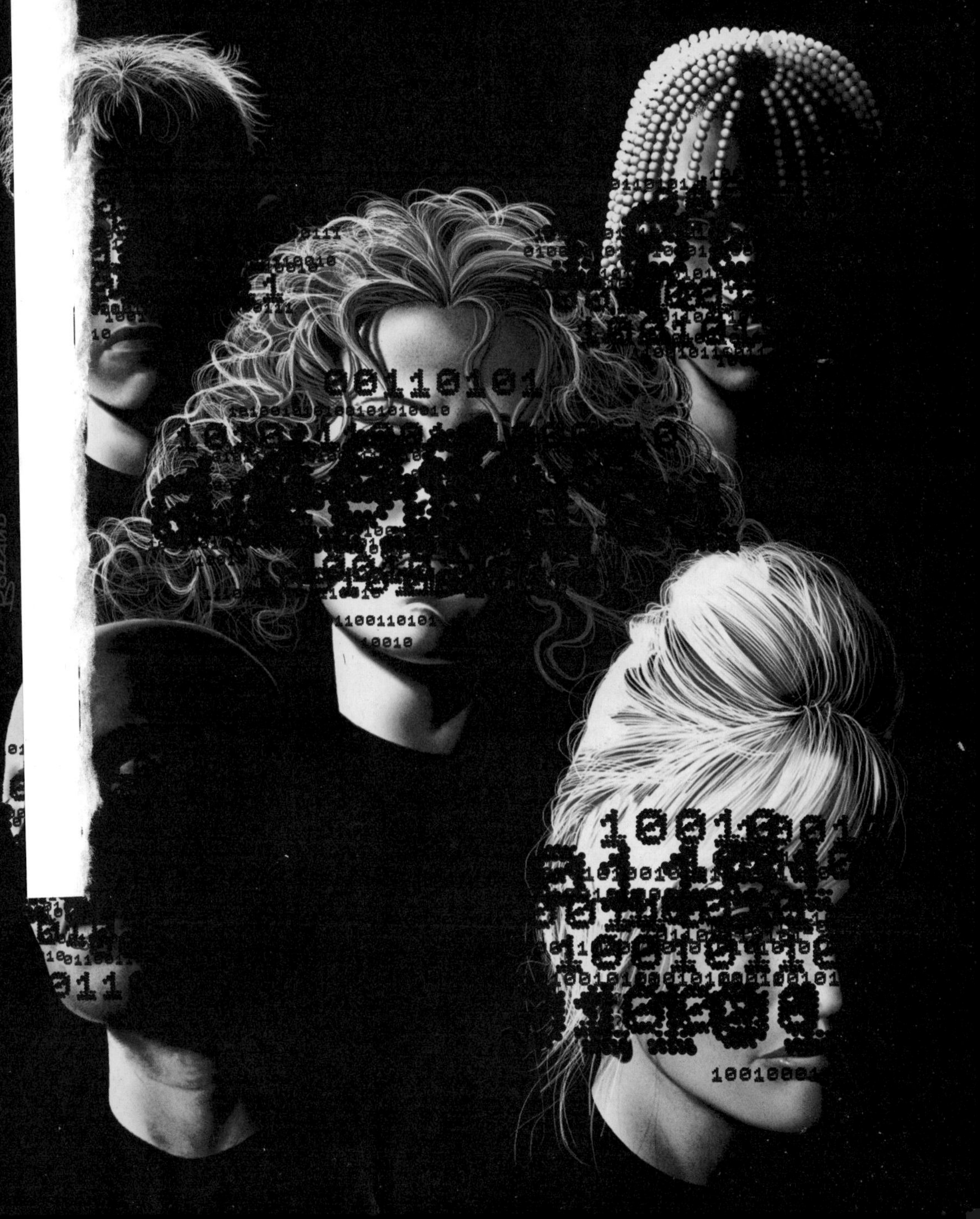
BOLLAND

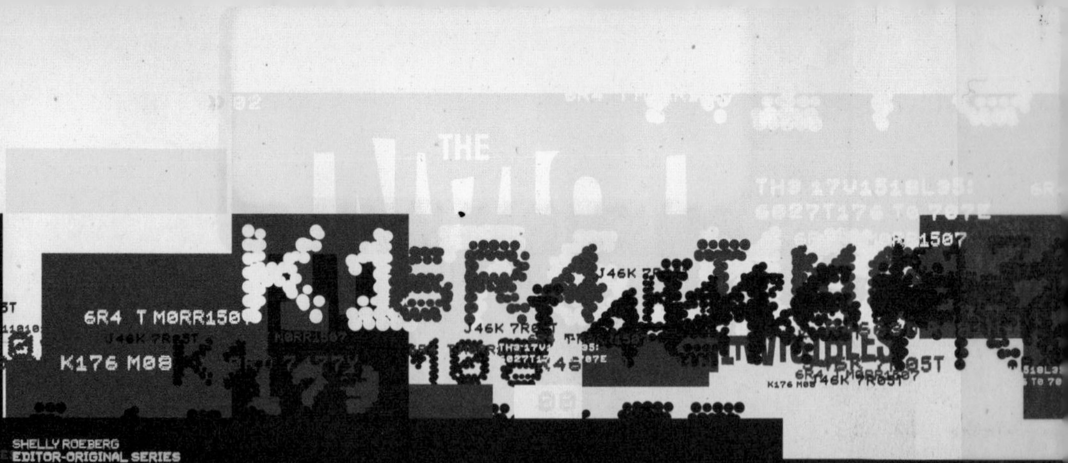

SHELLY ROEBERG
EDITOR-ORIGINAL SERIES

RICK TAYLOR
EDITOR

JIM SPIVEY
ASSOCIATE EDITOR

ROBBIN BROSTERMAN
DESIGN DIRECTOR - BOOKS

RIAN HUGHES
PULBLICATION DESIGN

KAREN BERGER
SENIOR VP - EXECUTIVE EDITOR, VERTIGO

BOB HARRAS
VP - EDITOR-IN-CHIEF

DIANE NELSON
PRESIDENT

DAN DIDIO AND JIM LEE
CO-PUBLISHERS

GEOFF JOHNS
CHIEF CREATIVE OFFICER

JOHN ROOD
EXECUTIVE VP - SALES, MARKETING AND BUSINESS DEVELOPMENT

AMY GENKINS
SENIOR VP - BUSINESS AND LEGAL AFFAIRS

NAIRI GARDINER
SENIOR VP - FINANCE

JEFF BOISON
VP - PUBLISHING OPERATIONS

MARK CHIARELLO
VP - ART DIRECTION AND DESIGN

JOHN CUNNINGHAM
VP - MARKETING

TERRI CUNNINGHAM
VP - TALENT RELATIONS AND SERVICES

ALISON GILL
SENIOR VP - MANUFACTURING AND OPERATIONS

HANK KANALZ
SENIOR VP - DIGITAL

JAY KOGAN
VP - BUSINESS AND LEGAL AFFAIRS, PUBLISHING

JACK MAHAN
VP - BUSINESS AFFAIRS, TALENT

NICK NAPOLITANO
VP - MANUFACTURING ADMINISTRATION

SUE POHJA
VP - BOOK SALES

COURTNEY SIMMONS
SENIOR VP - PUBLICITY

BOB WAYNE
SENIOR VP - SALES

THE INVISIBLES: COUNTING TO NONE

PUBLISHED BY DC COMICS.

DC COMICS, 1700 BROADWAY, NEW YORK, NY 10019
A WARNER BROS. ENTERTAINMENT COMPANY
PRINTED IN THE USA . FIFTH PRINTING.
ISBN: 978-1-56389-489-3
COVER ILLUSTRATION: BRIAN BOLLAND

LIBRARY OF CONGRESS CATALOGING-IN-PUBLICATION DATA

MORRISON, GRANT.
THE INVISIBLES. VOLUME 5, COUNTING TO NONE / GRANT MORRISON, PHIL JIMENEZ, JOHN STOKES, CHRIS WESTON.
PAGES CM
"ORIGINALLY PUBLISHED IN SINGLE MAGAZINE FORM AS THE INVISIBLES VOLUME TWO 5-13 AND VERTIGO WINTER'S EDGE 1."
ISBN 978-1-56389-489-3
1. GRAPHIC NOVELS. I. JIMENEZ, PHIL. II. STOKES, JOHN. III. WESTON, CHRIS, 1969- IV. TITLE. V. TITLE: COUNTING TO NONE.
PN6728.I58M6644 2013
741.5'973-DC23
2013000116

SUSTAINABLE FORESTRY INITIATIVE
Certified Chain of Custody
Promoting Sustainable Forestry
www.sfiprogram.org
SFI-01042
APPLIES TO TEXT STOCK ONLY

THE

THE STORY THUS FAR

›› **THE END IS THE BEGINNING.**

AFTER ALLOWING KING MOB A YEAR TO RECUPERATE FROM PSYCHIC AND PHYSICAL INJURIES SUSTAINED ON THEIR LAST ADVENTURE, THE INVISIBLES ARE BACK IN THE FRAY. ALONGSIDE JOLLY ROGER, AN INVISIBLE WHO ONCE TRAINED WITH KING MOB, THE TEAM LEFT MASON LANG'S LUXURIOUS HUDSON RIVER SAFEHOUSE TO LEAD AN ASSAULT ON A U.S. ARMY INSTALLATION IN DULCE, NEW MEXICO. OFFICIALLY, IT DIDN'T EXIST. UNOFFICIALLY, IT GUARDED A SECRET HIV VACCINE AND ROGER'S CAPTURED INVISIBLES CELL.

IN AND OUT. IT SHOULD HAVE BEEN EASY.

WITH RAGGED ROBIN NOW LEADING, THE INVISIBLES FOUND MORE THAN THE OBLIGATORY ARMY OF LETHAL DELTA FORCE COMMANDOS THEY ANTICIPATED: A CAPTURED ROSWELL ALIEN LIFEFORM, JOLLY ROGER'S GENETICALLY MUTATED TEAMMATES, AND THE DIABOLICAL MIND-CONTROLLING DWARF QUIMPER. THE INVISIBLES BARELY MADE IT OUT ALIVE BEFORE THE PLACE BLEW TO BLOODY HELL.

BUT THEY RETRIEVED THE HIV VACCINE. AND LIFE HAS RETURNED TO NORMAL...OR AS NORMAL AS IT CAN GET FOR A BAND OF MERRY ANARCHISTS ON THE FRONTLINES OF THE ULTIMATE CONSPIRACY—DEFENDING THE PLANET FROM THE ARCHONS, ANTI-BEINGS FROM BEYOND REALITY WAITING TO OVERWHELM **EVERYTHING**. THE INVISIBLES KNOW THAT THE ARCHONS ARE ALREADY SUBVERTING FREEDOM AND THOUGHT, PREPARING FOR AN UNIMAGINABLE APOCALYPSE IN THE NOT-SO-DISTANT FUTURE. IT'S ONLY A MATTER OF **STOPPING** THEM.

AND AS SCIENTISTS IN JAPAN APPROACH A MAJOR SCIENTIFIC BREAKTHROUGH THAT WILL CHANGE THE FACE OF REALITY, RAGGED ROBIN'S ABOUT TO COME CLEAN ON HER MYSTERIOUS ORIGINS, THE PURPOSE OF HER CRYPTIC PHOTOGRAPHS, AND WHY SHE ACCESSORIZES BY WEARING A BRACELET THAT TRANSMITS AN ANTI-NANOMACHINE FIELD.

THROUGH RAGGED ROBIN'S REVELATIONS, THE INVISIBLES ARE BEGINNING TO UNDERSTAND THAT THE FUTURE IS NOW.

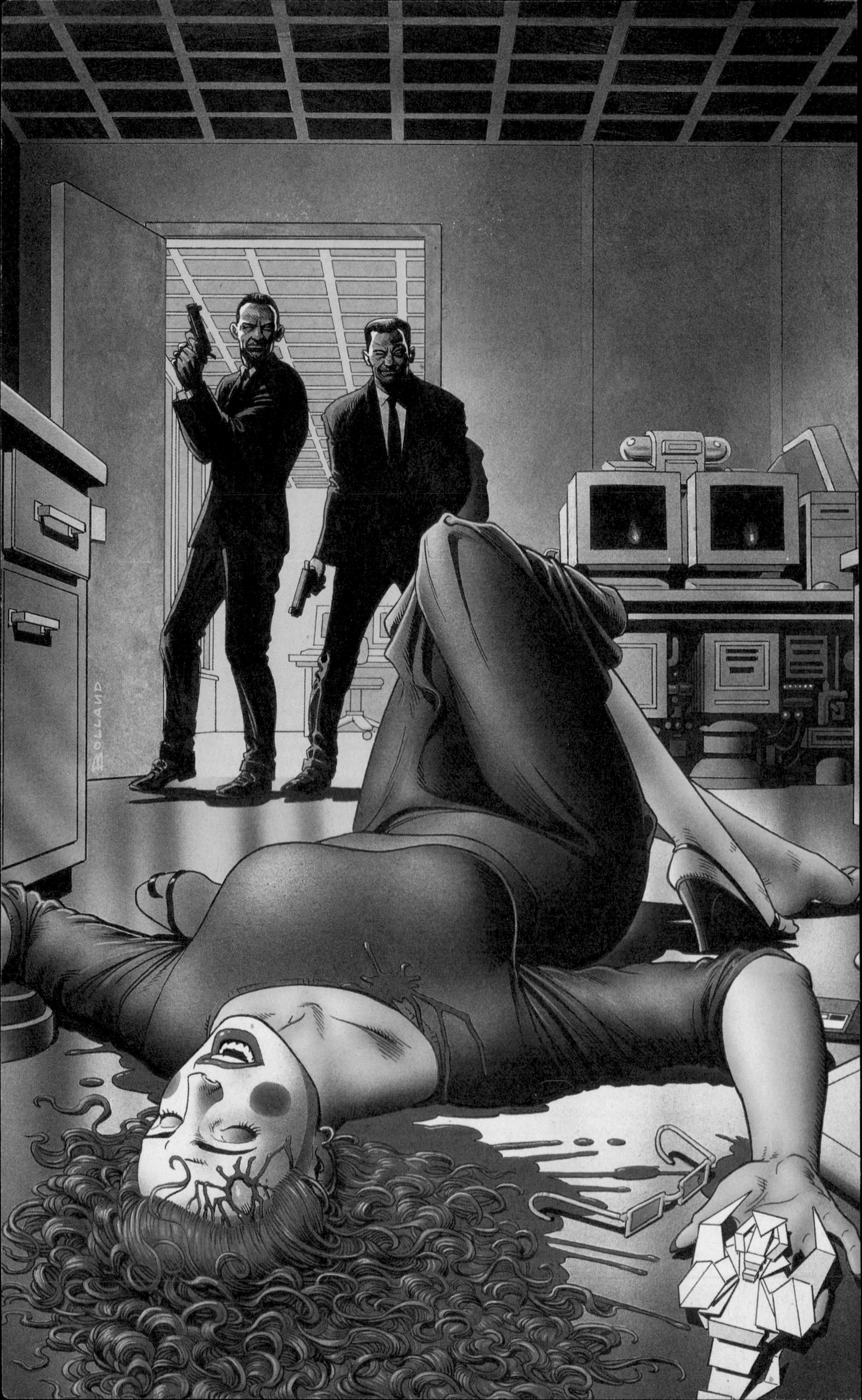
BOLLAND

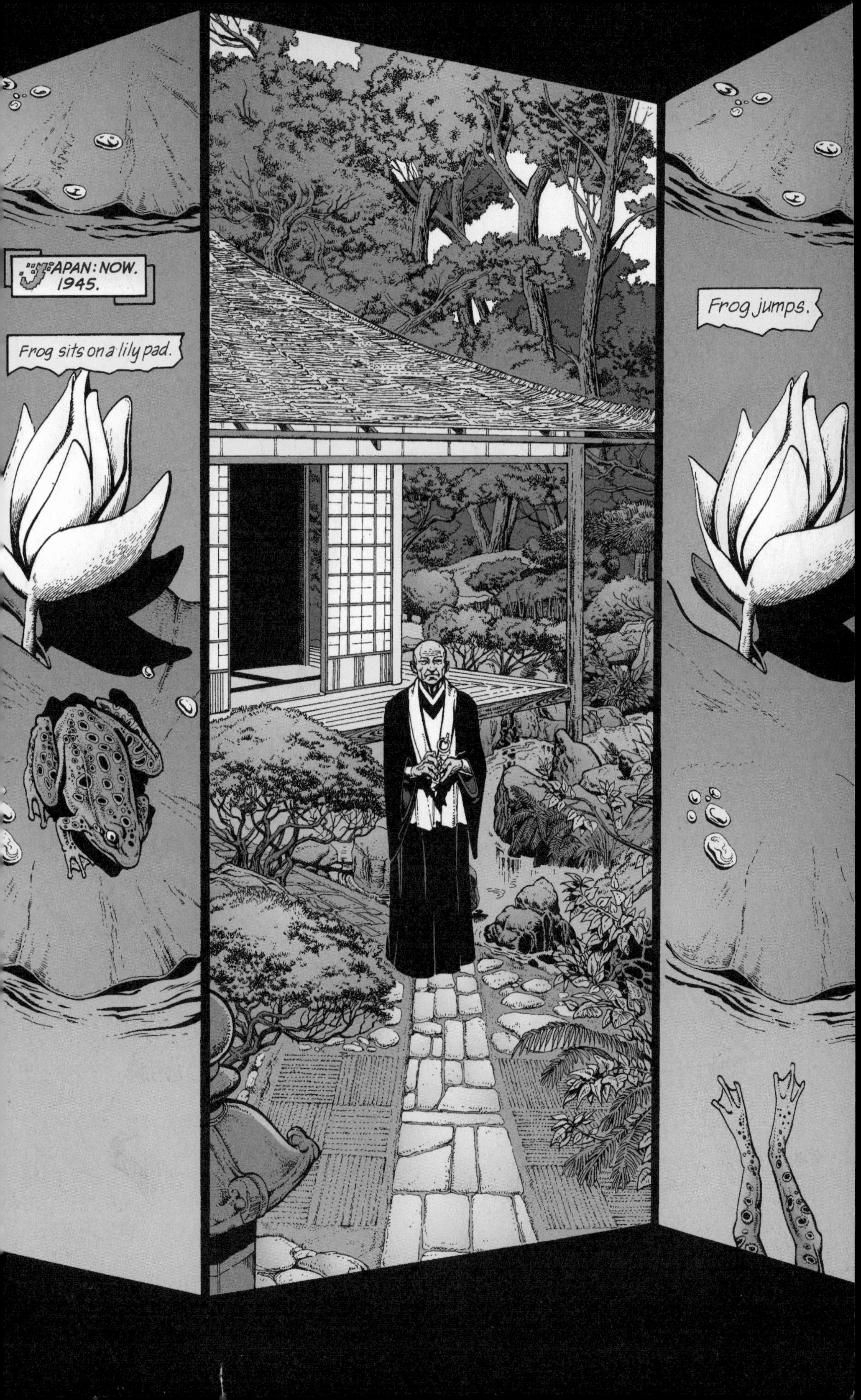
JAPAN: NOW. 1945.
Frog sits on a lily pad.
Frog jumps.

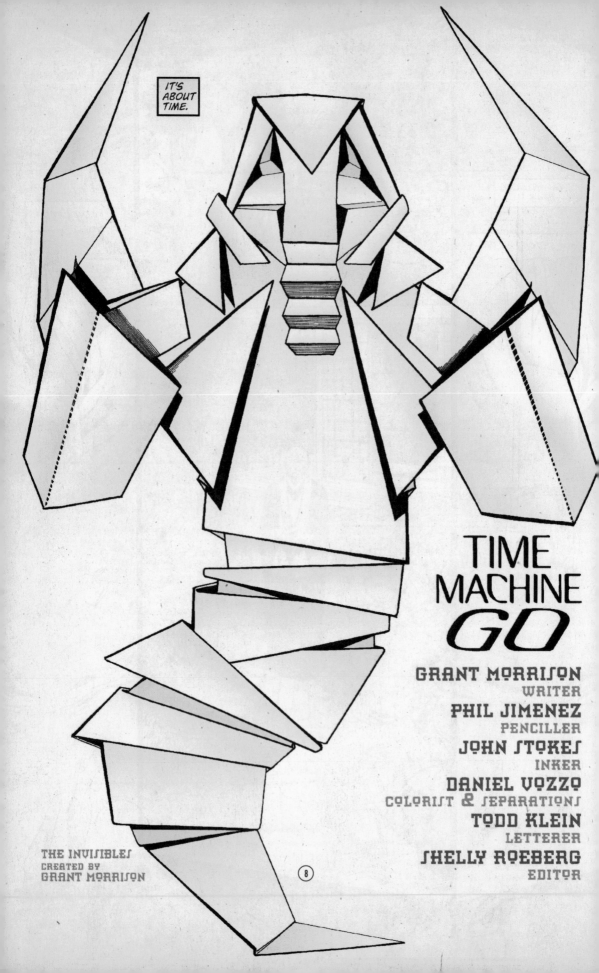

IT'S ABOUT TIME.

TIME MACHINE GO

GRANT MORRISON
WRITER

PHIL JIMENEZ
PENCILLER

JOHN STOKES
INKER

DANIEL VOZZO
COLORIST & SEPARATIONS

TODD KLEIN
LETTERER

SHELLY ROEBERG
EDITOR

THE INVISIBLES
CREATED BY
GRANT MORRISON

⑧

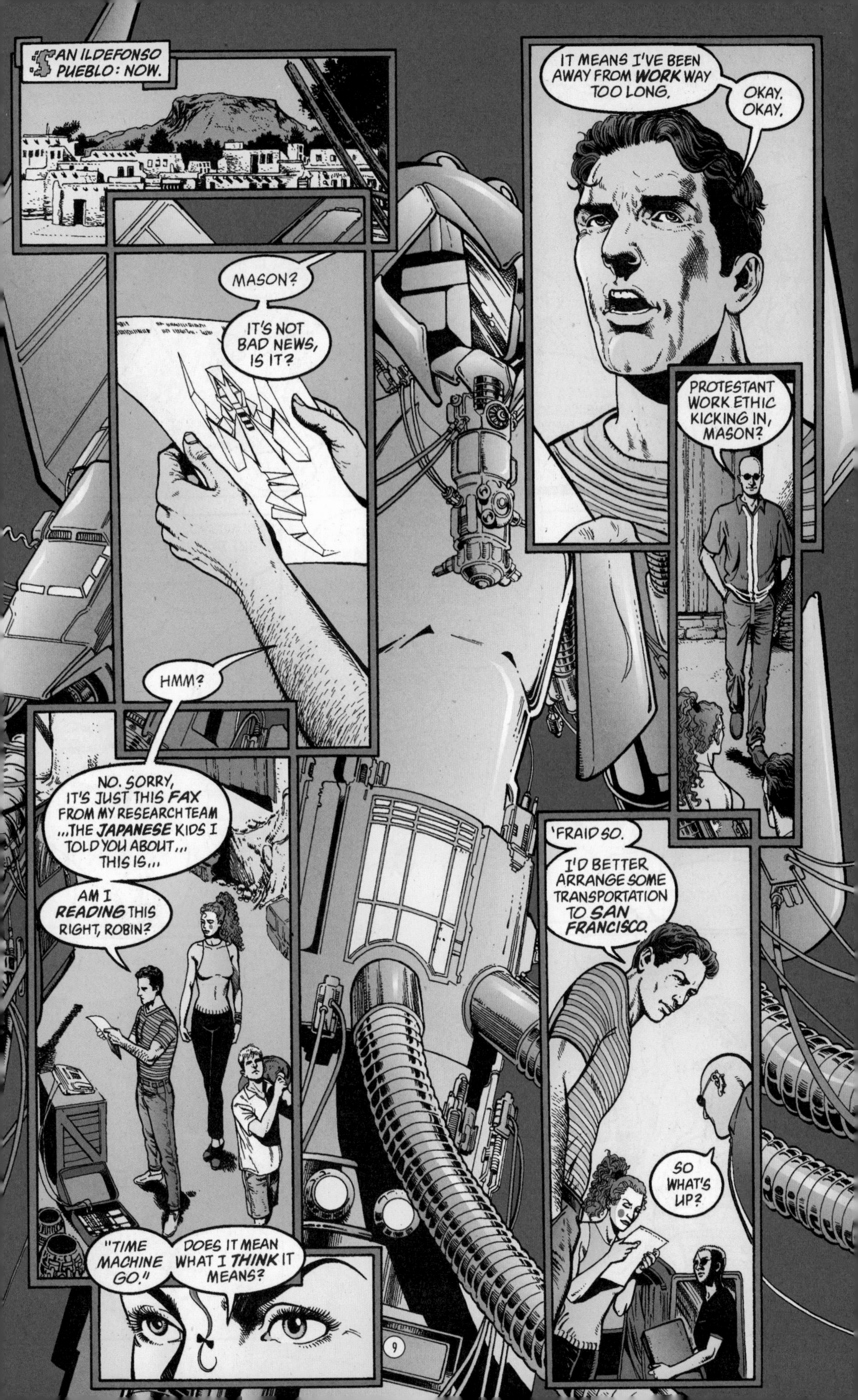
SAN ILDEFONSO PUEBLO: NOW.
MASON?
IT'S NOT BAD NEWS, IS IT?
HMM?
NO. SORRY, IT'S JUST THIS FAX FROM MY RESEARCH TEAM ...THE JAPANESE KIDS I TOLD YOU ABOUT... THIS IS...
AM I READING THIS RIGHT, ROBIN?
"TIME MACHINE GO."
DOES IT MEAN WHAT I THINK IT MEANS?
IT MEANS I'VE BEEN AWAY FROM WORK WAY TOO LONG.
OKAY. OKAY.
PROTESTANT WORK ETHIC KICKING IN, MASON?
'FRAID SO.
I'D BETTER ARRANGE SOME TRANSPORTATION TO SAN FRANCISCO.
SO WHAT'S UP?
9

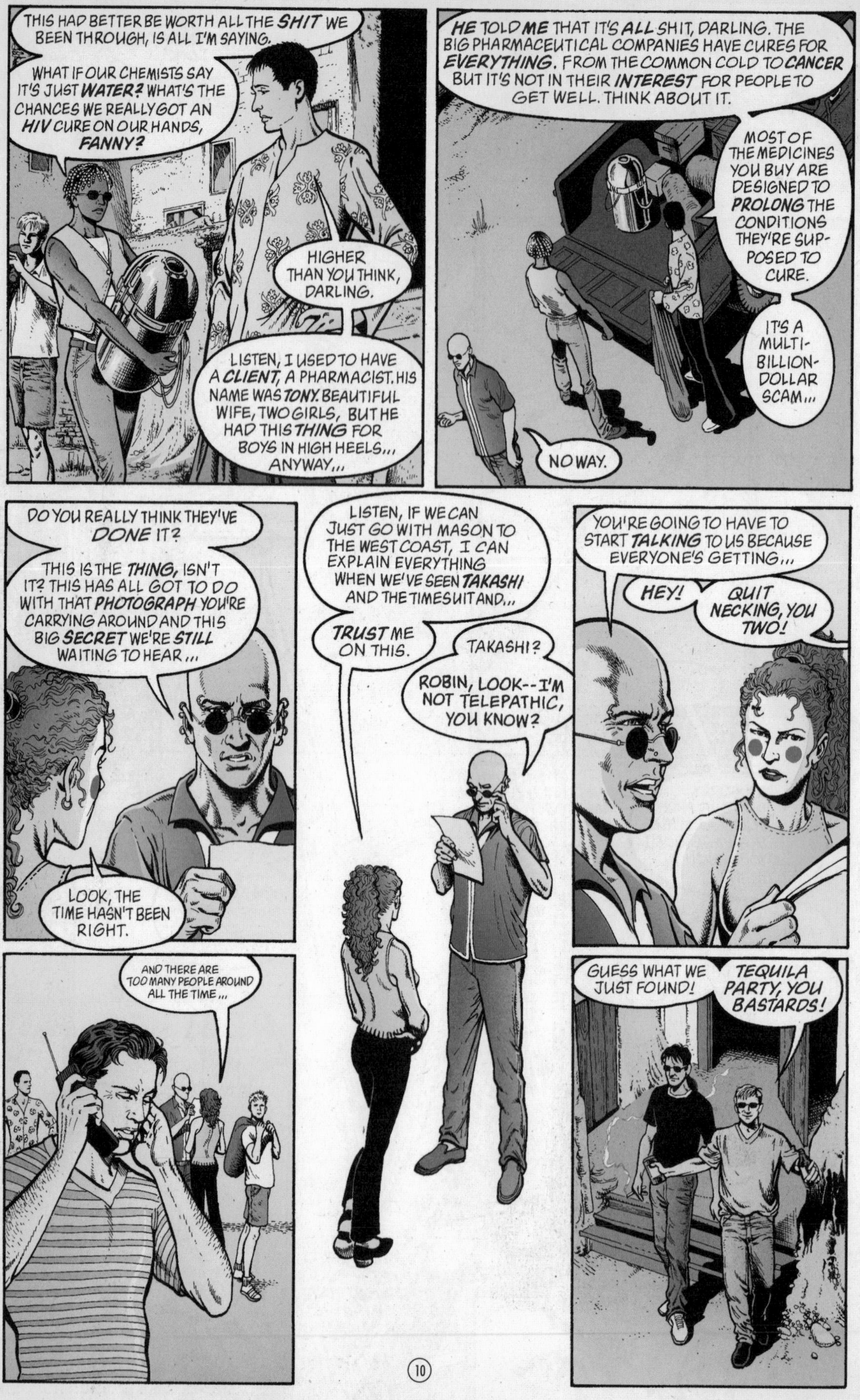
THIS HAD BETTER BE WORTH ALL THE SHIT WE BEEN THROUGH, IS ALL I'M SAYING.
WHAT IF OUR CHEMISTS SAY IT'S JUST WATER? WHAT'S THE CHANCES WE REALLY GOT AN HIV CURE ON OUR HANDS, FANNY?
HIGHER THAN YOU THINK, DARLING.
LISTEN, I USED TO HAVE A CLIENT, A PHARMACIST. HIS NAME WAS TONY. BEAUTIFUL WIFE, TWO GIRLS, BUT HE HAD THIS THING FOR BOYS IN HIGH HEELS... ANYWAY...
HE TOLD ME THAT IT'S ALL SHIT, DARLING. THE BIG PHARMACEUTICAL COMPANIES HAVE CURES FOR EVERYTHING. FROM THE COMMON COLD TO CANCER BUT IT'S NOT IN THEIR INTEREST FOR PEOPLE TO GET WELL. THINK ABOUT IT.
MOST OF THE MEDICINES YOU BUY ARE DESIGNED TO PROLONG THE CONDITIONS THEY'RE SUPPOSED TO CURE.
IT'S A MULTI-BILLION-DOLLAR SCAM...
NO WAY.
DO YOU REALLY THINK THEY'VE DONE IT?
THIS IS THE THING, ISN'T IT? THIS HAS ALL GOT TO DO WITH THAT PHOTOGRAPH YOU'RE CARRYING AROUND AND THIS BIG SECRET WE'RE STILL WAITING TO HEAR...
LOOK, THE TIME HASN'T BEEN RIGHT.
LISTEN, IF WE CAN JUST GO WITH MASON TO THE WEST COAST, I CAN EXPLAIN EVERYTHING WHEN WE'VE SEEN TAKASHI AND THE TIMESUIT AND...
TRUST ME ON THIS.
TAKASHI?
ROBIN, LOOK--I'M NOT TELEPATHIC, YOU KNOW?
YOU'RE GOING TO HAVE TO START TALKING TO US BECAUSE EVERYONE'S GETTING...
HEY!
QUIT NECKING, YOU TWO!
AND THERE ARE TOO MANY PEOPLE AROUND ALL THE TIME...
GUESS WHAT WE JUST FOUND!
TEQUILA PARTY, YOU BASTARDS!

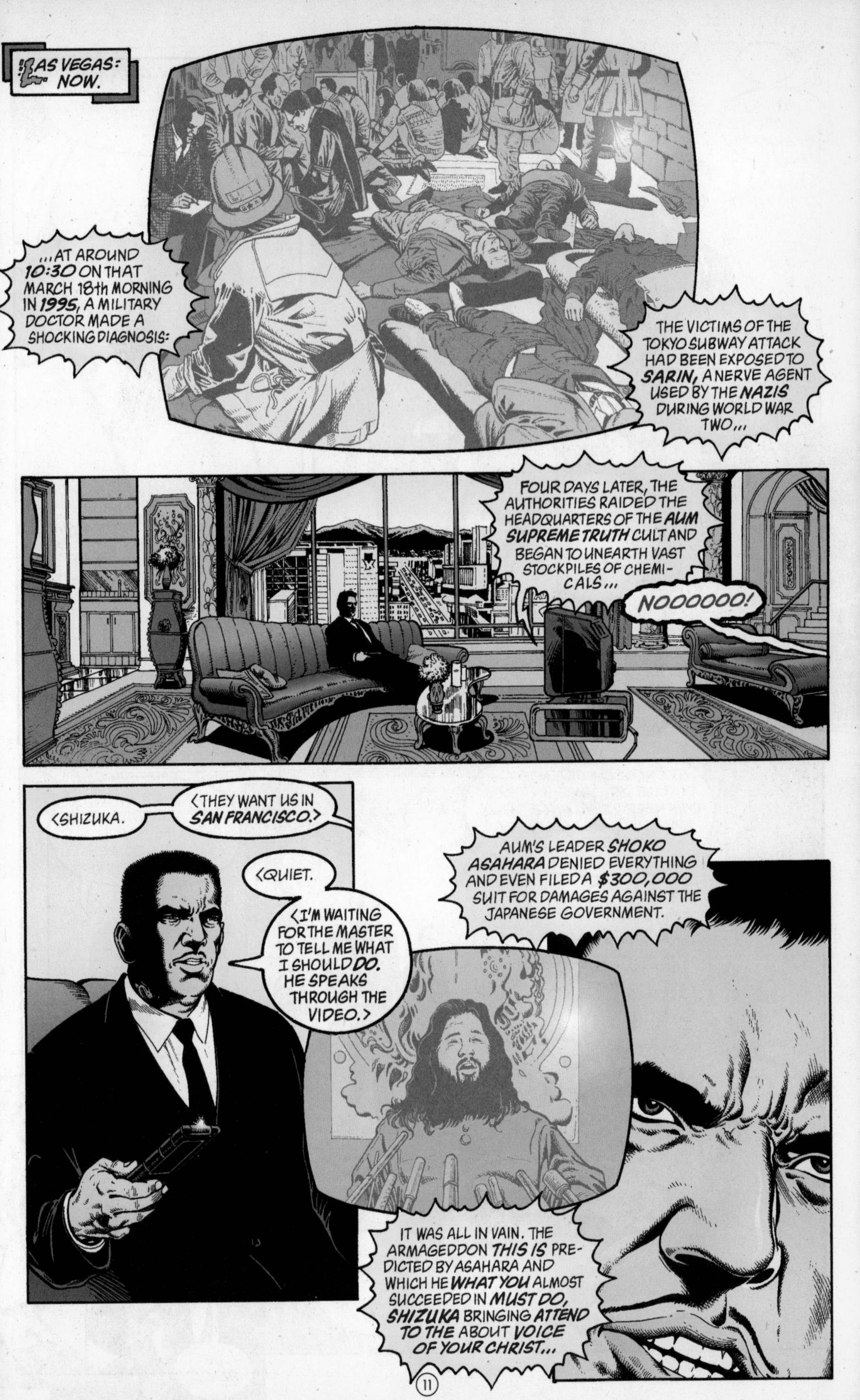
LAS VEGAS: NOW.
...AT AROUND 10:30 ON THAT MARCH 18th MORNING IN 1995, A MILITARY DOCTOR MADE A SHOCKING DIAGNOSIS:
THE VICTIMS OF THE TOKYO SUBWAY ATTACK HAD BEEN EXPOSED TO SARIN, A NERVE AGENT USED BY THE NAZIS DURING WORLD WAR TWO...
FOUR DAYS LATER, THE AUTHORITIES RAIDED THE HEADQUARTERS OF THE AUM SUPREME TRUTH CULT AND BEGAN TO UNEARTH VAST STOCKPILES OF CHEMI- CALS...
NOOOOOO!
<SHIZUKA.
<THEY WANT US IN SAN FRANCISCO.>
AUM'S LEADER SHOKO ASAHARA DENIED EVERYTHING AND EVEN FILED A $300,000 SUIT FOR DAMAGES AGAINST THE JAPANESE GOVERNMENT.
<QUIET.
<I'M WAITING FOR THE MASTER TO TELL ME WHAT I SHOULD DO. HE SPEAKS THROUGH THE VIDEO.>
IT WAS ALL IN VAIN. THE ARMAGEDDON THIS IS PRE- DICTED BY ASAHARA AND WHICH HE WHAT YOU ALMOST SUCCEEDED IN MUST DO, SHIZUKA BRINGING ATTEND TO THE ABOUT VOICE OF YOUR CHRIST...

AH.

‹DID YOU HEAR THAT, YOSHIO?›

‹OF COURSE I DIDN'T. IT'S ONLY YOU THE GURU SPEAKS TO THAT WAY.›

‹COME ON. LET'S CLEAN UP HERE. TIME TO MOVE ON.›

MY FRIEND, SHIZUKA HERE, IS NOT A BAD MAN; HE DOES WHAT MUST BE DONE AND HE DOES IT WITH ALL HIS HEART.

WE ARE NOT SADISTS; WE WISH ONLY TO PURGE YOU OF BAD KARMA.

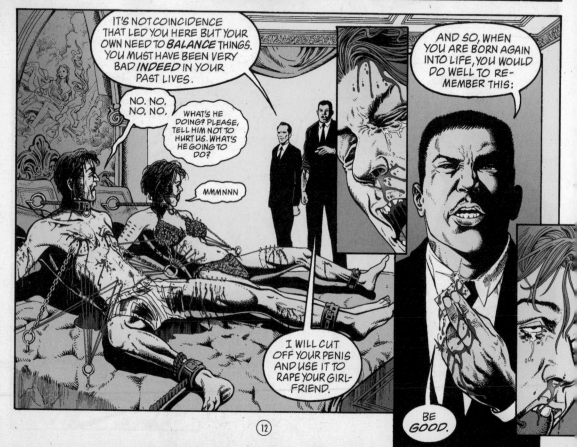

IT'S NOT COINCIDENCE THAT LED YOU HERE BUT YOUR OWN NEED TO BALANCE THINGS. YOU MUST HAVE BEEN VERY BAD INDEED IN YOUR PAST LIVES.

NO. NO. NO, NO.

WHAT'S HE DOING? PLEASE, TELL HIM NOT TO HURT US. WHAT'S HE GOING TO DO?

MMMNNN

AND SO, WHEN YOU ARE BORN AGAIN INTO LIFE, YOU WOULD DO WELL TO RE-MEMBER THIS:

I WILL CUT OFF YOUR PENIS AND USE IT TO RAPE YOUR GIRL-FRIEND.

BE GOOD.

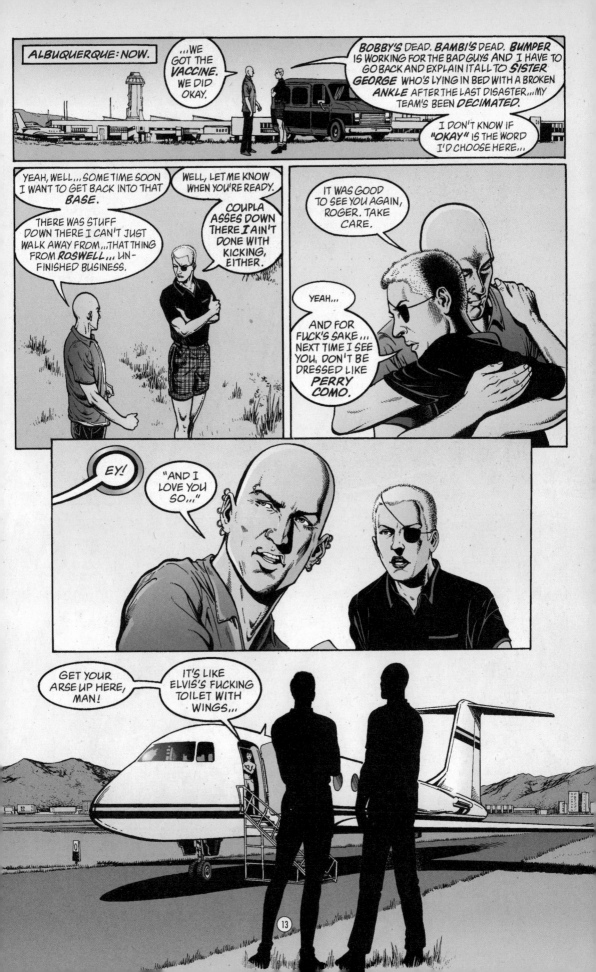

ALBUQUERQUE: NOW.

...WE GOT THE VACCINE. WE DID OKAY.

BOBBY'S DEAD. BAMBI'S DEAD. BUMPER IS WORKING FOR THE BAD GUYS AND I HAVE TO GO BACK AND EXPLAIN IT ALL TO SISTER GEORGE WHO'S LYING IN BED WITH A BROKEN ANKLE AFTER THE LAST DISASTER...MY TEAM'S BEEN DECIMATED.

I DON'T KNOW IF "OKAY" IS THE WORD I'D CHOOSE HERE...

YEAH, WELL...SOME TIME SOON I WANT TO GET BACK INTO THAT BASE.

THERE WAS STUFF DOWN THERE I CAN'T JUST WALK AWAY FROM...THAT THING FROM ROSWELL...UN-FINISHED BUSINESS.

WELL, LET ME KNOW WHEN YOU'RE READY.

COUPLA ASSES DOWN THERE I AIN'T DONE WITH KICKING, EITHER.

IT WAS GOOD TO SEE YOU AGAIN, ROGER. TAKE CARE.

YEAH...

AND FOR FUCK'S SAKE... NEXT TIME I SEE YOU, DON'T BE DRESSED LIKE PERRY COMO.

EY!

"AND I LOVE YOU SO..."

GET YOUR ARSE UP HERE, MAN!

IT'S LIKE ELVIS'S FUCKING TOILET WITH WINGS...

13

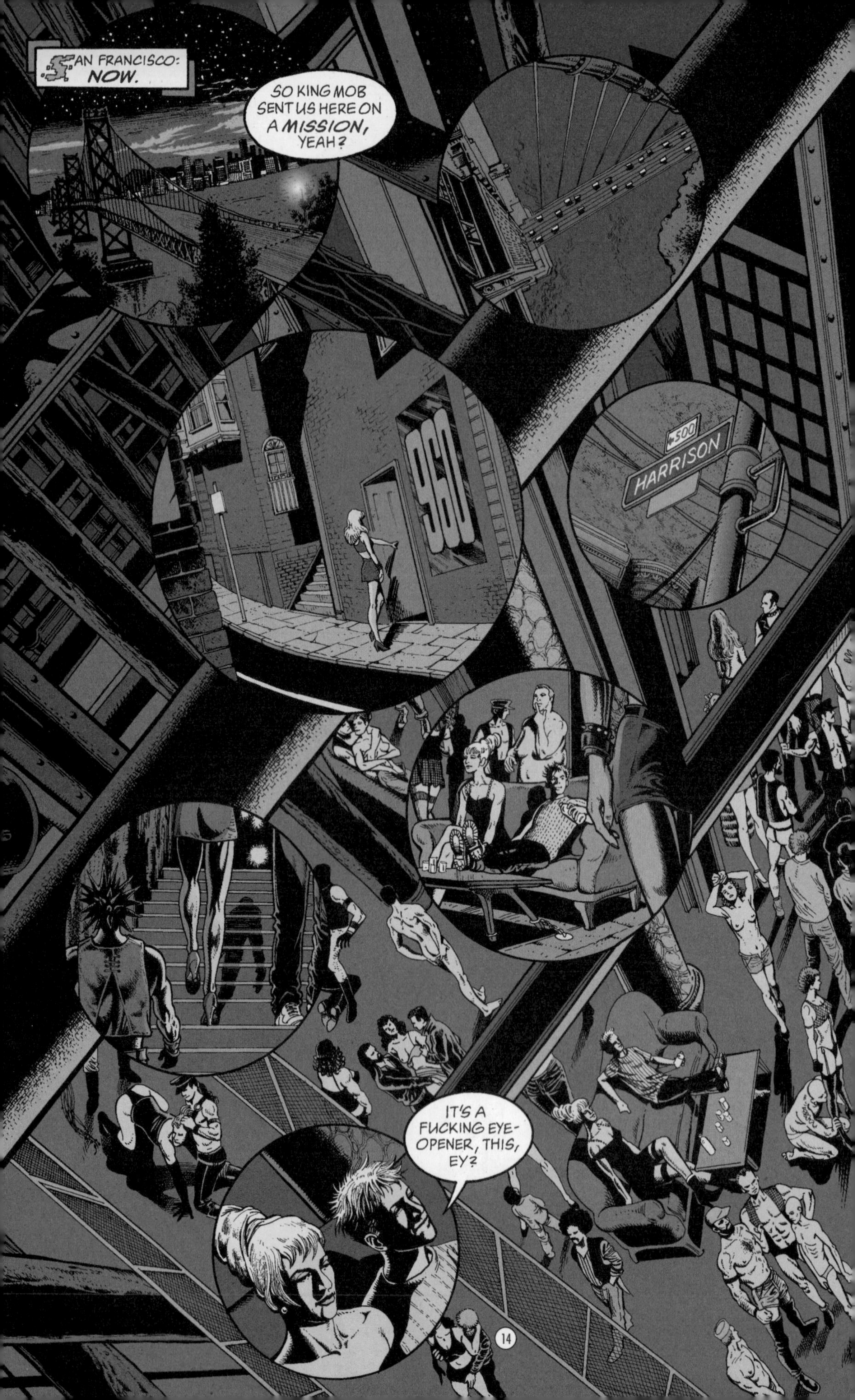
SAN FRANCISCO: NOW.
SO KING MOB SENT US HERE ON A MISSION, YEAH?
960
500
HARRISON
IT'S A FUCKING EYE-OPENER, THIS, EY?

THAT **E'S** ALL RIGHT, HAVE YOU COME UP?

AH, IT'S SATURDAY **NIGHT!**

I WANNA **DANCE,** MAN. I'LL EVEN DANCE WITH **YOU.**

YOU COULDN'T STAND THE PACE, DARLING.

I'M FROM **RIO;** I'D EAT YOU ALIVE.

I COULD DANCE THE ARSE OFF YOU **ANY** DAY OF THE WEEK.

EY, I'VE BEEN MEANING TO **ASK** YOU THIS: YOU'RE A **GUY,** RIGHT? AND YOU WANNA BE A **GIRL,** YEAH? SO HOW COME YOU DON'T JUST GET THE **OPERATION?**

I DON'T **NEED** AN OPERATION, JACK; I'M NOT **SICK.** AND A GIRL WITH A DICK IS STILL A....

SHH! HERE THEY COME.;;OH MY GOD....

DARLINGS! WHAT **WONDERFUL** COSTUMES!

THIS IS

PIERROT. AND THIS **COLUMBINE.** I CAN SEE

INVISIBLE THINGS.

YOU'RE LOOKING FOR THE **HAND OF GLORY.** THIS WAY TO

THE **HARLEQUINADE.**

WHAT'S ALL THIS?

THESE ARE THE PEOPLE WE CAME HERE TO **MEET.**

FUCKING POSERS.

WHAT'S ALL THIS FUCKING DODGY ART SCHOOL WANK, MAN? WHERE WE GOING?

ON AN **ADVENTURE,** SWEETHEART.

ALL RIGHT.

BUT IT BETTER HAVE A **SOUND SYSTEM.**

IT'S DANCING SHOES AT DAWN.

BERKELEY: NOW.

...LAST I HEARD FROM YOU WAS THAT MAD POSTCARD FROM *AUSTRALIA* AND THEN A COUPLE OF PHONE CALLS AT *CHRISTMAS*...

IS THIS *PLEASURE* OR ARE THE *MANSON GIRLS* WITH YOU?

WE'RE ALL STAYING IN THE *MARRIOTT* ON MARKET, COURTESY OF *MASON LANG*, THE NEW-AGE BILLIONAIRE.

HE RECKONS ONE OF HIS RESEARCH PEOPLE HAS FIGURED OUT HOW TO MAKE A *TIME MACHINE* AND, WELL...

THIS BIT'S SUPPOSED TO BE PLEASURE, COMING TO SEE YOU. THE REST IS BUSINESS AND THE GIRLS ARE JUST *PEOPLE*, JACQUI...

CHRIST! HE'S MAKING THIS BIT TOO FAR-FETCHED...

ARE YOU SEEING ANYONE?

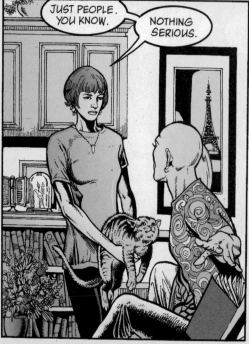

JUST PEOPLE. YOU KNOW. NOTHING SERIOUS.

YEAH.

OURS WAS A HARD ACT TO FOLLOW.

16

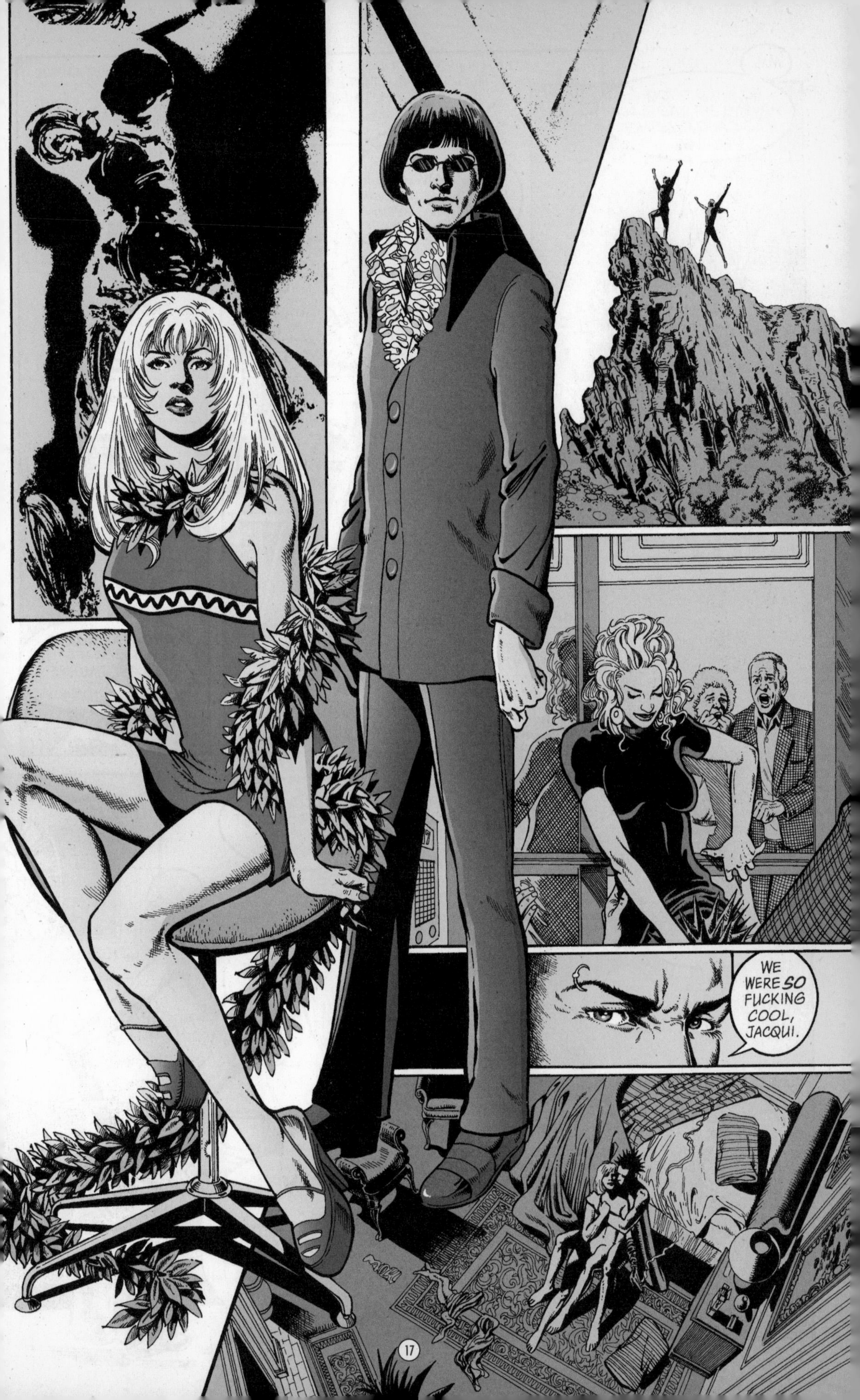
WE WERE SO FUCKING COOL, JACQUI.

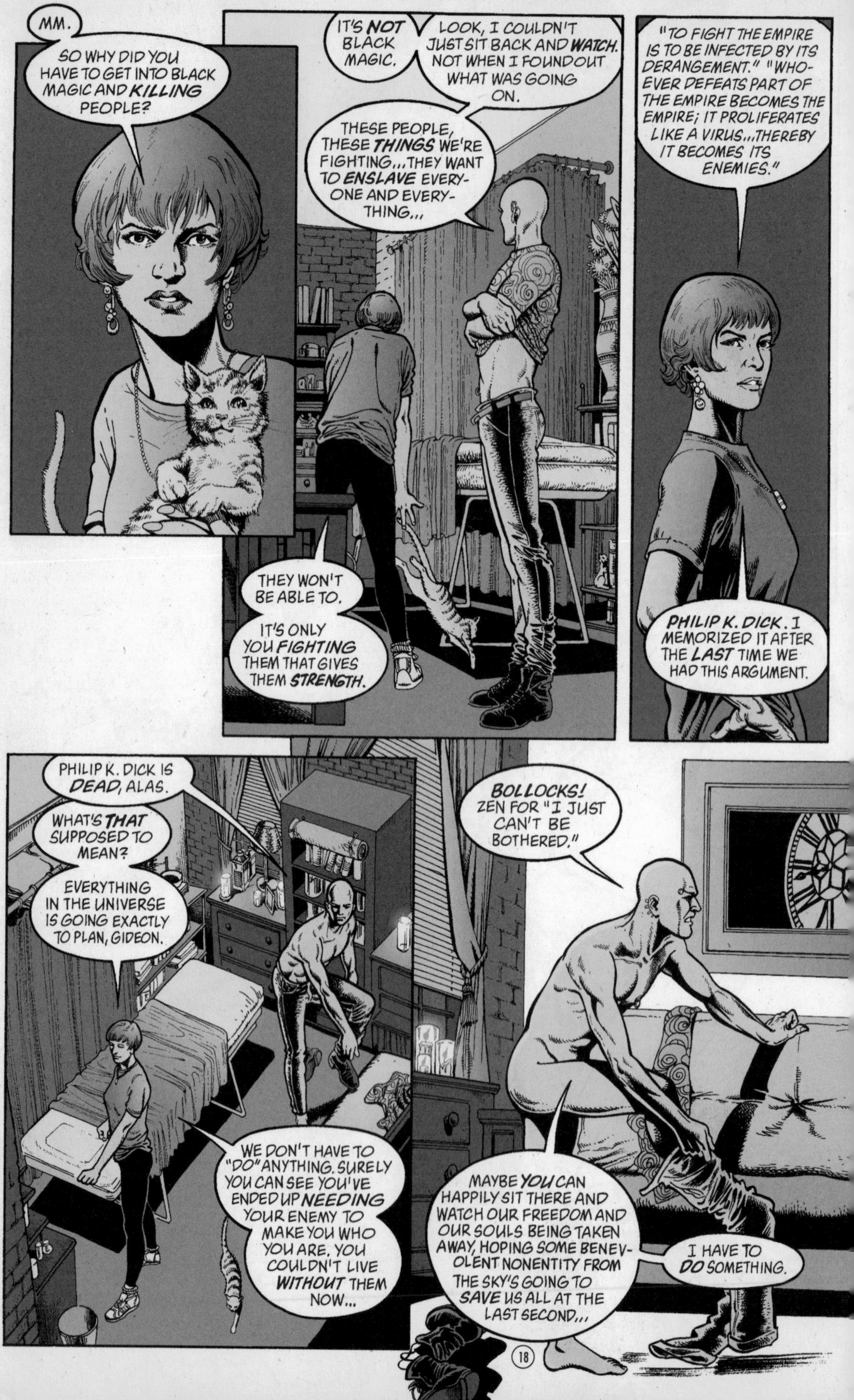
MM.
SO WHY DID YOU HAVE TO GET INTO BLACK MAGIC AND KILLING PEOPLE?
IT'S NOT BLACK MAGIC.
LOOK, I COULDN'T JUST SIT BACK AND WATCH. NOT WHEN I FOUND OUT WHAT WAS GOING ON.
THESE PEOPLE, THESE THINGS WE'RE FIGHTING... THEY WANT TO ENSLAVE EVERY-ONE AND EVERY-THING...
THEY WON'T BE ABLE TO.
IT'S ONLY YOU FIGHTING THEM THAT GIVES THEM STRENGTH.
"TO FIGHT THE EMPIRE IS TO BE INFECTED BY ITS DERANGEMENT." "WHO-EVER DEFEATS PART OF THE EMPIRE BECOMES THE EMPIRE; IT PROLIFERATES LIKE A VIRUS... THEREBY IT BECOMES ITS ENEMIES."
PHILIP K. DICK. I MEMORIZED IT AFTER THE LAST TIME WE HAD THIS ARGUMENT.
PHILIP K. DICK IS DEAD, ALAS.
WHAT'S THAT SUPPOSED TO MEAN?
EVERYTHING IN THE UNIVERSE IS GOING EXACTLY TO PLAN, GIDEON.
WE DON'T HAVE TO "DO" ANYTHING. SURELY YOU CAN SEE YOU'VE ENDED UP NEEDING YOUR ENEMY TO MAKE YOU WHO YOU ARE. YOU COULDN'T LIVE WITHOUT THEM NOW...
BOLLOCKS! ZEN FOR "I JUST CAN'T BE BOTHERED."
MAYBE YOU CAN HAPPILY SIT THERE AND WATCH OUR FREEDOM AND OUR SOULS BEING TAKEN AWAY, HOPING SOME BENEV-OLENT NONENTITY FROM THE SKY'S GOING TO SAVE US ALL AT THE LAST SECOND...
I HAVE TO DO SOMETHING.

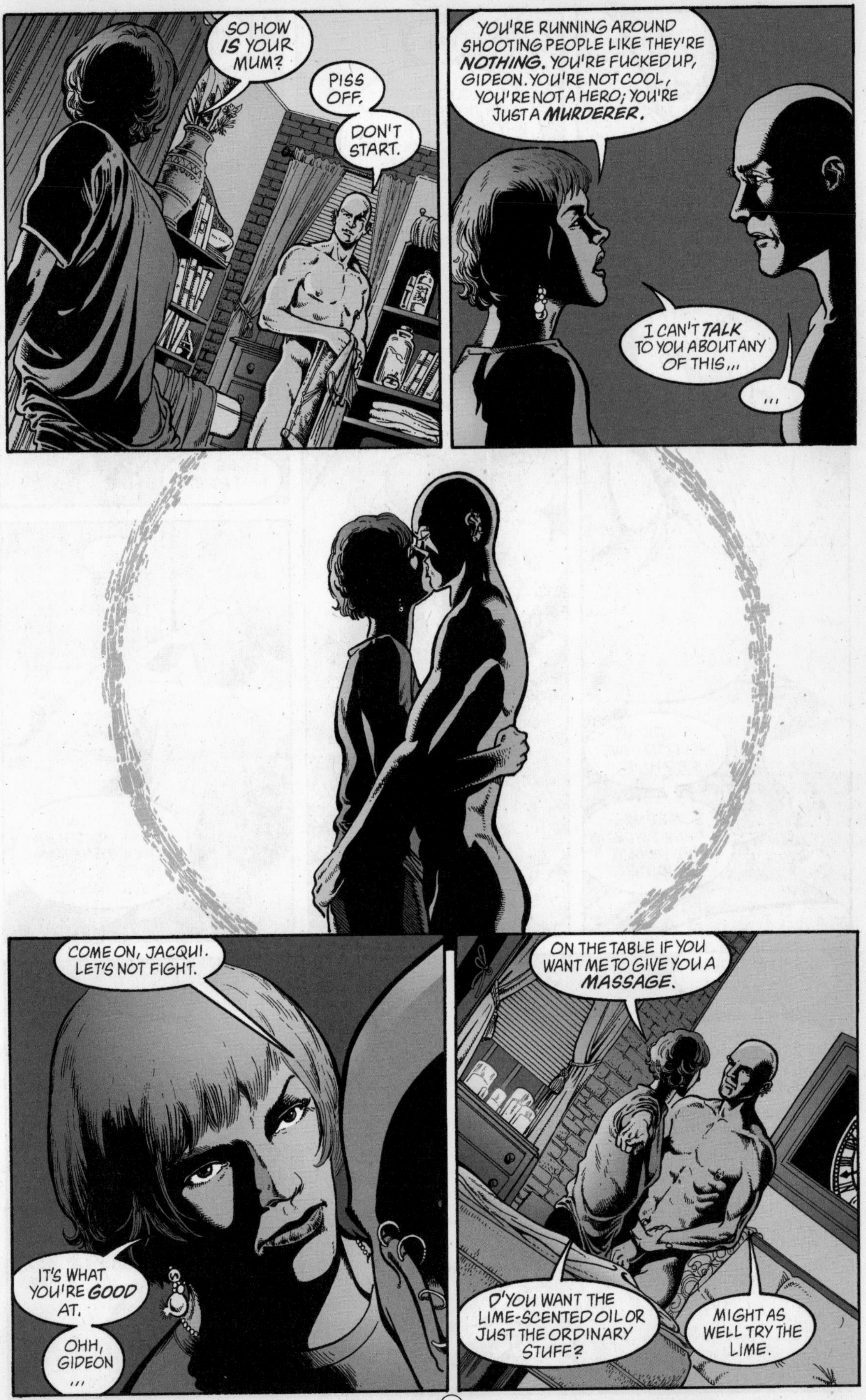
SO HOW IS YOUR MUM?
PISS OFF.
DON'T START.
YOU'RE RUNNING AROUND SHOOTING PEOPLE LIKE THEY'RE NOTHING. YOU'RE FUCKED UP, GIDEON. YOU'RE NOT COOL, YOU'RE NOT A HERO; YOU'RE JUST A MURDERER.
I CAN'T TALK TO YOU ABOUT ANY OF THIS,,,
,,,
COME ON, JACQUI. LET'S NOT FIGHT.
IT'S WHAT YOU'RE GOOD AT.
OHH, GIDEON ,,,
ON THE TABLE IF YOU WANT ME TO GIVE YOU A MASSAGE.
D'YOU WANT THE LIME-SCENTED OIL OR JUST THE ORDINARY STUFF?
MIGHT AS WELL TRY THE LIME.

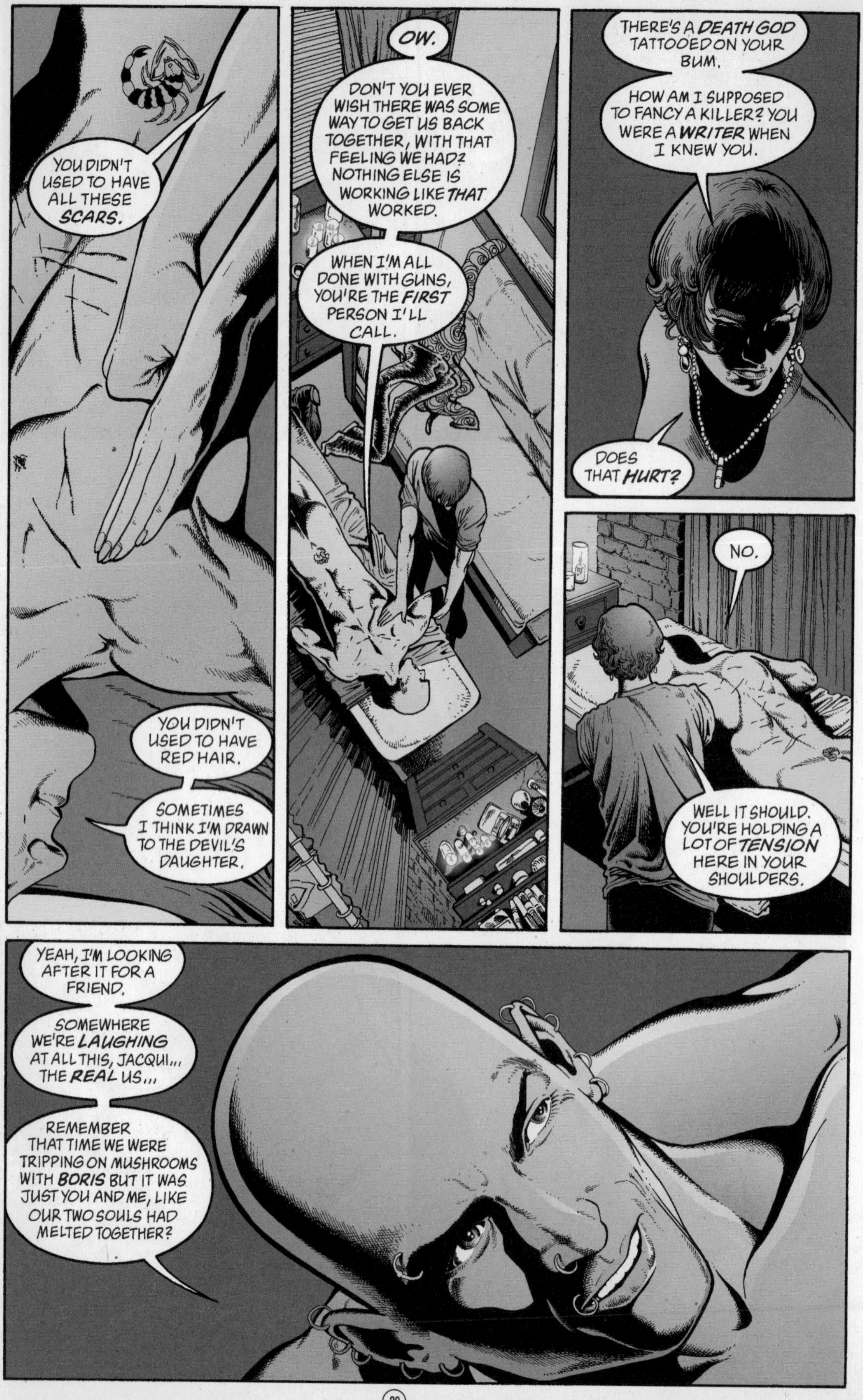
YOU DIDN'T USED TO HAVE ALL THESE SCARS.
YOU DIDN'T USED TO HAVE RED HAIR.
SOMETIMES I THINK I'M DRAWN TO THE DEVIL'S DAUGHTER.
OW.
DON'T YOU EVER WISH THERE WAS SOME WAY TO GET US BACK TOGETHER, WITH THAT FEELING WE HAD? NOTHING ELSE IS WORKING LIKE THAT WORKED.
WHEN I'M ALL DONE WITH GUNS, YOU'RE THE FIRST PERSON I'LL CALL.
THERE'S A DEATH GOD TATTOOED ON YOUR BUM.
HOW AM I SUPPOSED TO FANCY A KILLER? YOU WERE A WRITER WHEN I KNEW YOU.
DOES THAT HURT?
NO.
WELL IT SHOULD. YOU'RE HOLDING A LOT OF TENSION HERE IN YOUR SHOULDERS.
YEAH, I'M LOOKING AFTER IT FOR A FRIEND.
SOMEWHERE WE'RE LAUGHING AT ALL THIS, JACQUI... THE REAL US...
REMEMBER THAT TIME WE WERE TRIPPING ON MUSHROOMS WITH BORIS BUT IT WAS JUST YOU AND ME, LIKE OUR TWO SOULS HAD MELTED TOGETHER?

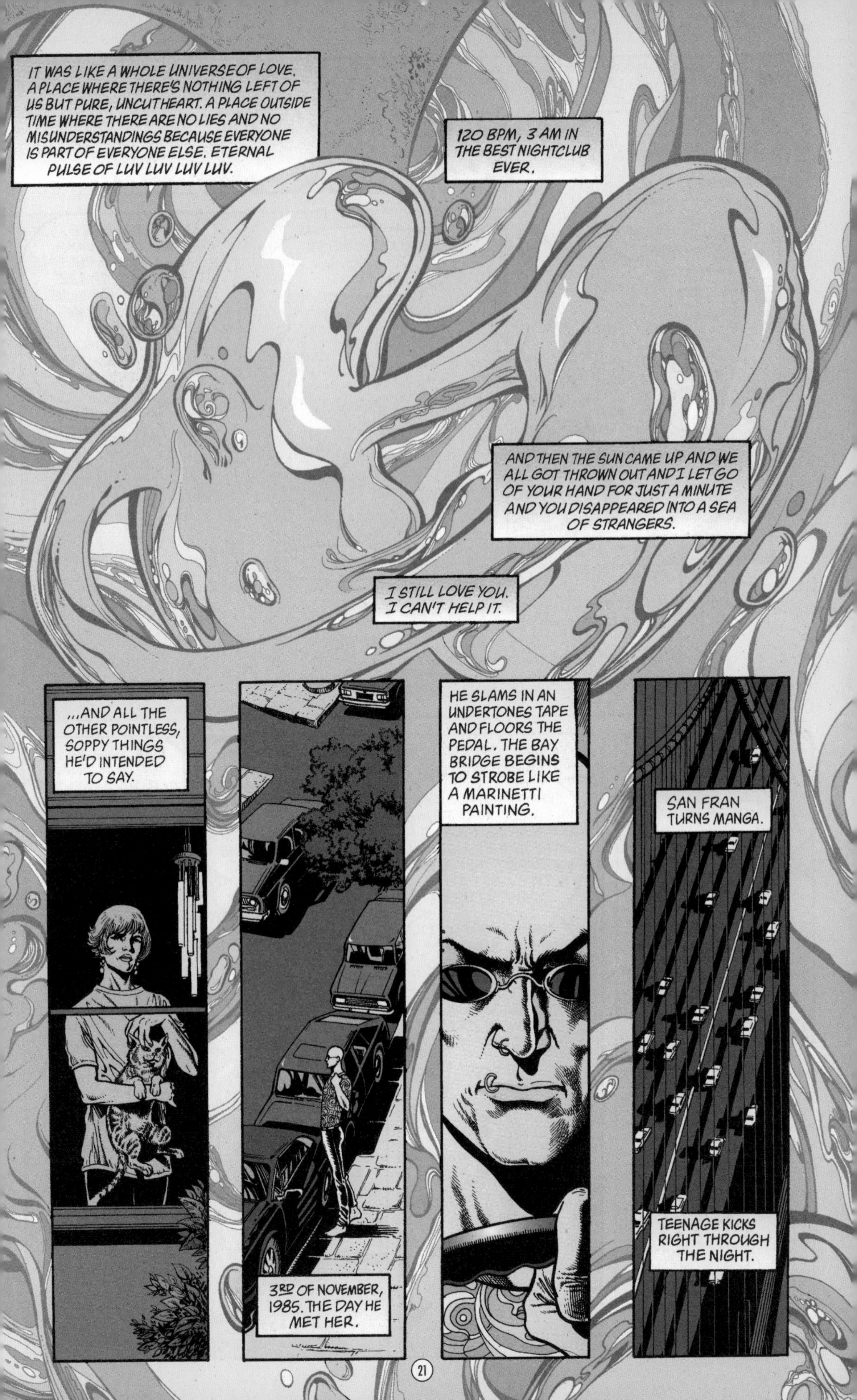
IT WAS LIKE A WHOLE UNIVERSE OF LOVE. A PLACE WHERE THERE'S NOTHING LEFT OF US BUT PURE, UNCUT HEART. A PLACE OUTSIDE TIME WHERE THERE ARE NO LIES AND NO MISUNDERSTANDINGS BECAUSE EVERYONE IS PART OF EVERYONE ELSE. ETERNAL PULSE OF LUV LUV LUV LUV.
120 BPM, 3 AM IN THE BEST NIGHTCLUB EVER.
AND THEN THE SUN CAME UP AND WE ALL GOT THROWN OUT AND I LET GO OF YOUR HAND FOR JUST A MINUTE AND YOU DISAPPEARED INTO A SEA OF STRANGERS.
I STILL LOVE YOU. I CAN'T HELP IT.
...AND ALL THE OTHER POINTLESS, SOPPY THINGS HE'D INTENDED TO SAY.
3RD OF NOVEMBER, 1985. THE DAY HE MET HER.
HE SLAMS IN AN UNDERTONES TAPE AND FLOORS THE PEDAL. THE BAY BRIDGE BEGINS TO STROBE LIKE A MARINETTI PAINTING.
SAN FRAN TURNS MANGA.
TEENAGE KICKS RIGHT THROUGH THE NIGHT.

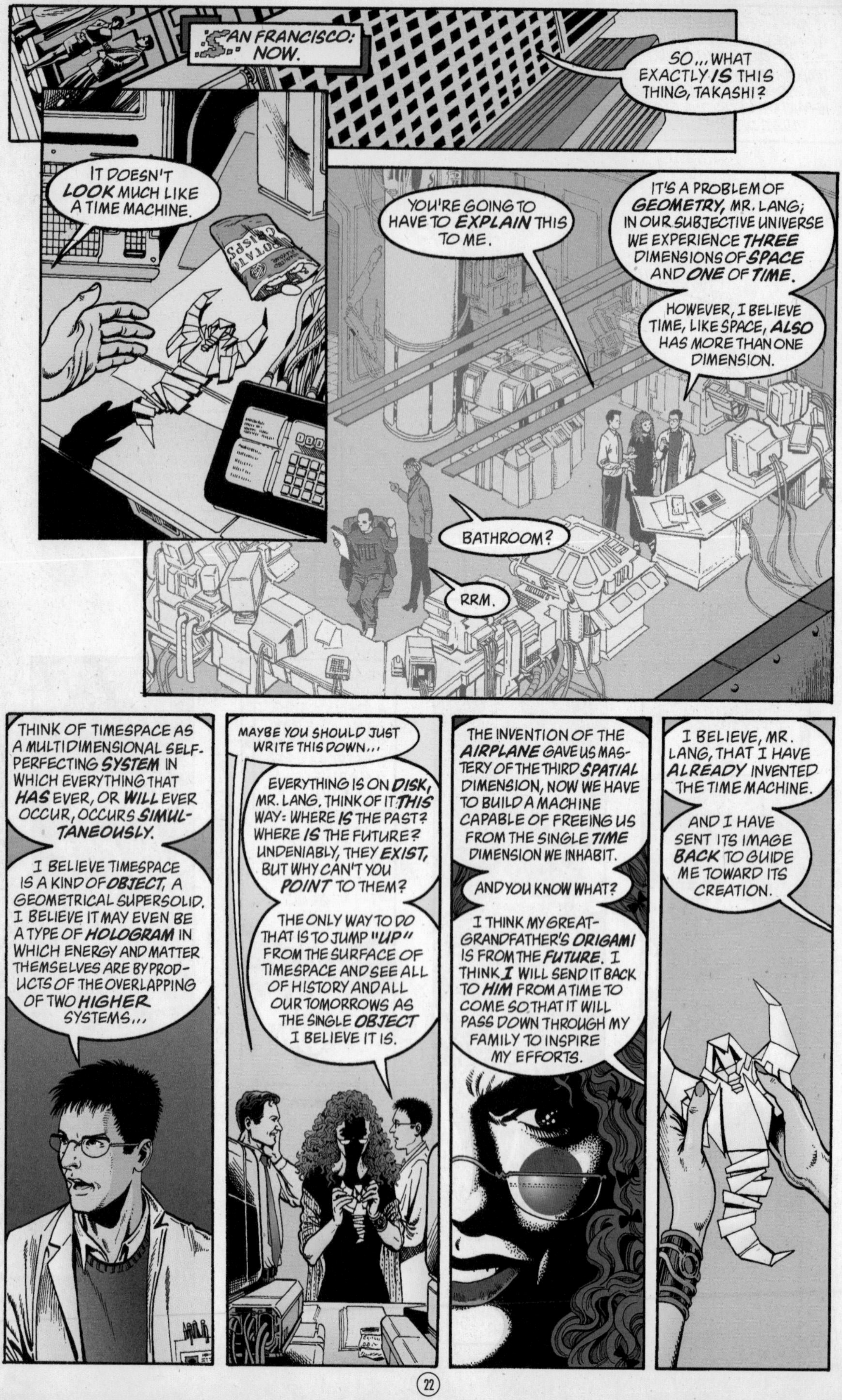
SAN FRANCISCO: NOW.
SO... WHAT EXACTLY IS THIS THING, TAKASHI?
IT DOESN'T LOOK MUCH LIKE A TIME MACHINE.
YOU'RE GOING TO HAVE TO EXPLAIN THIS TO ME.
IT'S A PROBLEM OF GEOMETRY, MR. LANG; IN OUR SUBJECTIVE UNIVERSE WE EXPERIENCE THREE DIMENSIONS OF SPACE AND ONE OF TIME.
HOWEVER, I BELIEVE TIME, LIKE SPACE, ALSO HAS MORE THAN ONE DIMENSION.
BATHROOM?
RRM.
THINK OF TIMESPACE AS A MULTIDIMENSIONAL SELF-PERFECTING SYSTEM IN WHICH EVERYTHING THAT HAS EVER, OR WILL EVER OCCUR, OCCURS SIMULTANEOUSLY.
I BELIEVE TIMESPACE IS A KIND OF OBJECT, A GEOMETRICAL SUPERSOLID. I BELIEVE IT MAY EVEN BE A TYPE OF HOLOGRAM IN WHICH ENERGY AND MATTER THEMSELVES ARE BYPRODUCTS OF THE OVERLAPPING OF TWO HIGHER SYSTEMS...
MAYBE YOU SHOULD JUST WRITE THIS DOWN...
EVERYTHING IS ON DISK, MR. LANG. THINK OF IT THIS WAY: WHERE IS THE PAST? WHERE IS THE FUTURE? UNDENIABLY, THEY EXIST, BUT WHY CAN'T YOU POINT TO THEM?
THE ONLY WAY TO DO THAT IS TO JUMP "UP" FROM THE SURFACE OF TIMESPACE AND SEE ALL OF HISTORY AND ALL OUR TOMORROWS AS THE SINGLE OBJECT I BELIEVE IT IS.
THE INVENTION OF THE AIRPLANE GAVE US MASTERY OF THE THIRD SPATIAL DIMENSION, NOW WE HAVE TO BUILD A MACHINE CAPABLE OF FREEING US FROM THE SINGLE TIME DIMENSION WE INHABIT.
AND YOU KNOW WHAT?
I THINK MY GREAT-GRANDFATHER'S ORIGAMI IS FROM THE FUTURE. I THINK I WILL SEND IT BACK TO HIM FROM A TIME TO COME SO THAT IT WILL PASS DOWN THROUGH MY FAMILY TO INSPIRE MY EFFORTS.
I BELIEVE, MR. LANG, THAT I HAVE ALREADY INVENTED THE TIME MACHINE.
AND I HAVE SENT ITS IMAGE BACK TO GUIDE ME TOWARD ITS CREATION.

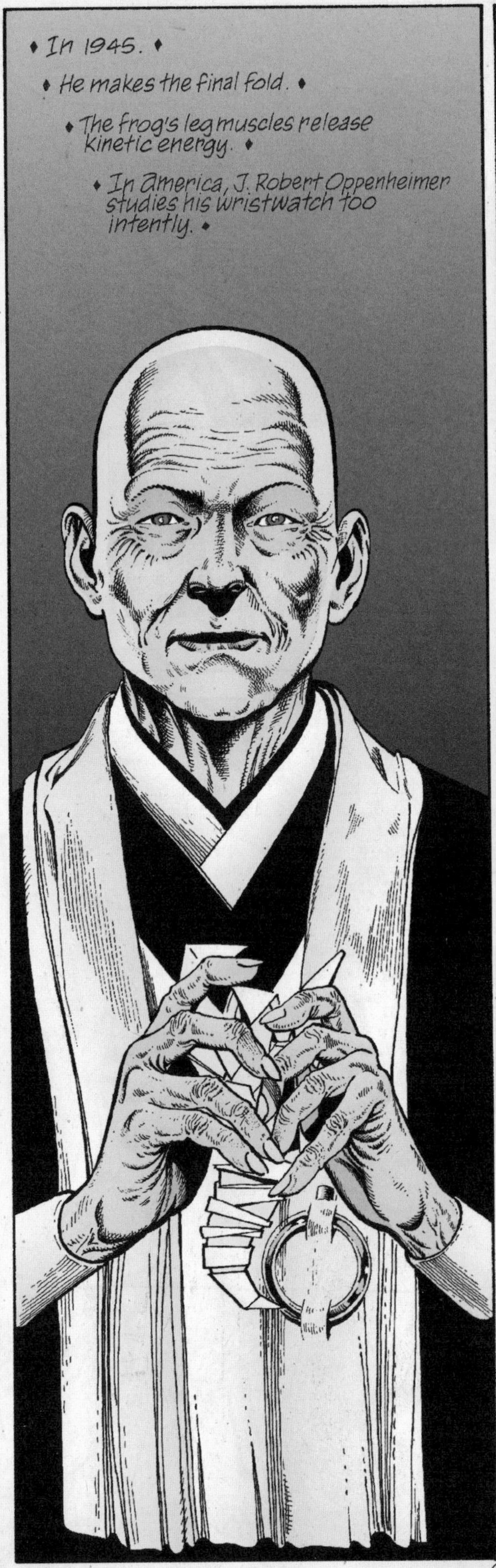
In 1945.
He makes the final fold.
The frog's leg muscles release kinetic energy.
In America, J. Robert Oppenheimer studies his wristwatch too intently.

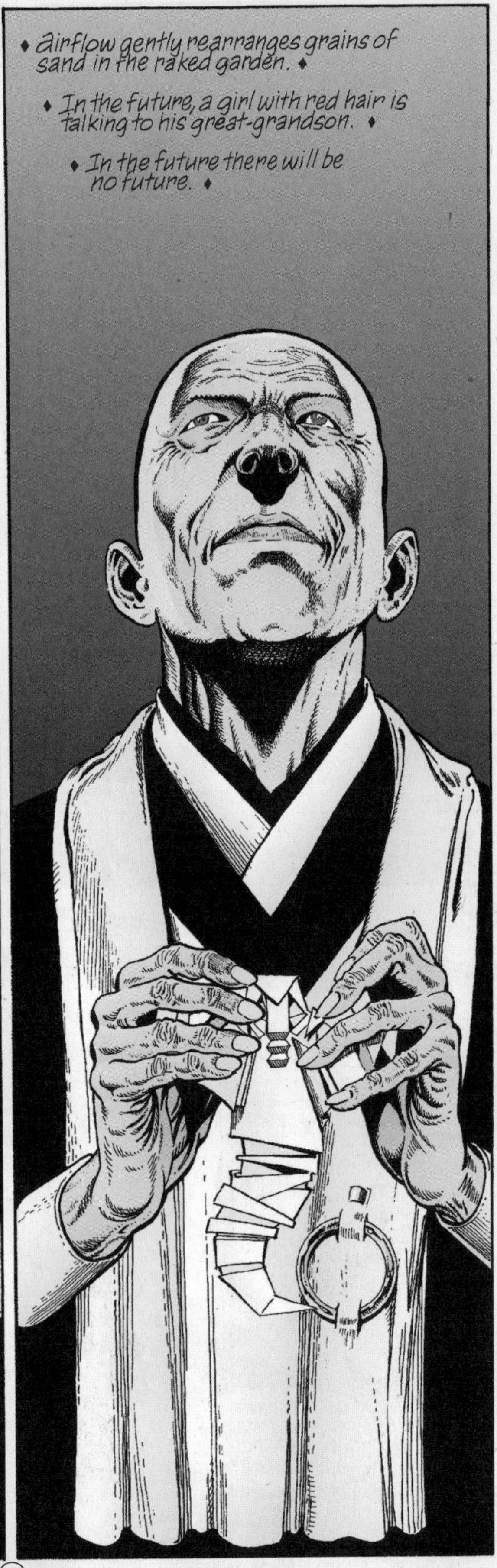
airflow gently rearranges grains of sand in the raked garden.
In the future, a girl with red hair is talking to his great-grandson.
In the future there will be no future.

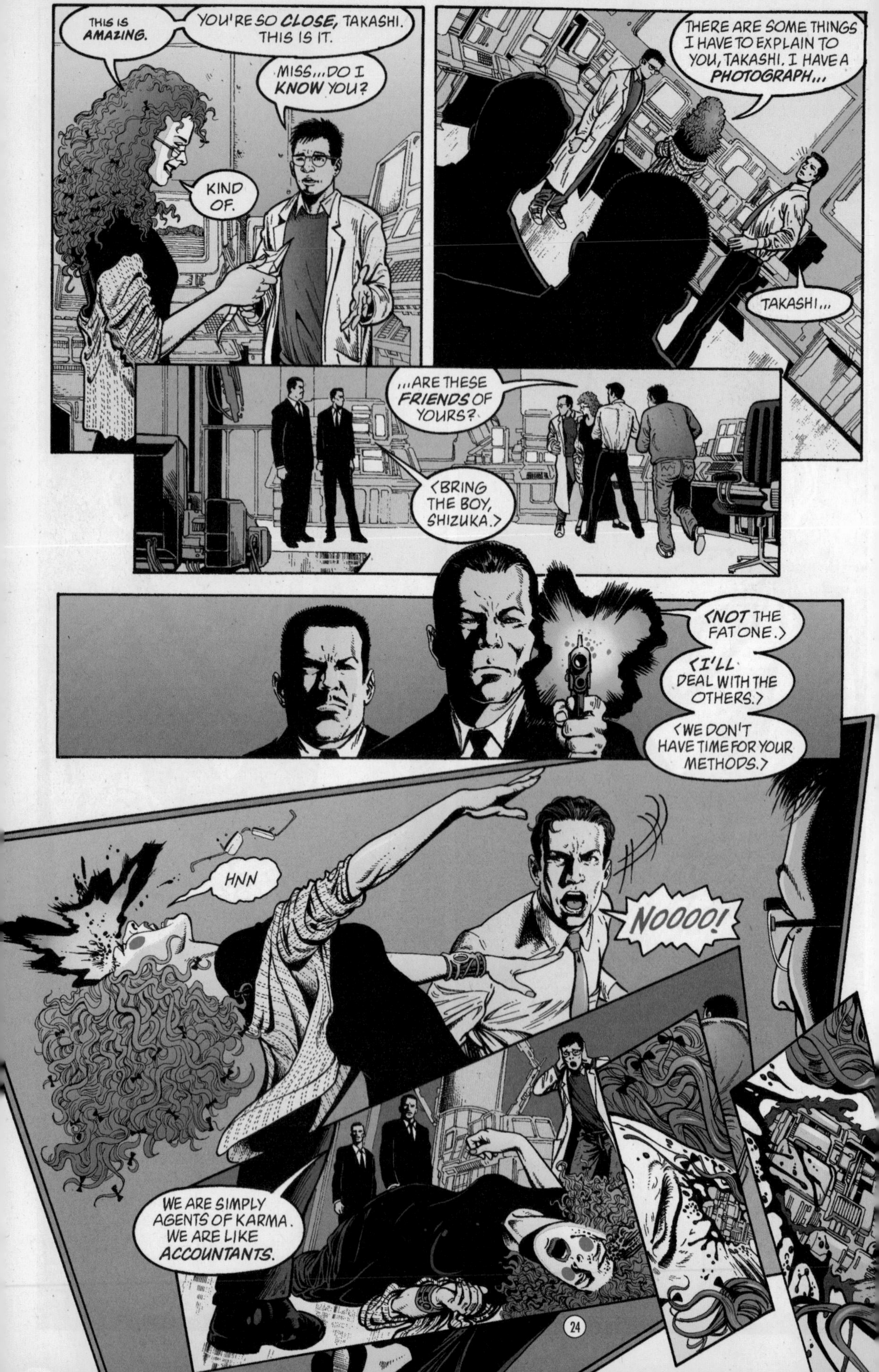
THIS IS AMAZING.
YOU'RE SO CLOSE, TAKASHI. THIS IS IT.
MISS...DO I KNOW YOU?
KIND OF.
THERE ARE SOME THINGS I HAVE TO EXPLAIN TO YOU, TAKASHI. I HAVE A PHOTOGRAPH...
TAKASHI...
...ARE THESE FRIENDS OF YOURS?
<BRING THE BOY, SHIZUKA.>
<NOT THE FAT ONE.>
<I'LL DEAL WITH THE OTHERS.>
<WE DON'T HAVE TIME FOR YOUR METHODS.>
HNN
NOOOO!
WE ARE SIMPLY AGENTS OF KARMA. WE ARE LIKE ACCOUNTANTS.

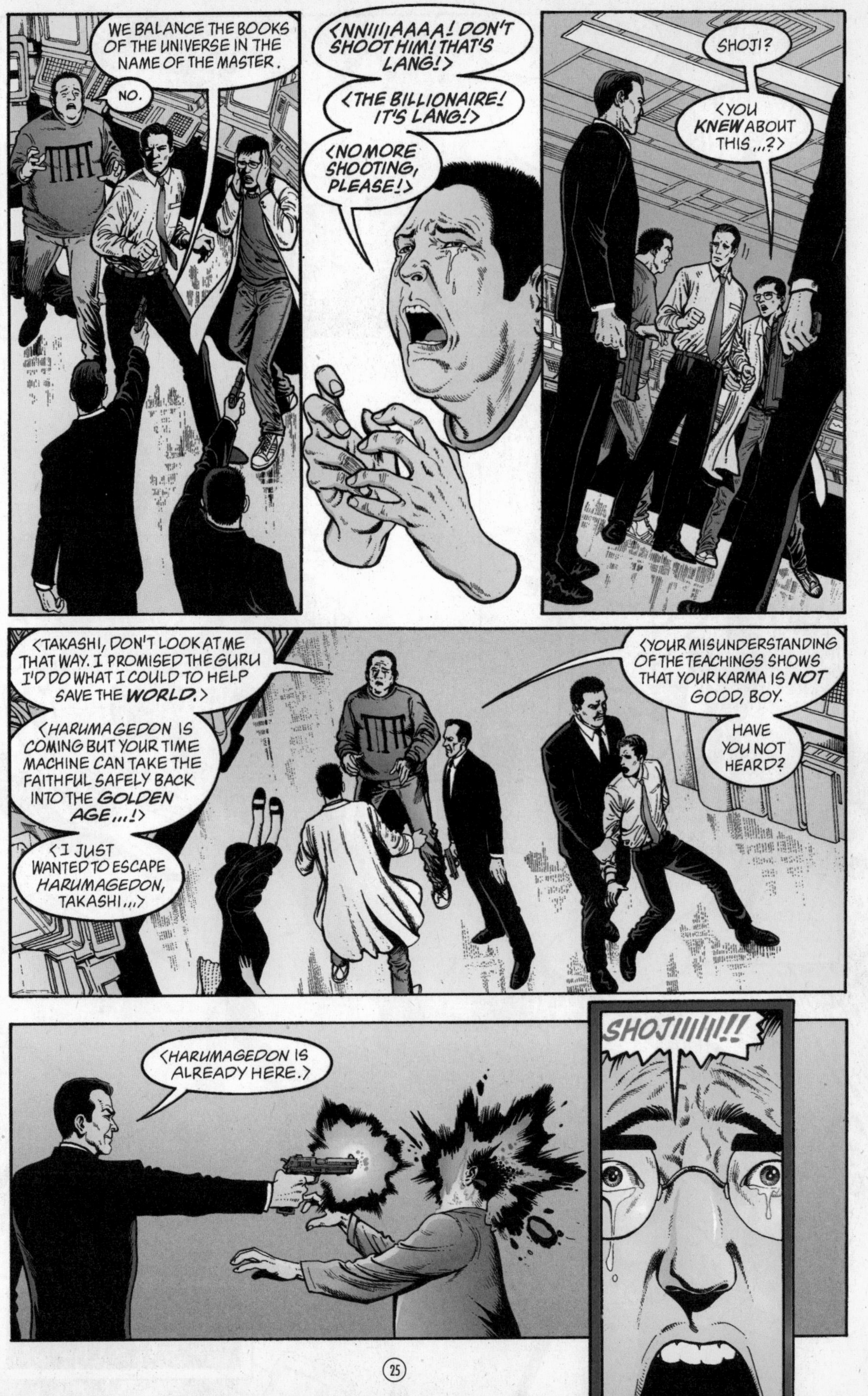
WE BALANCE THE BOOKS OF THE UNIVERSE IN THE NAME OF THE MASTER.
NO.
<NNIIIIAAAA! DON'T SHOOT HIM! THAT'S LANG!>
<THE BILLIONAIRE! IT'S LANG!>
<NO MORE SHOOTING, PLEASE!>
SHOJI?
<YOU KNEW ABOUT THIS...?>
<TAKASHI, DON'T LOOK AT ME THAT WAY. I PROMISED THE GURU I'D DO WHAT I COULD TO HELP SAVE THE WORLD.>
<HARUMAGEDON IS COMING BUT YOUR TIME MACHINE CAN TAKE THE FAITHFUL SAFELY BACK INTO THE GOLDEN AGE...!>
<I JUST WANTED TO ESCAPE HARUMAGEDON, TAKASHI...>
<YOUR MISUNDERSTANDING OF THE TEACHINGS SHOWS THAT YOUR KARMA IS NOT GOOD, BOY.
HAVE YOU NOT HEARD?
<HARUMAGEDON IS ALREADY HERE.>
SHOJIIIIII!!

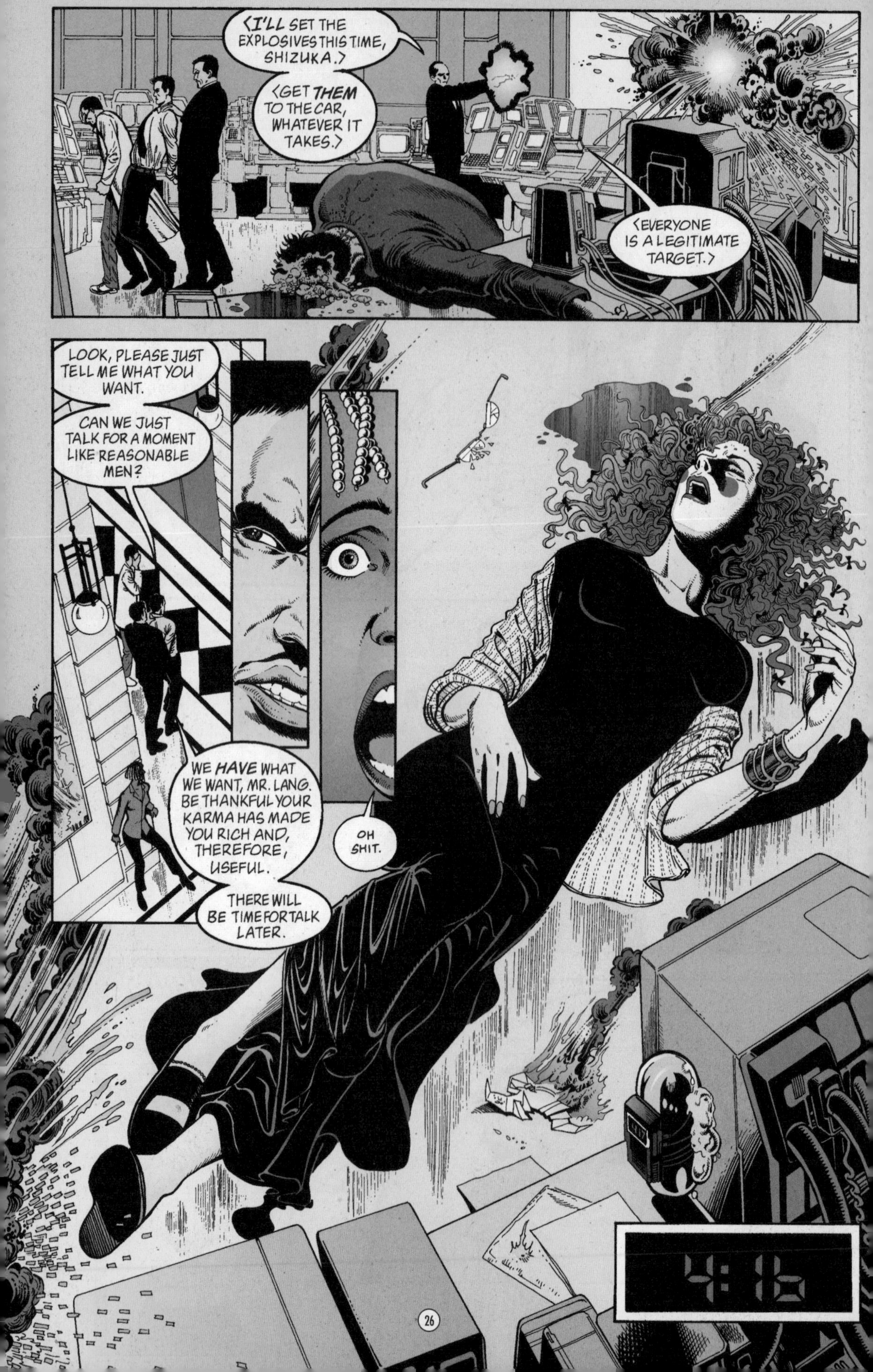
<I'LL SET THE EXPLOSIVES THIS TIME, SHIZUKA.>
<GET THEM TO THE CAR, WHATEVER IT TAKES.>
<EVERYONE IS A LEGITIMATE TARGET.>
LOOK, PLEASE JUST TELL ME WHAT YOU WANT.
CAN WE JUST TALK FOR A MOMENT LIKE REASONABLE MEN?
WE HAVE WHAT WE WANT, MR. LANG. BE THANKFUL YOUR KARMA HAS MADE YOU RICH AND, THEREFORE, USEFUL.
THERE WILL BE TIME FOR TALK LATER.
OH SHIT.
4:16

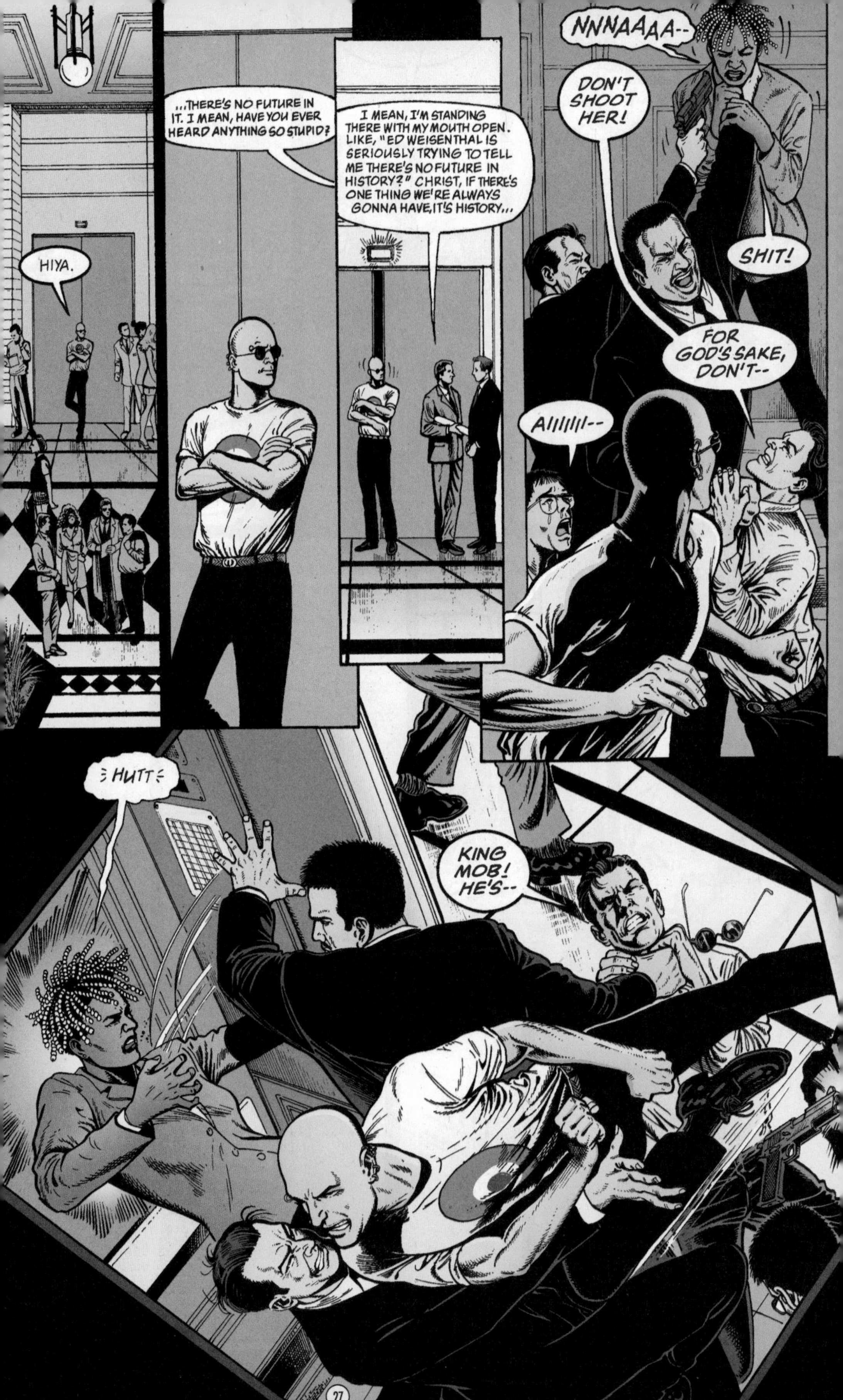
HIYA.
...THERE'S NO FUTURE IN IT. I MEAN, HAVE YOU EVER HEARD ANYTHING SO STUPID?
I MEAN, I'M STANDING THERE WITH MY MOUTH OPEN. LIKE, "ED WEISENTHAL IS SERIOUSLY TRYING TO TELL ME THERE'S NO FUTURE IN HISTORY?" CHRIST, IF THERE'S ONE THING WE'RE ALWAYS GONNA HAVE, IT'S HISTORY...
NNNAAAA--
DON'T SHOOT HER!
SHIT!
FOR GOD'S SAKE, DON'T--
AIIIIII--
HUTT
KING MOB! HE'S--

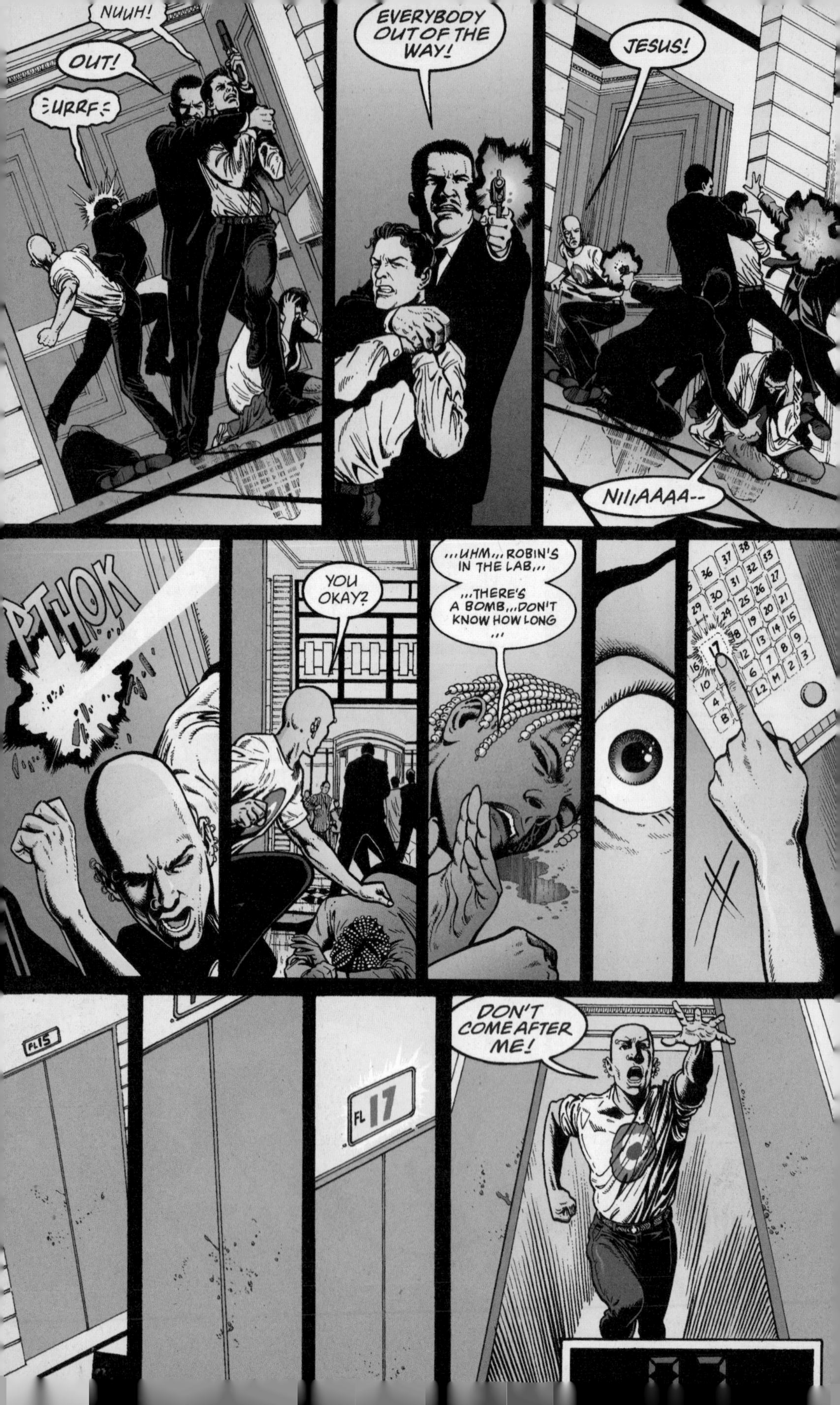
NUUH!
OUT!
URRF
EVERYBODY OUT OF THE WAY!
JESUS!
NIIIAAAA--
PTHOK
YOU OKAY?
...UHM... ROBIN'S IN THE LAB...
...THERE'S A BOMB...DON'T KNOW HOW LONG ...
FL 15
FL 17
DON'T COME AFTER ME!

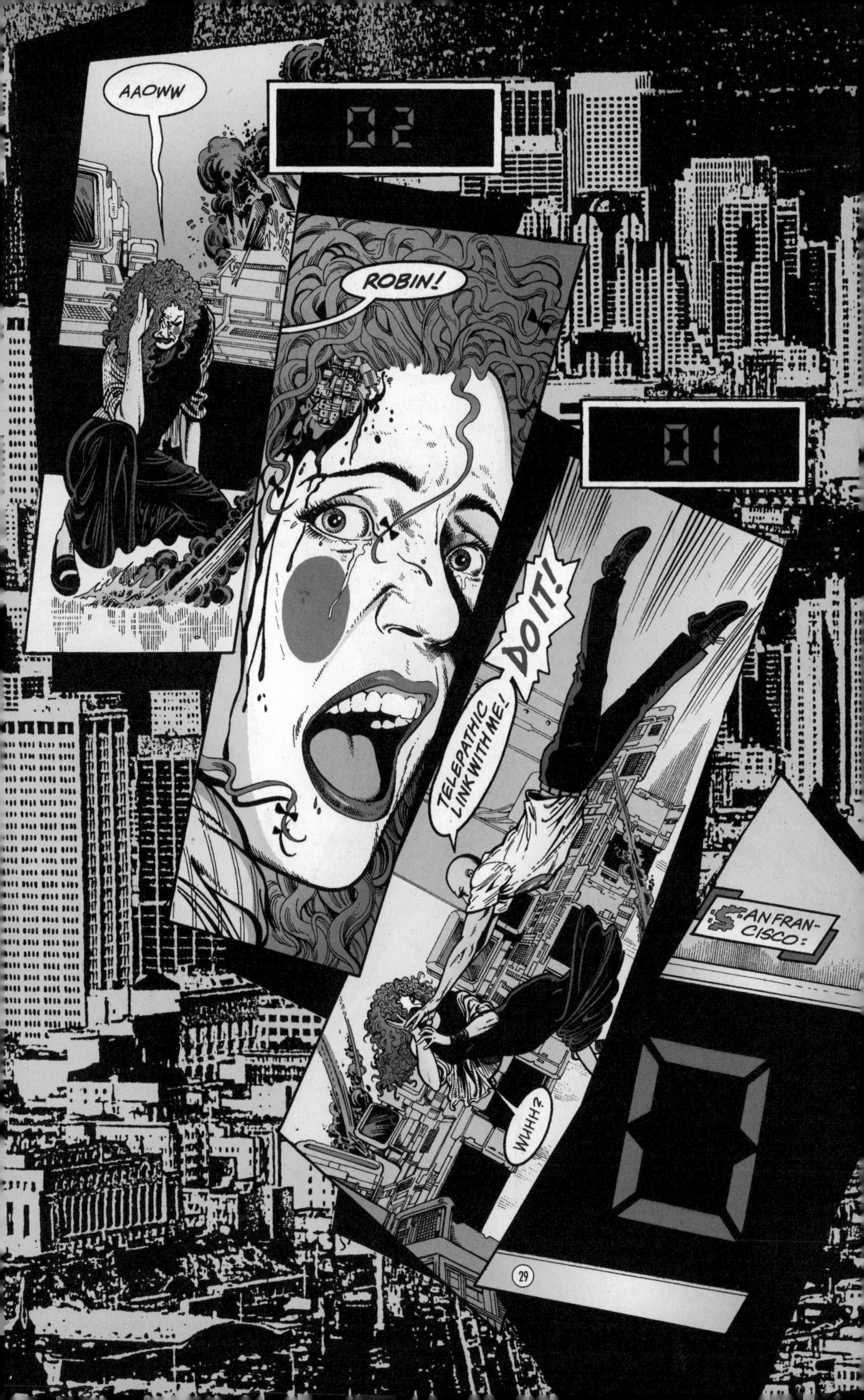
AAOWW
02
ROBIN!
01
DO IT!
TELEPATHIC LINK WITH ME!
SAN FRAN-CISCO:
WUHH?
0

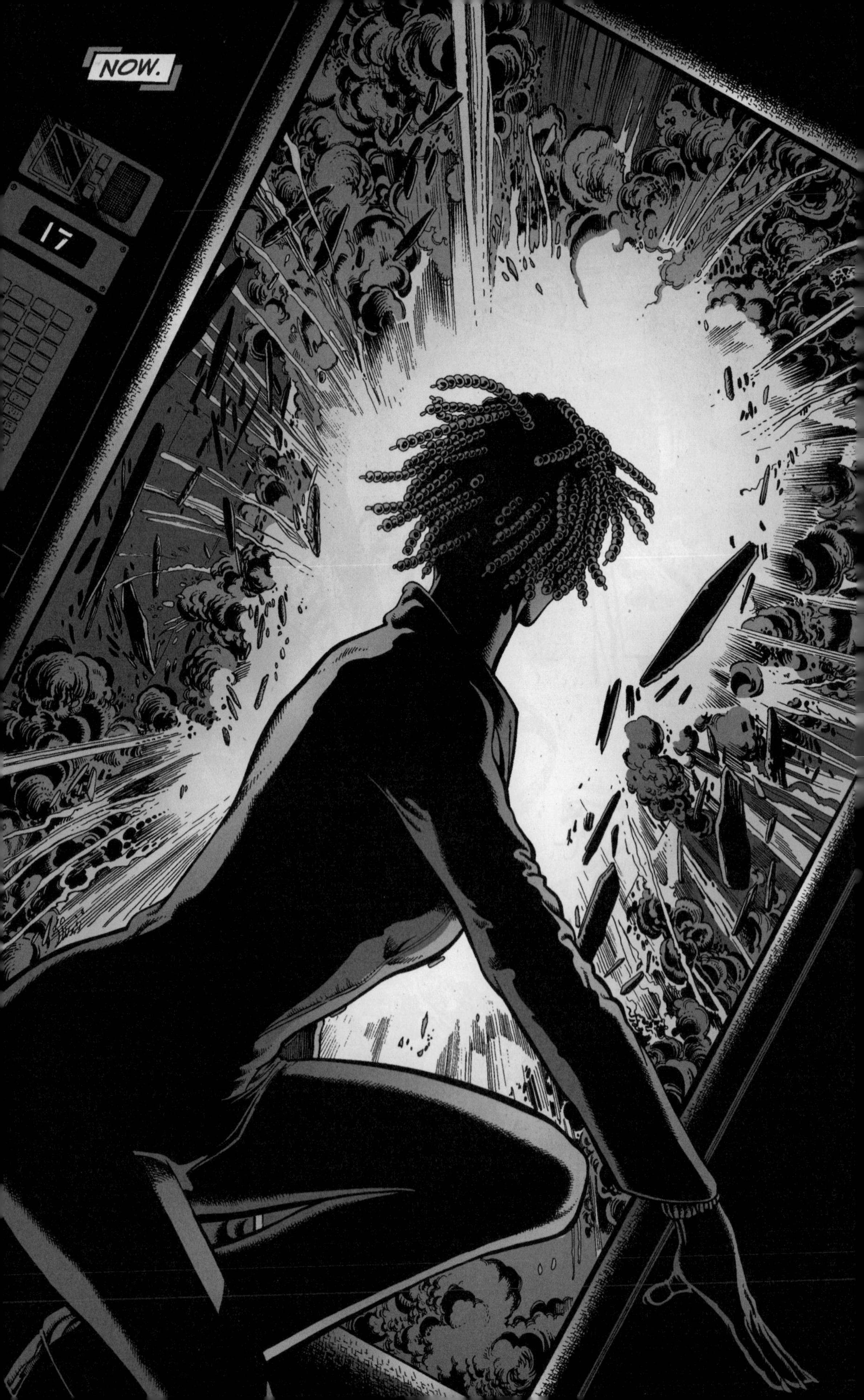
NOW.
17

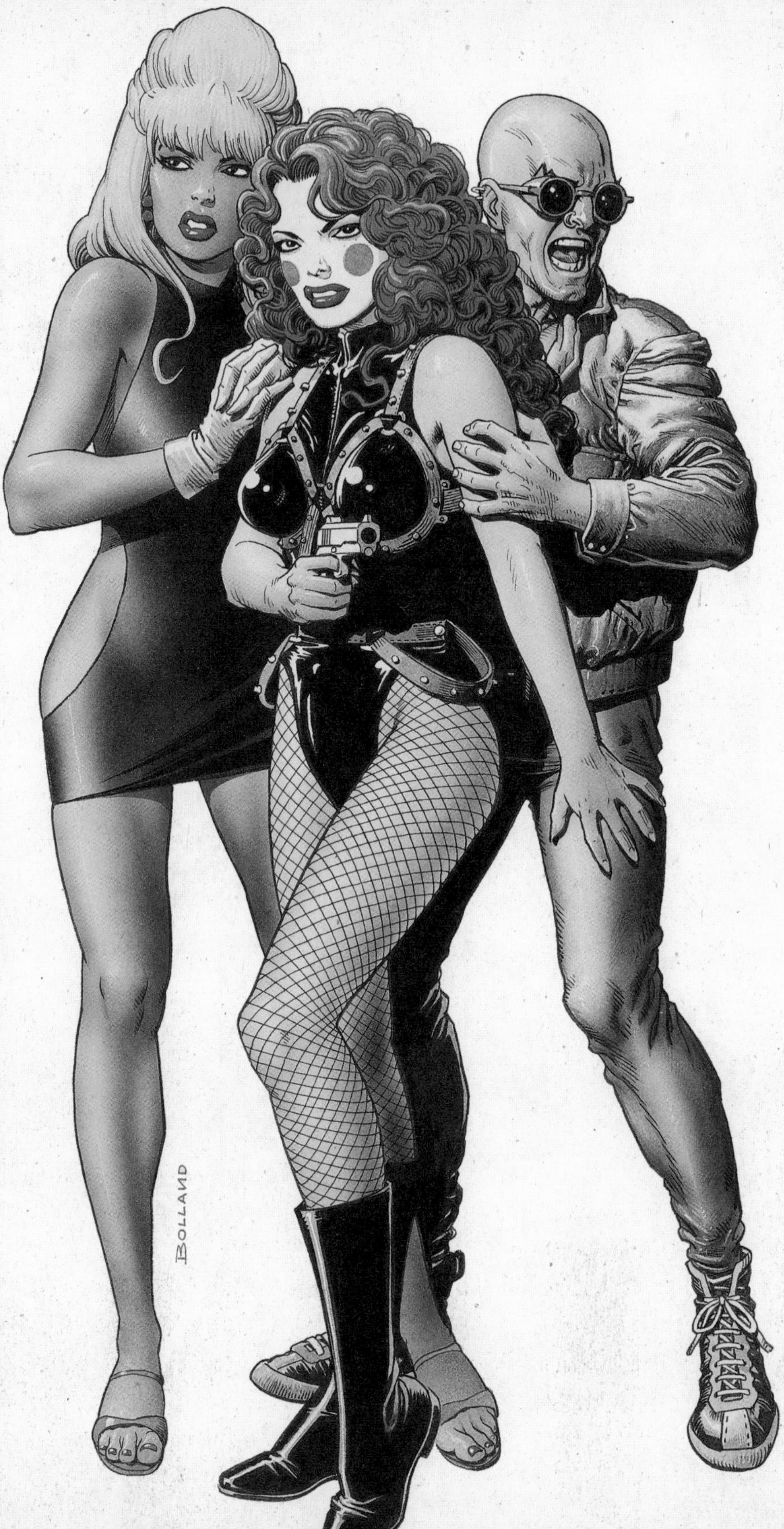
BOLLAND

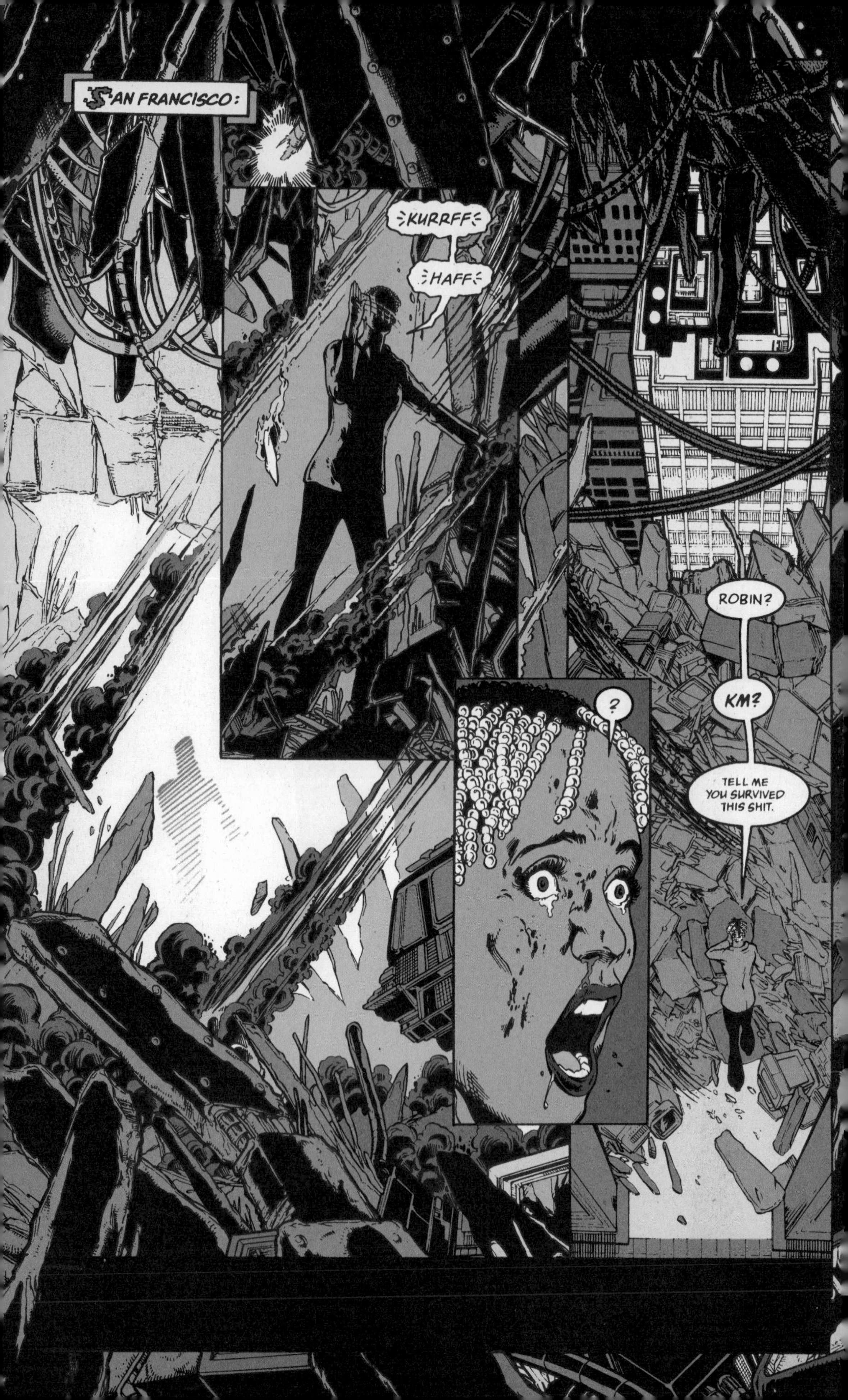
SAN FRANCISCO:
KURRFF
HAFF
?
ROBIN?
KM?
TELL ME YOU SURVIVED THIS SHIT.

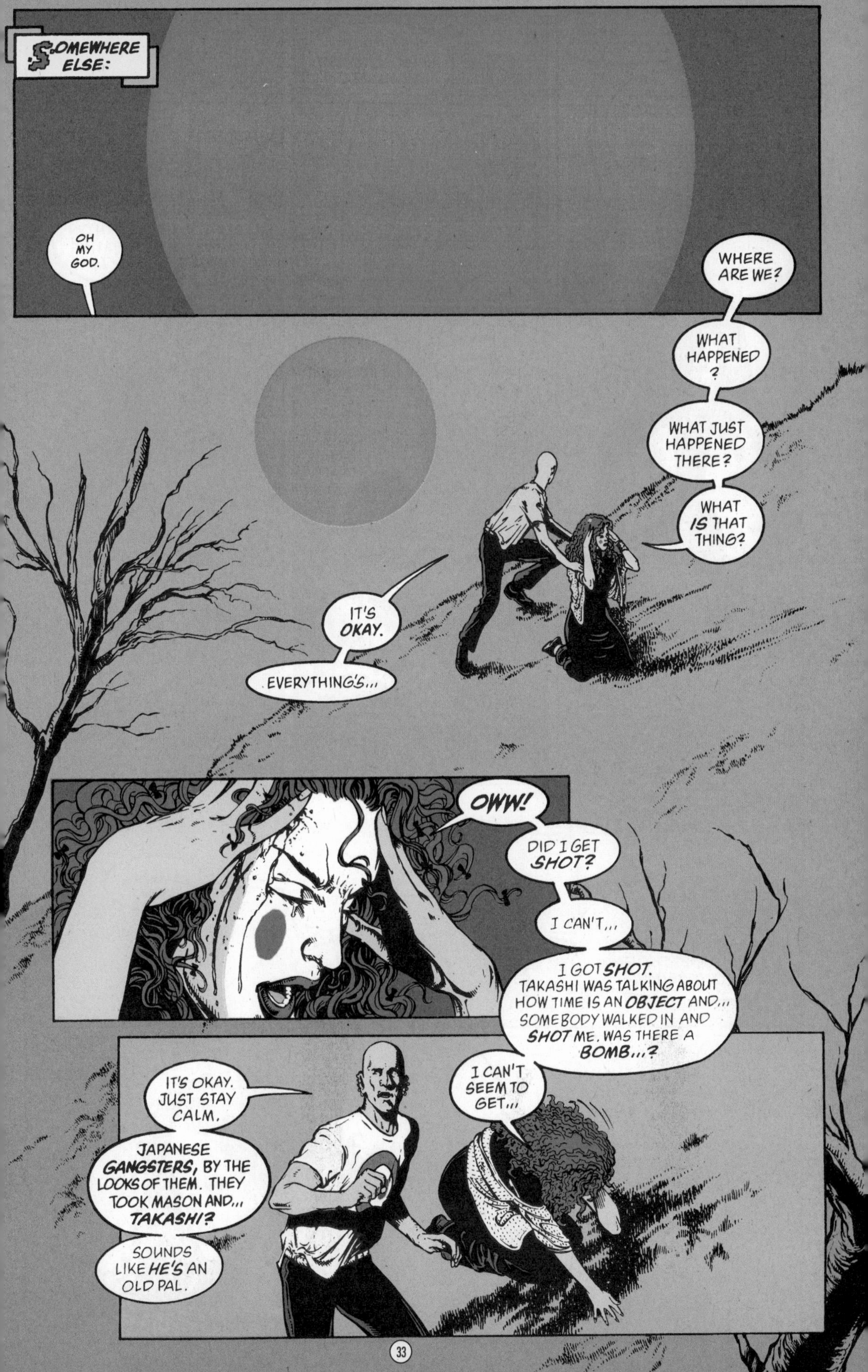
SOMEWHERE ELSE:
OH MY GOD.
WHERE ARE WE?
WHAT HAPPENED?
WHAT JUST HAPPENED THERE?
WHAT IS THAT THING?
IT'S OKAY.
EVERYTHING'S...
OWW!
DID I GET SHOT?
I CAN'T...
I GOT SHOT. TAKASHI WAS TALKING ABOUT HOW TIME IS AN OBJECT AND... SOMEBODY WALKED IN AND SHOT ME. WAS THERE A BOMB...?
I CAN'T SEEM TO GET...
IT'S OKAY. JUST STAY CALM.
JAPANESE GANGSTERS, BY THE LOOKS OF THEM. THEY TOOK MASON AND... TAKASHI?
SOUNDS LIKE HE'S AN OLD PAL.

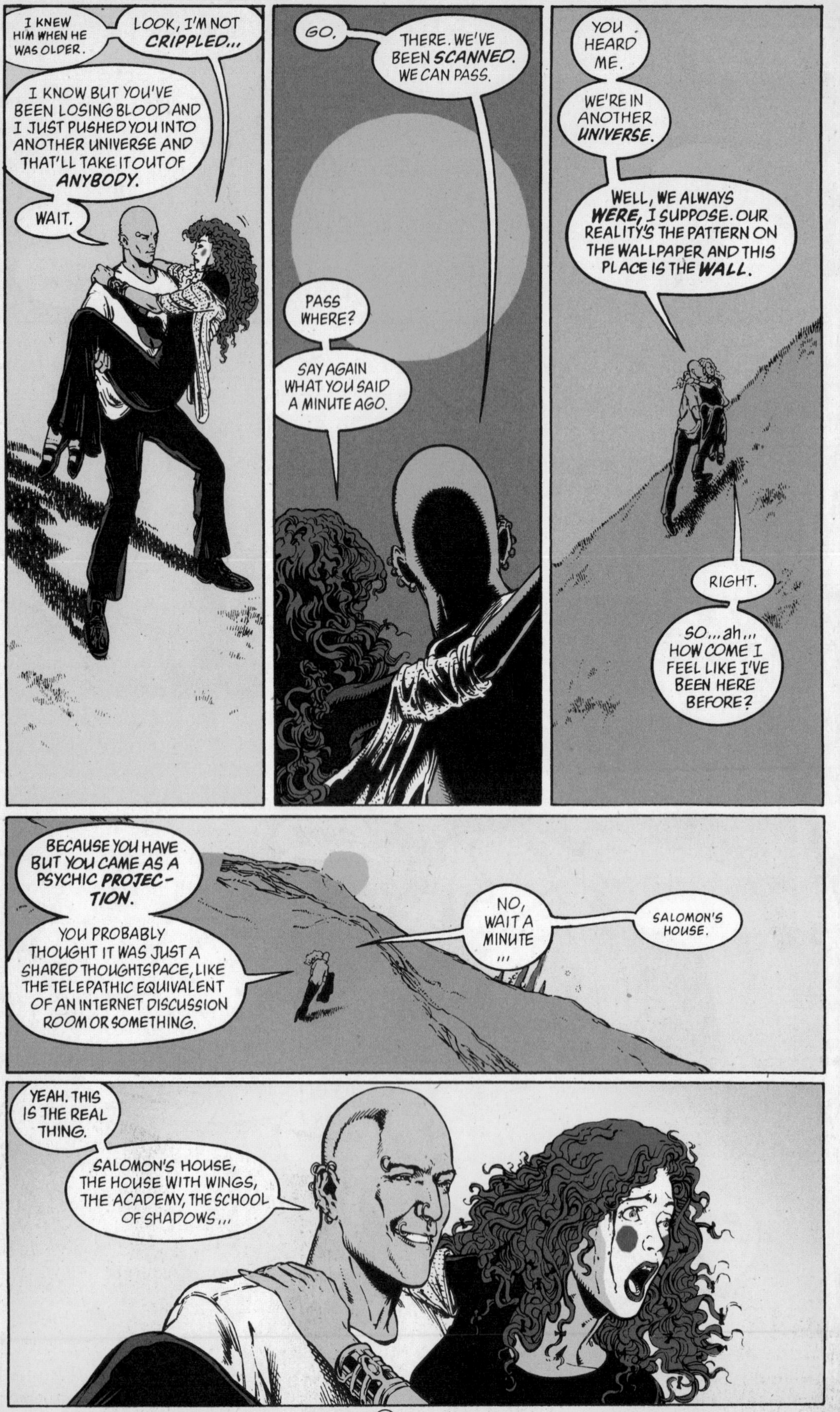

I KNEW HIM WHEN HE WAS OLDER.
LOOK, I'M NOT CRIPPLED...
I KNOW BUT YOU'VE BEEN LOSING BLOOD AND I JUST PUSHED YOU INTO ANOTHER UNIVERSE AND THAT'LL TAKE IT OUT OF ANYBODY.
WAIT.
GO.
THERE. WE'VE BEEN SCANNED. WE CAN PASS.
PASS WHERE?
SAY AGAIN WHAT YOU SAID A MINUTE AGO.
YOU HEARD ME.
WE'RE IN ANOTHER UNIVERSE.
WELL, WE ALWAYS WERE, I SUPPOSE. OUR REALITY'S THE PATTERN ON THE WALLPAPER AND THIS PLACE IS THE WALL.
RIGHT.
SO...ah... HOW COME I FEEL LIKE I'VE BEEN HERE BEFORE?
BECAUSE YOU HAVE BUT YOU CAME AS A PSYCHIC PROJEC-TION.
YOU PROBABLY THOUGHT IT WAS JUST A SHARED THOUGHTSPACE, LIKE THE TELEPATHIC EQUIVALENT OF AN INTERNET DISCUSSION ROOM OR SOMETHING.
NO, WAIT A MINUTE ...
SALOMON'S HOUSE.
YEAH. THIS IS THE REAL THING.
SALOMON'S HOUSE, THE HOUSE WITH WINGS, THE ACADEMY, THE SCHOOL OF SHADOWS...

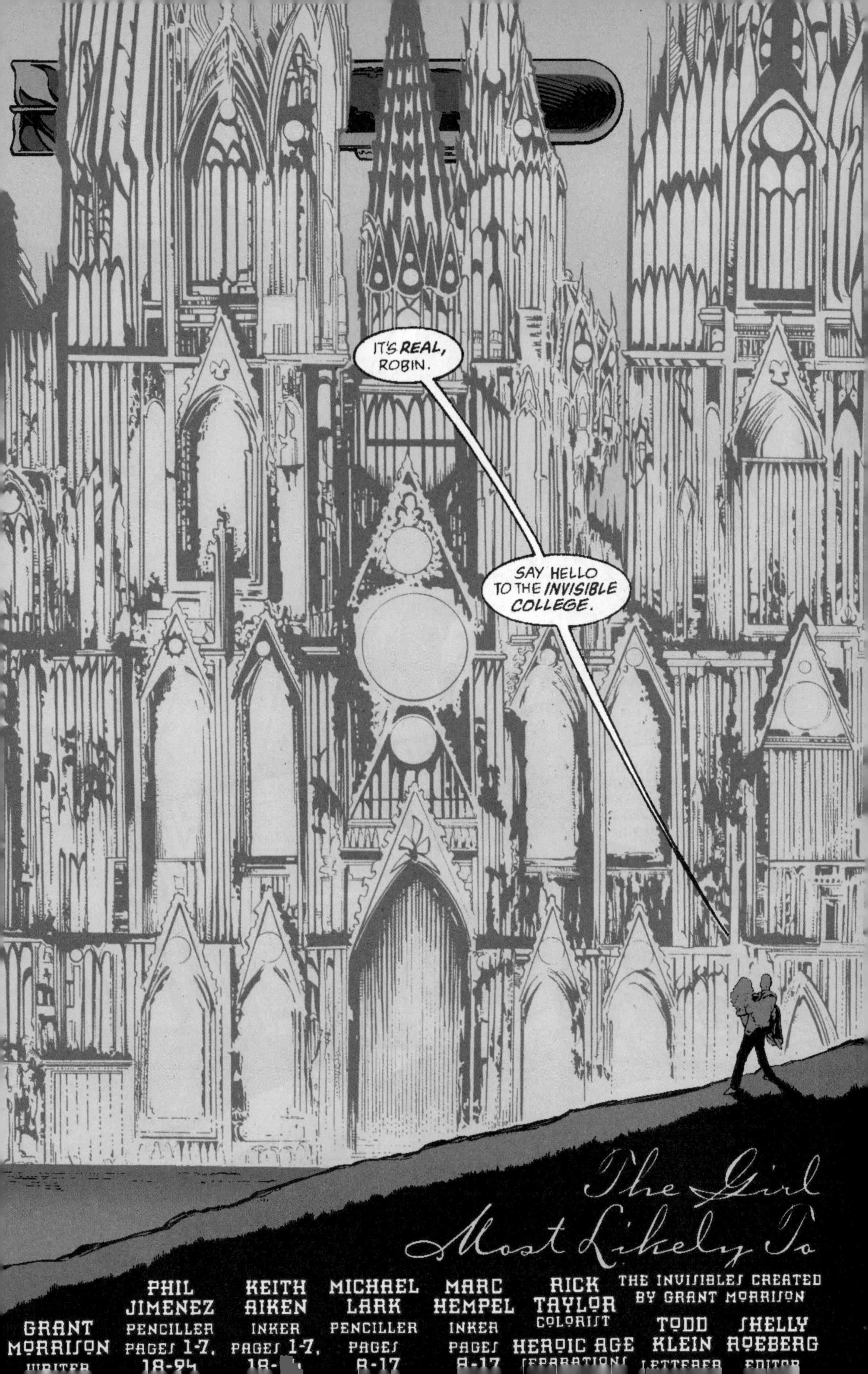
IT'S REAL, ROBIN.
SAY HELLO TO THE INVISIBLE COLLEGE.
The Girl Most Likely To
PHIL JIMENEZ PENCILLER PAGES 1-7,
KEITH AIKEN INKER PAGES 1-7,
MICHAEL LARK PENCILLER PAGES
MARC HEMPEL INKER PAGES
RICK TAYLOR COLORIST
HEROIC AGE
THE INVISIBLES CREATED BY GRANT MORRISON
GRANT MORRISON
TODD KLEIN
SHELLY ROEBERG

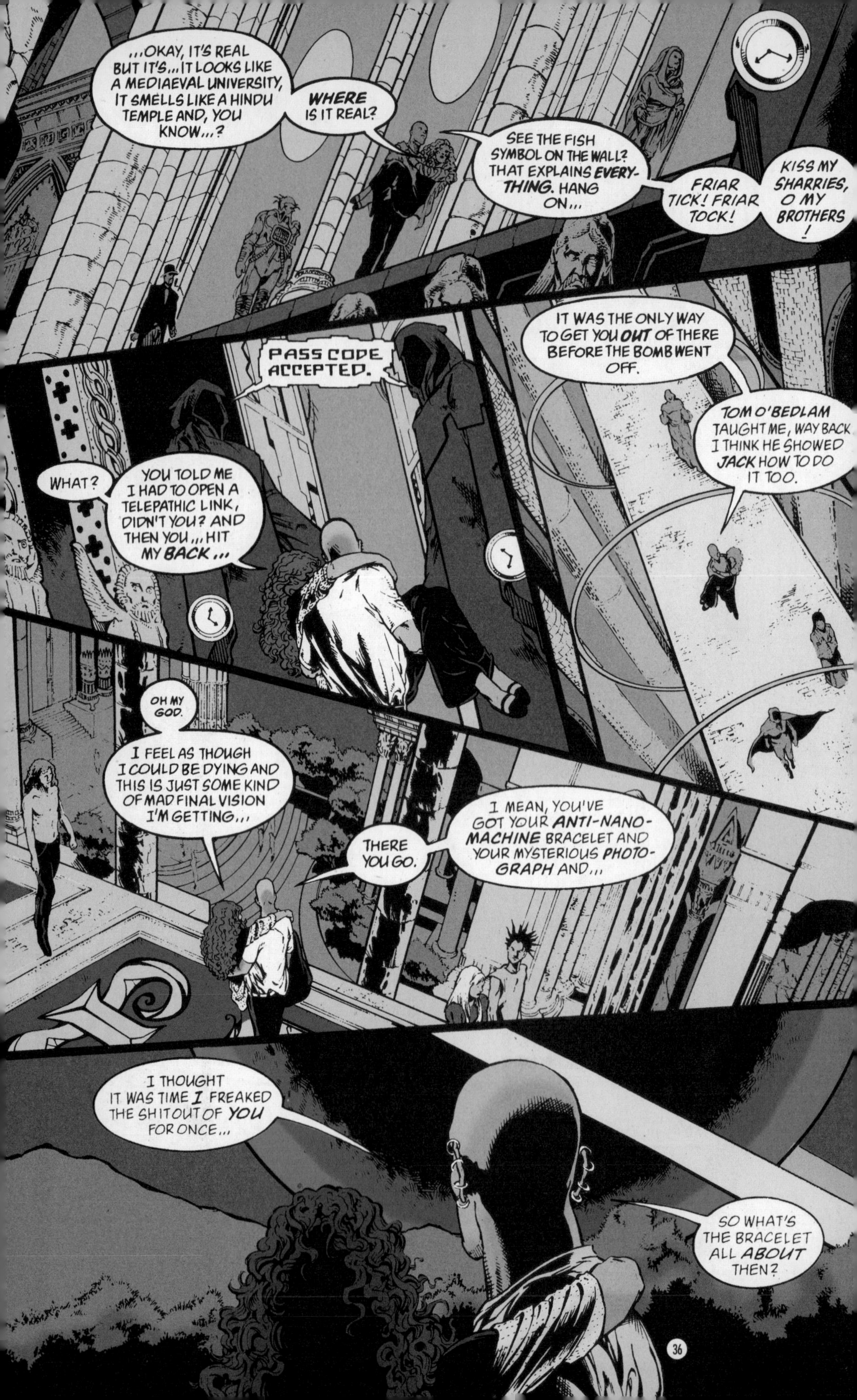
...OKAY, IT'S REAL BUT IT'S... IT LOOKS LIKE A MEDIAEVAL UNIVERSITY, IT SMELLS LIKE A HINDU TEMPLE AND, YOU KNOW...?
WHERE IS IT REAL?
SEE THE FISH SYMBOL ON THE WALL? THAT EXPLAINS EVERY-THING. HANG ON...
FRIAR TICK! FRIAR TOCK!
KISS MY SHARRIES, O MY BROTHERS!
PASS CODE ACCEPTED.
WHAT?
YOU TOLD ME I HAD TO OPEN A TELEPATHIC LINK, DIDN'T YOU? AND THEN YOU... HIT MY BACK...
IT WAS THE ONLY WAY TO GET YOU OUT OF THERE BEFORE THE BOMB WENT OFF.
TOM O'BEDLAM TAUGHT ME, WAY BACK I THINK HE SHOWED JACK HOW TO DO IT TOO.
OH MY GOD.
I FEEL AS THOUGH I COULD BE DYING AND THIS IS JUST SOME KIND OF MAD FINAL VISION I'M GETTING...
THERE YOU GO.
I MEAN, YOU'VE GOT YOUR ANTI-NANO-MACHINE BRACELET AND YOUR MYSTERIOUS PHOTO-GRAPH AND...
I THOUGHT IT WAS TIME I FREAKED THE SHIT OUT OF YOU FOR ONCE...
SO WHAT'S THE BRACELET ALL ABOUT THEN?

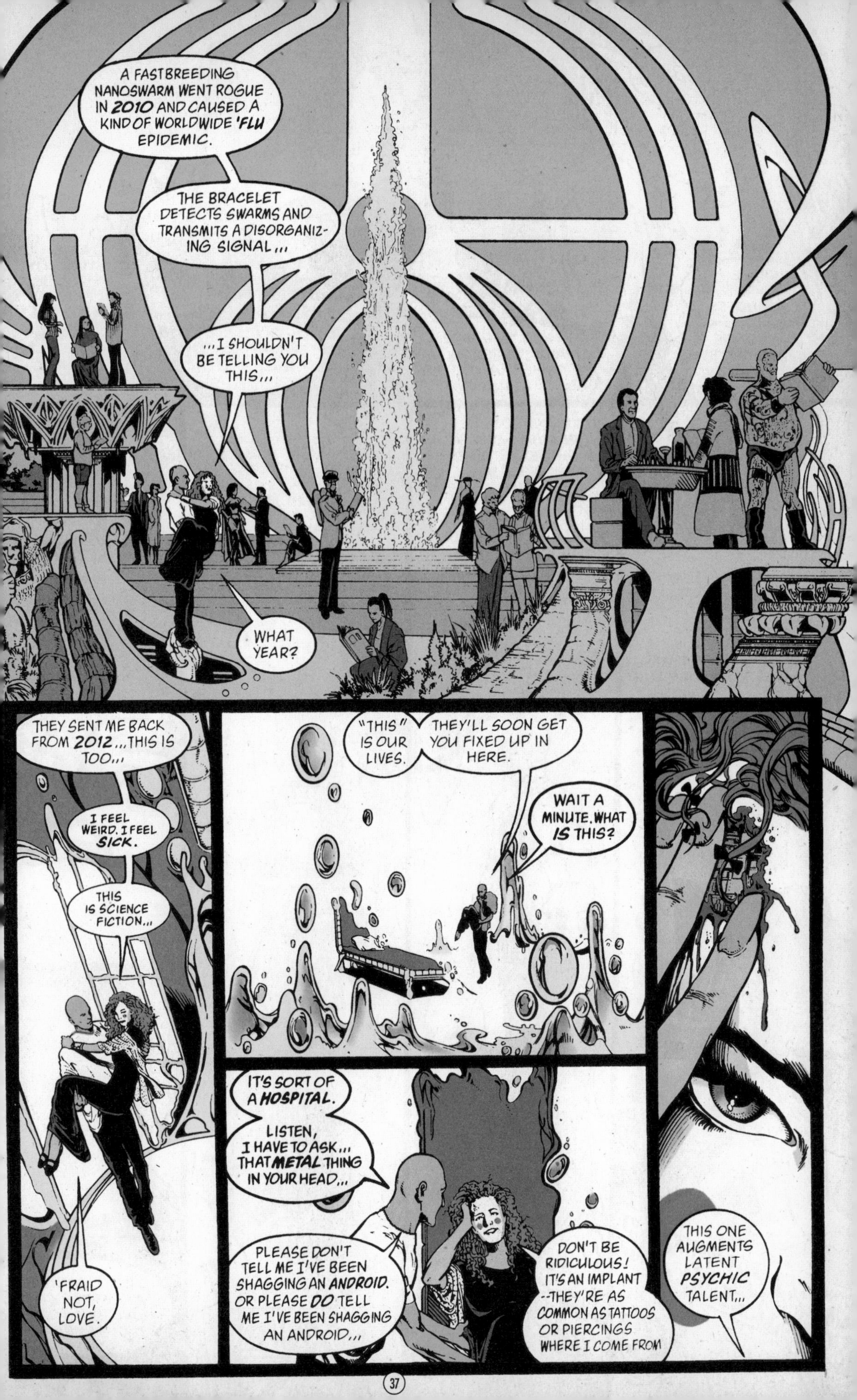
A FASTBREEDING NANOSWARM WENT ROGUE IN 2010 AND CAUSED A KIND OF WORLDWIDE 'FLU EPIDEMIC.
THE BRACELET DETECTS SWARMS AND TRANSMITS A DISORGANIZ-ING SIGNAL...
...I SHOULDN'T BE TELLING YOU THIS...
WHAT YEAR?
THEY SENT ME BACK FROM 2012... THIS IS TOO...
I FEEL WEIRD. I FEEL SICK.
THIS IS SCIENCE FICTION...
'FRAID NOT, LOVE.
"THIS" IS OUR LIVES.
THEY'LL SOON GET YOU FIXED UP IN HERE.
WAIT A MINUTE. WHAT IS THIS?
IT'S SORT OF A HOSPITAL.
LISTEN, I HAVE TO ASK... THAT METAL THING IN YOUR HEAD...
PLEASE DON'T TELL ME I'VE BEEN SHAGGING AN ANDROID. OR PLEASE DO TELL ME I'VE BEEN SHAGGING AN ANDROID...
DON'T BE RIDICULOUS! IT'S AN IMPLANT --THEY'RE AS COMMON AS TATTOOS OR PIERCINGS WHERE I COME FROM
THIS ONE AUGMENTS LATENT PSYCHIC TALENT...

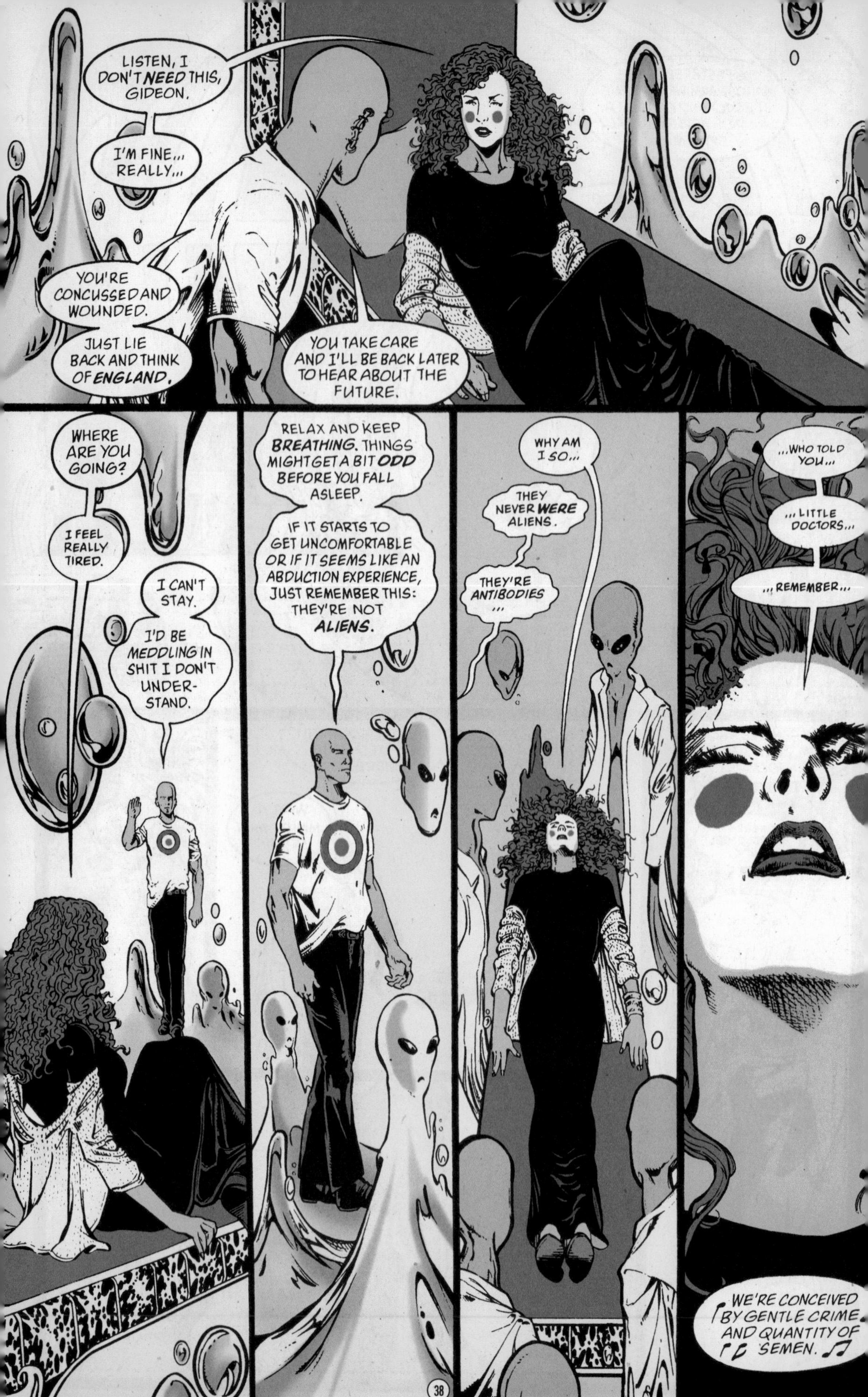
LISTEN, I DON'T NEED THIS, GIDEON.
I'M FINE... REALLY...
YOU'RE CONCUSSED AND WOUNDED.
JUST LIE BACK AND THINK OF ENGLAND.
YOU TAKE CARE AND I'LL BE BACK LATER TO HEAR ABOUT THE FUTURE.
WHERE ARE YOU GOING?
I FEEL REALLY TIRED.
I CAN'T STAY.
I'D BE MEDDLING IN SHIT I DON'T UNDER-STAND.
RELAX AND KEEP BREATHING. THINGS MIGHT GET A BIT ODD BEFORE YOU FALL ASLEEP.
IF IT STARTS TO GET UNCOMFORTABLE OR IF IT SEEMS LIKE AN ABDUCTION EXPERIENCE, JUST REMEMBER THIS: THEY'RE NOT ALIENS.
WHY AM I SO...
THEY NEVER WERE ALIENS.
THEY'RE ANTIBODIES ...
...WHO TOLD YOU...
...LITTLE DOCTORS...
...REMEMBER...
WE'RE CONCEIVED BY GENTLE CRIME AND QUANTITY OF SEMEN.

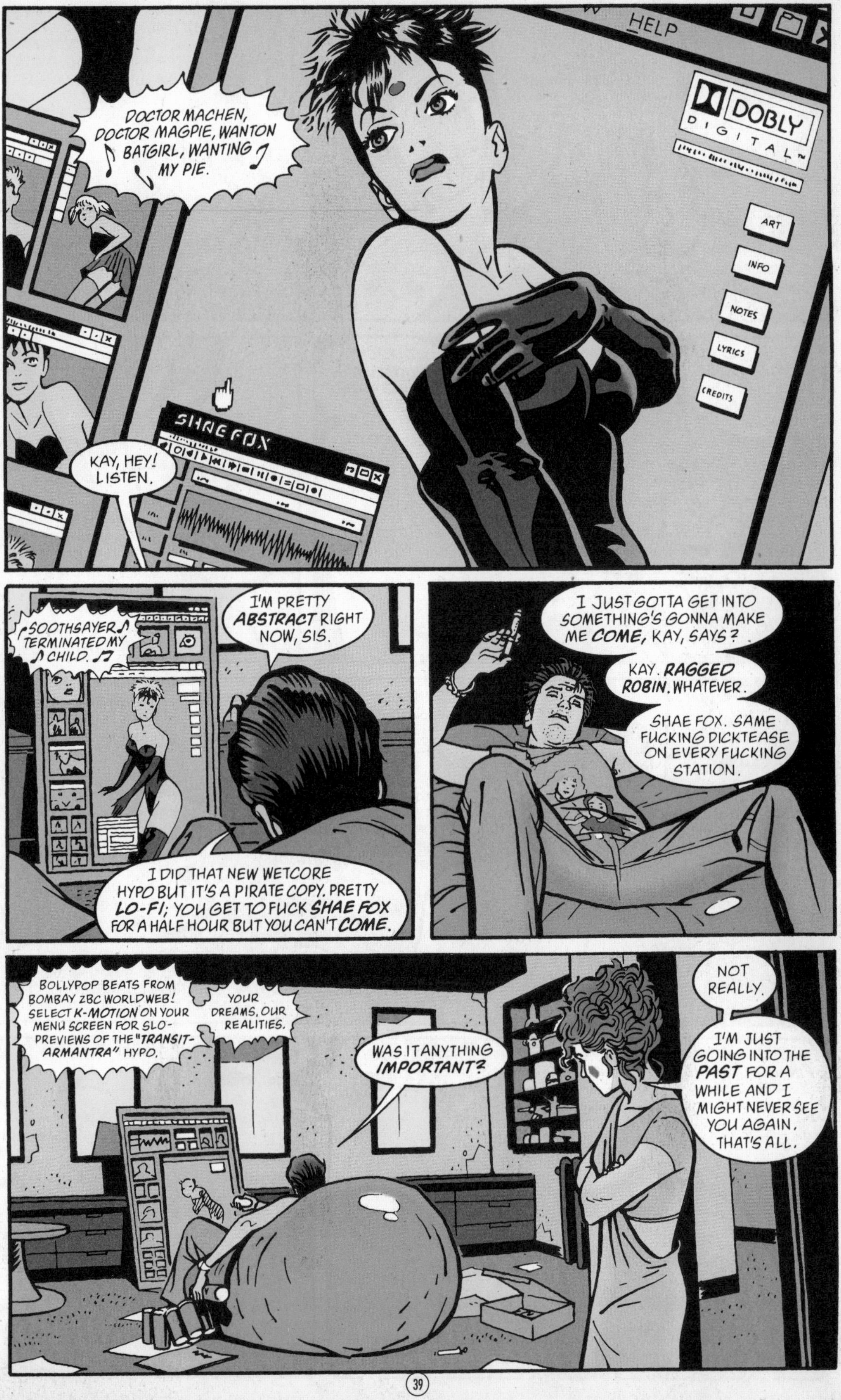
HELP
DOBLY DIGITAL™
DOCTOR MACHEN, DOCTOR MAGPIE, WANTON BATGIRL, WANTING MY PIE.
ART
INFO
NOTES
LYRICS
CREDITS
SHAE FOX
KAY, HEY! LISTEN.
SOOTHSAYER TERMINATED MY CHILD.
I'M PRETTY ABSTRACT RIGHT NOW, SIS.
I DID THAT NEW WETCORE HYPO BUT IT'S A PIRATE COPY. PRETTY LO-FI; YOU GET TO FUCK SHAE FOX FOR A HALF HOUR BUT YOU CAN'T COME.
I JUST GOTTA GET INTO SOMETHING'S GONNA MAKE ME COME, KAY, SAYS?
KAY. RAGGED ROBIN. WHATEVER.
SHAE FOX. SAME FUCKING DICKTEASE ON EVERY FUCKING STATION.
BOLLYPOP BEATS FROM BOMBAY ZBC WORLDWEB! SELECT K-MOTION ON YOUR MENU SCREEN FOR SLO-PREVIEWS OF THE "TRANSIT-ARMANTRA" HYPO.
YOUR DREAMS, OUR REALITIES.
WAS IT ANYTHING IMPORTANT?
NOT REALLY.
I'M JUST GOING INTO THE PAST FOR A WHILE AND I MIGHT NEVER SEE YOU AGAIN. THAT'S ALL.

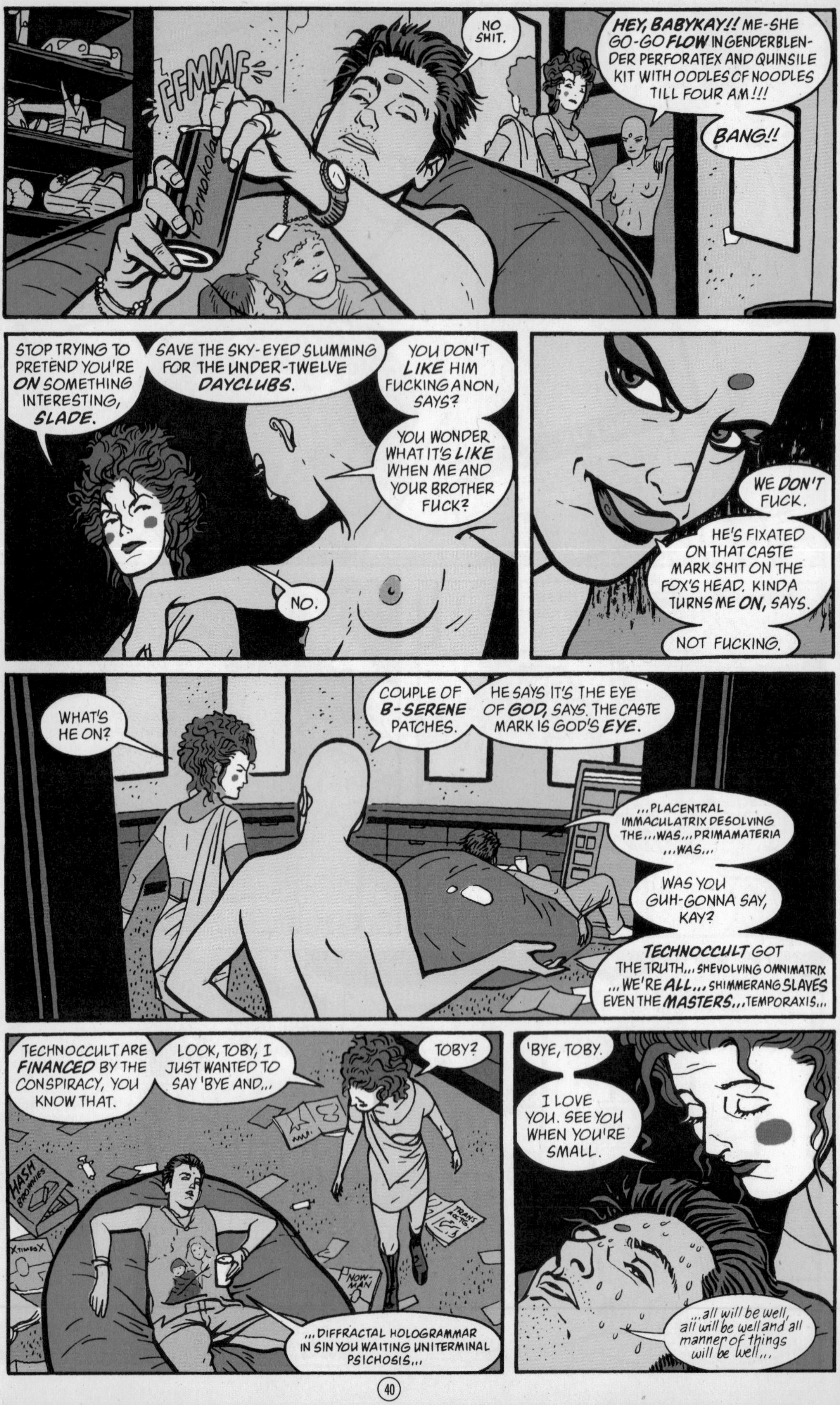
FFMMF
NO SHIT.
HEY, BABYKAY!! ME-SHE GO-GO FLOW IN GENDERBLENDER PERFORATEX AND QUINSILE KIT WITH OODLES OF NOODLES TILL FOUR AM!!!
BANG!!
STOP TRYING TO PRETEND YOU'RE ON SOMETHING INTERESTING, SLADE.
SAVE THE SKY-EYED SLUMMING FOR THE UNDER-TWELVE DAYCLUBS.
YOU DON'T LIKE HIM FUCKING A NON, SAYS?
YOU WONDER WHAT IT'S LIKE WHEN ME AND YOUR BROTHER FUCK?
NO.
WE DON'T FUCK.
HE'S FIXATED ON THAT CASTE MARK SHIT ON THE FOX'S HEAD. KINDA TURNS ME ON, SAYS.
NOT FUCKING.
WHAT'S HE ON?
COUPLE OF B-SERENE PATCHES.
HE SAYS IT'S THE EYE OF GOD, SAYS. THE CASTE MARK IS GOD'S EYE.
...PLACENTRAL IMMACULATRIX DESOLVING THE...WAS...PRIMAMATERIA ...WAS...
WAS YOU GUH-GONNA SAY, KAY?
TECHNOCCULT GOT THE TRUTH... SHEVOLVING OMNIMATRIX ...WE'RE ALL... SHIMMERANG SLAVES EVEN THE MASTERS...TEMPORAXIS...
TECHNOCCULT ARE FINANCED BY THE CONSPIRACY, YOU KNOW THAT.
LOOK, TOBY, I JUST WANTED TO SAY 'BYE AND...
TOBY?
HASH BROWNIES
TRANS ACTS
NOW-MAN
...DIFFRACTAL HOLOGRAMMAR IN SIN YOU WAITING UNITERMINAL PSICHOSIS...
'BYE, TOBY.
I LOVE YOU. SEE YOU WHEN YOU'RE SMALL.
...all will be well, all will be well and all manner of things will be well...

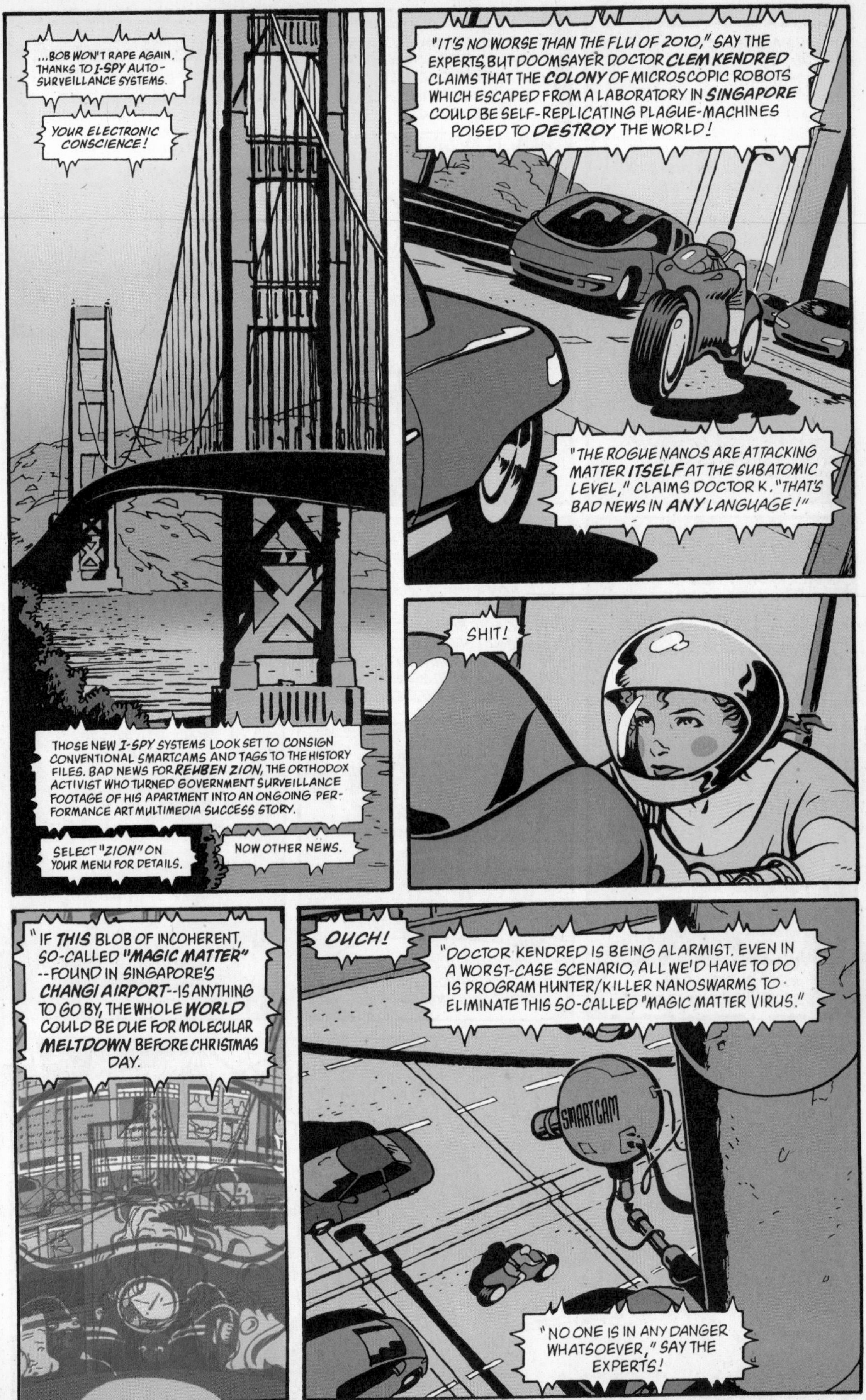
...BOB WON'T RAPE AGAIN, THANKS TO I-SPY AUTO-SURVEILLANCE SYSTEMS.
YOUR ELECTRONIC CONSCIENCE!
THOSE NEW I-SPY SYSTEMS LOOK SET TO CONSIGN CONVENTIONAL SMARTCAMS AND TAGS TO THE HISTORY FILES. BAD NEWS FOR REUBEN ZION, THE ORTHODOX ACTIVIST WHO TURNED GOVERNMENT SURVEILLANCE FOOTAGE OF HIS APARTMENT INTO AN ONGOING PERFORMANCE ART MULTIMEDIA SUCCESS STORY.
SELECT "ZION" ON YOUR MENU FOR DETAILS.
NOW OTHER NEWS.
"IT'S NO WORSE THAN THE FLU OF 2010," SAY THE EXPERTS, BUT DOOMSAYER DOCTOR CLEM KENDRED CLAIMS THAT THE COLONY OF MICROSCOPIC ROBOTS WHICH ESCAPED FROM A LABORATORY IN SINGAPORE COULD BE SELF-REPLICATING PLAGUE-MACHINES POISED TO DESTROY THE WORLD!
"THE ROGUE NANOS ARE ATTACKING MATTER ITSELF AT THE SUBATOMIC LEVEL," CLAIMS DOCTOR K. "THAT'S BAD NEWS IN ANY LANGUAGE!"
SHIT!
"IF THIS BLOB OF INCOHERENT, SO-CALLED "MAGIC MATTER" --FOUND IN SINGAPORE'S CHANGI AIRPORT--IS ANYTHING TO GO BY, THE WHOLE WORLD COULD BE DUE FOR MOLECULAR MELTDOWN BEFORE CHRISTMAS DAY.
OUCH!
"DOCTOR KENDRED IS BEING ALARMIST. EVEN IN A WORST-CASE SCENARIO, ALL WE'D HAVE TO DO IS PROGRAM HUNTER/KILLER NANOSWARMS TO ELIMINATE THIS SO-CALLED "MAGIC MATTER VIRUS."
SMARTCAM
"NO ONE IS IN ANY DANGER WHATSOEVER," SAY THE EXPERTS!

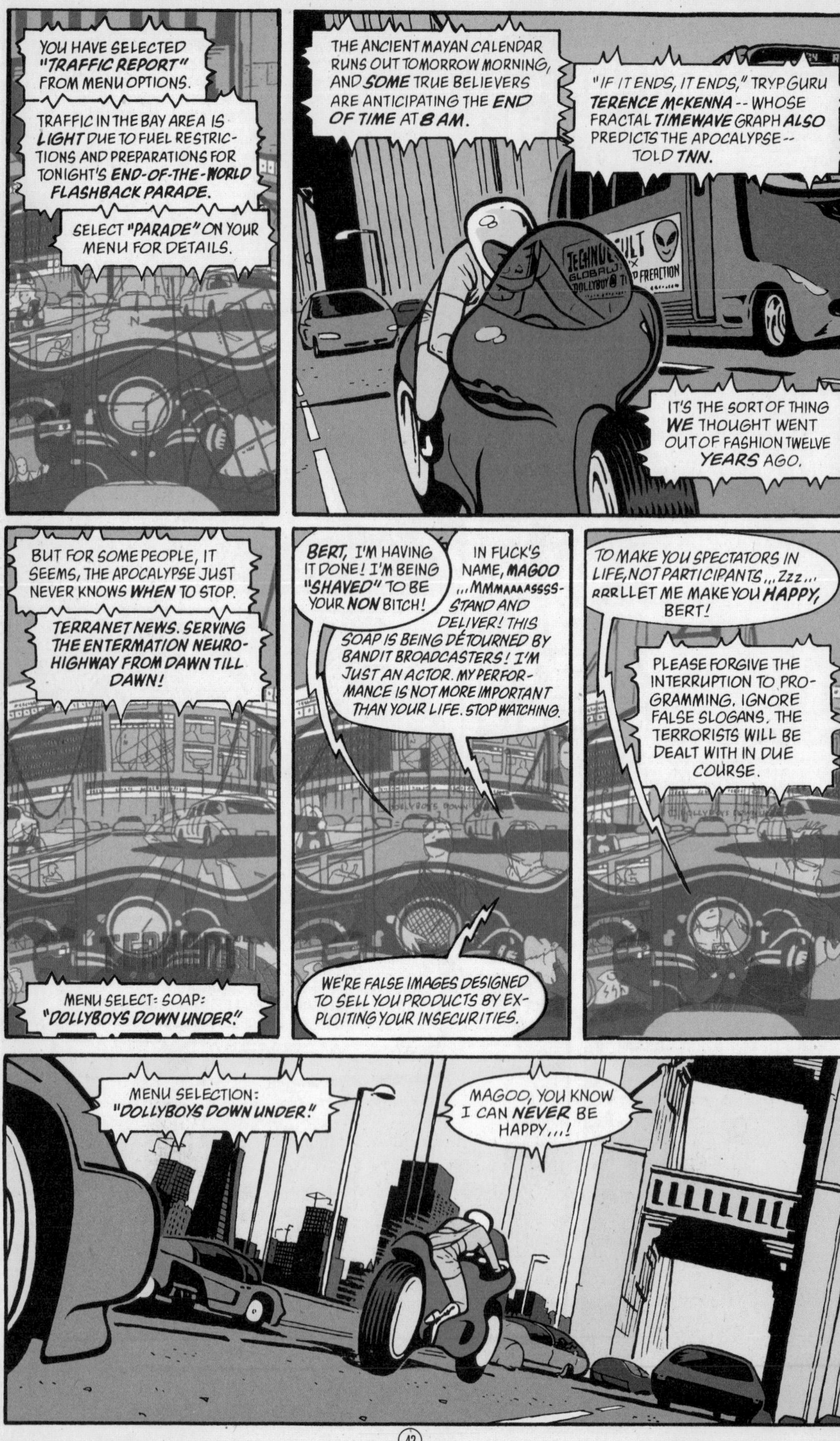
YOU HAVE SELECTED "TRAFFIC REPORT" FROM MENU OPTIONS.
TRAFFIC IN THE BAY AREA IS LIGHT DUE TO FUEL RESTRICTIONS AND PREPARATIONS FOR TONIGHT'S END-OF-THE-WORLD FLASHBACK PARADE.
SELECT "PARADE" ON YOUR MENU FOR DETAILS.
THE ANCIENT MAYAN CALENDAR RUNS OUT TOMORROW MORNING, AND SOME TRUE BELIEVERS ARE ANTICIPATING THE END OF TIME AT 8 AM.
"IF IT ENDS, IT ENDS," TRYP GURU TERENCE McKENNA -- WHOSE FRACTAL TIMEWAVE GRAPH ALSO PREDICTS THE APOCALYPSE -- TOLD TNN.
IT'S THE SORT OF THING WE THOUGHT WENT OUT OF FASHION TWELVE YEARS AGO.
BUT FOR SOME PEOPLE, IT SEEMS, THE APOCALYPSE JUST NEVER KNOWS WHEN TO STOP.
TERRANET NEWS. SERVING THE ENTERMATION NEURO-HIGHWAY FROM DAWN TILL DAWN!
MENU SELECT: SOAP: "DOLLYBOYS DOWN UNDER."
BERT, I'M HAVING IT DONE! I'M BEING "SHAVED" TO BE YOUR NON BITCH!
IN FUCK'S NAME, MAGOO ...MMMAAAAASSSS-STAND AND DELIVER! THIS SOAP IS BEING DÉTOURNED BY BANDIT BROADCASTERS! I'M JUST AN ACTOR. MY PERFORMANCE IS NOT MORE IMPORTANT THAN YOUR LIFE. STOP WATCHING.
WE'RE FALSE IMAGES DESIGNED TO SELL YOU PRODUCTS BY EXPLOITING YOUR INSECURITIES.
TO MAKE YOU SPECTATORS IN LIFE, NOT PARTICIPANTS... Zzz... RRRLLET ME MAKE YOU HAPPY, BERT!
PLEASE FORGIVE THE INTERRUPTION TO PROGRAMMING. IGNORE FALSE SLOGANS. THE TERRORISTS WILL BE DEALT WITH IN DUE COURSE.
MENU SELECTION: "DOLLYBOYS DOWN UNDER."
MAGOO, YOU KNOW I CAN NEVER BE HAPPY...!

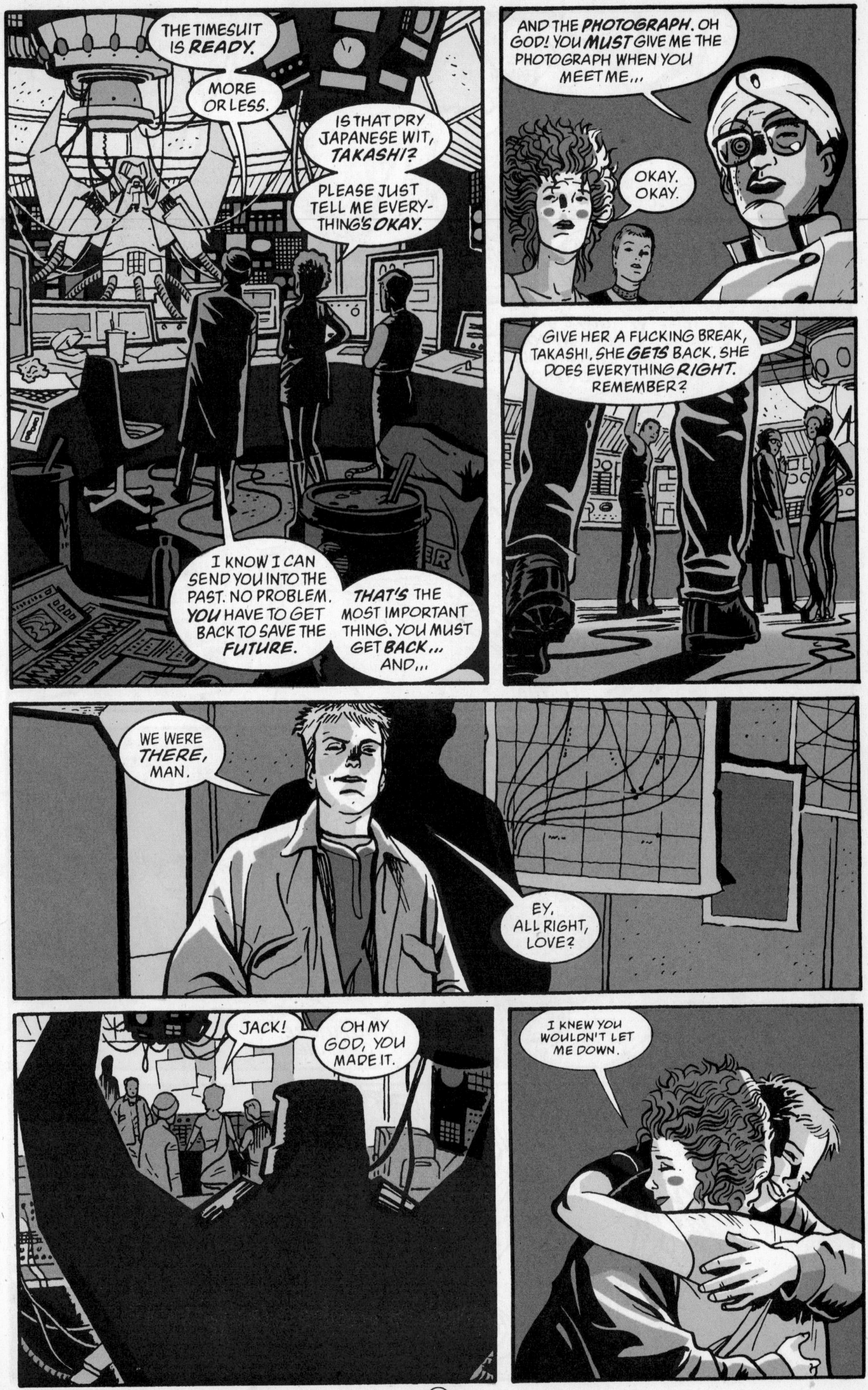
THE TIMESUIT IS READY.
MORE OR LESS.
IS THAT DRY JAPANESE WIT, TAKASHI?
PLEASE JUST TELL ME EVERY-THING'S OKAY.
I KNOW I CAN SEND YOU INTO THE PAST. NO PROBLEM. YOU HAVE TO GET BACK TO SAVE THE FUTURE.
THAT'S THE MOST IMPORTANT THING. YOU MUST GET BACK... AND...
AND THE PHOTOGRAPH. OH GOD! YOU MUST GIVE ME THE PHOTOGRAPH WHEN YOU MEET ME...
OKAY. OKAY.
GIVE HER A FUCKING BREAK, TAKASHI. SHE GETS BACK. SHE DOES EVERYTHING RIGHT. REMEMBER?
WE WERE THERE, MAN.
EY, ALL RIGHT, LOVE?
JACK!
OH MY GOD, YOU MADE IT.
I KNEW YOU WOULDN'T LET ME DOWN.

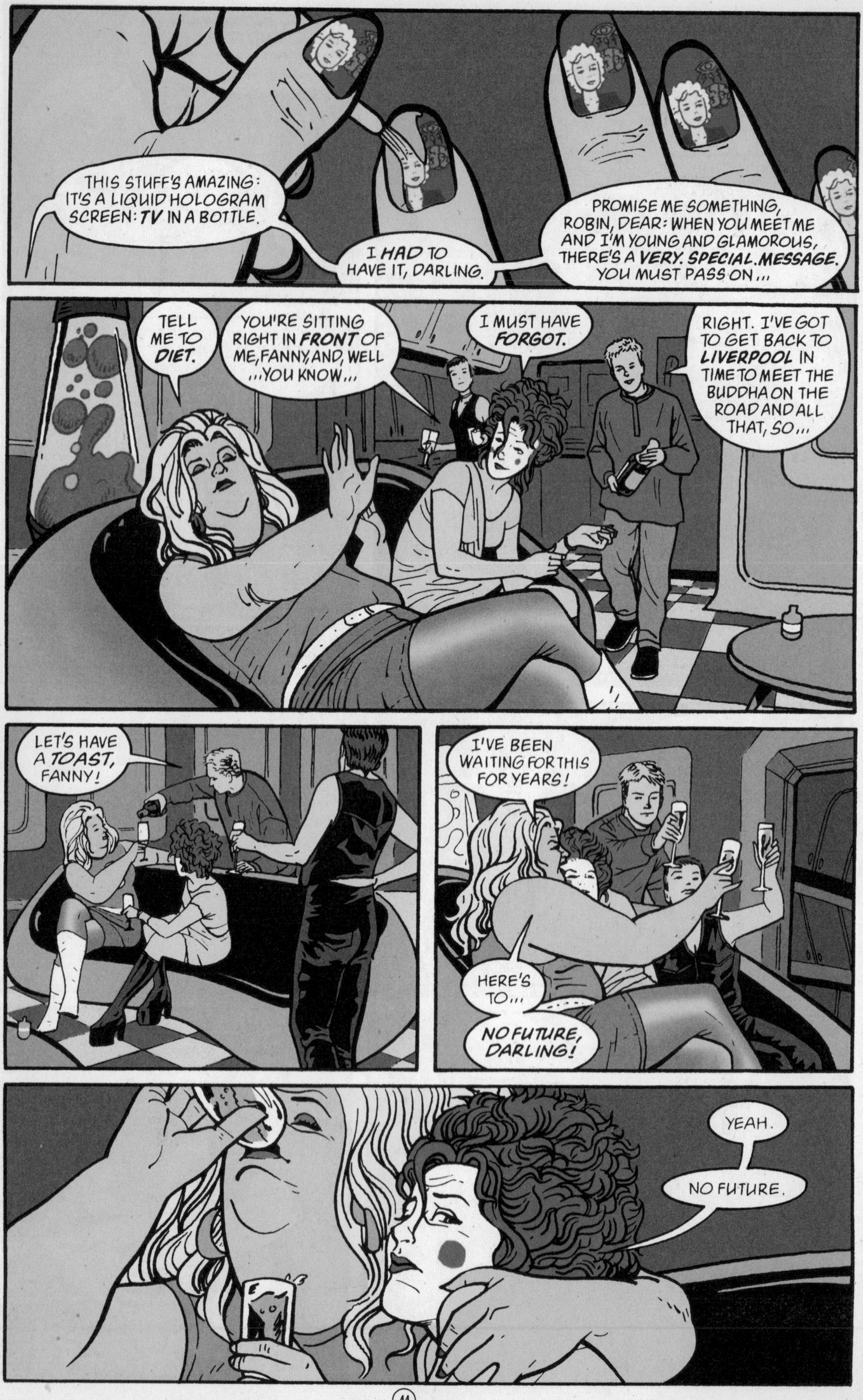

THIS STUFF'S AMAZING: IT'S A LIQUID HOLOGRAM SCREEN: TV IN A BOTTLE.
I HAD TO HAVE IT, DARLING.
PROMISE ME SOMETHING, ROBIN, DEAR: WHEN YOU MEET ME AND I'M YOUNG AND GLAMOROUS, THERE'S A VERY. SPECIAL. MESSAGE. YOU MUST PASS ON...
TELL ME TO DIET.
YOU'RE SITTING RIGHT IN FRONT OF ME, FANNY, AND, WELL ...YOU KNOW...
I MUST HAVE FORGOT.
RIGHT. I'VE GOT TO GET BACK TO LIVERPOOL IN TIME TO MEET THE BUDDHA ON THE ROAD AND ALL THAT, SO...
LET'S HAVE A TOAST, FANNY!
I'VE BEEN WAITING FOR THIS FOR YEARS!
HERE'S TO...
NO FUTURE, DARLING!
YEAH.
NO FUTURE.

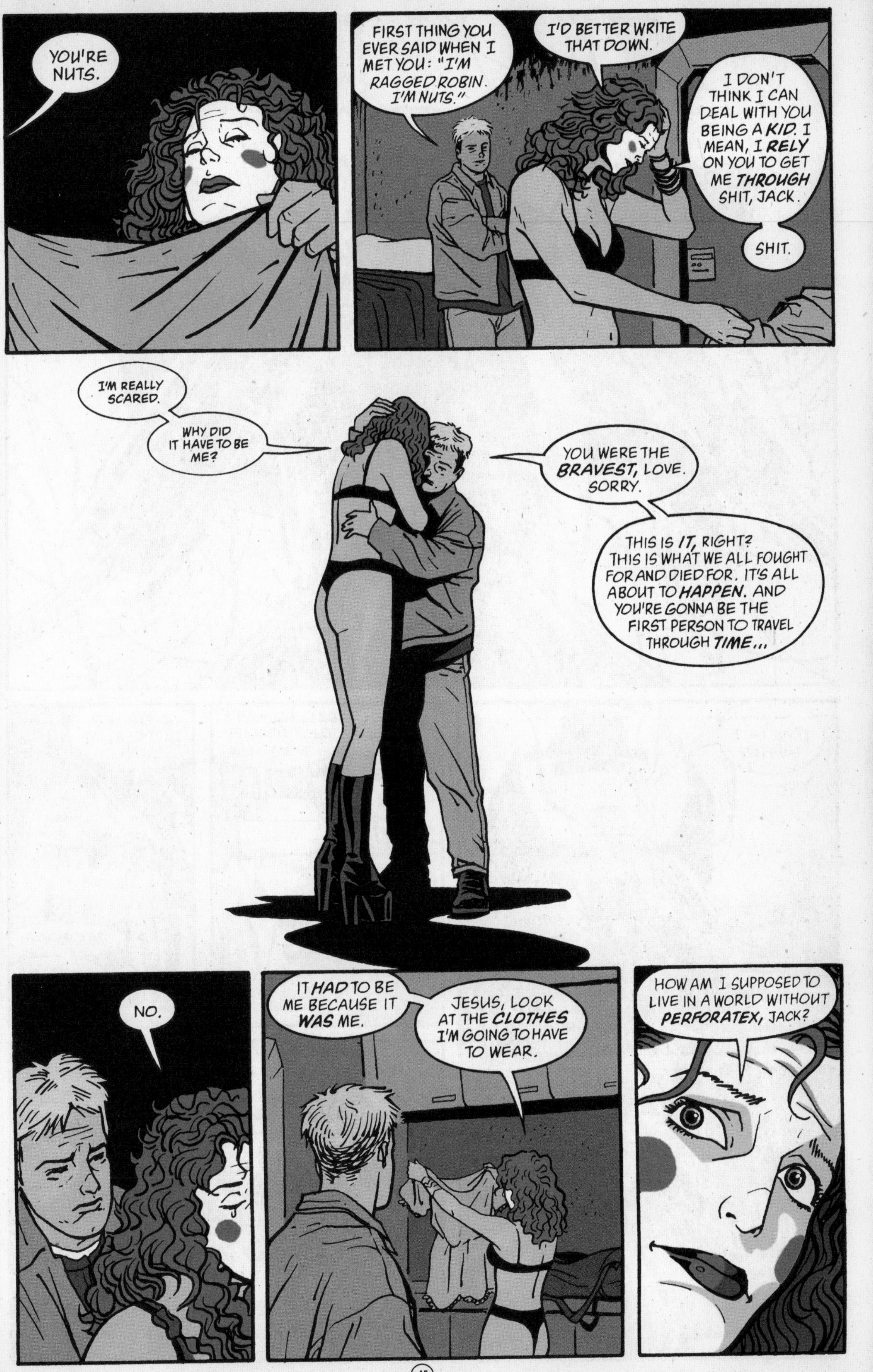
YOU'RE NUTS.
FIRST THING YOU EVER SAID WHEN I MET YOU: "I'M RAGGED ROBIN. I'M NUTS."
I'D BETTER WRITE THAT DOWN.
I DON'T THINK I CAN DEAL WITH YOU BEING A KID. I MEAN, I RELY ON YOU TO GET ME THROUGH SHIT, JACK.
SHIT.
I'M REALLY SCARED.
WHY DID IT HAVE TO BE ME?
YOU WERE THE BRAVEST, LOVE. SORRY.
THIS IS IT, RIGHT? THIS IS WHAT WE ALL FOUGHT FOR AND DIED FOR. IT'S ALL ABOUT TO HAPPEN. AND YOU'RE GONNA BE THE FIRST PERSON TO TRAVEL THROUGH TIME...
NO.
IT HAD TO BE ME BECAUSE IT WAS ME.
JESUS, LOOK AT THE CLOTHES I'M GOING TO HAVE TO WEAR.
HOW AM I SUPPOSED TO LIVE IN A WORLD WITHOUT PERFORATEX, JACK?

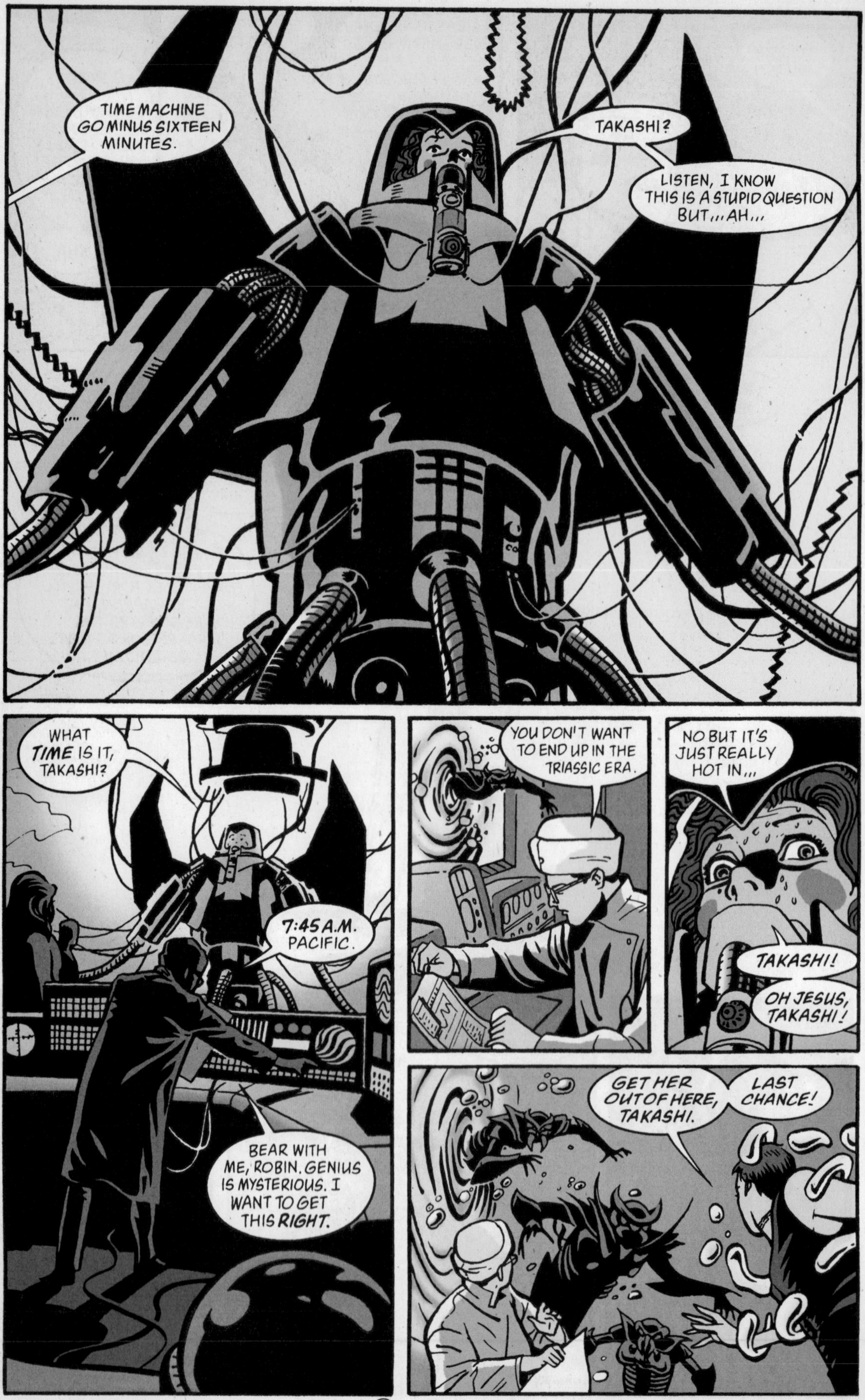
TIME MACHINE GO MINUS SIXTEEN MINUTES.
TAKASHI?
LISTEN, I KNOW THIS IS A STUPID QUESTION BUT,,, AH,,,
WHAT TIME IS IT, TAKASHI?
7:45 A.M. PACIFIC.
BEAR WITH ME, ROBIN. GENIUS IS MYSTERIOUS. I WANT TO GET THIS RIGHT.
YOU DON'T WANT TO END UP IN THE TRIASSIC ERA.
NO BUT IT'S JUST REALLY HOT IN,,,
TAKASHI!
OH JESUS, TAKASHI!
GET HER OUT OF HERE, TAKASHI.
LAST CHANCE!

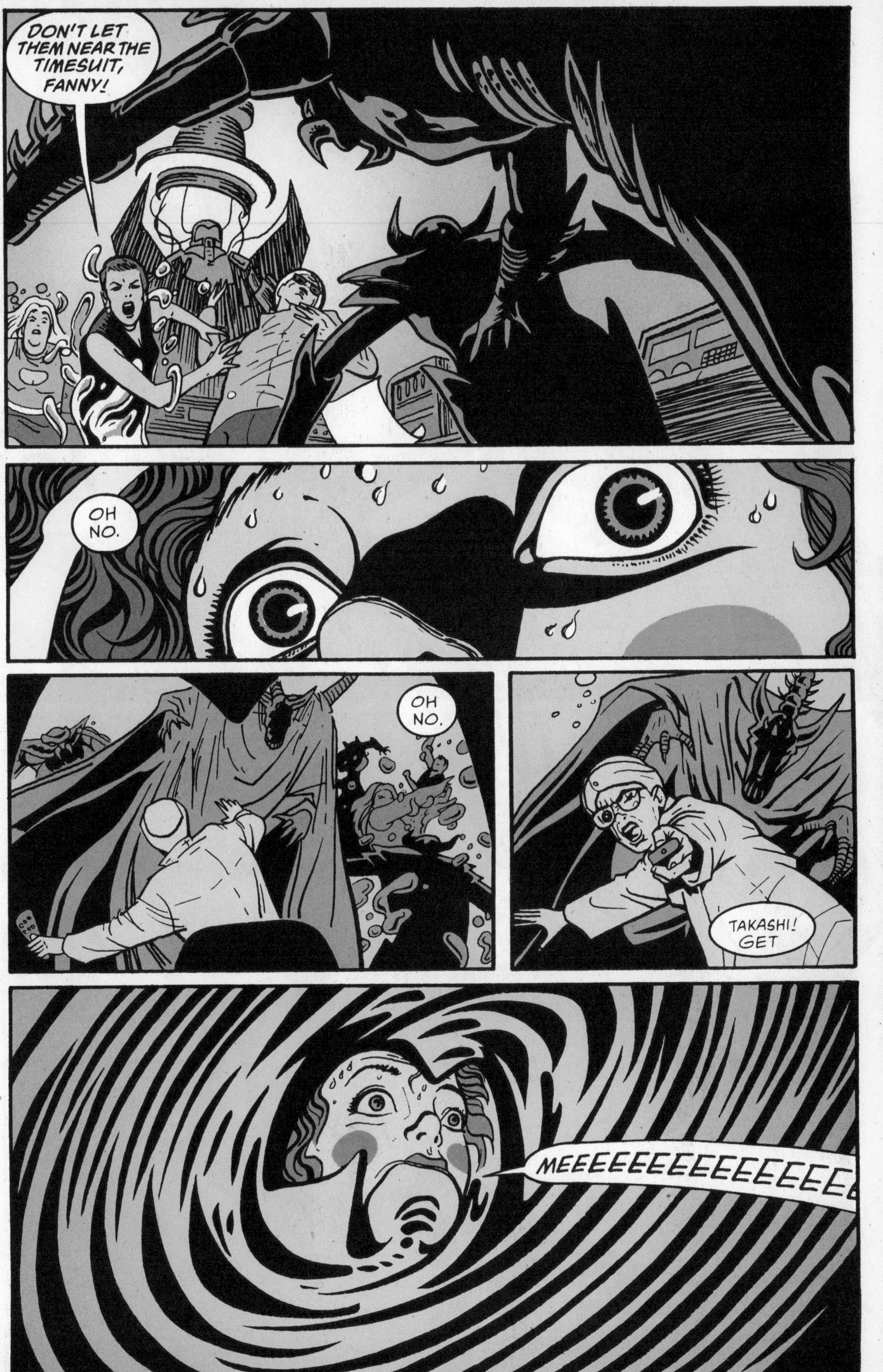
DON'T LET THEM NEAR THE TIMESUIT, FANNY!
OH NO.
OH NO.
TAKASHI! GET
MEEEEEEEEEEEEEEE

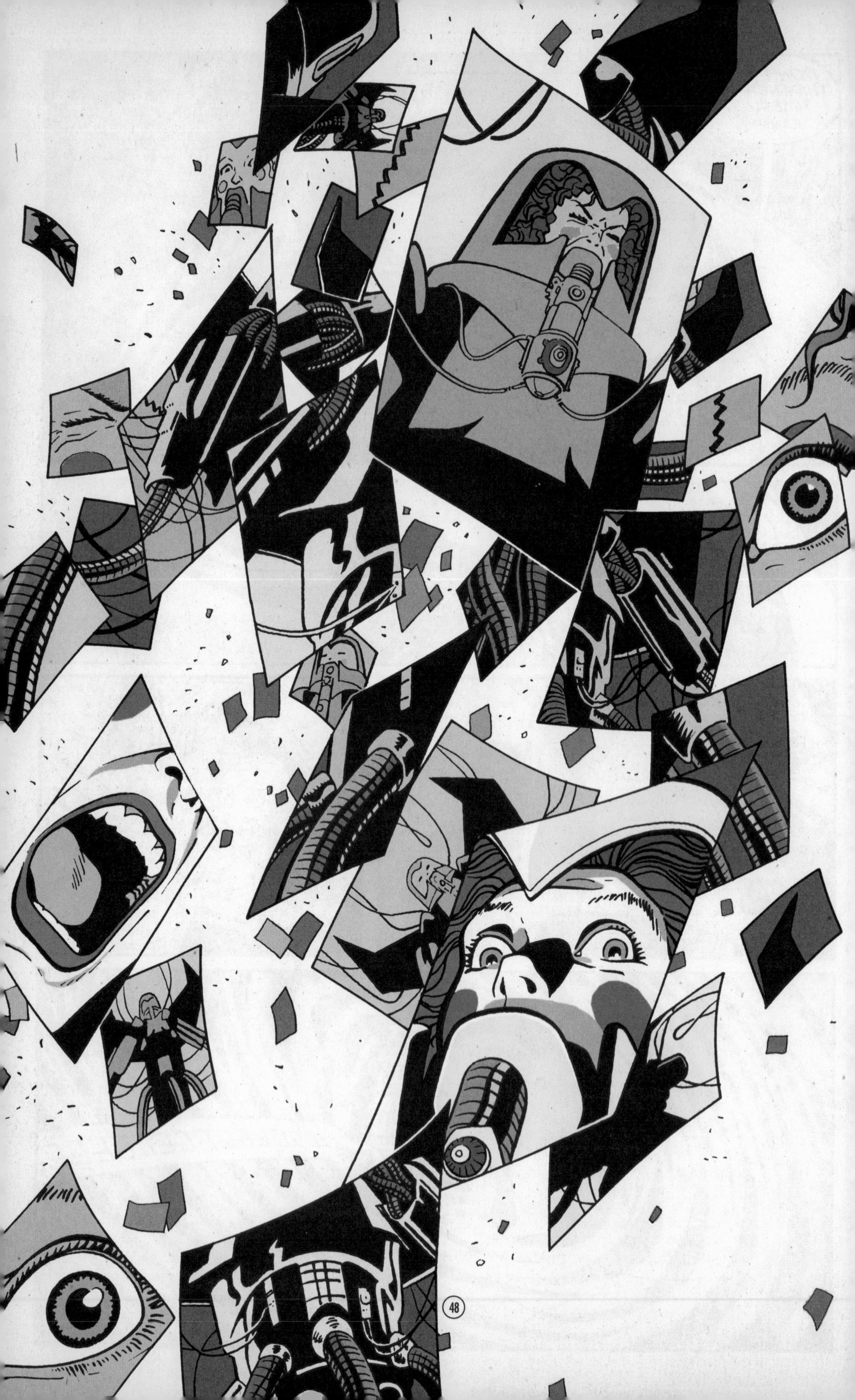

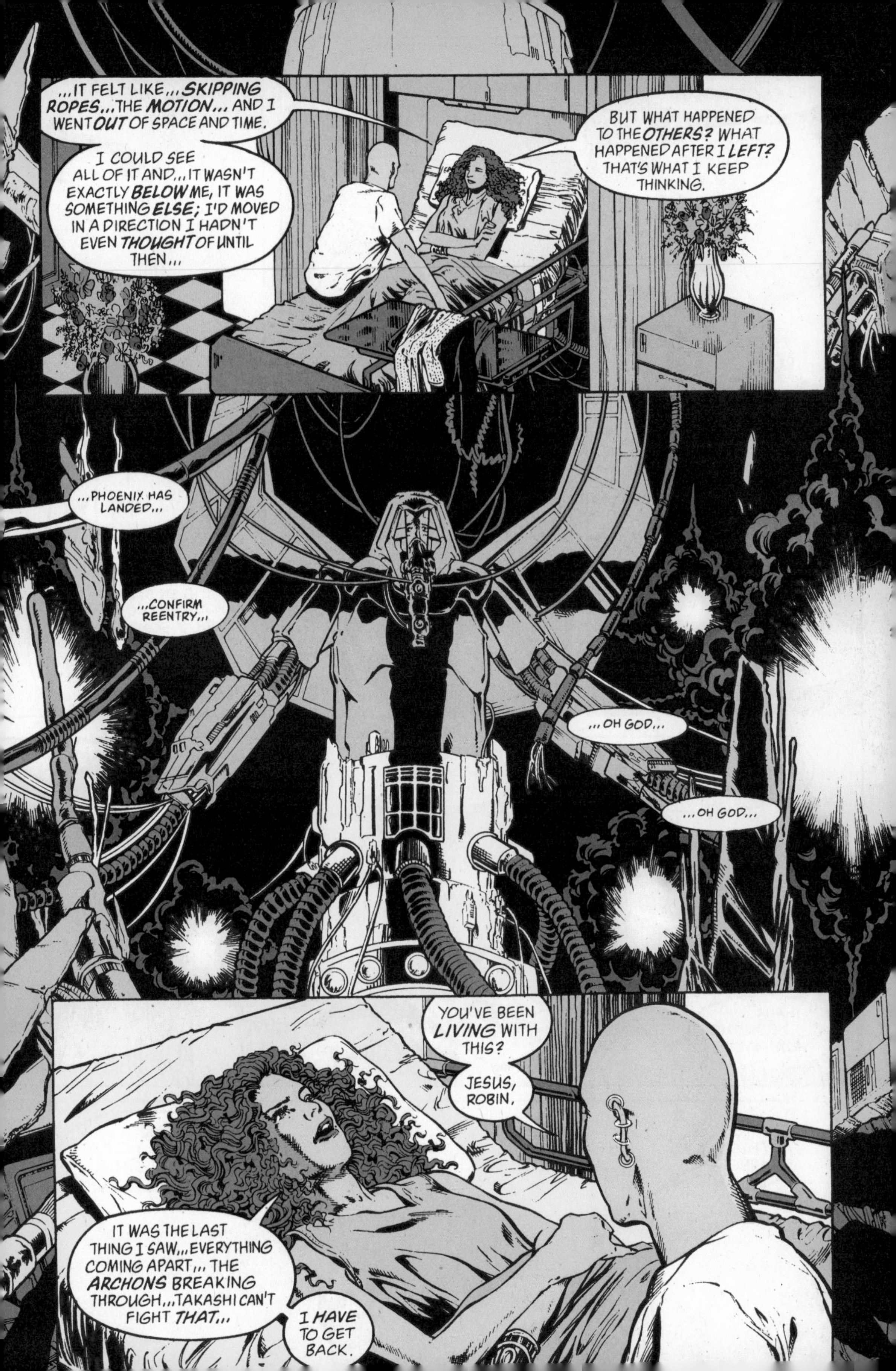
...IT FELT LIKE... SKIPPING ROPES... THE MOTION... AND I WENT OUT OF SPACE AND TIME.
I COULD SEE ALL OF IT AND... IT WASN'T EXACTLY BELOW ME, IT WAS SOMETHING ELSE; I'D MOVED IN A DIRECTION I HADN'T EVEN THOUGHT OF UNTIL THEN...
BUT WHAT HAPPENED TO THE OTHERS? WHAT HAPPENED AFTER I LEFT? THAT'S WHAT I KEEP THINKING.
...PHOENIX HAS LANDED...
...CONFIRM REENTRY...
...OH GOD...
...OH GOD...
YOU'VE BEEN LIVING WITH THIS?
JESUS, ROBIN.
IT WAS THE LAST THING I SAW... EVERYTHING COMING APART... THE ARCHONS BREAKING THROUGH... TAKASHI CAN'T FIGHT THAT...
I HAVE TO GET BACK.

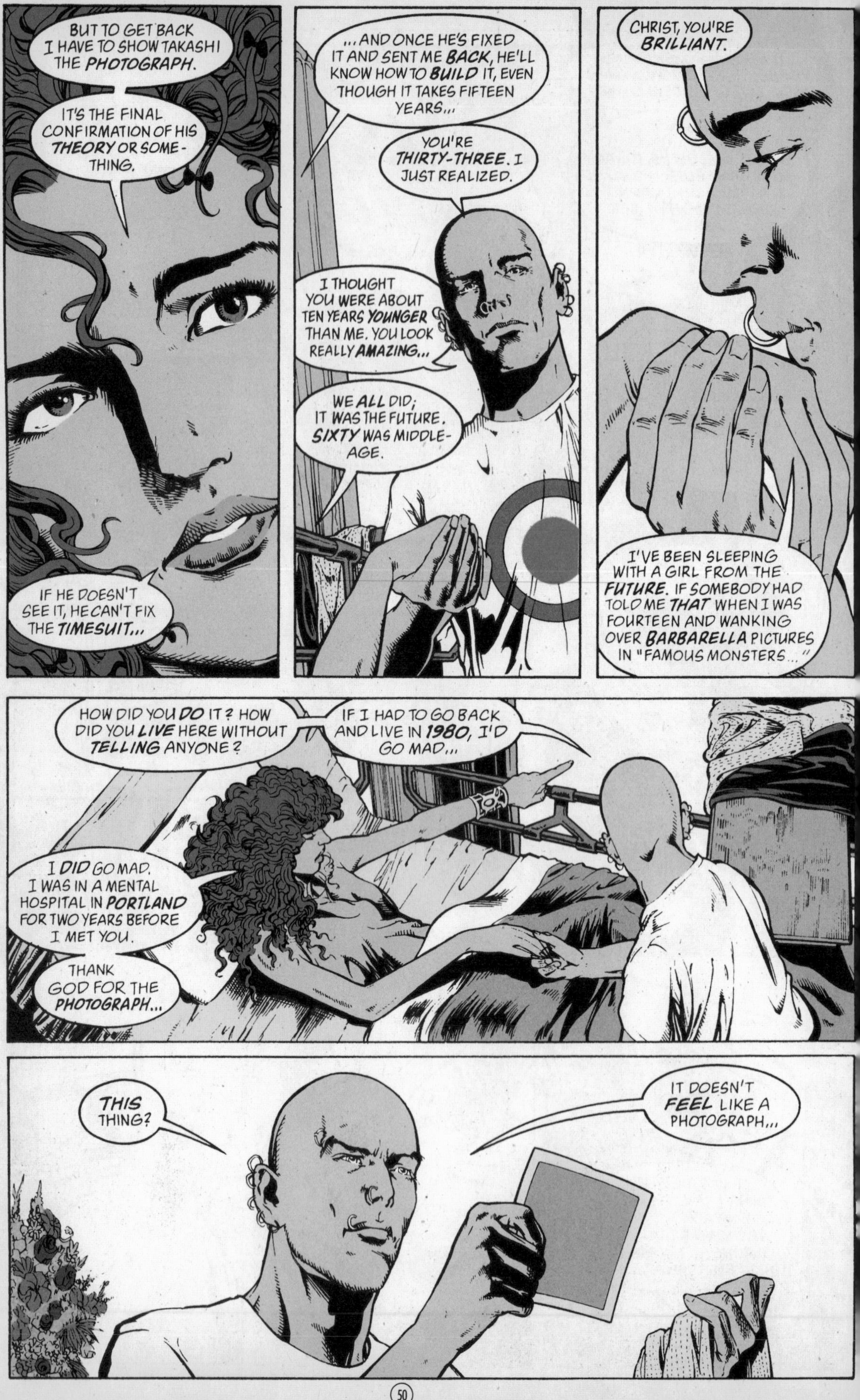

BUT TO GET BACK I HAVE TO SHOW TAKASHI THE PHOTOGRAPH.
IT'S THE FINAL CONFIRMATION OF HIS THEORY OR SOME-THING.
IF HE DOESN'T SEE IT, HE CAN'T FIX THE TIMESUIT...
...AND ONCE HE'S FIXED IT AND SENT ME BACK, HE'LL KNOW HOW TO BUILD IT, EVEN THOUGH IT TAKES FIFTEEN YEARS...
YOU'RE THIRTY-THREE. I JUST REALIZED.
I THOUGHT YOU WERE ABOUT TEN YEARS YOUNGER THAN ME. YOU LOOK REALLY AMAZING...
WE ALL DID; IT WAS THE FUTURE. SIXTY WAS MIDDLE-AGE.
CHRIST, YOU'RE BRILLIANT.
I'VE BEEN SLEEPING WITH A GIRL FROM THE FUTURE. IF SOMEBODY HAD TOLD ME THAT WHEN I WAS FOURTEEN AND WANKING OVER BARBARELLA PICTURES IN "FAMOUS MONSTERS..."
HOW DID YOU DO IT? HOW DID YOU LIVE HERE WITHOUT TELLING ANYONE?
IF I HAD TO GO BACK AND LIVE IN 1980, I'D GO MAD...
I DID GO MAD. I WAS IN A MENTAL HOSPITAL IN PORTLAND FOR TWO YEARS BEFORE I MET YOU.
THANK GOD FOR THE PHOTOGRAPH...
THIS THING?
IT DOESN'T FEEL LIKE A PHOTOGRAPH...

WHAT'S THE STORY, RAGS? WHAT WAS GOING ON WHEN WE WERE IN *NEW MEXICO* THAT DAY?

I WATCHED MY PARENTS TAKE A PHOTOGRAPH OF ME WHEN I WAS EIGHT. I *REMEMBERED* THE LADY ON THE ROOF.

I CONFIRMED TAKASHI'S THEORY, LIKE I SAID.

IN *2009*, WHEN I MET HIM, TAKASHI ASKED ME IF I HAD A PHOTOGRAPH OF MYSELF AS A CHILD IN *NEW MEXICO*. THEN *HE* SHOWED ME AN OLD, CRACKED ENLARGEMENT OF THE SKY, FROM A SHOT OF *NEW ZEALAND*, IN 1990. THAT ONE YOU'RE HOLDING.

IT WAS IN *BOTH* PICTURES: THE EXACT SAME *CLOUD* FORMATION.

THEY FIXED MY HEAD?

YEAH. SO YEAH, I WAS SAYING...

TAKASHI STARTED TALKING ABOUT HOW FRACTAL PATTERNS *REPEAT* THEMSELVES THROUGH TIME, LIKE THE BACKGROUNDS IN *CARTOONS*.

HE TOLD ME THE ENTIRE UNIVERSE WAS MUCH *SIMPLER* THAN WE THOUGHT.

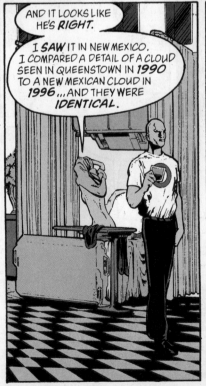

AND IT LOOKS LIKE HE'S *RIGHT*.

I *SAW* IT IN NEW MEXICO. I COMPARED A DETAIL OF A CLOUD SEEN IN QUEENSTOWN IN *1990* TO A NEW MEXICAN CLOUD IN *1996*...AND THEY WERE *IDENTICAL*.

"BARBARELLA."

THAT'S WHAT I LOVE ABOUT YOU; YOU'RE SO *SHALLOW*.

THAT'S ME, BABE.

LISTEN...YOU MUST KNOW WHAT *HAPPENS* TO ALL OF US...

YEAH.

I DO.

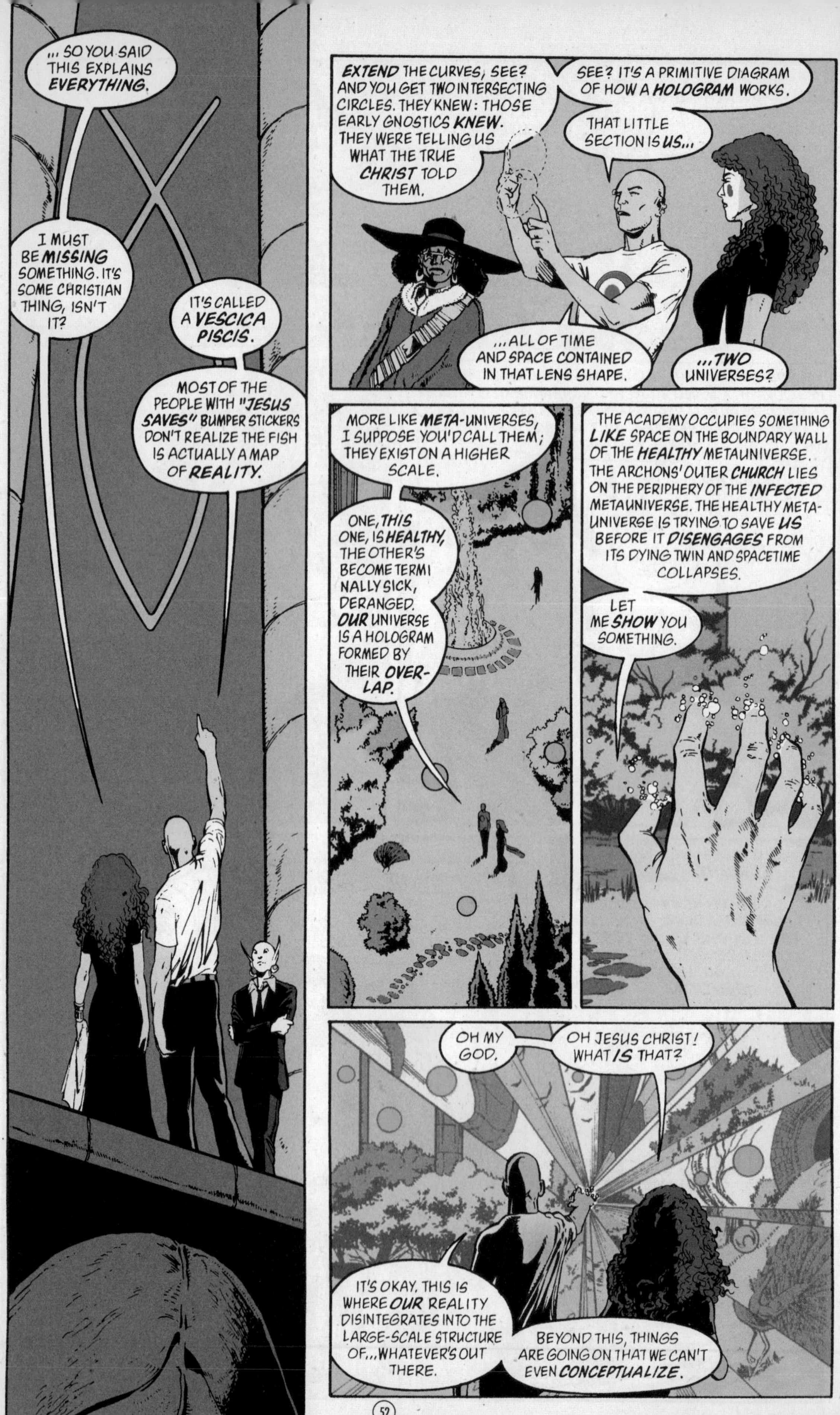

... SO YOU SAID THIS EXPLAINS EVERYTHING.
I MUST BE MISSING SOMETHING. IT'S SOME CHRISTIAN THING, ISN'T IT?
IT'S CALLED A VESCICA PISCIS.
MOST OF THE PEOPLE WITH "JESUS SAVES" BUMPER STICKERS DON'T REALIZE THE FISH IS ACTUALLY A MAP OF REALITY.
EXTEND THE CURVES, SEE? AND YOU GET TWO INTERSECTING CIRCLES. THEY KNEW: THOSE EARLY GNOSTICS KNEW. THEY WERE TELLING US WHAT THE TRUE CHRIST TOLD THEM.
SEE? IT'S A PRIMITIVE DIAGRAM OF HOW A HOLOGRAM WORKS.
THAT LITTLE SECTION IS US...
...ALL OF TIME AND SPACE CONTAINED IN THAT LENS SHAPE.
...TWO UNIVERSES?
MORE LIKE META-UNIVERSES, I SUPPOSE YOU'D CALL THEM; THEY EXIST ON A HIGHER SCALE.
ONE, THIS ONE, IS HEALTHY, THE OTHER'S BECOME TERMI NALLY SICK, DERANGED. OUR UNIVERSE IS A HOLOGRAM FORMED BY THEIR OVER-LAP.
THE ACADEMY OCCUPIES SOMETHING LIKE SPACE ON THE BOUNDARY WALL OF THE HEALTHY METAUNIVERSE. THE ARCHONS' OUTER CHURCH LIES ON THE PERIPHERY OF THE INFECTED METAUNIVERSE. THE HEALTHY META-UNIVERSE IS TRYING TO SAVE US BEFORE IT DISENGAGES FROM ITS DYING TWIN AND SPACETIME COLLAPSES.
LET ME SHOW YOU SOMETHING.
OH MY GOD.
OH JESUS CHRIST! WHAT IS THAT?
IT'S OKAY. THIS IS WHERE OUR REALITY DISINTEGRATES INTO THE LARGE-SCALE STRUCTURE OF... WHATEVER'S OUT THERE.
BEYOND THIS, THINGS ARE GOING ON THAT WE CAN'T EVEN CONCEPTUALIZE.

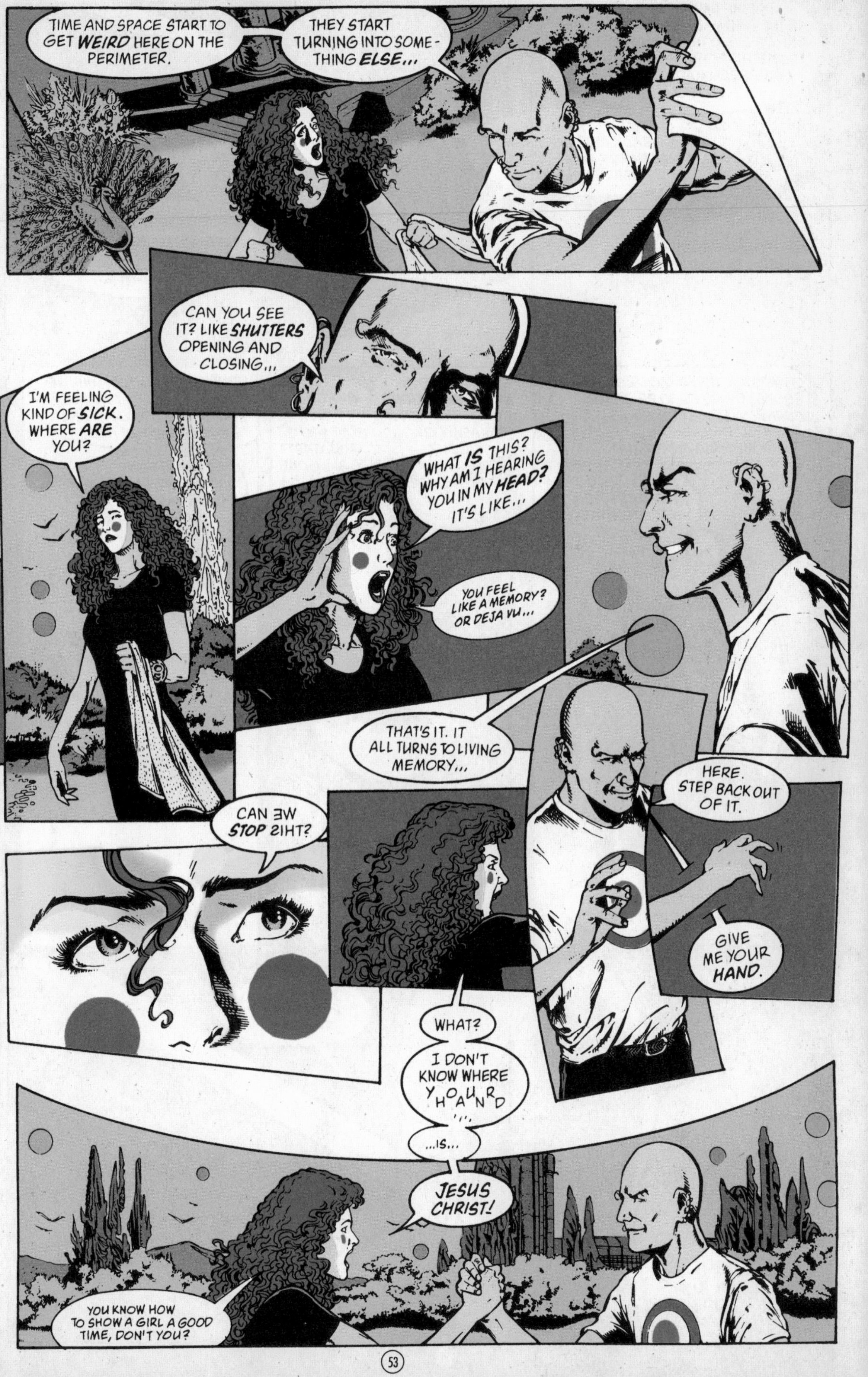

TIME AND SPACE START TO GET WEIRD HERE ON THE PERIMETER.
THEY START TURNING INTO SOME-THING ELSE...
CAN YOU SEE IT? LIKE SHUTTERS OPENING AND CLOSING...
I'M FEELING KIND OF SICK. WHERE ARE YOU?
WHAT IS THIS? WHY AM I HEARING YOU IN MY HEAD? IT'S LIKE...
YOU FEEL LIKE A MEMORY? OR DEJA VU...
THAT'S IT. IT ALL TURNS TO LIVING MEMORY...
CAN ƎW STOP ƧIHT?
HERE. STEP BACK OUT OF IT.
GIVE ME YOUR HAND.
WHAT?
I DON'T KNOW WHERE YHOAUNRD
...IS...
JESUS CHRIST!
YOU KNOW HOW TO SHOW A GIRL A GOOD TIME, DON'T YOU?

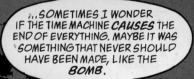

...SOMETIMES I WONDER IF THE TIME MACHINE *CAUSES* THE END OF EVERYTHING. MAYBE IT WAS SOMETHING THAT NEVER SHOULD HAVE BEEN MADE, LIKE THE *BOMB.*

WHAT IF I HAVE TO GO BACK AND THE ENEMY HAS *WON?* WHAT DO I *DO?* IT'S TERRIFYING ME.

I DON'T THINK THEY WIN. THE ANTIBODIES ARE APPEARING *EVERY-WHERE* IN OUR WORLD NOW.

I JUST DON'T KNOW IF *WE* WIN EITHER. I'M SHOOTING PEOPLE AND IT NEVER SEEMS TO *END...*

IT WAS ALL THOSE *MOORCOCK* BOOKS; I WANTED TO BE *JERRY CORNELIUS,* THE ENGLISH ASSASSIN. I WANTED THE GUNS AND THE CARS AND THE GIRLS AND THE CHAOS...

SHIT.

I'VE ENDED UP A *MURDERER.* MY KARMA'S A BLOODY *MINEFIELD...*

WHY DOES THIS HAVE TO BE *US?* DON'T YOU SOMETIMES WISH YOU JUST DIDN'T *KNOW?*

I MEAN, THOSE MEN WERE *SERIOUS.* WHAT IF THEY *KILL* TAKASHI? OR MASON?

WHAT IF IT'S ALL GONE WRONG? CHRIST, WHAT IF IT'S ALL GONE *RIGHT?* WHICH IS *WORSE?*

WHAT DO WE *DO?*

ROBIN, WE *WANTED* THIS. WE WANTED TO BE SPECIAL AND IMPORTANT AND COOL AND *LOOK!* HERE WE ARE.

SO WHAT CAN WE DO BUT LIE IN THE BEDS WE MADE.

YOU SAVE THE FUTURE FROM THE PAST.

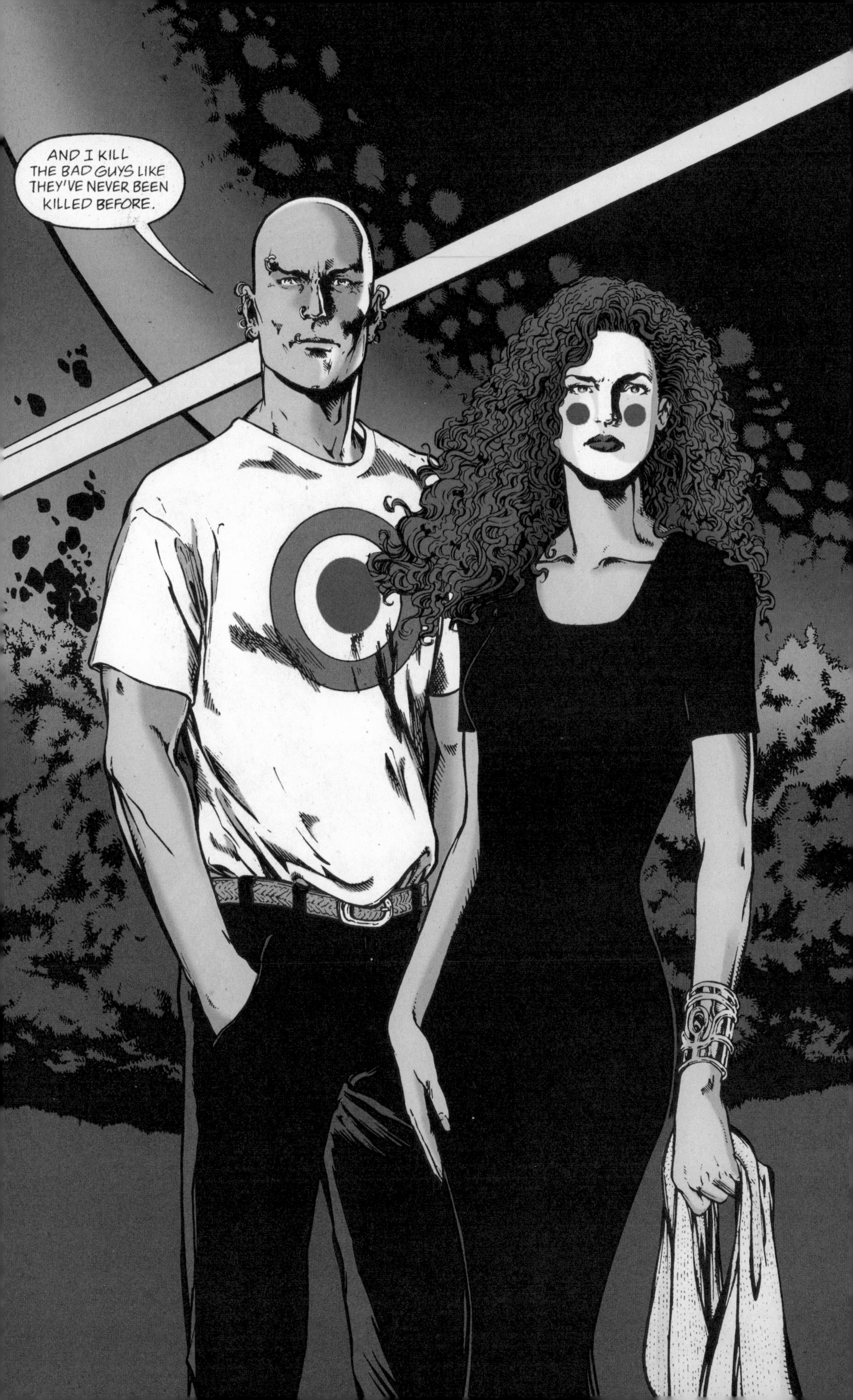
AND I KILL THE BAD GUYS LIKE THEY'VE NEVER BEEN KILLED BEFORE.

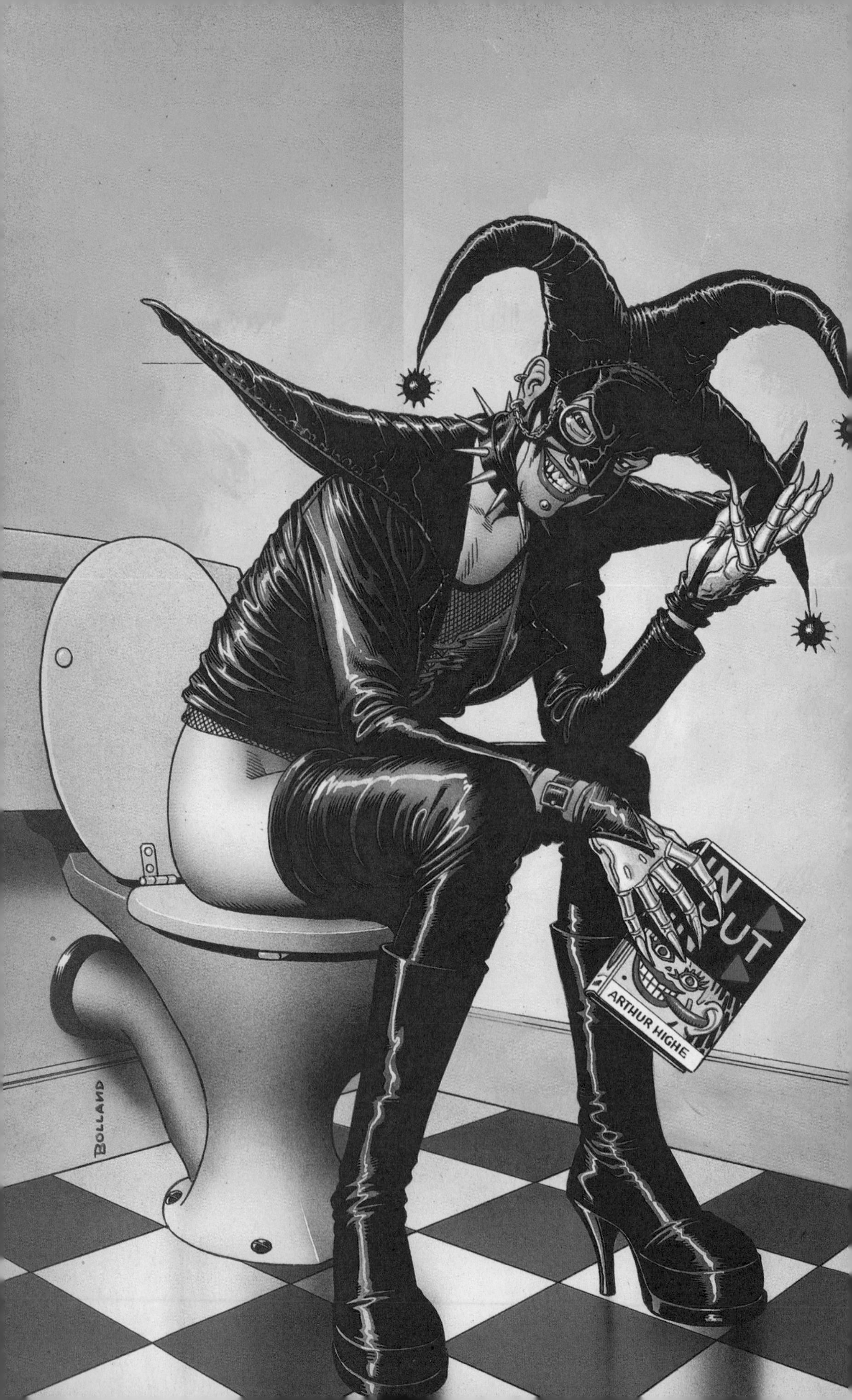

IN
ARTHUR HIGHE
BOLLAND

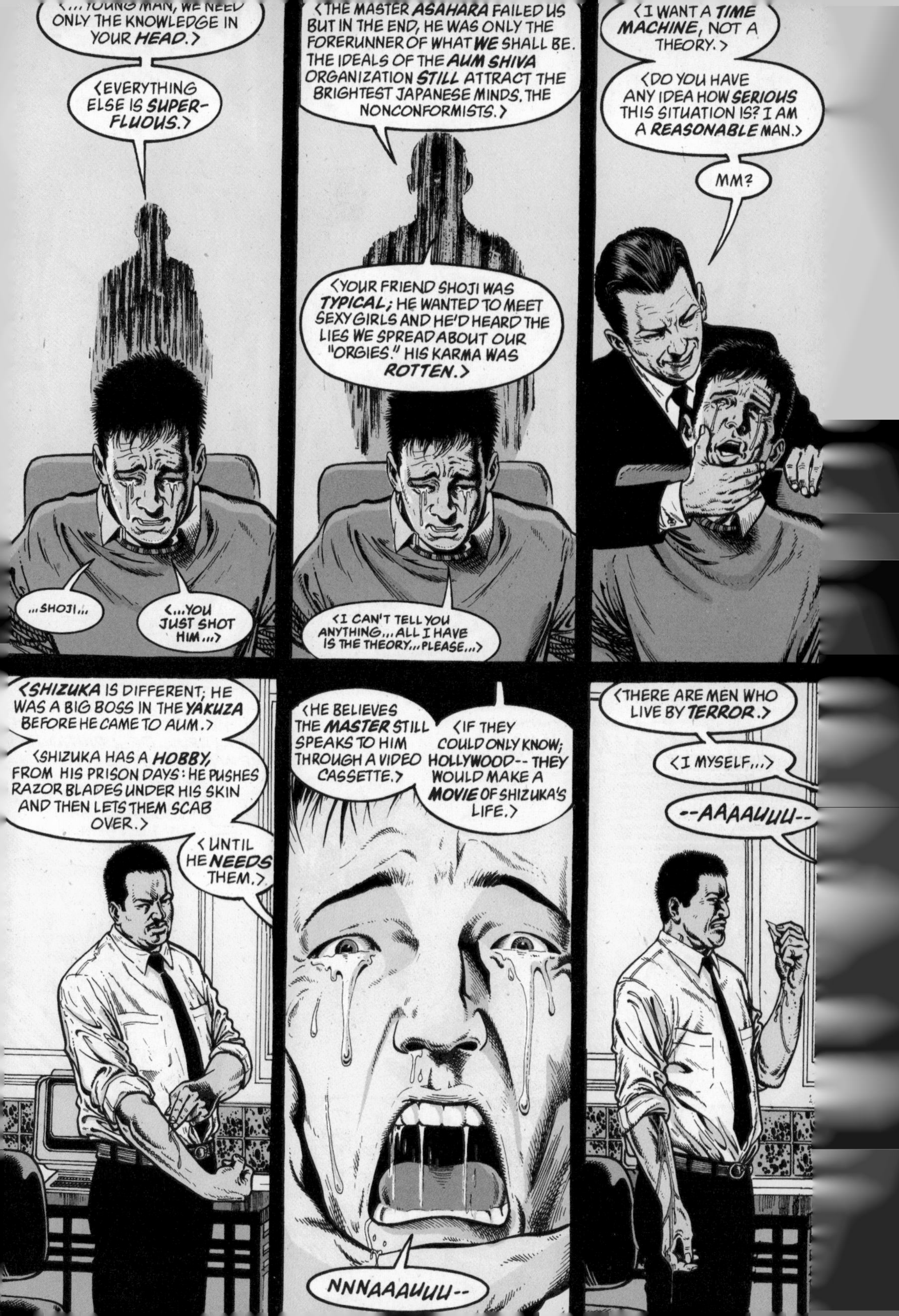

<...YOUNG MAN, WE NEED ONLY THE KNOWLEDGE IN YOUR HEAD.>
<EVERYTHING ELSE IS SUPERFLUOUS.>
...SHOJI...
<...YOU JUST SHOT HIM...>
<THE MASTER ASAHARA FAILED US BUT IN THE END, HE WAS ONLY THE FORERUNNER OF WHAT WE SHALL BE. THE IDEALS OF THE AUM SHIVA ORGANIZATION STILL ATTRACT THE BRIGHTEST JAPANESE MINDS. THE NONCONFORMISTS.>
<YOUR FRIEND SHOJI WAS TYPICAL; HE WANTED TO MEET SEXY GIRLS AND HE'D HEARD THE LIES WE SPREAD ABOUT OUR "ORGIES." HIS KARMA WAS ROTTEN.>
<I CAN'T TELL YOU ANYTHING... ALL I HAVE IS THE THEORY... PLEASE...>
<I WANT A TIME MACHINE, NOT A THEORY.>
<DO YOU HAVE ANY IDEA HOW SERIOUS THIS SITUATION IS? I AM A REASONABLE MAN.>
MM?
<SHIZUKA IS DIFFERENT; HE WAS A BIG BOSS IN THE YAKUZA BEFORE HE CAME TO AUM.>
<SHIZUKA HAS A HOBBY, FROM HIS PRISON DAYS: HE PUSHES RAZOR BLADES UNDER HIS SKIN AND THEN LETS THEM SCAB OVER.>
<UNTIL HE NEEDS THEM.>
<HE BELIEVES THE MASTER STILL SPEAKS TO HIM THROUGH A VIDEO CASSETTE.>
<IF THEY COULD ONLY KNOW; HOLLYWOOD-- THEY WOULD MAKE A MOVIE OF SHIZUKA'S LIFE.>
NNNAAAUUU--
<THERE ARE MEN WHO LIVE BY TERROR.>
<I MYSELF...>
--AAAAUUU--

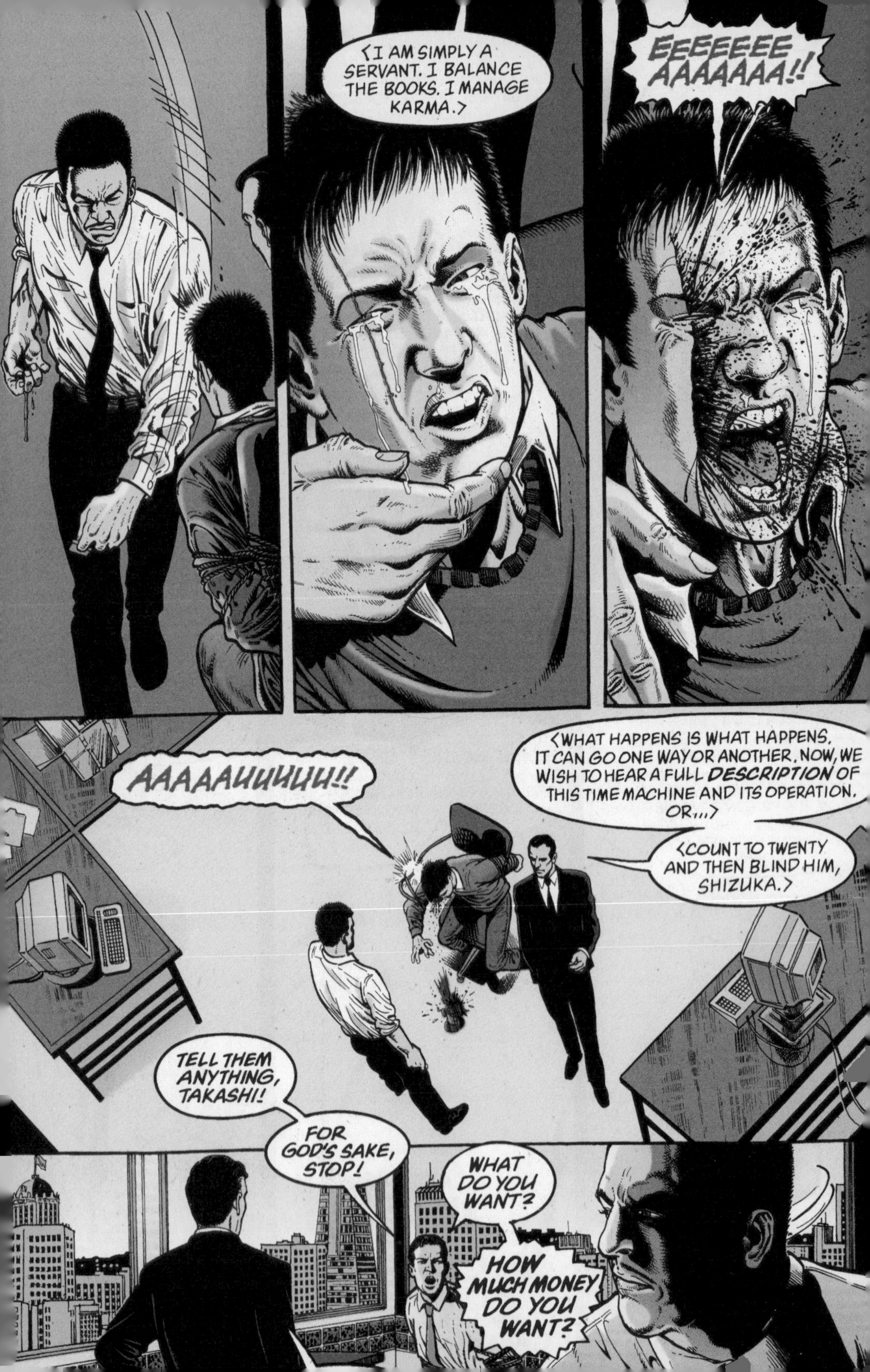

‹I AM SIMPLY A SERVANT. I BALANCE THE BOOKS. I MANAGE KARMA.›
EEEEEEE AAAAAAA!!
AAAAAUUUUU!!
‹WHAT HAPPENS IS WHAT HAPPENS. IT CAN GO ONE WAY OR ANOTHER. NOW, WE WISH TO HEAR A FULL DESCRIPTION OF THIS TIME MACHINE AND ITS OPERATION. OR...›
‹COUNT TO TWENTY AND THEN BLIND HIM, SHIZUKA.›
TELL THEM ANYTHING, TAKASHI!
FOR GOD'S SAKE, STOP!
WHAT DO YOU WANT?
HOW MUCH MONEY DO YOU WANT?

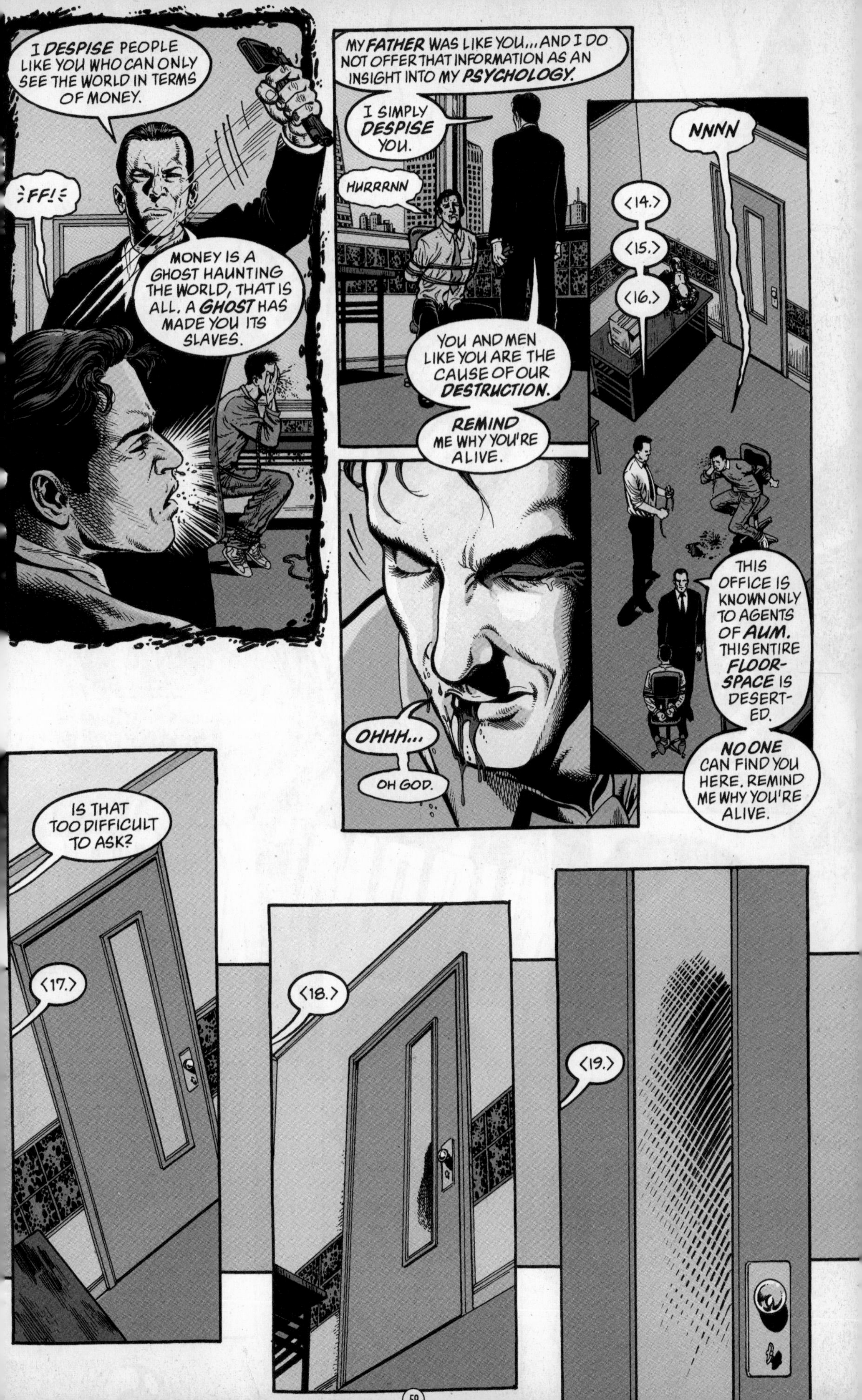
I DESPISE PEOPLE LIKE YOU WHO CAN ONLY SEE THE WORLD IN TERMS OF MONEY.
FF!
MONEY IS A GHOST HAUNTING THE WORLD, THAT IS ALL. A GHOST HAS MADE YOU ITS SLAVES.
MY FATHER WAS LIKE YOU... AND I DO NOT OFFER THAT INFORMATION AS AN INSIGHT INTO MY PSYCHOLOGY.
I SIMPLY DESPISE YOU.
HURRRNN
YOU AND MEN LIKE YOU ARE THE CAUSE OF OUR DESTRUCTION.
REMIND ME WHY YOU'RE ALIVE.
OHHH...
OH GOD.
NNNN
<14.>
<15.>
<16.>
THIS OFFICE IS KNOWN ONLY TO AGENTS OF AUM. THIS ENTIRE FLOOR-SPACE IS DESERT-ED.
NO ONE CAN FIND YOU HERE. REMIND ME WHY YOU'RE ALIVE.
IS THAT TOO DIFFICULT TO ASK?
<17.>
<18.>
<19.>

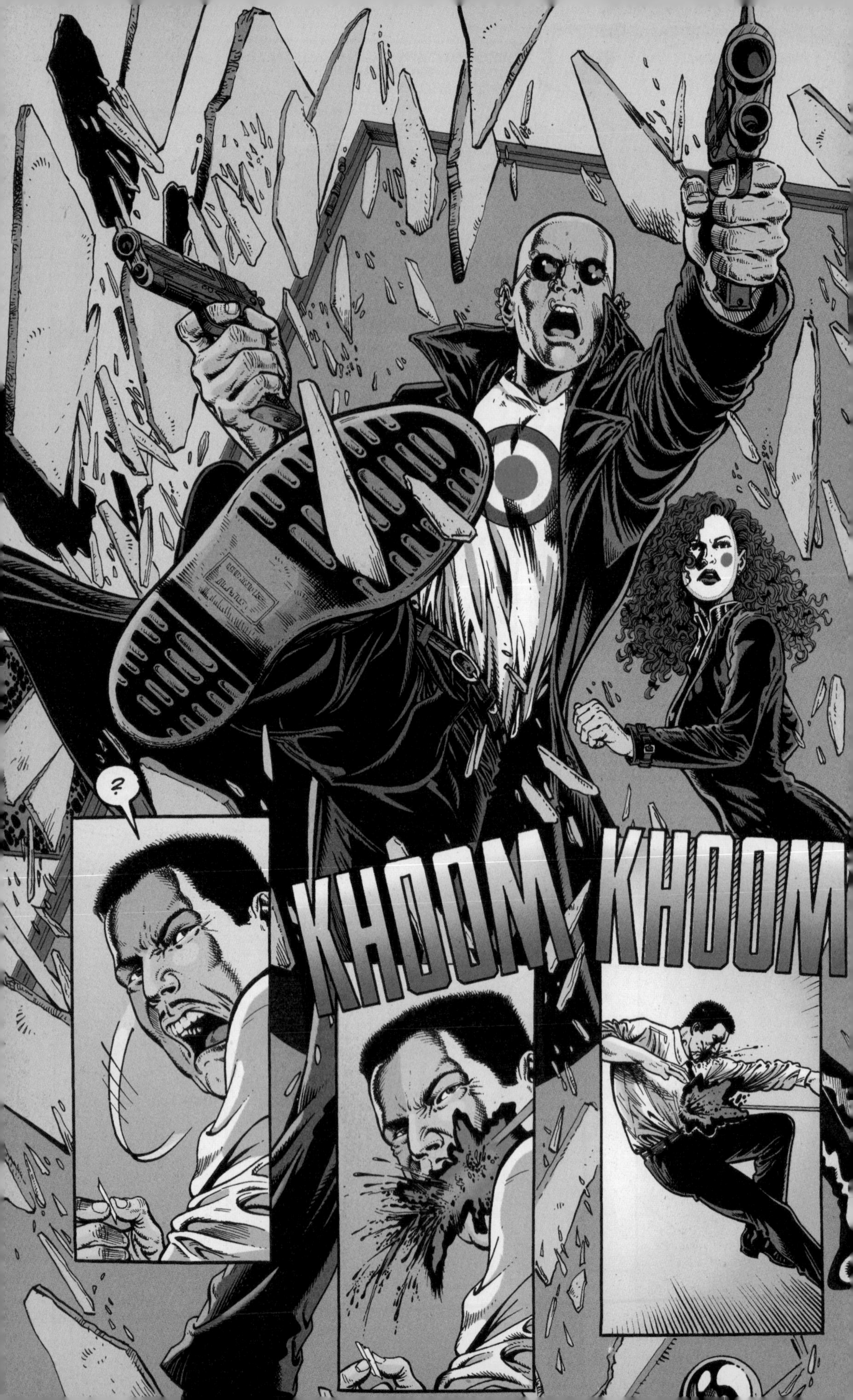
?
KHOOM KHOOM

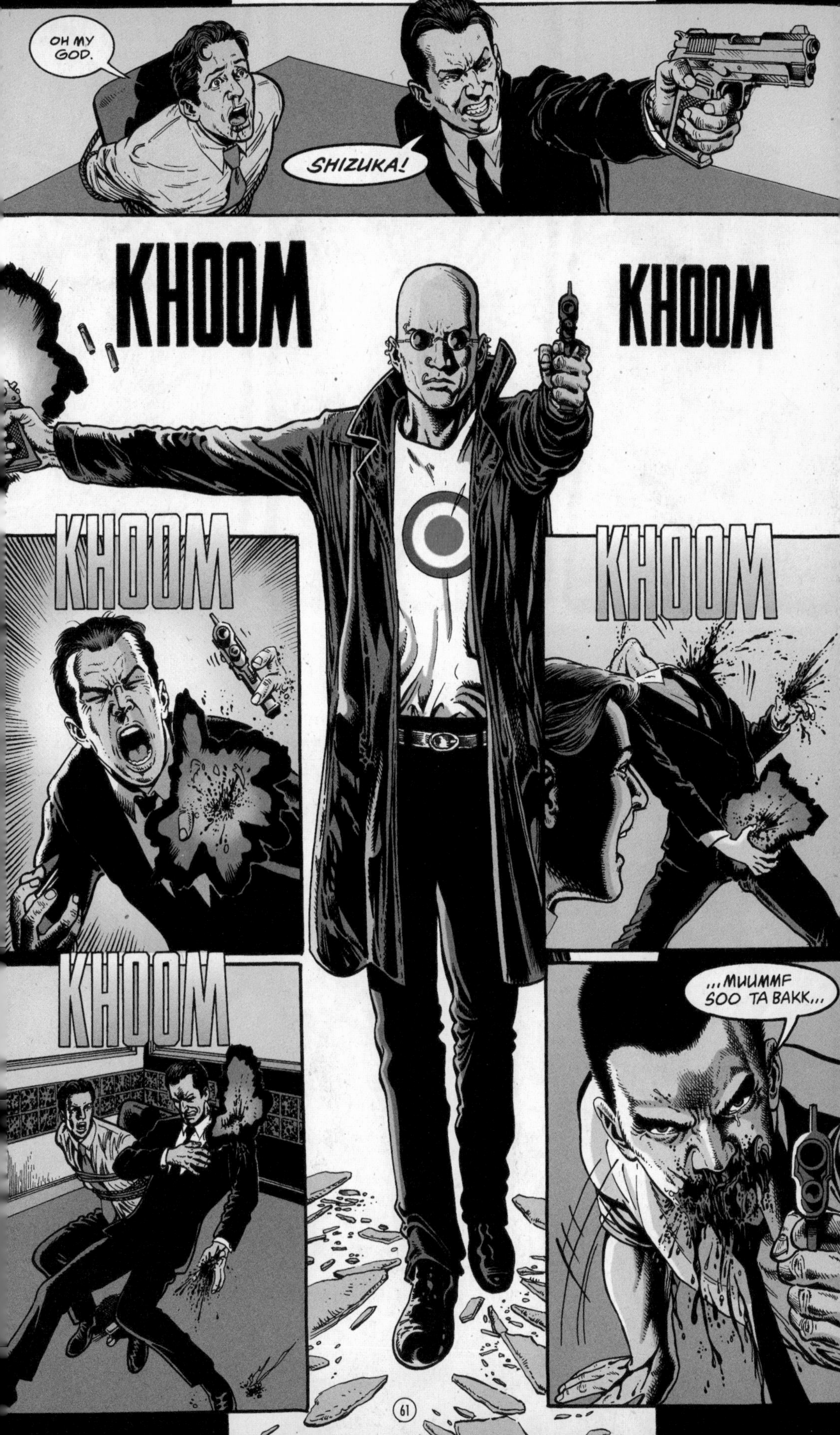
OH MY GOD.
SHIZUKA!
KHOOM
KHOOM
KHOOM
KHOOM
KHOOM
...MUUMMF SOO TA BAKK...

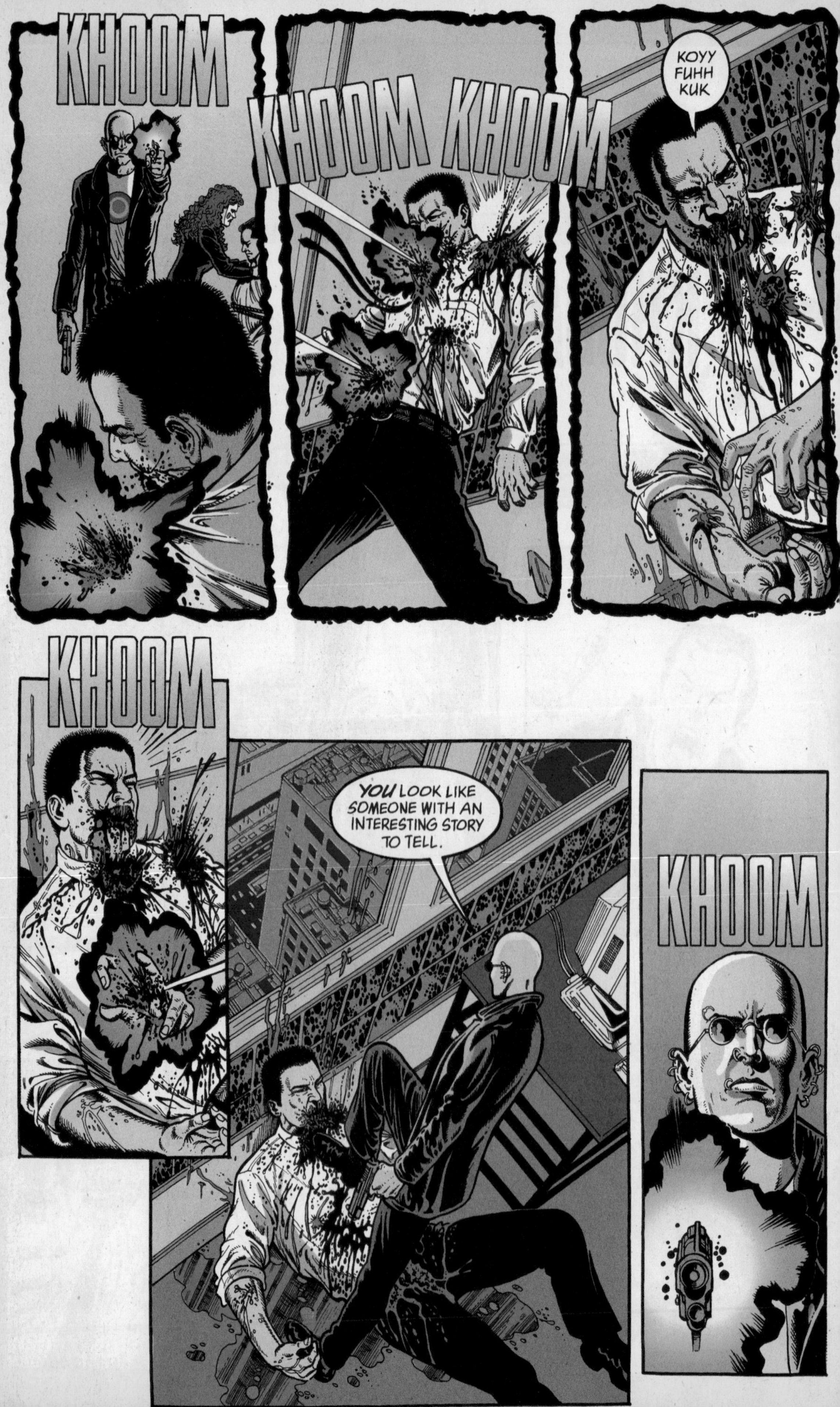
KHOOM
KHOOM KHOOM
KOYY FUHH KUK
KHOOM
YOU LOOK LIKE SOMEONE WITH AN INTERESTING STORY TO TELL.
KHOOM

THE SOUND OF THE ATOM SPLITTING

GRANT MORRISON
WRITER

PHIL JIMENEZ
PENCILLER

JOHN STOKES
INKER

DANIEL VOZZO
COLORIST

HEROIC AGE
SEPARATIONS

TODD KLEIN
LETTERER

SHELLY ROEBERG
EDITOR

THE INVISIBLES CREATED
BY GRANT MORRISON

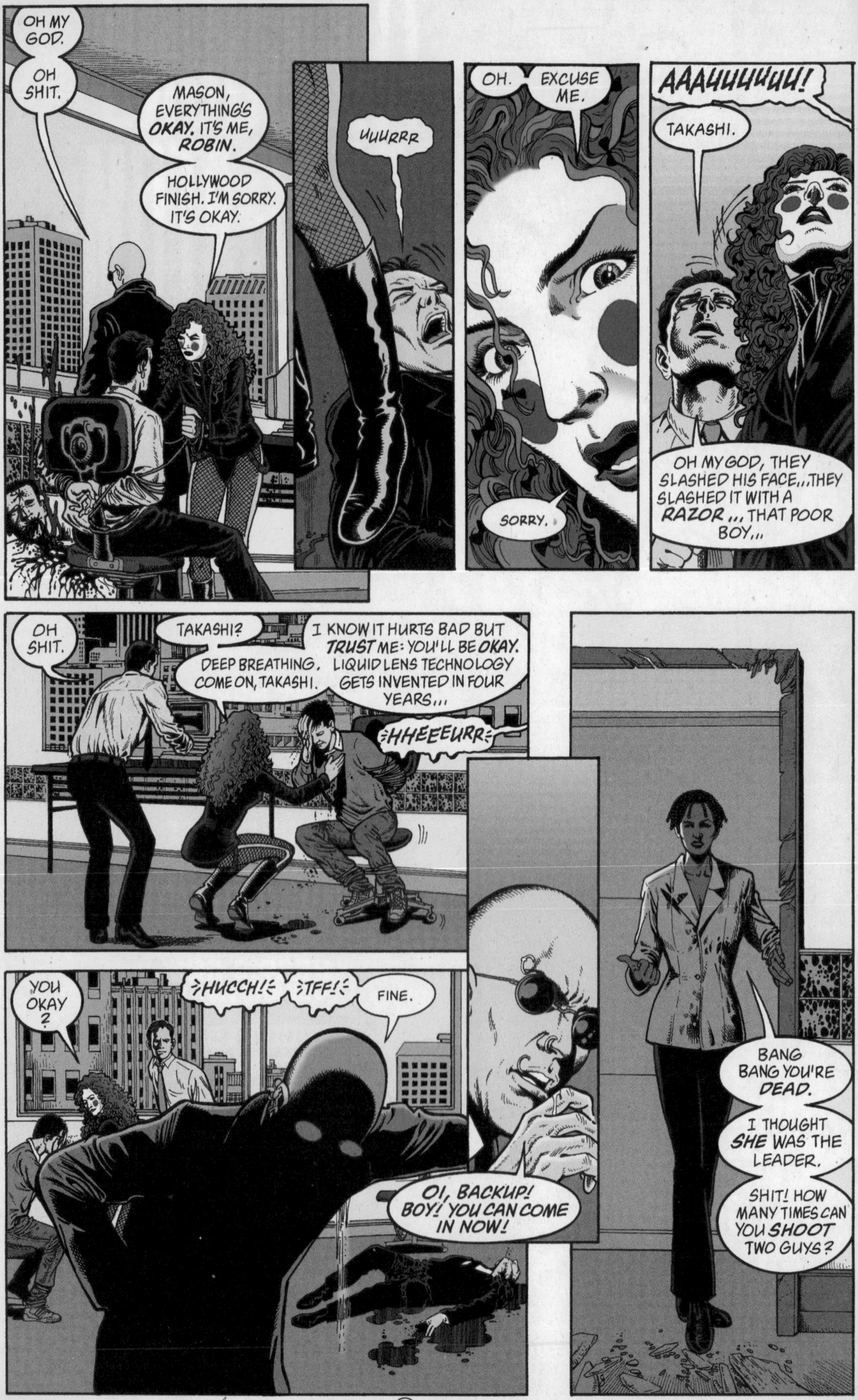
OH MY GOD.
OH SHIT.
MASON, EVERYTHING'S OKAY. IT'S ME, ROBIN.
HOLLYWOOD FINISH. I'M SORRY. IT'S OKAY.
UUURRR
OH.
EXCUSE ME.
SORRY.
AAAUUUUUU!
TAKASHI.
OH MY GOD, THEY SLASHED HIS FACE... THEY SLASHED IT WITH A RAZOR... THAT POOR BOY...
OH SHIT.
TAKASHI?
DEEP BREATHING. COME ON, TAKASHI.
I KNOW IT HURTS BAD BUT TRUST ME: YOU'LL BE OKAY. LIQUID LENS TECHNOLOGY GETS INVENTED IN FOUR YEARS...
HHEEEURR
YOU OKAY?
HUCCH!
TFF!
FINE.
OI, BACKUP! BOY! YOU CAN COME IN NOW!
BANG BANG YOU'RE DEAD.
I THOUGHT SHE WAS THE LEADER.
SHIT! HOW MANY TIMES CAN YOU SHOOT TWO GUYS?

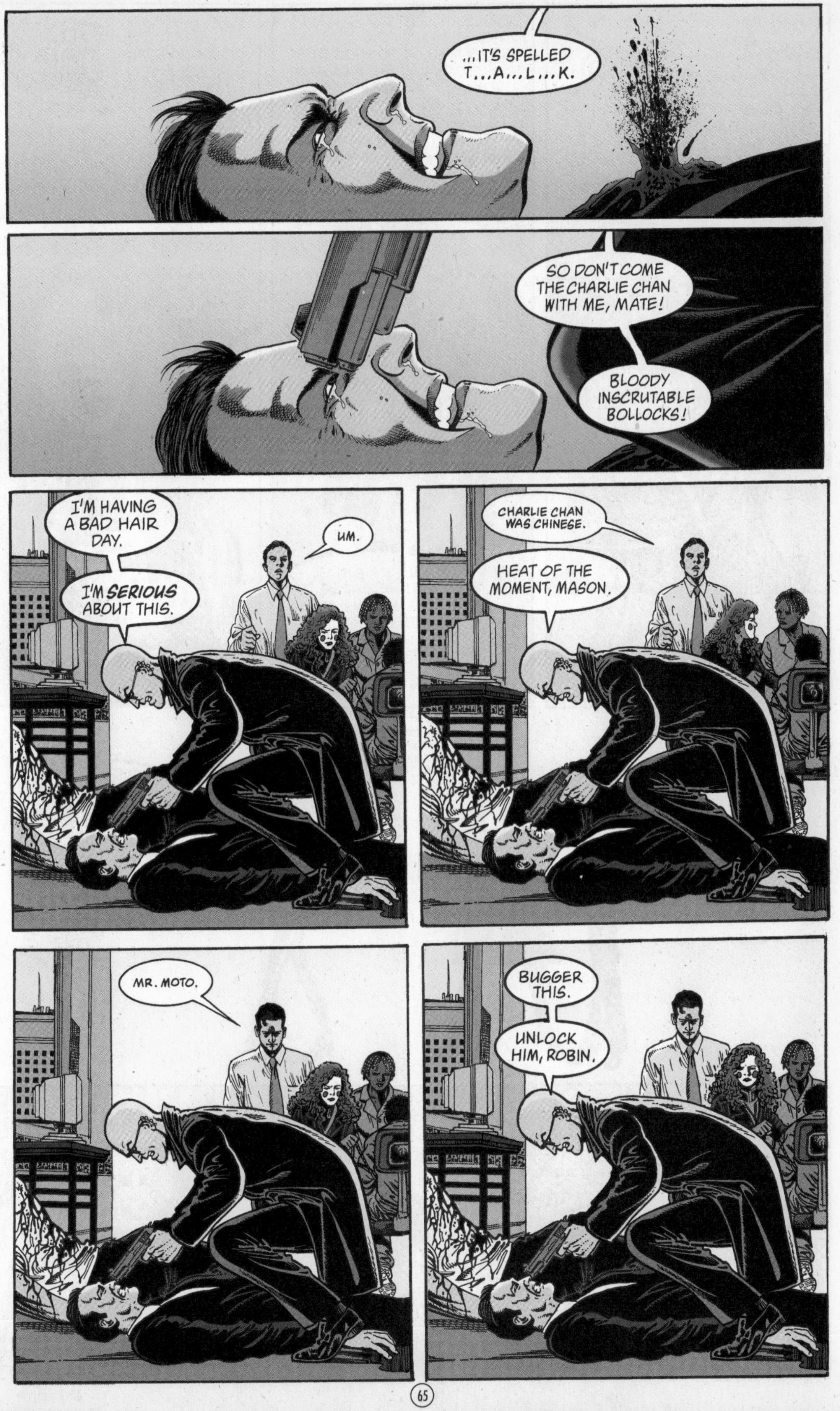
...IT'S SPELLED T...A...L...K.
SO DON'T COME THE CHARLIE CHAN WITH ME, MATE!
BLOODY INSCRUTABLE BOLLOCKS!
I'M HAVING A BAD HAIR DAY.
I'M SERIOUS ABOUT THIS.
UM.
CHARLIE CHAN WAS CHINESE.
HEAT OF THE MOMENT, MASON.
MR. MOTO.
BUGGER THIS.
UNLOCK HIM, ROBIN.

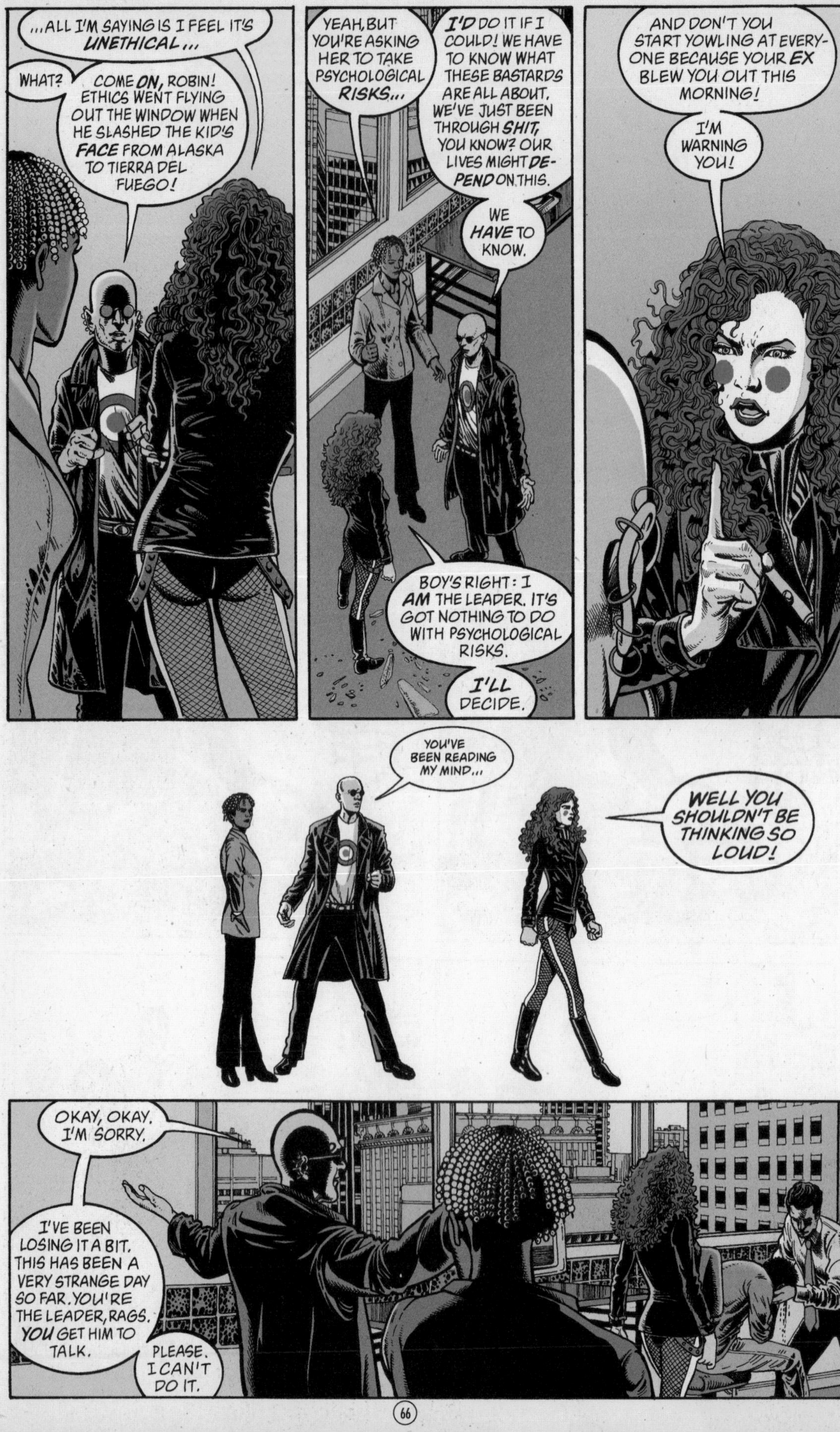
...ALL I'M SAYING IS I FEEL IT'S UNETHICAL...
WHAT?
COME ON, ROBIN! ETHICS WENT FLYING OUT THE WINDOW WHEN HE SLASHED THE KID'S FACE FROM ALASKA TO TIERRA DEL FUEGO!
YEAH, BUT YOU'RE ASKING HER TO TAKE PSYCHOLOGICAL RISKS...
I'D DO IT IF I COULD! WE HAVE TO KNOW WHAT THESE BASTARDS ARE ALL ABOUT. WE'VE JUST BEEN THROUGH SHIT, YOU KNOW? OUR LIVES MIGHT DEPEND ON THIS.
WE HAVE TO KNOW.
BOY'S RIGHT: I AM THE LEADER. IT'S GOT NOTHING TO DO WITH PSYCHOLOGICAL RISKS.
I'LL DECIDE.
AND DON'T YOU START YOWLING AT EVERYONE BECAUSE YOUR EX BLEW YOU OUT THIS MORNING!
I'M WARNING YOU!
YOU'VE BEEN READING MY MIND...
WELL YOU SHOULDN'T BE THINKING SO LOUD!
OKAY, OKAY. I'M SORRY.
I'VE BEEN LOSING IT A BIT. THIS HAS BEEN A VERY STRANGE DAY SO FAR. YOU'RE THE LEADER, RAGS. YOU GET HIM TO TALK.
PLEASE. I CAN'T DO IT.

I'D BETTER UNLOCK HIM THEN, HUH?

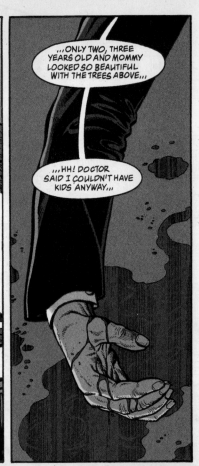

...ONLY TWO, THREE YEARS OLD AND MOMMY LOOKED SO BEAUTIFUL WITH THE TREES ABOVE...

...HH! DOCTOR SAID I COULDN'T HAVE KIDS ANYWAY...

STICK TO THE *POINT*, YOSHIO, IT'S EASIER THAT WAY.

...THE TIME MACHINE TO TAKE US INTO THE FUTURE... THERE TO WATCH HARUMAGEDON AS IT OCCURS... AND TO RETURN WITH THE PERFECT KNOWLEDGE OF HOW TO BRING IT ABOUT...

BUT I HAVE LEARNED SOMETHING NEW...HARUMAGEDON ISN'T COMING... IT IS HERE ALREADY...THIS IS HOW THE COLLAPSE APPEARS TO THOSE CONDEMNED TO LIVE IN IT...

HARUMAGEDON IS HAPPENING NOW.

67

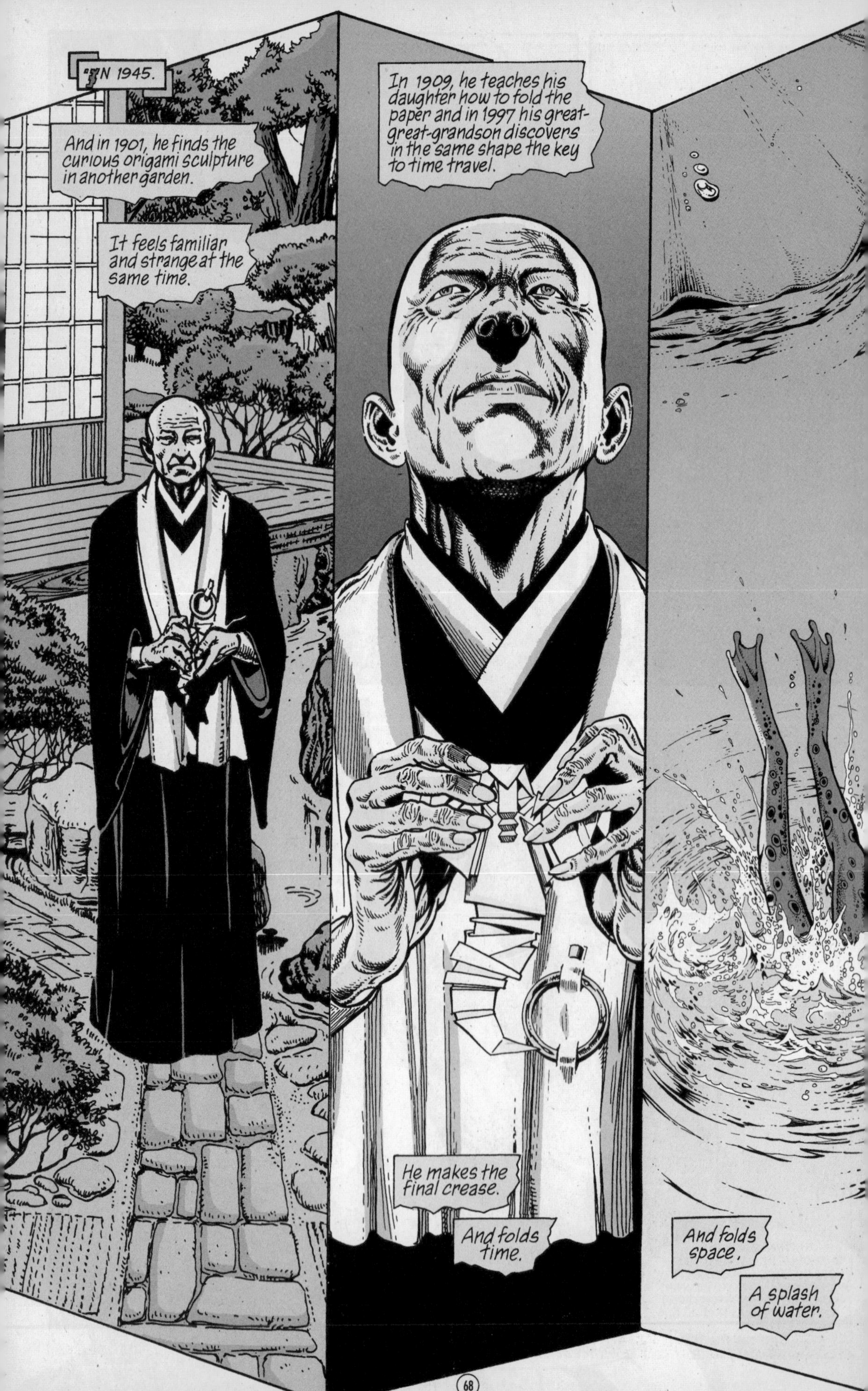
"IN 1945.
And in 1901, he finds the curious origami sculpture in another garden.
It feels familiar and strange at the same time.
In 1909, he teaches his daughter how to fold the paper and in 1997 his great-great-grandson discovers in the same shape the key to time travel.
He makes the final crease.
And folds time.
And folds space.
A splash of water.

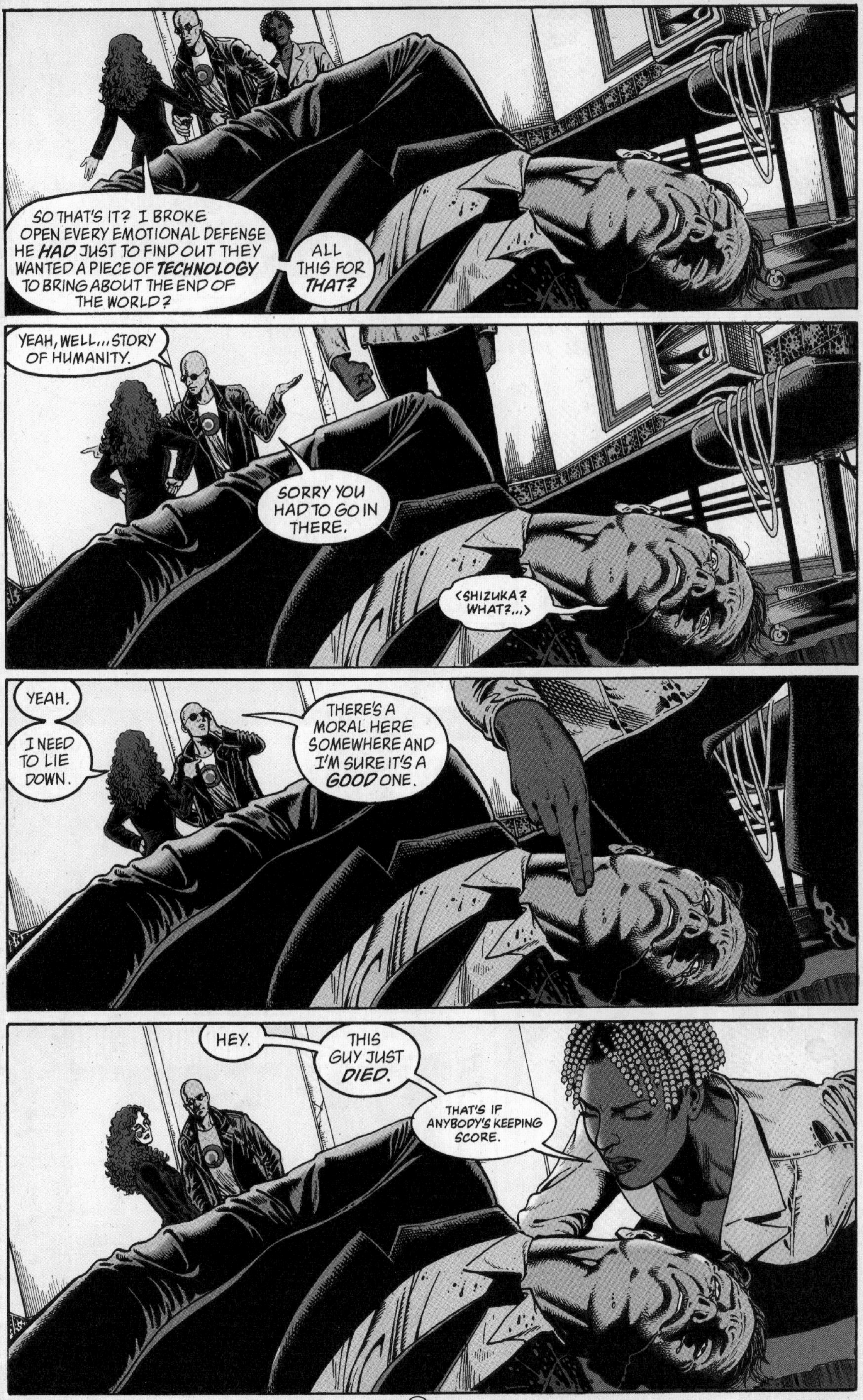
SO THAT'S IT? I BROKE OPEN EVERY EMOTIONAL DEFENSE HE HAD JUST TO FIND OUT THEY WANTED A PIECE OF TECHNOLOGY TO BRING ABOUT THE END OF THE WORLD?
ALL THIS FOR THAT?
YEAH, WELL... STORY OF HUMANITY.
SORRY YOU HAD TO GO IN THERE.
<SHIZUKA? WHAT?...>
YEAH.
I NEED TO LIE DOWN.
THERE'S A MORAL HERE SOMEWHERE AND I'M SURE IT'S A GOOD ONE.
HEY.
THIS GUY JUST DIED.
THAT'S IF ANYBODY'S KEEPING SCORE.

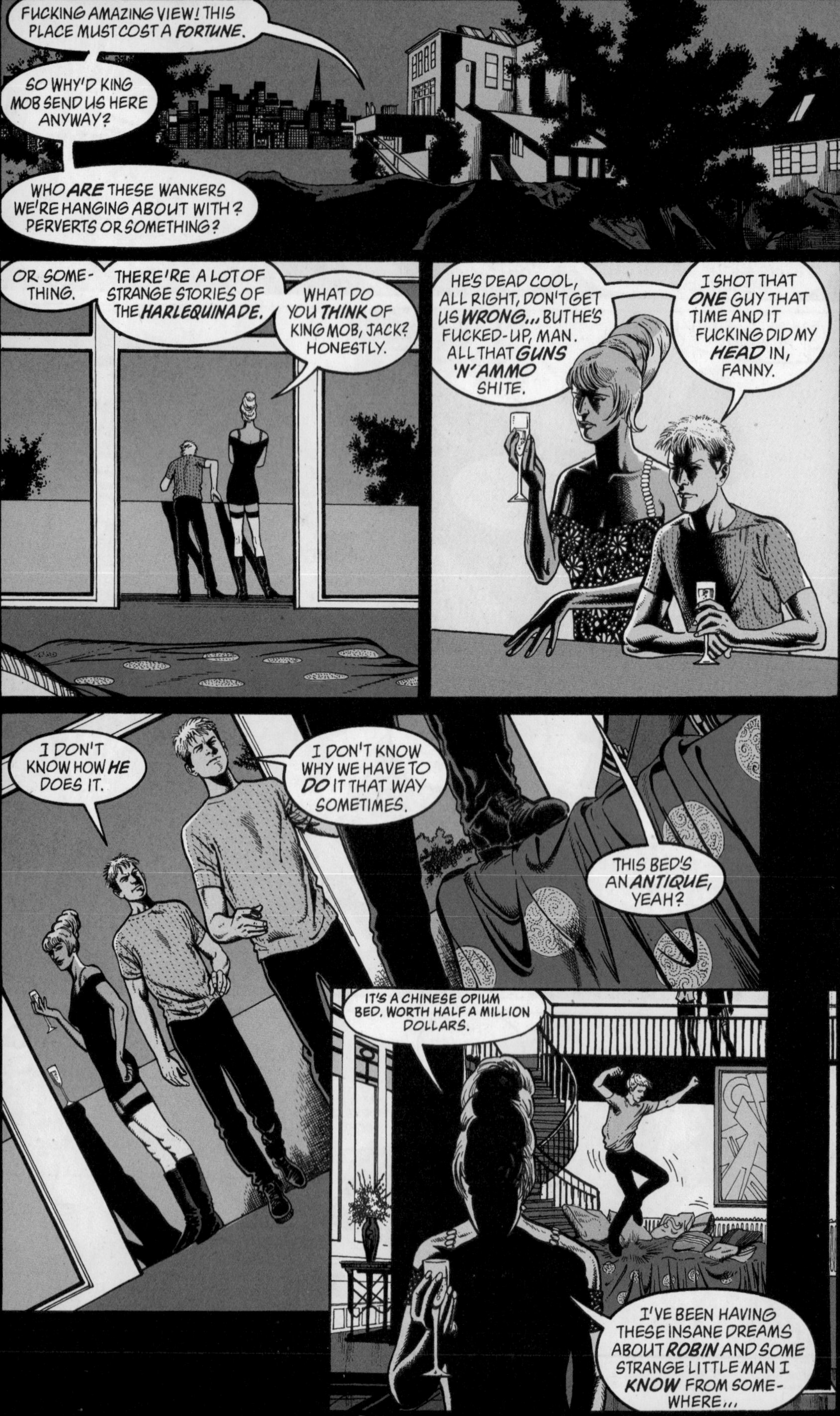
FUCKING AMAZING VIEW! THIS PLACE MUST COST A FORTUNE.
SO WHY'D KING MOB SEND US HERE ANYWAY?
WHO ARE THESE WANKERS WE'RE HANGING ABOUT WITH? PERVERTS OR SOMETHING?
OR SOME-THING.
THERE'RE A LOT OF STRANGE STORIES OF THE HARLEQUINADE.
WHAT DO YOU THINK OF KING MOB, JACK? HONESTLY.
HE'S DEAD COOL, ALL RIGHT, DON'T GET US WRONG... BUT HE'S FUCKED-UP, MAN. ALL THAT GUNS 'N' AMMO SHITE.
I SHOT THAT ONE GUY THAT TIME AND IT FUCKING DID MY HEAD IN, FANNY.
I DON'T KNOW HOW HE DOES IT.
I DON'T KNOW WHY WE HAVE TO DO IT THAT WAY SOMETIMES.
THIS BED'S AN ANTIQUE, YEAH?
IT'S A CHINESE OPIUM BED. WORTH HALF A MILLION DOLLARS.
I'VE BEEN HAVING THESE INSANE DREAMS ABOUT ROBIN AND SOME STRANGE LITTLE MAN I KNOW FROM SOME-WHERE...

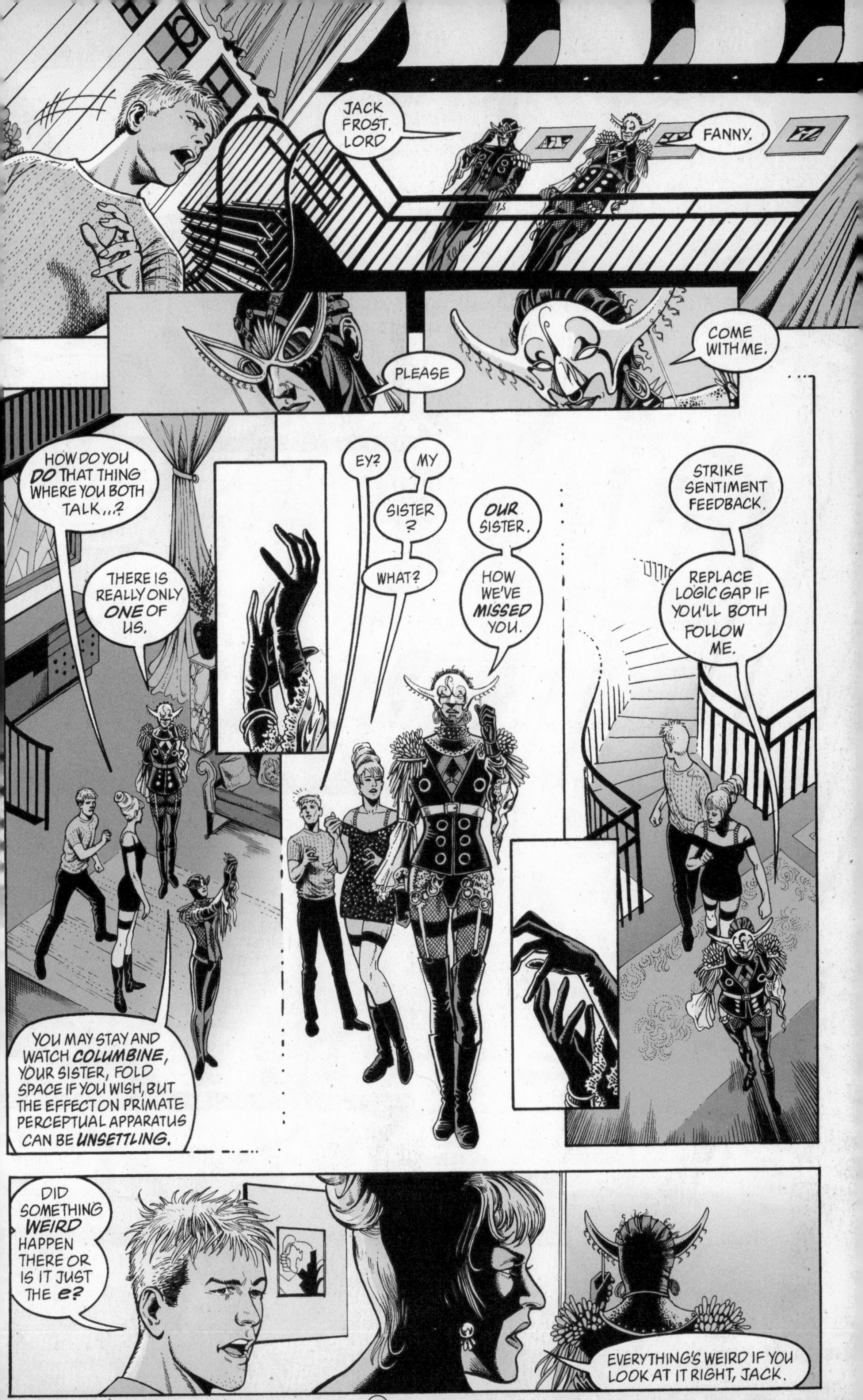
JACK FROST, LORD
FANNY.
PLEASE
COME WITH ME.
HOW DO YOU DO THAT THING WHERE YOU BOTH TALK...?
THERE IS REALLY ONLY ONE OF US.
YOU MAY STAY AND WATCH COLUMBINE, YOUR SISTER, FOLD SPACE IF YOU WISH, BUT THE EFFECT ON PRIMATE PERCEPTUAL APPARATUS CAN BE UNSETTLING.
EY?
MY
SISTER?
WHAT?
OUR SISTER.
HOW WE'VE MISSED YOU.
STRIKE SENTIMENT FEEDBACK.
REPLACE LOGIC GAP IF YOU'LL BOTH FOLLOW ME.
DID SOMETHING WEIRD HAPPEN THERE OR IS IT JUST THE e?
EVERYTHING'S WEIRD IF YOU LOOK AT IT RIGHT, JACK.

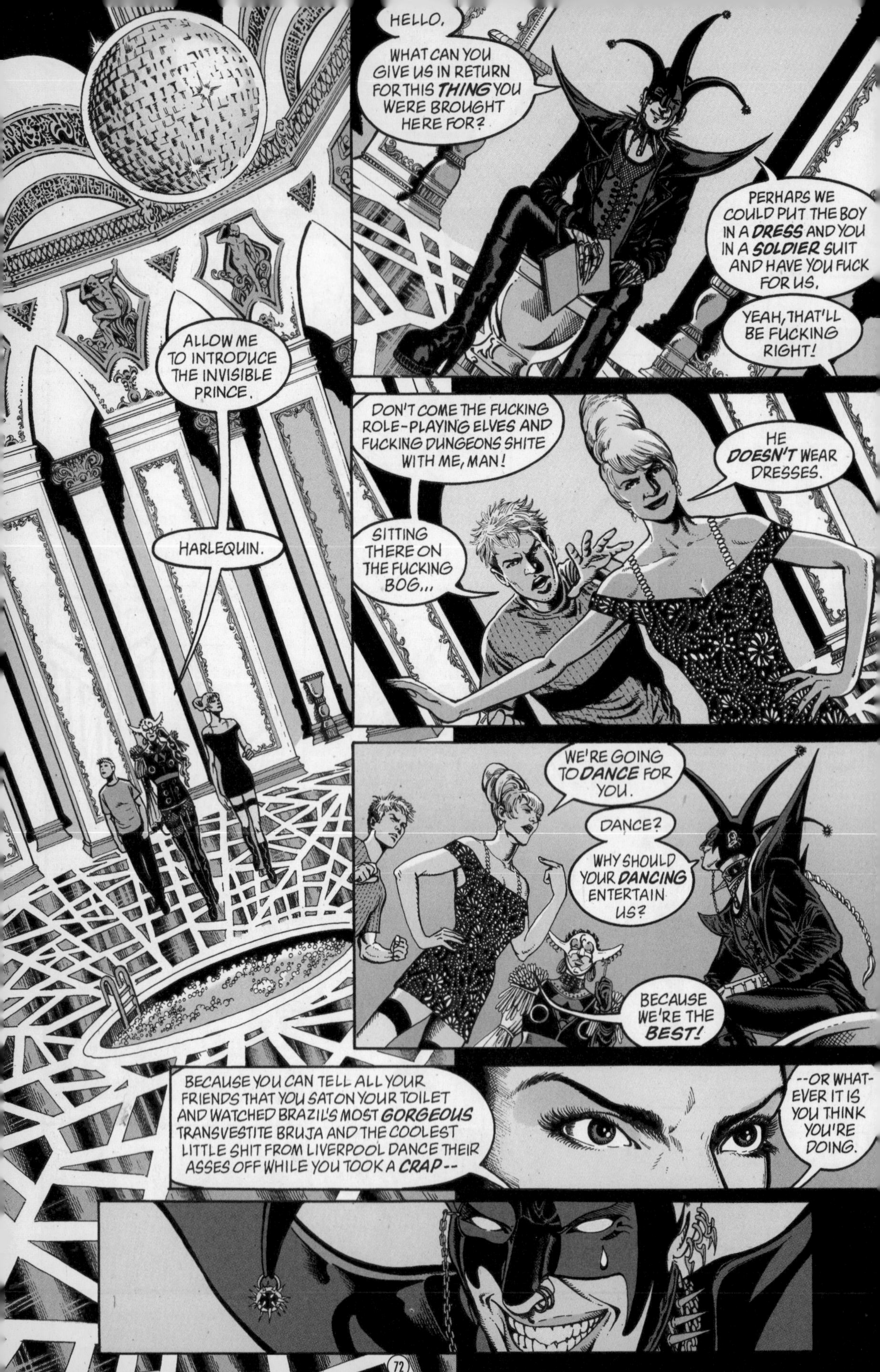
ALLOW ME TO INTRODUCE THE INVISIBLE PRINCE.
HARLEQUIN.
HELLO.
WHAT CAN YOU GIVE US IN RETURN FOR THIS THING YOU WERE BROUGHT HERE FOR?
PERHAPS WE COULD PUT THE BOY IN A DRESS AND YOU IN A SOLDIER SUIT AND HAVE YOU FUCK FOR US.
YEAH, THAT'LL BE FUCKING RIGHT!
DON'T COME THE FUCKING ROLE-PLAYING ELVES AND FUCKING DUNGEONS SHITE WITH ME, MAN!
SITTING THERE ON THE FUCKING BOG...
HE DOESN'T WEAR DRESSES.
WE'RE GOING TO DANCE FOR YOU.
DANCE?
WHY SHOULD YOUR DANCING ENTERTAIN US?
BECAUSE WE'RE THE BEST!
BECAUSE YOU CAN TELL ALL YOUR FRIENDS THAT YOU SAT ON YOUR TOILET AND WATCHED BRAZIL'S MOST GORGEOUS TRANSVESTITE BRUJA AND THE COOLEST LITTLE SHIT FROM LIVERPOOL DANCE THEIR ASSES OFF WHILE YOU TOOK A CRAP--
--OR WHATEVER IT IS YOU THINK YOU'RE DOING.

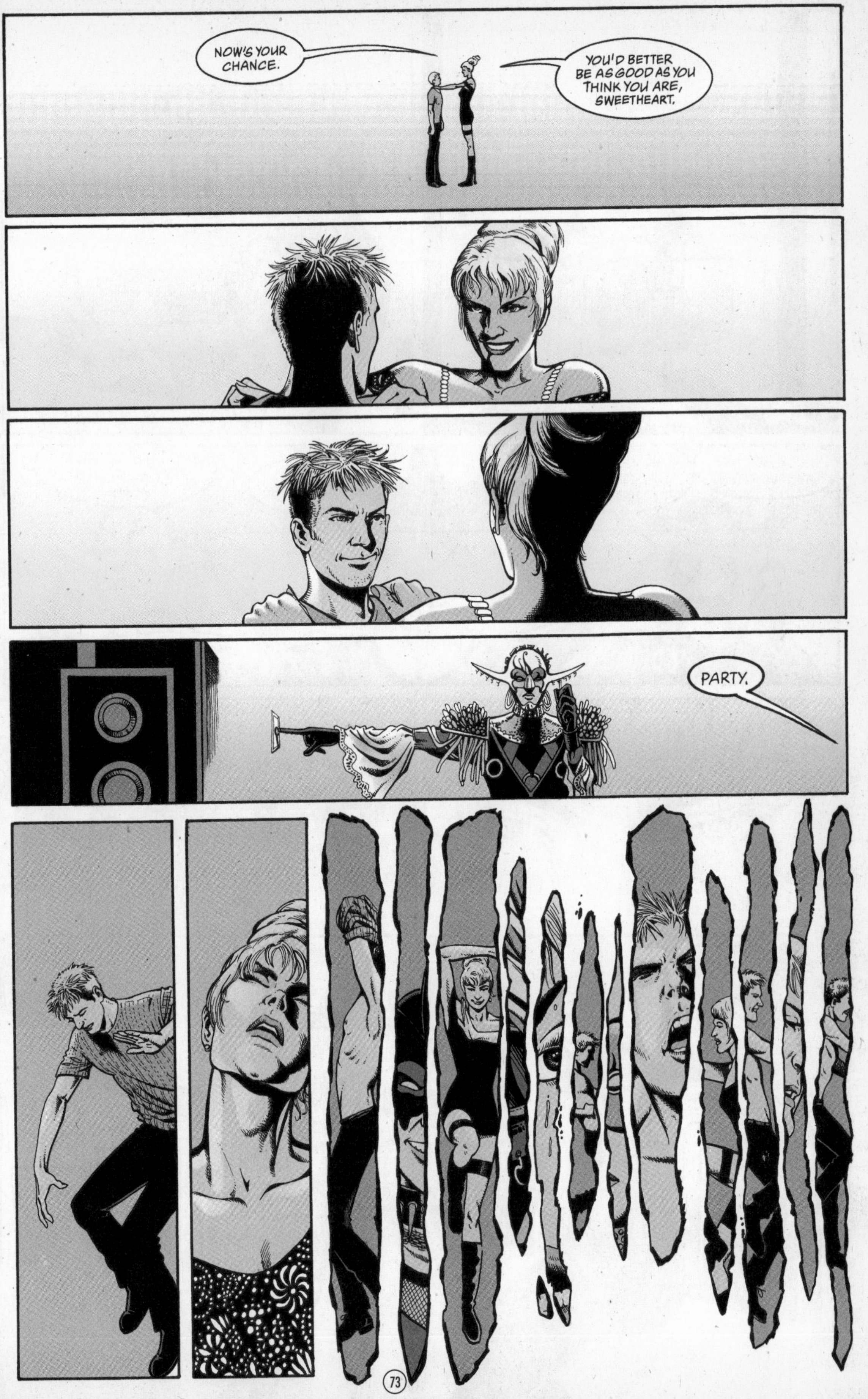
NOW'S YOUR CHANCE.
YOU'D BETTER BE AS GOOD AS YOU THINK YOU ARE, SWEETHEART.
PARTY.

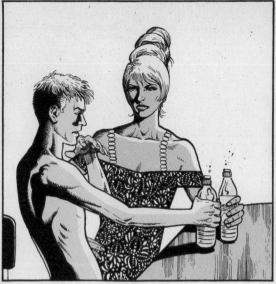

THESE TWO ARE MY FAVORITES.

CAN YOU SEE THE DAZZLE ALL AROUND?

HOW STRANGE.

SAD LIKE FAR AWAY. LIKE CHILDREN FAR AWAY.

"THEY TALK IN EMOTIONAL AGGREGATES."

WHUDDAWHU

DDAWHUDDA

WHUDDA HUDDA UDDAW

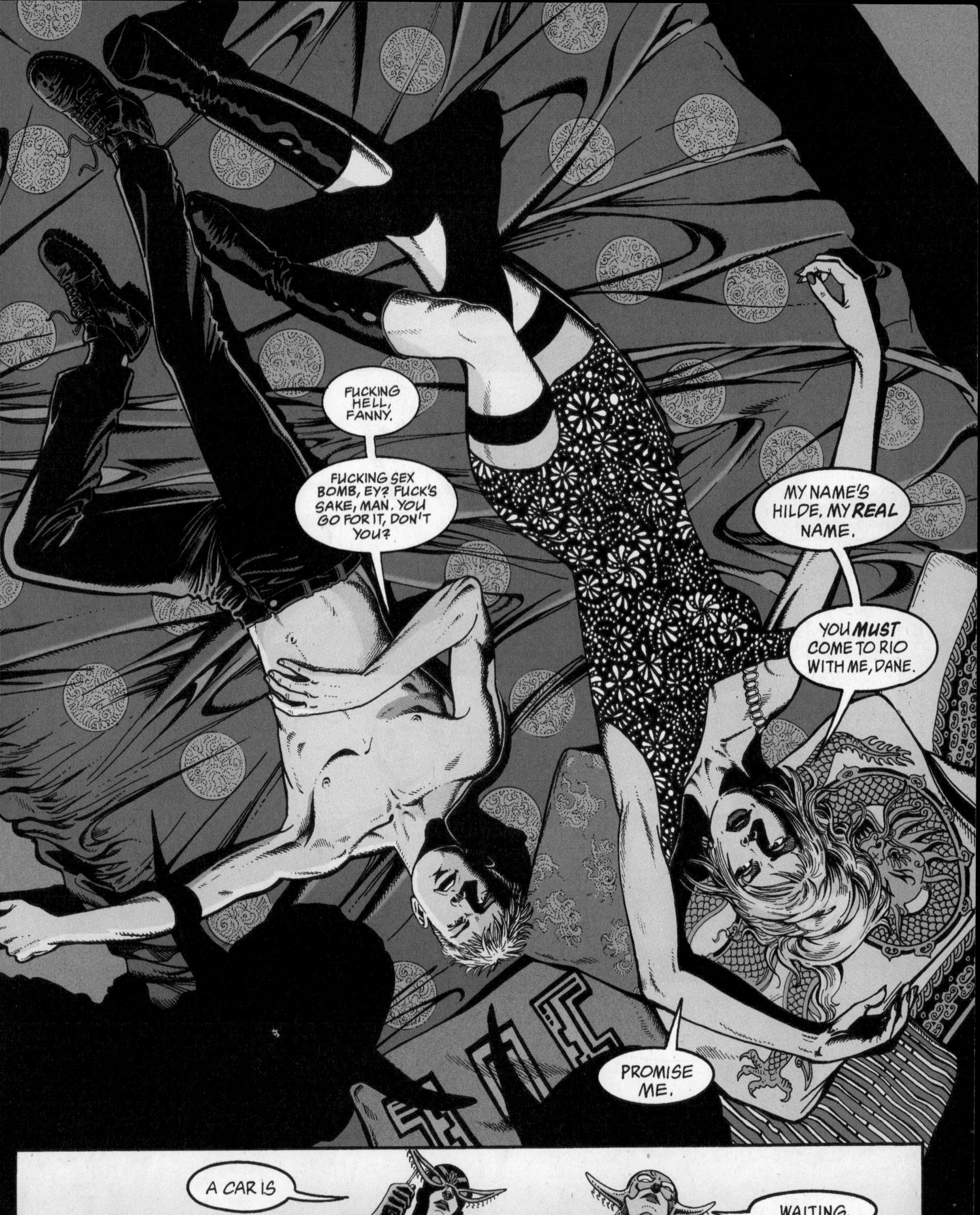
FUCKING HELL, FANNY.
FUCKING SEX BOMB, EY? FUCK'S SAKE, MAN. YOU GO FOR IT, DON'T YOU?
MY NAME'S HILDE. MY **REAL** NAME.
YOU **MUST** COME TO RIO WITH ME, DANE.
PROMISE ME.

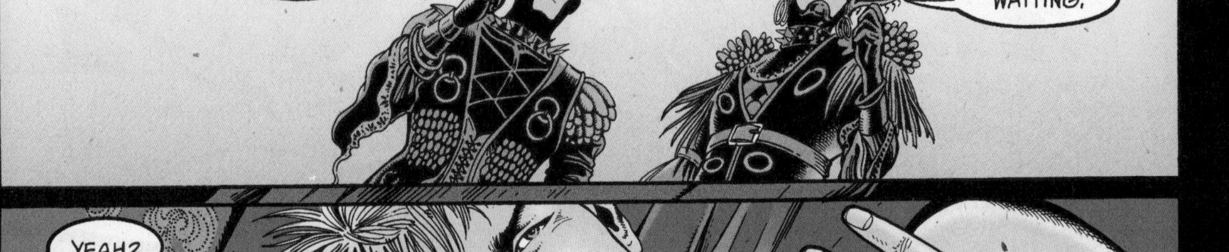
A CAR IS
WAITING.

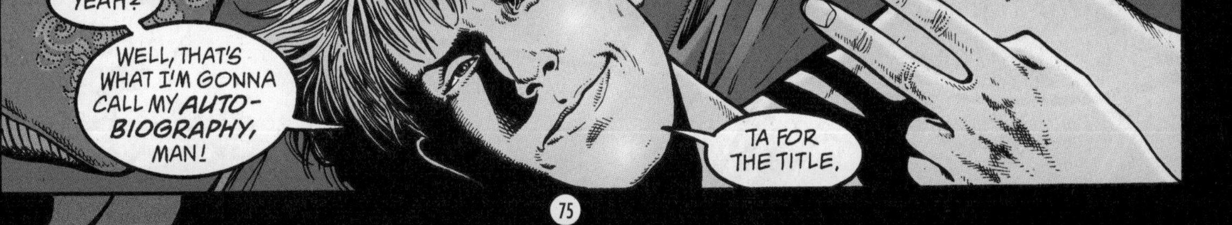
YEAH?
WELL, THAT'S WHAT I'M GONNA CALL MY **AUTO-BIOGRAPHY,** MAN!
TA FOR THE TITLE.

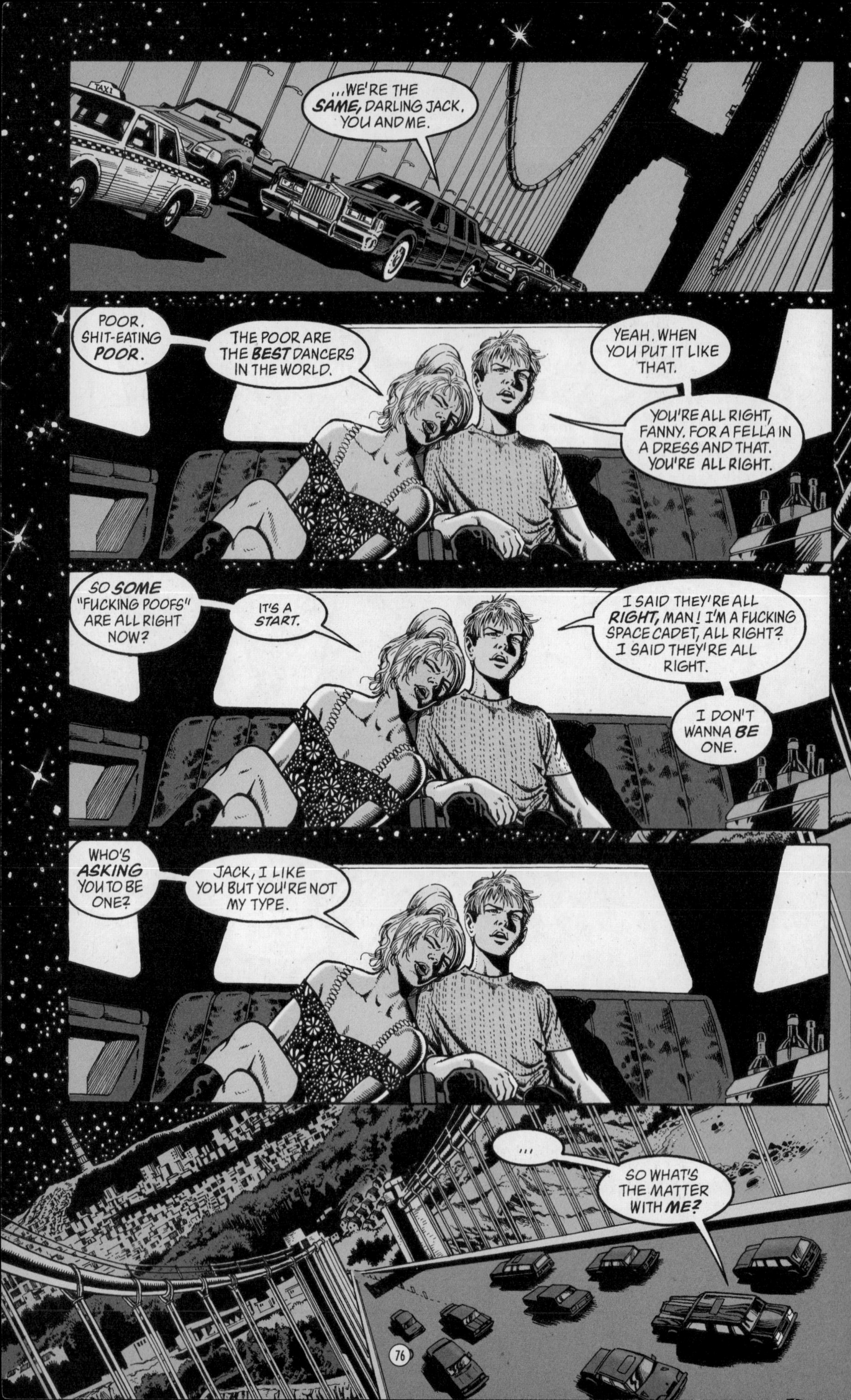

TAXI
...WE'RE THE SAME, DARLING JACK. YOU AND ME.
POOR. SHIT-EATING POOR.
THE POOR ARE THE BEST DANCERS IN THE WORLD.
YEAH. WHEN YOU PUT IT LIKE THAT.
YOU'RE ALL RIGHT, FANNY. FOR A FELLA IN A DRESS AND THAT. YOU'RE ALL RIGHT.
SO SOME "FUCKING POOFS" ARE ALL RIGHT NOW?
IT'S A START.
I SAID THEY'RE ALL RIGHT, MAN! I'M A FUCKING SPACE CADET, ALL RIGHT? I SAID THEY'RE ALL RIGHT.
I DON'T WANNA BE ONE.
WHO'S ASKING YOU TO BE ONE?
JACK, I LIKE YOU BUT YOU'RE NOT MY TYPE.
...
SO WHAT'S THE MATTER WITH ME?

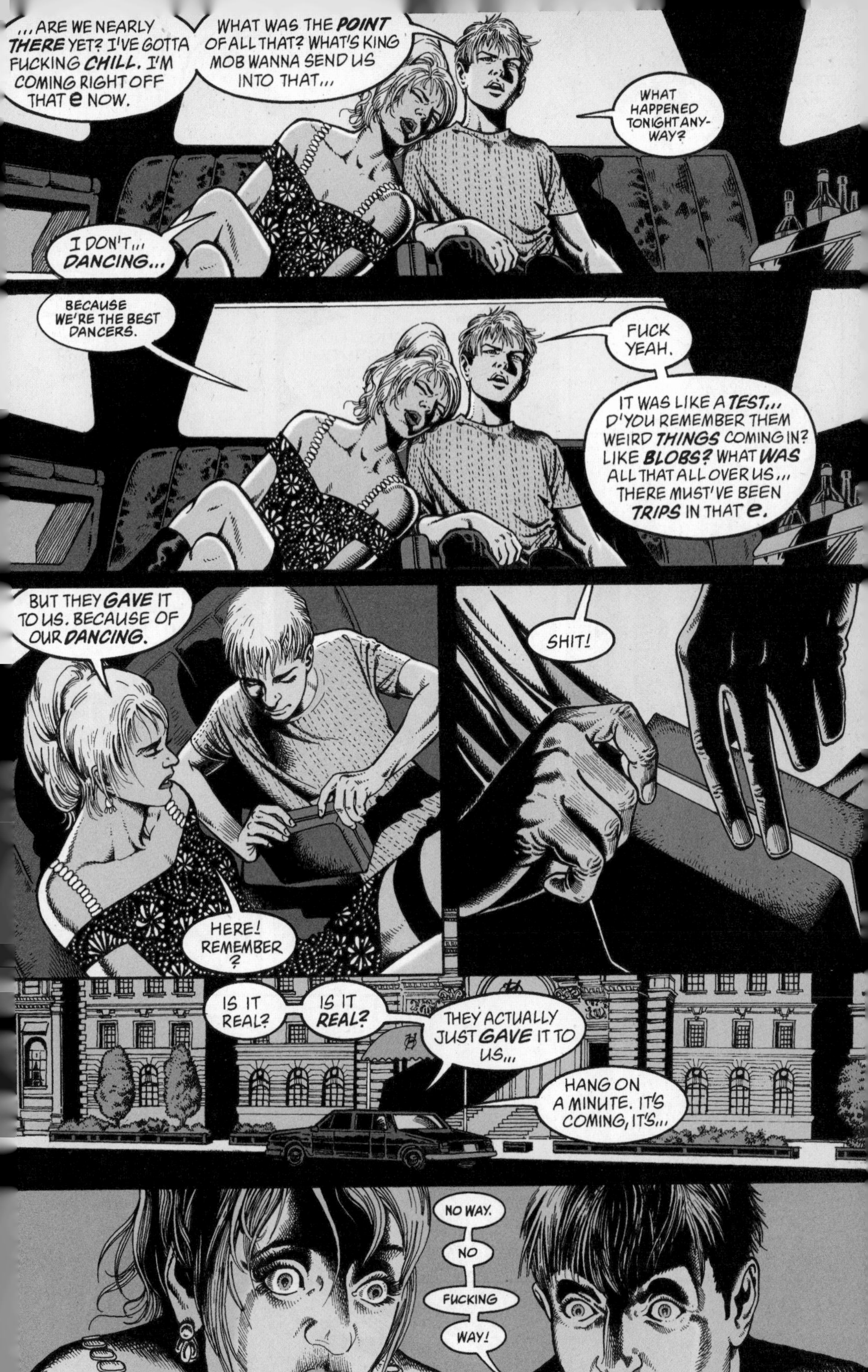
...ARE WE NEARLY THERE YET? I'VE GOTTA FUCKING CHILL. I'M COMING RIGHT OFF THAT e NOW.
WHAT WAS THE POINT OF ALL THAT? WHAT'S KING MOB WANNA SEND US INTO THAT...
WHAT HAPPENED TONIGHT ANYWAY?
I DON'T... DANCING...
BECAUSE WE'RE THE BEST DANCERS.
FUCK YEAH.
IT WAS LIKE A TEST... D'YOU REMEMBER THEM WEIRD THINGS COMING IN? LIKE BLOBS? WHAT WAS ALL THAT ALL OVER US... THERE MUST'VE BEEN TRIPS IN THAT e.
BUT THEY GAVE IT TO US. BECAUSE OF OUR DANCING.
HERE! REMEMBER?
SHIT!
IS IT REAL?
IS IT REAL?
THEY ACTUALLY JUST GAVE IT TO US...
HANG ON A MINUTE. IT'S COMING, IT'S...
NO WAY.
NO
FUCKING
WAY!

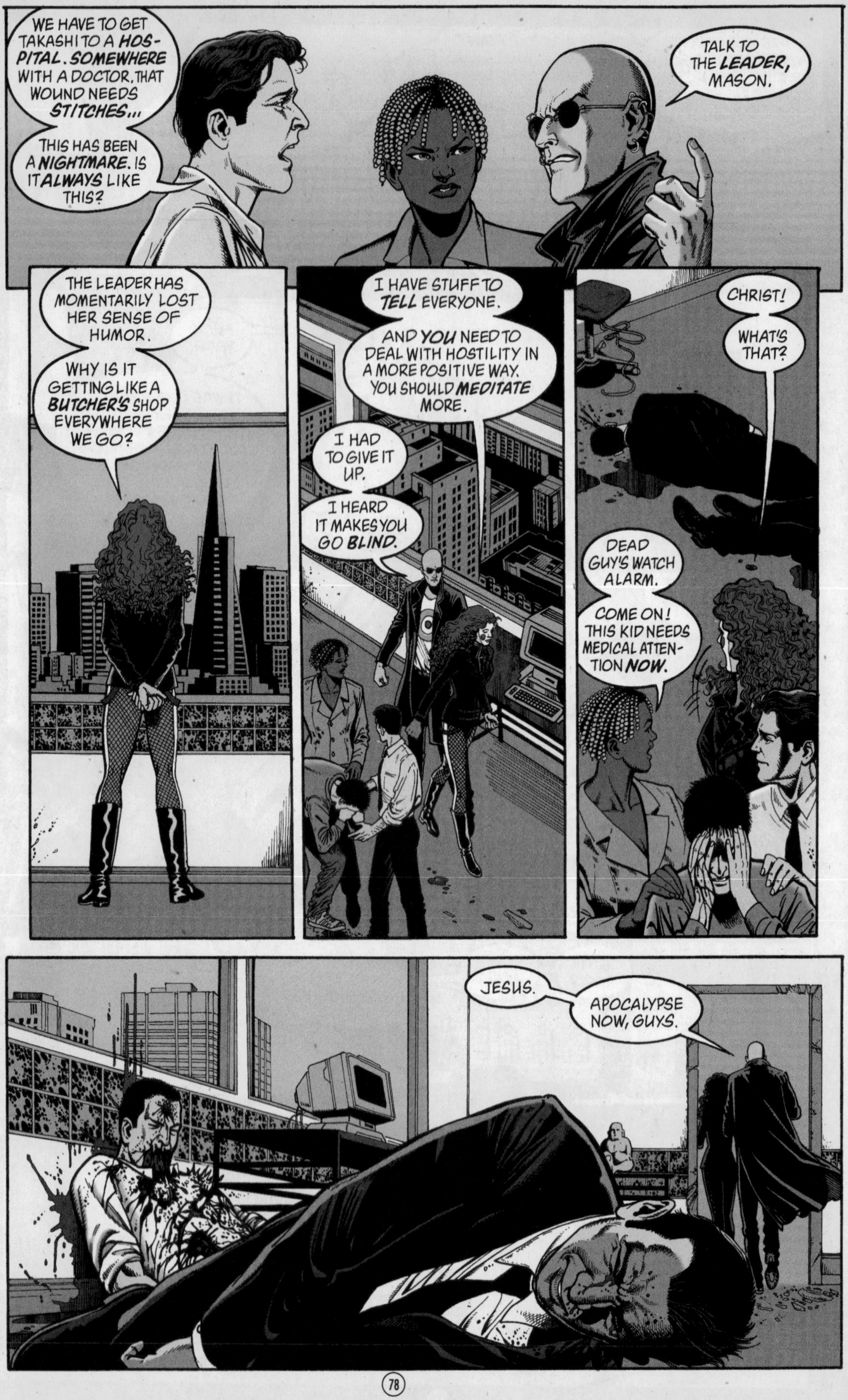
WE HAVE TO GET TAKASHI TO A HOS-PITAL. SOMEWHERE WITH A DOCTOR. THAT WOUND NEEDS STITCHES...
THIS HAS BEEN A NIGHTMARE. IS IT ALWAYS LIKE THIS?
TALK TO THE LEADER, MASON.
THE LEADER HAS MOMENTARILY LOST HER SENSE OF HUMOR.
WHY IS IT GETTING LIKE A BUTCHER'S SHOP EVERYWHERE WE GO?
I HAVE STUFF TO TELL EVERYONE.
AND YOU NEED TO DEAL WITH HOSTILITY IN A MORE POSITIVE WAY. YOU SHOULD MEDITATE MORE.
I HAD TO GIVE IT UP.
I HEARD IT MAKES YOU GO BLIND.
CHRIST!
WHAT'S THAT?
DEAD GUY'S WATCH ALARM.
COME ON! THIS KID NEEDS MEDICAL ATTEN-TION NOW.
JESUS.
APOCALYPSE NOW, GUYS.

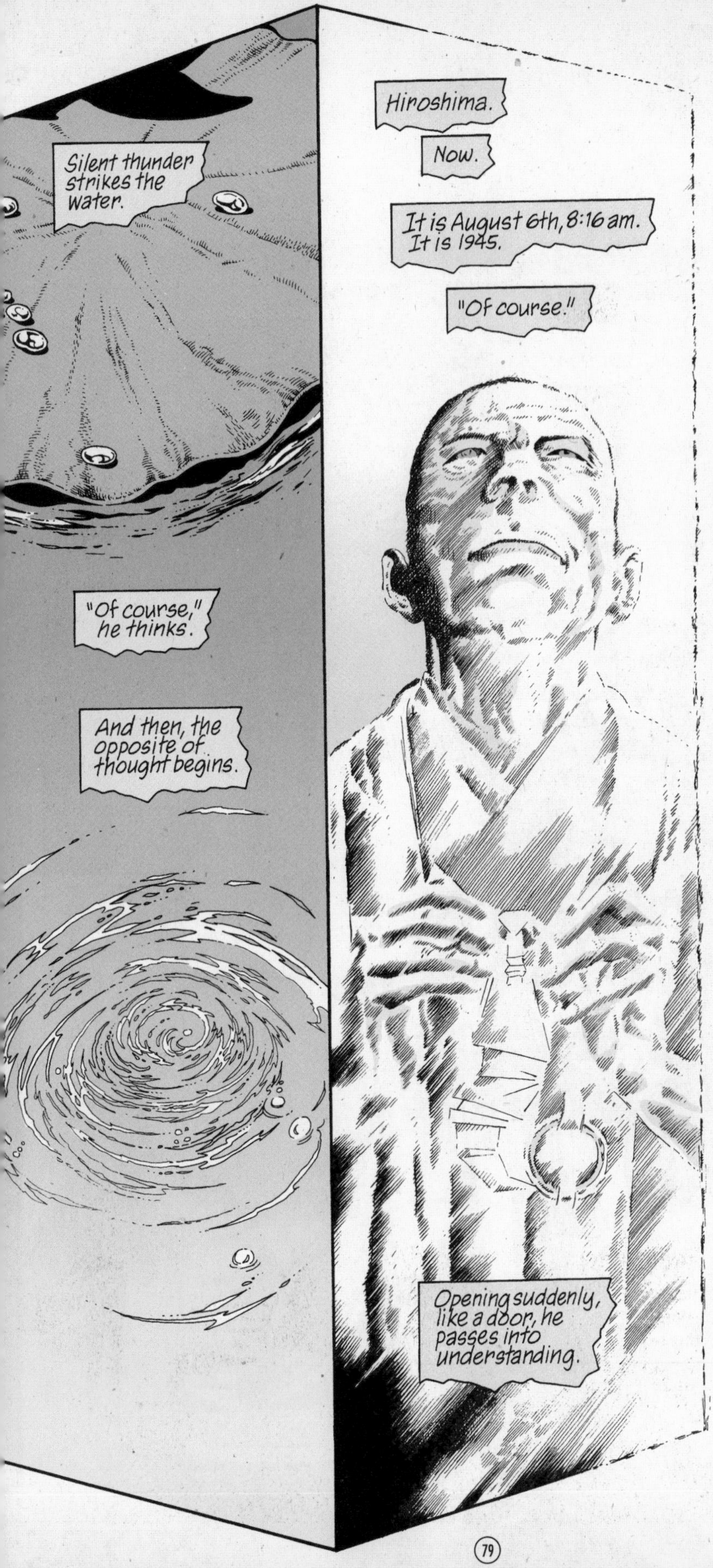
Silent thunder strikes the water.
Hiroshima.
Now.
It is August 6th, 8:16 am. It is 1945.
"Of course."
"Of course," he thinks.
And then, the opposite of thought begins.
Opening suddenly, like a door, he passes into understanding.

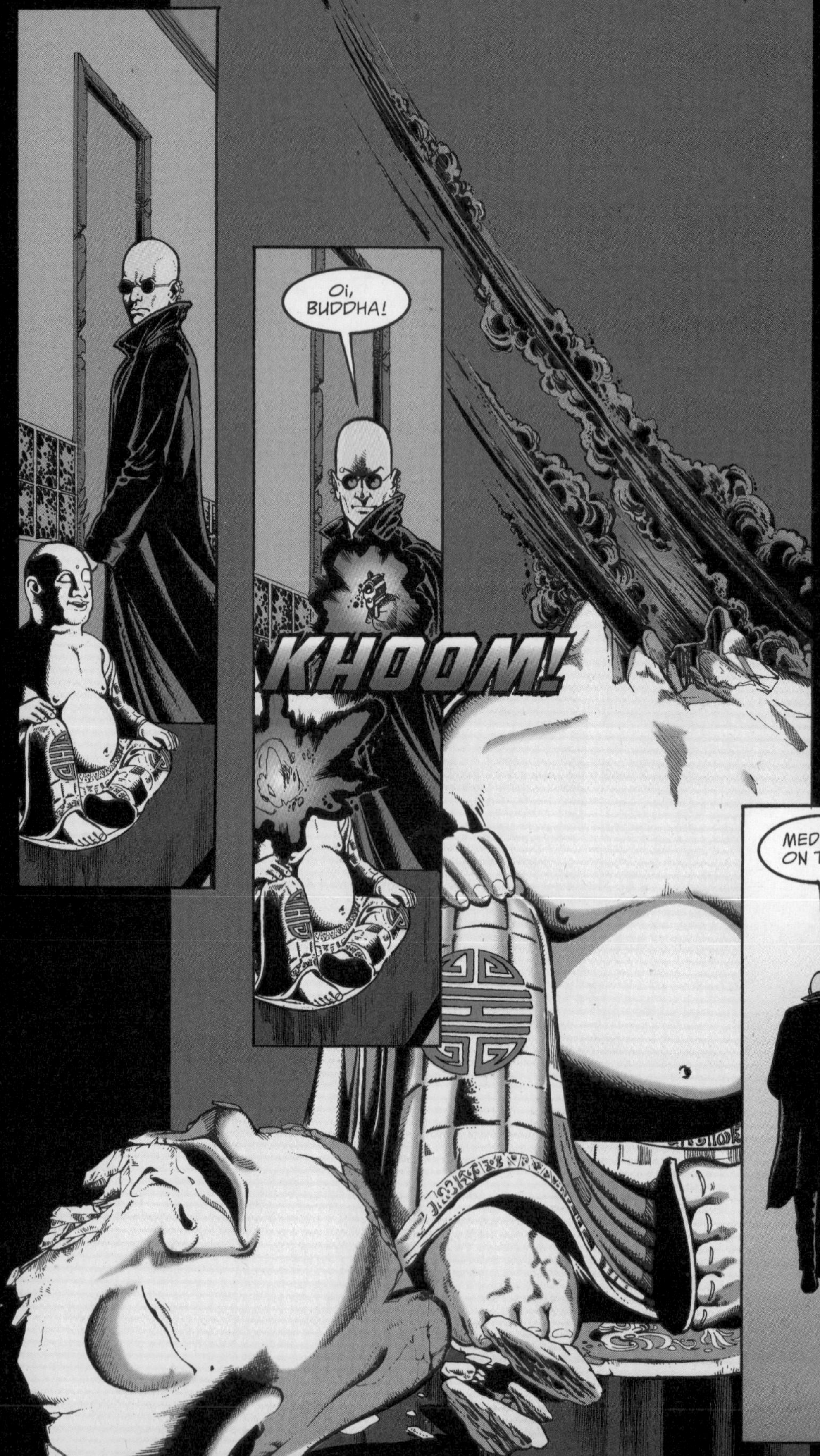
Oi, BUDDHA!
KHOOM!
MEDITATE ON THAT.

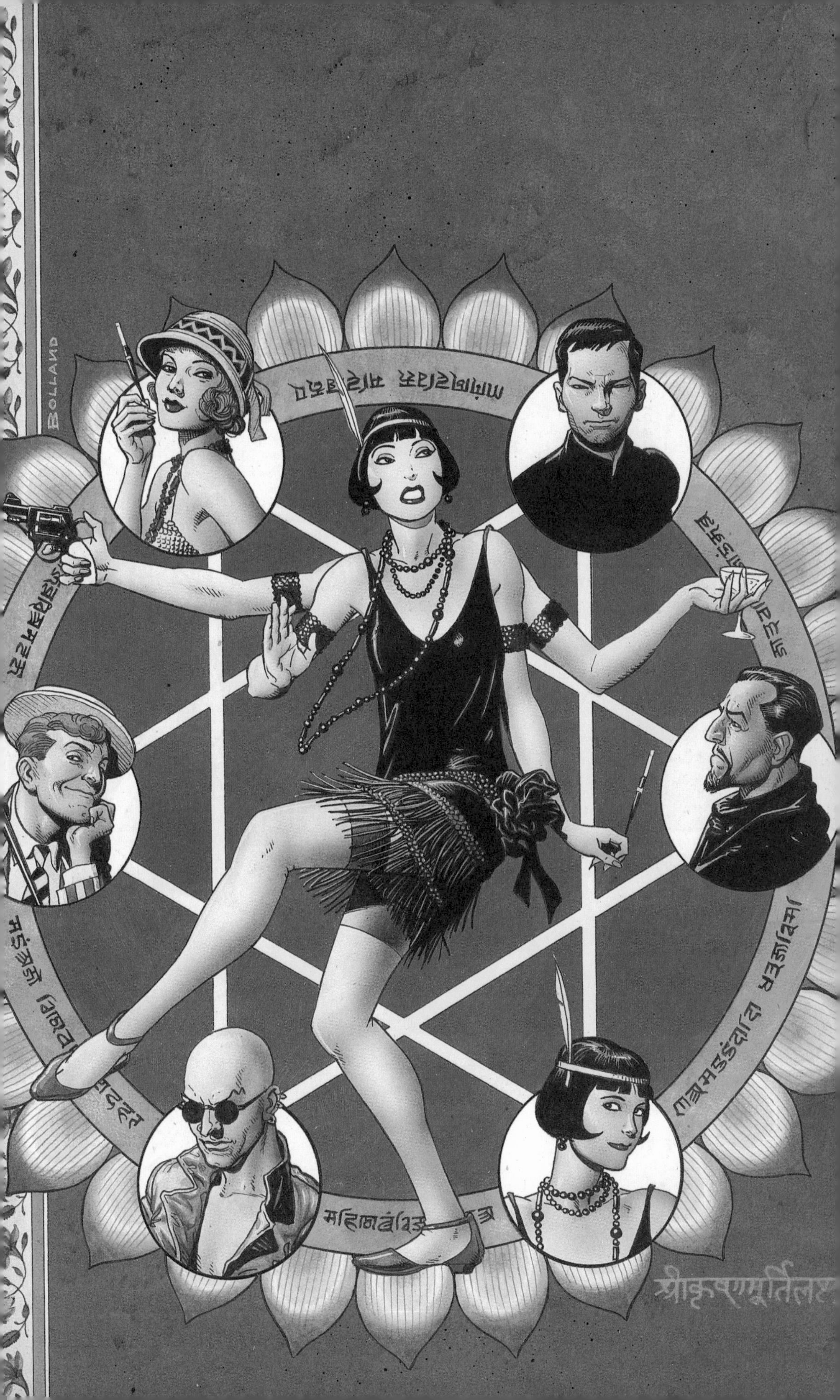
BOLLAND

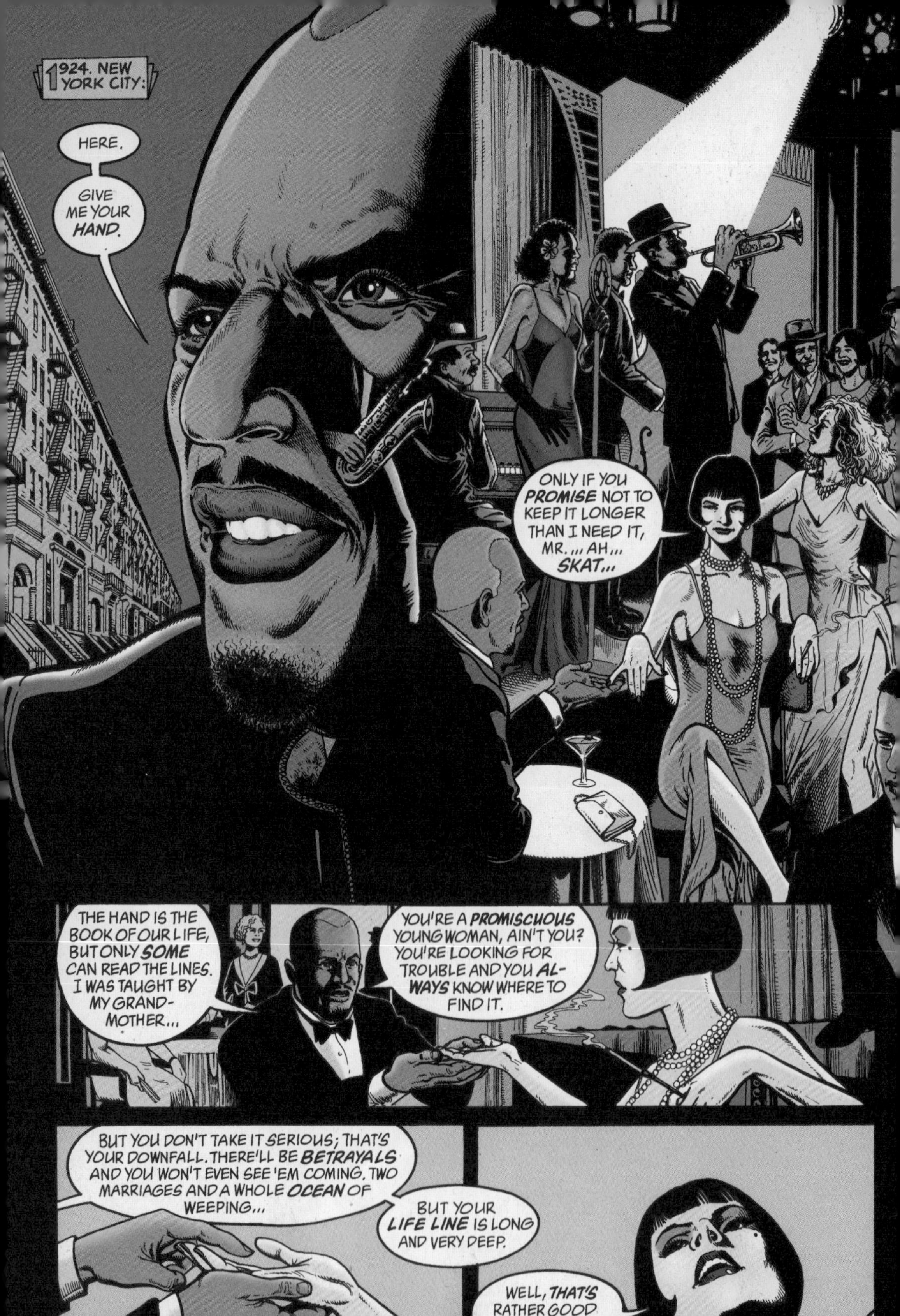
1924. NEW YORK CITY:
HERE.
GIVE ME YOUR HAND.
ONLY IF YOU PROMISE NOT TO KEEP IT LONGER THAN I NEED IT, MR. ... AH ... SKAT...
THE HAND IS THE BOOK OF OUR LIFE, BUT ONLY SOME CAN READ THE LINES. I WAS TAUGHT BY MY GRAND-MOTHER...
YOU'RE A PROMISCUOUS YOUNG WOMAN, AIN'T YOU? YOU'RE LOOKING FOR TROUBLE AND YOU AL-WAYS KNOW WHERE TO FIND IT.
BUT YOU DON'T TAKE IT SERIOUS; THAT'S YOUR DOWNFALL. THERE'LL BE BETRAYALS AND YOU WON'T EVEN SEE 'EM COMING. TWO MARRIAGES AND A WHOLE OCEAN OF WEEPING...
BUT YOUR LIFE LINE IS LONG AND VERY DEEP.
WELL, THAT'S RATHER GOOD NEWS, ISN'T IT?

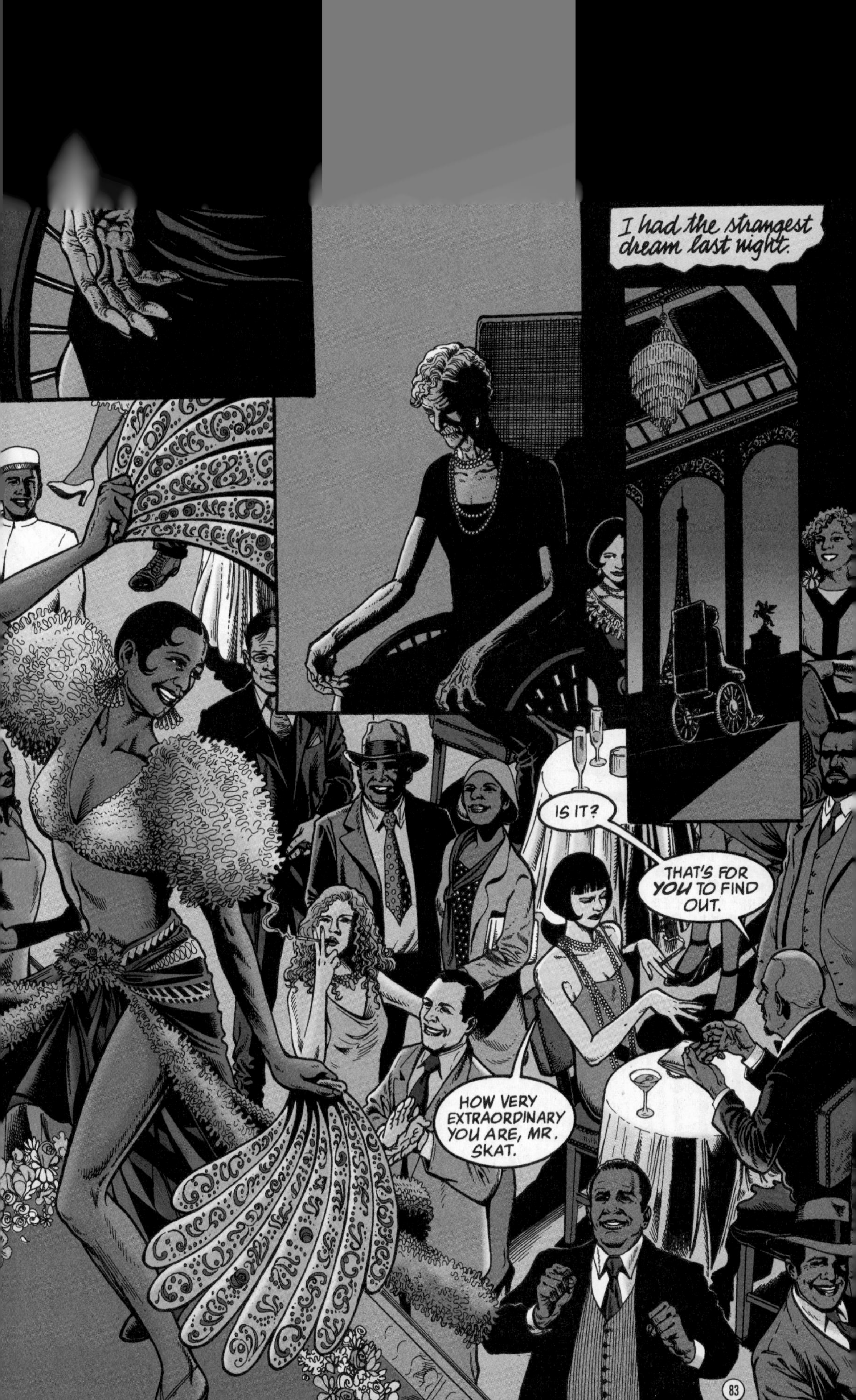
I had the strangest dream last night.
IS IT?
THAT'S FOR YOU TO FIND OUT.
HOW VERY EXTRAORDINARY YOU ARE, MR. SKAT.

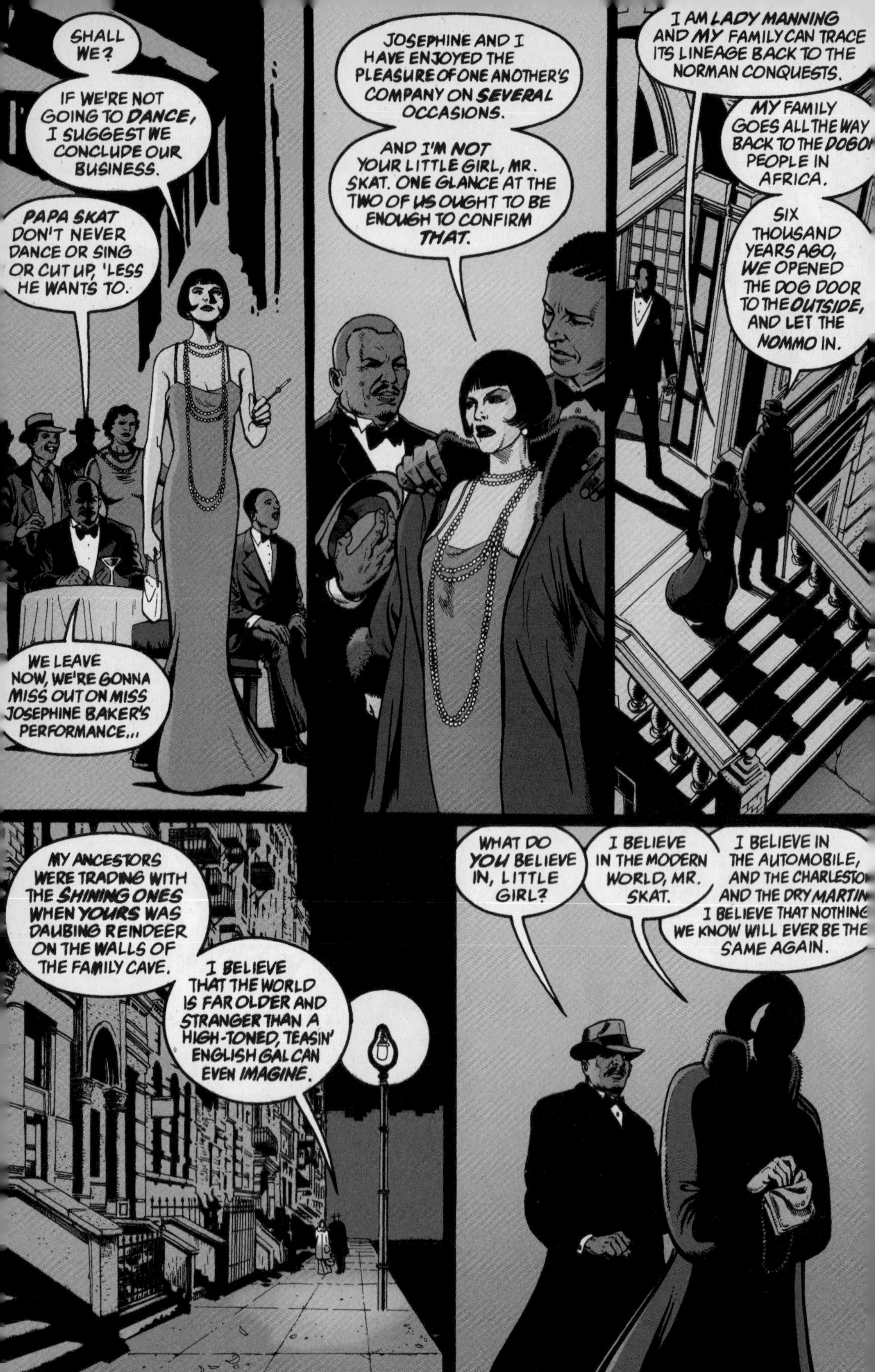
SHALL WE?
IF WE'RE NOT GOING TO DANCE, I SUGGEST WE CONCLUDE OUR BUSINESS.
PAPA SKAT DON'T NEVER DANCE OR SING OR CUT UP, 'LESS HE WANTS TO.
WE LEAVE NOW, WE'RE GONNA MISS OUT ON MISS JOSEPHINE BAKER'S PERFORMANCE...
JOSEPHINE AND I HAVE ENJOYED THE PLEASURE OF ONE ANOTHER'S COMPANY ON SEVERAL OCCASIONS.
AND I'M NOT YOUR LITTLE GIRL, MR. SKAT. ONE GLANCE AT THE TWO OF US OUGHT TO BE ENOUGH TO CONFIRM THAT.
I AM LADY MANNING AND MY FAMILY CAN TRACE ITS LINEAGE BACK TO THE NORMAN CONQUESTS.
MY FAMILY GOES ALL THE WAY BACK TO THE DOGON PEOPLE IN AFRICA.
SIX THOUSAND YEARS AGO, WE OPENED THE DOG DOOR TO THE OUTSIDE, AND LET THE NOMMO IN.
MY ANCESTORS WERE TRADING WITH THE SHINING ONES WHEN YOURS WAS DAUBING REINDEER ON THE WALLS OF THE FAMILY CAVE.
I BELIEVE THAT THE WORLD IS FAR OLDER AND STRANGER THAN A HIGH-TONED, TEASIN' ENGLISH GAL CAN EVEN IMAGINE.
WHAT DO YOU BELIEVE IN, LITTLE GIRL?
I BELIEVE IN THE MODERN WORLD, MR. SKAT.
I BELIEVE IN THE AUTOMOBILE, AND THE CHARLESTON AND THE DRY MARTINI. I BELIEVE THAT NOTHING WE KNOW WILL EVER BE THE SAME AGAIN.

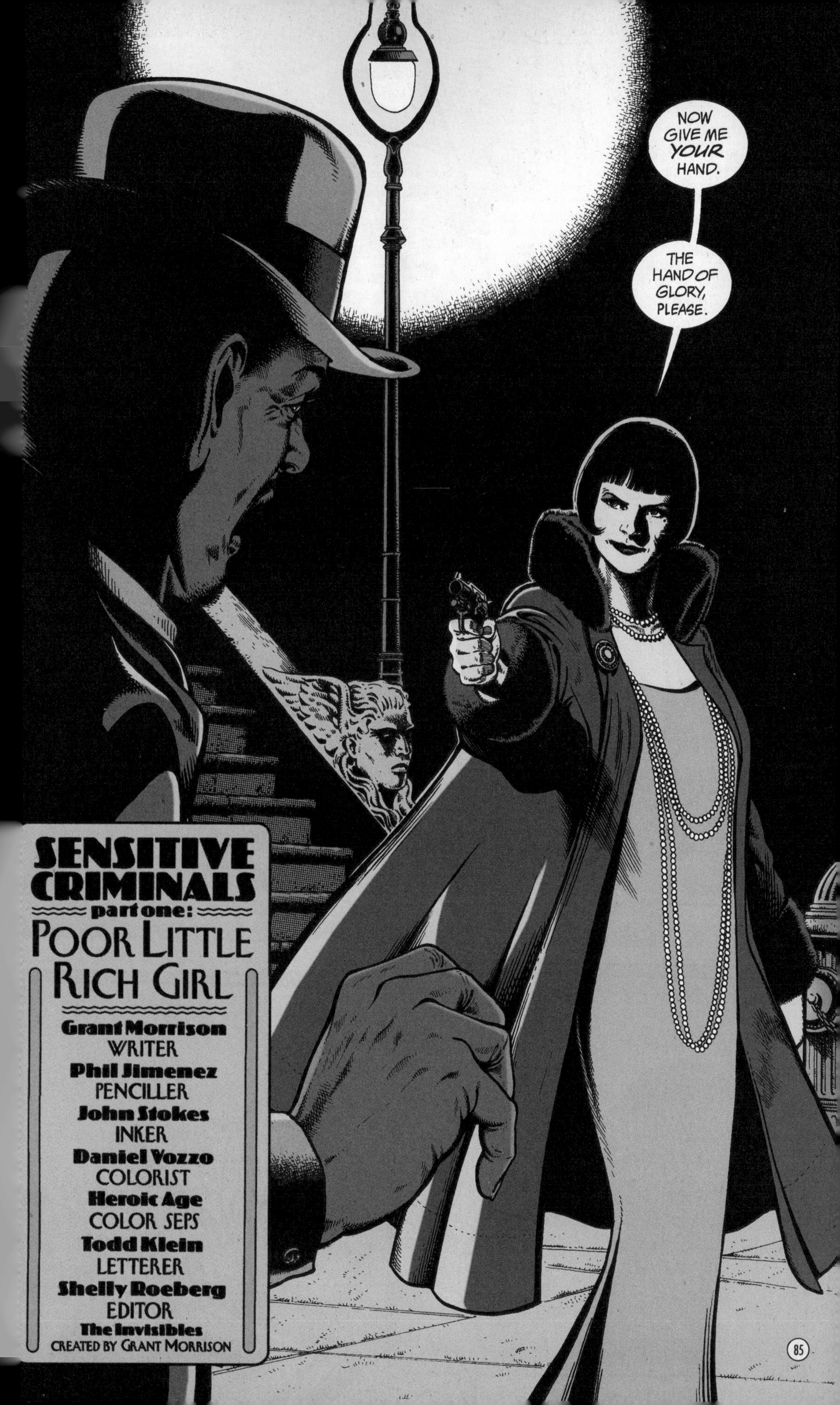
NOW GIVE ME YOUR HAND.
THE HAND OF GLORY, PLEASE.
SENSITIVE CRIMINALS
part one:
POOR LITTLE RICH GIRL
Grant Morrison
WRITER
Phil Jimenez
PENCILLER
John Stokes
INKER
Daniel Vozzo
COLORIST
Heroic Age
COLOR SEPS
Todd Klein
LETTERER
Shelly Roeberg
EDITOR
The Invisibles
CREATED BY GRANT MORRISON

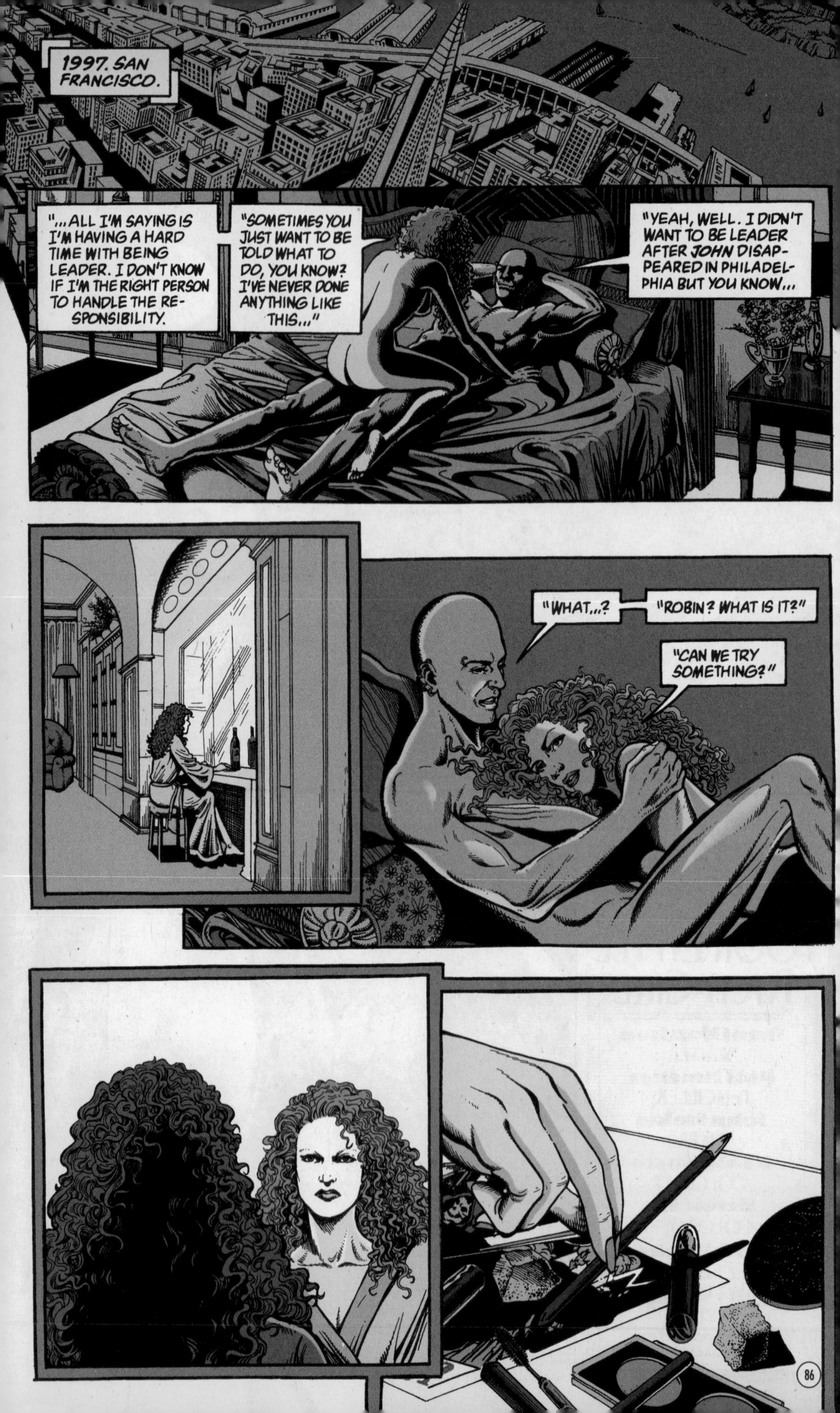
1997. SAN FRANCISCO.
"...ALL I'M SAYING IS I'M HAVING A HARD TIME WITH BEING LEADER. I DON'T KNOW IF I'M THE RIGHT PERSON TO HANDLE THE RE-SPONSIBILITY.
"SOMETIMES YOU JUST WANT TO BE TOLD WHAT TO DO, YOU KNOW? I'VE NEVER DONE ANYTHING LIKE THIS..."
"YEAH, WELL. I DIDN'T WANT TO BE LEADER AFTER JOHN DISAP-PEARED IN PHILADEL-PHIA BUT YOU KNOW...
"WHAT...?
"ROBIN? WHAT IS IT?"
"CAN WE TRY SOMETHING?"

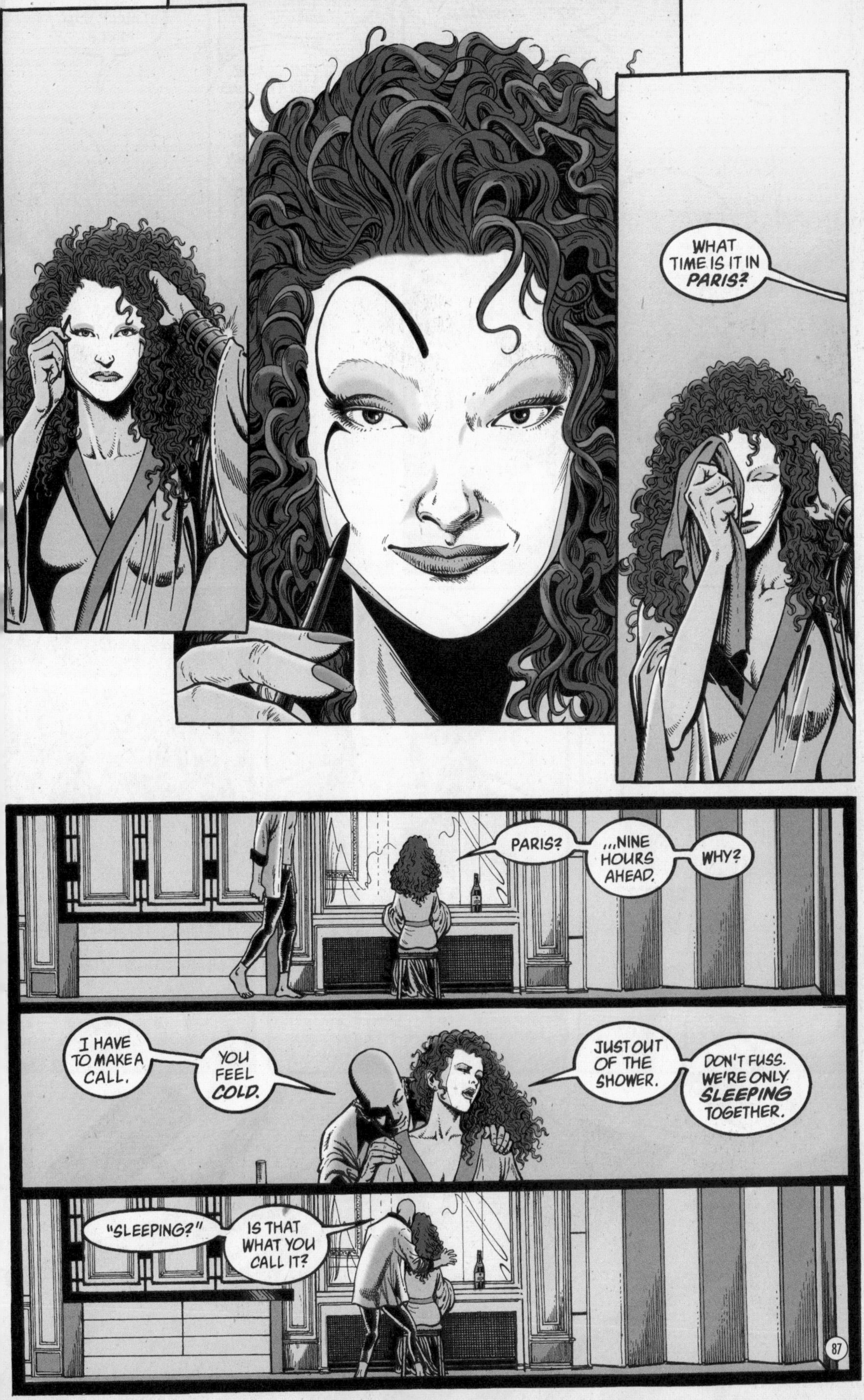
WHAT TIME IS IT IN PARIS?
PARIS?
...NINE HOURS AHEAD.
WHY?
I HAVE TO MAKE A CALL.
YOU FEEL COLD.
JUST OUT OF THE SHOWER.
DON'T FUSS. WE'RE ONLY SLEEPING TOGETHER.
"SLEEPING?"
IS THAT WHAT YOU CALL IT?

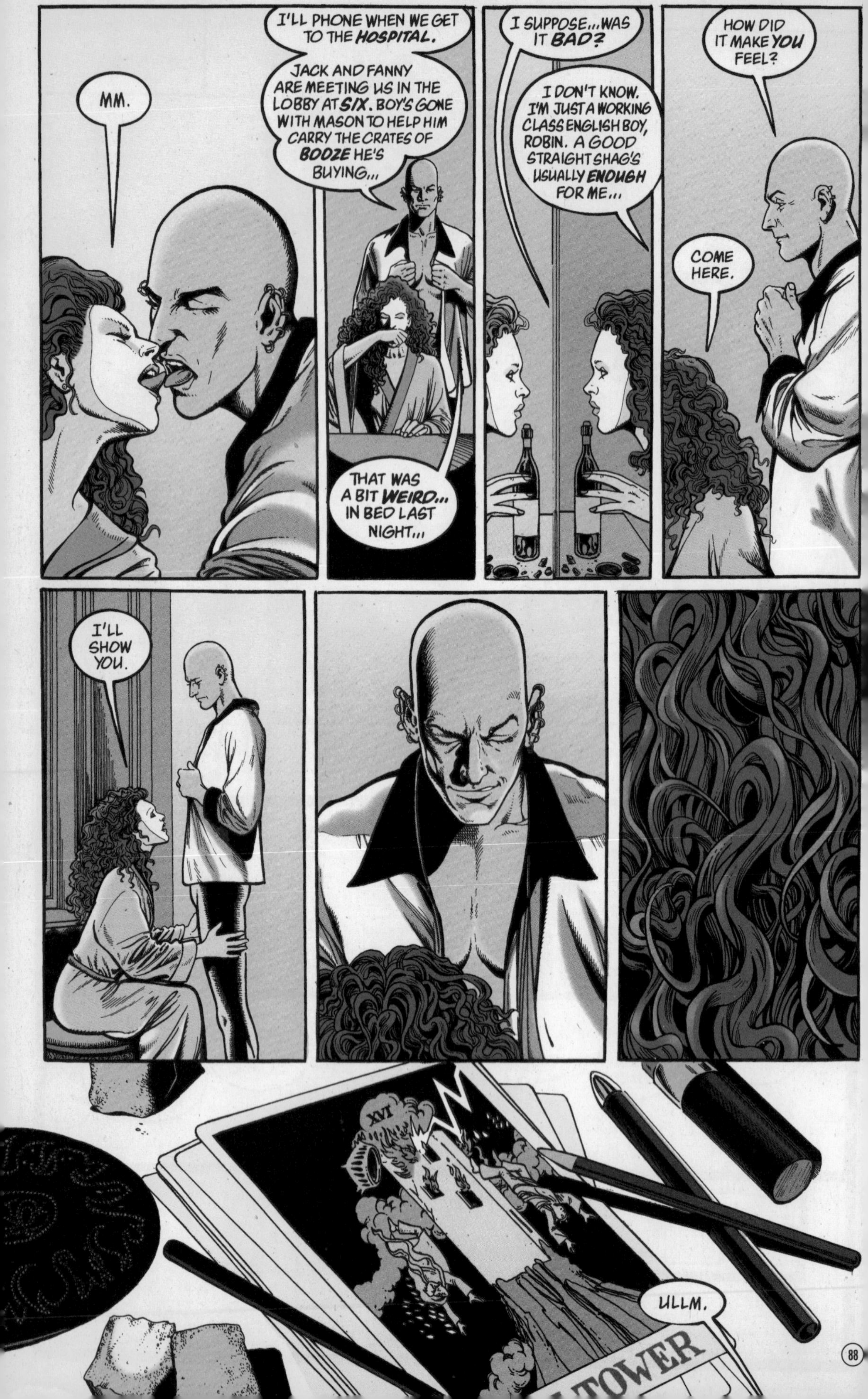
MM.
I'LL PHONE WHEN WE GET TO THE HOSPITAL.
JACK AND FANNY ARE MEETING US IN THE LOBBY AT SIX. BOY'S GONE WITH MASON TO HELP HIM CARRY THE CRATES OF BOOZE HE'S BUYING...
THAT WAS A BIT WEIRD... IN BED LAST NIGHT...
I SUPPOSE... WAS IT BAD?
I DON'T KNOW. I'M JUST A WORKING CLASS ENGLISH BOY, ROBIN. A GOOD STRAIGHT SHAG'S USUALLY ENOUGH FOR ME...
HOW DID IT MAKE YOU FEEL?
COME HERE.
I'LL SHOW YOU.
XVI
ULLM.
TOWER

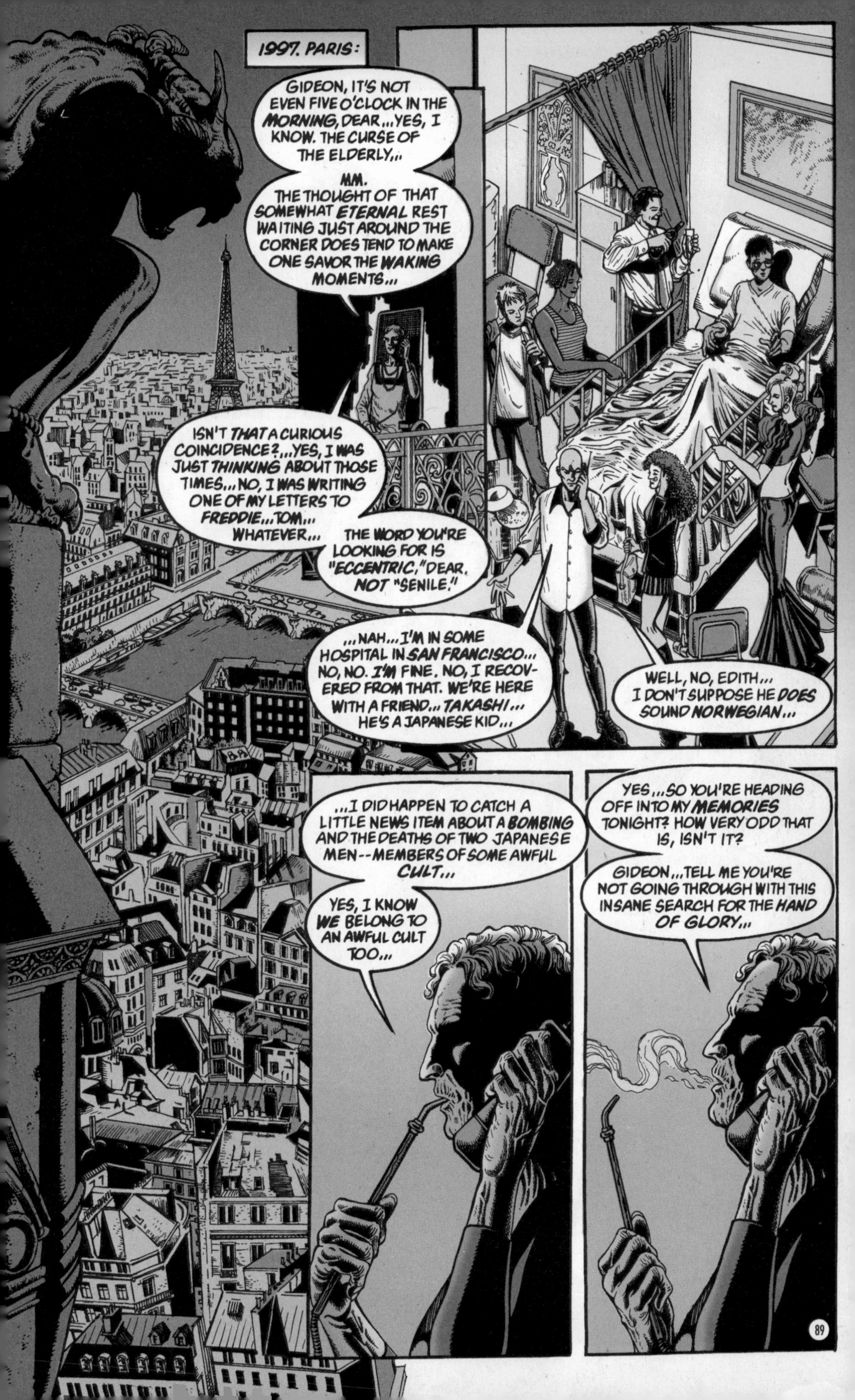
1997. PARIS:
GIDEON, IT'S NOT EVEN FIVE O'CLOCK IN THE MORNING, DEAR... YES, I KNOW. THE CURSE OF THE ELDERLY...
MM. THE THOUGHT OF THAT SOMEWHAT ETERNAL REST WAITING JUST AROUND THE CORNER DOES TEND TO MAKE ONE SAVOR THE WAKING MOMENTS...
ISN'T THAT A CURIOUS COINCIDENCE?...YES, I WAS JUST THINKING ABOUT THOSE TIMES... NO, I WAS WRITING ONE OF MY LETTERS TO FREDDIE...TOM... WHATEVER...
THE WORD YOU'RE LOOKING FOR IS "ECCENTRIC," DEAR. NOT "SENILE."
...NAH...I'M IN SOME HOSPITAL IN SAN FRANCISCO... NO, NO. I'M FINE. NO, I RECOVERED FROM THAT. WE'RE HERE WITH A FRIEND... TAKASHI... HE'S A JAPANESE KID...
WELL, NO, EDITH... I DON'T SUPPOSE HE DOES SOUND NORWEGIAN...
...I DID HAPPEN TO CATCH A LITTLE NEWS ITEM ABOUT A BOMBING AND THE DEATHS OF TWO JAPANESE MEN--MEMBERS OF SOME AWFUL CULT...
YES, I KNOW WE BELONG TO AN AWFUL CULT TOO...
YES... SO YOU'RE HEADING OFF INTO MY MEMORIES TONIGHT? HOW VERY ODD THAT IS, ISN'T IT?
GIDEON... TELL ME YOU'RE NOT GOING THROUGH WITH THIS INSANE SEARCH FOR THE HAND OF GLORY...

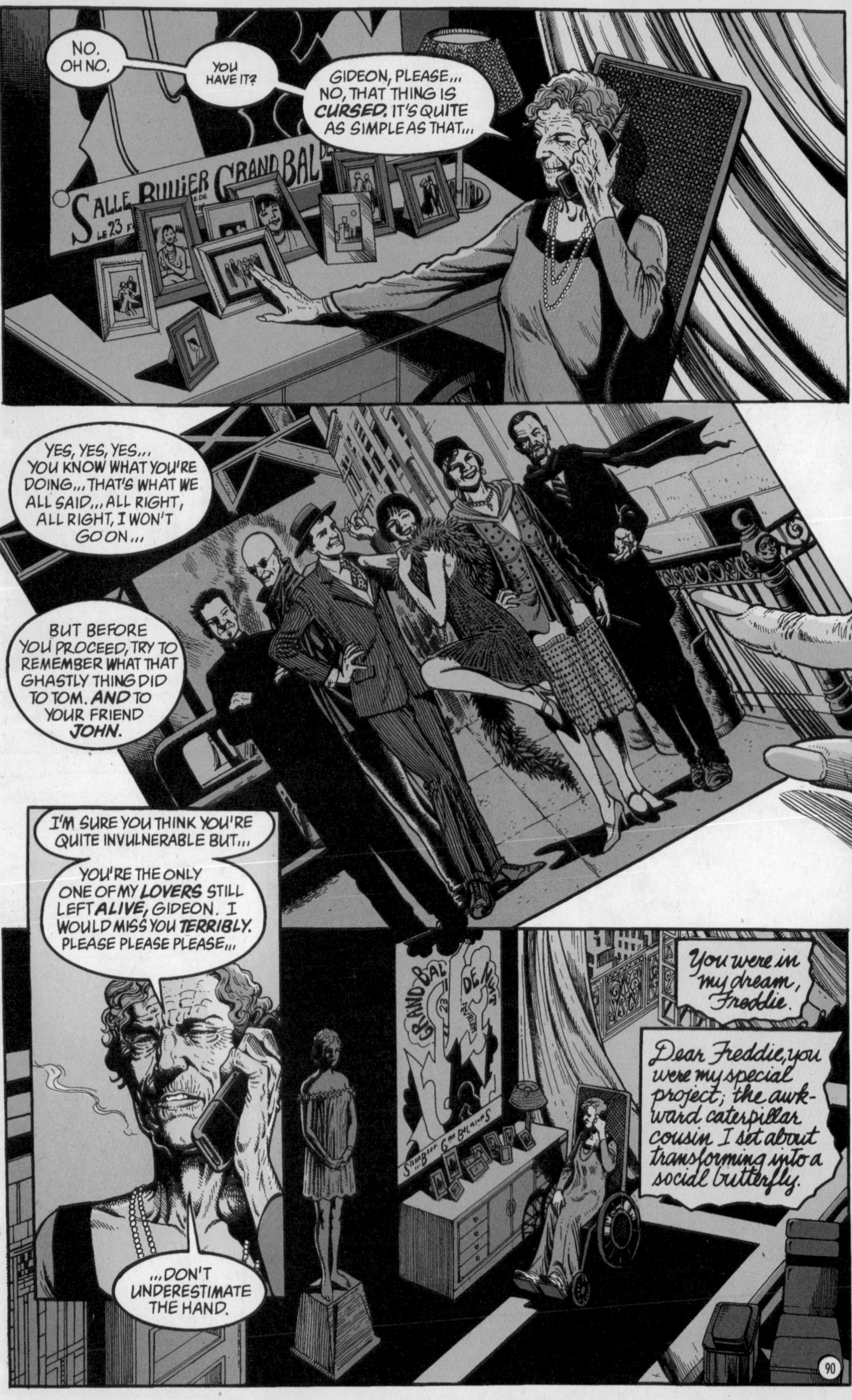
NO. OH NO.
YOU HAVE IT?
GIDEON, PLEASE... NO, THAT THING IS CURSED. IT'S QUITE AS SIMPLE AS THAT...
SALLE BULLIER GRAND BAL
YES, YES, YES... YOU KNOW WHAT YOU'RE DOING... THAT'S WHAT WE ALL SAID... ALL RIGHT, ALL RIGHT, I WON'T GO ON...
BUT BEFORE YOU PROCEED, TRY TO REMEMBER WHAT THAT GHASTLY THING DID TO TOM. AND TO YOUR FRIEND JOHN.
I'M SURE YOU THINK YOU'RE QUITE INVULNERABLE BUT...
YOU'RE THE ONLY ONE OF MY LOVERS STILL LEFT ALIVE, GIDEON. I WOULD MISS YOU TERRIBLY. PLEASE PLEASE PLEASE...
GRAND BAL DE NUIT 23
You were in my dream, Freddie.
Dear Freddie, you were my special project; the awk-ward caterpillar cousin I set about transforming into a social butterfly.
...DON'T UNDERESTIMATE THE HAND.

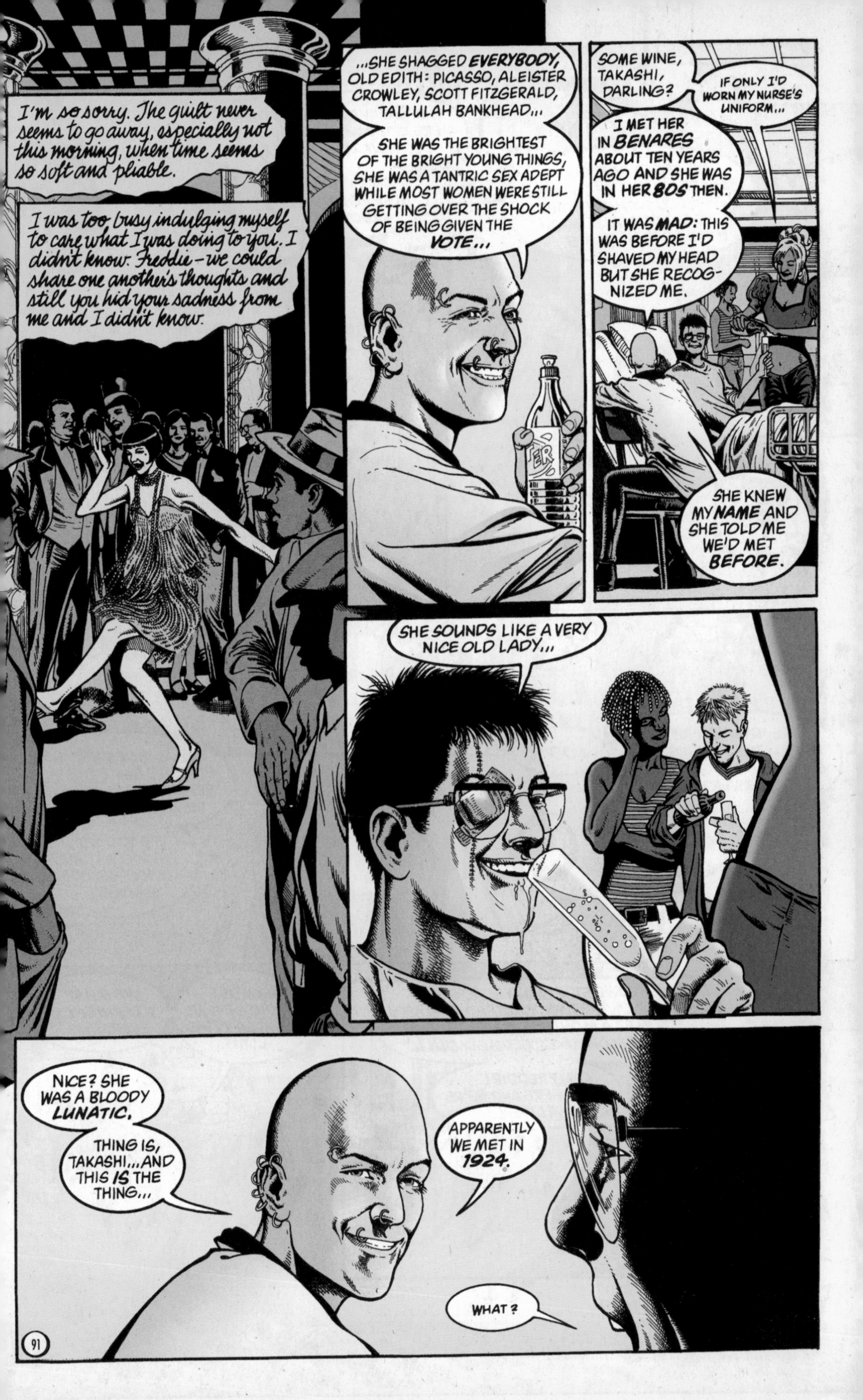
I'm so sorry. The guilt never seems to go away, especially not this morning, when time seems so soft and pliable.
I was too busy indulging myself to care what I was doing to you. I didn't know. Freddie - we could share one another's thoughts and still you hid your sadness from me and I didn't know.
...SHE SHAGGED EVERYBODY, OLD EDITH: PICASSO, ALEISTER CROWLEY, SCOTT FITZGERALD, TALLULAH BANKHEAD...
SHE WAS THE BRIGHTEST OF THE BRIGHT YOUNG THINGS, SHE WAS A TANTRIC SEX ADEPT WHILE MOST WOMEN WERE STILL GETTING OVER THE SHOCK OF BEING GIVEN THE VOTE...
SOME WINE, TAKASHI, DARLING?
IF ONLY I'D WORN MY NURSE'S UNIFORM...
I MET HER IN BENARES ABOUT TEN YEARS AGO AND SHE WAS IN HER 80S THEN.
IT WAS MAD: THIS WAS BEFORE I'D SHAVED MY HEAD BUT SHE RECOGNIZED ME.
SHE KNEW MY NAME AND SHE TOLD ME WE'D MET BEFORE.
SHE SOUNDS LIKE A VERY NICE OLD LADY...
NICE? SHE WAS A BLOODY LUNATIC.
THING IS, TAKASHI...AND THIS IS THE THING...
APPARENTLY WE MET IN 1924.
WHAT?

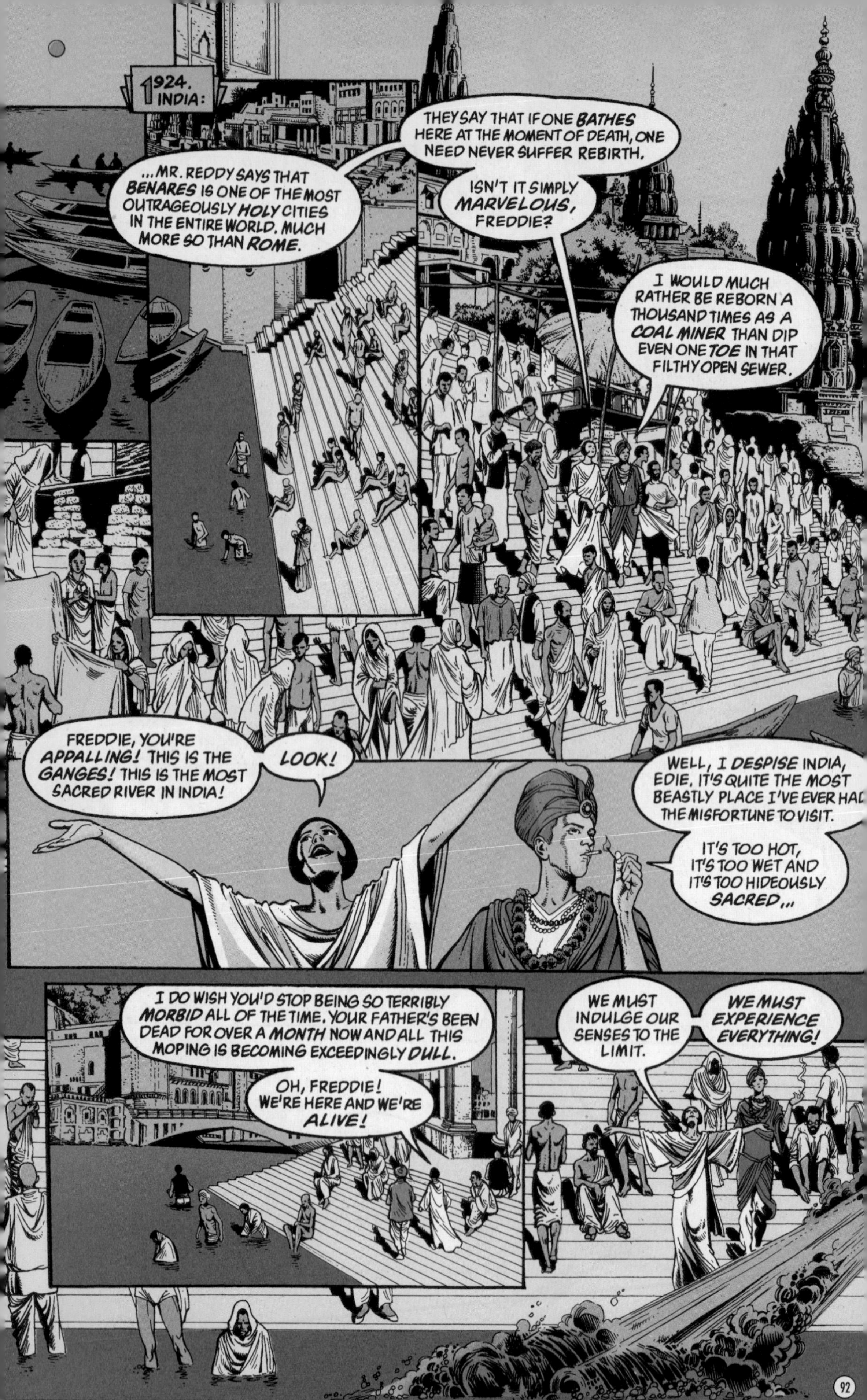

1924. INDIA:
...MR. REDDY SAYS THAT BENARES IS ONE OF THE MOST OUTRAGEOUSLY HOLY CITIES IN THE ENTIRE WORLD. MUCH MORE SO THAN ROME.
THEY SAY THAT IF ONE BATHES HERE AT THE MOMENT OF DEATH, ONE NEED NEVER SUFFER REBIRTH.
ISN'T IT SIMPLY MARVELOUS, FREDDIE?
I WOULD MUCH RATHER BE REBORN A THOUSAND TIMES AS A COAL MINER THAN DIP EVEN ONE TOE IN THAT FILTHY OPEN SEWER.
FREDDIE, YOU'RE APPALLING! THIS IS THE GANGES! THIS IS THE MOST SACRED RIVER IN INDIA!
LOOK!
WELL, I DESPISE INDIA, EDIE. IT'S QUITE THE MOST BEASTLY PLACE I'VE EVER HAD THE MISFORTUNE TO VISIT.
IT'S TOO HOT, IT'S TOO WET AND IT'S TOO HIDEOUSLY SACRED...
I DO WISH YOU'D STOP BEING SO TERRIBLY MORBID ALL OF THE TIME. YOUR FATHER'S BEEN DEAD FOR OVER A MONTH NOW AND ALL THIS MOPING IS BECOMING EXCEEDINGLY DULL.
OH, FREDDIE! WE'RE HERE AND WE'RE ALIVE!
WE MUST INDULGE OUR SENSES TO THE LIMIT.
WE MUST EXPERIENCE EVERYTHING!

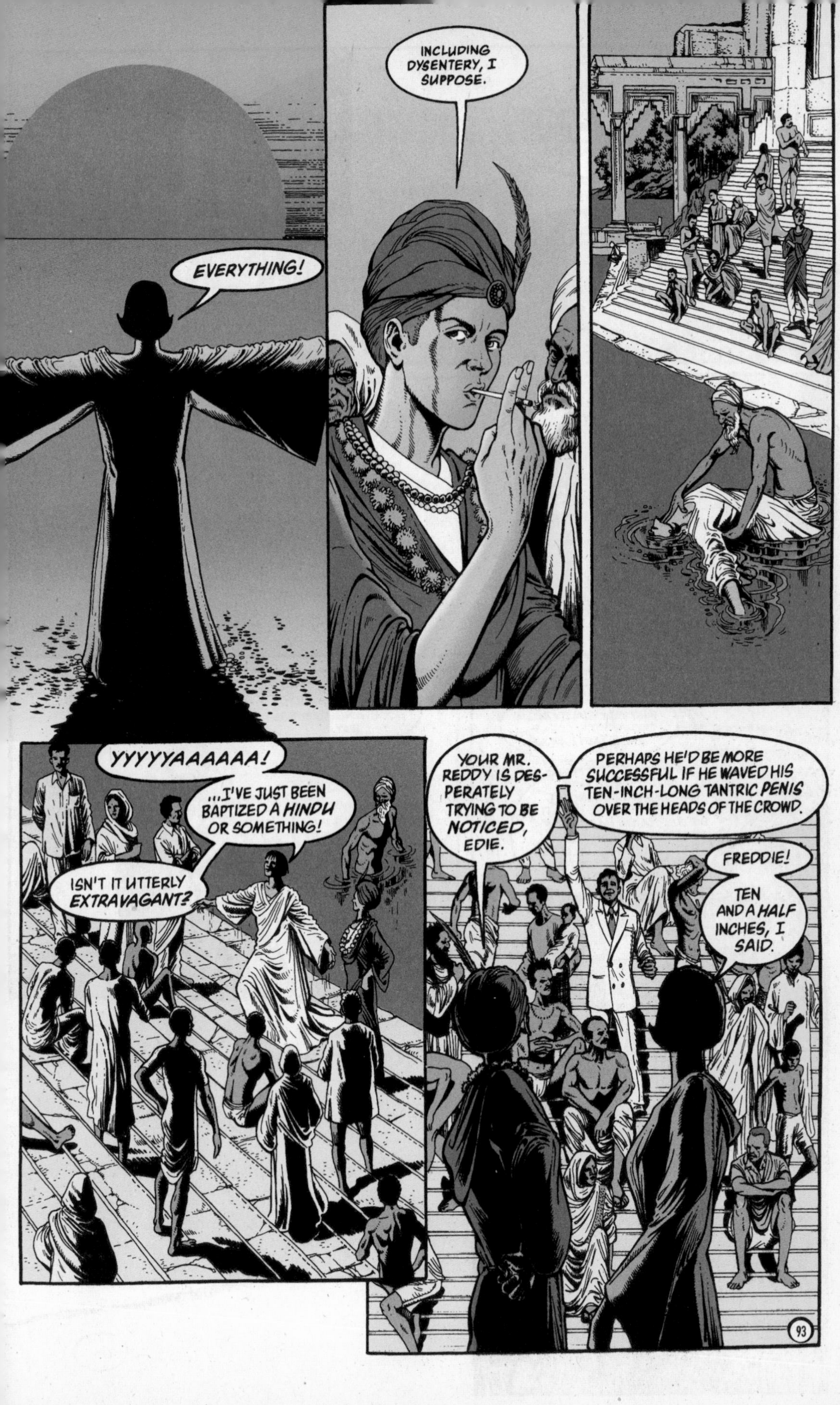
EVERYTHING!
INCLUDING DYSENTERY, I SUPPOSE.
YYYYYAAAAAA!
...I'VE JUST BEEN BAPTIZED A HINDU OR SOMETHING!
ISN'T IT UTTERLY EXTRAVAGANT?
YOUR MR. REDDY IS DESPERATELY TRYING TO BE NOTICED, EDIE.
PERHAPS HE'D BE MORE SUCCESSFUL IF HE WAVED HIS TEN-INCH-LONG TANTRIC PENIS OVER THE HEADS OF THE CROWD.
FREDDIE!
TEN AND A HALF INCHES, I SAID.

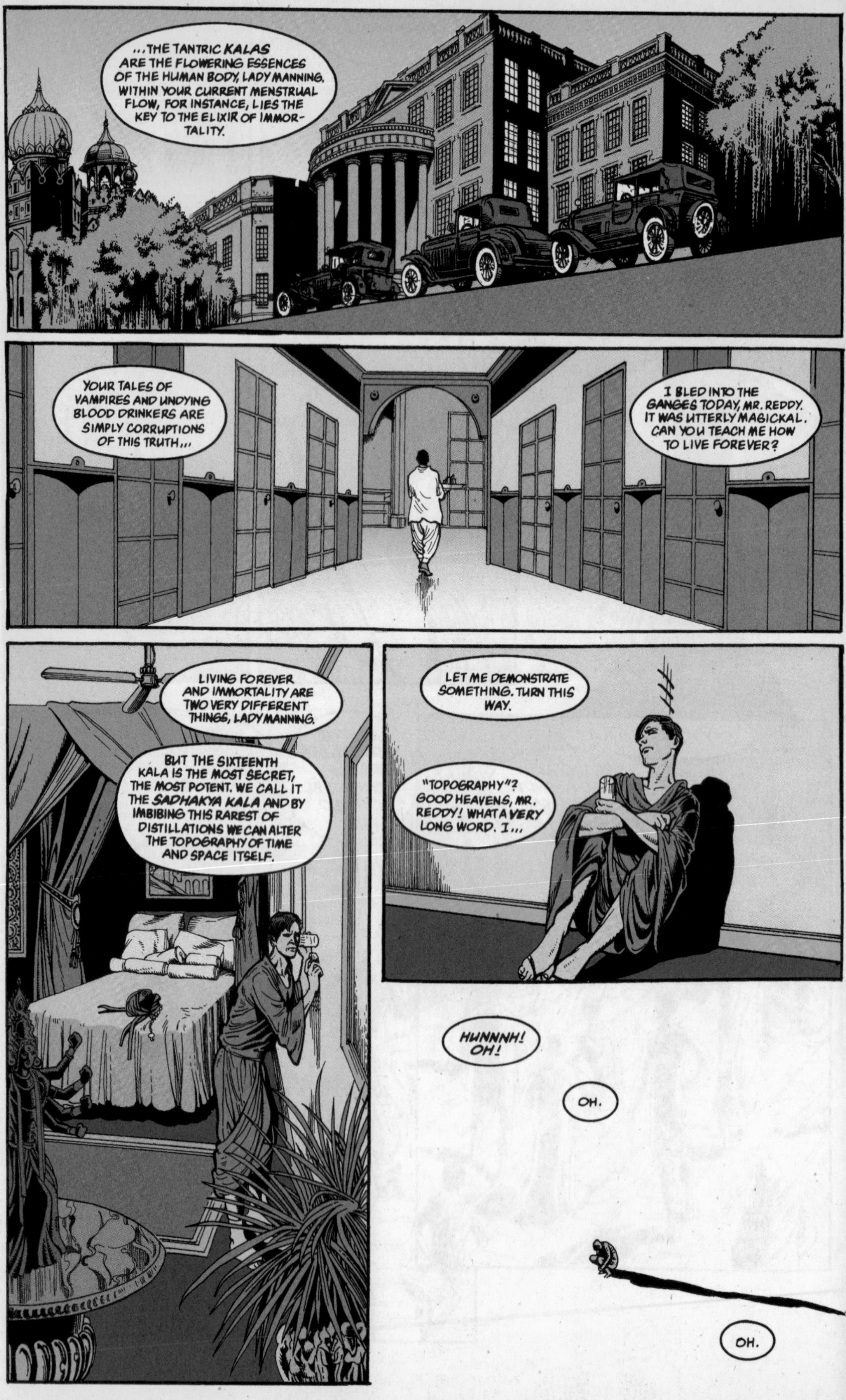
...THE TANTRIC KALAS ARE THE FLOWERING ESSENCES OF THE HUMAN BODY, LADY MANNING. WITHIN YOUR CURRENT MENSTRUAL FLOW, FOR INSTANCE, LIES THE KEY TO THE ELIXIR OF IMMORTALITY.
YOUR TALES OF VAMPIRES AND UNDYING BLOOD DRINKERS ARE SIMPLY CORRUPTIONS OF THIS TRUTH...
I BLED INTO THE GANGES TODAY, MR. REDDY. IT WAS UTTERLY MAGICKAL. CAN YOU TEACH ME HOW TO LIVE FOREVER?
LIVING FOREVER AND IMMORTALITY ARE TWO VERY DIFFERENT THINGS, LADY MANNING.
BUT THE SIXTEENTH KALA IS THE MOST SECRET, THE MOST POTENT. WE CALL IT THE SADHAKYA KALA AND BY IMBIBING THIS RAREST OF DISTILLATIONS WE CAN ALTER THE TOPOGRAPHY OF TIME AND SPACE ITSELF.
LET ME DEMONSTRATE SOMETHING. TURN THIS WAY.
"TOPOGRAPHY"? GOOD HEAVENS, MR. REDDY! WHAT A VERY LONG WORD. I...
HUNNNH! OH!
OH.
OH.

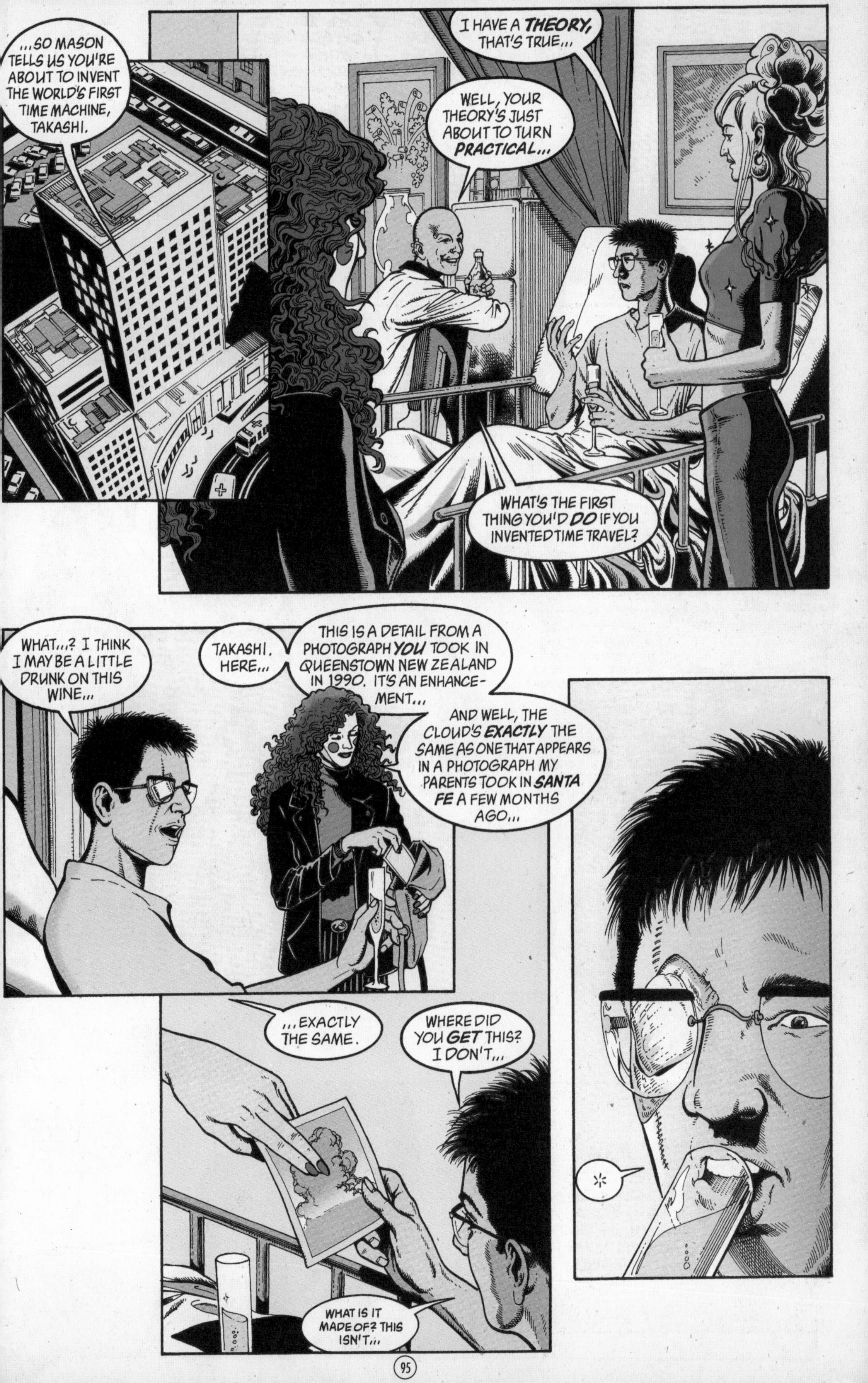
...SO MASON TELLS US YOU'RE ABOUT TO INVENT THE WORLD'S FIRST TIME MACHINE, TAKASHI.
I HAVE A THEORY, THAT'S TRUE...
WELL, YOUR THEORY'S JUST ABOUT TO TURN PRACTICAL...
WHAT'S THE FIRST THING YOU'D DO IF YOU INVENTED TIME TRAVEL?
WHAT...? I THINK I MAY BE A LITTLE DRUNK ON THIS WINE...
TAKASHI. HERE...
THIS IS A DETAIL FROM A PHOTOGRAPH YOU TOOK IN QUEENSTOWN NEW ZEALAND IN 1990. IT'S AN ENHANCEMENT...
AND WELL, THE CLOUD'S EXACTLY THE SAME AS ONE THAT APPEARS IN A PHOTOGRAPH MY PARENTS TOOK IN SANTA FE A FEW MONTHS AGO...
...EXACTLY THE SAME.
WHERE DID YOU GET THIS? I DON'T...
WHAT IS IT MADE OF? THIS ISN'T...

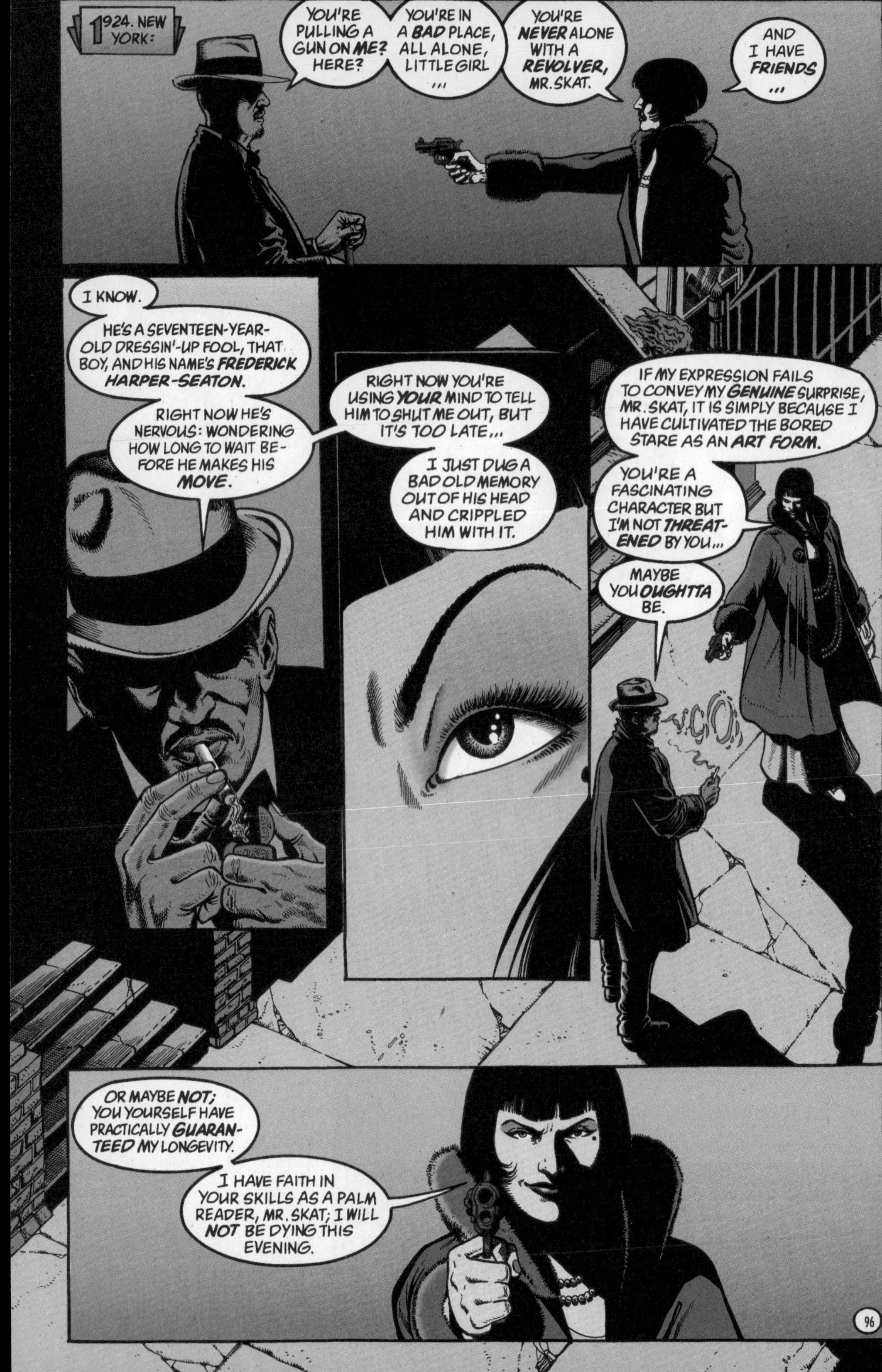
1924. NEW YORK:
YOU'RE PULLING A GUN ON ME? HERE?
YOU'RE IN A BAD PLACE, ALL ALONE, LITTLE GIRL ...
YOU'RE NEVER ALONE WITH A REVOLVER, MR. SKAT.
AND I HAVE FRIENDS ...
I KNOW.
HE'S A SEVENTEEN-YEAR-OLD DRESSIN'-UP FOOL, THAT BOY, AND HIS NAME'S FREDERICK HARPER-SEATON.
RIGHT NOW HE'S NERVOUS: WONDERING HOW LONG TO WAIT BEFORE HE MAKES HIS MOVE.
RIGHT NOW YOU'RE USING YOUR MIND TO TELL HIM TO SHUT ME OUT, BUT IT'S TOO LATE...
I JUST DUG A BAD OLD MEMORY OUT OF HIS HEAD AND CRIPPLED HIM WITH IT.
IF MY EXPRESSION FAILS TO CONVEY MY GENUINE SURPRISE, MR. SKAT, IT IS SIMPLY BECAUSE I HAVE CULTIVATED THE BORED STARE AS AN ART FORM.
YOU'RE A FASCINATING CHARACTER BUT I'M NOT THREATENED BY YOU...
MAYBE YOU OUGHTTA BE.
OR MAYBE NOT; YOU YOURSELF HAVE PRACTICALLY GUARANTEED MY LONGEVITY.
I HAVE FAITH IN YOUR SKILLS AS A PALM READER, MR. SKAT; I WILL NOT BE DYING THIS EVENING.

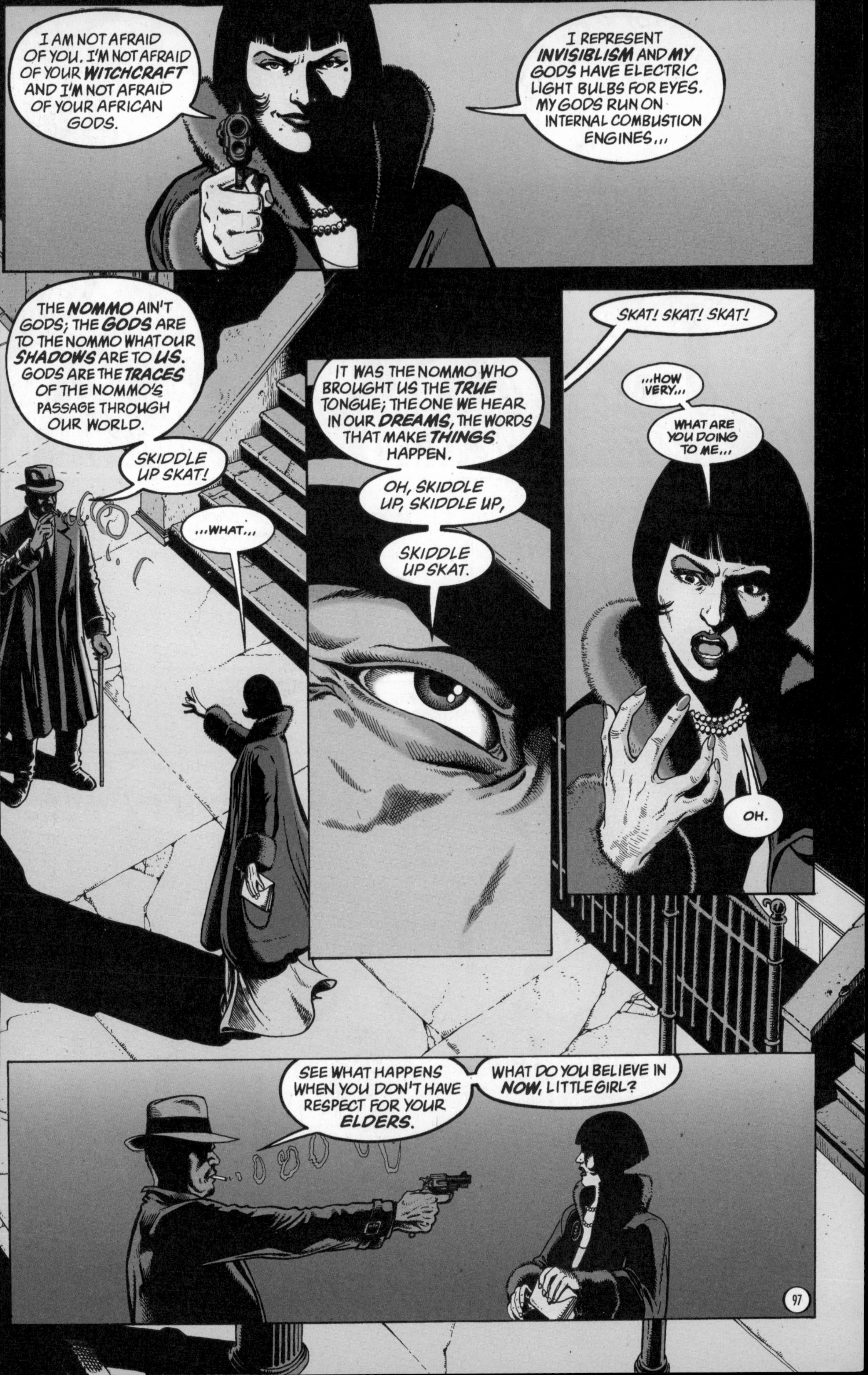
I AM NOT AFRAID OF YOU. I'M NOT AFRAID OF YOUR WITCHCRAFT AND I'M NOT AFRAID OF YOUR AFRICAN GODS.
I REPRESENT INVISIBLISM AND MY GODS HAVE ELECTRIC LIGHT BULBS FOR EYES. MY GODS RUN ON INTERNAL COMBUSTION ENGINES...
THE NOMMO AIN'T GODS; THE GODS ARE TO THE NOMMO WHAT OUR SHADOWS ARE TO US. GODS ARE THE TRACES OF THE NOMMO'S PASSAGE THROUGH OUR WORLD.
SKIDDLE UP SKAT!
...WHAT...
IT WAS THE NOMMO WHO BROUGHT US THE TRUE TONGUE; THE ONE WE HEAR IN OUR DREAMS, THE WORDS THAT MAKE THINGS HAPPEN.
OH, SKIDDLE UP, SKIDDLE UP,
SKIDDLE UP SKAT.
SKAT! SKAT! SKAT!
...HOW VERY...
WHAT ARE YOU DOING TO ME...
OH.
SEE WHAT HAPPENS WHEN YOU DON'T HAVE RESPECT FOR YOUR ELDERS.
WHAT DO YOU BELIEVE IN NOW, LITTLE GIRL?

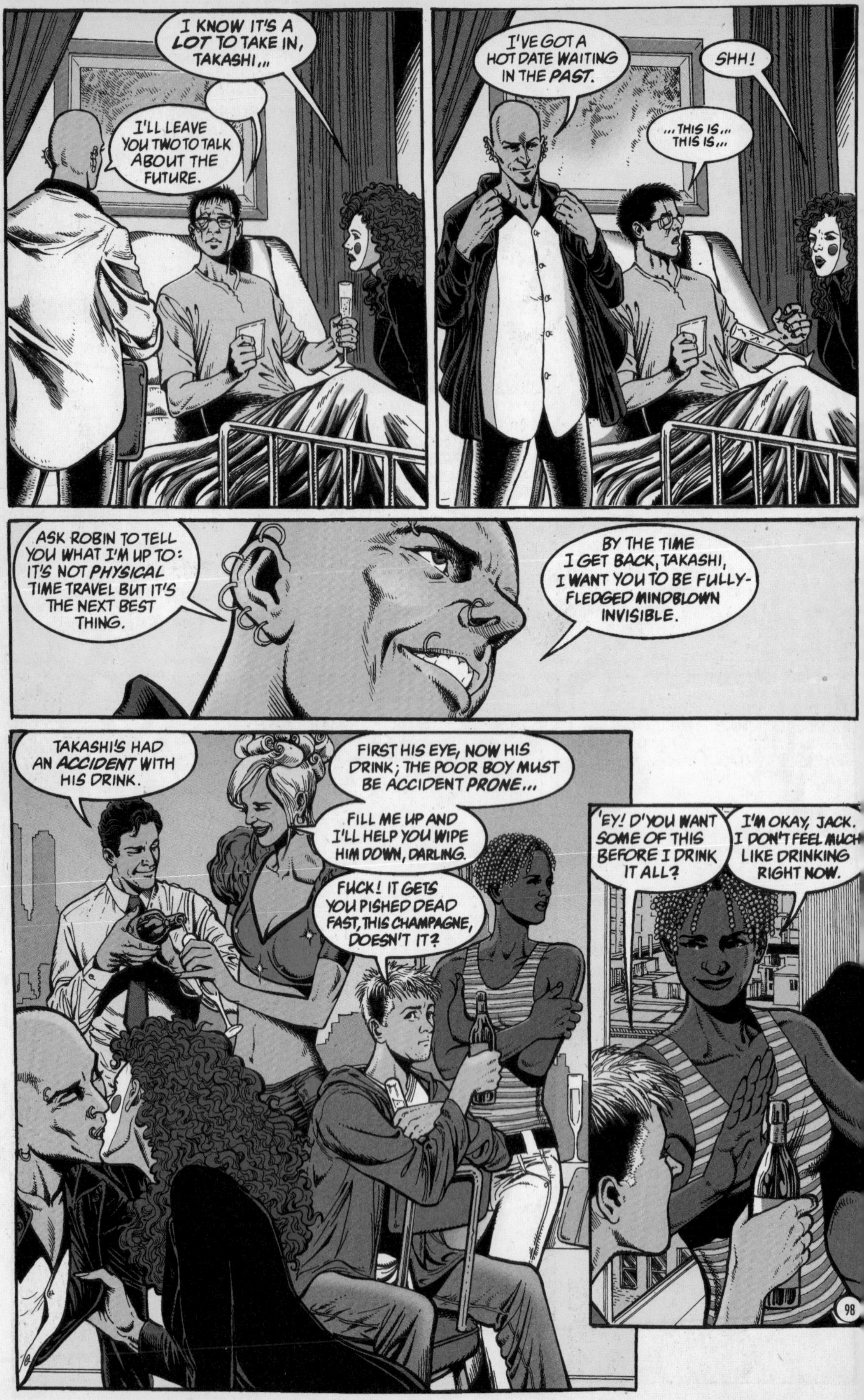
I KNOW IT'S A LOT TO TAKE IN, TAKASHI...
I'LL LEAVE YOU TWO TO TALK ABOUT THE FUTURE.
I'VE GOT A HOT DATE WAITING IN THE PAST.
SHH!
...THIS IS... THIS IS...
ASK ROBIN TO TELL YOU WHAT I'M UP TO: IT'S NOT PHYSICAL TIME TRAVEL BUT IT'S THE NEXT BEST THING.
BY THE TIME I GET BACK, TAKASHI, I WANT YOU TO BE FULLY-FLEDGED MINDBLOWN INVISIBLE.
TAKASHI'S HAD AN ACCIDENT WITH HIS DRINK.
FIRST HIS EYE, NOW HIS DRINK; THE POOR BOY MUST BE ACCIDENT PRONE...
FILL ME UP AND I'LL HELP YOU WIPE HIM DOWN, DARLING.
FUCK! IT GETS YOU PISHED DEAD FAST, THIS CHAMPAGNE, DOESN'T IT?
'EY! D'YOU WANT SOME OF THIS BEFORE I DRINK IT ALL?
I'M OKAY, JACK. I DON'T FEEL MUCH LIKE DRINKING RIGHT NOW.

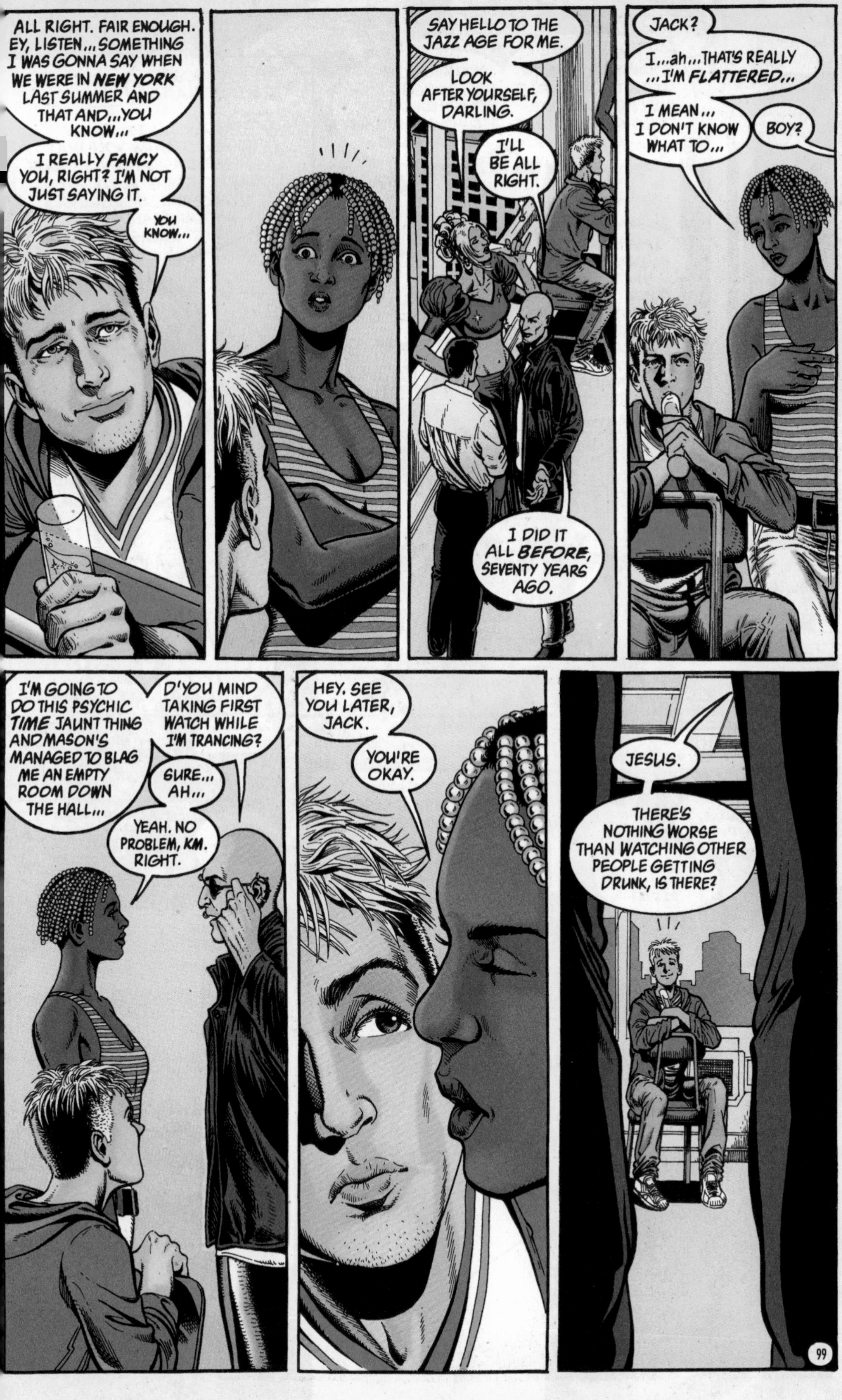
ALL RIGHT. FAIR ENOUGH. EY, LISTEN... SOMETHING I WAS GONNA SAY WHEN WE WERE IN NEW YORK LAST SUMMER AND THAT AND... YOU KNOW...
I REALLY FANCY YOU, RIGHT? I'M NOT JUST SAYING IT.
YOU KNOW...
SAY HELLO TO THE JAZZ AGE FOR ME.
LOOK AFTER YOURSELF, DARLING.
I'LL BE ALL RIGHT.
I DID IT ALL BEFORE, SEVENTY YEARS AGO.
JACK?
I...ah... THAT'S REALLY ...I'M FLATTERED...
I MEAN... I DON'T KNOW WHAT TO...
BOY?
I'M GOING TO DO THIS PSYCHIC TIME JAUNT THING AND MASON'S MANAGED TO BLAG ME AN EMPTY ROOM DOWN THE HALL...
D'YOU MIND TAKING FIRST WATCH WHILE I'M TRANCING?
SURE... AH...
YEAH. NO PROBLEM, KM. RIGHT.
HEY. SEE YOU LATER, JACK.
YOU'RE OKAY.
JESUS.
THERE'S NOTHING WORSE THAN WATCHING OTHER PEOPLE GETTING DRUNK, IS THERE?

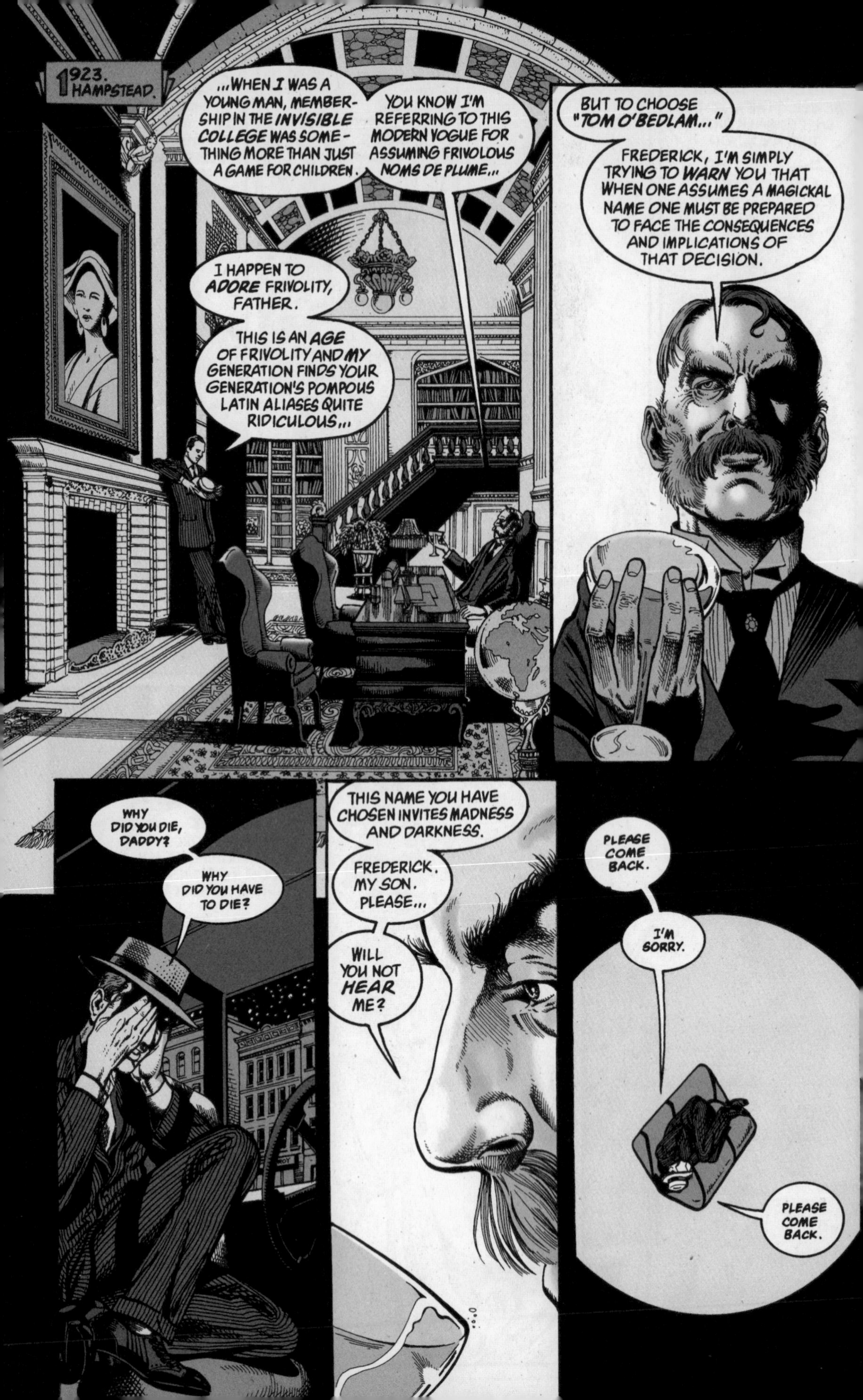
1923. HAMPSTEAD.
...WHEN I WAS A YOUNG MAN, MEMBERSHIP IN THE INVISIBLE COLLEGE WAS SOMETHING MORE THAN JUST A GAME FOR CHILDREN.
YOU KNOW I'M REFERRING TO THIS MODERN VOGUE FOR ASSUMING FRIVOLOUS NOMS DE PLUME...
I HAPPEN TO ADORE FRIVOLITY, FATHER.
THIS IS AN AGE OF FRIVOLITY AND MY GENERATION FINDS YOUR GENERATION'S POMPOUS LATIN ALIASES QUITE RIDICULOUS...
BUT TO CHOOSE "TOM O'BEDLAM..."
FREDERICK, I'M SIMPLY TRYING TO WARN YOU THAT WHEN ONE ASSUMES A MAGICKAL NAME ONE MUST BE PREPARED TO FACE THE CONSEQUENCES AND IMPLICATIONS OF THAT DECISION.
WHY DID YOU DIE, DADDY?
WHY DID YOU HAVE TO DIE?
THIS NAME YOU HAVE CHOSEN INVITES MADNESS AND DARKNESS.
FREDERICK. MY SON. PLEASE...
WILL YOU NOT HEAR ME?
PLEASE COME BACK.
I'M SORRY.
PLEASE COME BACK.

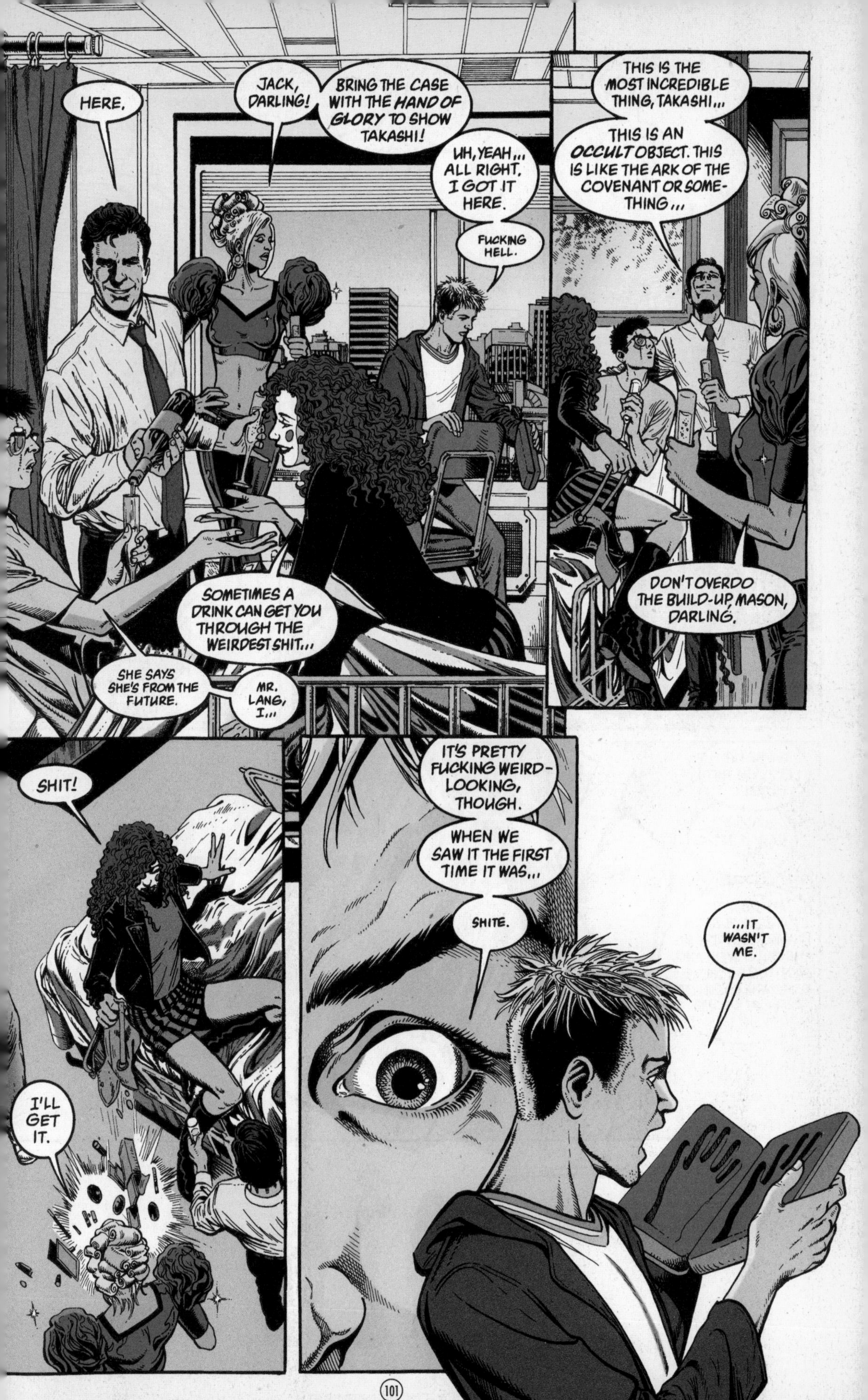
HERE.
JACK, DARLING!
BRING THE CASE WITH THE *HAND OF GLORY* TO SHOW TAKASHI!
UH, YEAH... ALL RIGHT. I GOT IT HERE.
FUCKING HELL.
SOMETIMES A DRINK CAN GET YOU THROUGH THE WEIRDEST SHIT...
SHE SAYS SHE'S FROM THE FUTURE.
MR. LANG, I...
THIS IS THE MOST INCREDIBLE THING, TAKASHI...
THIS IS AN *OCCULT* OBJECT. THIS IS LIKE THE ARK OF THE COVENANT OR SOMETHING...
DON'T OVERDO THE BUILD-UP, MASON, DARLING.
SHIT!
I'LL GET IT.
IT'S PRETTY FUCKING WEIRD-LOOKING, THOUGH.
WHEN WE SAW IT THE FIRST TIME IT WAS...
SHITE.
...IT WASN'T ME.

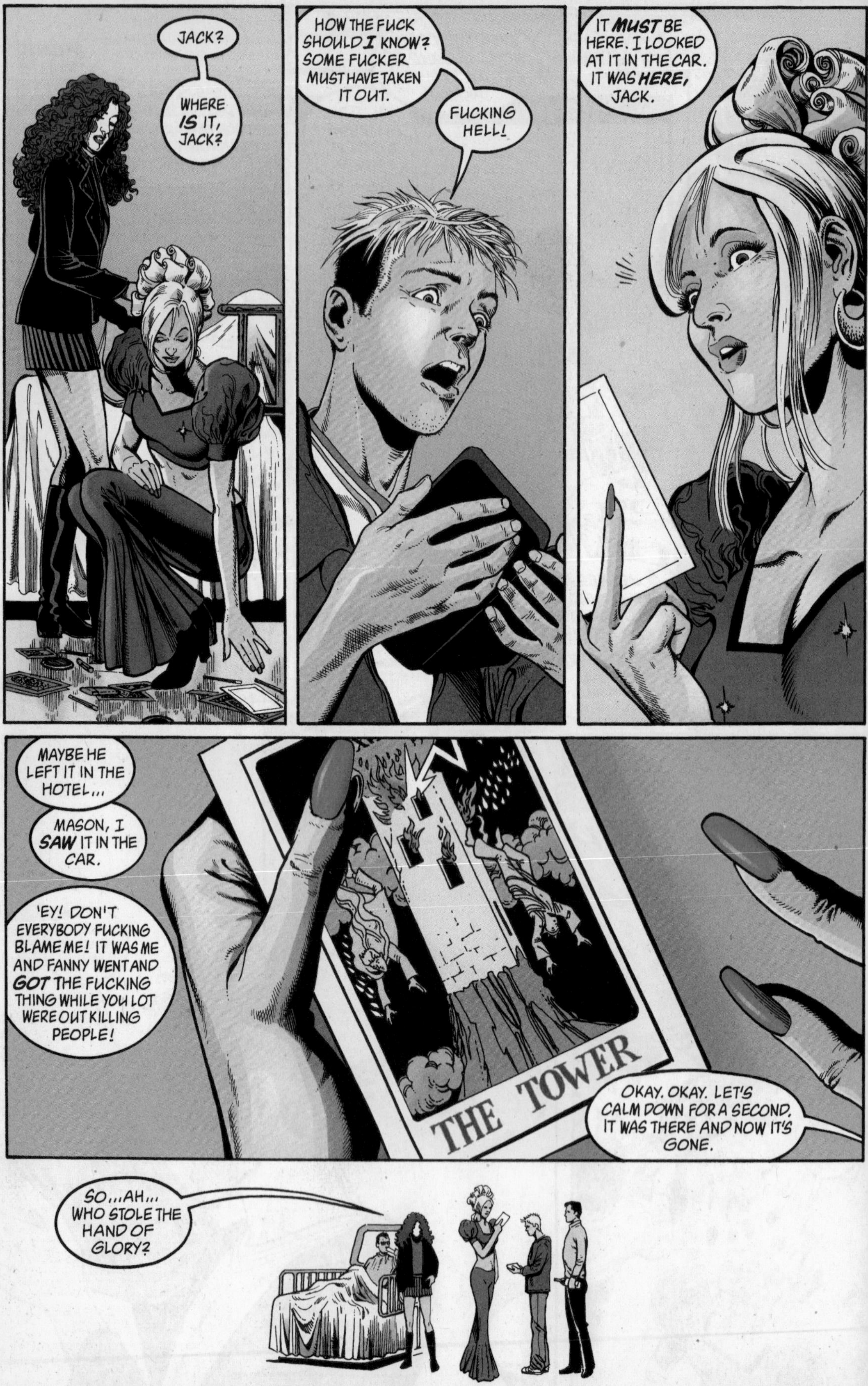
JACK?
WHERE IS IT, JACK?
HOW THE FUCK SHOULD I KNOW? SOME FUCKER MUST HAVE TAKEN IT OUT.
FUCKING HELL!
IT MUST BE HERE. I LOOKED AT IT IN THE CAR. IT WAS HERE, JACK.
MAYBE HE LEFT IT IN THE HOTEL...
MASON, I SAW IT IN THE CAR.
'EY! DON'T EVERYBODY FUCKING BLAME ME! IT WAS ME AND FANNY WENT AND GOT THE FUCKING THING WHILE YOU LOT WERE OUT KILLING PEOPLE!
THE TOWER
OKAY. OKAY. LET'S CALM DOWN FOR A SECOND. IT WAS THERE AND NOW IT'S GONE.
SO...AH... WHO STOLE THE HAND OF GLORY?

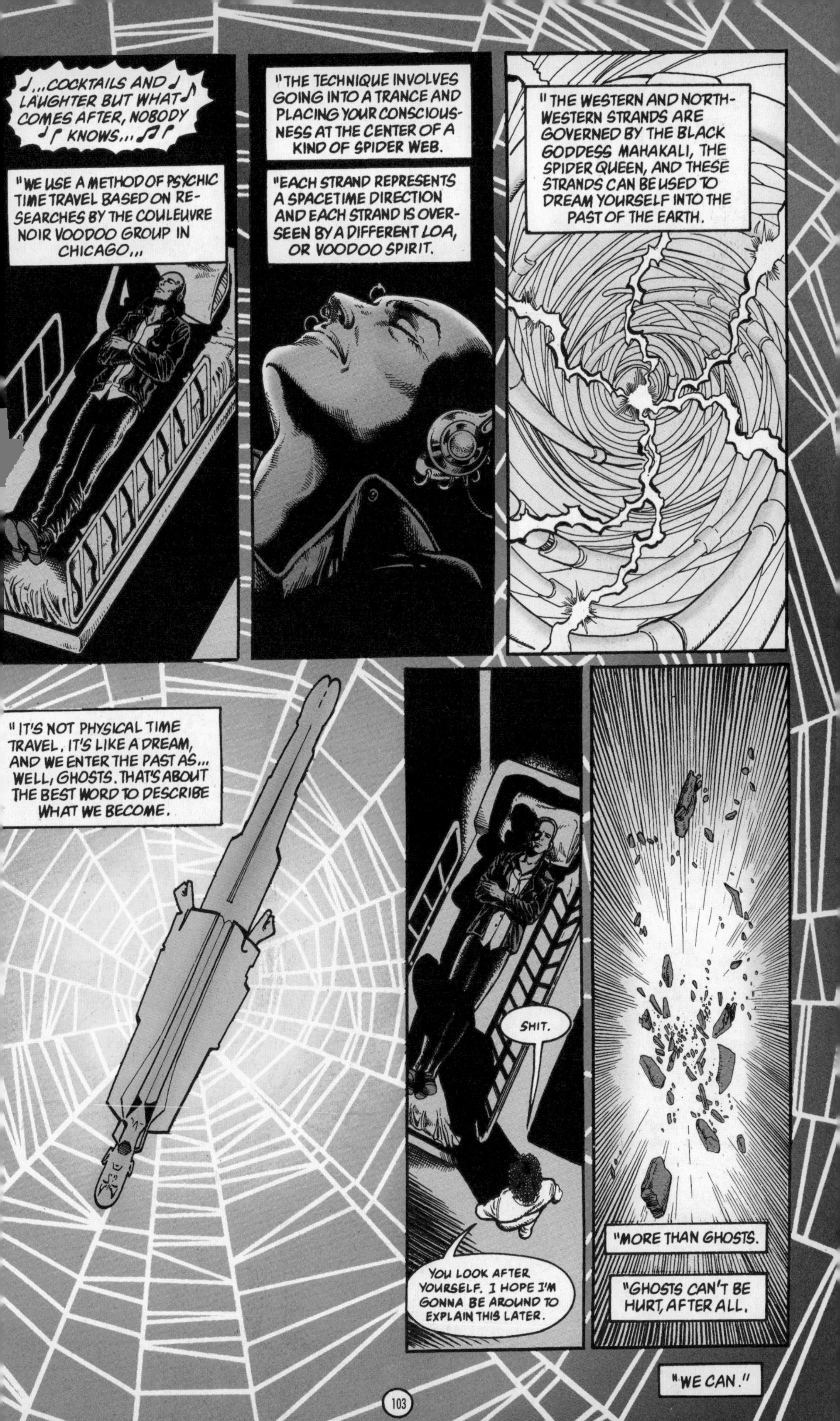
♩...COCKTAILS AND ♩ LAUGHTER BUT WHAT ♪ COMES AFTER, NOBODY ♩♪ KNOWS... ♫♪
"WE USE A METHOD OF PSYCHIC TIME TRAVEL BASED ON RESEARCHES BY THE COULEUVRE NOIR VOODOO GROUP IN CHICAGO...
"THE TECHNIQUE INVOLVES GOING INTO A TRANCE AND PLACING YOUR CONSCIOUSNESS AT THE CENTER OF A KIND OF SPIDER WEB.
"EACH STRAND REPRESENTS A SPACETIME DIRECTION AND EACH STRAND IS OVERSEEN BY A DIFFERENT LOA, OR VOODOO SPIRIT.
"THE WESTERN AND NORTH-WESTERN STRANDS ARE GOVERNED BY THE BLACK GODDESS MAHAKALI, THE SPIDER QUEEN, AND THESE STRANDS CAN BE USED TO DREAM YOURSELF INTO THE PAST OF THE EARTH.
"IT'S NOT PHYSICAL TIME TRAVEL, IT'S LIKE A DREAM, AND WE ENTER THE PAST AS... WELL, GHOSTS. THAT'S ABOUT THE BEST WORD TO DESCRIBE WHAT WE BECOME.
SHIT.
YOU LOOK AFTER YOURSELF. I HOPE I'M GONNA BE AROUND TO EXPLAIN THIS LATER.
"MORE THAN GHOSTS.
"GHOSTS CAN'T BE HURT, AFTER ALL.
"WE CAN."

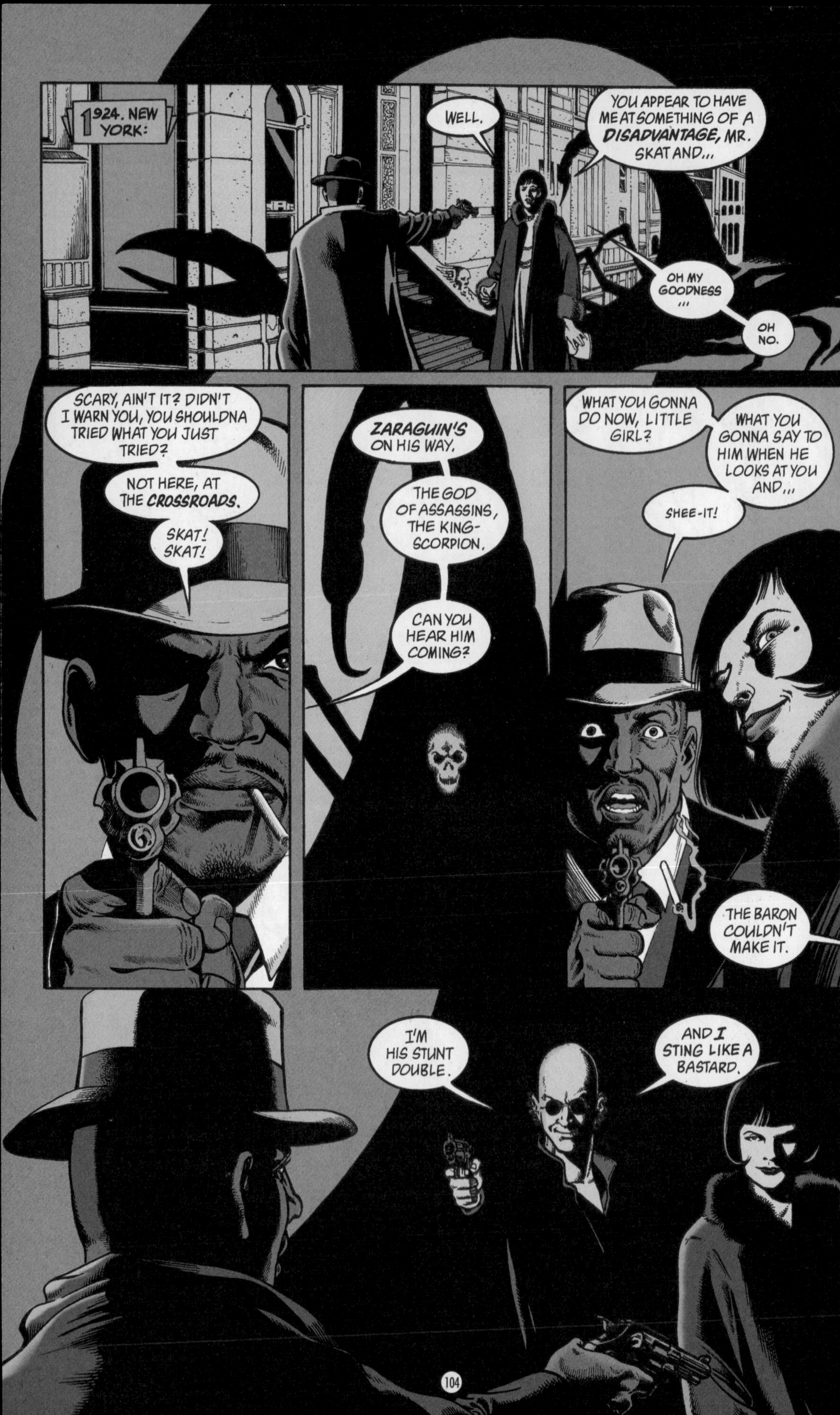
1924. NEW YORK:
WELL.
YOU APPEAR TO HAVE ME AT SOMETHING OF A DISADVANTAGE, MR. SKAT AND...
OH MY GOODNESS...
OH NO.
SCARY, AIN'T IT? DIDN'T I WARN YOU, YOU SHOULDNA TRIED WHAT YOU JUST TRIED?
NOT HERE, AT THE CROSSROADS.
SKAT! SKAT!
ZARAGUIN'S ON HIS WAY.
THE GOD OF ASSASSINS, THE KING-SCORPION.
CAN YOU HEAR HIM COMING?
WHAT YOU GONNA DO NOW, LITTLE GIRL?
WHAT YOU GONNA SAY TO HIM WHEN HE LOOKS AT YOU AND...
SHEE-IT!
THE BARON COULDN'T MAKE IT.
I'M HIS STUNT DOUBLE.
AND I STING LIKE A BASTARD.

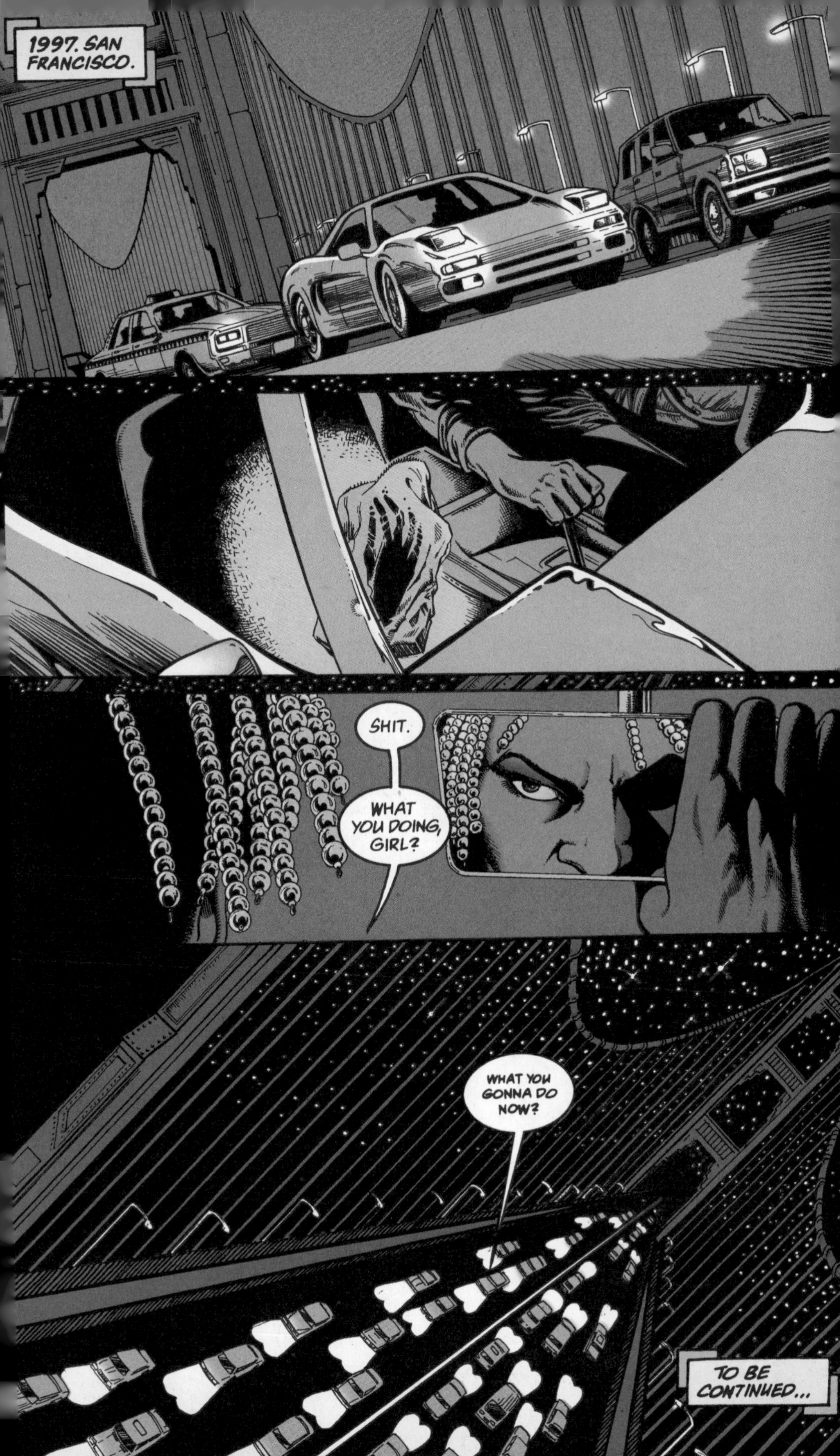
1997. SAN FRANCISCO.
SHIT.
WHAT YOU DOING, GIRL?
WHAT YOU GONNA DO NOW?
TO BE CONTINUED...

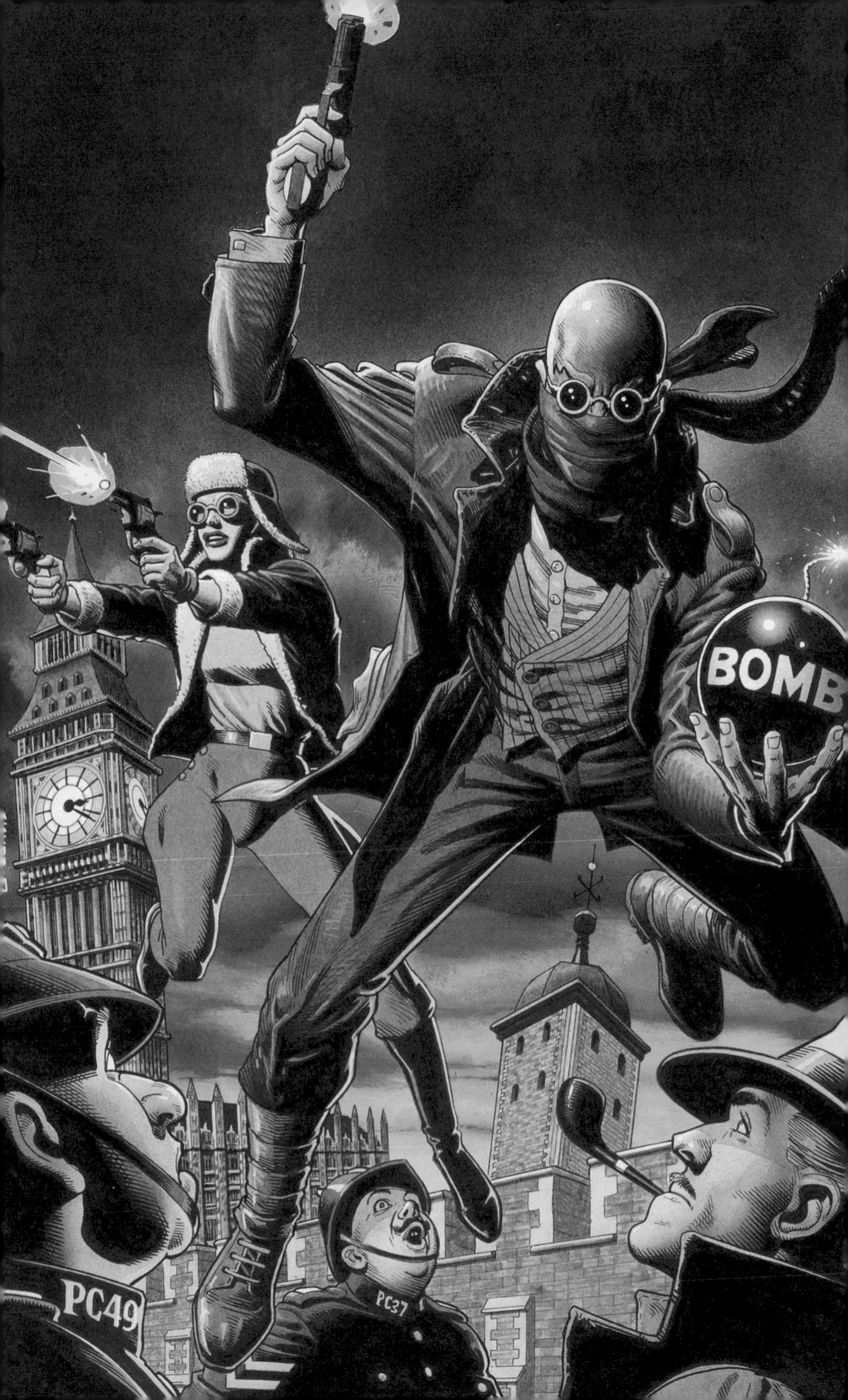
BOMB
PC49
PC37

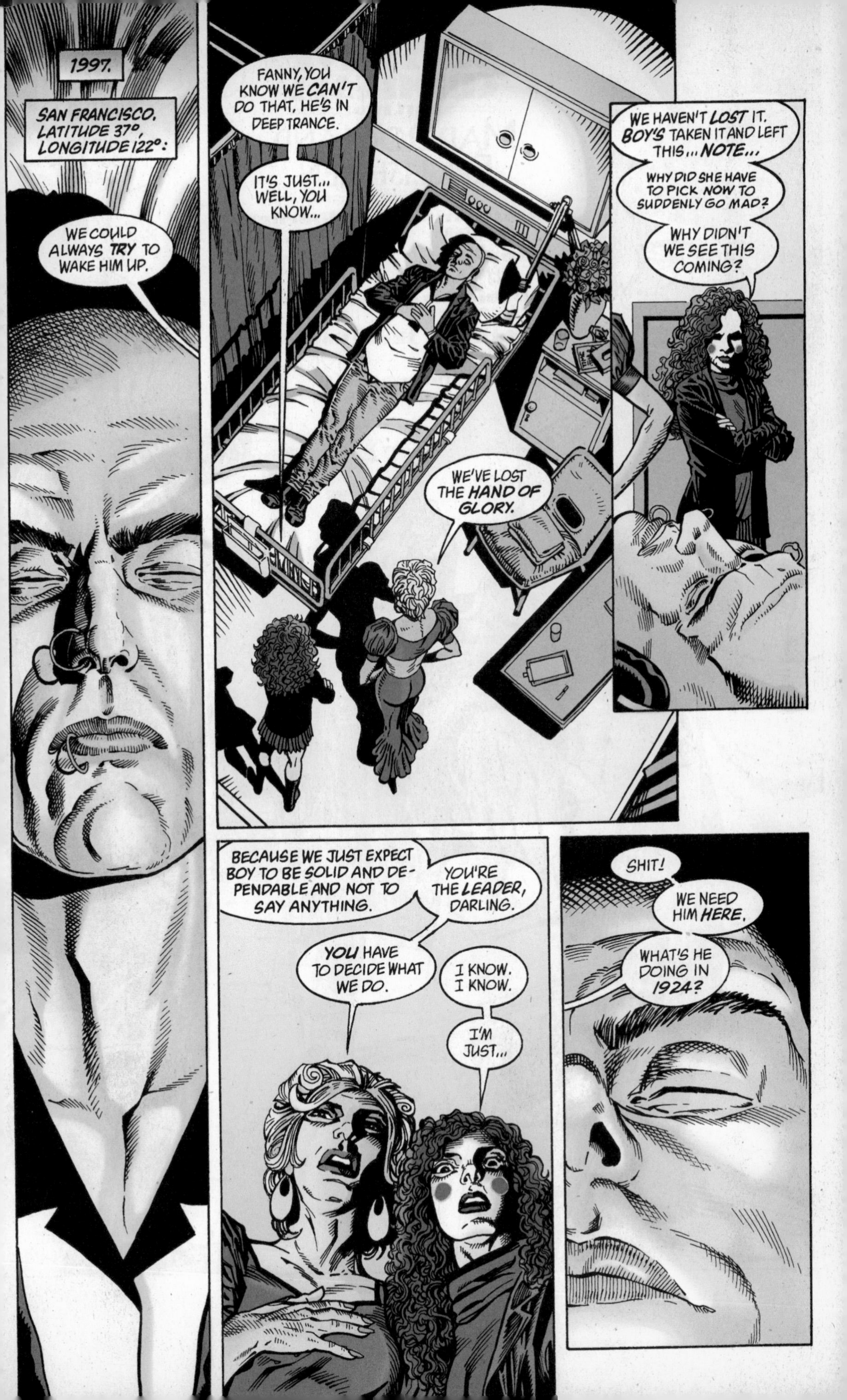
1997.
SAN FRANCISCO. LATITUDE 37°, LONGITUDE 122°:
WE COULD ALWAYS TRY TO WAKE HIM UP.
FANNY, YOU KNOW WE CAN'T DO THAT. HE'S IN DEEP TRANCE.
IT'S JUST... WELL, YOU KNOW...
WE'VE LOST THE HAND OF GLORY.
WE HAVEN'T LOST IT. BOY'S TAKEN IT AND LEFT THIS... NOTE...
WHY DID SHE HAVE TO PICK NOW TO SUDDENLY GO MAD?
WHY DIDN'T WE SEE THIS COMING?
BECAUSE WE JUST EXPECT BOY TO BE SOLID AND DEPENDABLE AND NOT TO SAY ANYTHING.
YOU'RE THE LEADER, DARLING.
YOU HAVE TO DECIDE WHAT WE DO.
I KNOW. I KNOW.
I'M JUST...
SHIT!
WE NEED HIM HERE.
WHAT'S HE DOING IN 1924?

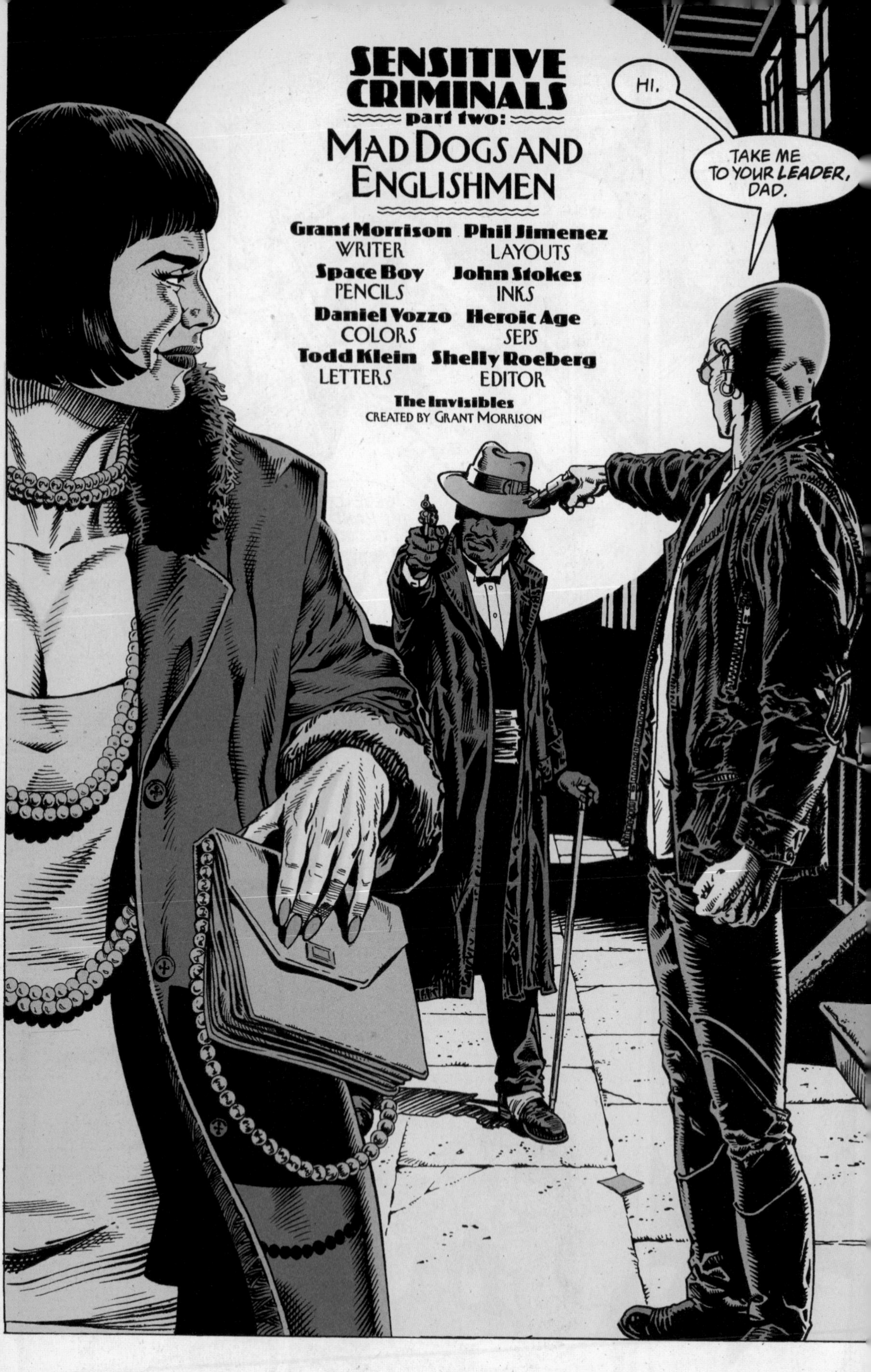
SENSITIVE CRIMINALS
part two:
MAD DOGS AND ENGLISHMEN
Grant Morrison WRITER
Phil Jimenez LAYOUTS
Space Boy PENCILS
John Stokes INKS
Daniel Vozzo COLORS
Heroic Age SEPS
Todd Klein LETTERS
Shelly Roeberg EDITOR
The Invisibles CREATED BY GRANT MORRISON
HI.
TAKE ME TO YOUR LEADER, DAD.

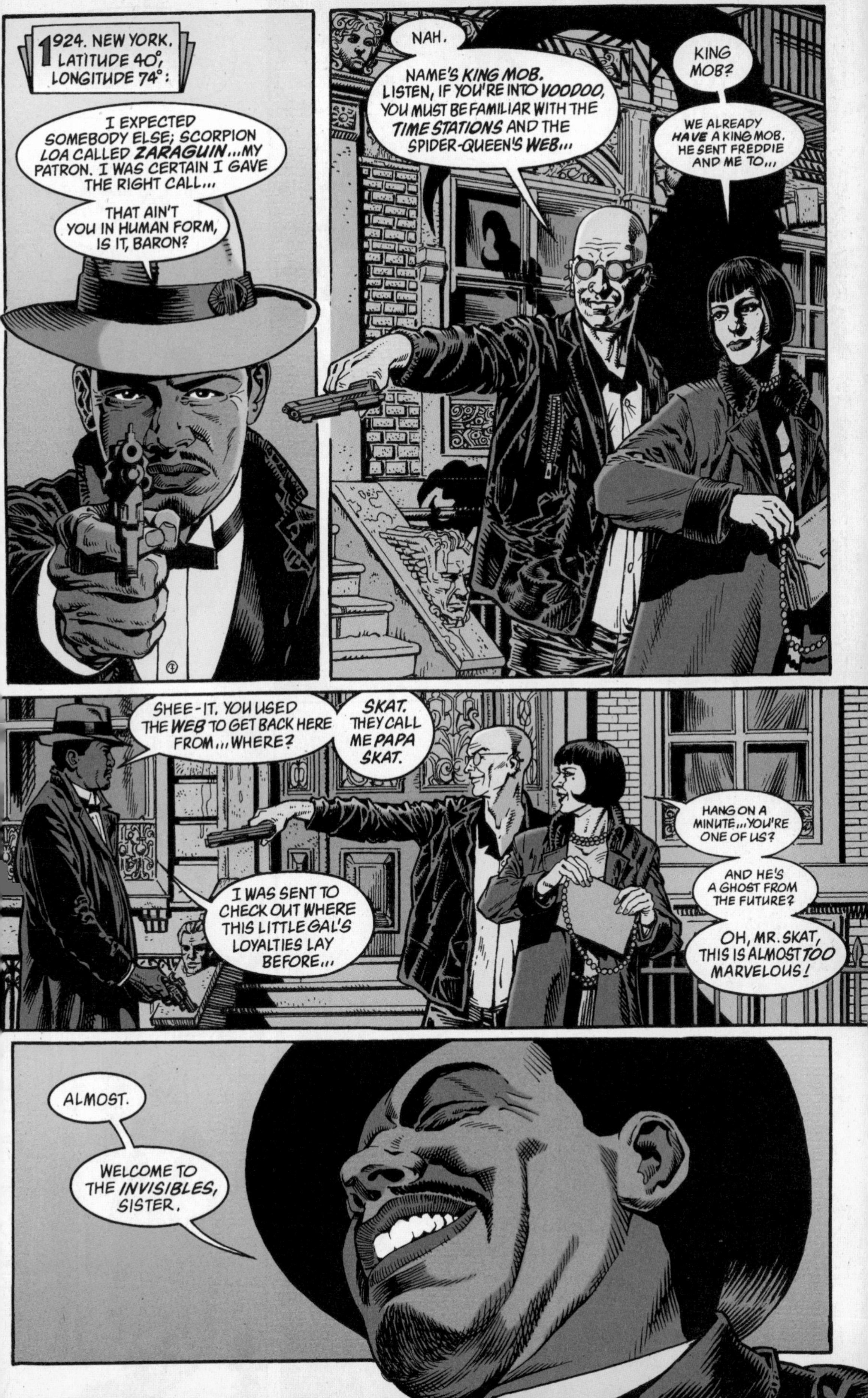
1924. NEW YORK. LATITUDE 40°, LONGITUDE 74°:
I EXPECTED SOMEBODY ELSE; SCORPION LOA CALLED ZARAGUIN...MY PATRON. I WAS CERTAIN I GAVE THE RIGHT CALL...
THAT AIN'T YOU IN HUMAN FORM, IS IT, BARON?
NAH.
NAME'S KING MOB. LISTEN, IF YOU'RE INTO VOODOO, YOU MUST BE FAMILIAR WITH THE TIME STATIONS AND THE SPIDER-QUEEN'S WEB...
KING MOB?
WE ALREADY HAVE A KING MOB. HE SENT FREDDIE AND ME TO...
SHEE-IT. YOU USED THE WEB TO GET BACK HERE FROM...WHERE?
SKAT. THEY CALL ME PAPA SKAT.
I WAS SENT TO CHECK OUT WHERE THIS LITTLE GAL'S LOYALTIES LAY BEFORE...
HANG ON A MINUTE...YOU'RE ONE OF US?
AND HE'S A GHOST FROM THE FUTURE?
OH, MR. SKAT, THIS IS ALMOST TOO MARVELOUS!
ALMOST.
WELCOME TO THE INVISIBLES, SISTER.

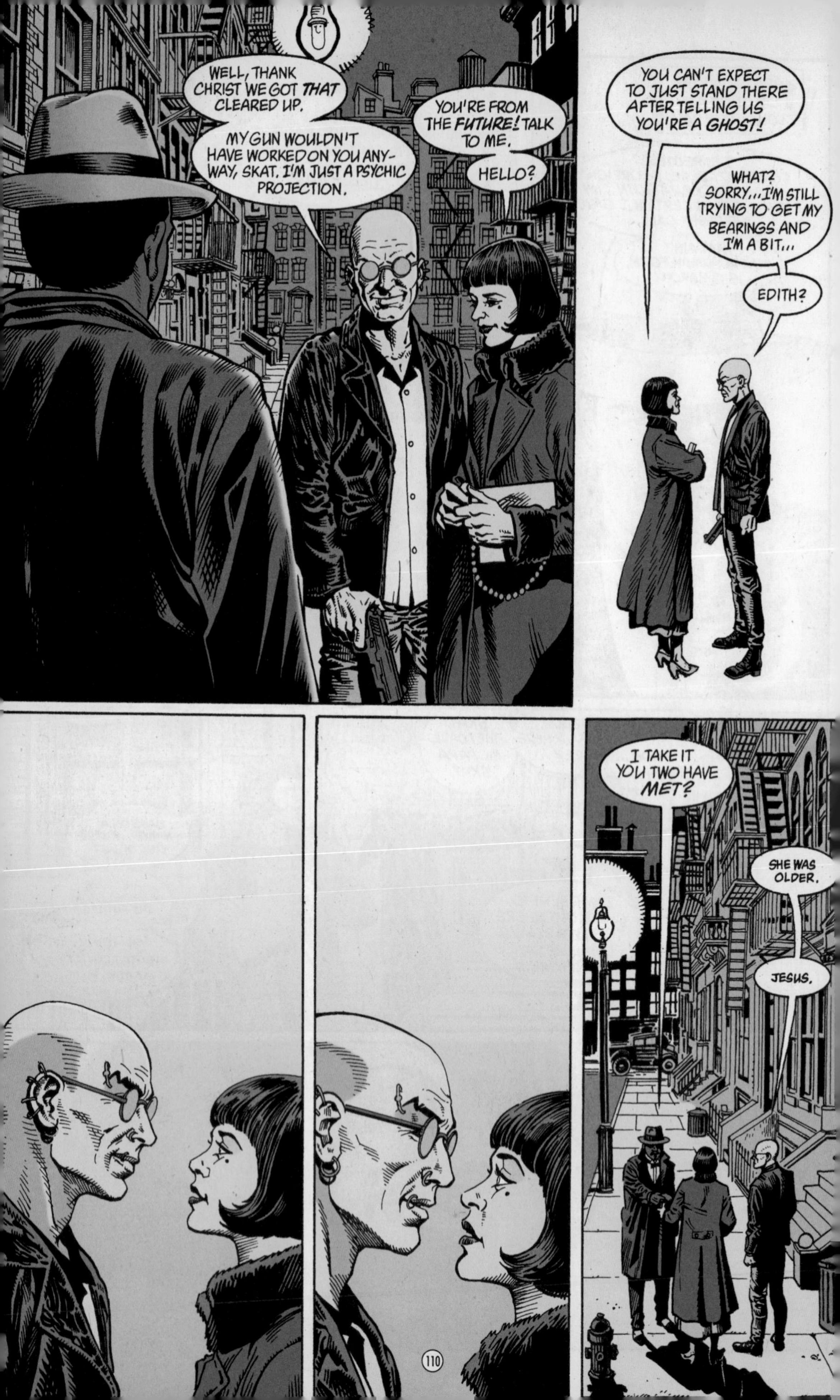
WELL, THANK CHRIST WE GOT THAT CLEARED UP.
MY GUN WOULDN'T HAVE WORKED ON YOU ANY-WAY, SKAT. I'M JUST A PSYCHIC PROJECTION.
YOU'RE FROM THE FUTURE! TALK TO ME.
HELLO?
YOU CAN'T EXPECT TO JUST STAND THERE AFTER TELLING US YOU'RE A GHOST!
WHAT? SORRY... I'M STILL TRYING TO GET MY BEARINGS AND I'M A BIT...
EDITH?
I TAKE IT YOU TWO HAVE MET?
SHE WAS OLDER.
JESUS.

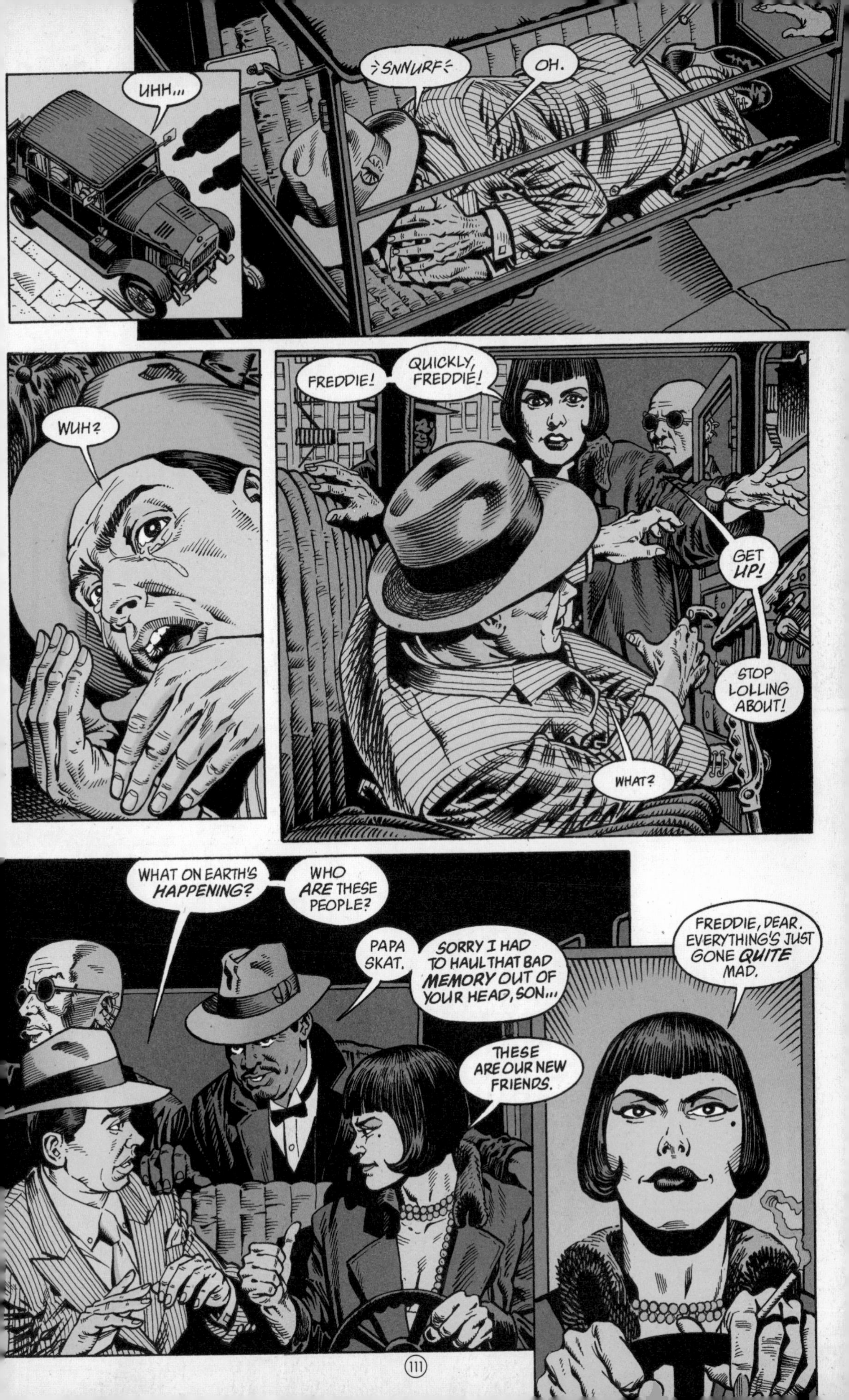
UHH...
SNNURF
OH.
WUH?
FREDDIE!
QUICKLY, FREDDIE!
GET UP!
STOP LOLLING ABOUT!
WHAT?
WHAT ON EARTH'S HAPPENING?
WHO ARE THESE PEOPLE?
PAPA SKAT.
SORRY I HAD TO HAUL THAT BAD MEMORY OUT OF YOUR HEAD, SON...
THESE ARE OUR NEW FRIENDS.
FREDDIE, DEAR. EVERYTHING'S JUST GONE QUITE MAD.

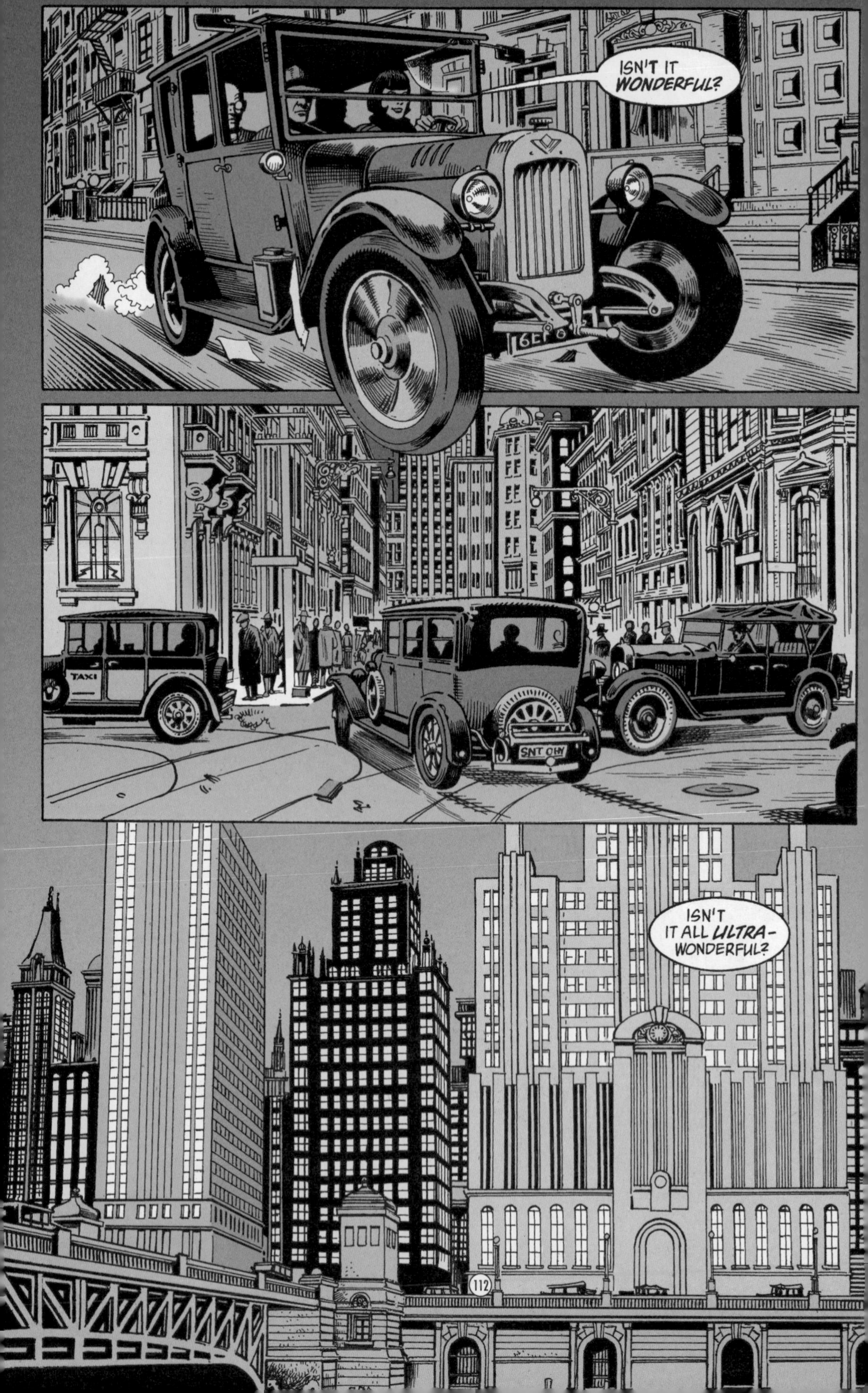
ISN'T IT WONDERFUL?
TAXI
ISN'T IT ALL ULTRA-WONDERFUL?

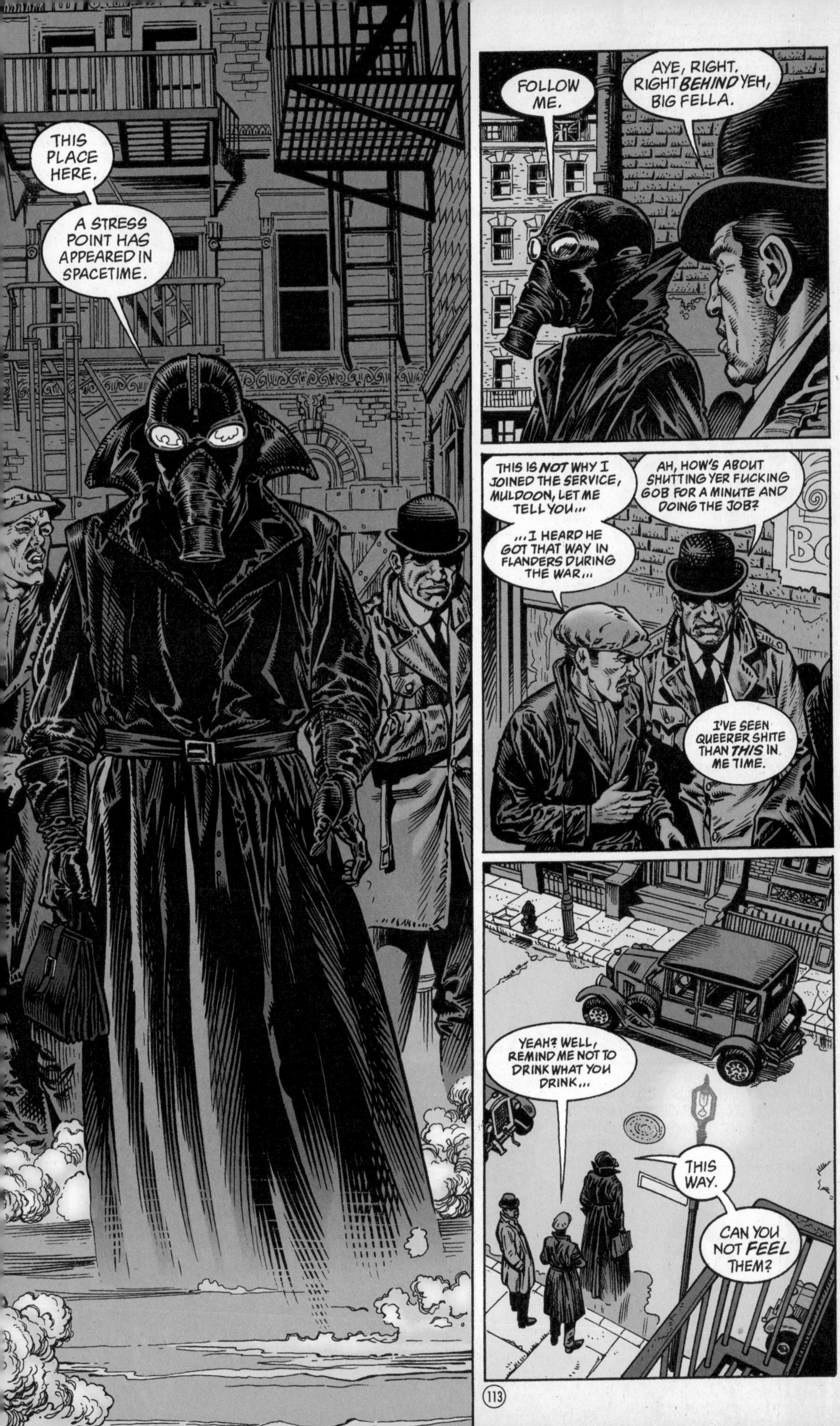
THIS PLACE HERE.
A STRESS POINT HAS APPEARED IN SPACETIME.
FOLLOW ME.
AYE, RIGHT. RIGHT BEHIND YEH, BIG FELLA.
THIS IS NOT WHY I JOINED THE SERVICE, MULDOON, LET ME TELL YOU...
...I HEARD HE GOT THAT WAY IN FLANDERS DURING THE WAR...
AH, HOW'S ABOUT SHUTTING YER FUCKING GOB FOR A MINUTE AND DOING THE JOB?
I'VE SEEN QUEERER SHITE THAN THIS IN ME TIME.
YEAH? WELL, REMIND ME NOT TO DRINK WHAT YOU DRINK...
THIS WAY.
CAN YOU NOT FEEL THEM?

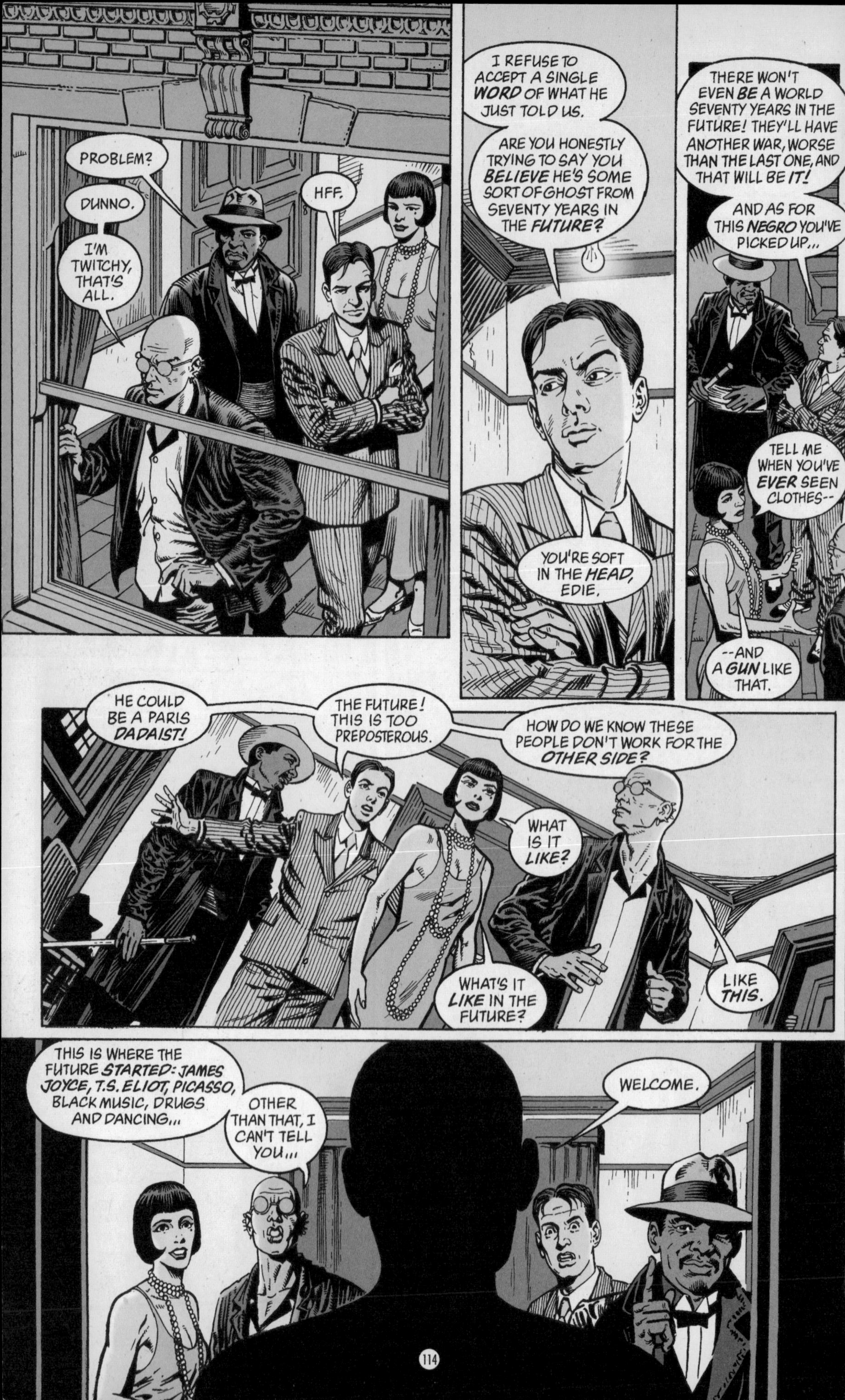
PROBLEM?
DUNNO.
I'M TWITCHY, THAT'S ALL.
HFF.
I REFUSE TO ACCEPT A SINGLE WORD OF WHAT HE JUST TOLD US.
ARE YOU HONESTLY TRYING TO SAY YOU BELIEVE HE'S SOME SORT OF GHOST FROM SEVENTY YEARS IN THE FUTURE?
YOU'RE SOFT IN THE HEAD, EDIE.
THERE WON'T EVEN BE A WORLD SEVENTY YEARS IN THE FUTURE! THEY'LL HAVE ANOTHER WAR, WORSE THAN THE LAST ONE, AND THAT WILL BE IT!
AND AS FOR THIS NEGRO YOU'VE PICKED UP...
TELL ME WHEN YOU'VE EVER SEEN CLOTHES--
--AND A GUN LIKE THAT.
HE COULD BE A PARIS DADAIST!
THE FUTURE! THIS IS TOO PREPOSTEROUS.
HOW DO WE KNOW THESE PEOPLE DON'T WORK FOR THE OTHER SIDE?
WHAT IS IT LIKE?
WHAT'S IT LIKE IN THE FUTURE?
LIKE THIS.
THIS IS WHERE THE FUTURE STARTED: JAMES JOYCE, T.S. ELIOT, PICASSO, BLACK MUSIC, DRUGS AND DANCING...
OTHER THAN THAT, I CAN'T TELL YOU...
WELCOME.

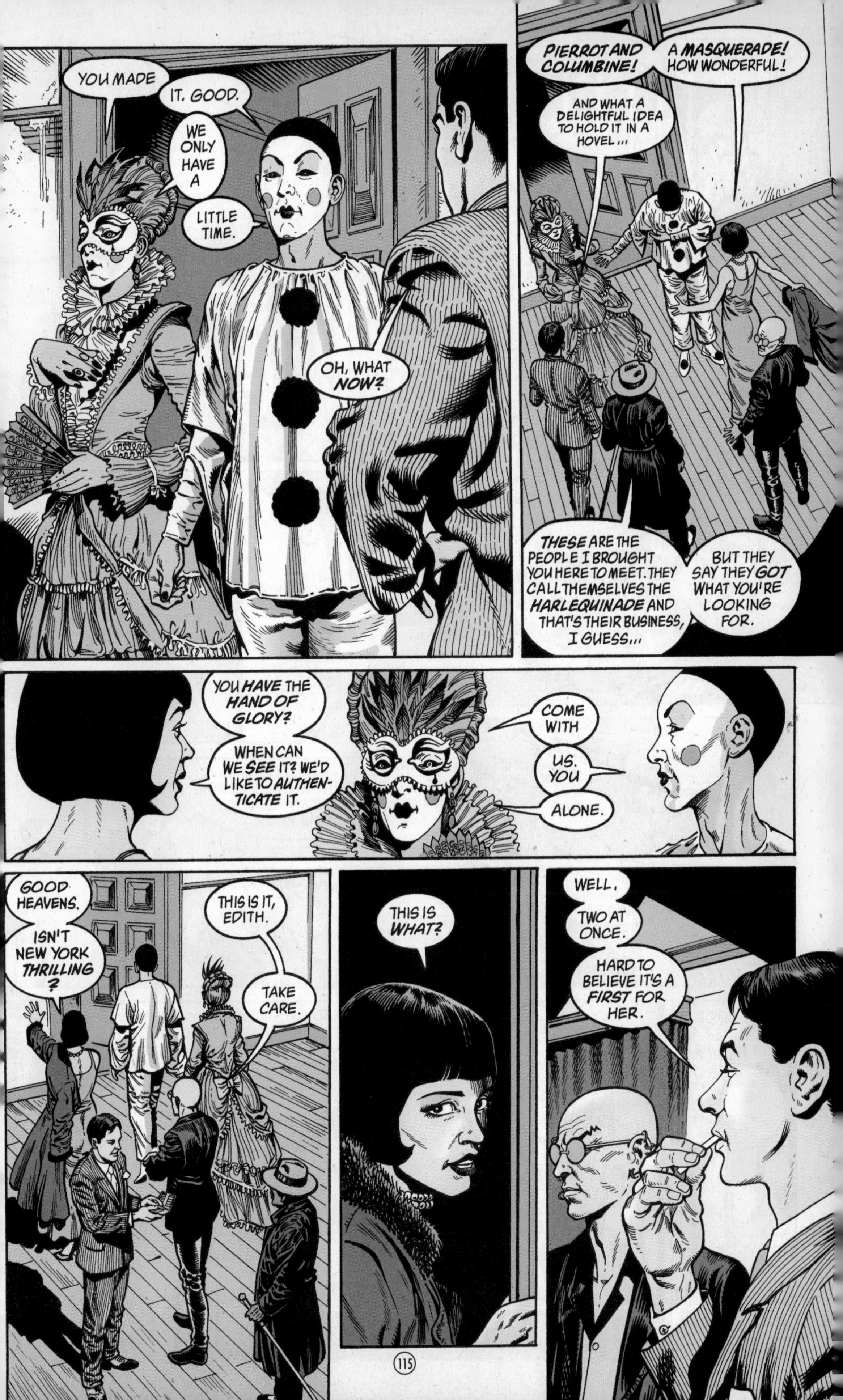
YOU MADE
IT. GOOD.
WE ONLY HAVE A
LITTLE TIME.
OH, WHAT NOW?
PIERROT AND COLUMBINE!
A MASQUERADE! HOW WONDERFUL!
AND WHAT A DELIGHTFUL IDEA TO HOLD IT IN A HOVEL...
THESE ARE THE PEOPLE I BROUGHT YOU HERE TO MEET. THEY CALL THEMSELVES THE HARLEQUINADE AND THAT'S THEIR BUSINESS, I GUESS...
BUT THEY SAY THEY GOT WHAT YOU'RE LOOKING FOR.
YOU HAVE THE HAND OF GLORY?
WHEN CAN WE SEE IT? WE'D LIKE TO AUTHENTICATE IT.
COME WITH
US. YOU
ALONE.
GOOD HEAVENS.
ISN'T NEW YORK THRILLING?
THIS IS IT, EDITH.
TAKE CARE.
THIS IS WHAT?
WELL,
TWO AT ONCE.
HARD TO BELIEVE IT'S A FIRST FOR HER.

YOU'RE *TOM,* YEAH?

NICE SUIT.

YES IT IS, ISN'T IT?

HOW DO YOU KNOW MY NAME IN THE *ORDER?* IF YOU'RE FROM THE FUTURE....

SHH!

WHAT KIND OF A THING IS *THAT?*

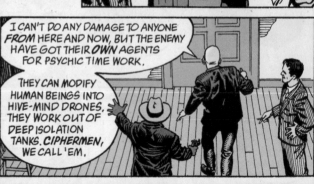

I CAN'T DO ANY DAMAGE TO ANYONE *FROM* HERE AND NOW, BUT THE ENEMY HAVE GOT THEIR *OWN* AGENTS FOR PSYCHIC TIME WORK.

THEY CAN MODIFY HUMAN BEINGS INTO HIVE-MIND DRONES. THEY WORK OUT OF DEEP ISOLATION TANKS. *CIPHERMEN,* WE CALL 'EM.

IT DOESN'T MATTER. LEAVE THEM TO *ME.*

CAN YOU HANDLE THE FLESH AND BLOOD?

SURE. GONNA HAVE TO SET *SOME* KIND OF OFFERING ON ZARAGUIN'S TABLE, AND HE LIKES THEM *RAW....*

ELEVATOR'S COMING THIS WAY.

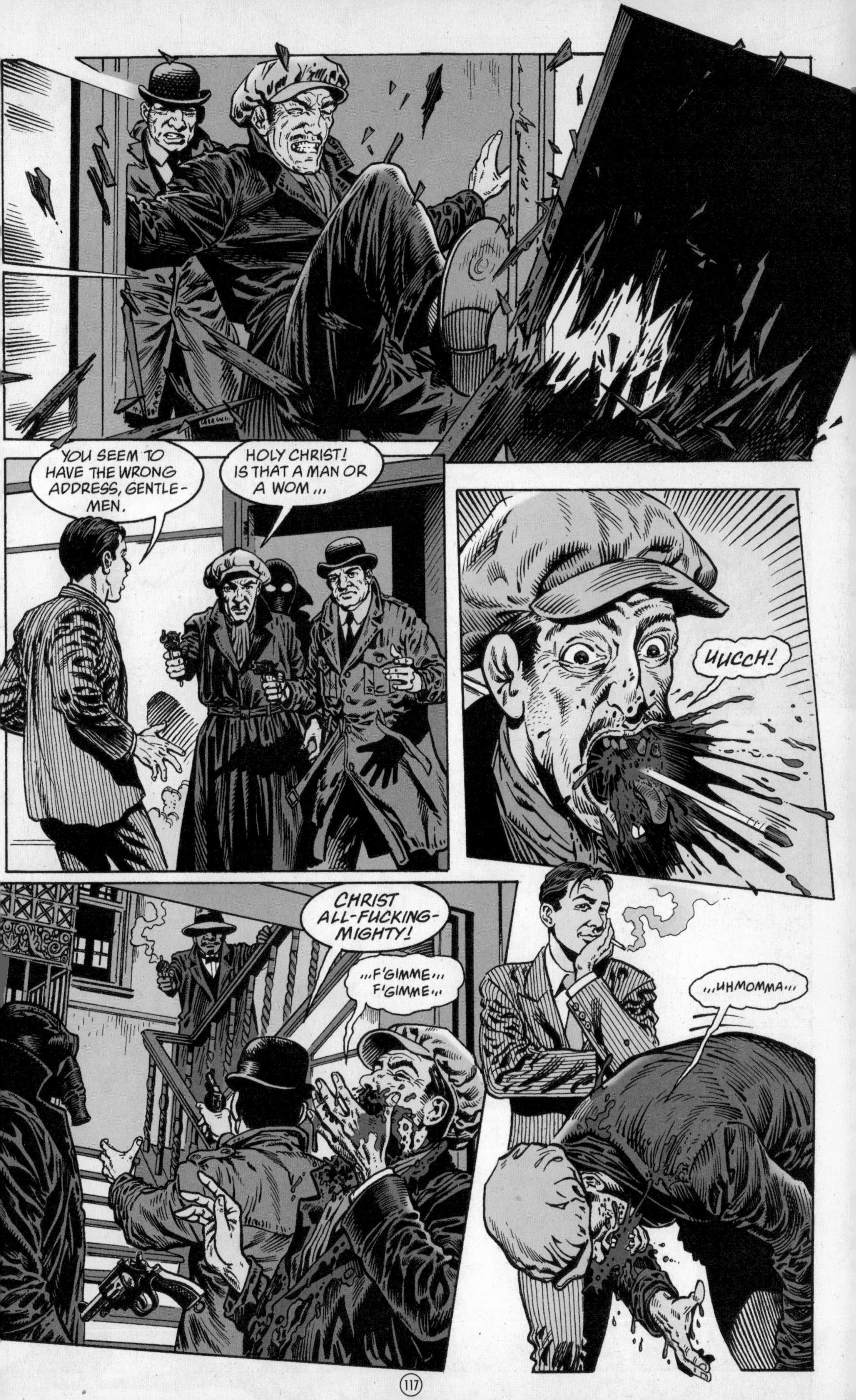
YOU SEEM TO HAVE THE WRONG ADDRESS, GENTLE-MEN.
HOLY CHRIST! IS THAT A MAN OR A WOM...
UUCCH!
CHRIST ALL-FUCKING-MIGHTY!
...F'GIMME... F'GIMME...
...UHMOMMA...

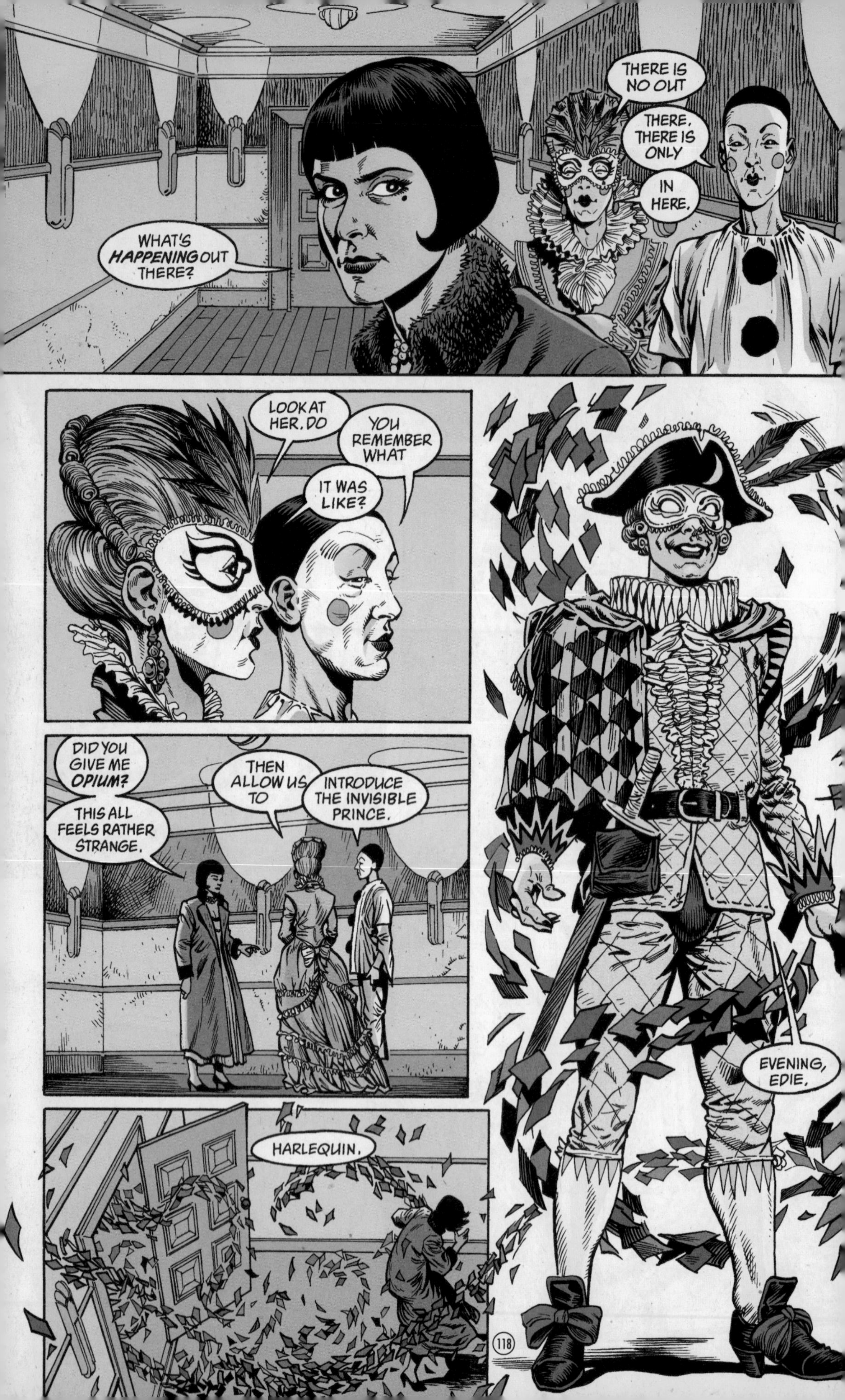
WHAT'S HAPPENING OUT THERE?
THERE IS NO OUT
THERE, THERE IS ONLY
IN HERE.
LOOK AT HER. DO
YOU REMEMBER WHAT
IT WAS LIKE?
DID YOU GIVE ME OPIUM?
THIS ALL FEELS RATHER STRANGE.
THEN ALLOW US TO
INTRODUCE THE INVISIBLE PRINCE.
HARLEQUIN.
EVENING, EDIE.

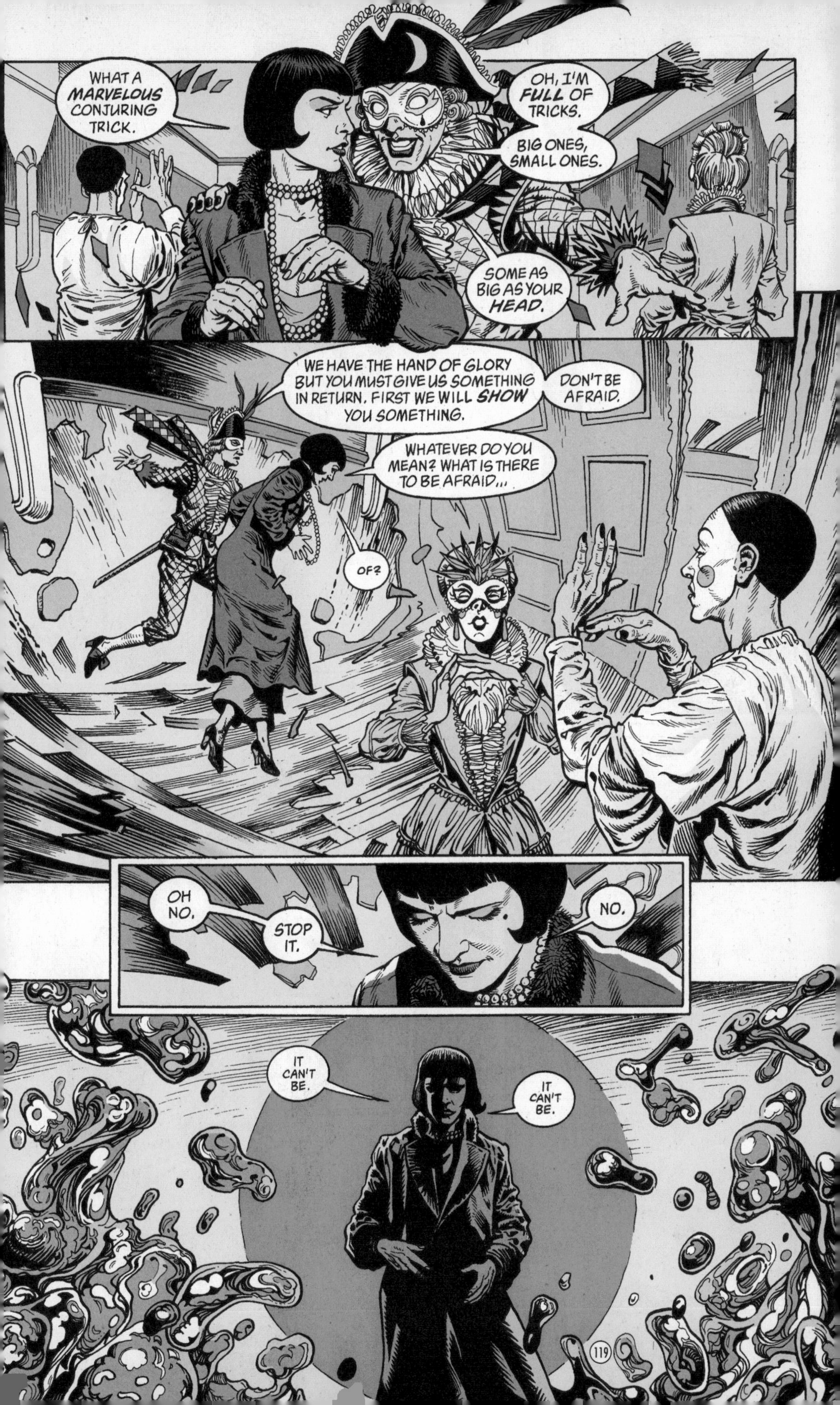
WHAT A MARVELOUS CONJURING TRICK.
OH, I'M FULL OF TRICKS.
BIG ONES, SMALL ONES.
SOME AS BIG AS YOUR HEAD.
WE HAVE THE HAND OF GLORY BUT YOU MUST GIVE US SOMETHING IN RETURN. FIRST WE WILL SHOW YOU SOMETHING.
DON'T BE AFRAID.
WHATEVER DO YOU MEAN? WHAT IS THERE TO BE AFRAID...
OF?
OH NO.
STOP IT.
NO.
IT CAN'T BE.
IT CAN'T BE.

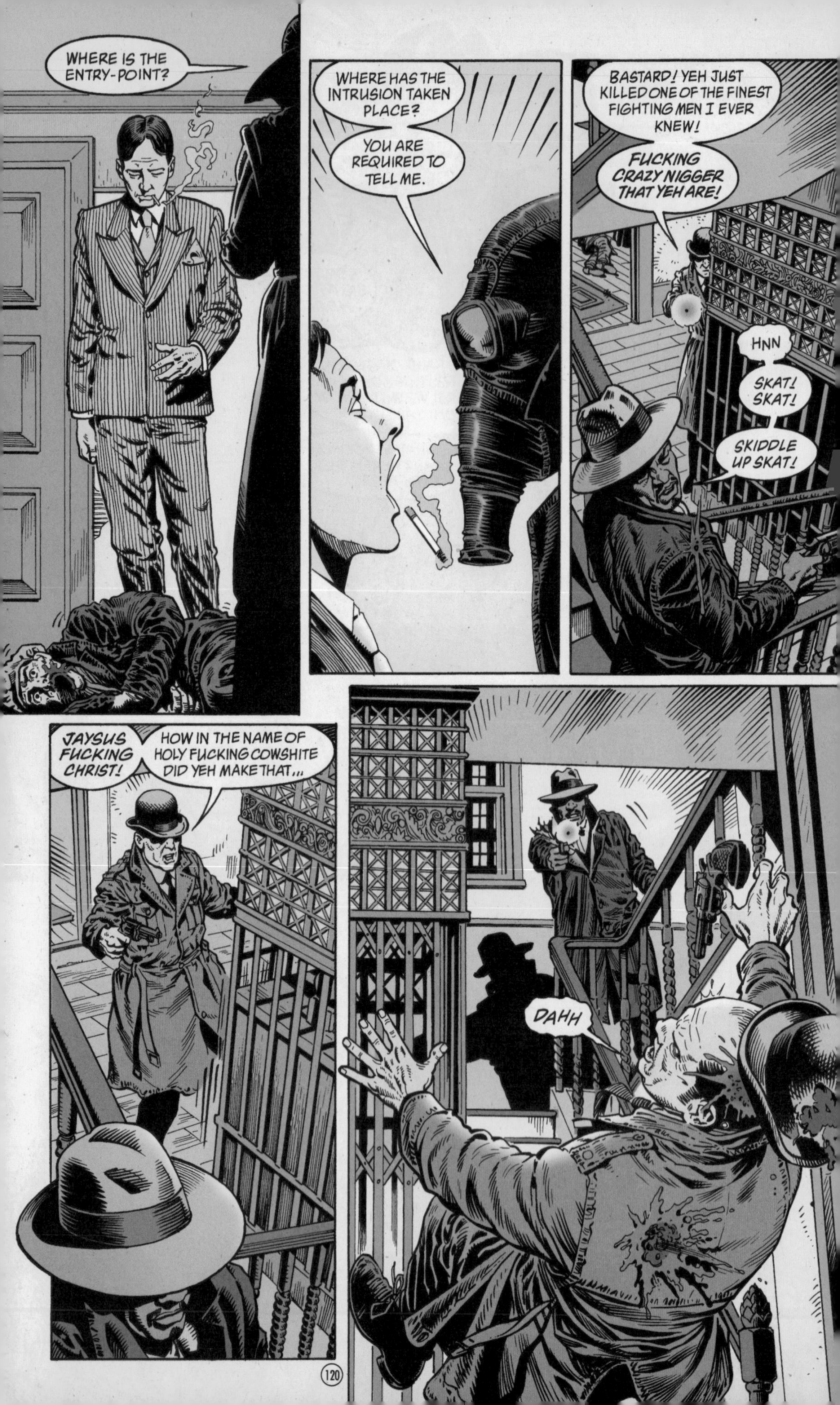

WHERE IS THE ENTRY-POINT?
WHERE HAS THE INTRUSION TAKEN PLACE?
YOU ARE REQUIRED TO TELL ME.
BASTARD! YEH JUST KILLED ONE OF THE FINEST FIGHTING MEN I EVER KNEW!
FUCKING CRAZY NIGGER THAT YEH ARE!
HNN
SKAT! SKAT!
SKIDDLE UP SKAT!
JAYSUS FUCKING CHRIST!
HOW IN THE NAME OF HOLY FUCKING COWSHITE DID YEH MAKE THAT...
DAHH

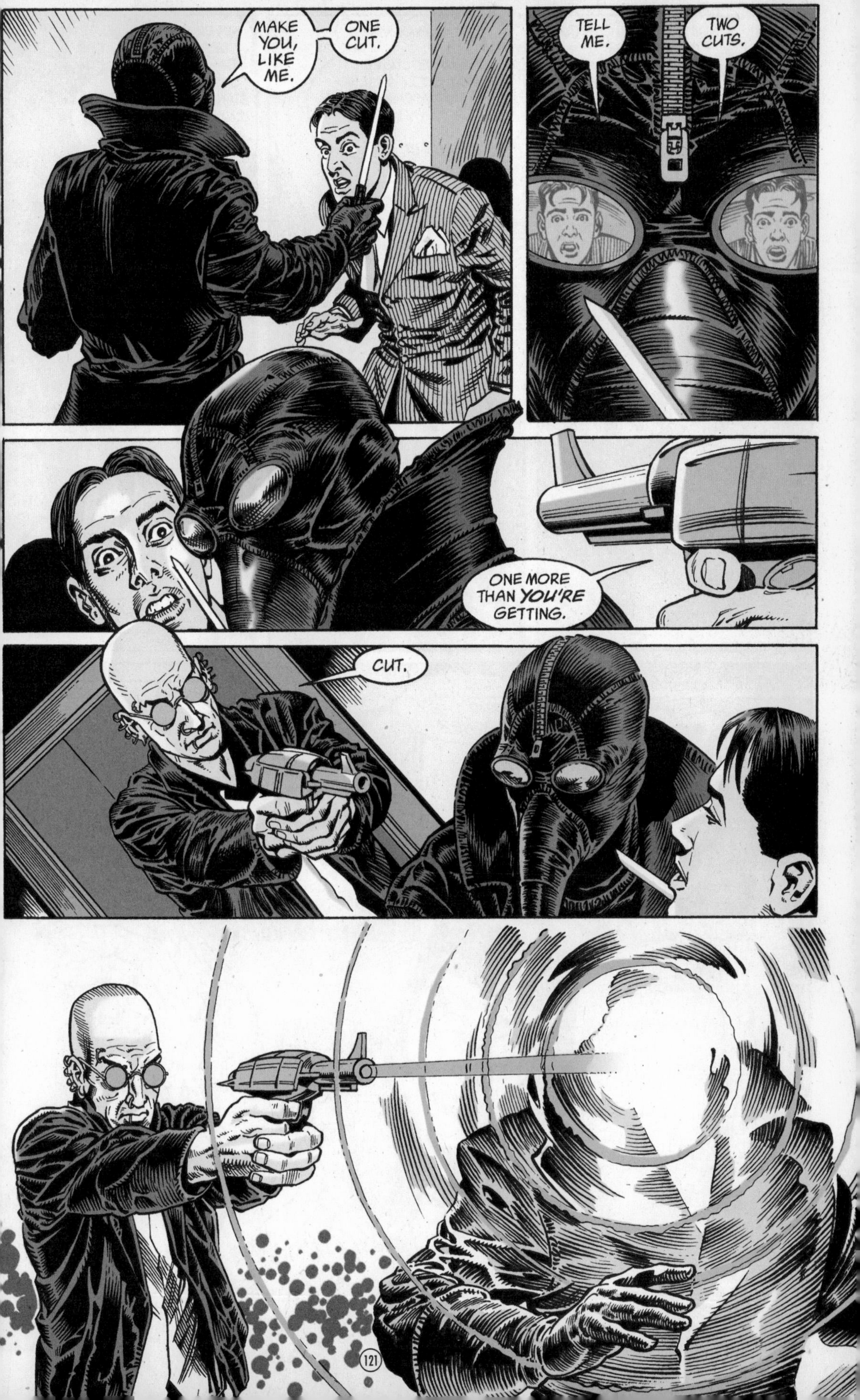
MAKE YOU, LIKE ME.
ONE CUT.
TELL ME.
TWO CUTS.
ONE MORE THAN *YOU'RE* GETTING.
CUT.

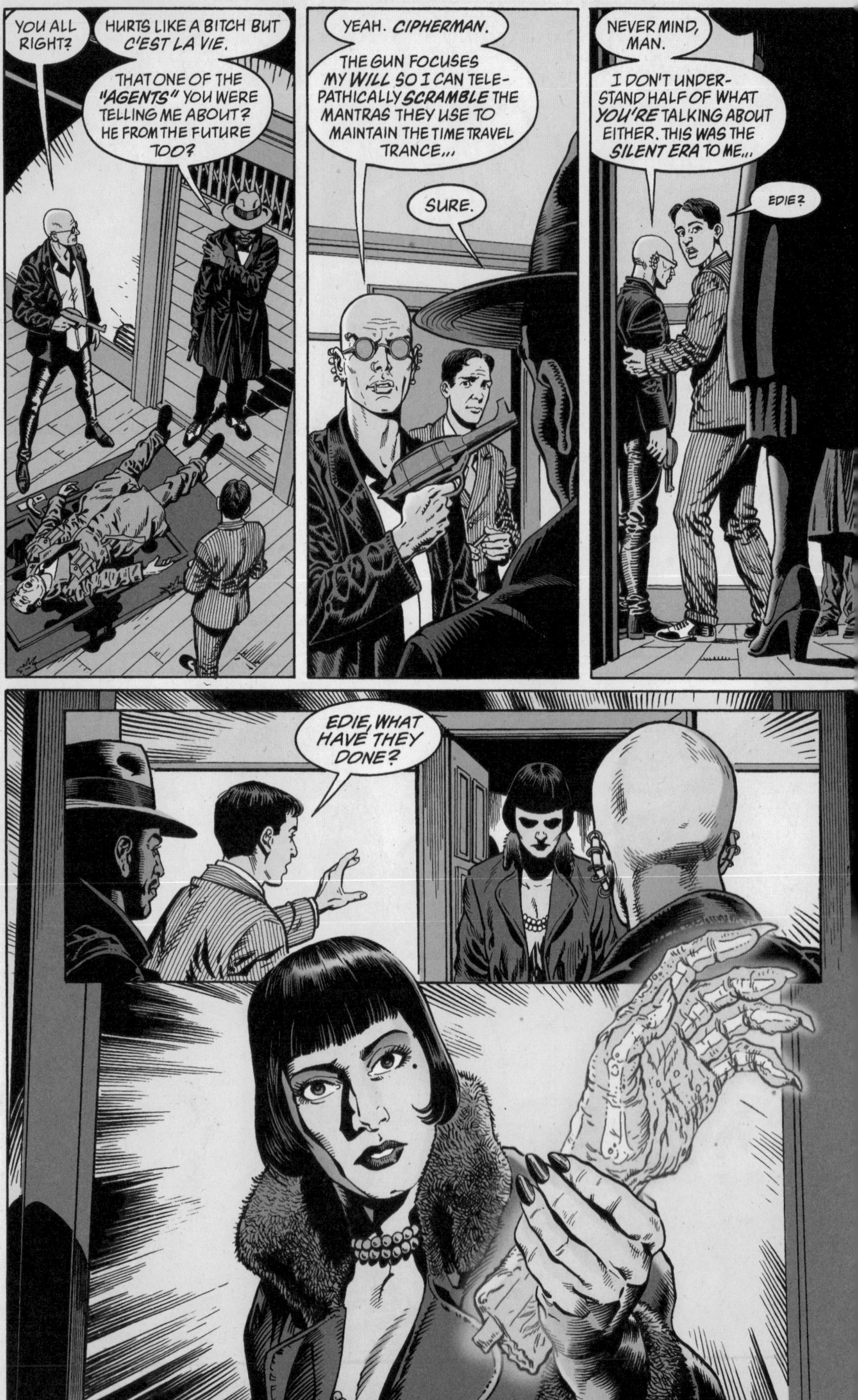
YOU ALL RIGHT?
HURTS LIKE A BITCH BUT C'EST LA VIE.
THAT ONE OF THE "AGENTS" YOU WERE TELLING ME ABOUT? HE FROM THE FUTURE TOO?
YEAH. CIPHERMAN.
THE GUN FOCUSES MY WILL SO I CAN TELE-PATHICALLY SCRAMBLE THE MANTRAS THEY USE TO MAINTAIN THE TIME TRAVEL TRANCE...
SURE.
NEVER MIND, MAN.
I DON'T UNDER-STAND HALF OF WHAT YOU'RE TALKING ABOUT EITHER. THIS WAS THE SILENT ERA TO ME...
EDIE?
EDIE, WHAT HAVE THEY DONE?

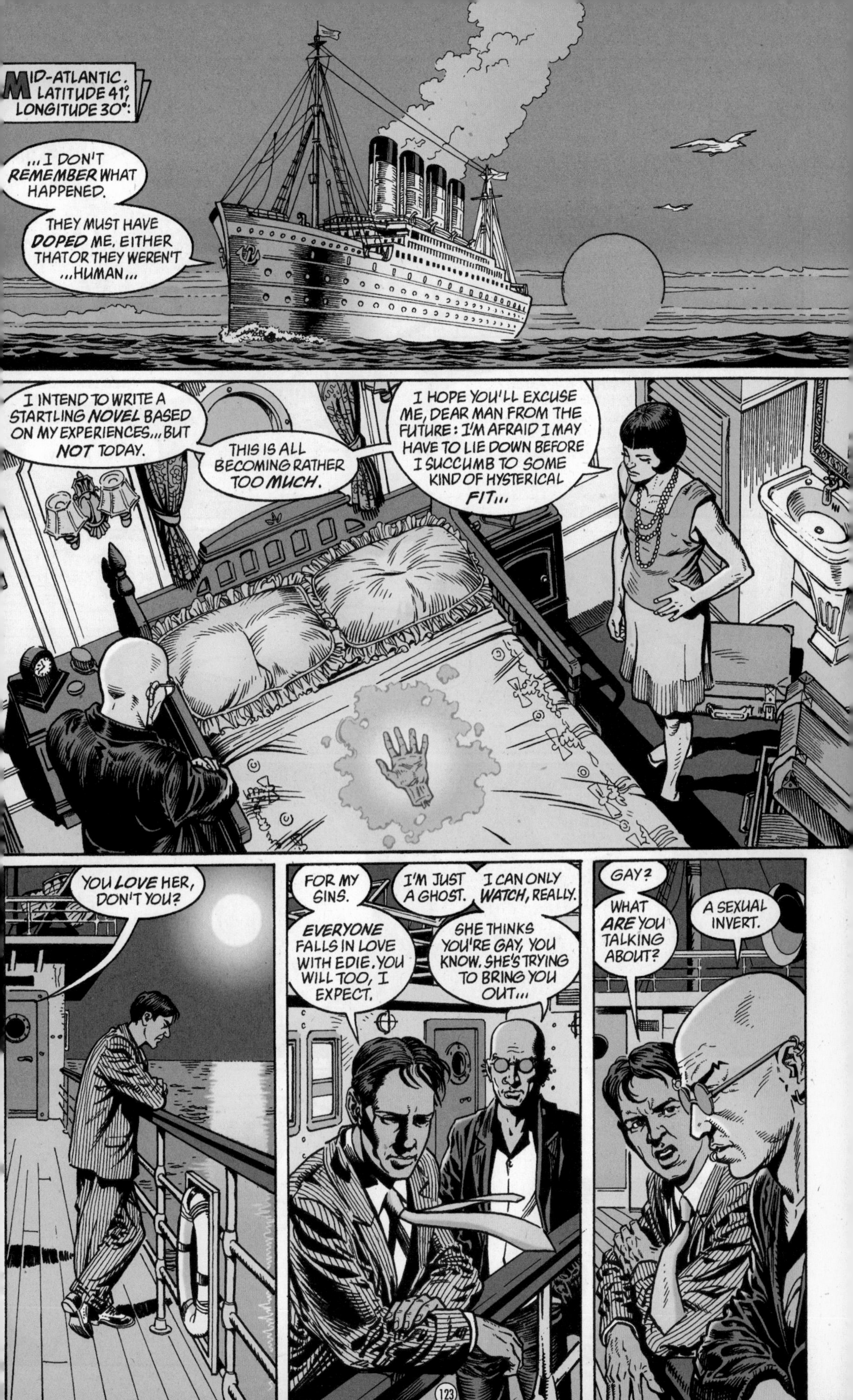
MID-ATLANTIC. LATITUDE 41°, LONGITUDE 30°:
...I DON'T REMEMBER WHAT HAPPENED.
THEY MUST HAVE DOPED ME. EITHER THAT OR THEY WEREN'T ...HUMAN...
I INTEND TO WRITE A STARTLING NOVEL BASED ON MY EXPERIENCES... BUT NOT TODAY.
THIS IS ALL BECOMING RATHER TOO MUCH.
I HOPE YOU'LL EXCUSE ME, DEAR MAN FROM THE FUTURE: I'M AFRAID I MAY HAVE TO LIE DOWN BEFORE I SUCCUMB TO SOME KIND OF HYSTERICAL FIT...
YOU LOVE HER, DON'T YOU?
FOR MY SINS.
EVERYONE FALLS IN LOVE WITH EDIE. YOU WILL TOO, I EXPECT.
I'M JUST A GHOST.
I CAN ONLY WATCH, REALLY.
SHE THINKS YOU'RE GAY, YOU KNOW. SHE'S TRYING TO BRING YOU OUT...
GAY?
WHAT ARE YOU TALKING ABOUT?
A SEXUAL INVERT.

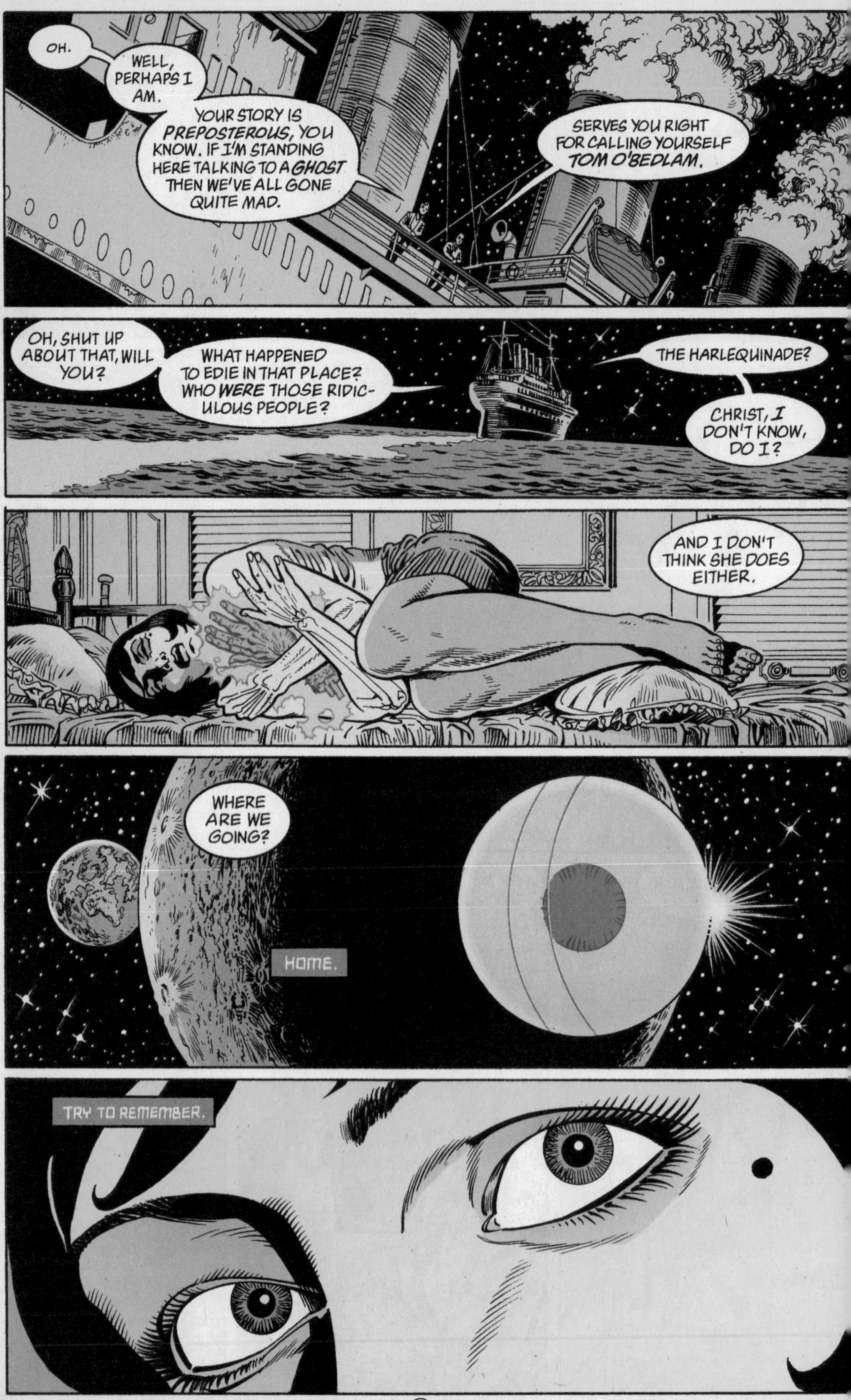
OH.
WELL, PERHAPS I AM.
YOUR STORY IS PREPOSTEROUS, YOU KNOW. IF I'M STANDING HERE TALKING TO A GHOST THEN WE'VE ALL GONE QUITE MAD.
SERVES YOU RIGHT FOR CALLING YOURSELF TOM O'BEDLAM.
OH, SHUT UP ABOUT THAT, WILL YOU?
WHAT HAPPENED TO EDIE IN THAT PLACE? WHO WERE THOSE RIDICULOUS PEOPLE?
THE HARLEQUINADE?
CHRIST, I DON'T KNOW, DO I?
AND I DON'T THINK SHE DOES EITHER.
WHERE ARE WE GOING?
HOME.
TRY TO REMEMBER.

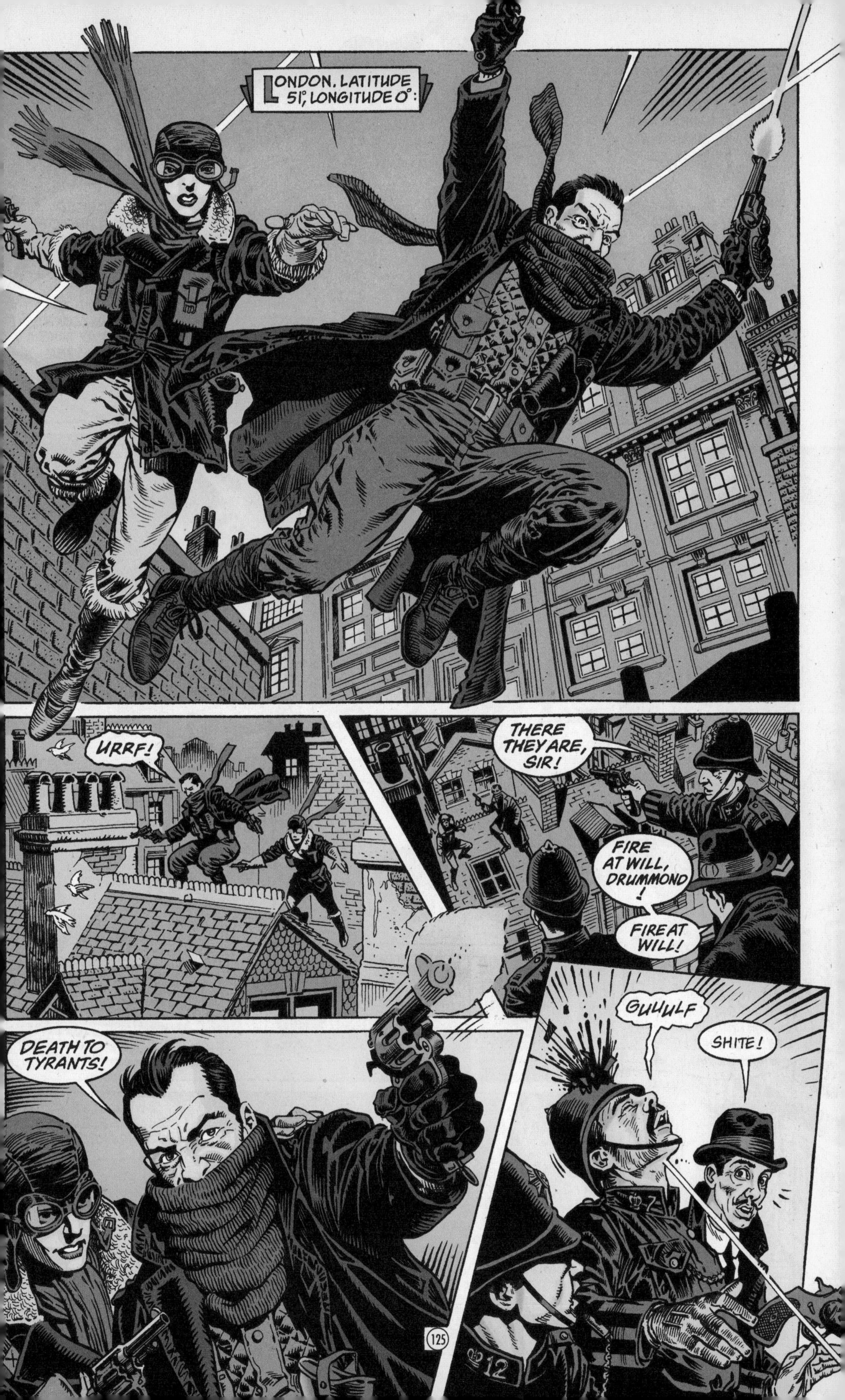
LONDON. LATITUDE 51°, LONGITUDE 0°:
URRF!
THERE THEY ARE, SIR!
FIRE AT WILL, DRUMMOND!
FIRE AT WILL!
DEATH TO TYRANTS!
GUUULF
SHITE!

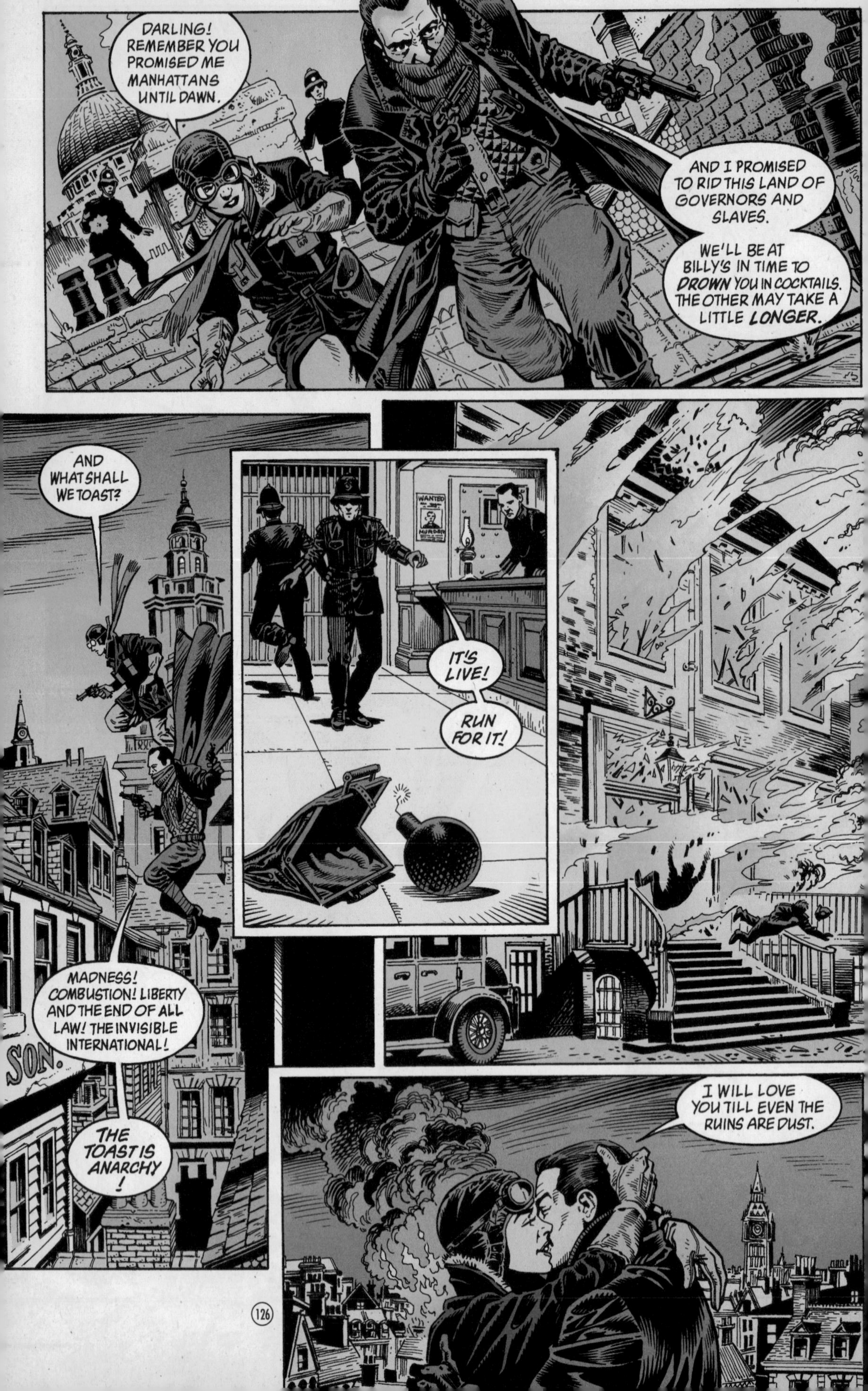
DARLING! REMEMBER YOU PROMISED ME MANHATTANS UNTIL DAWN.
AND I PROMISED TO RID THIS LAND OF GOVERNORS AND SLAVES.
WE'LL BE AT BILLY'S IN TIME TO DROWN YOU IN COCKTAILS. THE OTHER MAY TAKE A LITTLE LONGER.
AND WHAT SHALL WE TOAST?
WANTED
MURDER
IT'S LIVE!
RUN FOR IT!
MADNESS! COMBUSTION! LIBERTY AND THE END OF ALL LAW! THE INVISIBLE INTERNATIONAL!
THE TOAST IS ANARCHY!
SON.
I WILL LOVE YOU TILL EVEN THE RUINS ARE DUST.

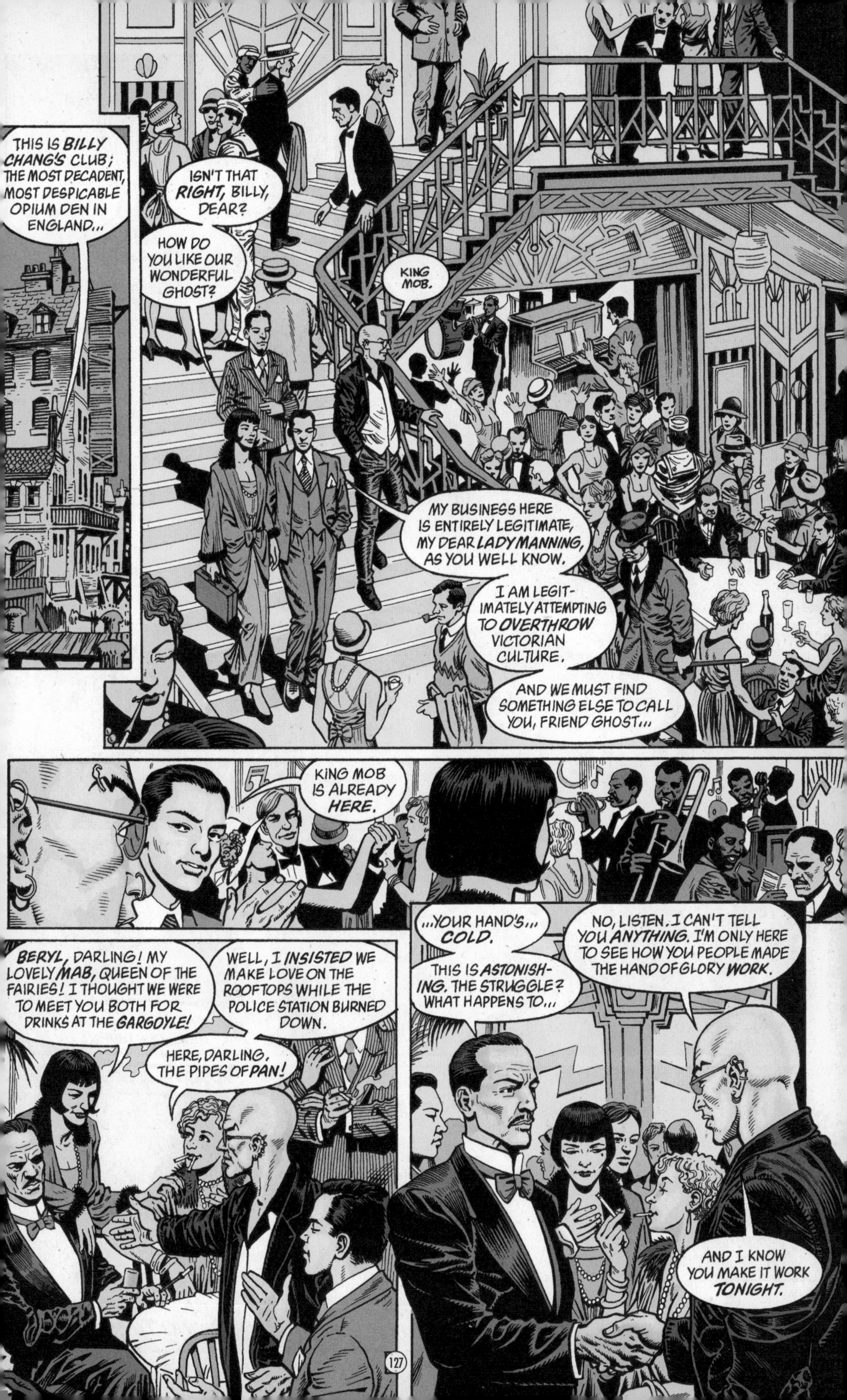
THIS IS BILLY CHANG'S CLUB; THE MOST DECADENT, MOST DESPICABLE OPIUM DEN IN ENGLAND...
ISN'T THAT RIGHT, BILLY, DEAR?
HOW DO YOU LIKE OUR WONDERFUL GHOST?
KING MOB.
MY BUSINESS HERE IS ENTIRELY LEGITIMATE, MY DEAR LADY MANNING, AS YOU WELL KNOW.
I AM LEGITIMATELY ATTEMPTING TO OVERTHROW VICTORIAN CULTURE.
AND WE MUST FIND SOMETHING ELSE TO CALL YOU, FRIEND GHOST...
KING MOB IS ALREADY HERE.
BERYL, DARLING! MY LOVELY MAB, QUEEN OF THE FAIRIES! I THOUGHT WE WERE TO MEET YOU BOTH FOR DRINKS AT THE GARGOYLE!
WELL, I INSISTED WE MAKE LOVE ON THE ROOFTOPS WHILE THE POLICE STATION BURNED DOWN.
HERE, DARLING, THE PIPES OF PAN!
...YOUR HAND'S... COLD.
THIS IS ASTONISHING. THE STRUGGLE? WHAT HAPPENS TO...
NO, LISTEN. I CAN'T TELL YOU ANYTHING. I'M ONLY HERE TO SEE HOW YOU PEOPLE MADE THE HAND OF GLORY WORK.
AND I KNOW YOU MAKE IT WORK TONIGHT.

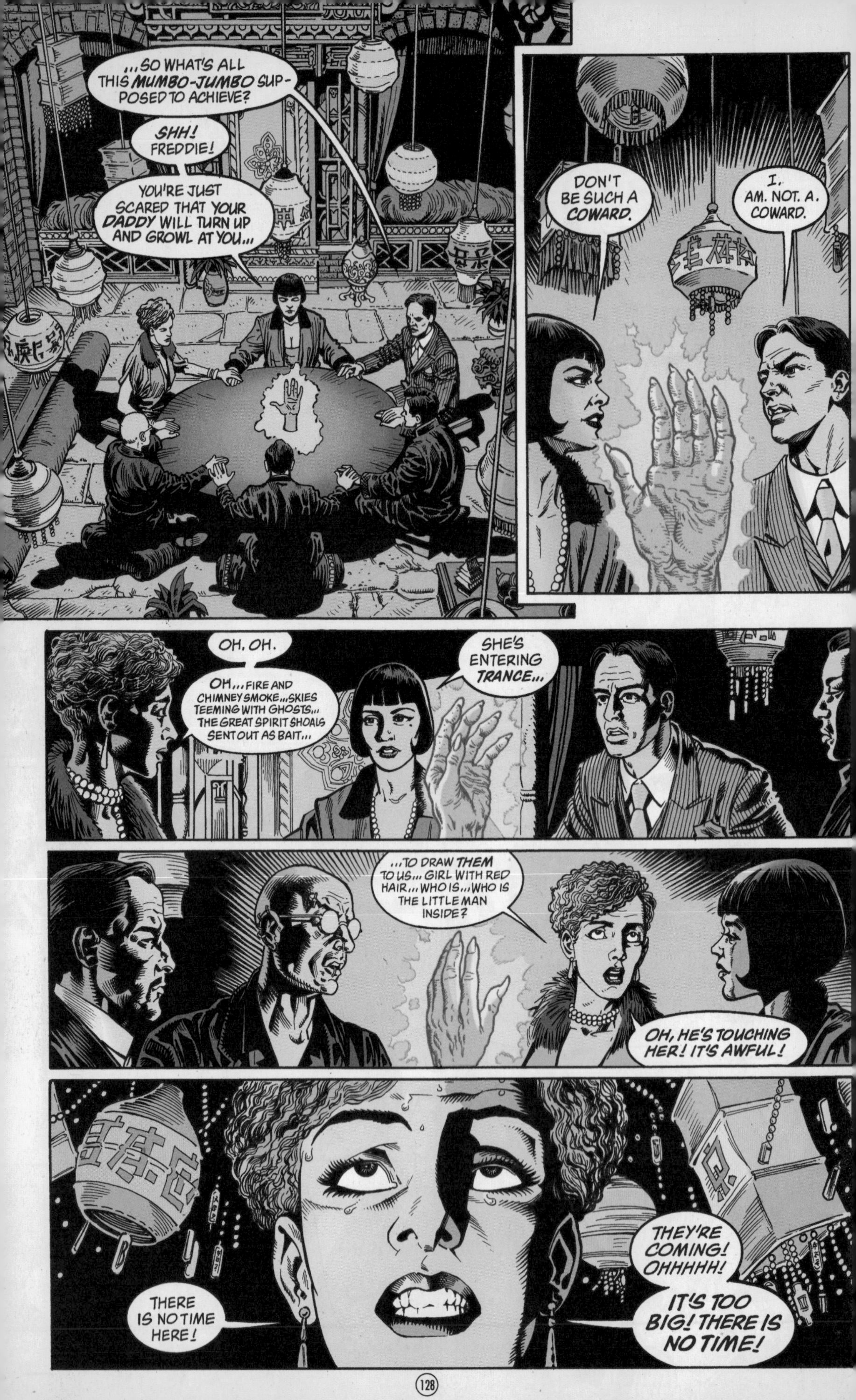
...SO WHAT'S ALL THIS MUMBO-JUMBO SUPPOSED TO ACHIEVE?
SHH! FREDDIE!
YOU'RE JUST SCARED THAT YOUR DADDY WILL TURN UP AND GROWL AT YOU...
DON'T BE SUCH A COWARD.
I. AM. NOT. A. COWARD.
OH. OH.
OH... FIRE AND CHIMNEY SMOKE... SKIES TEEMING WITH GHOSTS... THE GREAT SPIRIT SHOALS SENT OUT AS BAIT...
SHE'S ENTERING TRANCE...
...TO DRAW THEM TO US... GIRL WITH RED HAIR... WHO IS... WHO IS THE LITTLE MAN INSIDE?
OH, HE'S TOUCHING HER! IT'S AWFUL!
THERE IS NO TIME HERE!
THEY'RE COMING! OHHHHH!
IT'S TOO BIG! THERE IS NO TIME!

...GIRL WITH RED HAIR...?

THE FLAW! THE FRACTURE!

THE HOWLING DIAMOND!

THEY'RE COMING!

OH MY GOD.

STAY CALM.

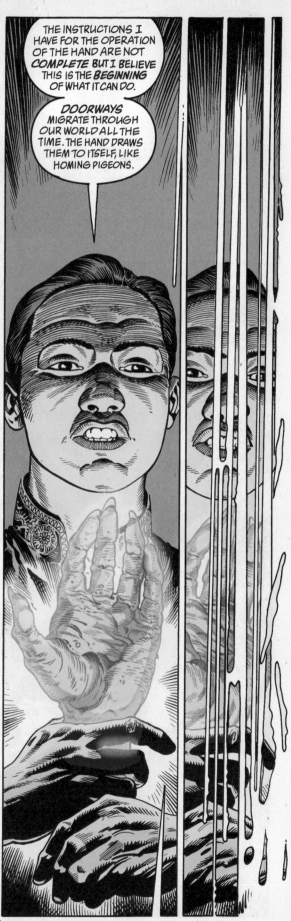

THE INSTRUCTIONS I HAVE FOR THE OPERATION OF THE HAND ARE NOT *COMPLETE* BUT I BELIEVE THIS IS THE *BEGINNING* OF WHAT IT CAN DO.

DOORWAYS MIGRATE THROUGH OUR WORLD ALL THE TIME. THE HAND DRAWS THEM TO ITSELF, LIKE HOMING PIGEONS.

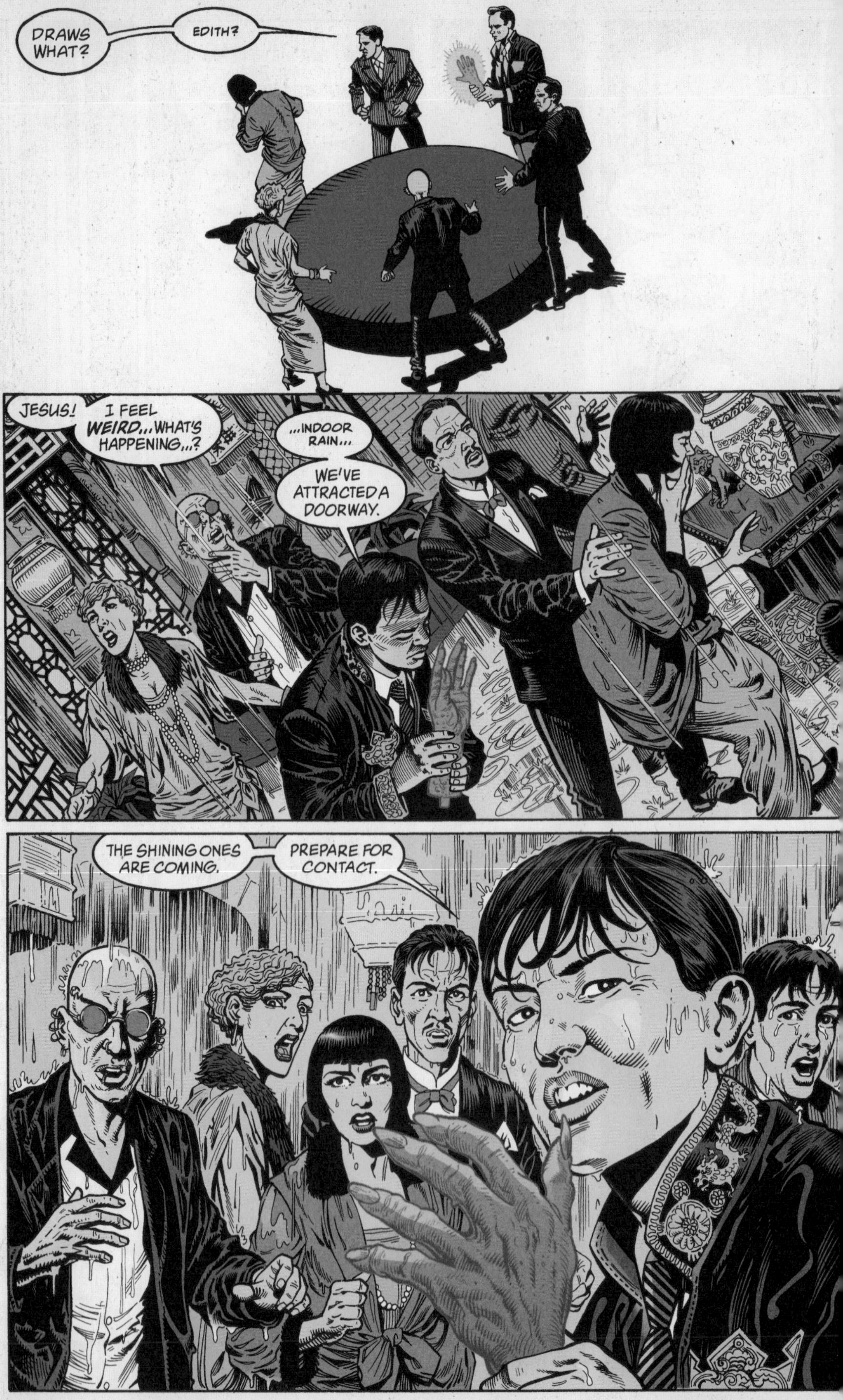
DRAWS WHAT?
EDITH?
JESUS!
I FEEL WEIRD... WHAT'S HAPPENING...?
...INDOOR RAIN...
WE'VE ATTRACTED A DOORWAY.
THE SHINING ONES ARE COMING.
PREPARE FOR CONTACT.

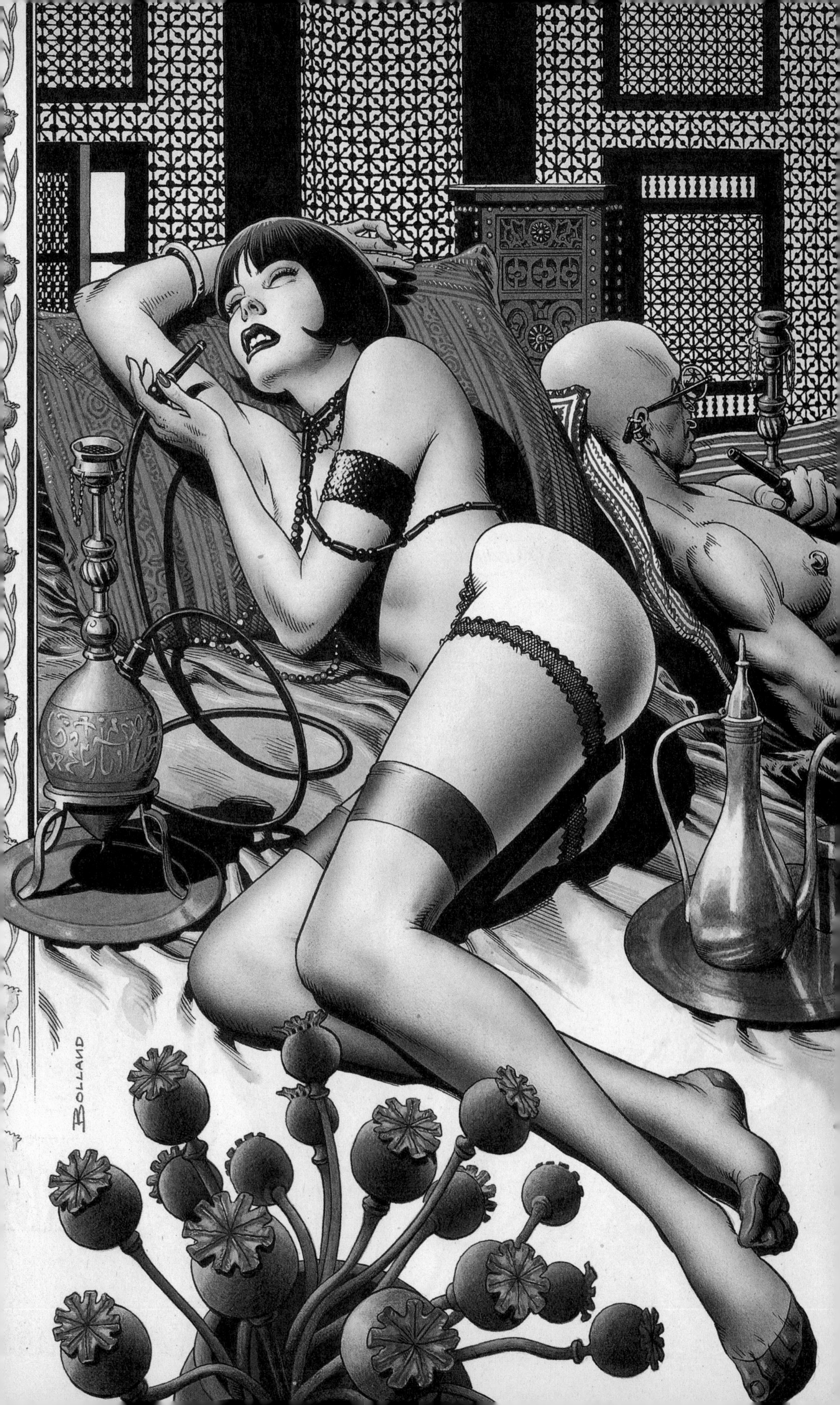
BOLLAND

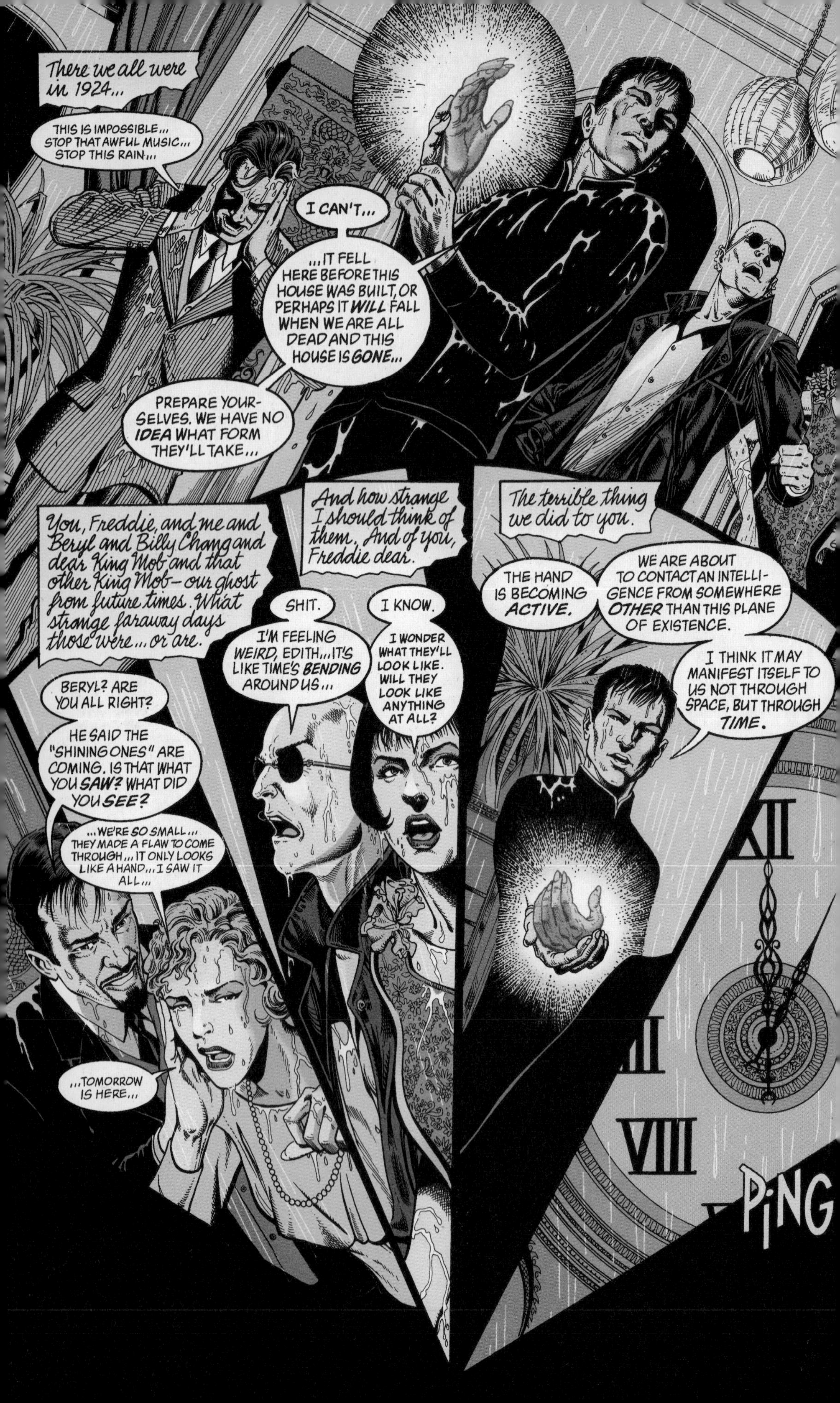
There we all were in 1924...
THIS IS IMPOSSIBLE... STOP THAT AWFUL MUSIC... STOP THIS RAIN...
I CAN'T...
...IT FELL HERE BEFORE THIS HOUSE WAS BUILT, OR PERHAPS IT WILL FALL WHEN WE ARE ALL DEAD AND THIS HOUSE IS GONE...
PREPARE YOURSELVES. WE HAVE NO IDEA WHAT FORM THEY'LL TAKE...
You, Freddie, and me and Beryl and Billy Chang and dear King Mob and that other King Mob — our ghost from future times. What strange faraway days those were... or are.
BERYL? ARE YOU ALL RIGHT?
HE SAID THE "SHINING ONES" ARE COMING. IS THAT WHAT YOU SAW? WHAT DID YOU SEE?
...WE'RE SO SMALL... THEY MADE A FLAW TO COME THROUGH... IT ONLY LOOKS LIKE A HAND... I SAW IT ALL...
...TOMORROW IS HERE...
And how strange I should think of them. And of you, Freddie dear.
SHIT.
I'M FEELING WEIRD, EDITH... IT'S LIKE TIME'S BENDING AROUND US...
I KNOW.
I WONDER WHAT THEY'LL LOOK LIKE. WILL THEY LOOK LIKE ANYTHING AT ALL?
The terrible thing we did to you.
THE HAND IS BECOMING ACTIVE.
WE ARE ABOUT TO CONTACT AN INTELLIGENCE FROM SOMEWHERE OTHER THAN THIS PLANE OF EXISTENCE.
I THINK IT MAY MANIFEST ITSELF TO US NOT THROUGH SPACE, BUT THROUGH TIME.
PING

SEN SIT IVE CRI MIN ALS

part three

PARISIAN · PIERROT.

And through time it came.

Grant Morrison WRITER

Phil Jimenez PENCILLER

John Stokes INKER

Daniel Vozzo COLORIST

Heroic Age COLOR SEPS

Todd Klein LETTERER

Shelly Roeberg EDITOR

The Invisibles CREATED BY GRANT MORRISON

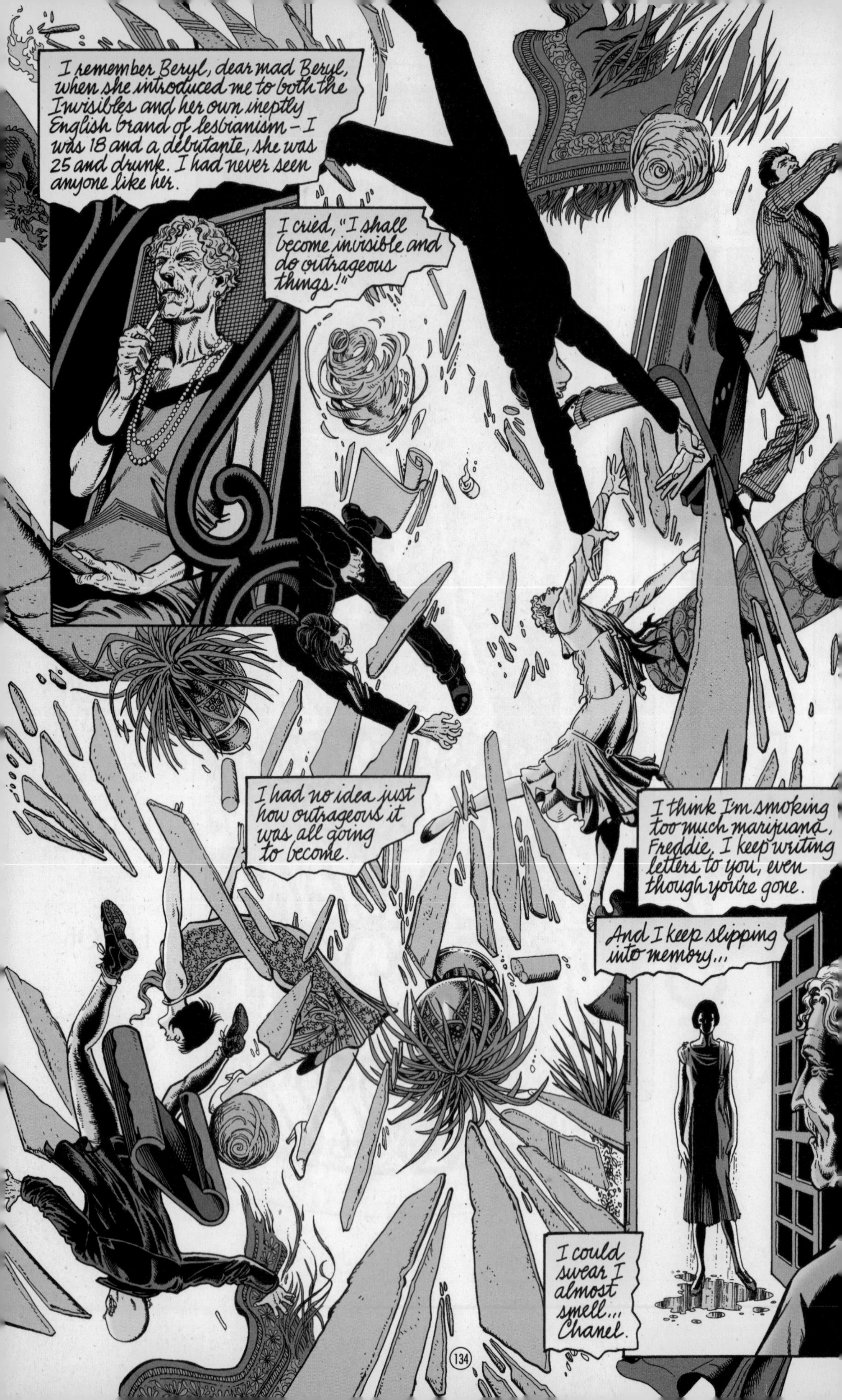
I remember Beryl, dear mad Beryl, when she introduced me to both the Invisibles and her own ineptly English brand of lesbianism – I was 18 and a debutante, she was 25 and drunk. I had never seen anyone like her.
I cried, "I shall become invisible and do outrageous things!"
I had no idea just how outrageous it was all going to become.
I think I'm smoking too much marijuana, Freddie. I keep writing letters to you, even though you're gone.
And I keep slipping into memory...
I could swear I almost smell... Chanel.

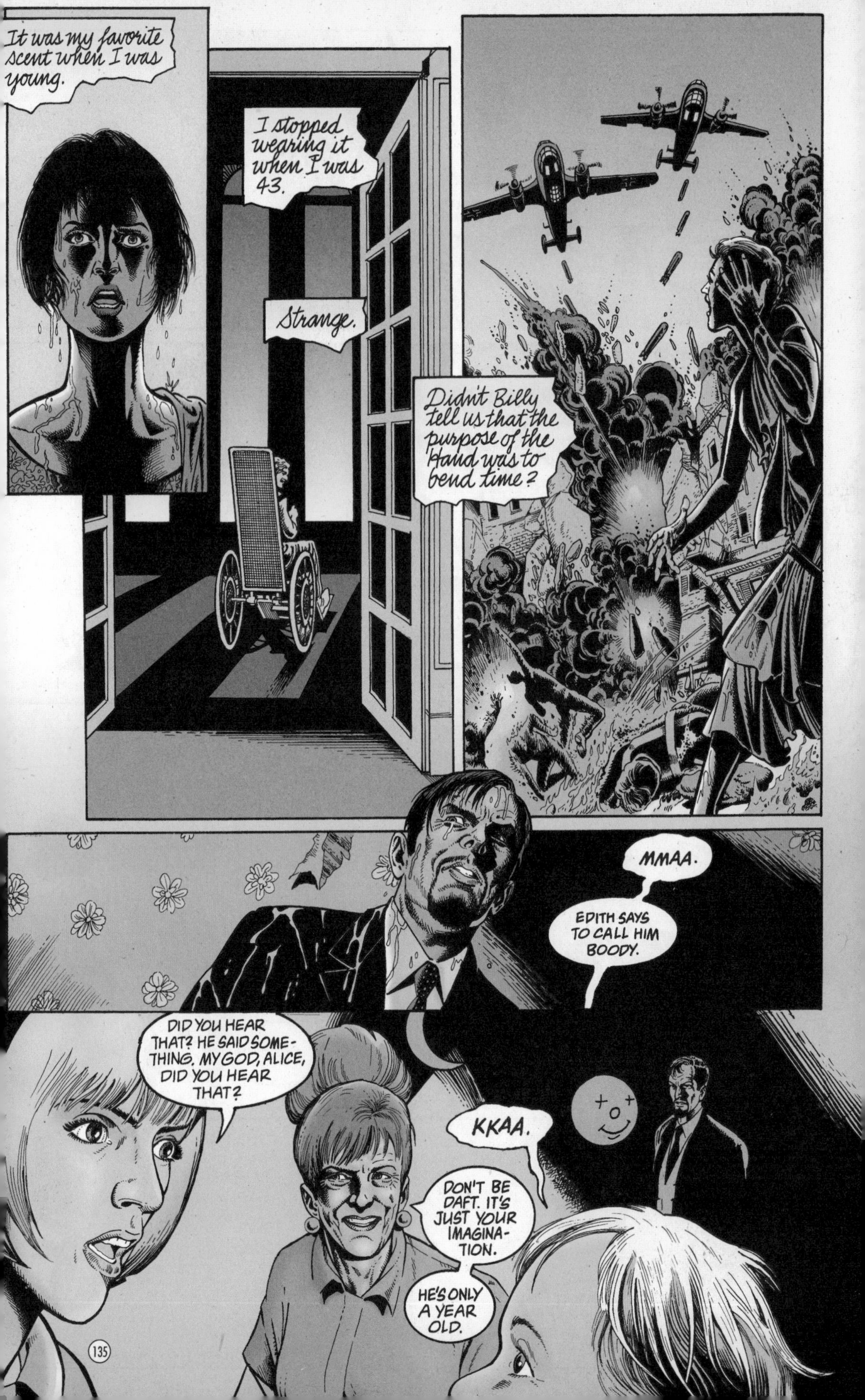

It was my favorite scent when I was young.
I stopped wearing it when I was 43.
Strange.
Didn't Billy tell us that the purpose of the Hand was to bend time?
MMAA.
EDITH SAYS TO CALL HIM BOODY.
DID YOU HEAR THAT? HE SAID SOME-THING. MY GOD, ALICE, DID YOU HEAR THAT?
KKAA.
DON'T BE DAFT. IT'S JUST YOUR IMAGINA-TION.
HE'S ONLY A YEAR OLD.

THEY'LL USE IT. RUSSIANS, AMERICANS, I DON'T CARE. THEY BUILT THE ATOM BOMB TO USE IT.

THE REAL WAR'S BETWEEN JAZZ AND ROCK 'N' ROLL.

TELL THAT TO KRUSHCHEV.

IF HE WAS HERE I WOULD.

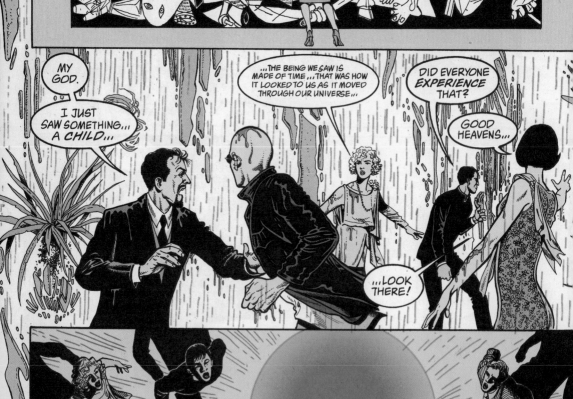

MY GOD.

I JUST SAW SOMETHING... A *CHILD*...

...THE BEING WE SAW IS MADE OF TIME... THAT WAS HOW IT LOOKED TO US AS IT MOVED THROUGH OUR UNIVERSE...

DID EVERYONE *EXPERIENCE* THAT?

GOOD HEAVENS...

...LOOK THERE!

...WHAT A MARVELOUS EVENING THIS HAS TURNED OUT TO BE.

And then something happened. And no one could ever remember what, could they, Freddie?

Then it was the next day...

ST. DUNSTAN'S IN-THE-EAST.

ACCORDING TO BILLY, THIS IS THE BEST PLACE IN *LONDON* TO REV UP THE HAND. "*TIME IS THIN AROUND ST. DUNSTAN'S*," HE CLAIMS. HE CAN BE SO UTTERLY *POETIC* AT TIMES.

I DON'T FEEL *COMFORTABLE* WITH THIS AT ALL.

THINGS ARE *HAPPENING* AROUND THIS OBJECT...

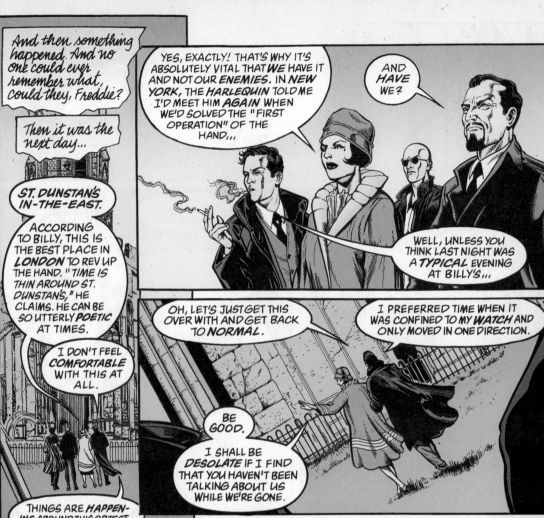

YES, EXACTLY! THAT'S WHY IT'S ABSOLUTELY VITAL THAT *WE* HAVE IT AND NOT OUR *ENEMIES*. IN *NEW YORK*, THE *HARLEQUIN* TOLD ME I'D MEET HIM *AGAIN* WHEN WE'D SOLVED THE "FIRST OPERATION" OF THE HAND,...

AND *HAVE* WE?

WELL, UNLESS YOU THINK LAST NIGHT WAS A *TYPICAL* EVENING AT BILLY'S...

OH, LET'S JUST GET THIS OVER WITH AND GET BACK TO *NORMAL*.

I PREFERRED TIME WHEN IT WAS CONFINED TO MY *WATCH* AND ONLY MOVED IN ONE DIRECTION.

BE GOOD.

I SHALL BE *DESOLATE* IF I FIND THAT YOU HAVEN'T BEEN TALKING ABOUT US WHILE WE'RE GONE.

WON'T IT BE *ENTRANCING* IF IT *WORKS*, FREDDIE? LEGEND HAS IT THAT THE HAND OF GLORY CAN ACTUALLY MAKE ONE *TRULY* INVISIBLE.

I RATHER THINK IT DOES A LITTLE MORE THAN THAT. SOMETHING HAPPENED LAST NIGHT.

THIS IS *SERIOUS*, EDIE.

STOP FRETTING.

WE HAVE *PAN* AND *DIONYSUS* ON OUR SIDE, FREDDIE DEAR.

AND WE MUST BE *INCANDESCENT* WHEN WE FACE THE HARLEQUIN. ANYTHING LESS WILL BE FATAL.

THAT'S EASY FOR YOU TO SAY.

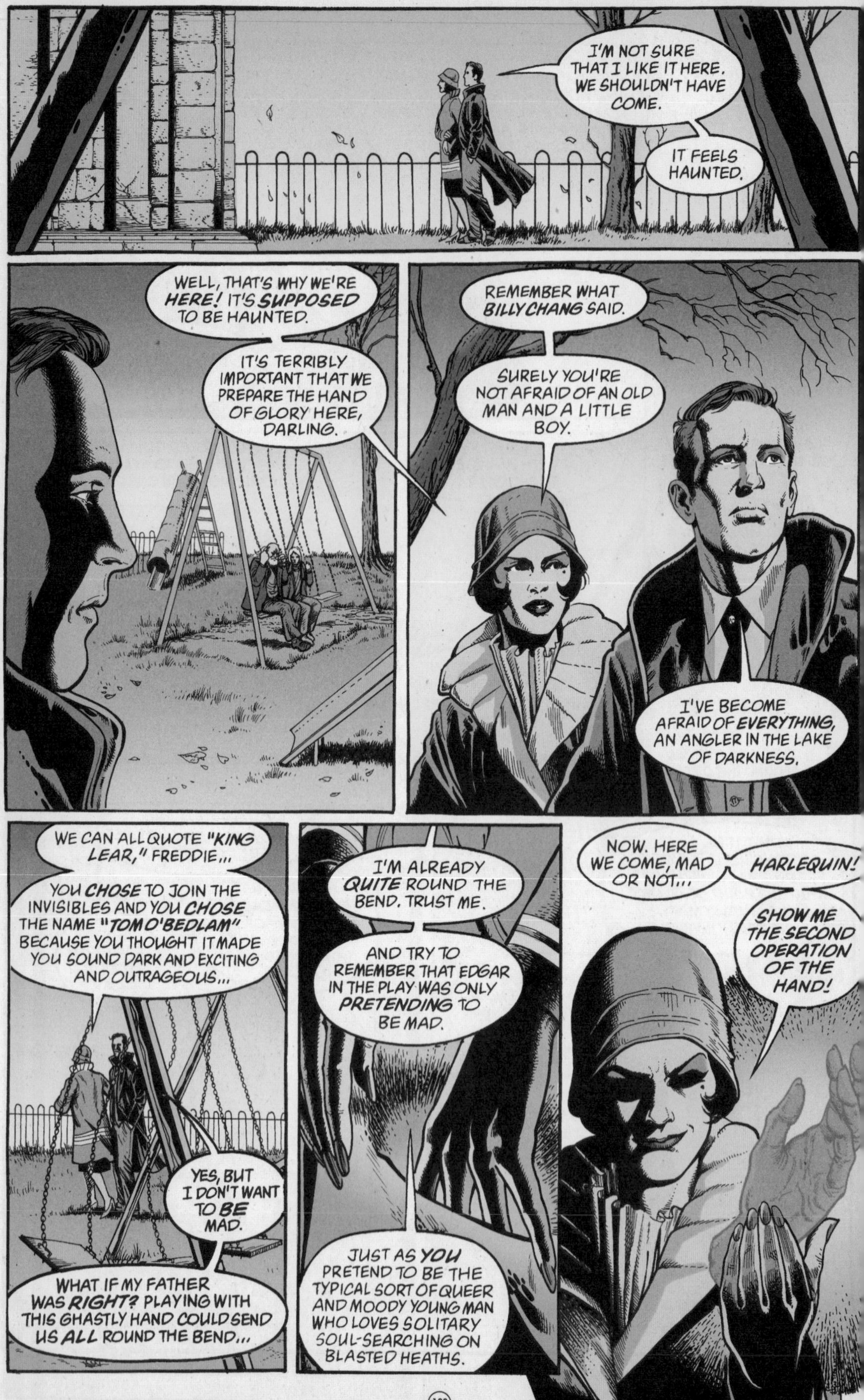

I'M NOT SURE THAT I LIKE IT HERE. WE SHOULDN'T HAVE COME.
IT FEELS HAUNTED.
WELL, THAT'S WHY WE'RE **HERE!** IT'S **SUPPOSED** TO BE HAUNTED.
IT'S TERRIBLY IMPORTANT THAT WE PREPARE THE HAND OF GLORY HERE, DARLING.
REMEMBER WHAT **BILLY CHANG** SAID.
SURELY YOU'RE NOT AFRAID OF AN OLD MAN AND A LITTLE BOY.
I'VE BECOME AFRAID OF **EVERYTHING**, AN ANGLER IN THE LAKE OF DARKNESS.
WE CAN ALL QUOTE **"KING LEAR,"** FREDDIE...
YOU **CHOSE** TO JOIN THE INVISIBLES AND YOU **CHOSE** THE NAME **"TOM O'BEDLAM"** BECAUSE YOU THOUGHT IT MADE YOU SOUND DARK AND EXCITING AND OUTRAGEOUS...
YES, BUT I DON'T WANT TO **BE** MAD.
WHAT IF MY FATHER WAS **RIGHT?** PLAYING WITH THIS GHASTLY HAND **COULD** SEND US **ALL** ROUND THE BEND...
I'M ALREADY **QUITE** ROUND THE BEND. TRUST ME.
AND TRY TO REMEMBER THAT EDGAR IN THE PLAY WAS ONLY **PRETENDING** TO BE MAD.
JUST AS **YOU** PRETEND TO BE THE TYPICAL SORT OF QUEER AND MOODY YOUNG MAN WHO LOVES SOLITARY SOUL-SEARCHING ON BLASTED HEATHS.
NOW. HERE WE COME, MAD OR NOT...
HARLEQUIN!
SHOW ME THE SECOND OPERATION OF THE HAND!

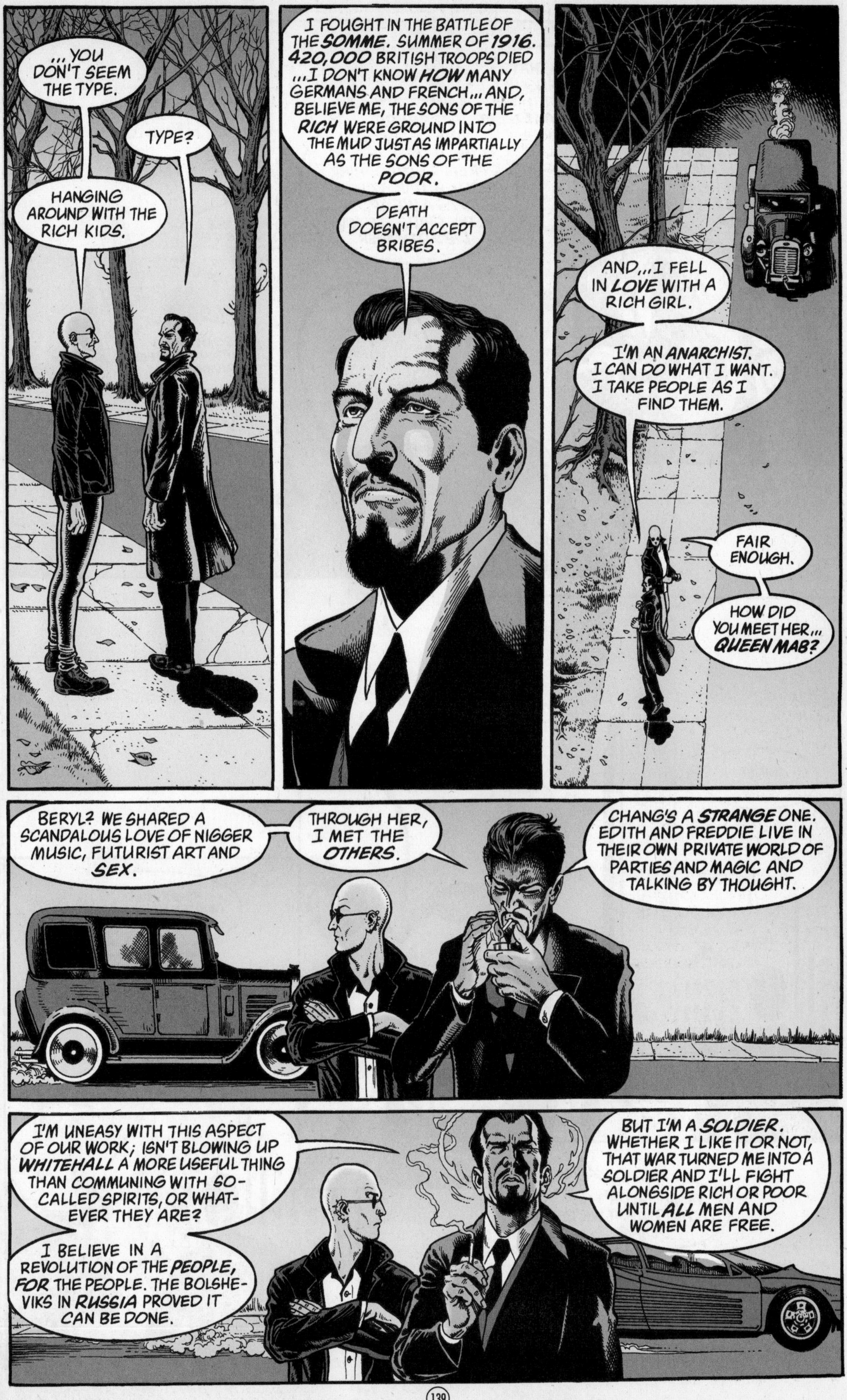

...YOU DON'T SEEM THE TYPE.
TYPE?
HANGING AROUND WITH THE RICH KIDS.
I FOUGHT IN THE BATTLE OF THE SOMME. SUMMER OF 1916. 420,000 BRITISH TROOPS DIED ...I DON'T KNOW HOW MANY GERMANS AND FRENCH... AND, BELIEVE ME, THE SONS OF THE RICH WERE GROUND INTO THE MUD JUST AS IMPARTIALLY AS THE SONS OF THE POOR.
DEATH DOESN'T ACCEPT BRIBES.
AND... I FELL IN LOVE WITH A RICH GIRL.
I'M AN ANARCHIST. I CAN DO WHAT I WANT. I TAKE PEOPLE AS I FIND THEM.
FAIR ENOUGH.
HOW DID YOU MEET HER... QUEEN MAB?
BERYL? WE SHARED A SCANDALOUS LOVE OF NIGGER MUSIC, FUTURIST ART AND SEX.
THROUGH HER, I MET THE OTHERS.
CHANG'S A STRANGE ONE. EDITH AND FREDDIE LIVE IN THEIR OWN PRIVATE WORLD OF PARTIES AND MAGIC AND TALKING BY THOUGHT.
I'M UNEASY WITH THIS ASPECT OF OUR WORK; ISN'T BLOWING UP WHITEHALL A MORE USEFUL THING THAN COMMUNING WITH SO-CALLED SPIRITS, OR WHATEVER THEY ARE?
I BELIEVE IN A REVOLUTION OF THE PEOPLE, FOR THE PEOPLE. THE BOLSHEVIKS IN RUSSIA PROVED IT CAN BE DONE.
BUT I'M A SOLDIER. WHETHER I LIKE IT OR NOT, THAT WAR TURNED ME INTO A SOLDIER AND I'LL FIGHT ALONGSIDE RICH OR POOR UNTIL ALL MEN AND WOMEN ARE FREE.

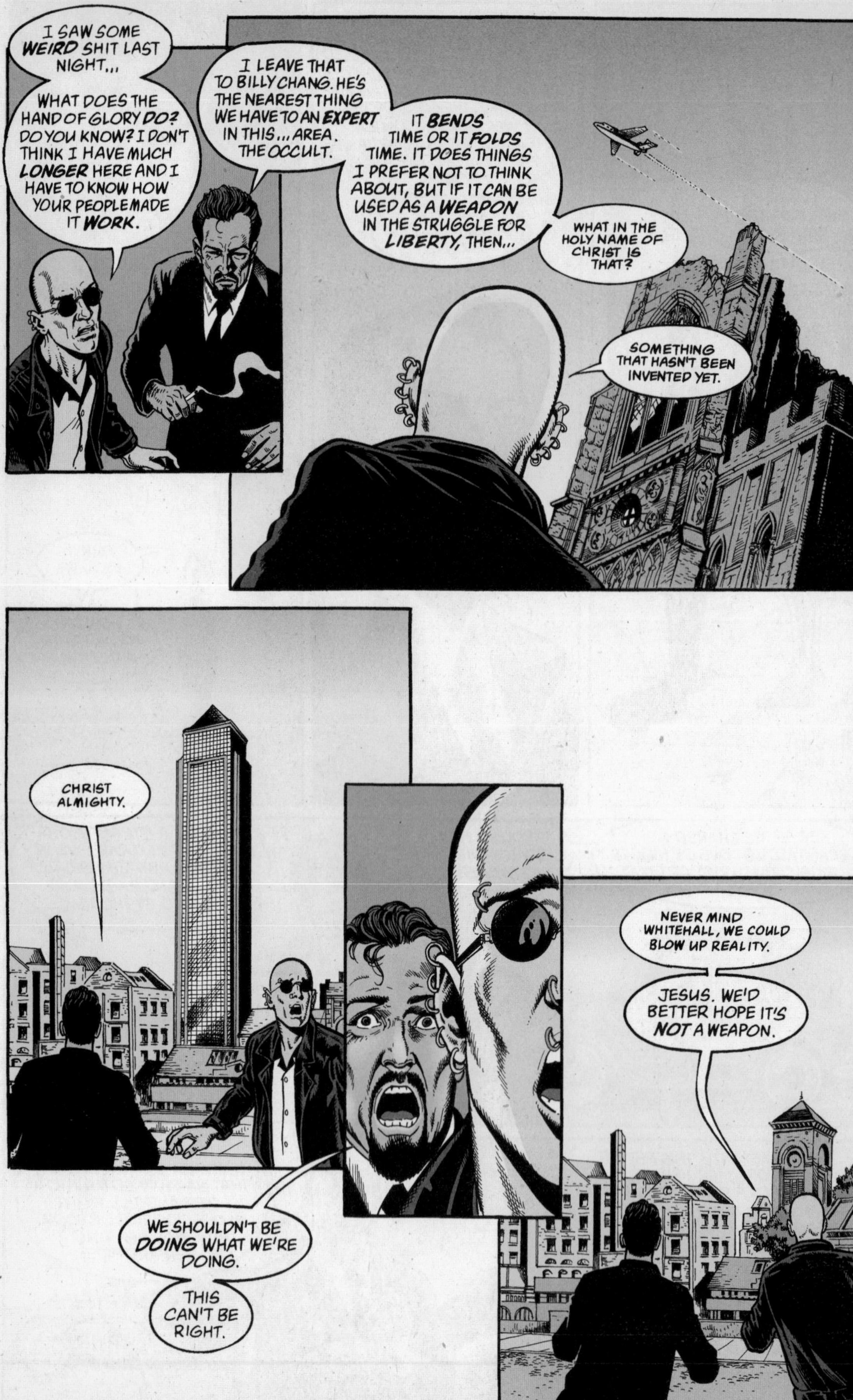

I SAW SOME WEIRD SHIT LAST NIGHT...
WHAT DOES THE HAND OF GLORY DO? DO YOU KNOW? I DON'T THINK I HAVE MUCH LONGER HERE AND I HAVE TO KNOW HOW YOUR PEOPLE MADE IT WORK.
I LEAVE THAT TO BILLY CHANG. HE'S THE NEAREST THING WE HAVE TO AN EXPERT IN THIS... AREA. THE OCCULT.
IT BENDS TIME OR IT FOLDS TIME. IT DOES THINGS I PREFER NOT TO THINK ABOUT, BUT IF IT CAN BE USED AS A WEAPON IN THE STRUGGLE FOR LIBERTY, THEN...
WHAT IN THE HOLY NAME OF CHRIST IS THAT?
SOMETHING THAT HASN'T BEEN INVENTED YET.
CHRIST ALMIGHTY.
WE SHOULDN'T BE DOING WHAT WE'RE DOING.
THIS CAN'T BE RIGHT.
NEVER MIND WHITEHALL, WE COULD BLOW UP REALITY.
JESUS. WE'D BETTER HOPE IT'S NOT A WEAPON.

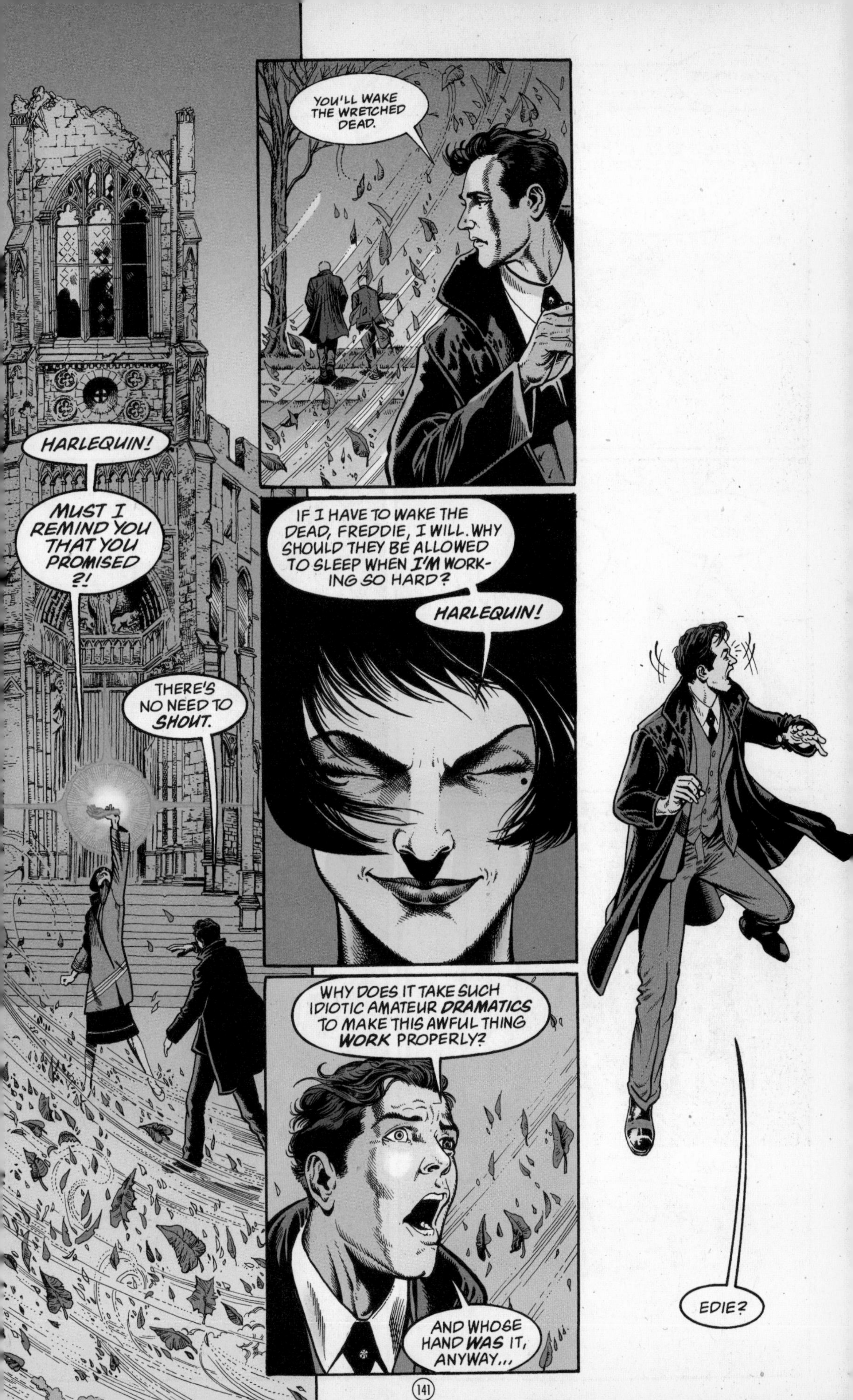
HARLEQUIN!
MUST I REMIND YOU THAT YOU PROMISED ?!
THERE'S NO NEED TO SHOUT.
YOU'LL WAKE THE WRETCHED DEAD.
IF I HAVE TO WAKE THE DEAD, FREDDIE, I WILL. WHY SHOULD THEY BE ALLOWED TO SLEEP WHEN I'M WORKING SO HARD?
HARLEQUIN!
WHY DOES IT TAKE SUCH IDIOTIC AMATEUR DRAMATICS TO MAKE THIS AWFUL THING WORK PROPERLY?
AND WHOSE HAND WAS IT, ANYWAY...
EDIE?

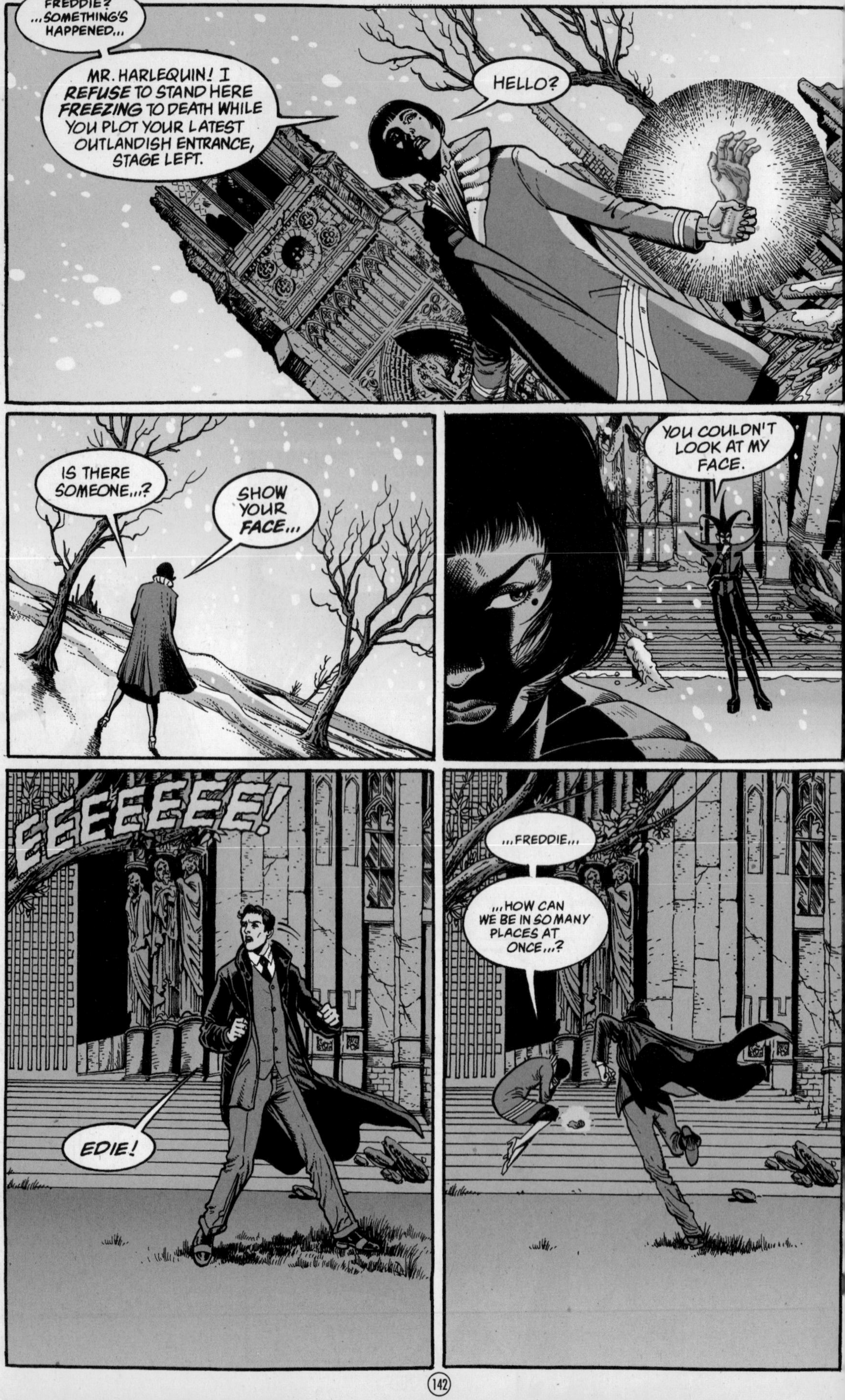

FREDDIE? ...SOMETHING'S HAPPENED...
MR. HARLEQUIN! I REFUSE TO STAND HERE FREEZING TO DEATH WHILE YOU PLOT YOUR LATEST OUTLANDISH ENTRANCE, STAGE LEFT.
HELLO?
IS THERE SOMEONE...?
SHOW YOUR FACE...
YOU COULDN'T LOOK AT MY FACE.
EEEEEEE!
EDIE!
...FREDDIE...
...HOW CAN WE BE IN SO MANY PLACES AT ONCE...?

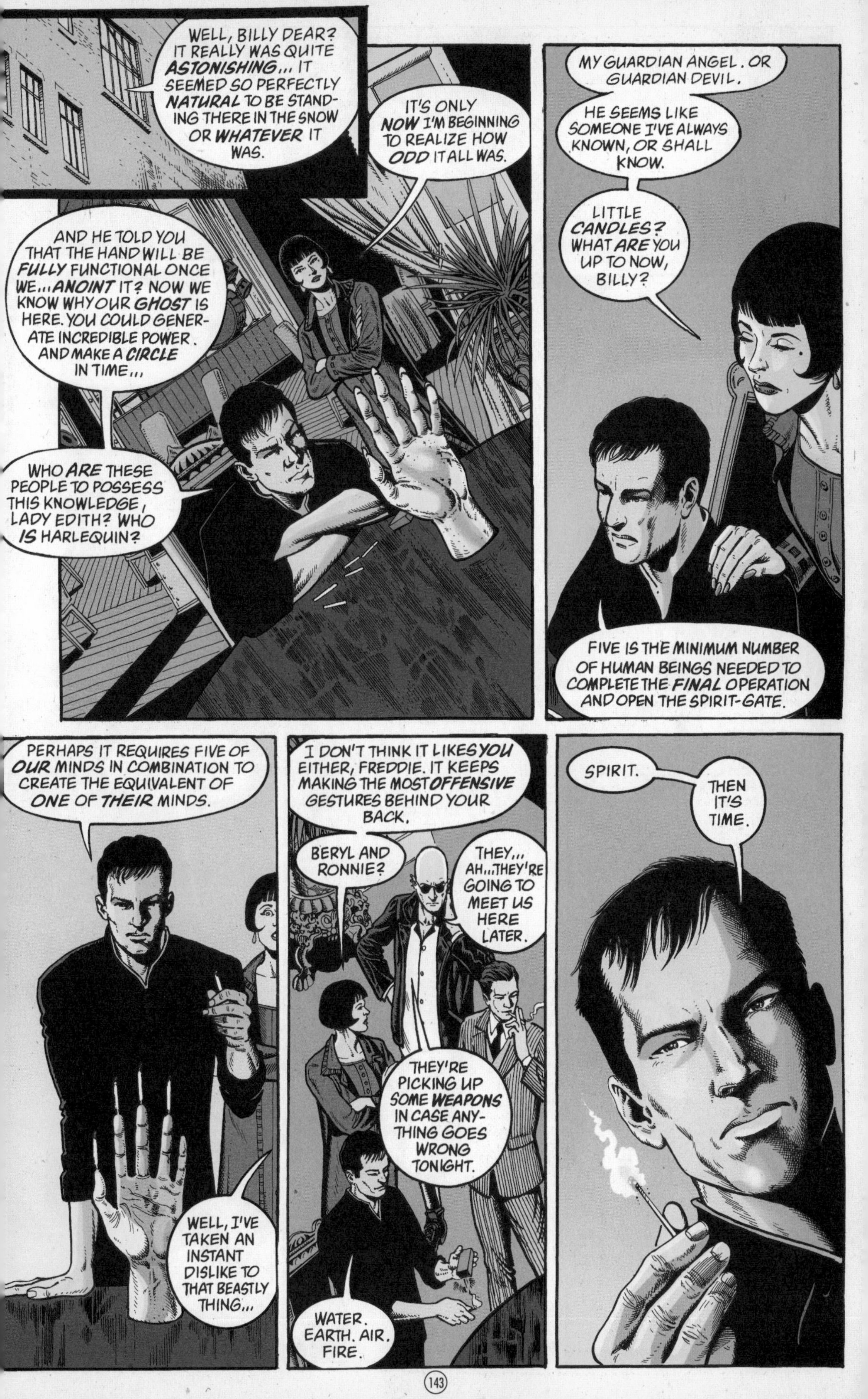
WELL, BILLY DEAR? IT REALLY WAS QUITE ASTONISHING... IT SEEMED SO PERFECTLY NATURAL TO BE STANDING THERE IN THE SNOW OR WHATEVER IT WAS.
IT'S ONLY NOW I'M BEGINNING TO REALIZE HOW ODD IT ALL WAS.
AND HE TOLD YOU THAT THE HAND WILL BE FULLY FUNCTIONAL ONCE WE...ANOINT IT? NOW WE KNOW WHY OUR GHOST IS HERE. YOU COULD GENERATE INCREDIBLE POWER. AND MAKE A CIRCLE IN TIME...
WHO ARE THESE PEOPLE TO POSSESS THIS KNOWLEDGE, LADY EDITH? WHO IS HARLEQUIN?
MY GUARDIAN ANGEL. OR GUARDIAN DEVIL.
HE SEEMS LIKE SOMEONE I'VE ALWAYS KNOWN, OR SHALL KNOW.
LITTLE CANDLES? WHAT ARE YOU UP TO NOW, BILLY?
FIVE IS THE MINIMUM NUMBER OF HUMAN BEINGS NEEDED TO COMPLETE THE FINAL OPERATION AND OPEN THE SPIRIT-GATE.
PERHAPS IT REQUIRES FIVE OF OUR MINDS IN COMBINATION TO CREATE THE EQUIVALENT OF ONE OF THEIR MINDS.
WELL, I'VE TAKEN AN INSTANT DISLIKE TO THAT BEASTLY THING...
I DON'T THINK IT LIKES YOU EITHER, FREDDIE. IT KEEPS MAKING THE MOST OFFENSIVE GESTURES BEHIND YOUR BACK.
BERYL AND RONNIE?
THEY... AH...THEY'RE GOING TO MEET US HERE LATER.
THEY'RE PICKING UP SOME WEAPONS IN CASE ANYTHING GOES WRONG TONIGHT.
WATER. EARTH. AIR. FIRE.
SPIRIT.
THEN IT'S TIME.

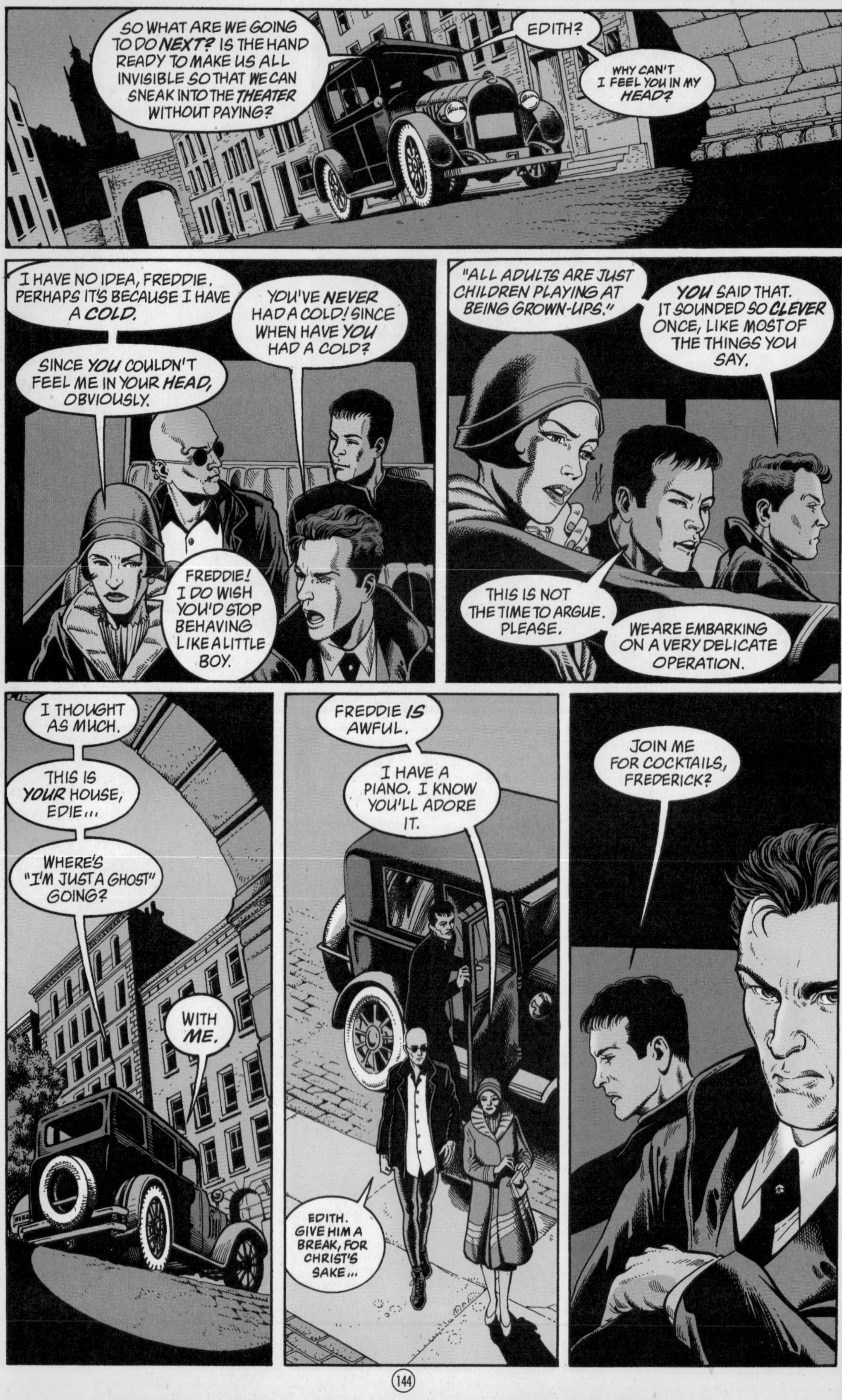

SO WHAT ARE WE GOING TO DO NEXT? IS THE HAND READY TO MAKE US ALL INVISIBLE SO THAT WE CAN SNEAK INTO THE THEATER WITHOUT PAYING?
EDITH?
WHY CAN'T I FEEL YOU IN MY HEAD?
I HAVE NO IDEA, FREDDIE. PERHAPS IT'S BECAUSE I HAVE A COLD.
YOU'VE NEVER HAD A COLD! SINCE WHEN HAVE YOU HAD A COLD?
SINCE YOU COULDN'T FEEL ME IN YOUR HEAD, OBVIOUSLY.
FREDDIE! I DO WISH YOU'D STOP BEHAVING LIKE A LITTLE BOY.
"ALL ADULTS ARE JUST CHILDREN PLAYING AT BEING GROWN-UPS."
YOU SAID THAT. IT SOUNDED SO CLEVER ONCE, LIKE MOST OF THE THINGS YOU SAY.
THIS IS NOT THE TIME TO ARGUE. PLEASE.
WE ARE EMBARKING ON A VERY DELICATE OPERATION.
I THOUGHT AS MUCH.
THIS IS YOUR HOUSE, EDIE...
WHERE'S "I'M JUST A GHOST" GOING?
WITH ME.
FREDDIE IS AWFUL.
I HAVE A PIANO. I KNOW YOU'LL ADORE IT.
EDITH. GIVE HIM A BREAK, FOR CHRIST'S SAKE...
JOIN ME FOR COCKTAILS, FREDERICK?

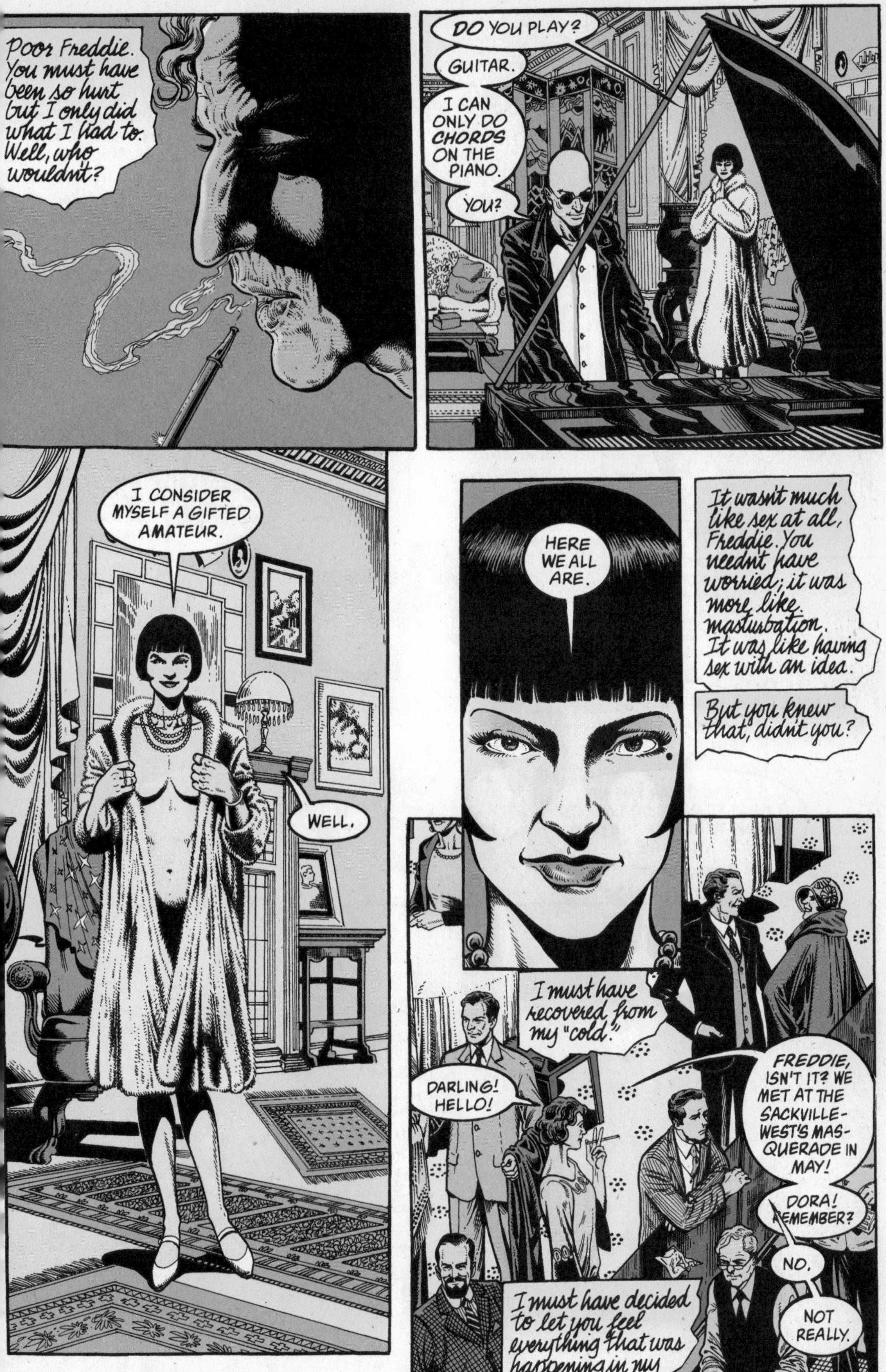
Poor Freddie. You must have been so hurt but I only did what I had to. Well, who wouldn't?
DO YOU PLAY?
GUITAR.
I CAN ONLY DO CHORDS ON THE PIANO.
YOU?
I CONSIDER MYSELF A GIFTED AMATEUR.
WELL.
HERE WE ALL ARE.
It wasn't much like sex at all, Freddie. You needn't have worried; it was more like masturbation. It was like having sex with an idea.
But you knew that, didn't you?
I must have recovered from my "cold."
DARLING! HELLO!
FREDDIE, ISN'T IT? WE MET AT THE SACKVILLE-WEST'S MASQUERADE IN MAY!
DORA! REMEMBER?
NO.
NOT REALLY.
I must have decided to let you feel everything that was happening in my head.

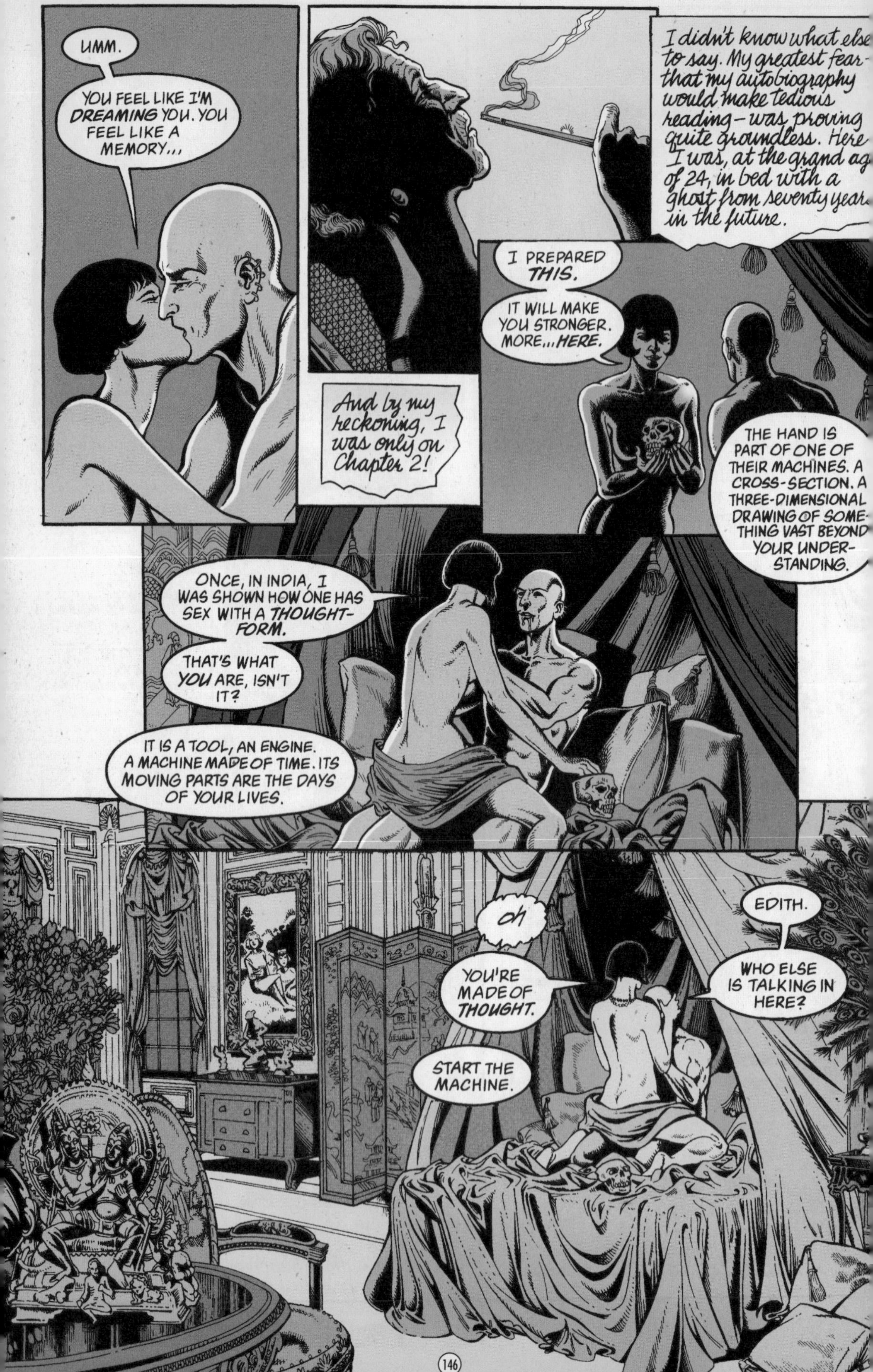
UMM.
YOU FEEL LIKE I'M DREAMING YOU. YOU FEEL LIKE A MEMORY...
I didn't know what else to say. My greatest fear that my autobiography would make tedious reading—was proving quite groundless. Here I was, at the grand age of 24, in bed with a ghost from seventy years in the future.
And by my reckoning, I was only on Chapter 2!
I PREPARED THIS.
IT WILL MAKE YOU STRONGER. MORE... HERE.
THE HAND IS PART OF ONE OF THEIR MACHINES. A CROSS-SECTION. A THREE-DIMENSIONAL DRAWING OF SOMETHING VAST BEYOND YOUR UNDERSTANDING.
ONCE, IN INDIA, I WAS SHOWN HOW ONE HAS SEX WITH A THOUGHT-FORM.
THAT'S WHAT YOU ARE, ISN'T IT?
IT IS A TOOL, AN ENGINE. A MACHINE MADE OF TIME. ITS MOVING PARTS ARE THE DAYS OF YOUR LIVES.
oh
YOU'RE MADE OF THOUGHT.
START THE MACHINE.
EDITH.
WHO ELSE IS TALKING IN HERE?

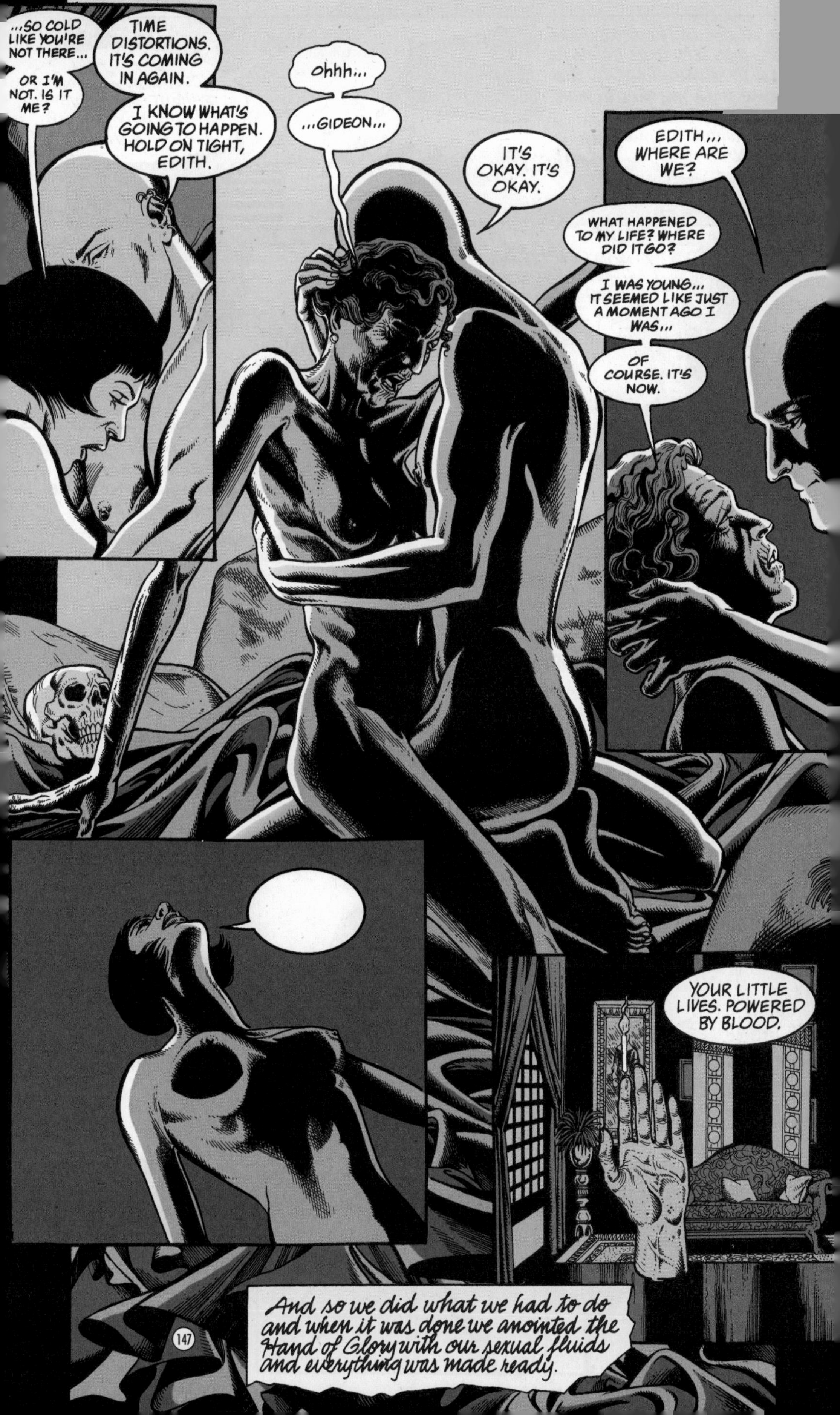
...SO COLD LIKE YOU'RE NOT THERE...
OR I'M NOT. IS IT ME?
TIME DISTORTIONS. IT'S COMING IN AGAIN.
I KNOW WHAT'S GOING TO HAPPEN. HOLD ON TIGHT, EDITH.
ohhh...
...GIDEON...
IT'S OKAY. IT'S OKAY.
EDITH... WHERE ARE WE?
WHAT HAPPENED TO MY LIFE? WHERE DID IT GO?
I WAS YOUNG... IT SEEMED LIKE JUST A MOMENT AGO I WAS...
OF COURSE. IT'S NOW.
YOUR LITTLE LIVES. POWERED BY BLOOD.
And so we did what we had to do and when it was done we anointed the Hand of Glory with our sexual fluids and everything was made ready.

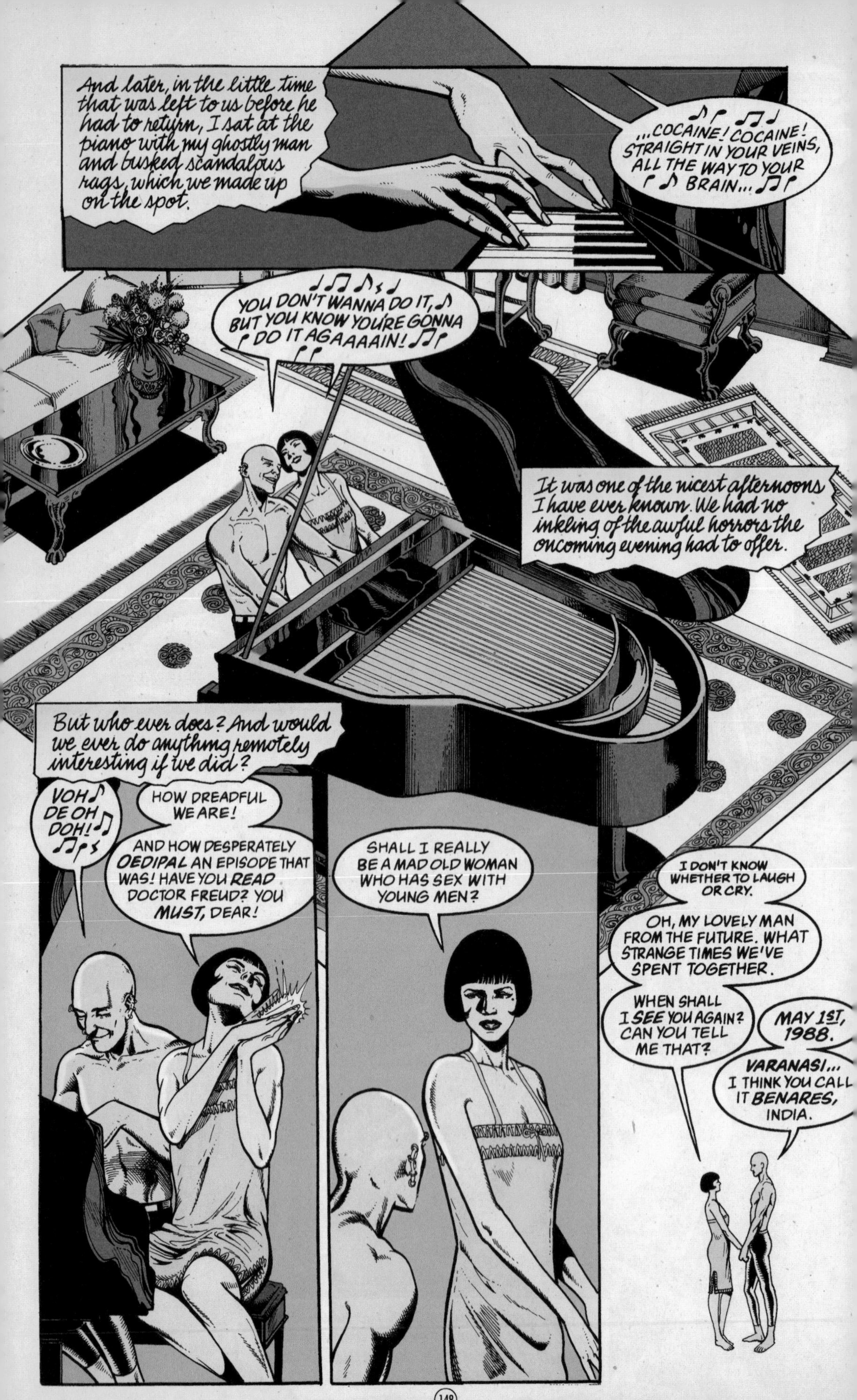

And later, in the little time that was left to us before he had to return, I sat at the piano with my ghostly man and busked scandalous rags, which we made up on the spot.
...COCAINE! COCAINE! STRAIGHT IN YOUR VEINS, ALL THE WAY TO YOUR BRAIN...
YOU DON'T WANNA DO IT, BUT YOU KNOW YOU'RE GONNA DO IT AGAAAAIN!
It was one of the nicest afternoons I have ever known. We had no inkling of the awful horrors the oncoming evening had to offer.
But who ever does? And would we ever do anything remotely interesting if we did?
VOH DE OH DOH!
HOW DREADFUL WE ARE!
AND HOW DESPERATELY OEDIPAL AN EPISODE THAT WAS! HAVE YOU READ DOCTOR FREUD? YOU MUST, DEAR!
SHALL I REALLY BE A MAD OLD WOMAN WHO HAS SEX WITH YOUNG MEN?
I DON'T KNOW WHETHER TO LAUGH OR CRY.
OH, MY LOVELY MAN FROM THE FUTURE. WHAT STRANGE TIMES WE'VE SPENT TOGETHER.
WHEN SHALL I SEE YOU AGAIN? CAN YOU TELL ME THAT?
MAY 1ST, 1988.
VARANASI... I THINK YOU CALL IT BENARES, INDIA.

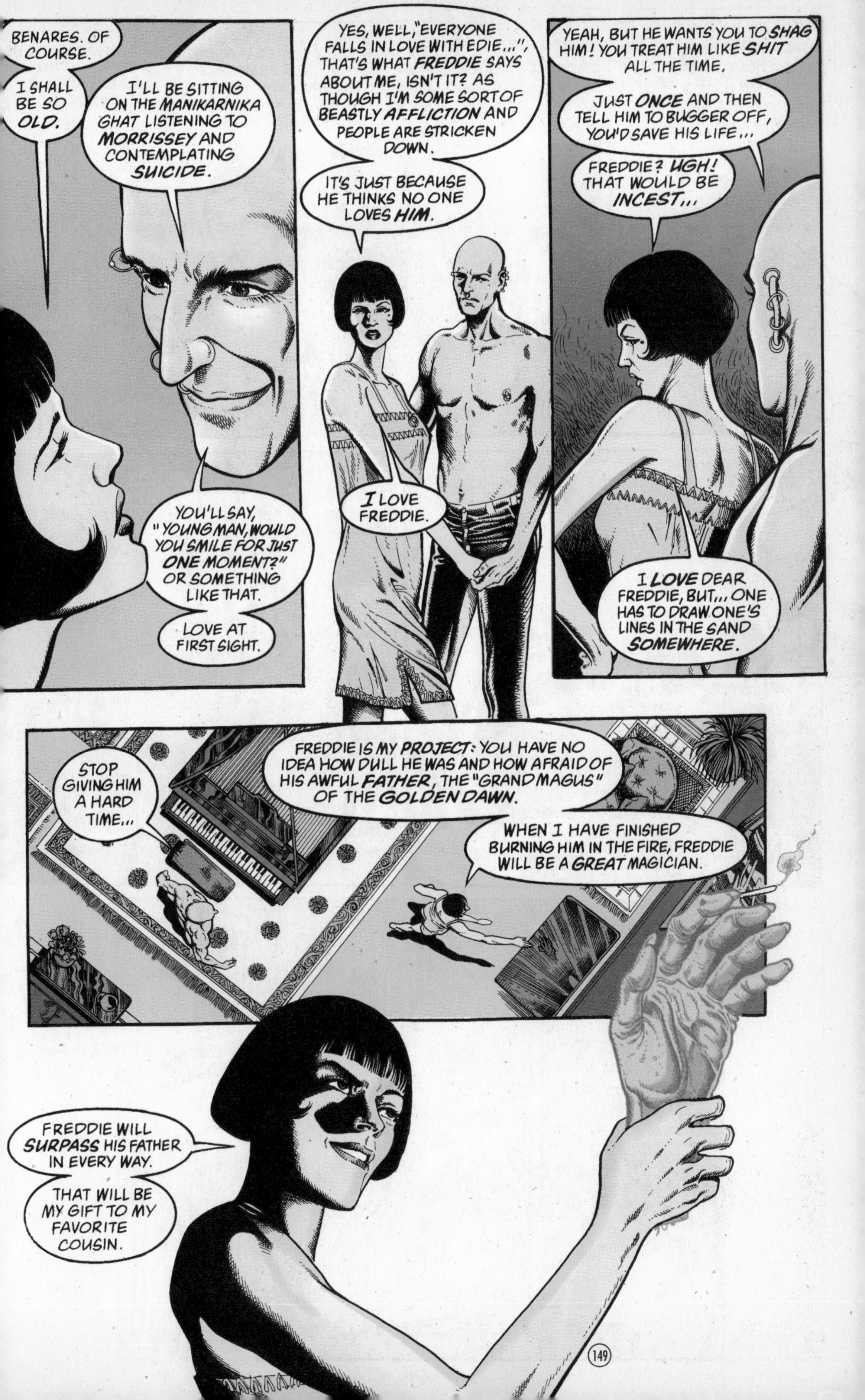
BENARES. OF COURSE.
I SHALL BE SO OLD.
I'LL BE SITTING ON THE MANIKARNIKA GHAT LISTENING TO MORRISSEY AND CONTEMPLATING SUICIDE.
YOU'LL SAY, "YOUNG MAN, WOULD YOU SMILE FOR JUST ONE MOMENT?" OR SOMETHING LIKE THAT.
LOVE AT FIRST SIGHT.
YES, WELL, "EVERYONE FALLS IN LOVE WITH EDIE...", THAT'S WHAT FREDDIE SAYS ABOUT ME, ISN'T IT? AS THOUGH I'M SOME SORT OF BEASTLY AFFLICTION AND PEOPLE ARE STRICKEN DOWN.
IT'S JUST BECAUSE HE THINKS NO ONE LOVES HIM.
I LOVE FREDDIE.
YEAH, BUT HE WANTS YOU TO SHAG HIM! YOU TREAT HIM LIKE SHIT ALL THE TIME.
JUST ONCE AND THEN TELL HIM TO BUGGER OFF, YOU'D SAVE HIS LIFE...
FREDDIE? UGH! THAT WOULD BE INCEST...
I LOVE DEAR FREDDIE, BUT... ONE HAS TO DRAW ONE'S LINES IN THE SAND SOMEWHERE.
STOP GIVING HIM A HARD TIME...
FREDDIE IS MY PROJECT: YOU HAVE NO IDEA HOW DULL HE WAS AND HOW AFRAID OF HIS AWFUL FATHER, THE "GRAND MAGUS" OF THE GOLDEN DAWN.
WHEN I HAVE FINISHED BURNING HIM IN THE FIRE, FREDDIE WILL BE A GREAT MAGICIAN.
FREDDIE WILL SURPASS HIS FATHER IN EVERY WAY.
THAT WILL BE MY GIFT TO MY FAVORITE COUSIN.

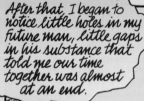

After that, I began to notice little holes in my future man, little gaps in his substance that told me our time together was almost at an end.

I felt a terrible pang at the thought of never seeing him again until I was so hideously old.

THIS WAS AN ULTRA-PERFECT IDEA, BILLY!

I WONDER IF OUR DEAR GHOST WILL BE *VISIBLE* ON THE PLATE? WOULDN'T IT BE THE STRANGEST THING EVER KNOWN IF HE *IS*?

INTO POSITION! I FEEL LIKE AN EXPLORER BEFORE VENTURING INTO UNCHARTED TERRITORY...

FREDDIE. *YOU MUST* STAND HERE WITH ME.

ALWAYS.

WELL THEN, I SUPPOSE I *MUST*, EDIE.

READY?

HELLO HISTORY.

EVERYTHING ALL RIGHT, COMRADE?

WOHH.

I'M PHASING IN AND OUT...

SMILE, EVERYBODY.

And that was that.

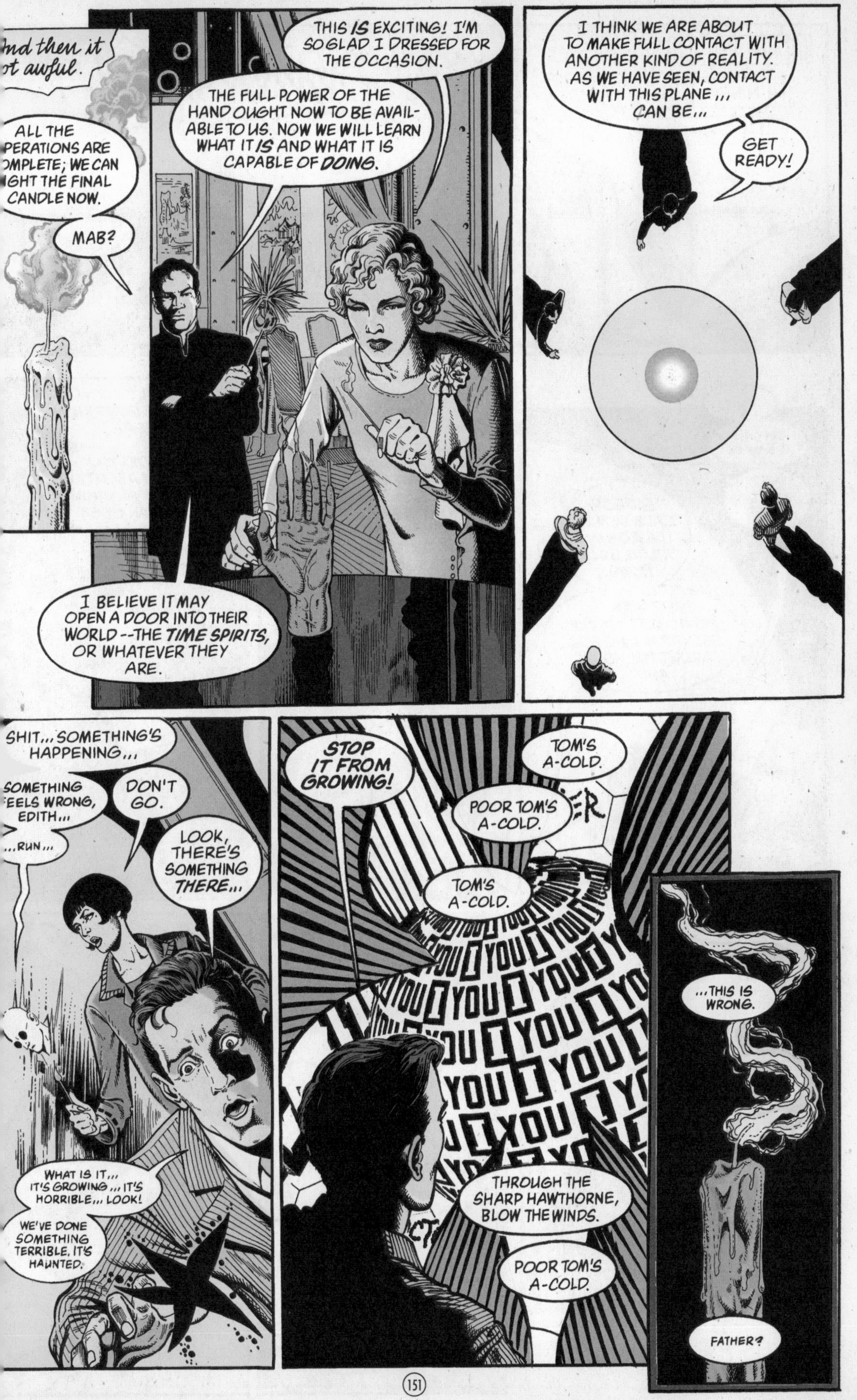
nd then it
ot awful.
ALL THE PERATIONS ARE OMPLETE; WE CAN IGHT THE FINAL CANDLE NOW.
MAB?
THIS IS EXCITING! I'M SO GLAD I DRESSED FOR THE OCCASION.
THE FULL POWER OF THE HAND OUGHT NOW TO BE AVAIL-ABLE TO US. NOW WE WILL LEARN WHAT IT IS AND WHAT IT IS CAPABLE OF DOING.
I BELIEVE IT MAY OPEN A DOOR INTO THEIR WORLD --THE TIME SPIRITS, OR WHATEVER THEY ARE.
I THINK WE ARE ABOUT TO MAKE FULL CONTACT WITH ANOTHER KIND OF REALITY. AS WE HAVE SEEN, CONTACT WITH THIS PLANE ... CAN BE...
GET READY!
SHIT... SOMETHING'S HAPPENING...
SOMETHING EELS WRONG, EDITH...
...RUN...
DON'T GO.
LOOK, THERE'S SOMETHING THERE...
WHAT IS IT... IT'S GROWING... IT'S HORRIBLE... LOOK!
WE'VE DONE SOMETHING TERRIBLE. IT'S HAUNTED.
STOP IT FROM GROWING!
TOM'S A-COLD.
POOR TOM'S A-COLD.
TOM'S A-COLD.
THROUGH THE SHARP HAWTHORNE, BLOW THE WINDS.
POOR TOM'S A-COLD.
...THIS IS WRONG.
FATHER?

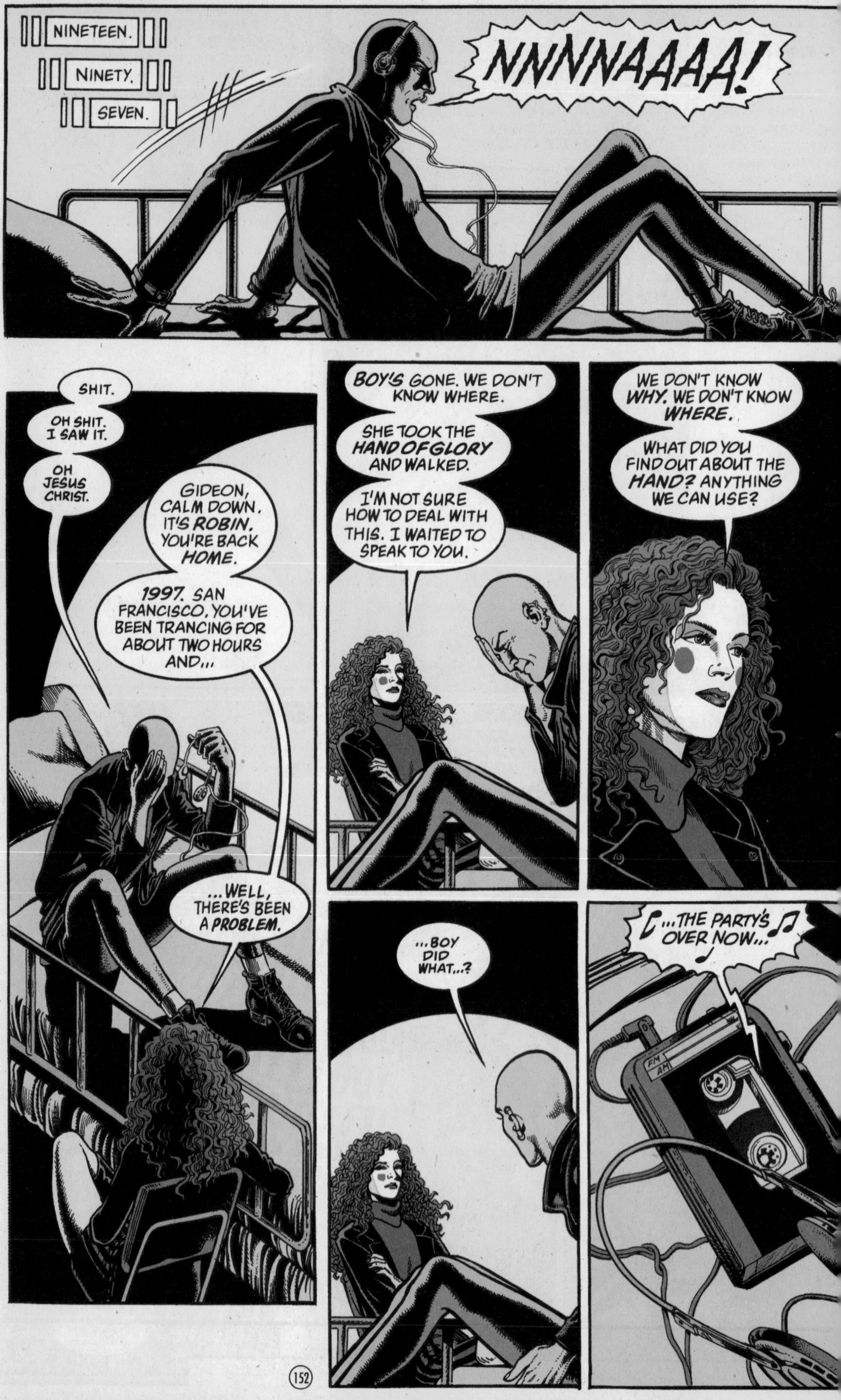
NINETEEN.
NINETY.
SEVEN.
NNNNAAAA!
SHIT.
OH SHIT. I SAW IT.
OH JESUS CHRIST.
GIDEON, CALM DOWN. IT'S ROBIN. YOU'RE BACK HOME.
1997. SAN FRANCISCO. YOU'VE BEEN TRANCING FOR ABOUT TWO HOURS AND...
...WELL, THERE'S BEEN A PROBLEM.
BOY'S GONE. WE DON'T KNOW WHERE.
SHE TOOK THE HAND OF GLORY AND WALKED.
I'M NOT SURE HOW TO DEAL WITH THIS. I WAITED TO SPEAK TO YOU.
WE DON'T KNOW WHY. WE DON'T KNOW WHERE.
WHAT DID YOU FIND OUT ABOUT THE HAND? ANYTHING WE CAN USE?
...BOY DID WHAT...?
...THE PARTY'S OVER NOW...
FM
AM

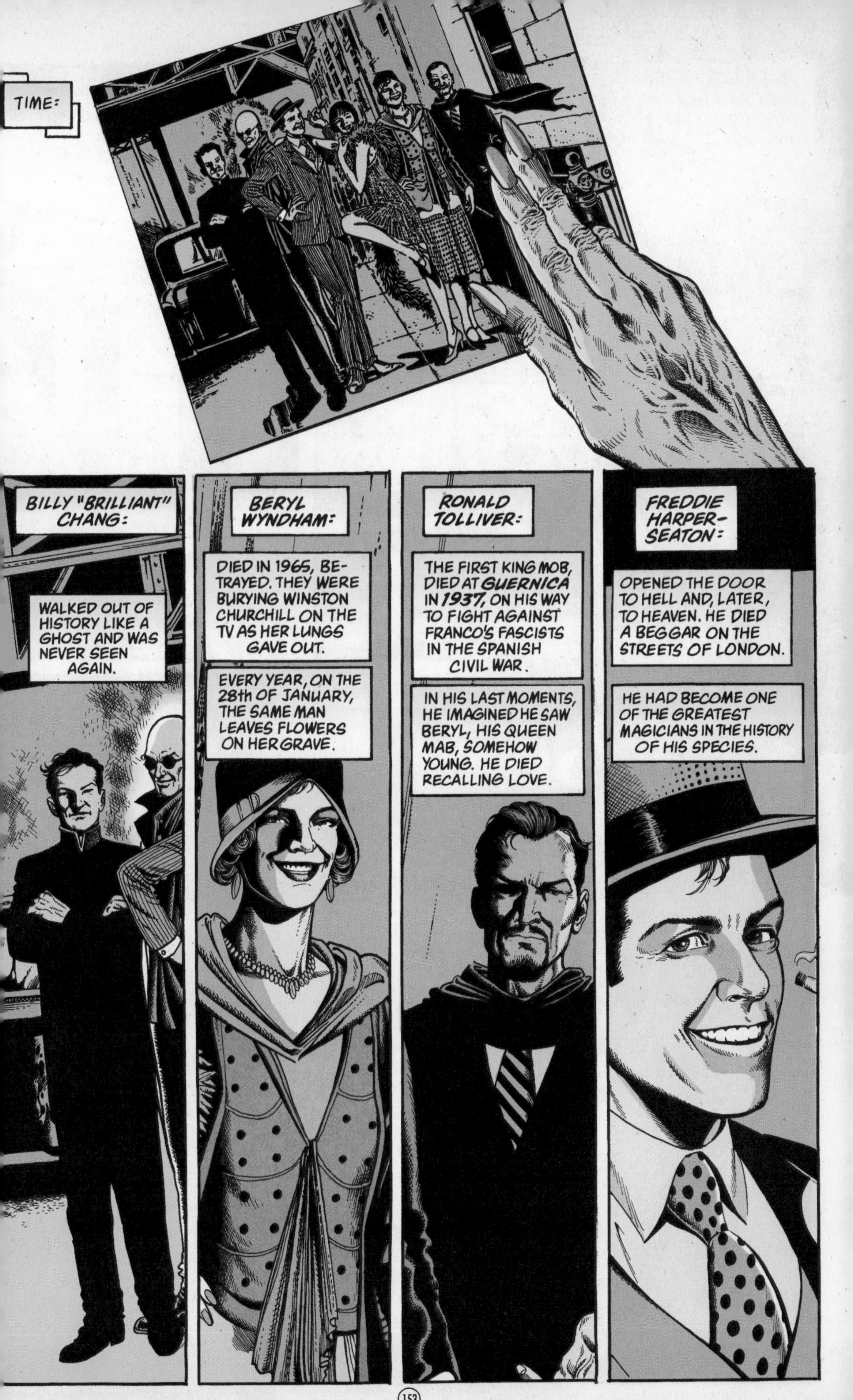
TIME:
BILLY "BRILLIANT" CHANG:
WALKED OUT OF HISTORY LIKE A GHOST AND WAS NEVER SEEN AGAIN.
BERYL WYNDHAM:
DIED IN 1965, BETRAYED. THEY WERE BURYING WINSTON CHURCHILL ON THE TV AS HER LUNGS GAVE OUT.
EVERY YEAR, ON THE 28th OF JANUARY, THE SAME MAN LEAVES FLOWERS ON HER GRAVE.
RONALD TOLLIVER:
THE FIRST KING MOB, DIED AT GUERNICA IN 1937, ON HIS WAY TO FIGHT AGAINST FRANCO'S FASCISTS IN THE SPANISH CIVIL WAR.
IN HIS LAST MOMENTS, HE IMAGINED HE SAW BERYL, HIS QUEEN MAB, SOMEHOW YOUNG. HE DIED RECALLING LOVE.
FREDDIE HARPER-SEATON:
OPENED THE DOOR TO HELL AND, LATER, TO HEAVEN. HE DIED A BEGGAR ON THE STREETS OF LONDON.
HE HAD BECOME ONE OF THE GREATEST MAGICIANS IN THE HISTORY OF HIS SPECIES.

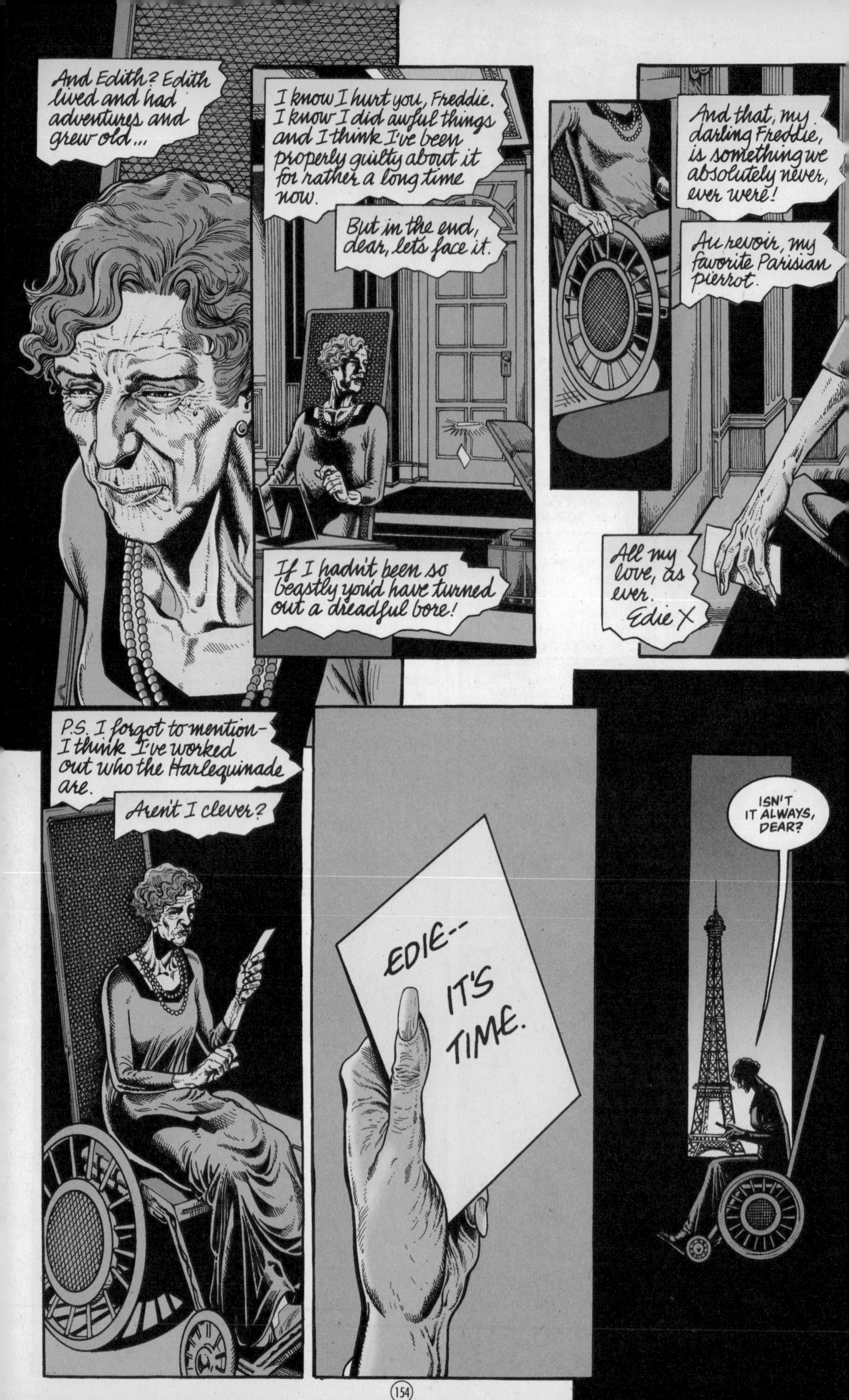
And Edith? Edith lived and had adventures and grew old...
I know I hurt you, Freddie. I know I did awful things and I think I've been properly guilty about it for rather a long time now.
But in the end, dear, lets face it.
If I hadn't been so beastly you'd have turned out a dreadful bore!
And that, my darling Freddie, is something we absolutely never, ever were!
Au revoir, my favorite Parisian pierrot.
All my love, as ever. Edie X
P.S. I forgot to mention- I think I've worked out who the Harlequinade are.
Aren't I clever?
EDIE-- IT'S TIME.
ISN'T IT ALWAYS, DEAR?

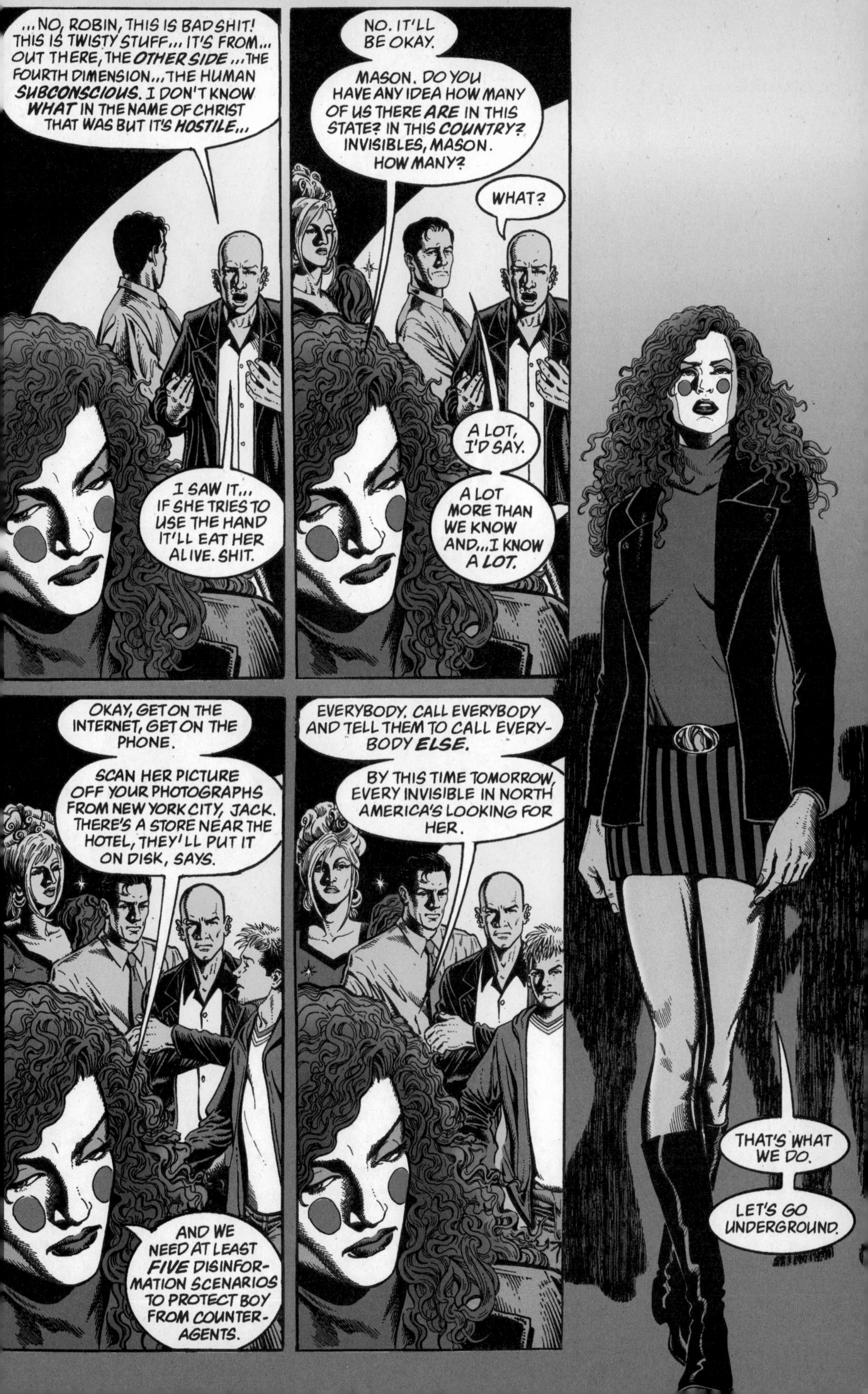

...NO, ROBIN, THIS IS BAD SHIT! THIS IS TWISTY STUFF... IT'S FROM... OUT THERE, THE OTHER SIDE ...THE FOURTH DIMENSION... THE HUMAN SUBCONSCIOUS. I DON'T KNOW WHAT IN THE NAME OF CHRIST THAT WAS BUT IT'S HOSTILE...
I SAW IT... IF SHE TRIES TO USE THE HAND IT'LL EAT HER ALIVE. SHIT.
NO. IT'LL BE OKAY.
MASON. DO YOU HAVE ANY IDEA HOW MANY OF US THERE ARE IN THIS STATE? IN THIS COUNTRY? INVISIBLES, MASON. HOW MANY?
WHAT?
A LOT, I'D SAY.
A LOT MORE THAN WE KNOW AND... I KNOW A LOT.
OKAY, GET ON THE INTERNET, GET ON THE PHONE.
SCAN HER PICTURE OFF YOUR PHOTOGRAPHS FROM NEW YORK CITY, JACK. THERE'S A STORE NEAR THE HOTEL, THEY'LL PUT IT ON DISK, SAYS.
AND WE NEED AT LEAST FIVE DISINFORMATION SCENARIOS TO PROTECT BOY FROM COUNTER-AGENTS.
EVERYBODY. CALL EVERYBODY AND TELL THEM TO CALL EVERYBODY ELSE.
BY THIS TIME TOMORROW, EVERY INVISIBLE IN NORTH AMERICA'S LOOKING FOR HER.
THAT'S WHAT WE DO.
LET'S GO UNDERGROUND.

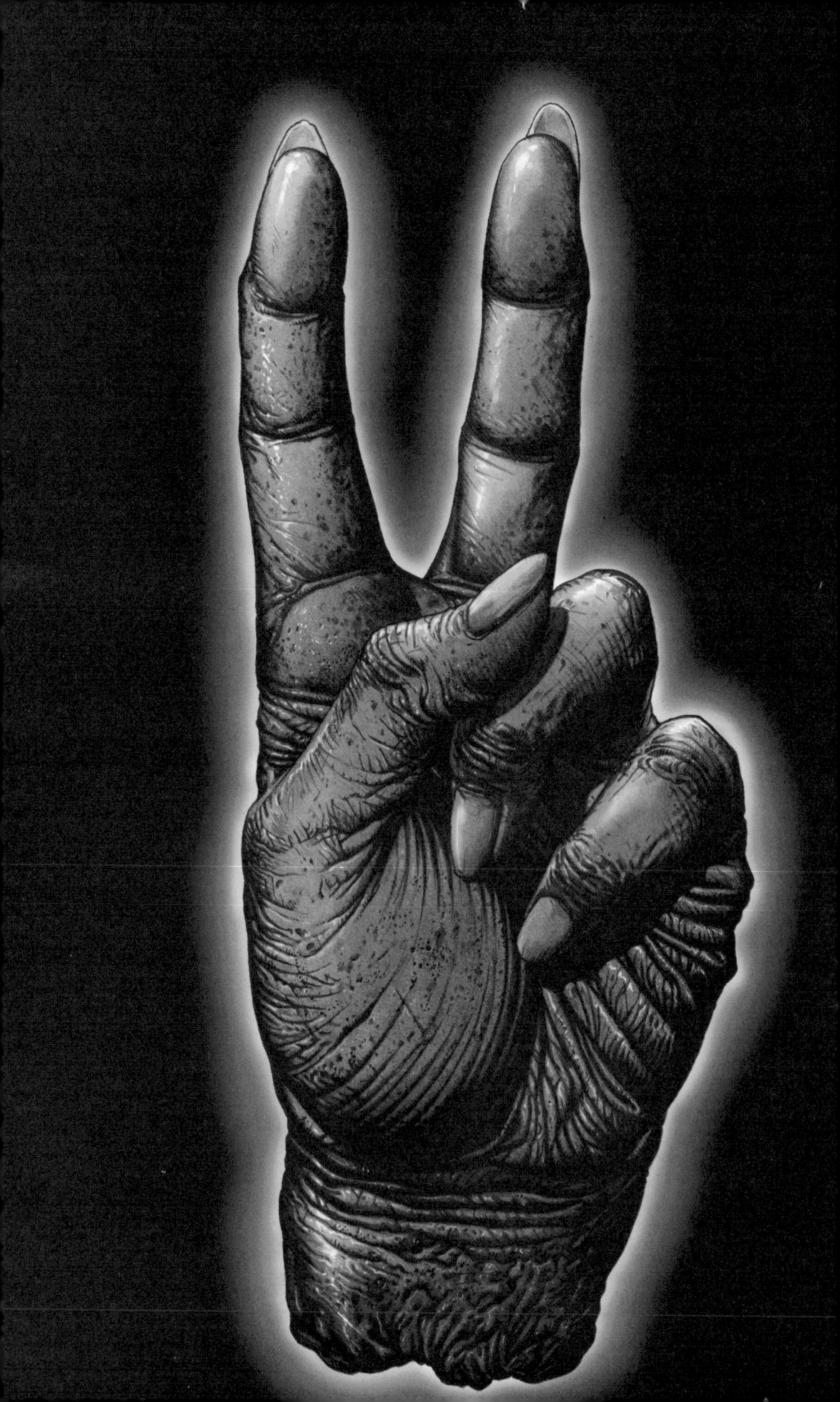

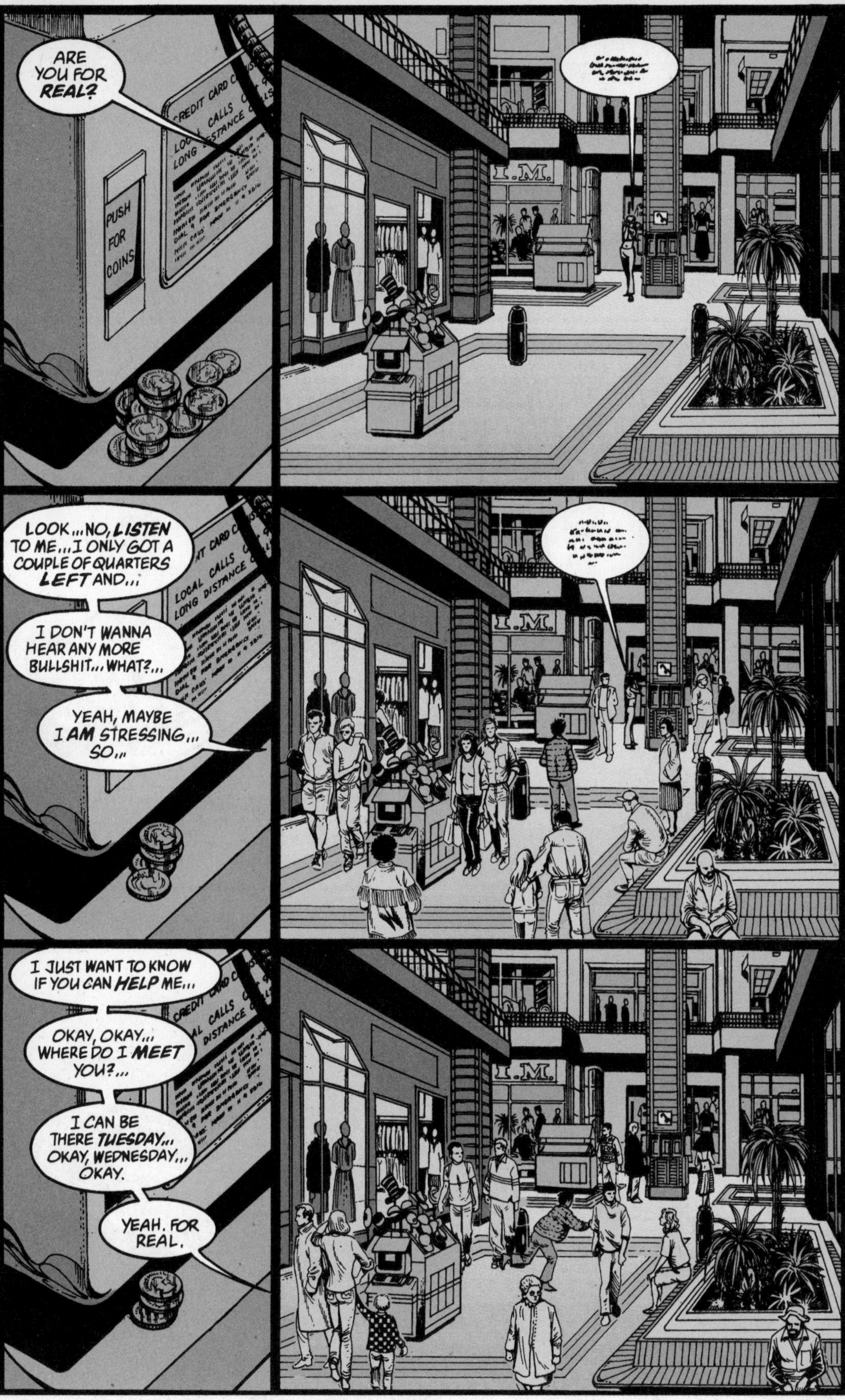

ARE YOU FOR REAL?
CREDIT CARD CALLS
LOCAL CALLS
LONG DISTANCE CALLS
PUSH FOR COINS
I.M.
LOOK... NO, LISTEN TO ME... I ONLY GOT A COUPLE OF QUARTERS LEFT AND...
I DON'T WANNA HEAR ANY MORE BULLSHIT... WHAT?...
YEAH, MAYBE I AM STRESSING... SO...
I JUST WANT TO KNOW IF YOU CAN HELP ME...
OKAY, OKAY... WHERE DO I MEET YOU?...
I CAN BE THERE TUESDAY... OKAY, WEDNESDAY... OKAY.
YEAH. FOR REAL.

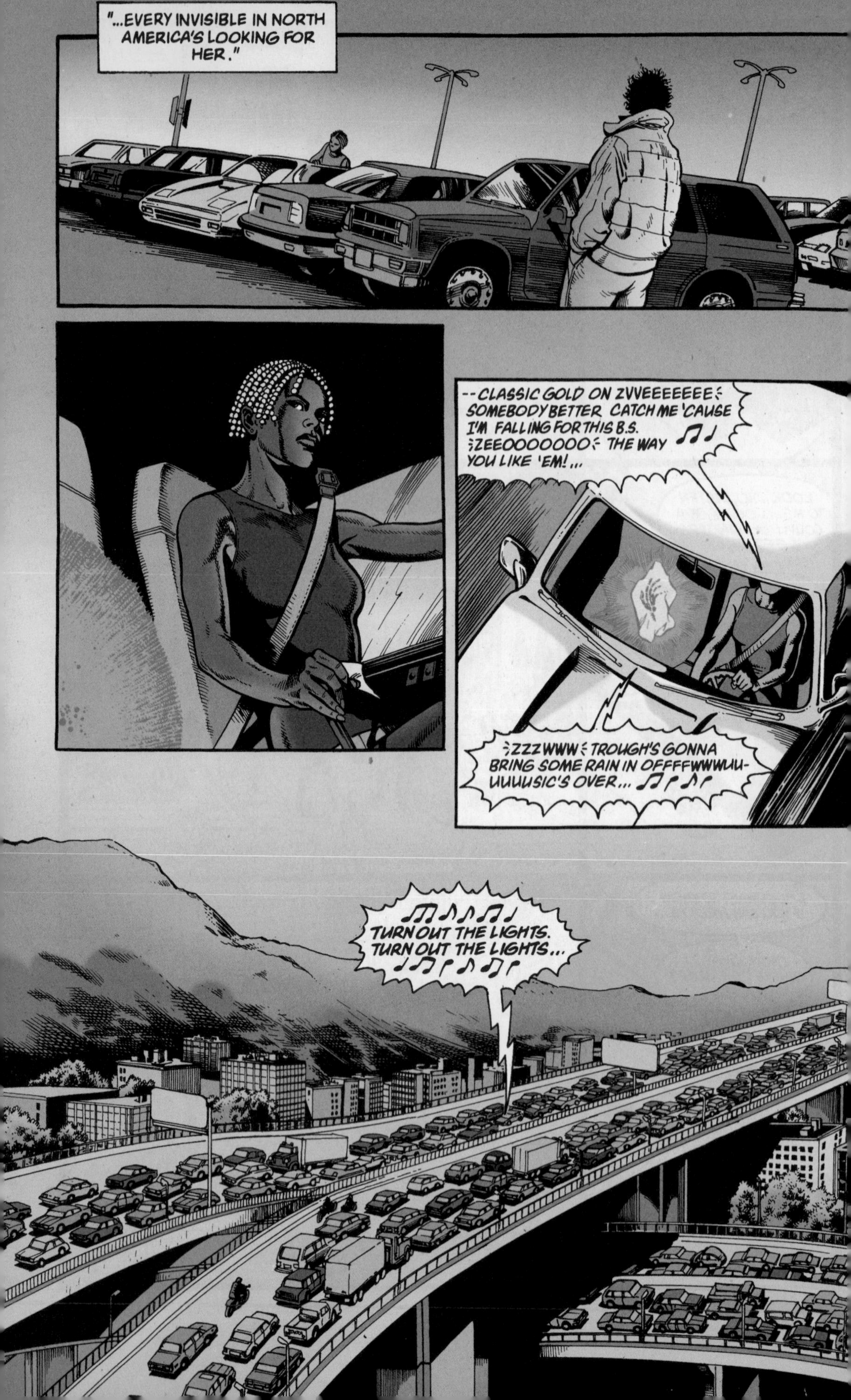
"...EVERY INVISIBLE IN NORTH AMERICA'S LOOKING FOR HER."
--CLASSIC GOLD ON ZVVEEEEEEE SOMEBODY BETTER CATCH ME 'CAUSE I'M FALLING FOR THIS B.S. ZEEOOOOOOO THE WAY YOU LIKE 'EM!...
ZZZWWW TROUGH'S GONNA BRING SOME RAIN IN OFFFFWWWUU-UUUUSIC'S OVER...
TURN OUT THE LIGHTS. TURN OUT THE LIGHTS...

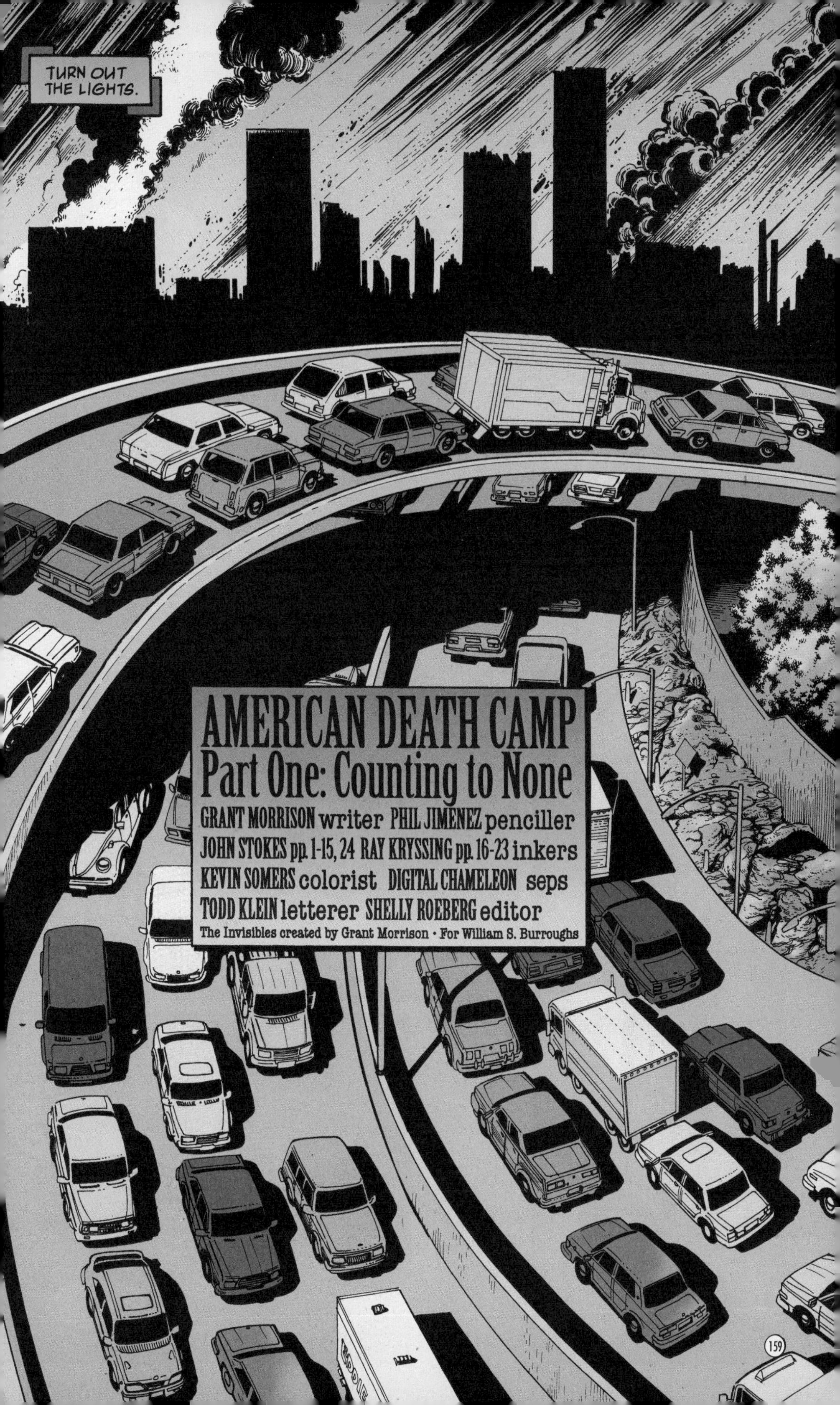

TURN OUT THE LIGHTS.
AMERICAN DEATH CAMP
Part One: Counting to None
GRANT MORRISON writer PHIL JIMENEZ penciller
JOHN STOKES pp. 1-15, 24 RAY KRYSSING pp. 16-23 inkers
KEVIN SOMERS colorist DIGITAL CHAMELEON seps
TODD KLEIN letterer SHELLY ROEBERG editor
The Invisibles created by Grant Morrison • For William S. Burroughs

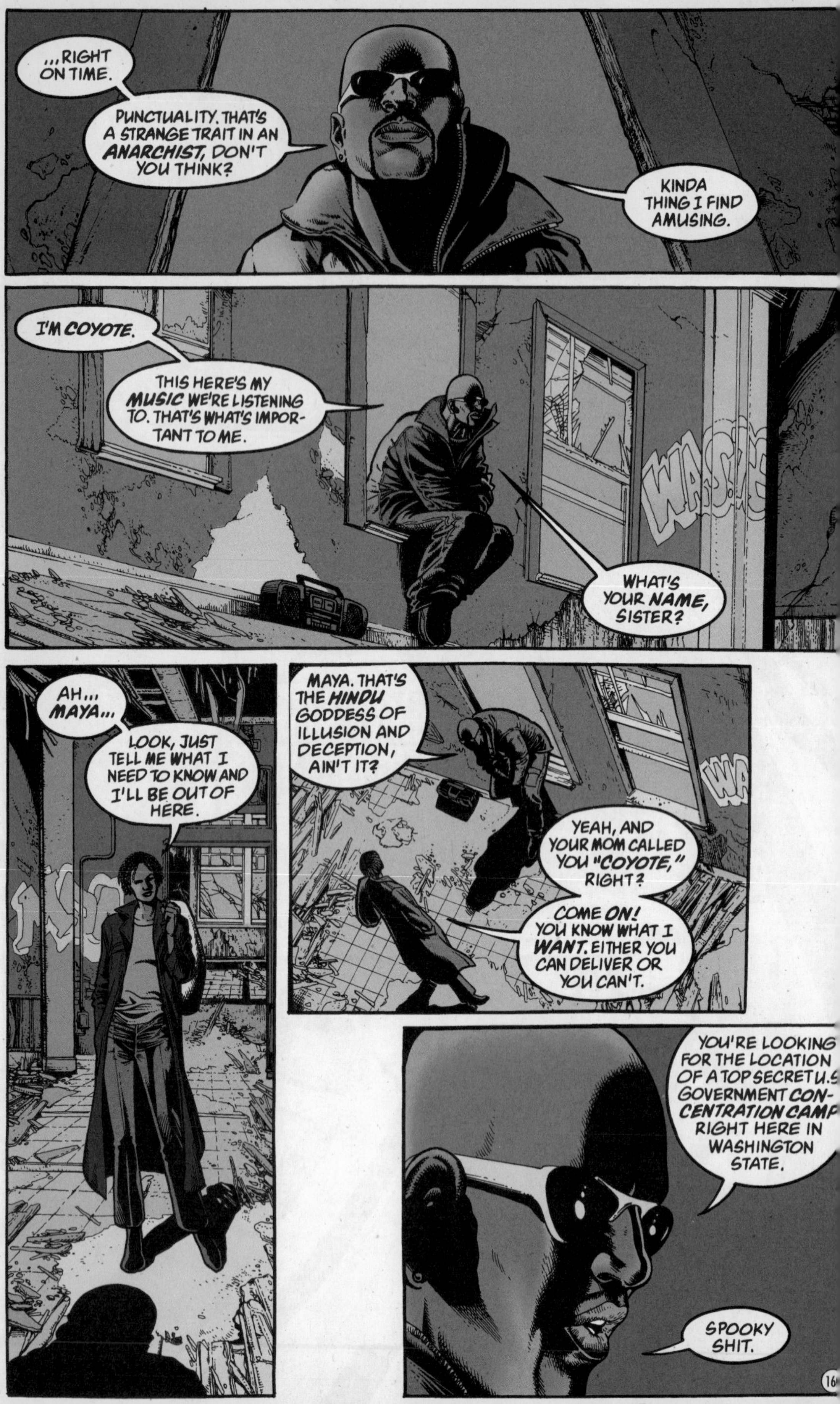
...RIGHT ON TIME.
PUNCTUALITY. THAT'S A STRANGE TRAIT IN AN ANARCHIST, DON'T YOU THINK?
KINDA THING I FIND AMUSING.
I'M COYOTE.
THIS HERE'S MY MUSIC WE'RE LISTENING TO. THAT'S WHAT'S IMPORTANT TO ME.
WHAT'S YOUR NAME, SISTER?
AH... MAYA...
LOOK, JUST TELL ME WHAT I NEED TO KNOW AND I'LL BE OUT OF HERE.
MAYA. THAT'S THE HINDU GODDESS OF ILLUSION AND DECEPTION, AIN'T IT?
YEAH, AND YOUR MOM CALLED YOU "COYOTE," RIGHT?
COME ON! YOU KNOW WHAT I WANT. EITHER YOU CAN DELIVER OR YOU CAN'T.
YOU'RE LOOKING FOR THE LOCATION OF A TOP SECRET U.S. GOVERNMENT CONCENTRATION CAMP RIGHT HERE IN WASHINGTON STATE.
SPOOKY SHIT.

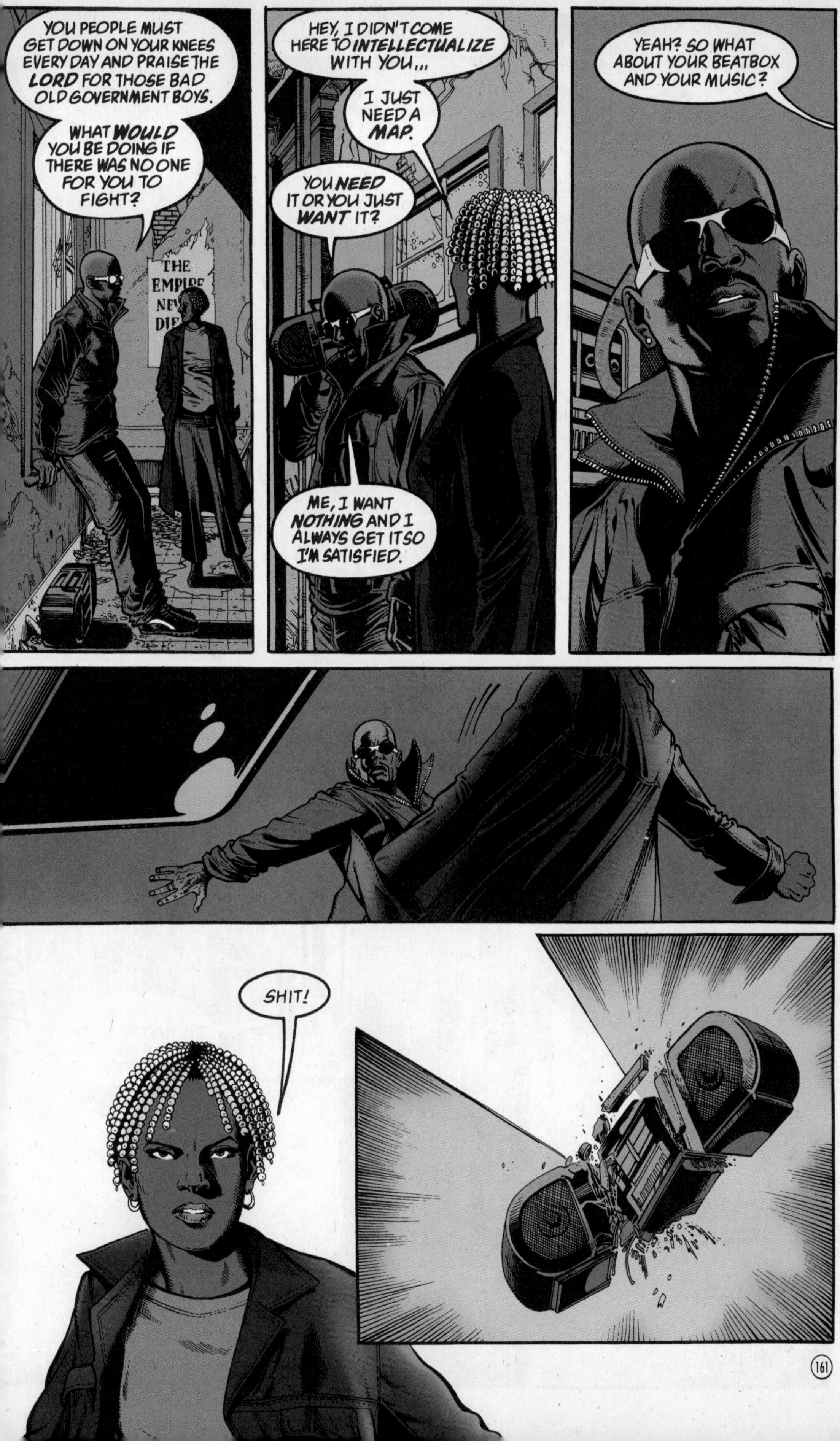
YOU PEOPLE MUST GET DOWN ON YOUR KNEES EVERY DAY AND PRAISE THE LORD FOR THOSE BAD OLD GOVERNMENT BOYS.
WHAT WOULD YOU BE DOING IF THERE WAS NO ONE FOR YOU TO FIGHT?
THE EMPIRE
HEY, I DIDN'T COME HERE TO INTELLECTUALIZE WITH YOU...
I JUST NEED A MAP.
YOU NEED IT OR YOU JUST WANT IT?
ME, I WANT NOTHING AND I ALWAYS GET IT SO I'M SATISFIED.
YEAH? SO WHAT ABOUT YOUR BEATBOX AND YOUR MUSIC?
SHIT!

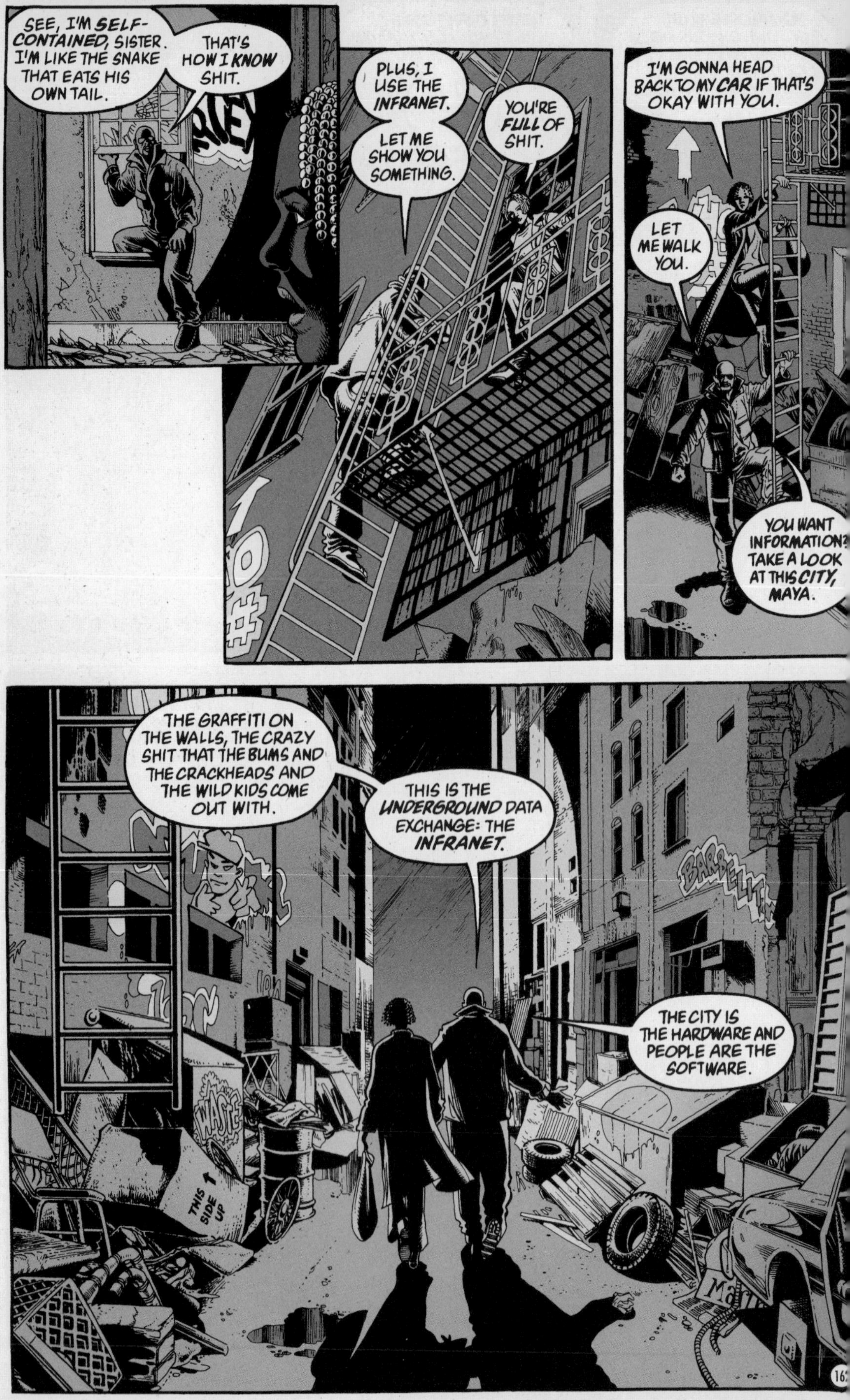

SEE, I'M SELF-CONTAINED, SISTER. I'M LIKE THE SNAKE THAT EATS HIS OWN TAIL.
THAT'S HOW I KNOW SHIT.
PLUS, I USE THE INFRANET.
LET ME SHOW YOU SOMETHING.
YOU'RE FULL OF SHIT.
I'M GONNA HEAD BACK TO MY CAR IF THAT'S OKAY WITH YOU.
LET ME WALK YOU.
YOU WANT INFORMATION? TAKE A LOOK AT THIS CITY, MAYA.
THE GRAFFITI ON THE WALLS, THE CRAZY SHIT THAT THE BUMS AND THE CRACKHEADS AND THE WILD KIDS COME OUT WITH.
THIS IS THE UNDERGROUND DATA EXCHANGE: THE INFRANET.
THE CITY IS THE HARDWARE AND PEOPLE ARE THE SOFTWARE.
WASTE
THIS SIDE UP

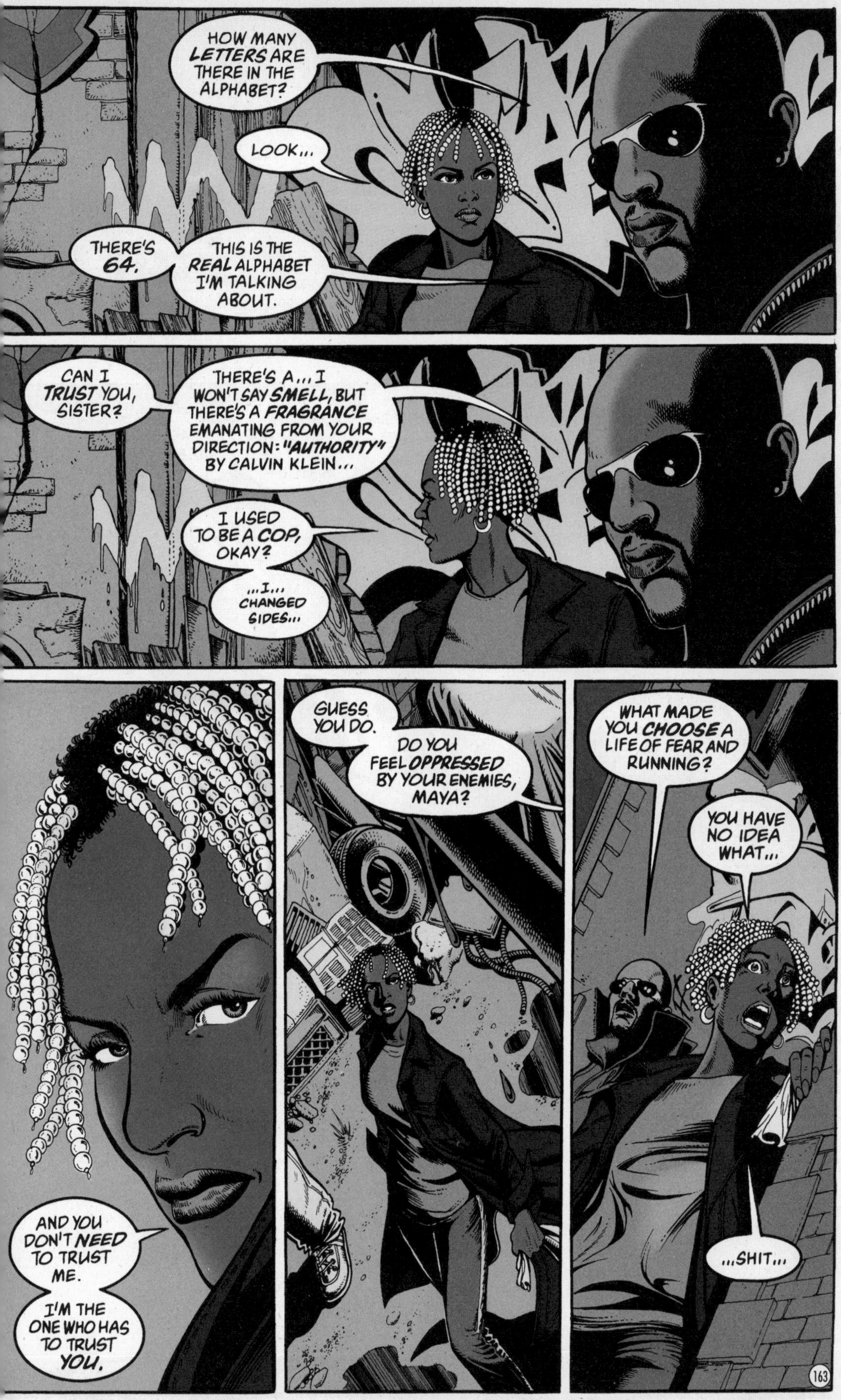

HOW MANY LETTERS ARE THERE IN THE ALPHABET?
LOOK...
THERE'S 64.
THIS IS THE REAL ALPHABET I'M TALKING ABOUT.
CAN I TRUST YOU, SISTER?
THERE'S A... I WON'T SAY SMELL, BUT THERE'S A FRAGRANCE EMANATING FROM YOUR DIRECTION: "AUTHORITY" BY CALVIN KLEIN...
I USED TO BE A COP, OKAY?
...I... CHANGED SIDES...
AND YOU DON'T NEED TO TRUST ME.
I'M THE ONE WHO HAS TO TRUST YOU.
GUESS YOU DO.
DO YOU FEEL OPPRESSED BY YOUR ENEMIES, MAYA?
WHAT MADE YOU CHOOSE A LIFE OF FEAR AND RUNNING?
YOU HAVE NO IDEA WHAT...
...SHIT...

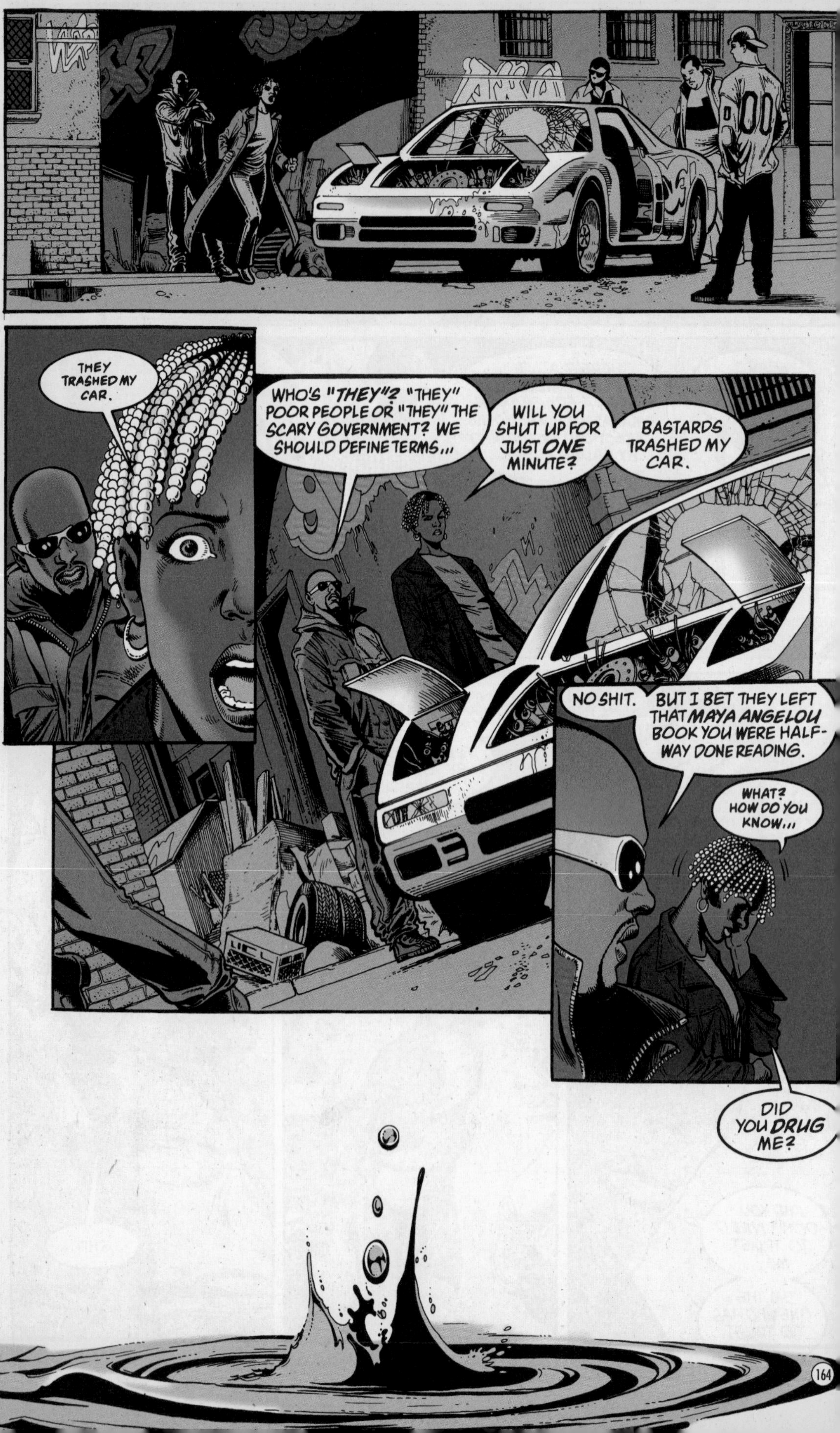
THEY TRASHED MY CAR.
WHO'S "THEY"? "THEY" POOR PEOPLE OR "THEY" THE SCARY GOVERNMENT? WE SHOULD DEFINE TERMS...
WILL YOU SHUT UP FOR JUST ONE MINUTE?
BASTARDS TRASHED MY CAR.
NO SHIT.
BUT I BET THEY LEFT THAT MAYA ANGELOU BOOK YOU WERE HALF-WAY DONE READING.
WHAT? HOW DO YOU KNOW...
DID YOU DRUG ME?

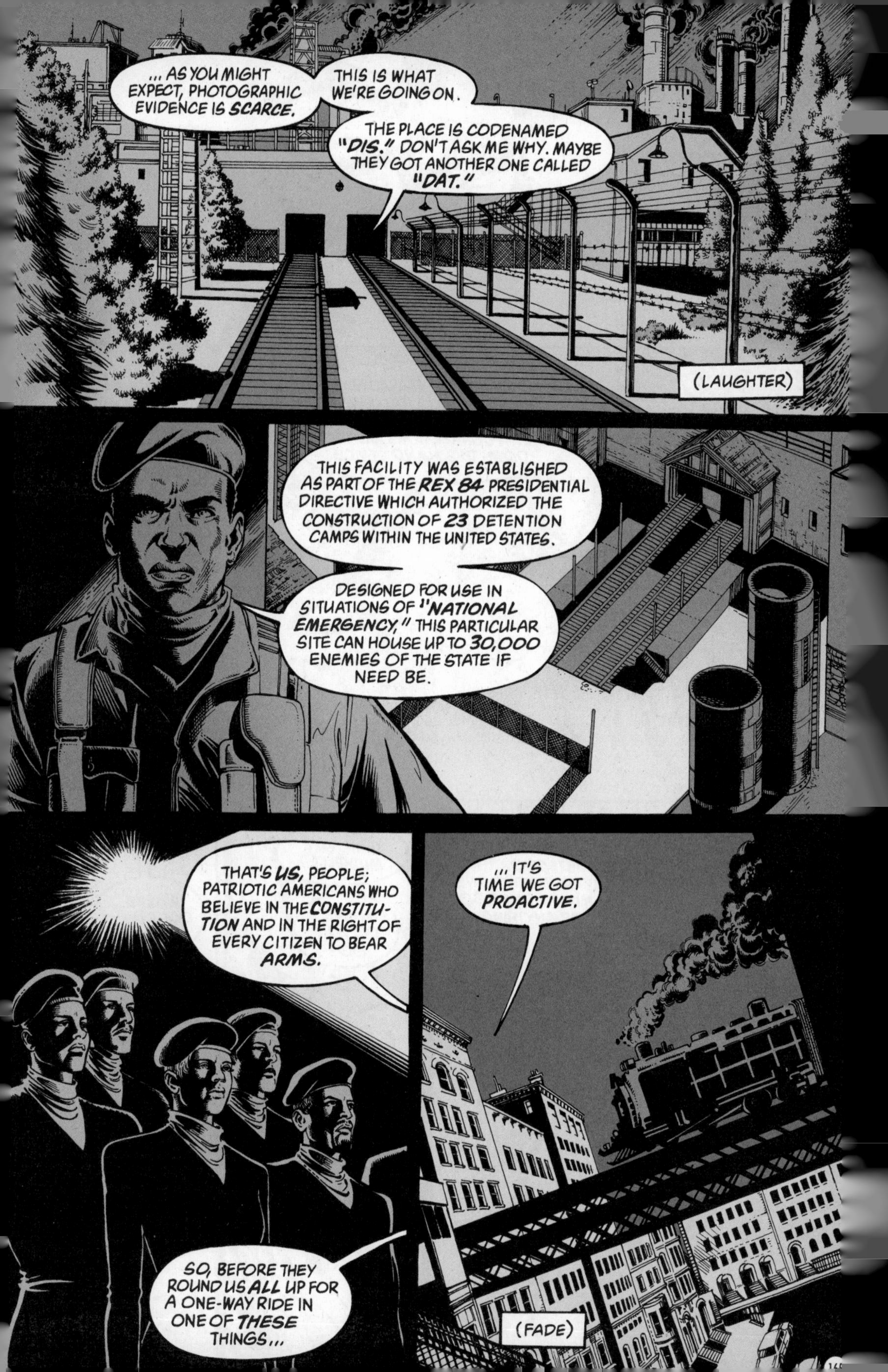
...AS YOU MIGHT EXPECT, PHOTOGRAPHIC EVIDENCE IS SCARCE.
THIS IS WHAT WE'RE GOING ON.
THE PLACE IS CODENAMED "DIS." DON'T ASK ME WHY. MAYBE THEY GOT ANOTHER ONE CALLED "DAT."
(LAUGHTER)
THIS FACILITY WAS ESTABLISHED AS PART OF THE REX 84 PRESIDENTIAL DIRECTIVE WHICH AUTHORIZED THE CONSTRUCTION OF 23 DETENTION CAMPS WITHIN THE UNITED STATES.
DESIGNED FOR USE IN SITUATIONS OF "NATIONAL EMERGENCY," THIS PARTICULAR SITE CAN HOUSE UP TO 30,000 ENEMIES OF THE STATE IF NEED BE.
THAT'S US, PEOPLE; PATRIOTIC AMERICANS WHO BELIEVE IN THE CONSTITUTION AND IN THE RIGHT OF EVERY CITIZEN TO BEAR ARMS.
SO, BEFORE THEY ROUND US ALL UP FOR A ONE-WAY RIDE IN ONE OF THESE THINGS...
...IT'S TIME WE GOT PROACTIVE.
(FADE)

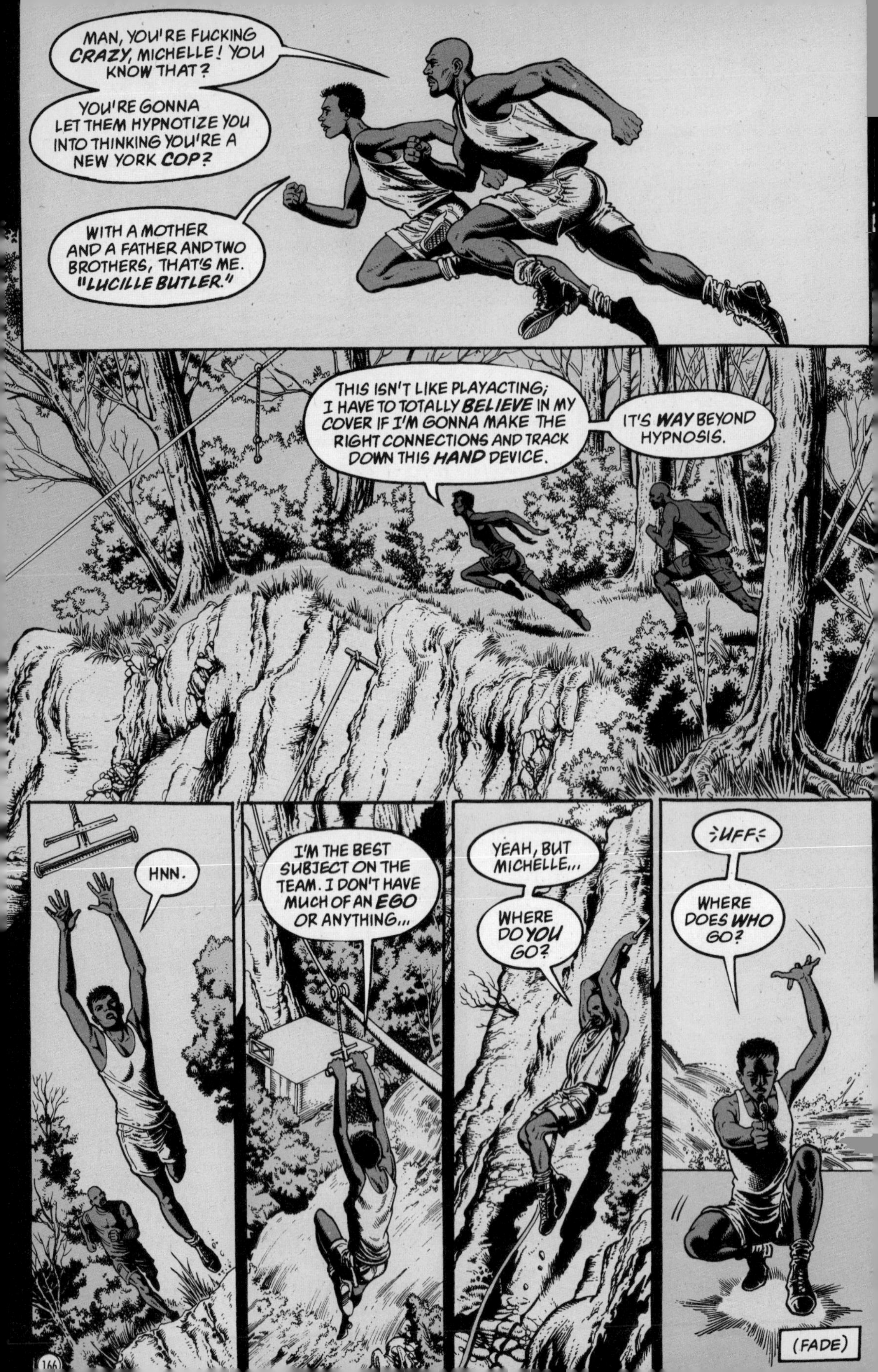
MAN, YOU'RE FUCKING CRAZY, MICHELLE! YOU KNOW THAT?
YOU'RE GONNA LET THEM HYPNOTIZE YOU INTO THINKING YOU'RE A NEW YORK COP?
WITH A MOTHER AND A FATHER AND TWO BROTHERS, THAT'S ME. "LUCILLE BUTLER."
THIS ISN'T LIKE PLAYACTING; I HAVE TO TOTALLY BELIEVE IN MY COVER IF I'M GONNA MAKE THE RIGHT CONNECTIONS AND TRACK DOWN THIS HAND DEVICE.
IT'S WAY BEYOND HYPNOSIS.
HNN.
I'M THE BEST SUBJECT ON THE TEAM. I DON'T HAVE MUCH OF AN EGO OR ANYTHING...
YEAH, BUT MICHELLE...
WHERE DO YOU GO?
UFF
WHERE DOES WHO GO?
(FADE)

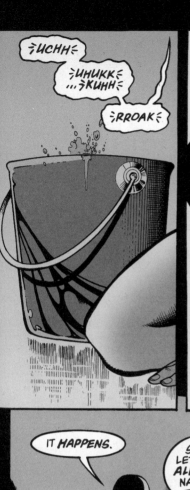

≥UCHH≤

≥UHUKK≤
....≥KUHH≤

≥RROAK≤

OHHH....

FEELING *BETTER?*

IT *HAPPENS.*

SEEING AND REMEMBERING LETTERS FROM THE *INVISIBLE ALPHABET* OFTEN TRIGGERS NAUSEA IN AGENTS WITH MULTIPLE COVER STORIES.

TRY TO STAY CALM. WE GOT TO YOU JUST IN TIME AND I'M HERE TO *HELP.*

HAVE YOU ANY IDEA WHAT'S BEEN *HAPPENING* TO YOU FOR THE LAST SEVEN YEARS?

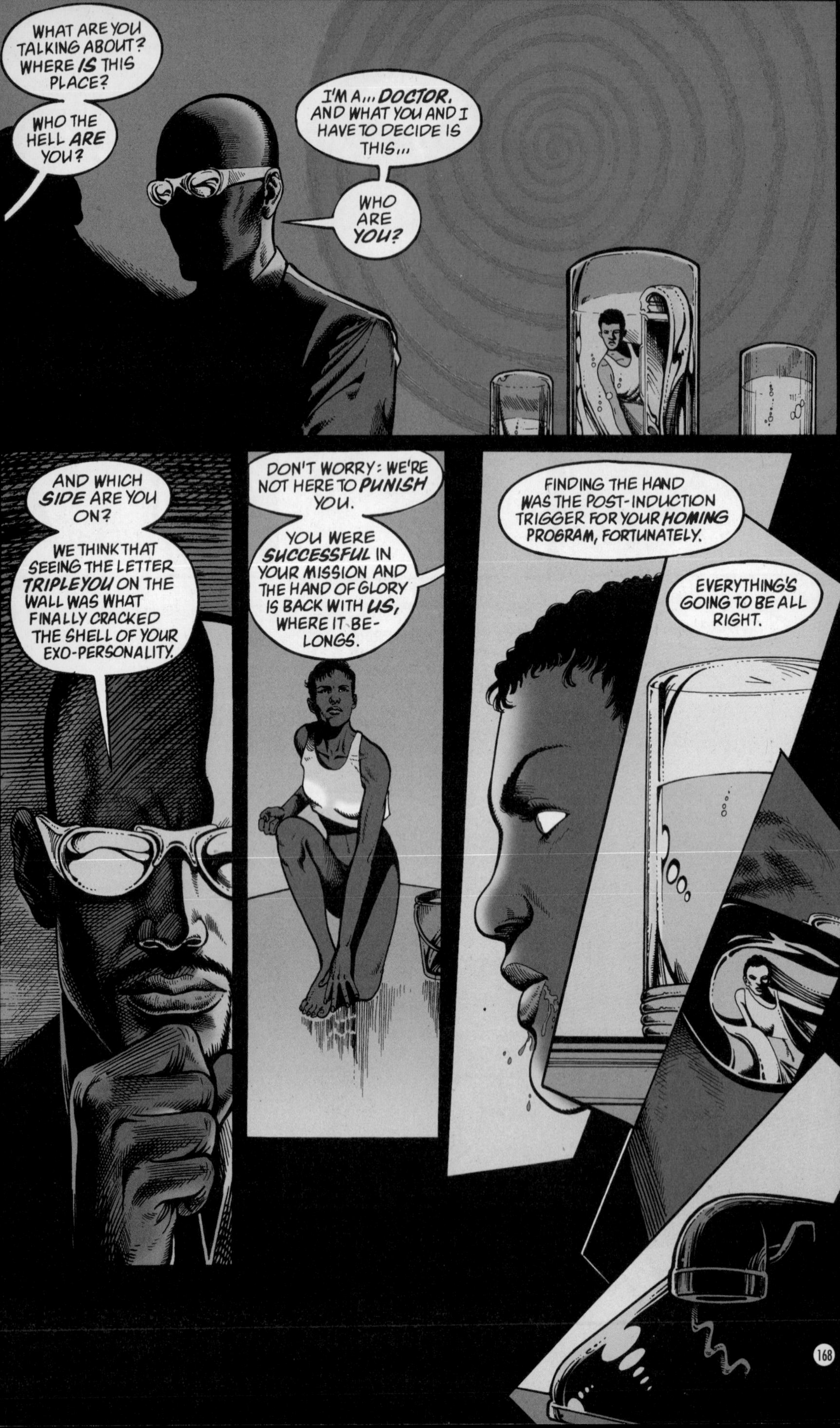
WHAT ARE YOU TALKING ABOUT? WHERE IS THIS PLACE?
WHO THE HELL ARE YOU?
I'M A... DOCTOR. AND WHAT YOU AND I HAVE TO DECIDE IS THIS...
WHO ARE YOU?
AND WHICH SIDE ARE YOU ON?
WE THINK THAT SEEING THE LETTER TRIPLEYOU ON THE WALL WAS WHAT FINALLY CRACKED THE SHELL OF YOUR EXO-PERSONALITY.
DON'T WORRY: WE'RE NOT HERE TO PUNISH YOU.
YOU WERE SUCCESSFUL IN YOUR MISSION AND THE HAND OF GLORY IS BACK WITH US, WHERE IT BE-LONGS.
FINDING THE HAND WAS THE POST-INDUCTION TRIGGER FOR YOUR HOMING PROGRAM, FORTUNATELY.
EVERYTHING'S GOING TO BE ALL RIGHT.

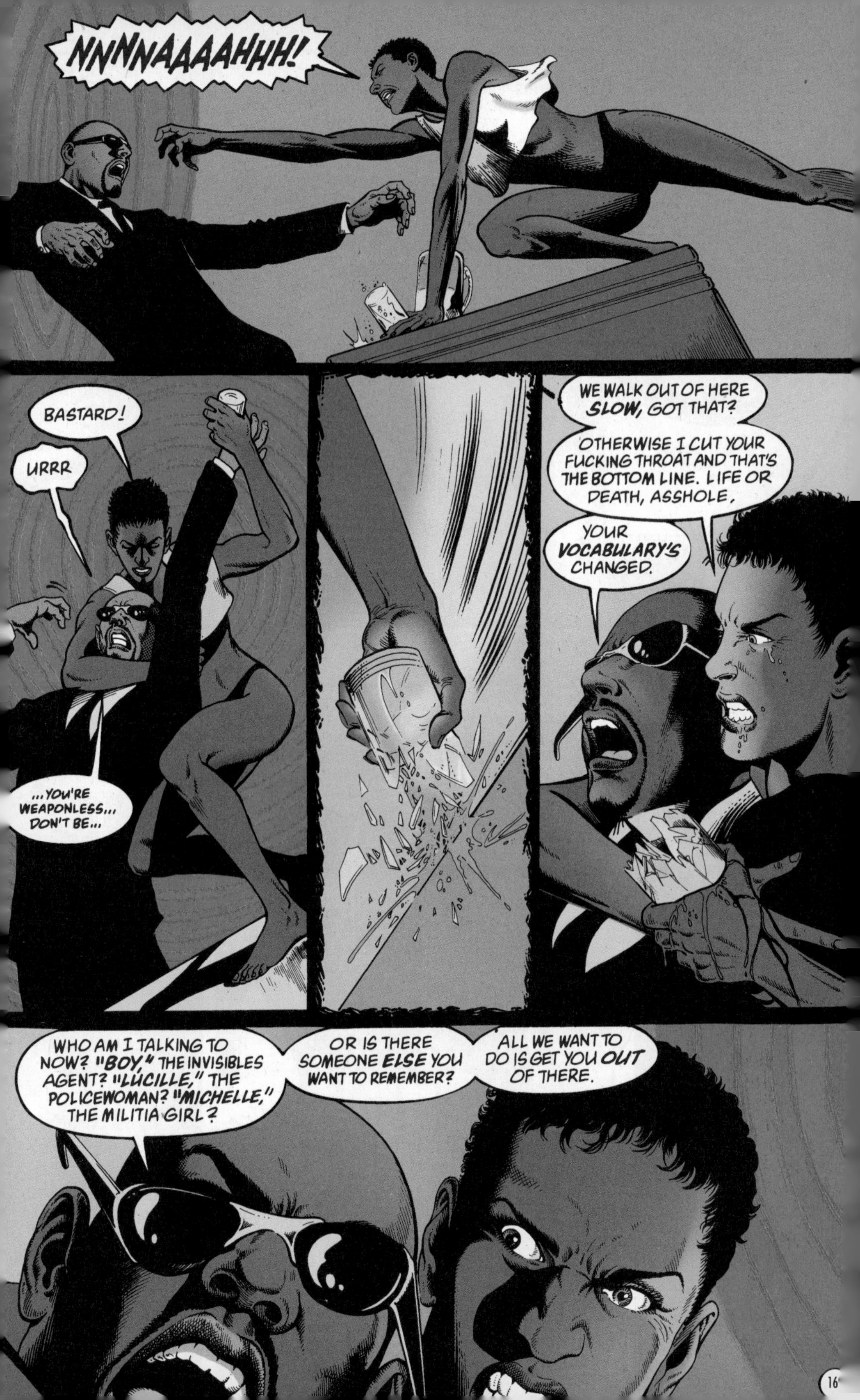
NNNNAAAAAHHH!
BASTARD!
URRR
...YOU'RE WEAPONLESS... DON'T BE...
WE WALK OUT OF HERE SLOW, GOT THAT?
OTHERWISE I CUT YOUR FUCKING THROAT AND THAT'S THE BOTTOM LINE. LIFE OR DEATH, ASSHOLE.
YOUR VOCABULARY'S CHANGED.
WHO AM I TALKING TO NOW? "BOY," THE INVISIBLES AGENT? "LUCILLE," THE POLICEWOMAN? "MICHELLE," THE MILITIA GIRL?
OR IS THERE SOMEONE ELSE YOU WANT TO REMEMBER?
ALL WE WANT TO DO IS GET YOU OUT OF THERE.

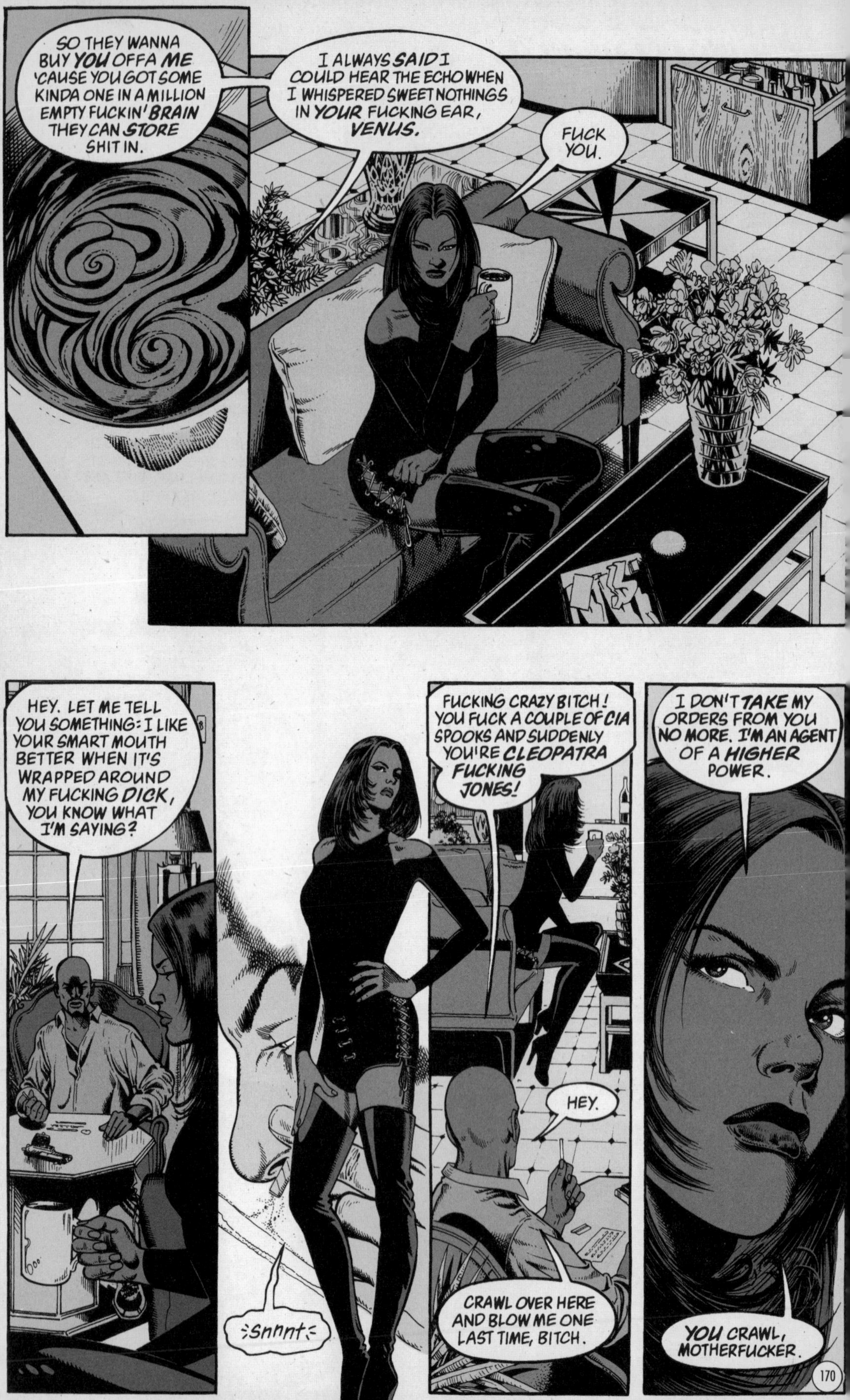
SO THEY WANNA BUY YOU OFFA ME 'CAUSE YOU GOT SOME KINDA ONE IN A MILLION EMPTY FUCKIN' BRAIN THEY CAN STORE SHIT IN.
I ALWAYS SAID I COULD HEAR THE ECHO WHEN I WHISPERED SWEET NOTHINGS IN YOUR FUCKING EAR, VENUS.
FUCK YOU.
HEY. LET ME TELL YOU SOMETHING: I LIKE YOUR SMART MOUTH BETTER WHEN IT'S WRAPPED AROUND MY FUCKING DICK, YOU KNOW WHAT I'M SAYING?
:SNNNT:
FUCKING CRAZY BITCH! YOU FUCK A COUPLE OF CIA SPOOKS AND SUDDENLY YOU'RE CLEOPATRA FUCKING JONES!
HEY.
CRAWL OVER HERE AND BLOW ME ONE LAST TIME, BITCH.
I DON'T TAKE MY ORDERS FROM YOU NO MORE. I'M AN AGENT OF A HIGHER POWER.
YOU CRAWL, MOTHERFUCKER.

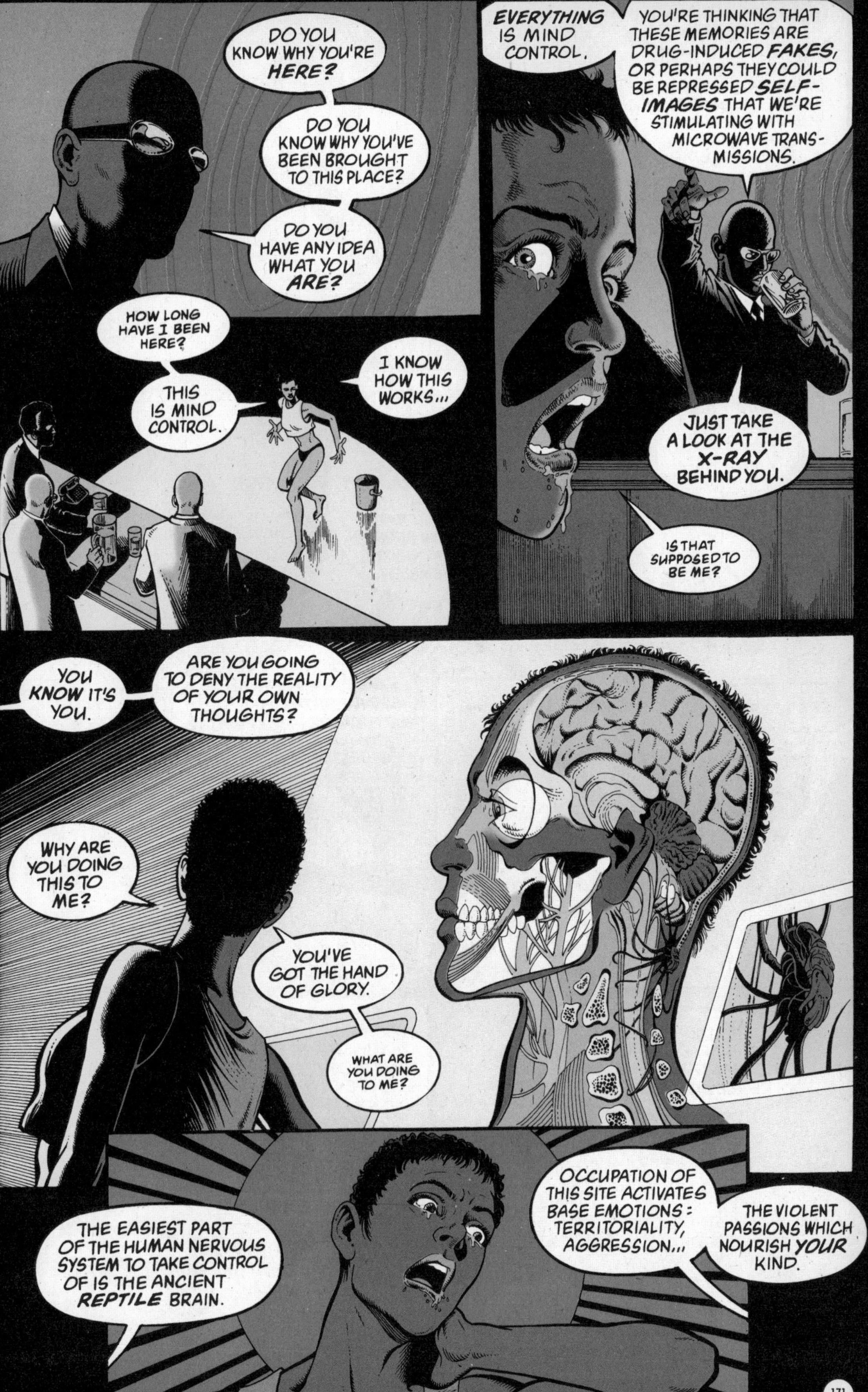
DO YOU KNOW WHY YOU'RE HERE?
DO YOU KNOW WHY YOU'VE BEEN BROUGHT TO THIS PLACE?
DO YOU HAVE ANY IDEA WHAT YOU ARE?
HOW LONG HAVE I BEEN HERE?
THIS IS MIND CONTROL.
I KNOW HOW THIS WORKS...
EVERYTHING IS MIND CONTROL.
YOU'RE THINKING THAT THESE MEMORIES ARE DRUG-INDUCED FAKES, OR PERHAPS THEY COULD BE REPRESSED SELF-IMAGES THAT WE'RE STIMULATING WITH MICROWAVE TRANS-MISSIONS.
JUST TAKE A LOOK AT THE X-RAY BEHIND YOU.
IS THAT SUPPOSED TO BE ME?
YOU KNOW IT'S YOU.
ARE YOU GOING TO DENY THE REALITY OF YOUR OWN THOUGHTS?
WHY ARE YOU DOING THIS TO ME?
YOU'VE GOT THE HAND OF GLORY.
WHAT ARE YOU DOING TO ME?
THE EASIEST PART OF THE HUMAN NERVOUS SYSTEM TO TAKE CONTROL OF IS THE ANCIENT REPTILE BRAIN.
OCCUPATION OF THIS SITE ACTIVATES BASE EMOTIONS: TERRITORIALITY, AGGRESSION...
THE VIOLENT PASSIONS WHICH NOURISH YOUR KIND.

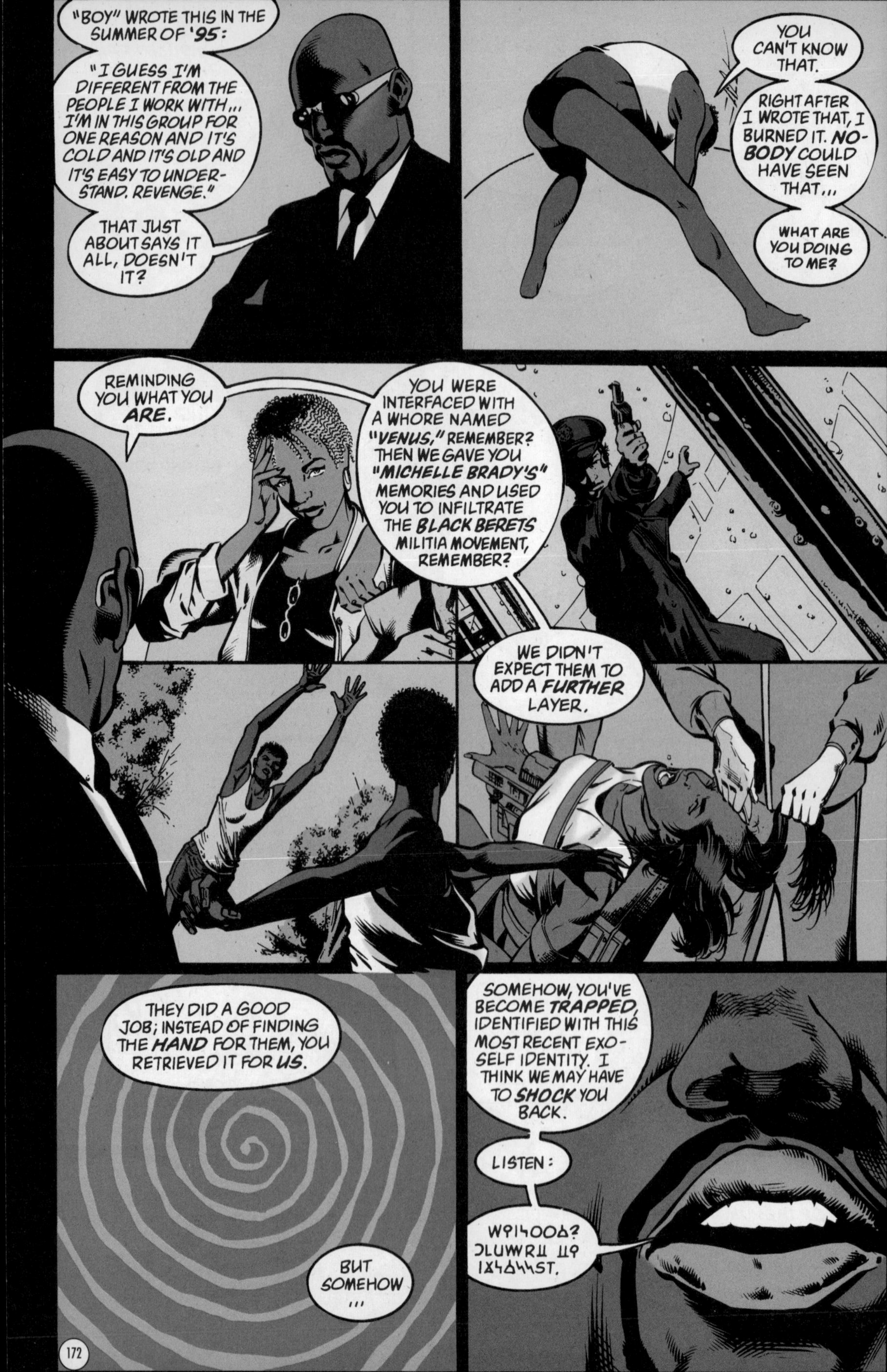
"BOY" WROTE THIS IN THE SUMMER OF '95:
"I GUESS I'M DIFFERENT FROM THE PEOPLE I WORK WITH... I'M IN THIS GROUP FOR ONE REASON AND IT'S COLD AND IT'S OLD AND IT'S EASY TO UNDERSTAND. REVENGE."
THAT JUST ABOUT SAYS IT ALL, DOESN'T IT?
YOU CAN'T KNOW THAT.
RIGHT AFTER I WROTE THAT, I BURNED IT. NOBODY COULD HAVE SEEN THAT...
WHAT ARE YOU DOING TO ME?
REMINDING YOU WHAT YOU ARE.
YOU WERE INTERFACED WITH A WHORE NAMED "VENUS," REMEMBER? THEN WE GAVE YOU "MICHELLE BRADY'S" MEMORIES AND USED YOU TO INFILTRATE THE BLACK BERETS MILITIA MOVEMENT, REMEMBER?
WE DIDN'T EXPECT THEM TO ADD A FURTHER LAYER.
THEY DID A GOOD JOB; INSTEAD OF FINDING THE HAND FOR THEM, YOU RETRIEVED IT FOR US.
BUT SOMEHOW ...
SOMEHOW, YOU'VE BECOME TRAPPED, IDENTIFIED WITH THIS MOST RECENT EXO-SELF IDENTITY. I THINK WE MAY HAVE TO SHOCK YOU BACK.
LISTEN:

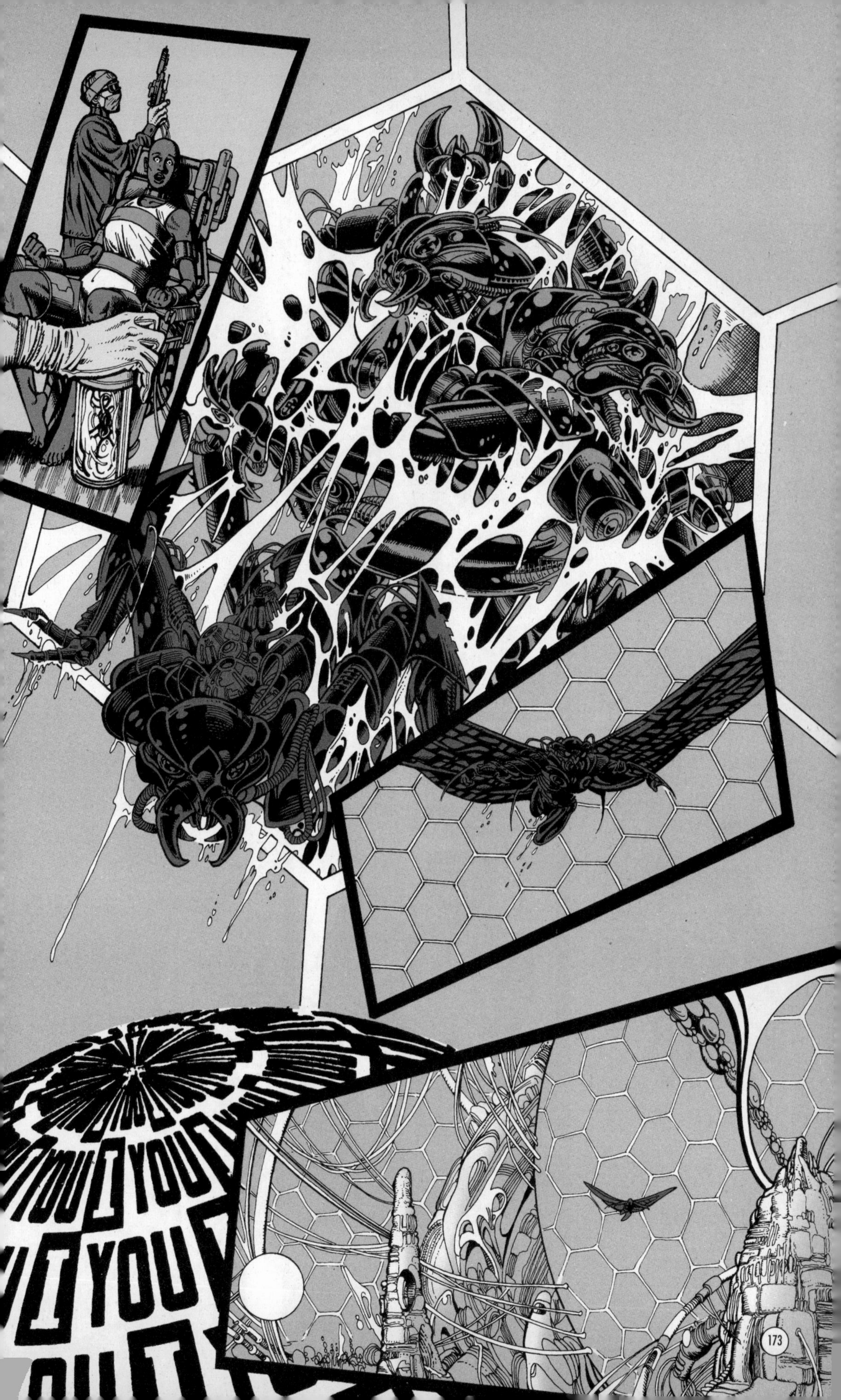
YOU I YOU
I YOU

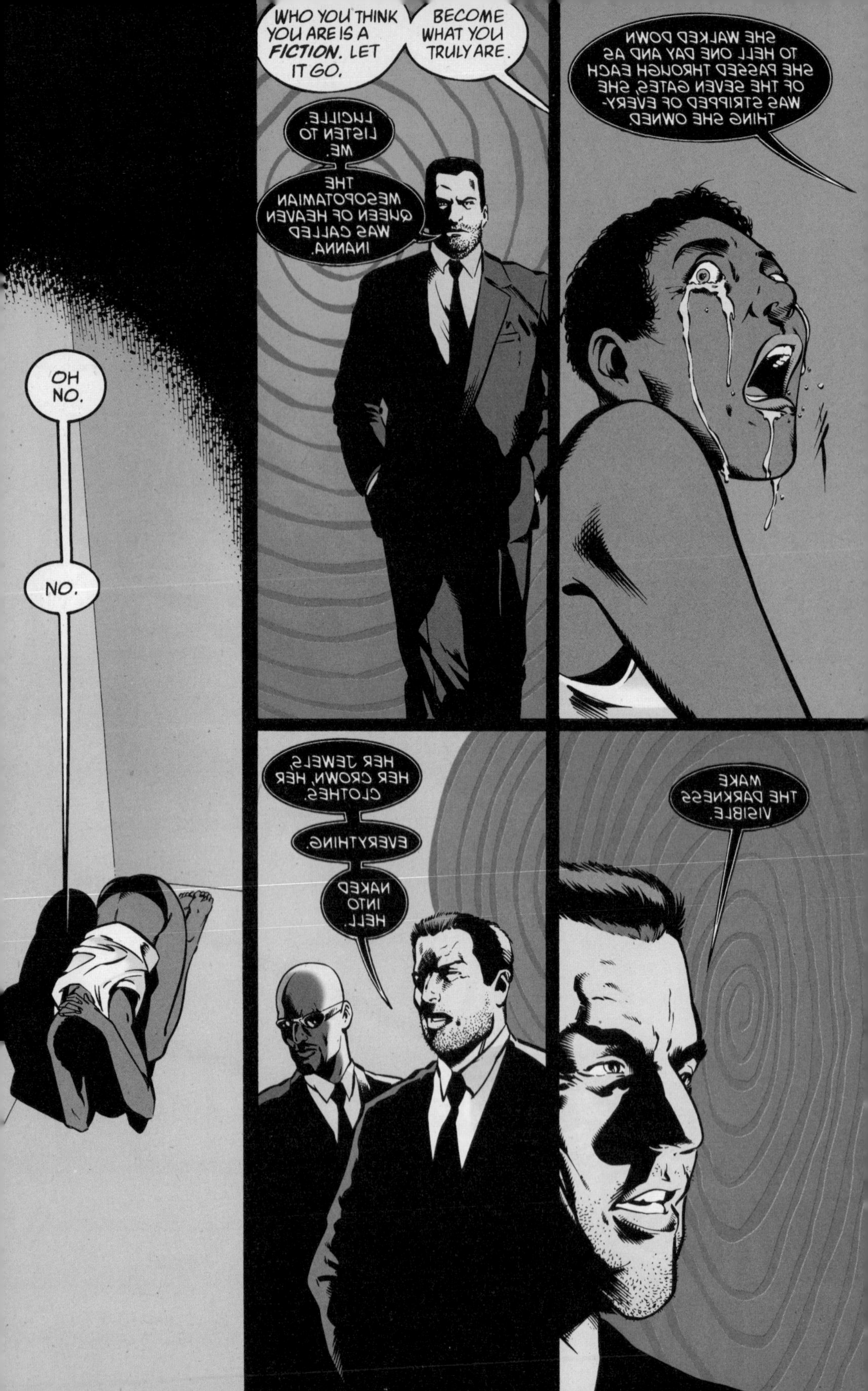

OH NO.
NO.
WHO YOU THINK YOU ARE IS A FICTION. LET IT GO.
BECOME WHAT YOU TRULY ARE.
LUCILLE. LISTEN TO ME.
THE MESOPOTAMIAN QUEEN OF HEAVEN WAS CALLED INANNA.
SHE WALKED DOWN TO HELL ONE DAY AND AS SHE PASSED THROUGH EACH OF THE SEVEN GATES, SHE WAS STRIPPED OF EVERY-THING SHE OWNED.
HER JEWELS, HER CROWN, HER CLOTHES.
EVERYTHING.
NAKED INTO HELL.
MAKE THE DARKNESS VISIBLE.

WUHH?

OH-KAY!

READINGS ARE STILL PRETTY HIGH. SHE MUST HAVE SHED ONLY RECENTLY.

NᏎᎯᎡᏏ! ᏆᏔᏏᏏᏎᏎᏚᎢ! ᏆᏔᏏᏏᏎᏎᏚᎢ!

AH, YOU'LL HAVE TO USE STANDARD ENGLISH ...WE...AH...

I BROUGHT YOUR UNIFORM.

MY UNIFORM.

LET'S MOVE IT OUT.

AND KEEP AN EYE ON HER: THERE COULD BE SOME VESTIGIAL PERSONA TRACES.

175

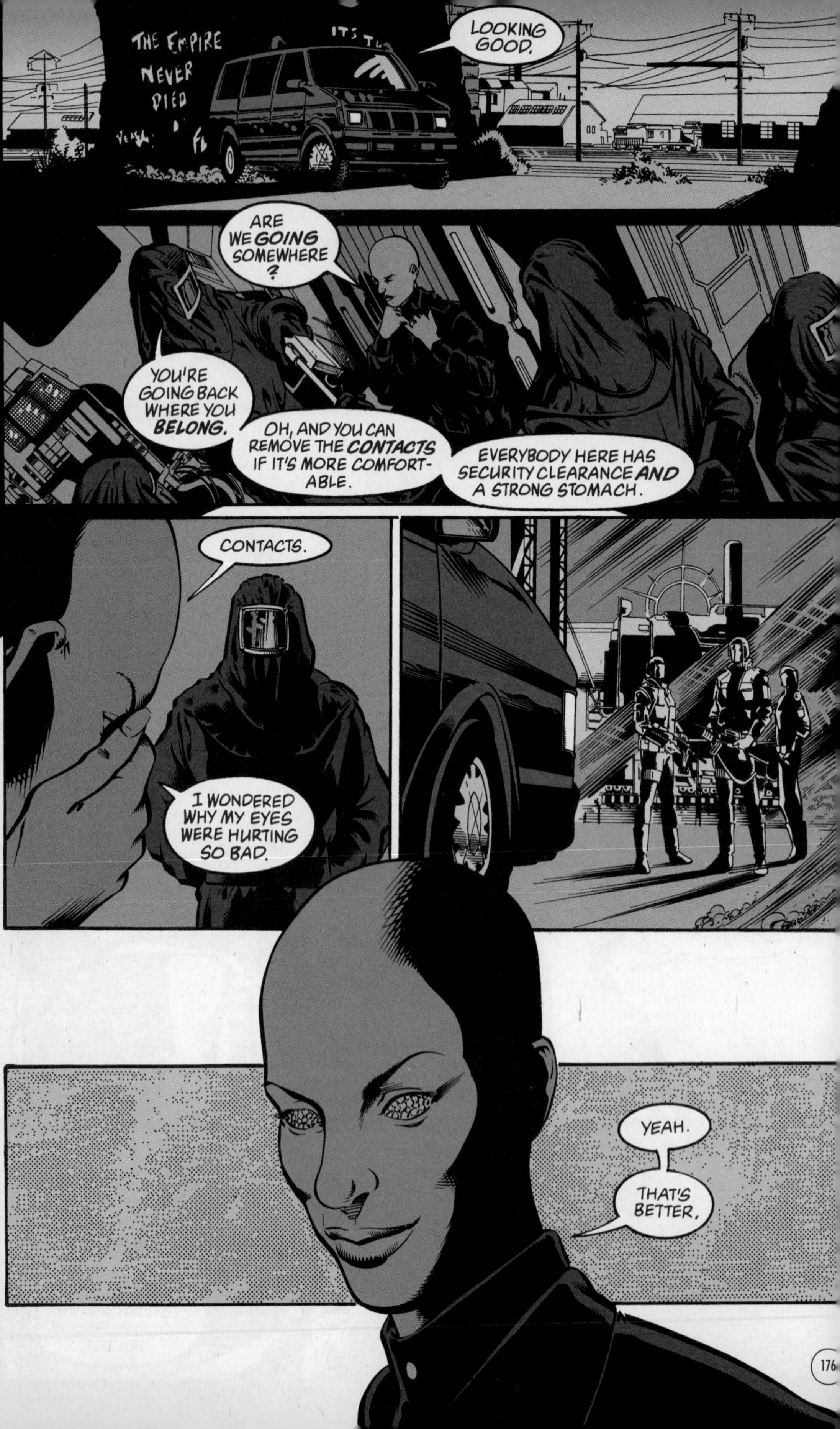
THE EMPIRE NEVER DIED
LOOKING GOOD.
ARE WE GOING SOMEWHERE?
YOU'RE GOING BACK WHERE YOU BELONG.
OH, AND YOU CAN REMOVE THE CONTACTS IF IT'S MORE COMFORTABLE.
EVERYBODY HERE HAS SECURITY CLEARANCE AND A STRONG STOMACH.
CONTACTS.
I WONDERED WHY MY EYES WERE HURTING SO BAD.
YEAH.
THAT'S BETTER.

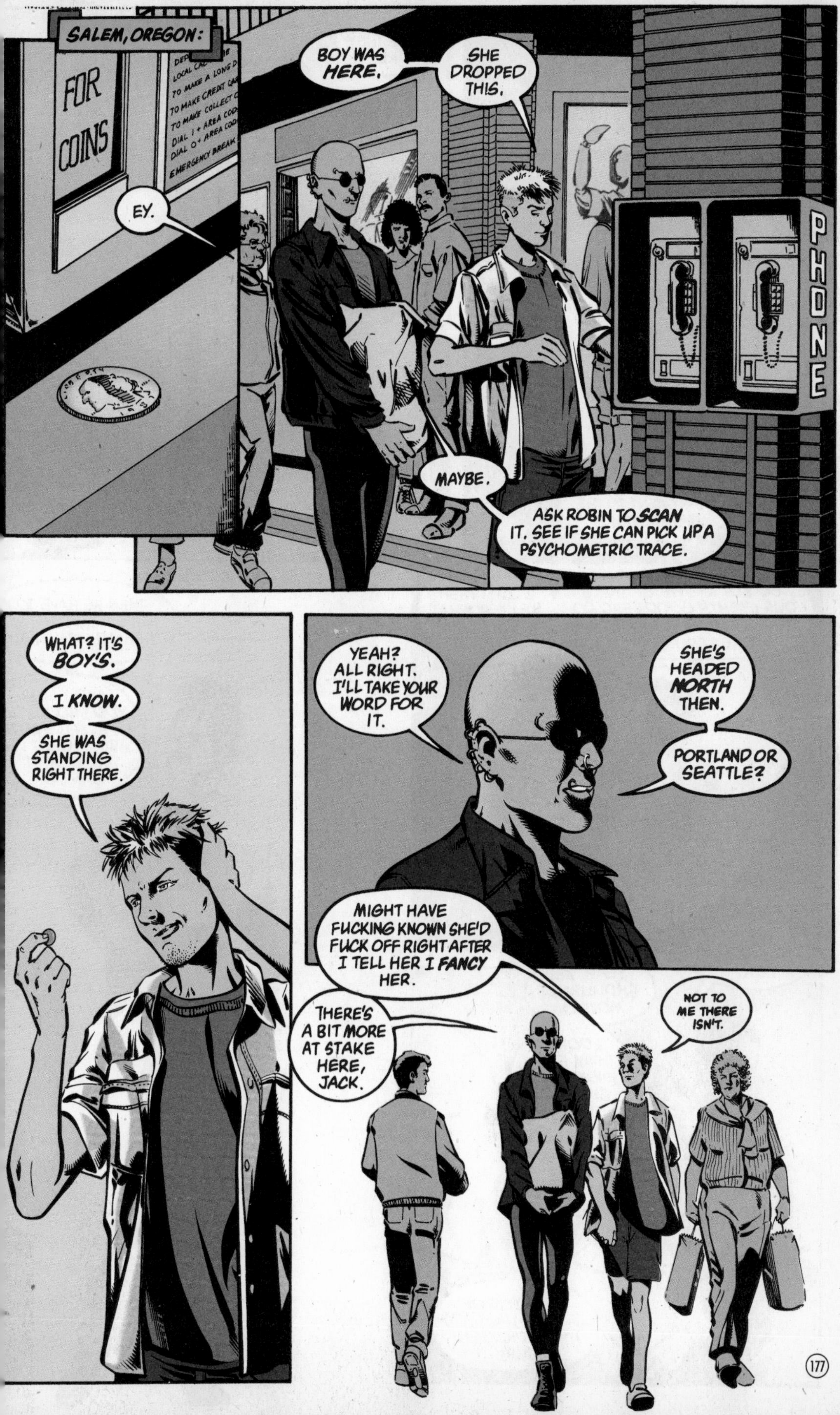
SALEM, OREGON:
FOR COINS
EY.
BOY WAS HERE.
SHE DROPPED THIS.
MAYBE.
ASK ROBIN TO SCAN IT. SEE IF SHE CAN PICK UP A PSYCHOMETRIC TRACE.
PHONE
WHAT? IT'S BOY'S.
I KNOW.
SHE WAS STANDING RIGHT THERE.
YEAH? ALL RIGHT. I'LL TAKE YOUR WORD FOR IT.
SHE'S HEADED NORTH THEN.
PORTLAND OR SEATTLE?
MIGHT HAVE FUCKING KNOWN SHE'D FUCK OFF RIGHT AFTER I TELL HER I FANCY HER.
THERE'S A BIT MORE AT STAKE HERE, JACK.
NOT TO ME THERE ISN'T.

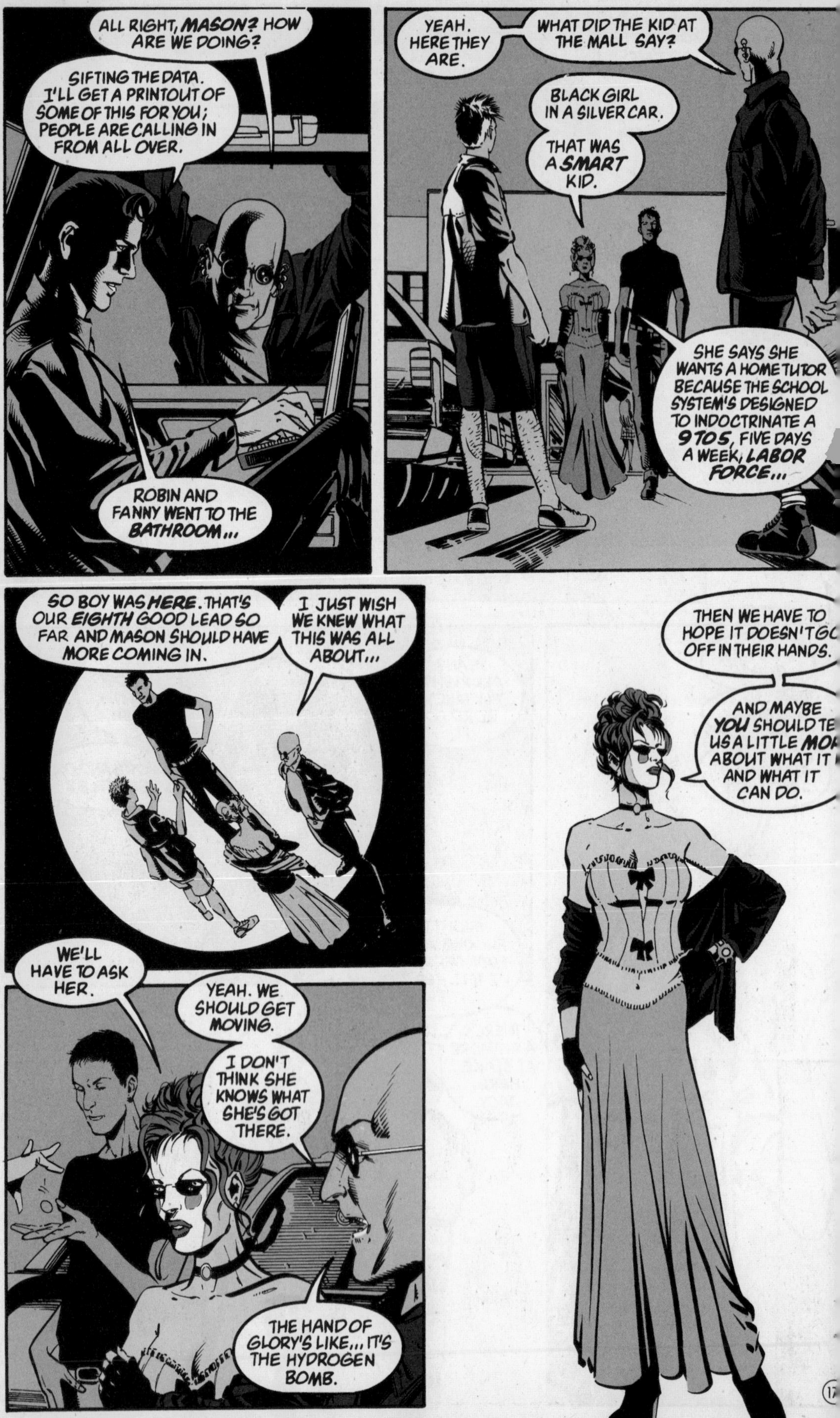
ALL RIGHT, MASON? HOW ARE WE DOING?
SIFTING THE DATA. I'LL GET A PRINTOUT OF SOME OF THIS FOR YOU; PEOPLE ARE CALLING IN FROM ALL OVER.
ROBIN AND FANNY WENT TO THE BATHROOM...
YEAH. HERE THEY ARE.
WHAT DID THE KID AT THE MALL SAY?
BLACK GIRL IN A SILVER CAR.
THAT WAS A SMART KID.
SHE SAYS SHE WANTS A HOME TUTOR BECAUSE THE SCHOOL SYSTEM'S DESIGNED TO INDOCTRINATE A 9 TO 5, FIVE DAYS A WEEK, LABOR FORCE...
SO BOY WAS HERE. THAT'S OUR EIGHTH GOOD LEAD SO FAR AND MASON SHOULD HAVE MORE COMING IN.
I JUST WISH WE KNEW WHAT THIS WAS ALL ABOUT...
WE'LL HAVE TO ASK HER.
YEAH. WE SHOULD GET MOVING.
I DON'T THINK SHE KNOWS WHAT SHE'S GOT THERE.
THE HAND OF GLORY'S LIKE... IT'S THE HYDROGEN BOMB.
THEN WE HAVE TO HOPE IT DOESN'T G
OFF IN THEIR HANDS.
AND MAYBE YOU SHOULD TE
US A LITTLE MO
ABOUT WHAT IT
AND WHAT IT CAN DO.

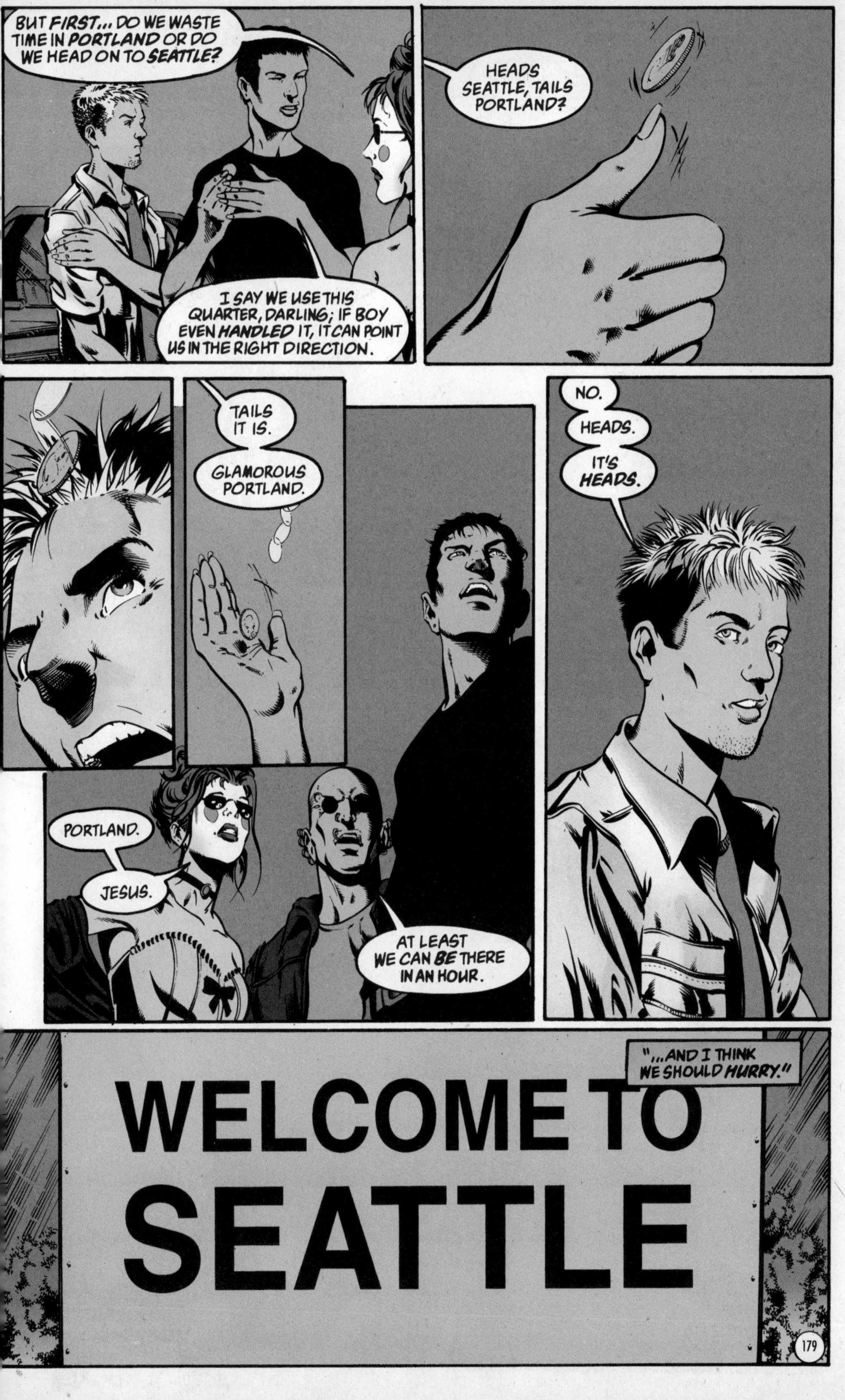
BUT FIRST... DO WE WASTE TIME IN PORTLAND OR DO WE HEAD ON TO SEATTLE?
I SAY WE USE THIS QUARTER, DARLING; IF BOY EVEN HANDLED IT, IT CAN POINT US IN THE RIGHT DIRECTION.
HEADS SEATTLE, TAILS PORTLAND?
TAILS IT IS.
GLAMOROUS PORTLAND.
PORTLAND.
JESUS.
AT LEAST WE CAN BE THERE IN AN HOUR.
NO.
HEADS.
IT'S HEADS.
"...AND I THINK WE SHOULD HURRY."
WELCOME TO SEATTLE

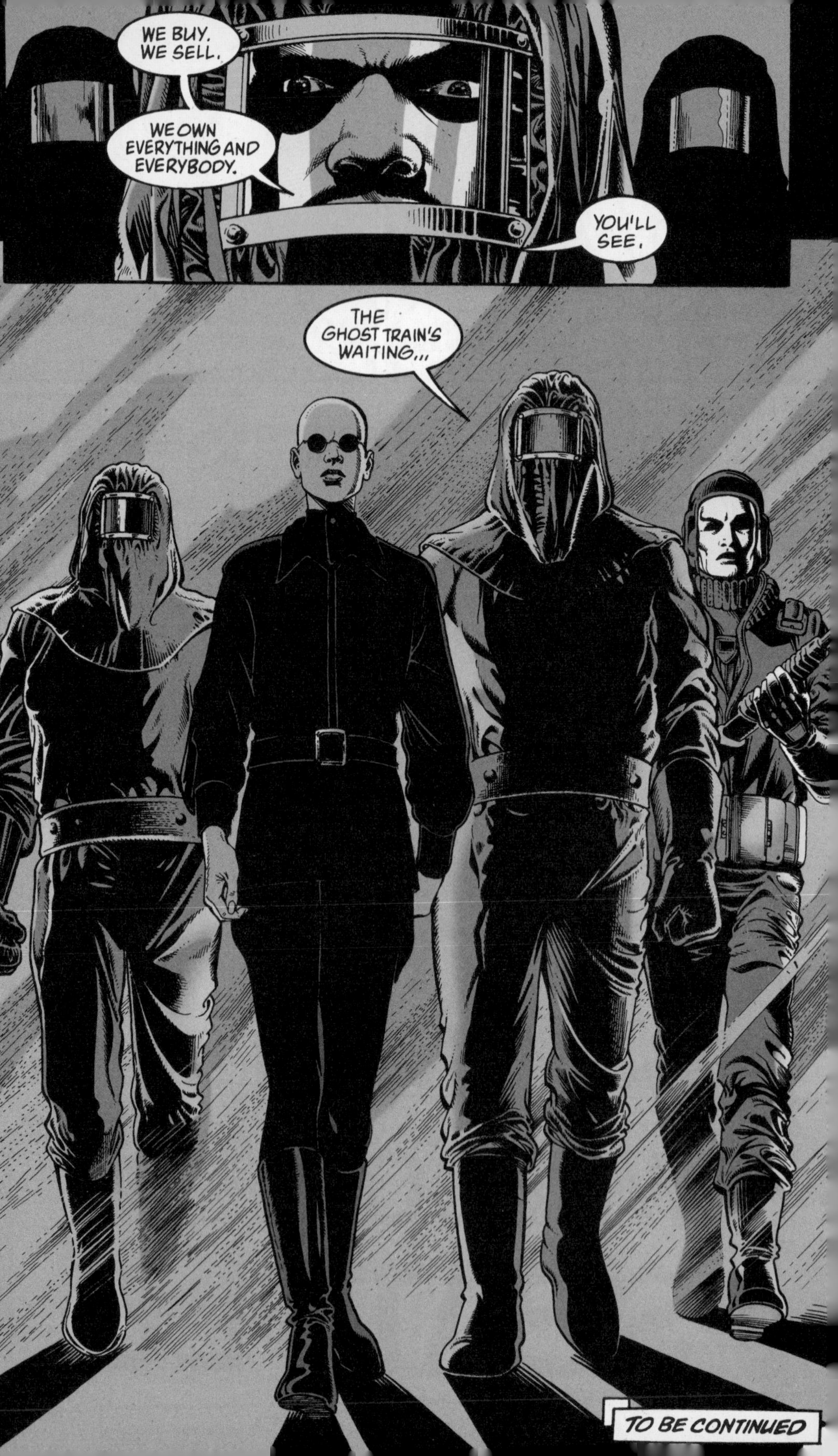
WE BUY. WE SELL.
WE OWN EVERYTHING AND EVERYBODY.
YOU'LL SEE.
THE GHOST TRAIN'S WAITING...
TO BE CONTINUED

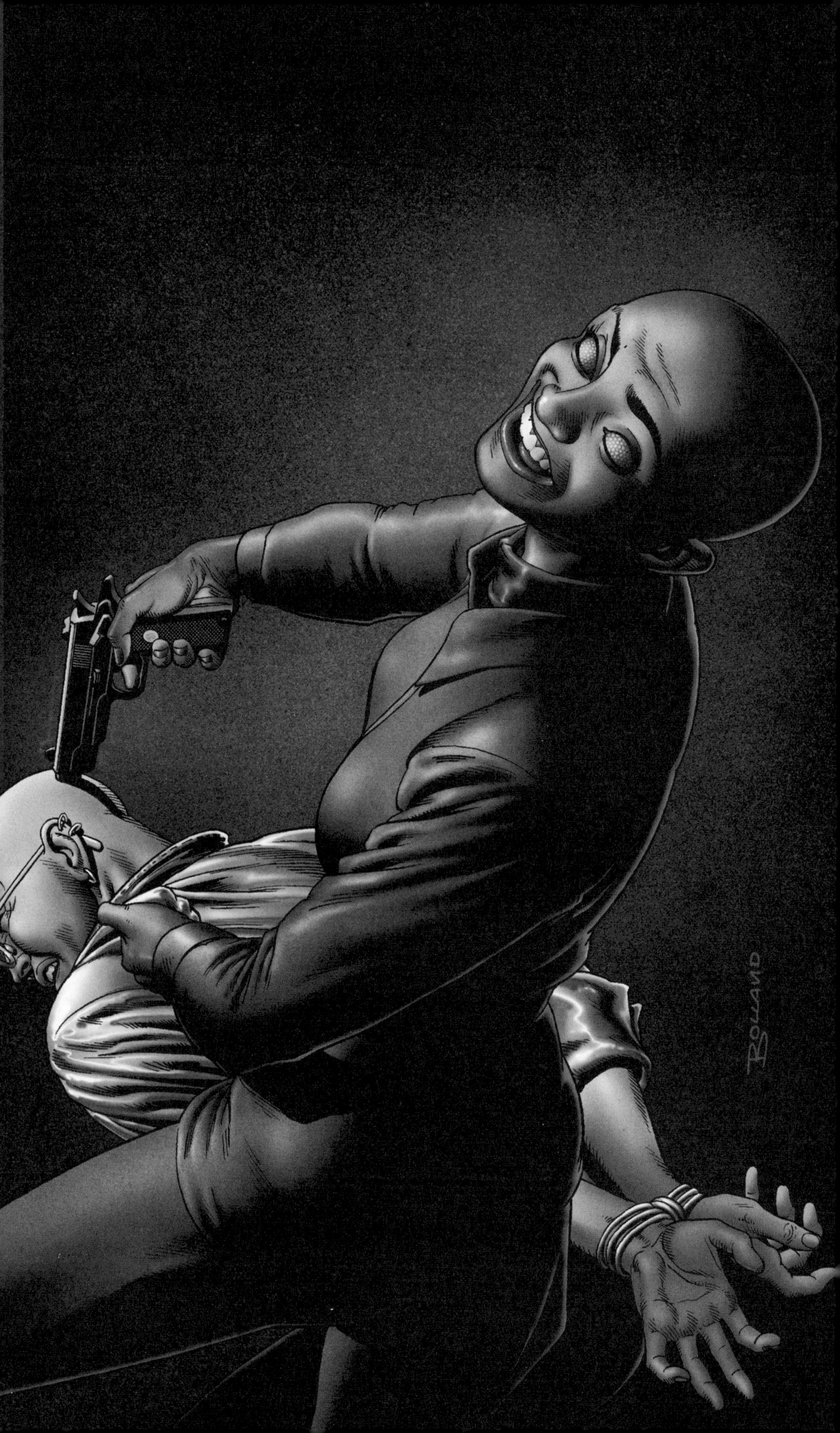
BOLLAND

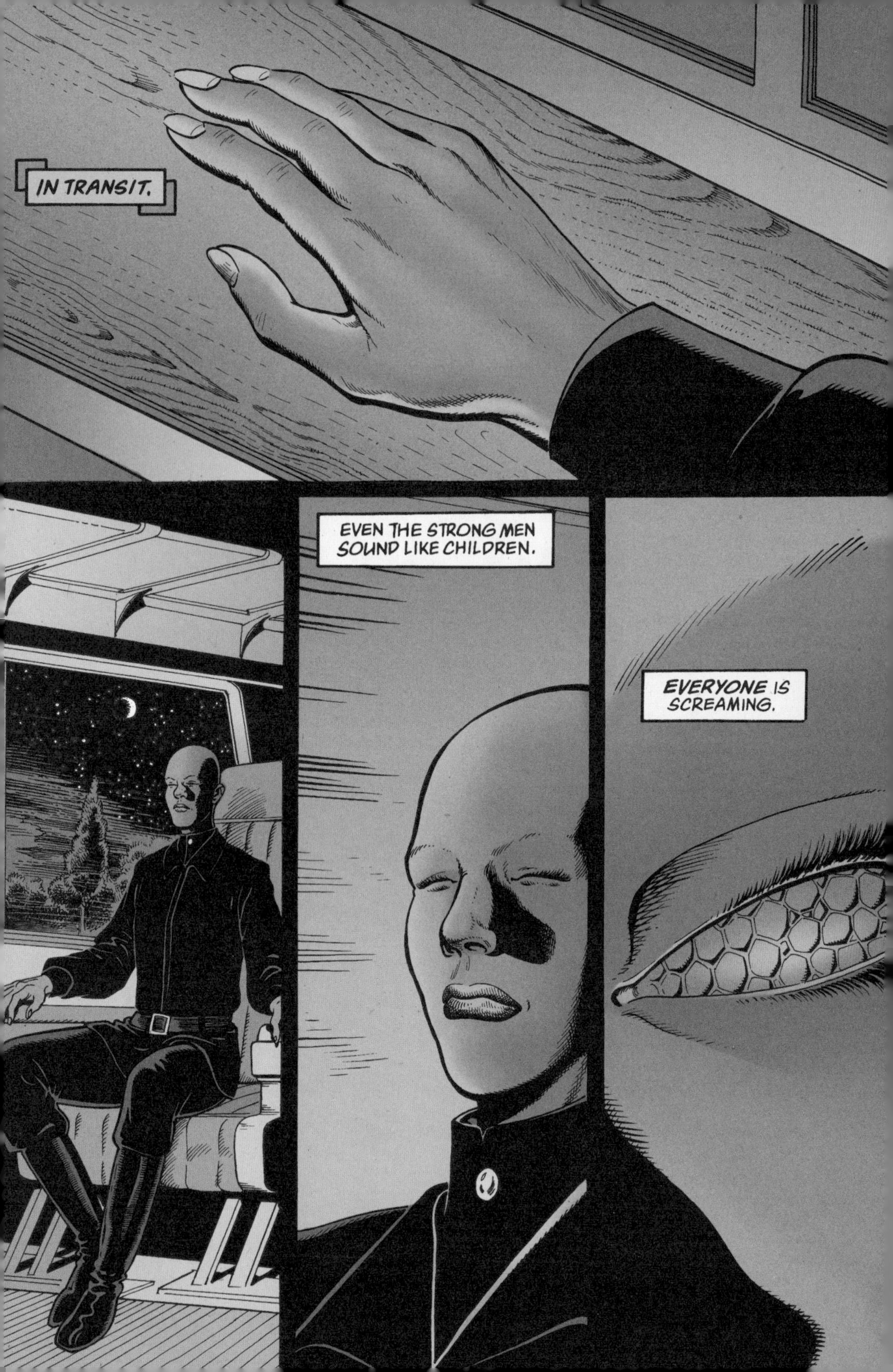
IN TRANSIT.
EVEN THE STRONG MEN SOUND LIKE CHILDREN.
EVERYONE IS SCREAMING.

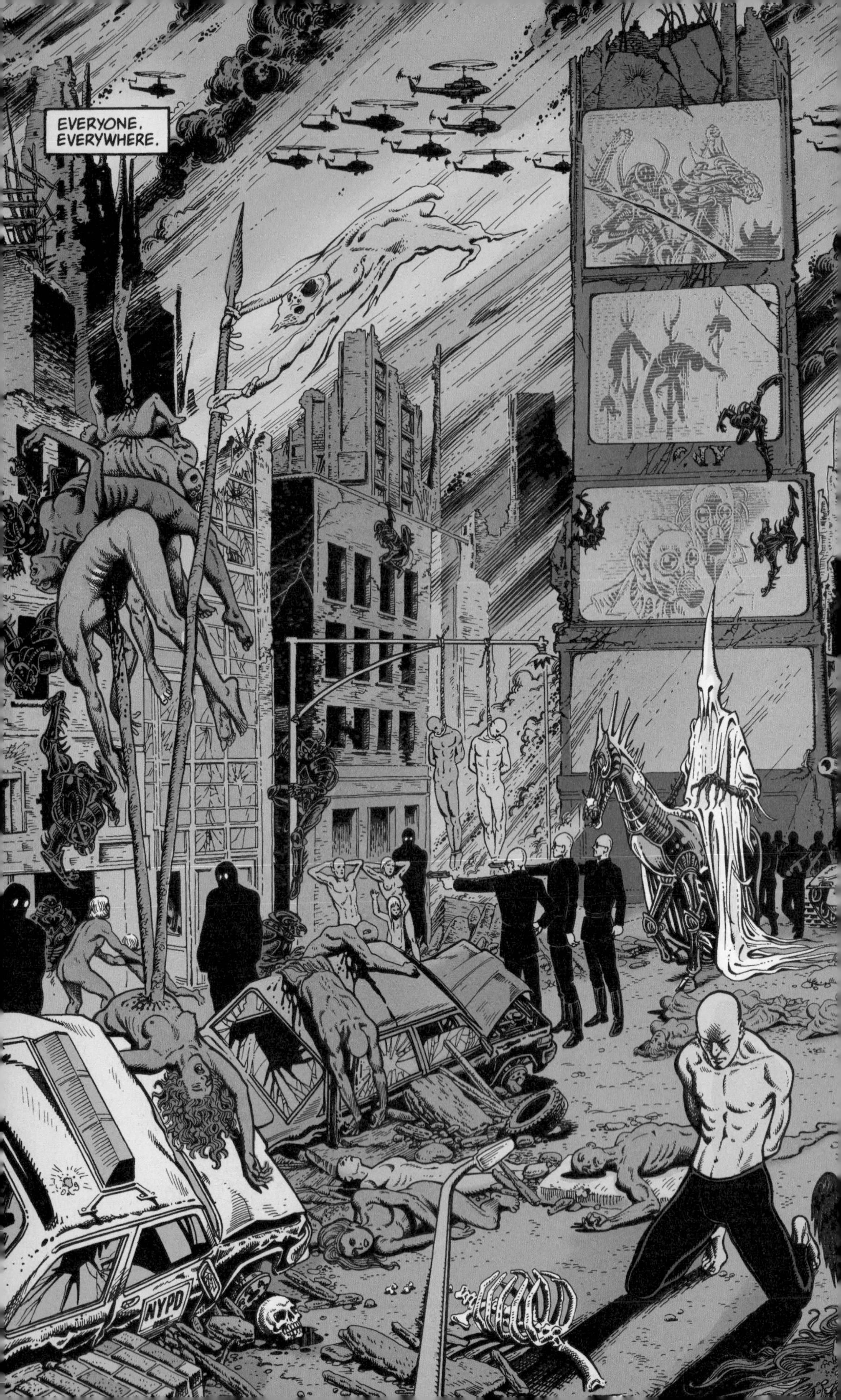
EVERYONE.
EVERYWHERE.
NYPD

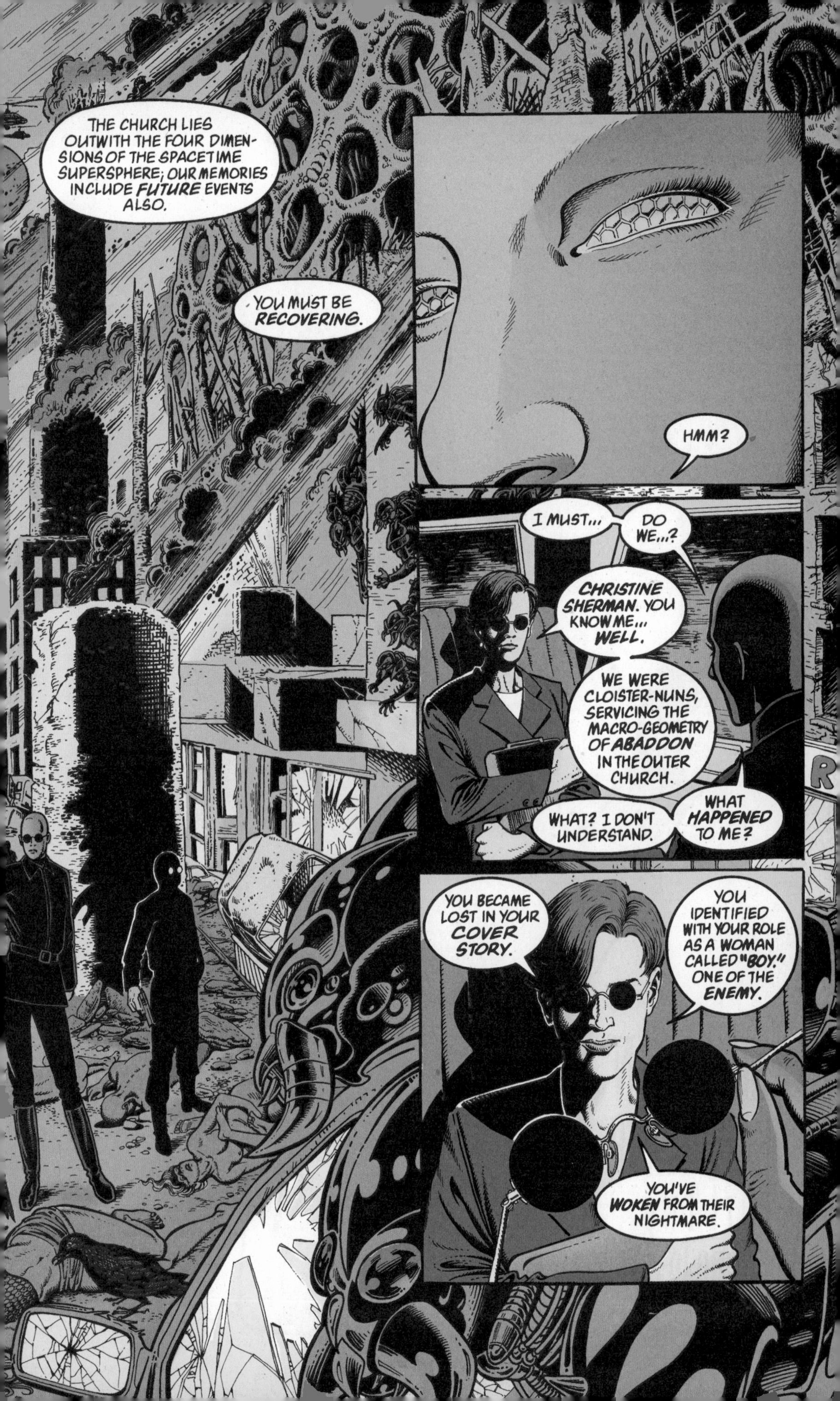

THE CHURCH LIES OUTWITH THE FOUR DIMENSIONS OF THE SPACETIME SUPERSPHERE; OUR MEMORIES INCLUDE FUTURE EVENTS ALSO.
YOU MUST BE RECOVERING.
HMM?
I MUST...
DO WE...?
CHRISTINE SHERMAN. YOU KNOW ME... WELL.
WE WERE CLOISTER-NUNS, SERVICING THE MACRO-GEOMETRY OF ABADDON IN THE OUTER CHURCH.
WHAT? I DON'T UNDERSTAND.
WHAT HAPPENED TO ME?
YOU BECAME LOST IN YOUR COVER STORY.
YOU IDENTIFIED WITH YOUR ROLE AS A WOMAN CALLED "BOY." ONE OF THE ENEMY.
YOU'VE WOKEN FROM THEIR NIGHTMARE.

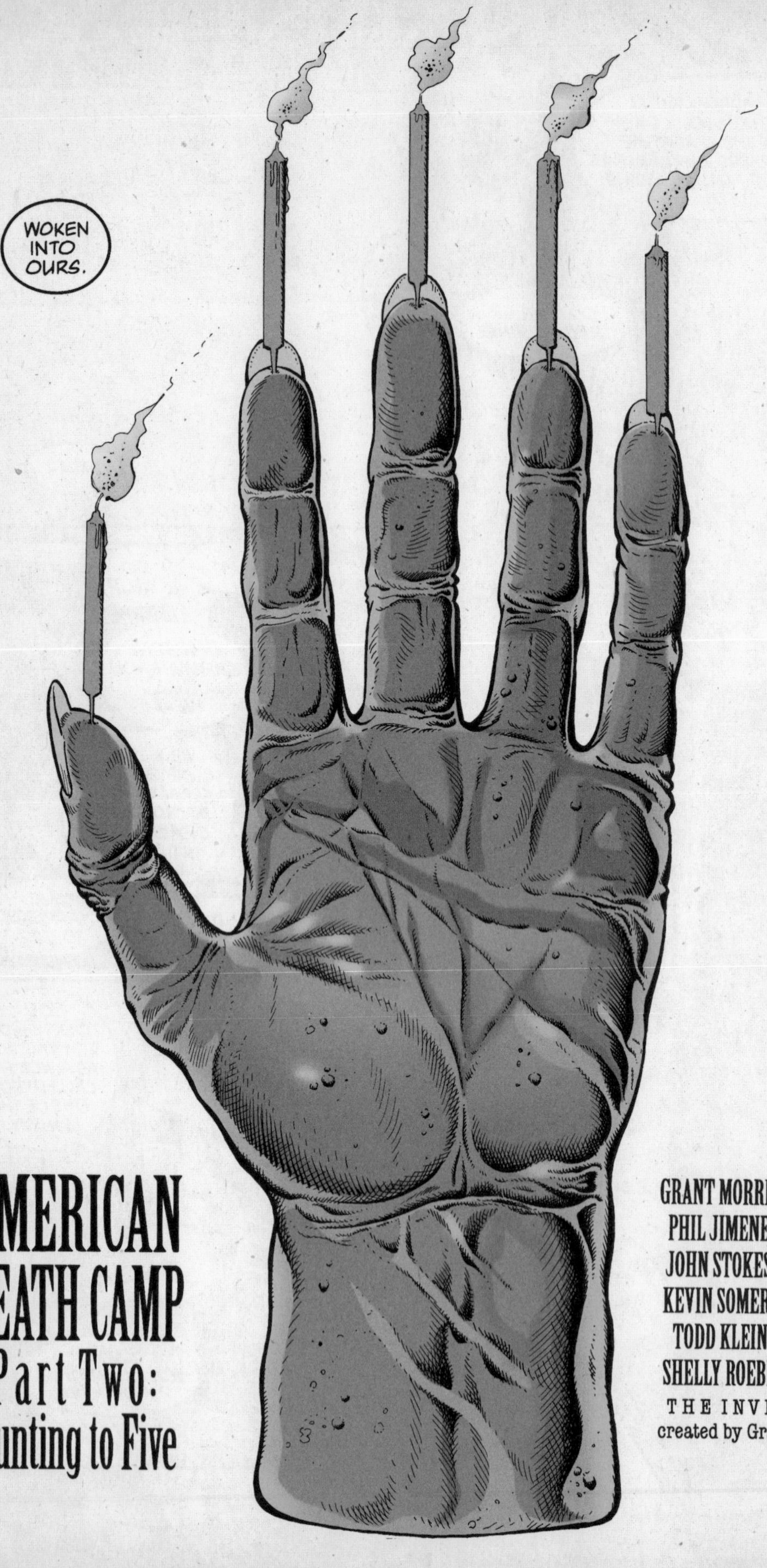
WOKEN INTO OURS.

AMERICAN DEATH CAMP
Part Two: Counting to Five

GRANT MORRISON writer
PHIL JIMENEZ layouts
JOHN STOKES finishes
KEVIN SOMERS colorist
TODD KLEIN letterer
SHELLY ROEBERG editor
THE INVISIBLES created by Grant Morrison

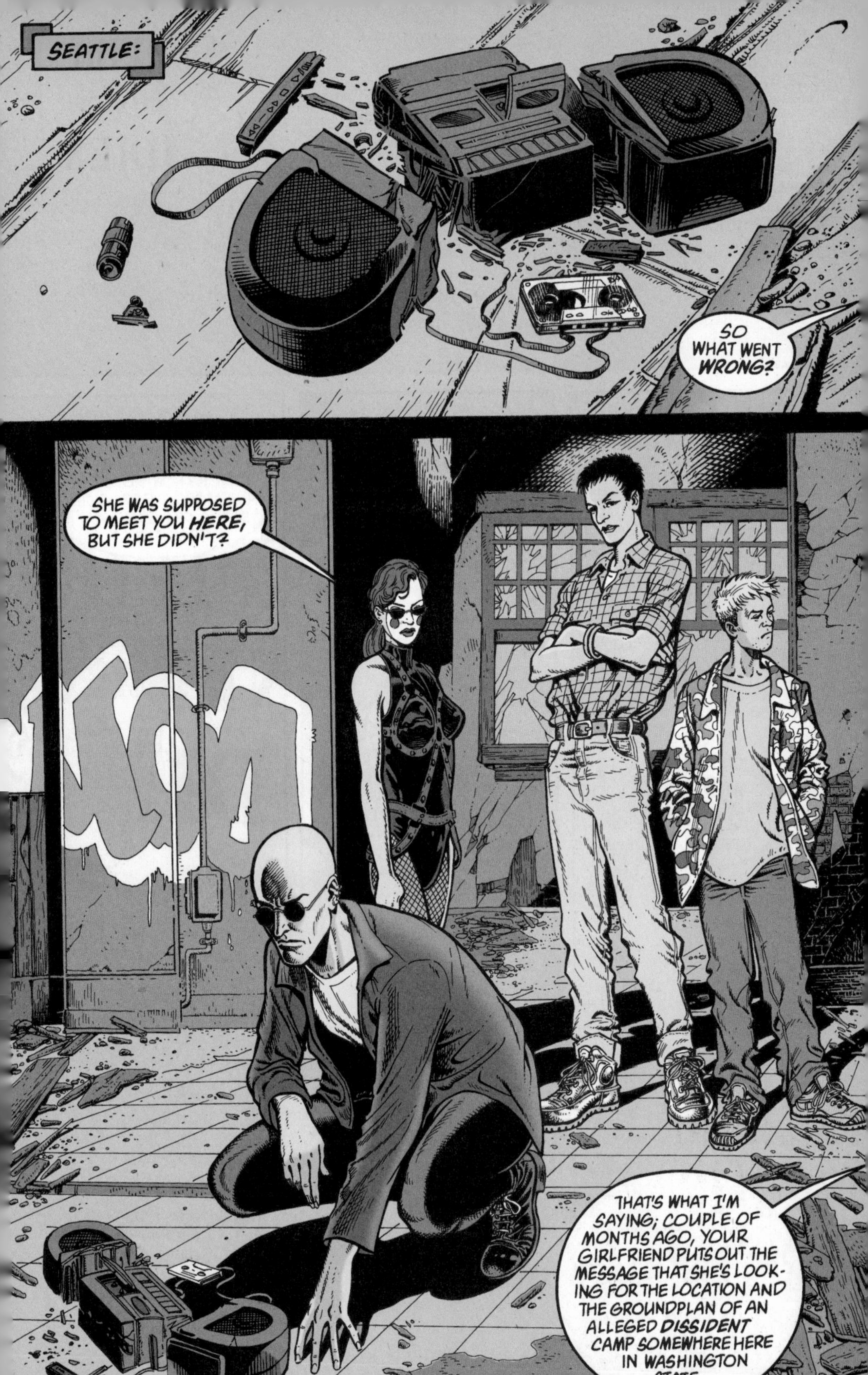
SEATTLE:
SO WHAT WENT WRONG?
SHE WAS SUPPOSED TO MEET YOU HERE, BUT SHE DIDN'T?
THAT'S WHAT I'M SAYING; COUPLE OF MONTHS AGO, YOUR GIRLFRIEND PUTS OUT THE MESSAGE THAT SHE'S LOOKING FOR THE LOCATION AND THE GROUNDPLAN OF AN ALLEGED DISSIDENT CAMP SOMEWHERE HERE IN WASHINGTON STATE...

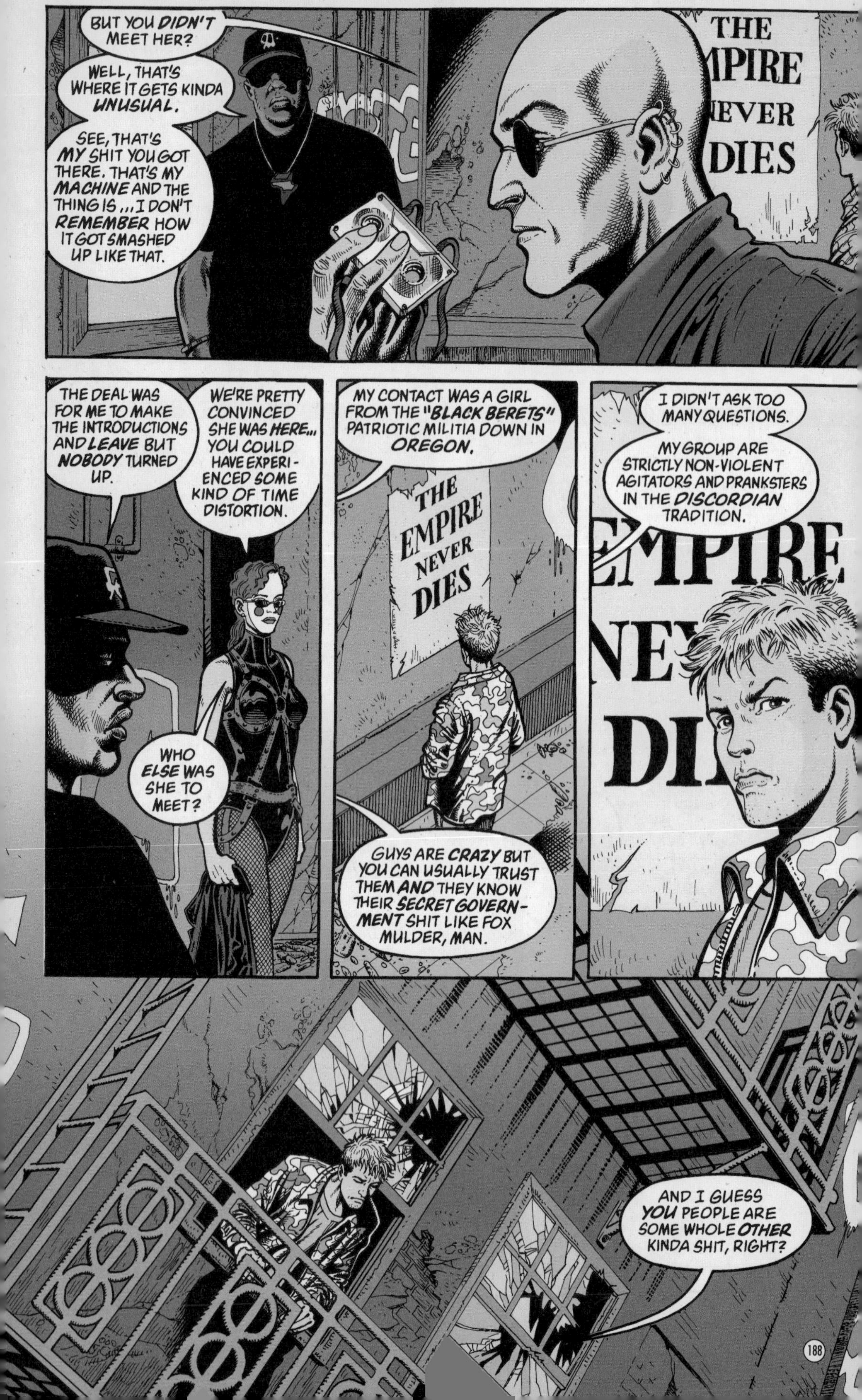
BUT YOU DIDN'T MEET HER?
WELL, THAT'S WHERE IT GETS KINDA UNUSUAL.
SEE, THAT'S MY SHIT YOU GOT THERE. THAT'S MY MACHINE AND THE THING IS ... I DON'T REMEMBER HOW IT GOT SMASHED UP LIKE THAT.
THE EMPIRE NEVER DIES
THE DEAL WAS FOR ME TO MAKE THE INTRODUCTIONS AND LEAVE BUT NOBODY TURNED UP.
WE'RE PRETTY CONVINCED SHE WAS HERE... YOU COULD HAVE EXPERIENCED SOME KIND OF TIME DISTORTION.
WHO ELSE WAS SHE TO MEET?
MY CONTACT WAS A GIRL FROM THE "BLACK BERETS" PATRIOTIC MILITIA DOWN IN OREGON.
THE EMPIRE NEVER DIES
GUYS ARE CRAZY BUT YOU CAN USUALLY TRUST THEM AND THEY KNOW THEIR SECRET GOVERNMENT SHIT LIKE FOX MULDER, MAN.
I DIDN'T ASK TOO MANY QUESTIONS.
MY GROUP ARE STRICTLY NON-VIOLENT AGITATORS AND PRANKSTERS IN THE DISCORDIAN TRADITION.
AND I GUESS YOU PEOPLE ARE SOME WHOLE OTHER KINDA SHIT, RIGHT?

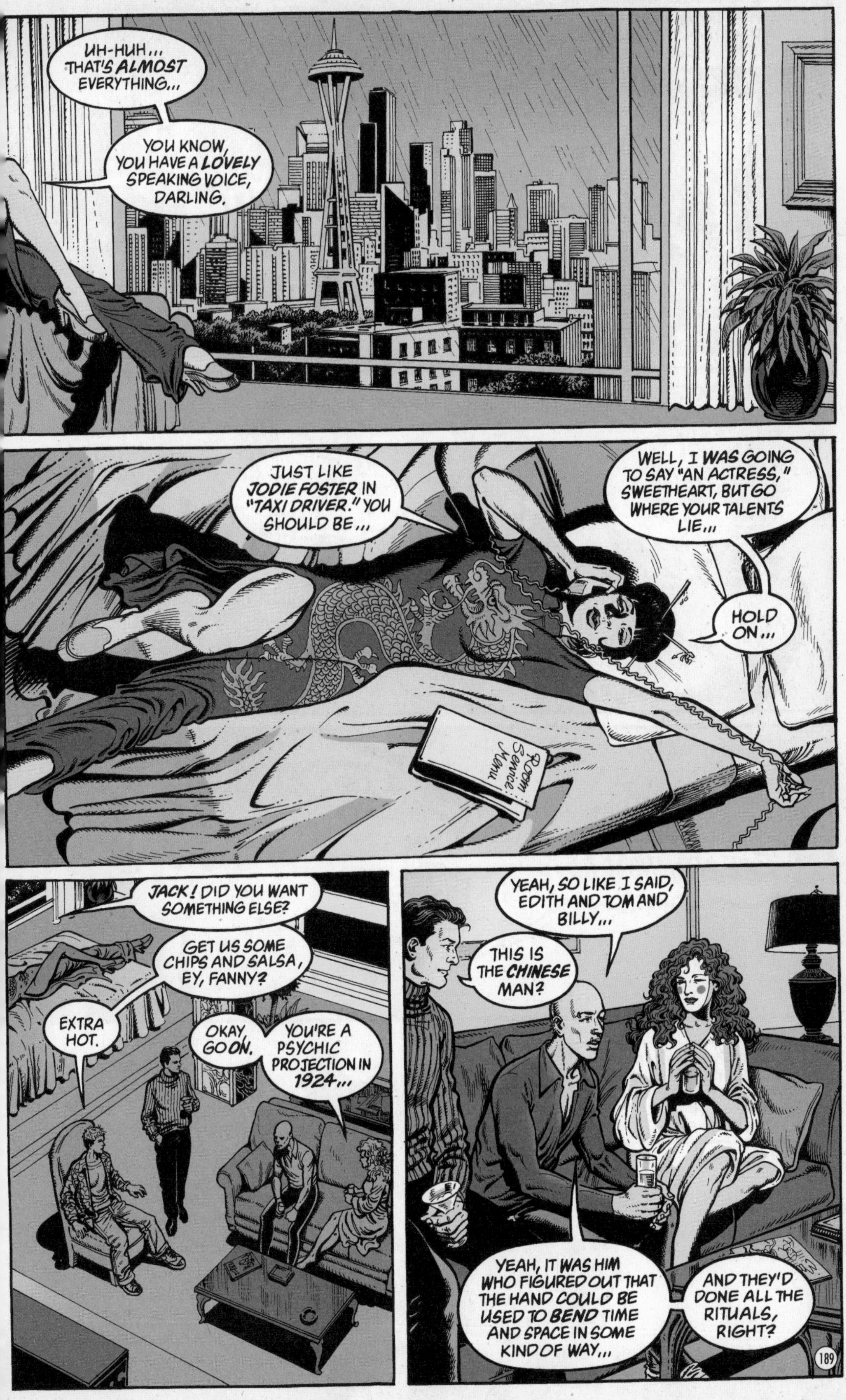
UH-HUH... THAT'S ALMOST EVERYTHING...
YOU KNOW, YOU HAVE A LOVELY SPEAKING VOICE, DARLING.
JUST LIKE JODIE FOSTER IN "TAXI DRIVER." YOU SHOULD BE...
WELL, I WAS GOING TO SAY "AN ACTRESS," SWEETHEART, BUT GO WHERE YOUR TALENTS LIE...
HOLD ON...
Room Service Menu
JACK! DID YOU WANT SOMETHING ELSE?
GET US SOME CHIPS AND SALSA, EY, FANNY?
EXTRA HOT.
OKAY, GO ON.
YOU'RE A PSYCHIC PROJECTION IN 1924...
YEAH, SO LIKE I SAID, EDITH AND TOM AND BILLY...
THIS IS THE CHINESE MAN?
YEAH, IT WAS HIM WHO FIGURED OUT THAT THE HAND COULD BE USED TO BEND TIME AND SPACE IN SOME KIND OF WAY...
AND THEY'D DONE ALL THE RITUALS, RIGHT?

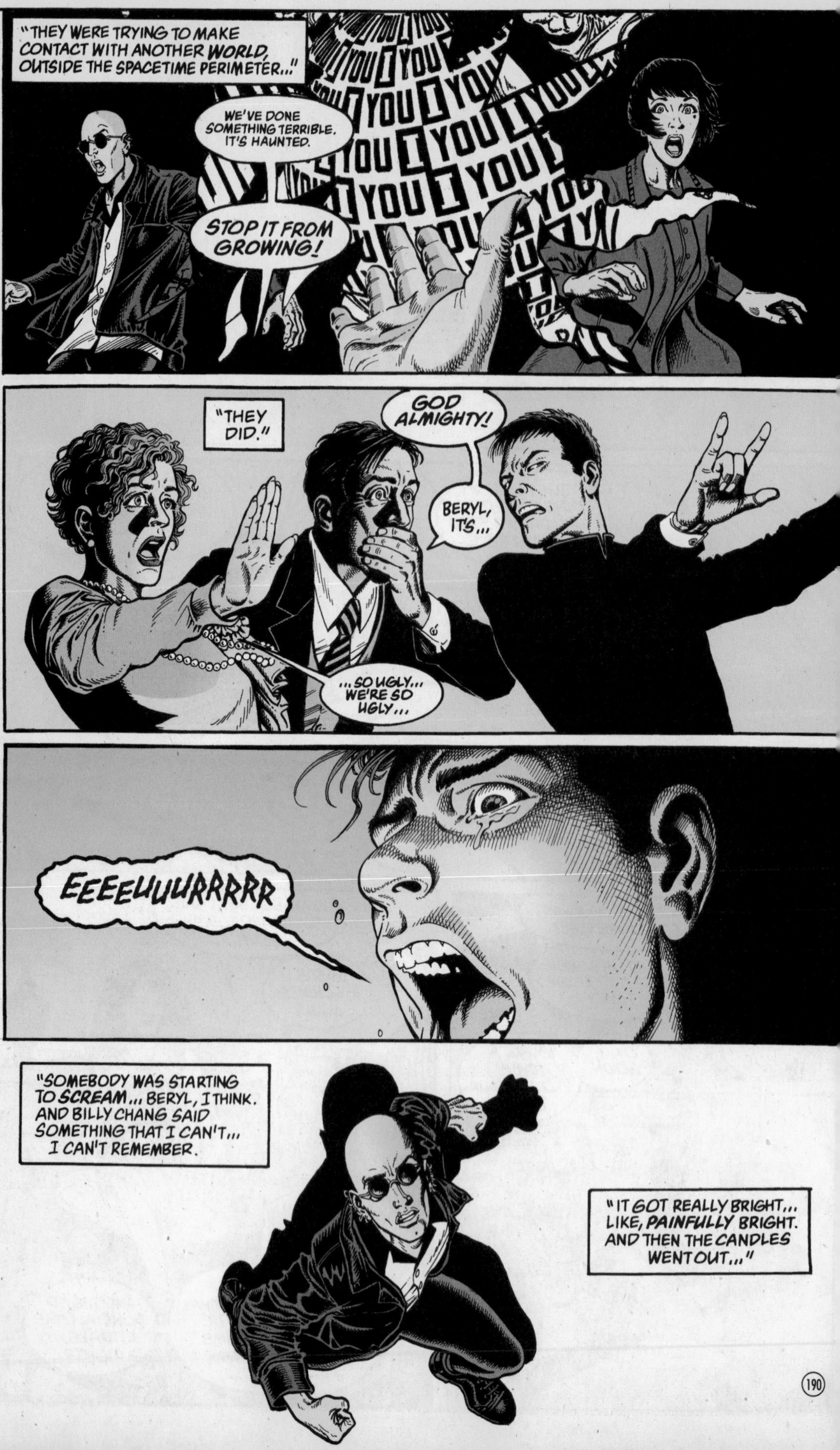
"THEY WERE TRYING TO MAKE CONTACT WITH ANOTHER WORLD, OUTSIDE THE SPACETIME PERIMETER..."
WE'VE DONE SOMETHING TERRIBLE. IT'S HAUNTED.
STOP IT FROM GROWING!
"THEY DID."
GOD ALMIGHTY!
BERYL, IT'S...
...SO UGLY... WE'RE SO UGLY...
EEEEUUURRRRR
"SOMEBODY WAS STARTING TO SCREAM... BERYL, I THINK. AND BILLY CHANG SAID SOMETHING THAT I CAN'T... I CAN'T REMEMBER.
"IT GOT REALLY BRIGHT... LIKE, PAINFULLY BRIGHT. AND THEN THE CANDLES WENT OUT..."

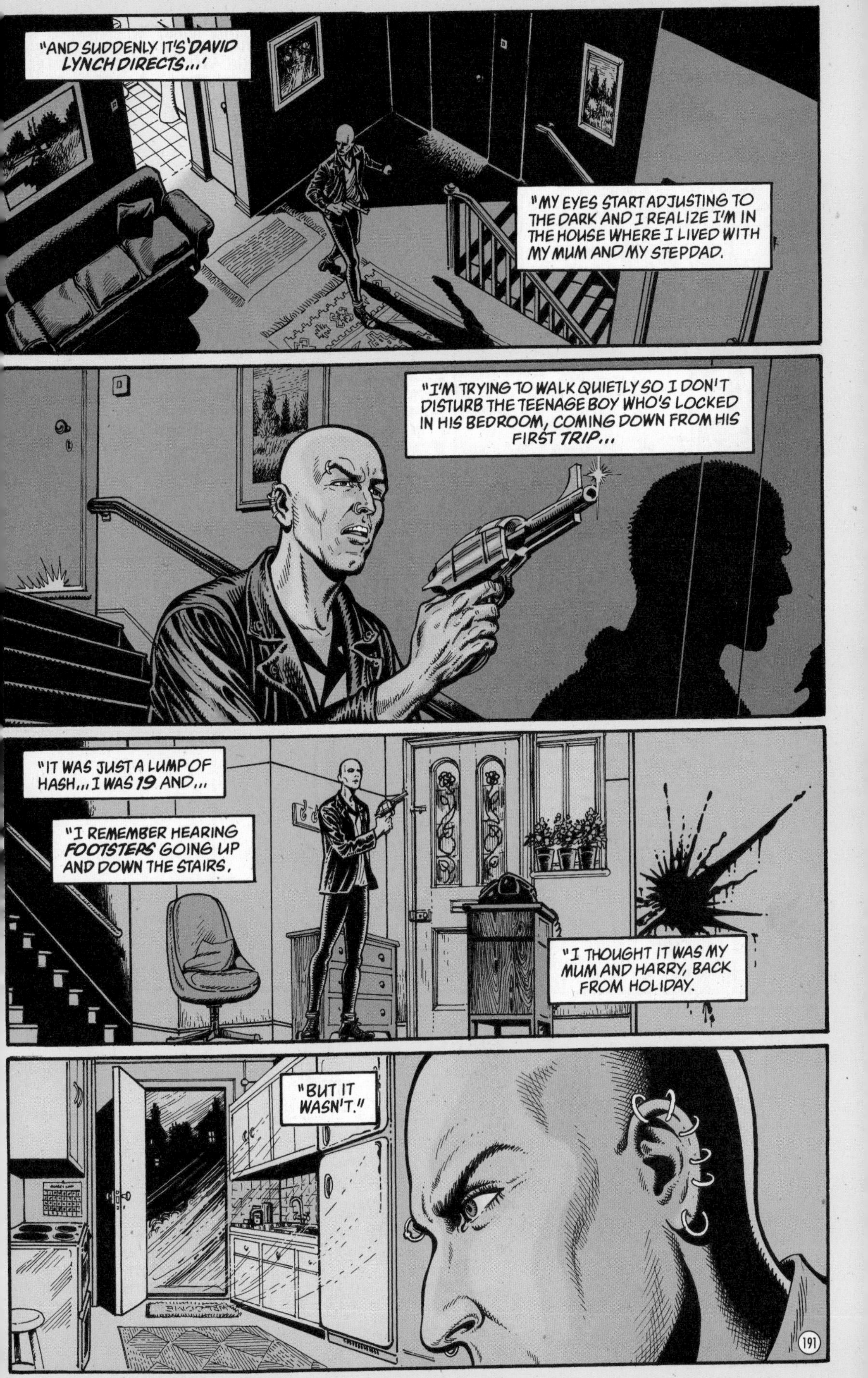
"AND SUDDENLY IT'S 'DAVID LYNCH DIRECTS...'
"MY EYES START ADJUSTING TO THE DARK AND I REALIZE I'M IN THE HOUSE WHERE I LIVED WITH MY MUM AND MY STEPDAD.
"I'M TRYING TO WALK QUIETLY SO I DON'T DISTURB THE TEENAGE BOY WHO'S LOCKED IN HIS BEDROOM, COMING DOWN FROM HIS FIRST TRIP...
"IT WAS JUST A LUMP OF HASH... I WAS 19 AND...
"I REMEMBER HEARING FOOTSTERS GOING UP AND DOWN THE STAIRS.
"I THOUGHT IT WAS MY MUM AND HARRY, BACK FROM HOLIDAY.
"BUT IT WASN'T."

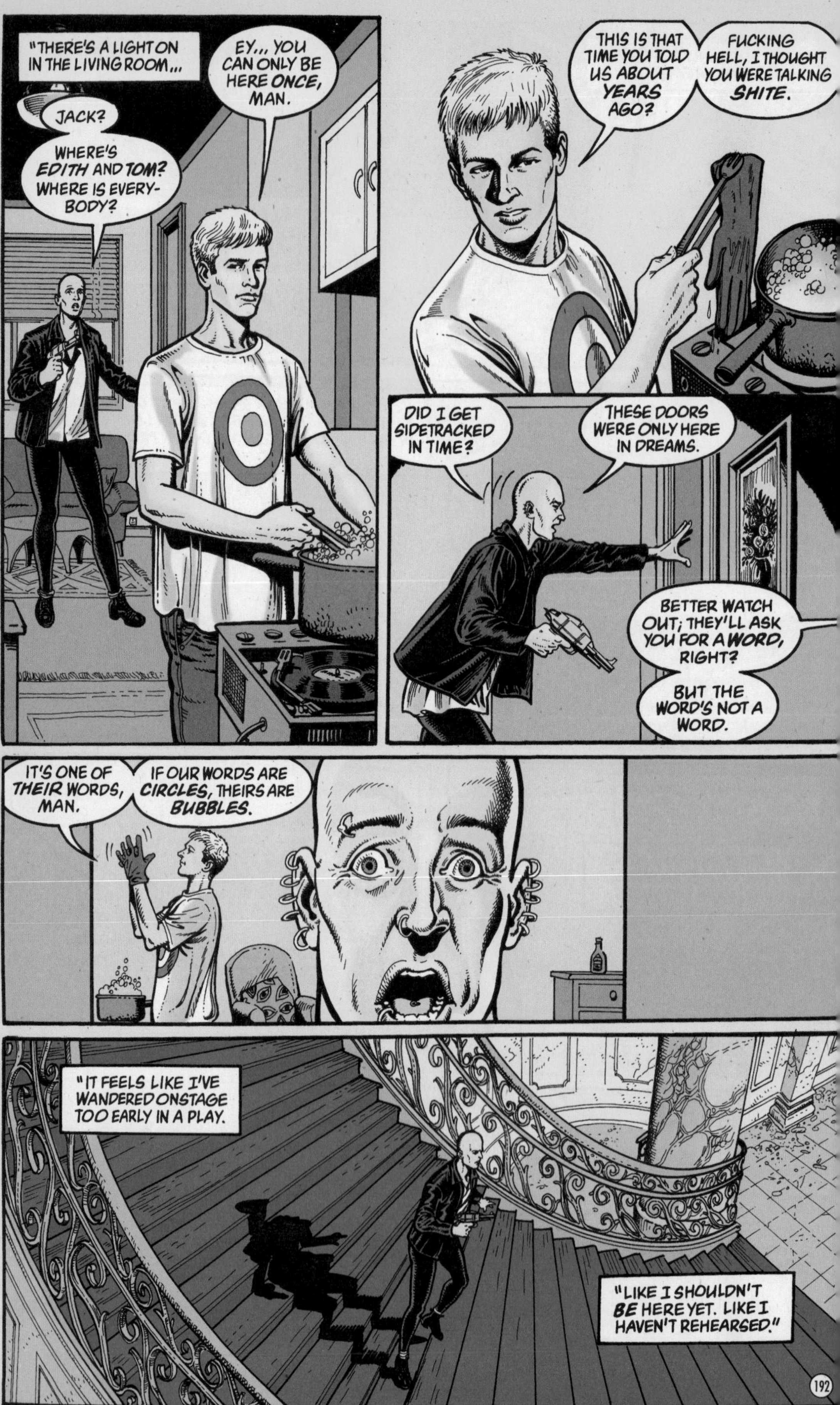
"THERE'S A LIGHT ON IN THE LIVING ROOM...
JACK?
WHERE'S EDITH AND TOM? WHERE IS EVERY-BODY?
EY... YOU CAN ONLY BE HERE ONCE, MAN.
THIS IS THAT TIME YOU TOLD US ABOUT YEARS AGO?
FUCKING HELL, I THOUGHT YOU WERE TALKING SHITE.
DID I GET SIDETRACKED IN TIME?
THESE DOORS WERE ONLY HERE IN DREAMS.
BETTER WATCH OUT; THEY'LL ASK YOU FOR A WORD, RIGHT?
BUT THE WORD'S NOT A WORD.
IT'S ONE OF THEIR WORDS, MAN.
IF OUR WORDS ARE CIRCLES, THEIRS ARE BUBBLES.
"IT FEELS LIKE I'VE WANDERED ONSTAGE TOO EARLY IN A PLAY.
"LIKE I SHOULDN'T BE HERE YET. LIKE I HAVEN'T REHEARSED."

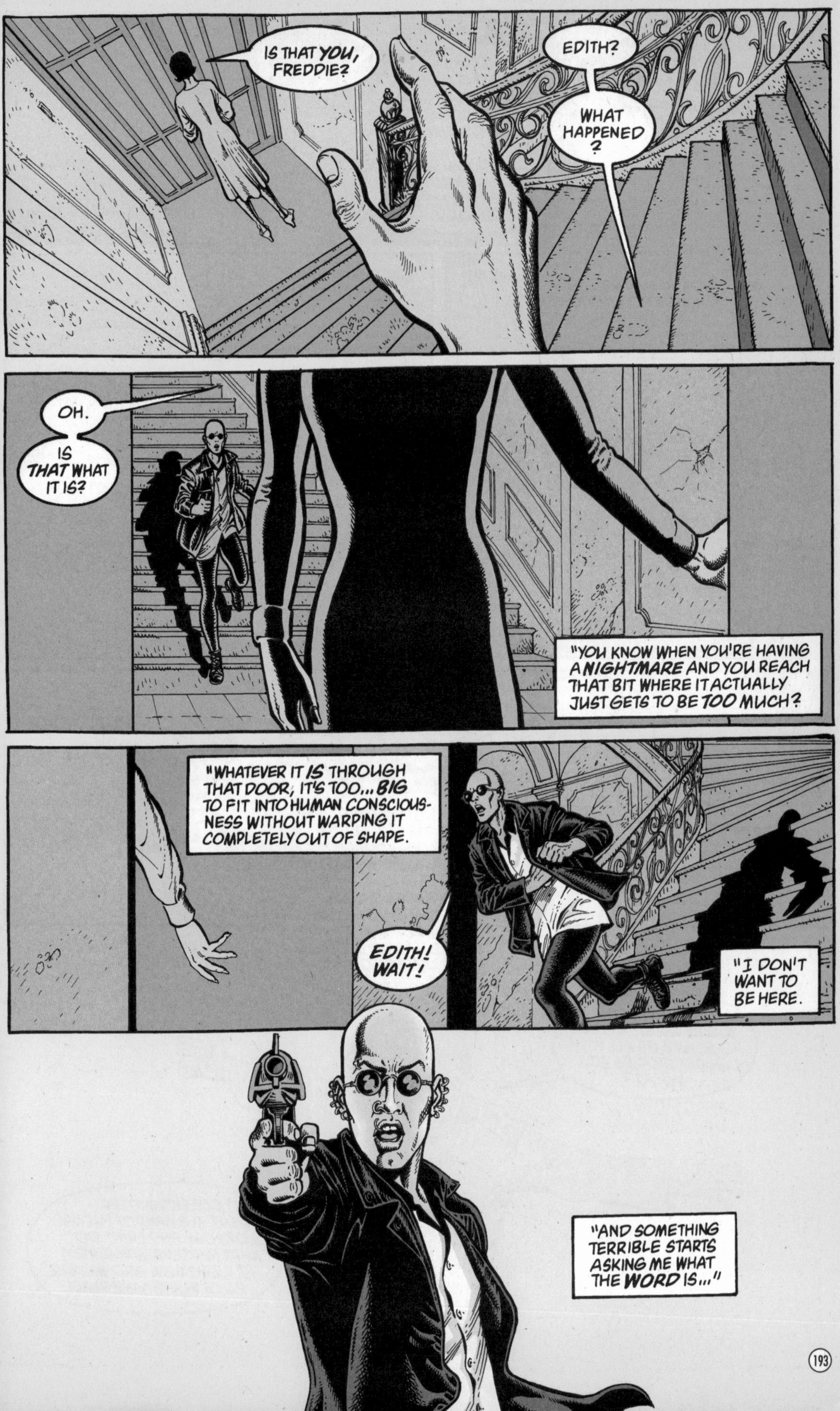
IS THAT YOU, FREDDIE?
EDITH?
WHAT HAPPENED ?
OH.
IS THAT WHAT IT IS?
"YOU KNOW WHEN YOU'RE HAVING A NIGHTMARE AND YOU REACH THAT BIT WHERE IT ACTUALLY JUST GETS TO BE TOO MUCH?
"WHATEVER IT IS THROUGH THAT DOOR, IT'S TOO... BIG TO FIT INTO HUMAN CONSCIOUSNESS WITHOUT WARPING IT COMPLETELY OUT OF SHAPE.
EDITH! WAIT!
"I DON'T WANT TO BE HERE.
"AND SOMETHING TERRIBLE STARTS ASKING ME WHAT THE WORD IS..."

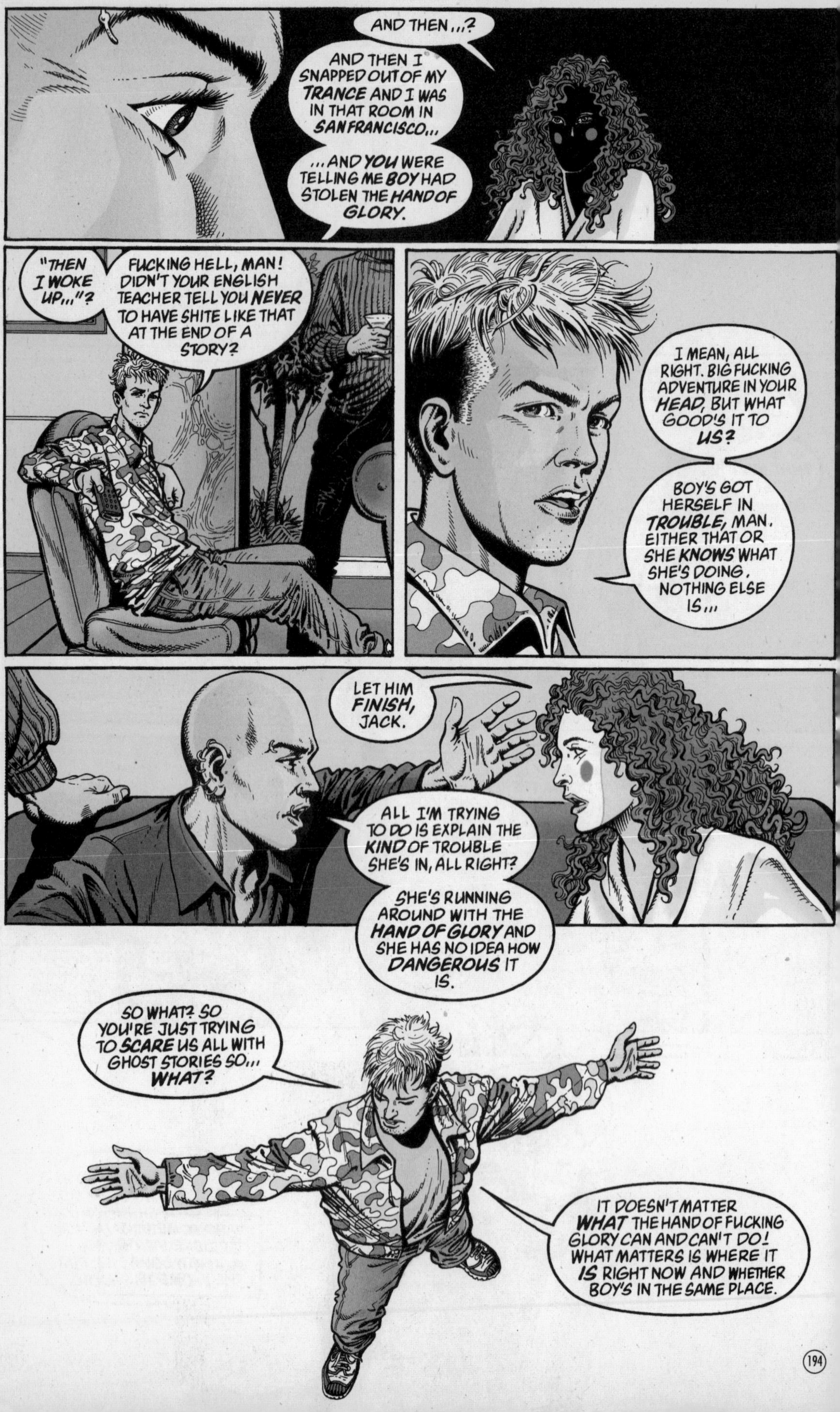
AND THEN...?
AND THEN I SNAPPED OUT OF MY TRANCE AND I WAS IN THAT ROOM IN SAN FRANCISCO...
...AND YOU WERE TELLING ME BOY HAD STOLEN THE HAND OF GLORY.
"THEN I WOKE UP..."?
FUCKING HELL, MAN! DIDN'T YOUR ENGLISH TEACHER TELL YOU NEVER TO HAVE SHITE LIKE THAT AT THE END OF A STORY?
I MEAN, ALL RIGHT. BIG FUCKING ADVENTURE IN YOUR HEAD, BUT WHAT GOOD'S IT TO US?
BOY'S GOT HERSELF IN TROUBLE, MAN. EITHER THAT OR SHE KNOWS WHAT SHE'S DOING. NOTHING ELSE IS...
LET HIM FINISH, JACK.
ALL I'M TRYING TO DO IS EXPLAIN THE KIND OF TROUBLE SHE'S IN, ALL RIGHT?
SHE'S RUNNING AROUND WITH THE HAND OF GLORY AND SHE HAS NO IDEA HOW DANGEROUS IT IS.
SO WHAT? SO YOU'RE JUST TRYING TO SCARE US ALL WITH GHOST STORIES SO... WHAT?
IT DOESN'T MATTER WHAT THE HAND OF FUCKING GLORY CAN AND CAN'T DO! WHAT MATTERS IS WHERE IT IS RIGHT NOW AND WHETHER BOY'S IN THE SAME PLACE.

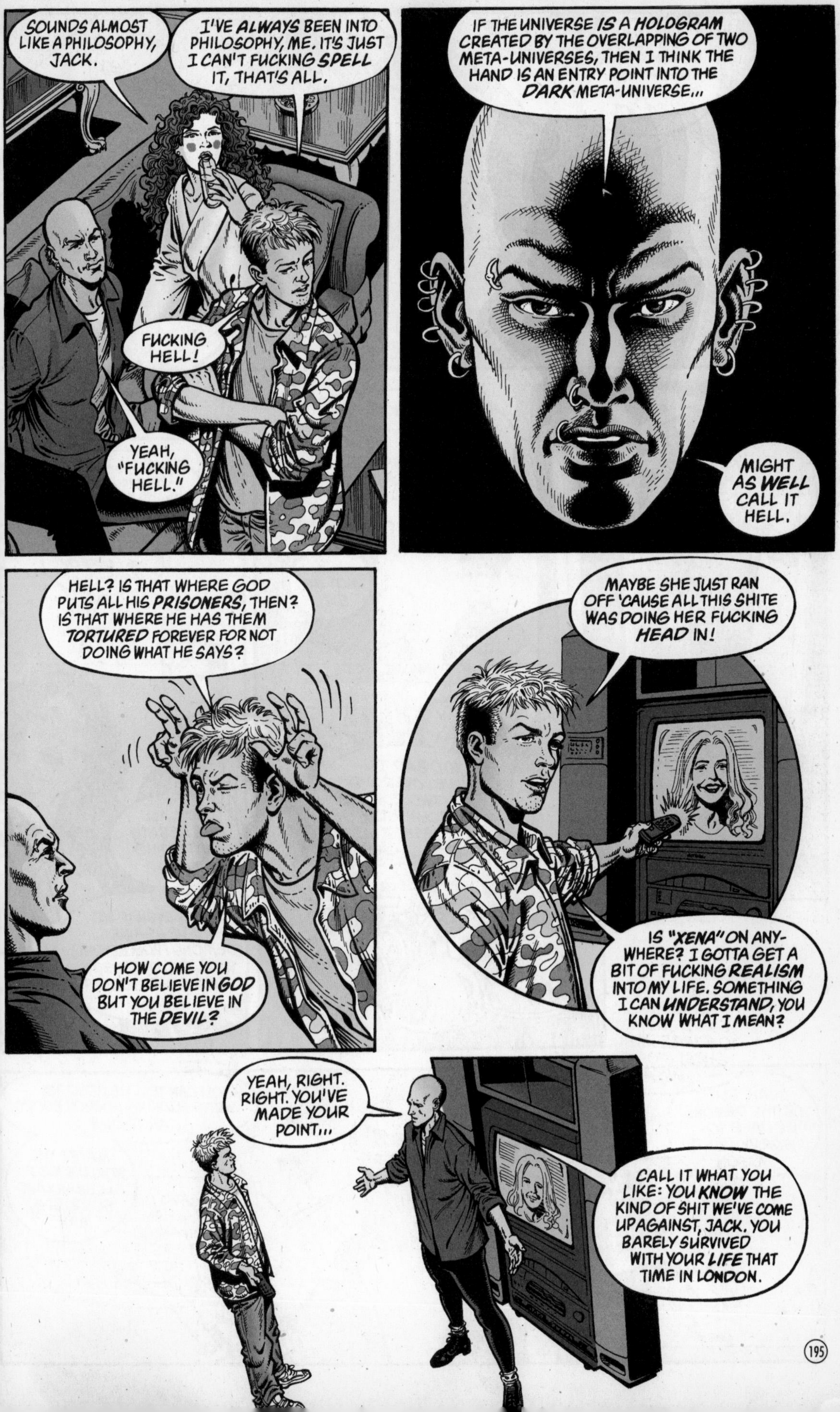
SOUNDS ALMOST LIKE A PHILOSOPHY, JACK.
I'VE ALWAYS BEEN INTO PHILOSOPHY, ME. IT'S JUST I CAN'T FUCKING SPELL IT, THAT'S ALL.
FUCKING HELL!
YEAH, "FUCKING HELL."
IF THE UNIVERSE IS A HOLOGRAM CREATED BY THE OVERLAPPING OF TWO META-UNIVERSES, THEN I THINK THE HAND IS AN ENTRY POINT INTO THE DARK META-UNIVERSE...
MIGHT AS WELL CALL IT HELL.
HELL? IS THAT WHERE GOD PUTS ALL HIS PRISONERS, THEN? IS THAT WHERE HE HAS THEM TORTURED FOREVER FOR NOT DOING WHAT HE SAYS?
HOW COME YOU DON'T BELIEVE IN GOD BUT YOU BELIEVE IN THE DEVIL?
MAYBE SHE JUST RAN OFF 'CAUSE ALL THIS SHITE WAS DOING HER FUCKING HEAD IN!
IS "XENA" ON ANY-WHERE? I GOTTA GET A BIT OF FUCKING REALISM INTO MY LIFE. SOMETHING I CAN UNDERSTAND, YOU KNOW WHAT I MEAN?
YEAH, RIGHT. RIGHT. YOU'VE MADE YOUR POINT...
CALL IT WHAT YOU LIKE: YOU KNOW THE KIND OF SHIT WE'VE COME UP AGAINST, JACK. YOU BARELY SURVIVED WITH YOUR LIFE THAT TIME IN LONDON.

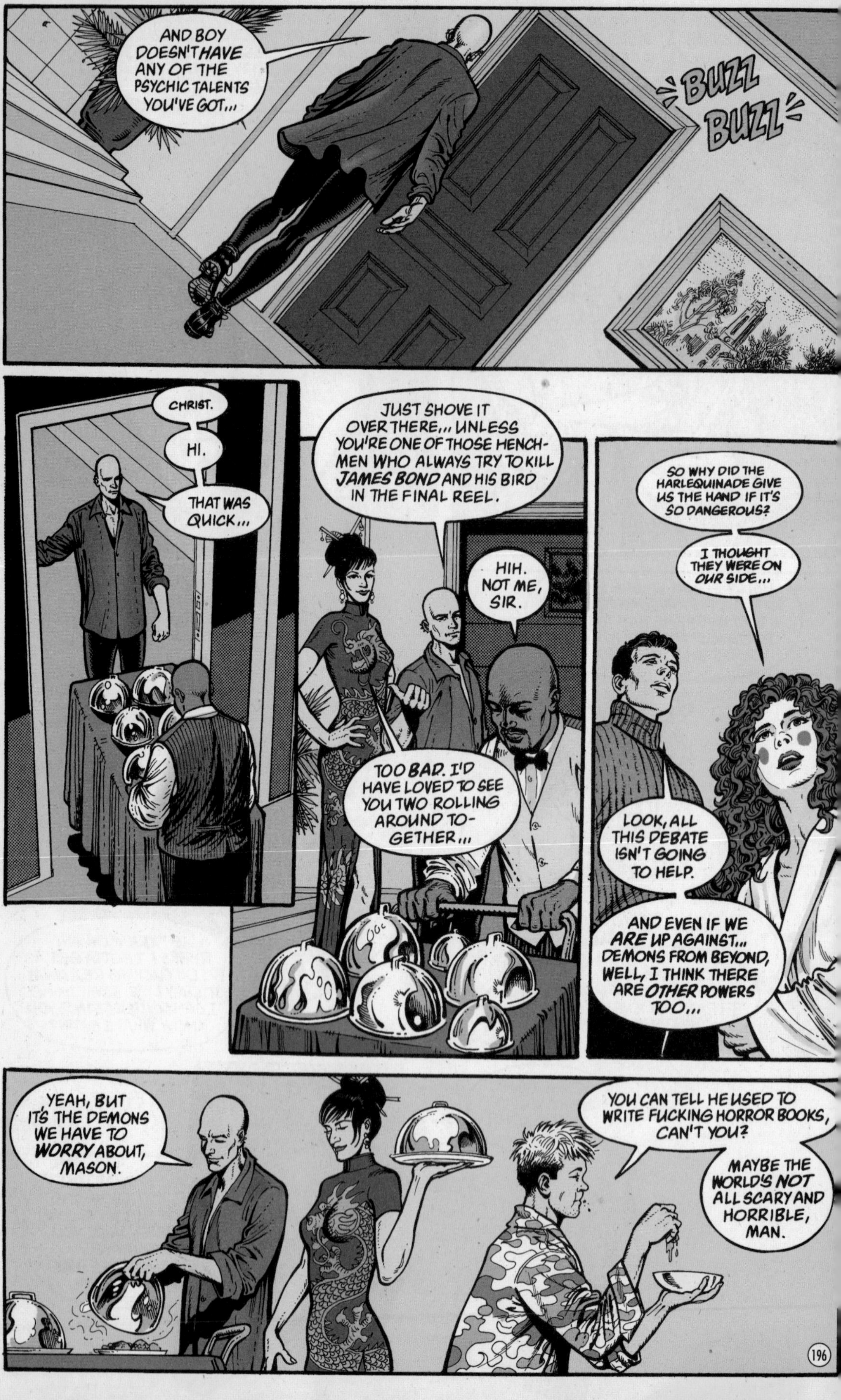
AND BOY DOESN'T HAVE ANY OF THE PSYCHIC TALENTS YOU'VE GOT...
BUZZ BUZZ
CHRIST.
HI.
THAT WAS QUICK...
JUST SHOVE IT OVER THERE... UNLESS YOU'RE ONE OF THOSE HENCH-MEN WHO ALWAYS TRY TO KILL JAMES BOND AND HIS BIRD IN THE FINAL REEL.
HIH. NOT ME, SIR.
TOO BAD. I'D HAVE LOVED TO SEE YOU TWO ROLLING AROUND TO-GETHER...
SO WHY DID THE HARLEQUINADE GIVE US THE HAND IF IT'S SO DANGEROUS?
I THOUGHT THEY WERE ON OUR SIDE...
LOOK, ALL THIS DEBATE ISN'T GOING TO HELP.
AND EVEN IF WE ARE UP AGAINST... DEMONS FROM BEYOND, WELL, I THINK THERE ARE OTHER POWERS TOO...
YEAH, BUT IT'S THE DEMONS WE HAVE TO WORRY ABOUT, MASON.
YOU CAN TELL HE USED TO WRITE FUCKING HORROR BOOKS, CAN'T YOU?
MAYBE THE WORLD'S NOT ALL SCARY AND HORRIBLE, MAN.

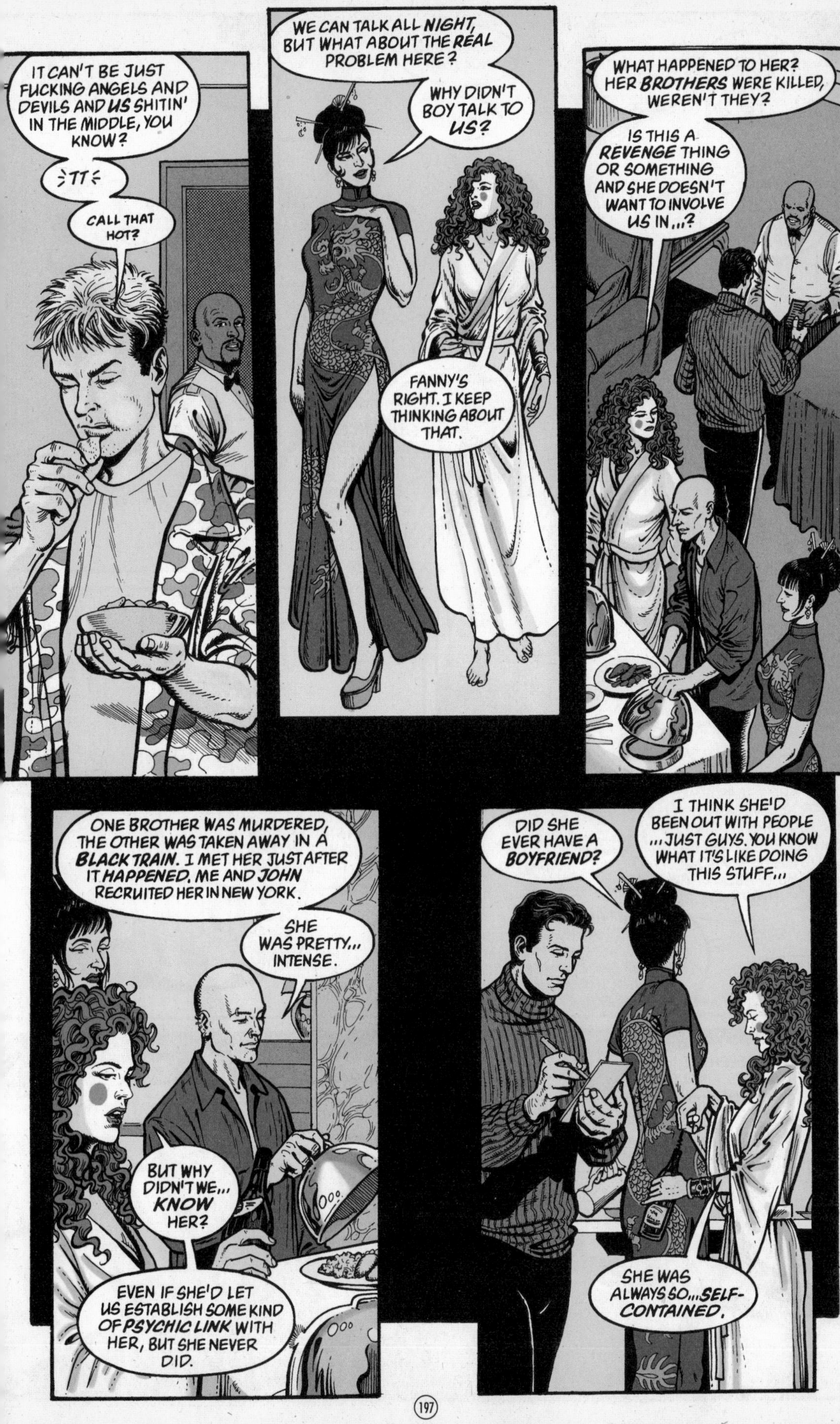
IT CAN'T BE JUST FUCKING ANGELS AND DEVILS AND US SHITIN' IN THE MIDDLE, YOU KNOW?
TT
CALL THAT HOT?
WE CAN TALK ALL NIGHT, BUT WHAT ABOUT THE REAL PROBLEM HERE?
WHY DIDN'T BOY TALK TO US?
FANNY'S RIGHT. I KEEP THINKING ABOUT THAT.
WHAT HAPPENED TO HER? HER BROTHERS WERE KILLED, WEREN'T THEY?
IS THIS A REVENGE THING OR SOMETHING AND SHE DOESN'T WANT TO INVOLVE US IN...?
ONE BROTHER WAS MURDERED, THE OTHER WAS TAKEN AWAY IN A BLACK TRAIN. I MET HER JUST AFTER IT HAPPENED. ME AND JOHN RECRUITED HER IN NEW YORK.
SHE WAS PRETTY... INTENSE.
BUT WHY DIDN'T WE... KNOW HER?
EVEN IF SHE'D LET US ESTABLISH SOME KIND OF PSYCHIC LINK WITH HER, BUT SHE NEVER DID.
DID SHE EVER HAVE A BOYFRIEND?
I THINK SHE'D BEEN OUT WITH PEOPLE ...JUST GUYS. YOU KNOW WHAT IT'S LIKE DOING THIS STUFF...
SHE WAS ALWAYS SO... SELF-CONTAINED.

UH...
THANKS.

...

ARE YOU GUYS A ROCK BAND?

SOMETHING LIKE THAT.

THANKS.

ALL RIGHT!

GUYS NEED ANYTHING, JUST CALL.

OKAY, LET'S GO BACK TO BASICS...

SHE'S SEARCHING FOR SOME KIND OF U.S. MILITARY INTERNMENT CAMP, BECAUSE MAYBE SHE'S HEARD SOMETHING ABOUT HER BROTHER...

...AND SHE KNOWS THE HAND HAS WEIRD, WITCHY POWERS, SO SHE'S PROBABLY THINKING SHE CAN USE IT TO GET HER THROUGH CAMP SECURITY.

BUT SOMETHING HAPPENS: WE KNOW SHE WAS IN THAT APARTMENT WHEN THE KID'S GHETTO BLASTER GOT SMASHED, RIGHT? BUT HE DIDN'T SEE IT...

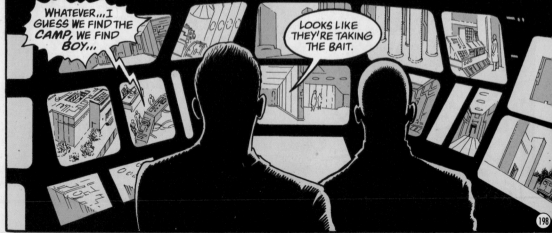

WHATEVER...I GUESS WE FIND THE CAMP, WE FIND BOY...

LOOKS LIKE THEY'RE TAKING THE BAIT.

198

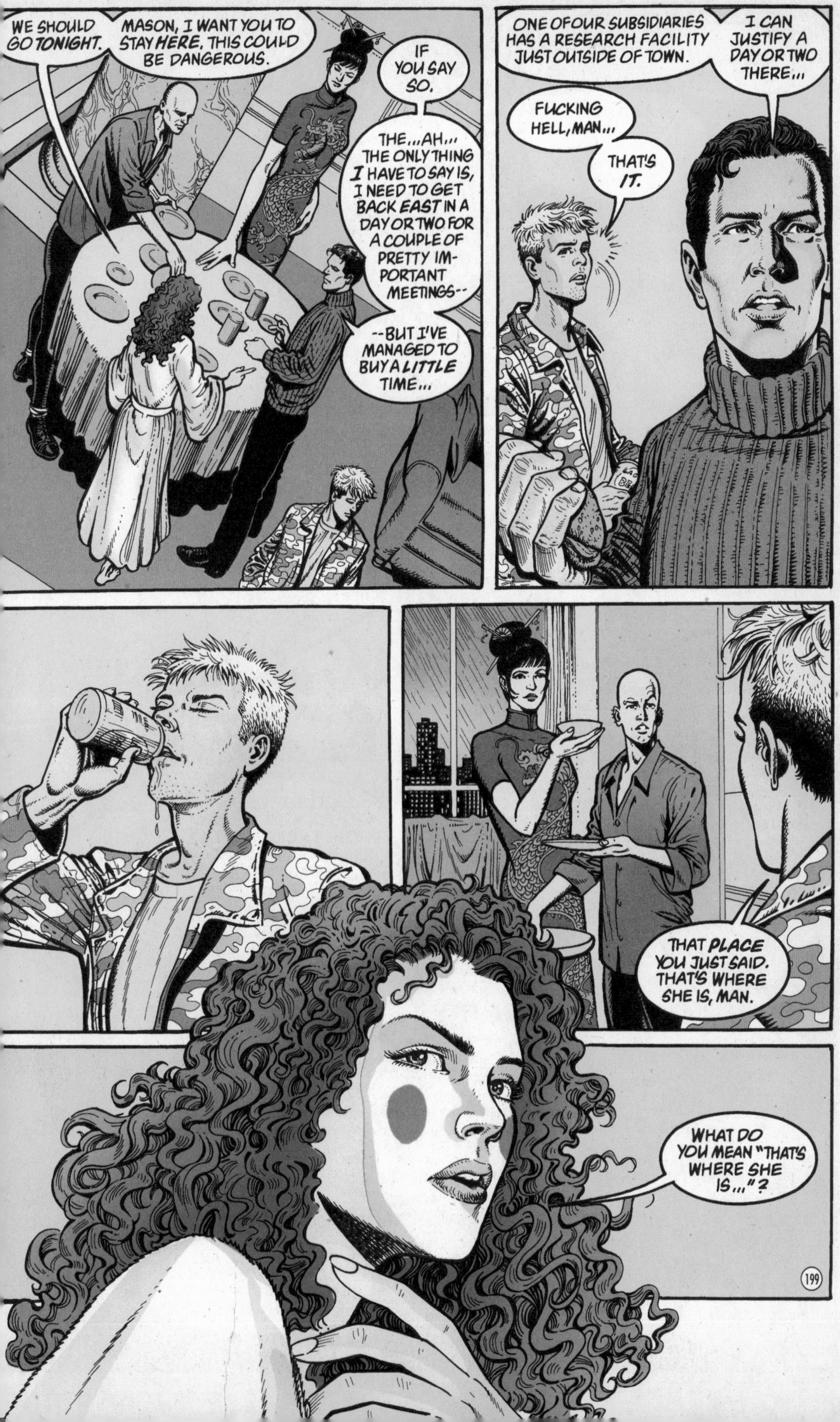
WE SHOULD GO TONIGHT.
MASON, I WANT YOU TO STAY HERE. THIS COULD BE DANGEROUS.
IF YOU SAY SO.
THE...AH... THE ONLY THING I HAVE TO SAY IS, I NEED TO GET BACK EAST IN A DAY OR TWO FOR A COUPLE OF PRETTY IMPORTANT MEETINGS--
--BUT I'VE MANAGED TO BUY A LITTLE TIME...
ONE OF OUR SUBSIDIARIES HAS A RESEARCH FACILITY JUST OUTSIDE OF TOWN.
I CAN JUSTIFY A DAY OR TWO THERE...
FUCKING HELL, MAN...
THAT'S IT.
THAT PLACE YOU JUST SAID. THAT'S WHERE SHE IS, MAN.
WHAT DO YOU MEAN "THAT'S WHERE SHE IS..."?

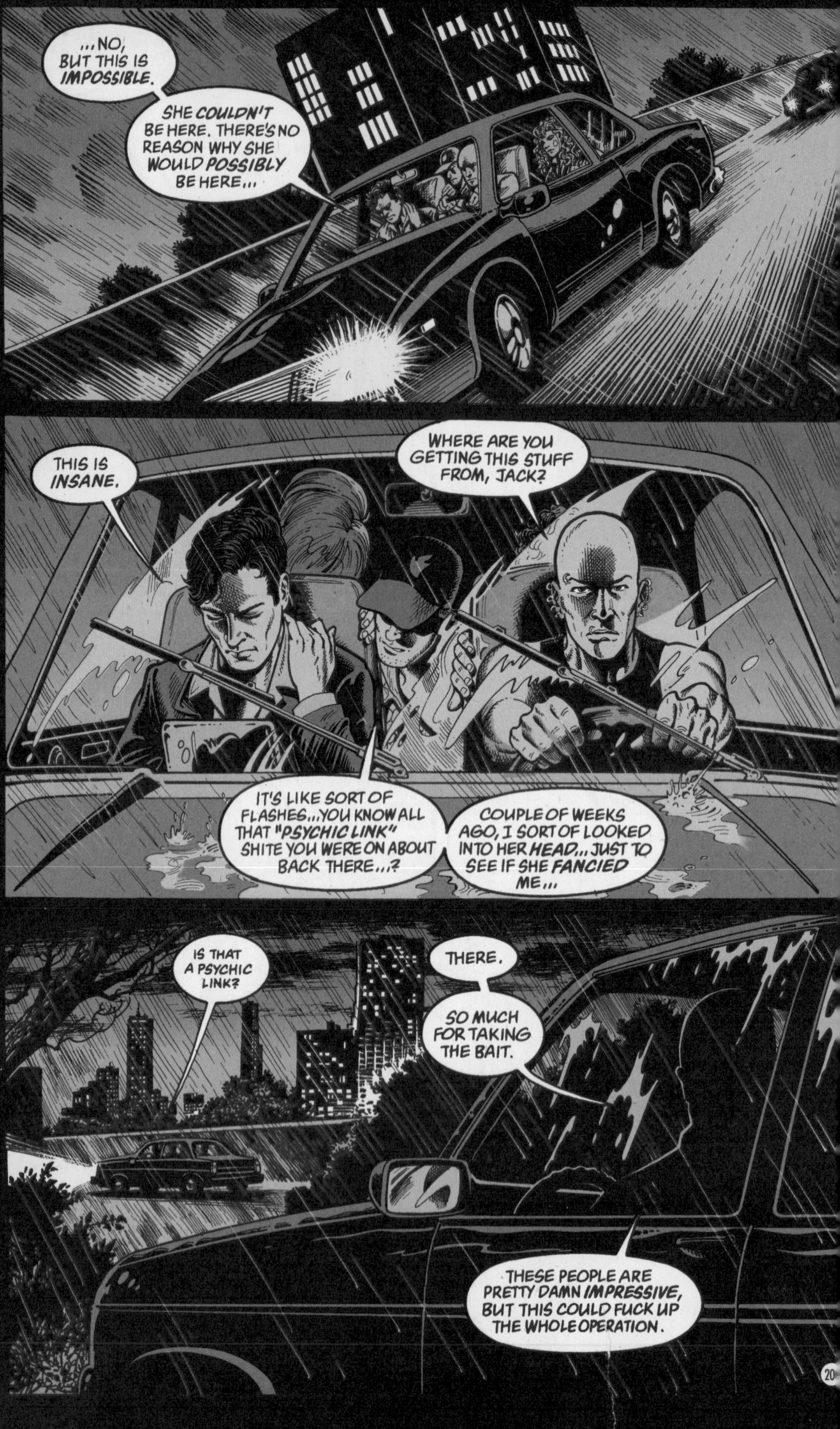
...NO, BUT THIS IS IMPOSSIBLE.
SHE COULDN'T BE HERE. THERE'S NO REASON WHY SHE WOULD POSSIBLY BE HERE...
THIS IS INSANE.
WHERE ARE YOU GETTING THIS STUFF FROM, JACK?
IT'S LIKE SORT OF FLASHES... YOU KNOW ALL THAT "PSYCHIC LINK" SHITE YOU WERE ON ABOUT BACK THERE...?
COUPLE OF WEEKS AGO, I SORT OF LOOKED INTO HER HEAD... JUST TO SEE IF SHE FANCIED ME...
IS THAT A PSYCHIC LINK?
THERE.
SO MUCH FOR TAKING THE BAIT.
THESE PEOPLE ARE PRETTY DAMN IMPRESSIVE, BUT THIS COULD FUCK UP THE WHOLE OPERATION.

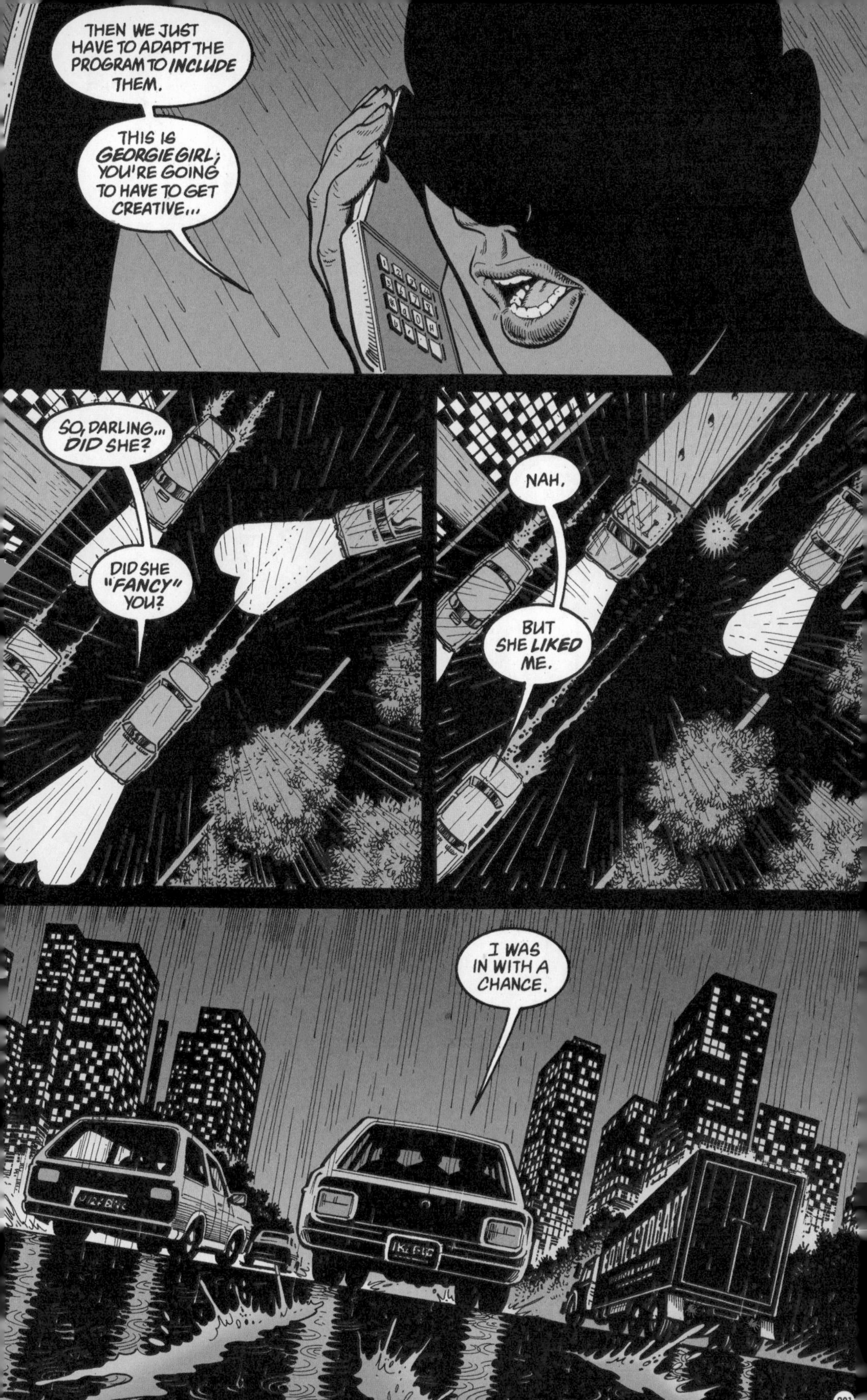
THEN WE JUST HAVE TO ADAPT THE PROGRAM TO INCLUDE THEM.
THIS IS GEORGIE GIRL; YOU'RE GOING TO HAVE TO GET CREATIVE...
SO, DARLING... DID SHE?
DID SHE "FANCY" YOU?
NAH.
BUT SHE LIKED ME.
I WAS IN WITH A CHANCE.
EDDIE STOBART

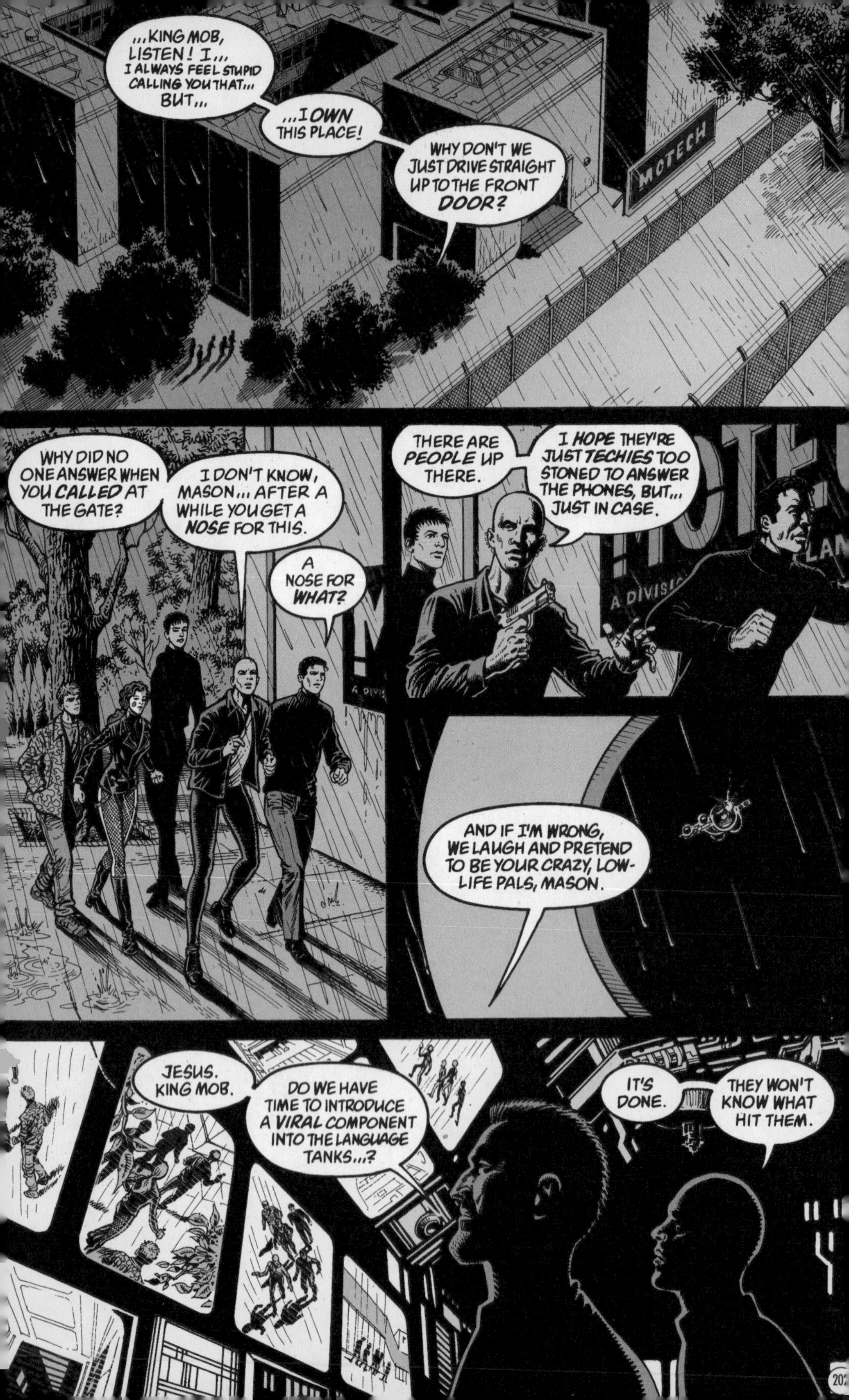
...KING MOB, LISTEN! I... I ALWAYS FEEL STUPID CALLING YOU THAT... BUT...
...I OWN THIS PLACE!
WHY DON'T WE JUST DRIVE STRAIGHT UP TO THE FRONT DOOR?
MOTECH
WHY DID NO ONE ANSWER WHEN YOU CALLED AT THE GATE?
I DON'T KNOW, MASON... AFTER A WHILE YOU GET A NOSE FOR THIS.
A NOSE FOR WHAT?
THERE ARE PEOPLE UP THERE.
I HOPE THEY'RE JUST TECHIES TOO STONED TO ANSWER THE PHONES, BUT... JUST IN CASE.
A DIVISI
AND IF I'M WRONG, WE LAUGH AND PRETEND TO BE YOUR CRAZY, LOW-LIFE PALS, MASON.
JESUS. KING MOB.
DO WE HAVE TIME TO INTRODUCE A VIRAL COMPONENT INTO THE LANGUAGE TANKS...?
IT'S DONE.
THEY WON'T KNOW WHAT HIT THEM.

MISTRESS.

WELCOME TO *DIS*.

DIS?

HER RECALL'S DOWN, HER SPINAL INTERFACE IS STILL IN SHOCK.

OUR QUOTAS ARE STILL GOOD HERE, MISTRESS; EXTERMINATION AND CONVERSION PROGRAMS ARE ALL ON SCHEDULE AND WITHIN BUDGET...

WE'LL BE ALL SET TO BEGIN THE WAR AND SUMMON THE KINGS BY MID-'99...

I'LL TAKE OVER HERE.

MR. KADMON, SIR.

A NEW BATCH OF *MERCHANDISE* IS ALMOST READY FOR RETURN TOMORROW EVENING.

SHOULD BE A QUIET JOURNEY; THEY COME IN *REBELS*, THEY GO HOME WORKING FOR US.

SO THEY *FOUND* YOU?

DO I KNOW YOU?

OF COURSE. PERHAPS THIS WILL HELP RESTORE YOU TO UNITY.

DAVAREES WODP·I·R OD DOIBAIS JAMCMAD.

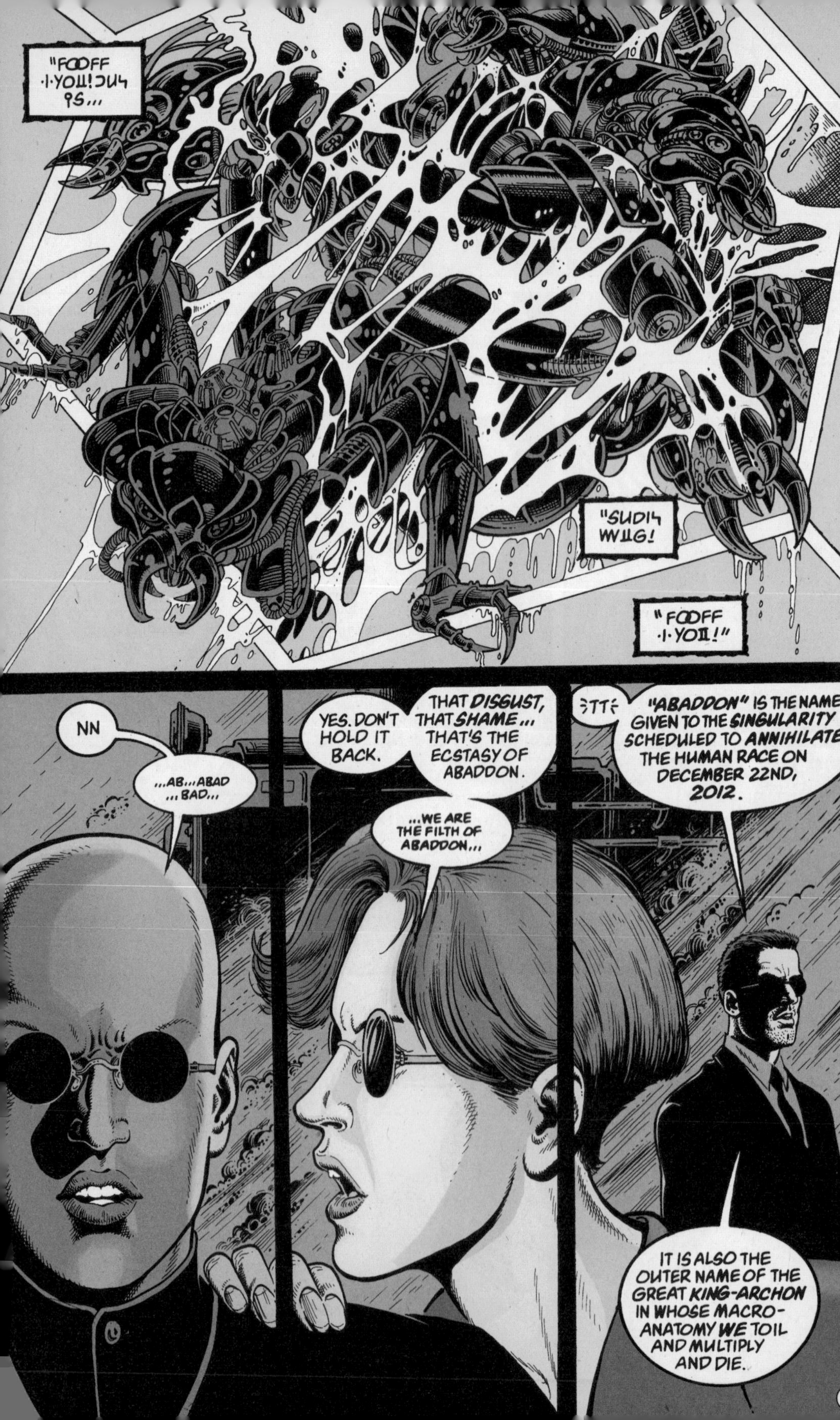

NN
...AB...ABAD ...BAD...
YES. DON'T HOLD IT BACK.
THAT DISGUST, THAT SHAME... THAT'S THE ECSTASY OF ABADDON.
...WE ARE THE FILTH OF ABADDON...
"ABADDON" IS THE NAME GIVEN TO THE SINGULARITY SCHEDULED TO ANNIHILATE THE HUMAN RACE ON DECEMBER 22ND, 2012.
IT IS ALSO THE OUTER NAME OF THE GREAT KING-ARCHON IN WHOSE MACRO-ANATOMY WE TOIL AND MULTIPLY AND DIE.

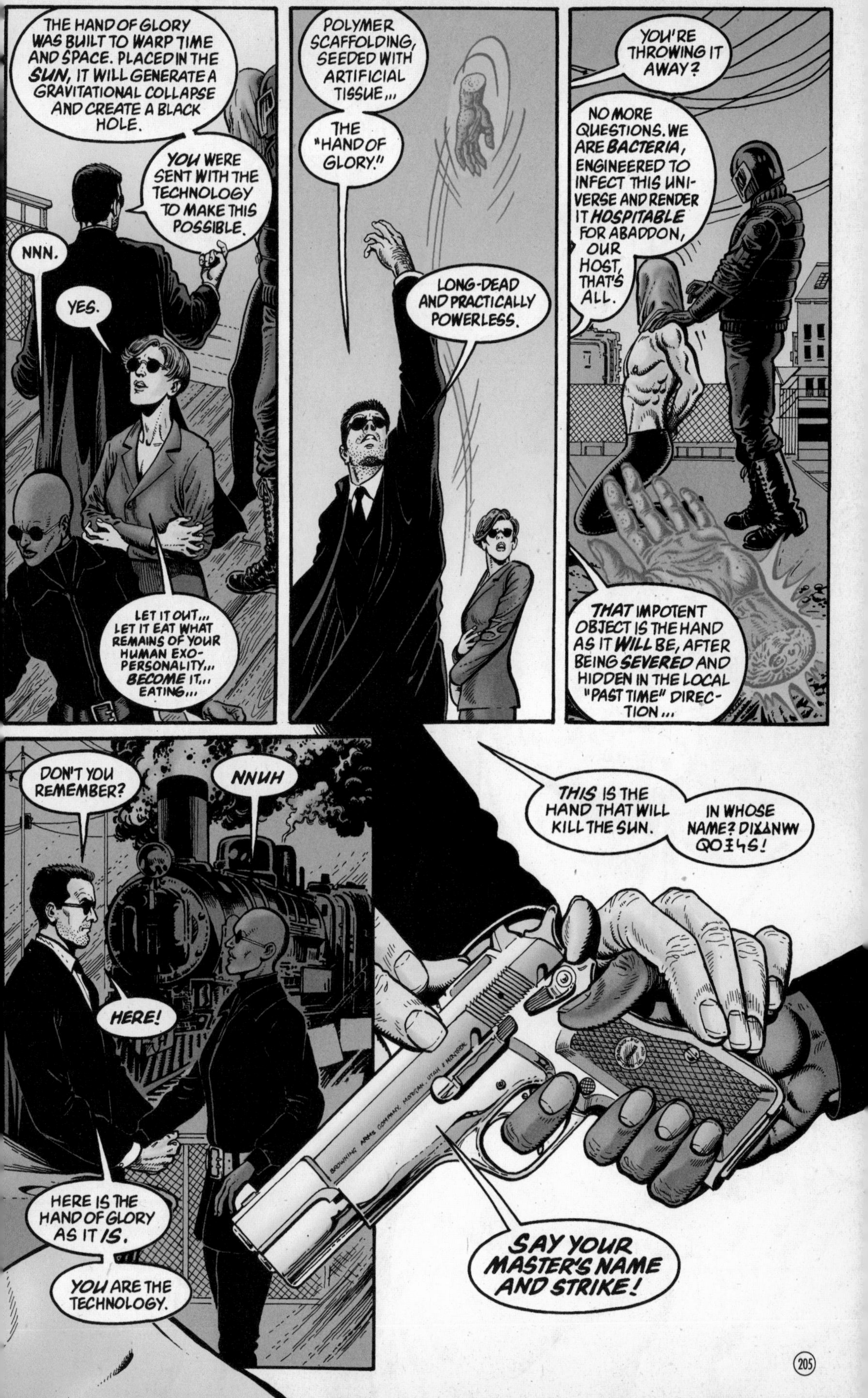
THE HAND OF GLORY WAS BUILT TO WARP TIME AND SPACE. PLACED IN THE SUN, IT WILL GENERATE A GRAVITATIONAL COLLAPSE AND CREATE A BLACK HOLE.
YOU WERE SENT WITH THE TECHNOLOGY TO MAKE THIS POSSIBLE.
NNN.
YES.
LET IT OUT... LET IT EAT WHAT REMAINS OF YOUR HUMAN EXO-PERSONALITY... BECOME IT... EATING...
POLYMER SCAFFOLDING, SEEDED WITH ARTIFICIAL TISSUE...
THE "HAND OF GLORY."
LONG-DEAD AND PRACTICALLY POWERLESS.
YOU'RE THROWING IT AWAY?
NO MORE QUESTIONS. WE ARE BACTERIA, ENGINEERED TO INFECT THIS UNIVERSE AND RENDER IT HOSPITABLE FOR ABADDON, OUR HOST, THAT'S ALL.
THAT IMPOTENT OBJECT IS THE HAND AS IT WILL BE, AFTER BEING SEVERED AND HIDDEN IN THE LOCAL "PAST TIME" DIRECTION...
DON'T YOU REMEMBER?
NNUH
HERE!
HERE IS THE HAND OF GLORY AS IT IS.
YOU ARE THE TECHNOLOGY.
THIS IS THE HAND THAT WILL KILL THE SUN.
IN WHOSE NAME?
SAY YOUR MASTER'S NAME AND STRIKE!

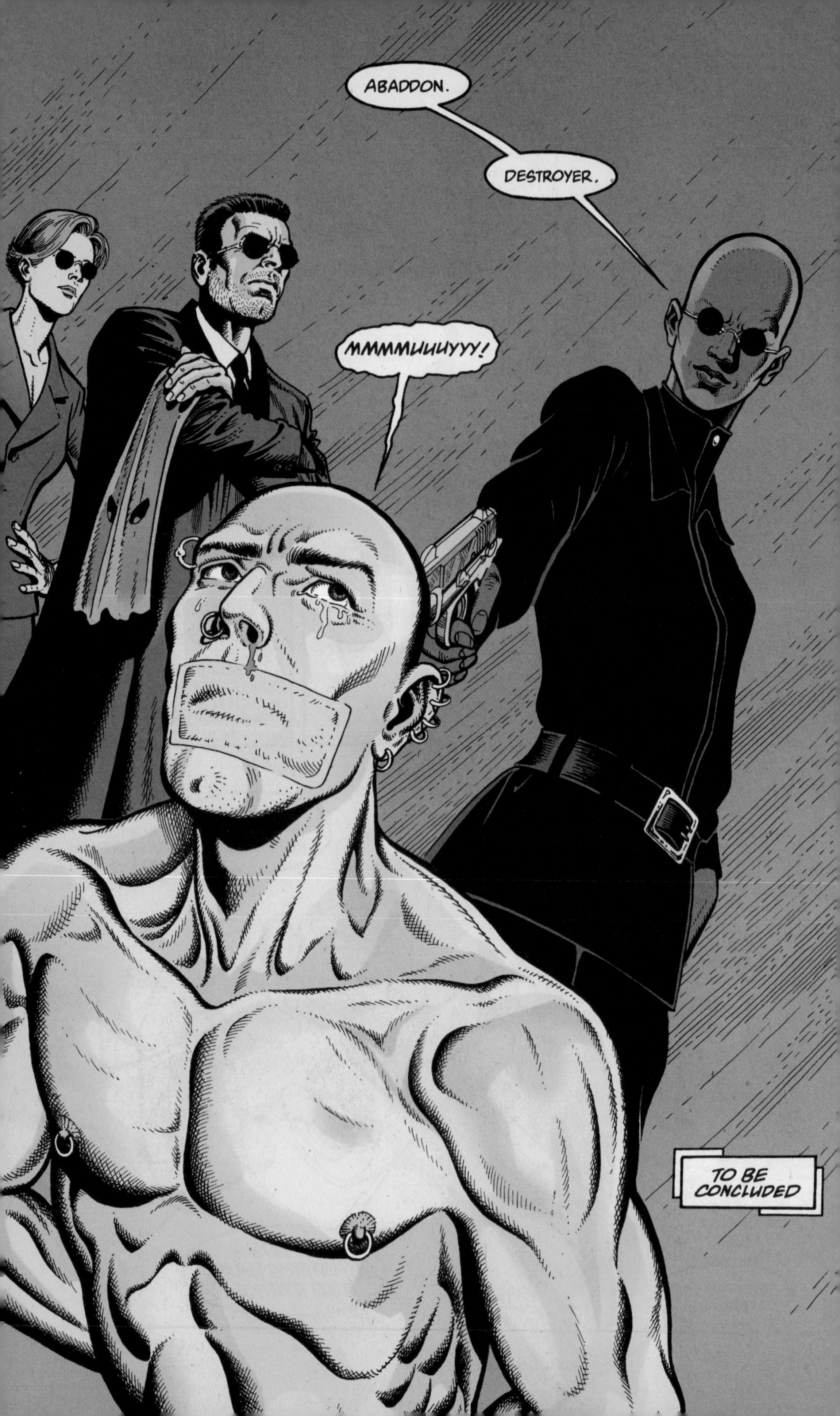
ABADDON.
DESTROYER.
MMMMUUUYYY!
TO BE CONCLUDED

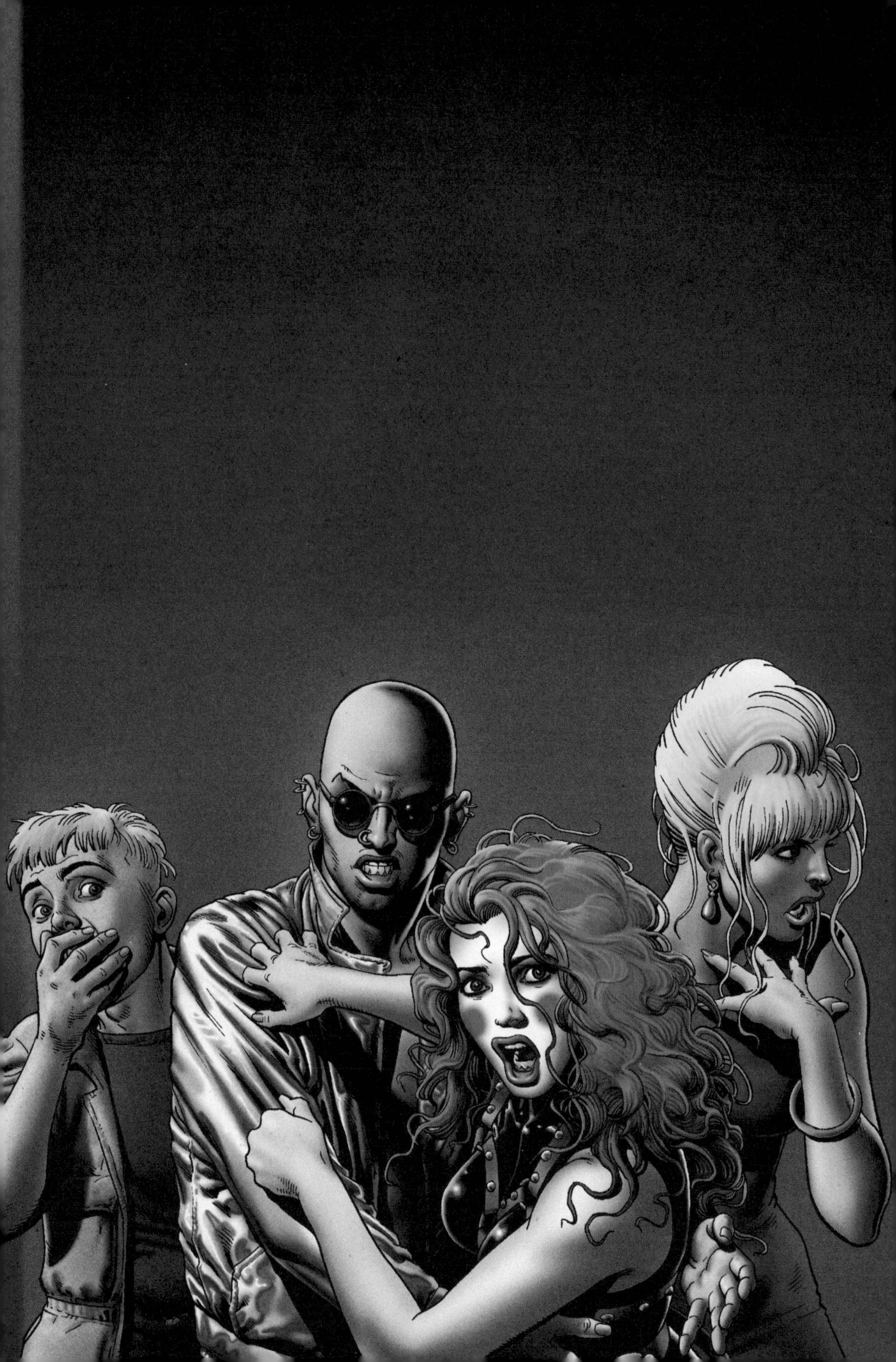

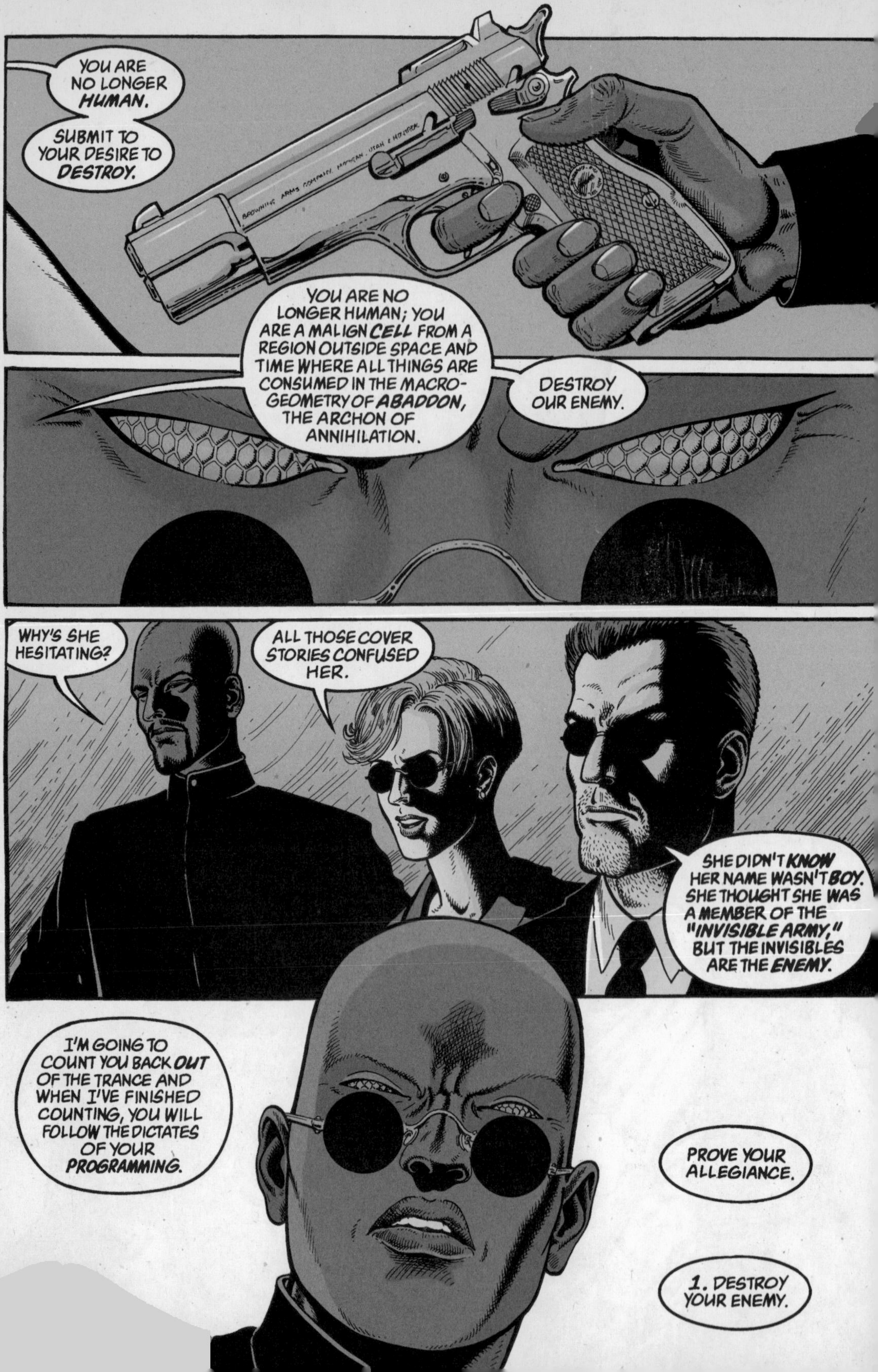

YOU ARE NO LONGER HUMAN.
SUBMIT TO YOUR DESIRE TO DESTROY.
BROWNING ARMS COMPANY, MORGAN, UTAH & MONTREAL
YOU ARE NO LONGER HUMAN; YOU ARE A MALIGN CELL FROM A REGION OUTSIDE SPACE AND TIME WHERE ALL THINGS ARE CONSUMED IN THE MACRO-GEOMETRY OF ABADDON, THE ARCHON OF ANNIHILATION.
DESTROY OUR ENEMY.
WHY'S SHE HESITATING?
ALL THOSE COVER STORIES CONFUSED HER.
SHE DIDN'T KNOW HER NAME WASN'T BOY. SHE THOUGHT SHE WAS A MEMBER OF THE "INVISIBLE ARMY," BUT THE INVISIBLES ARE THE ENEMY.
I'M GOING TO COUNT YOU BACK OUT OF THE TRANCE AND WHEN I'VE FINISHED COUNTING, YOU WILL FOLLOW THE DICTATES OF YOUR PROGRAMMING.
PROVE YOUR ALLEGIANCE.
1. DESTROY YOUR ENEMY.

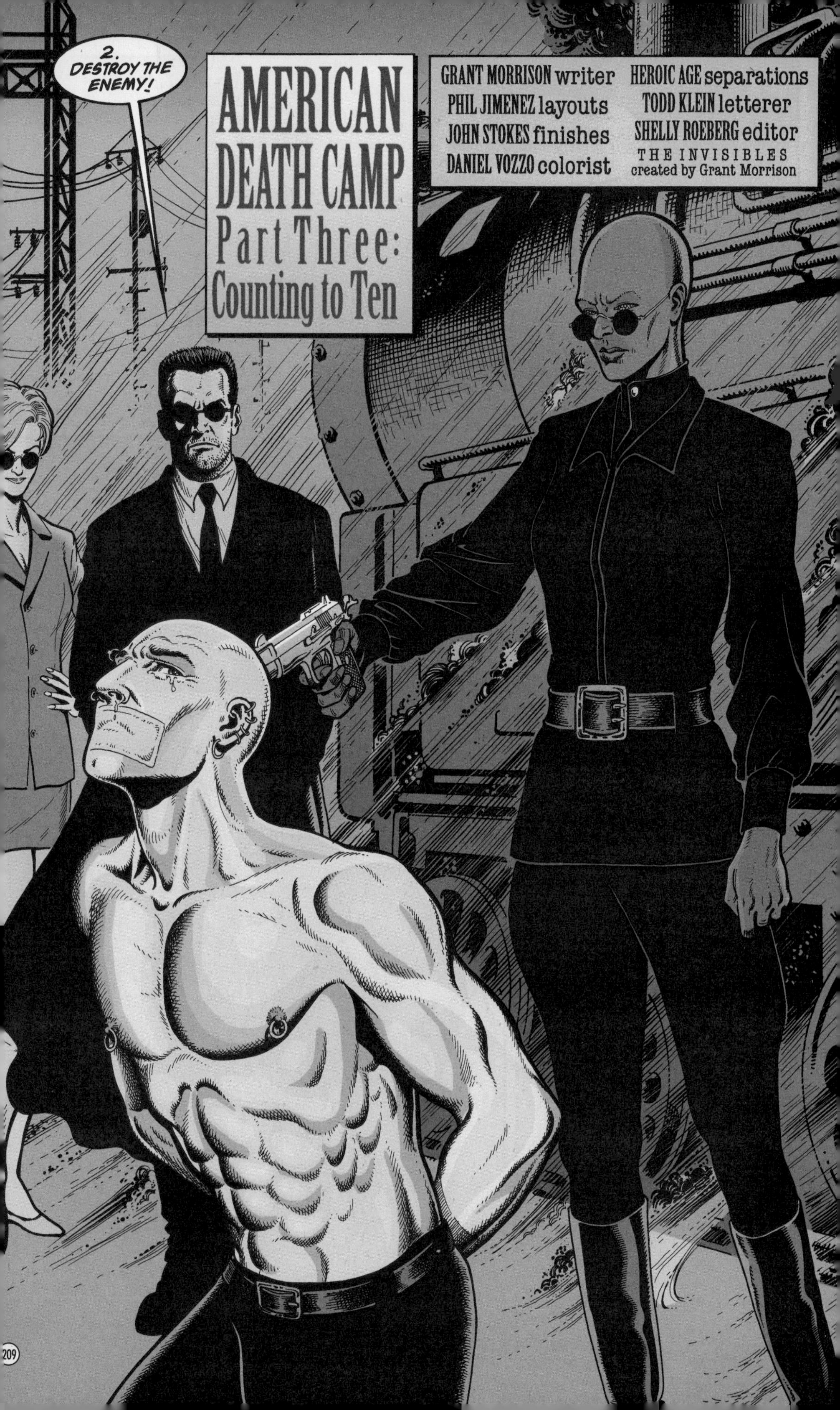

2. DESTROY THE ENEMY!
AMERICAN DEATH CAMP
Part Three: Counting to Ten
GRANT MORRISON writer
PHIL JIMENEZ layouts
JOHN STOKES finishes
DANIEL VOZZO colorist
HEROIC AGE separations
TODD KLEIN letterer
SHELLY ROEBERG editor
THE INVISIBLES created by Grant Morrison

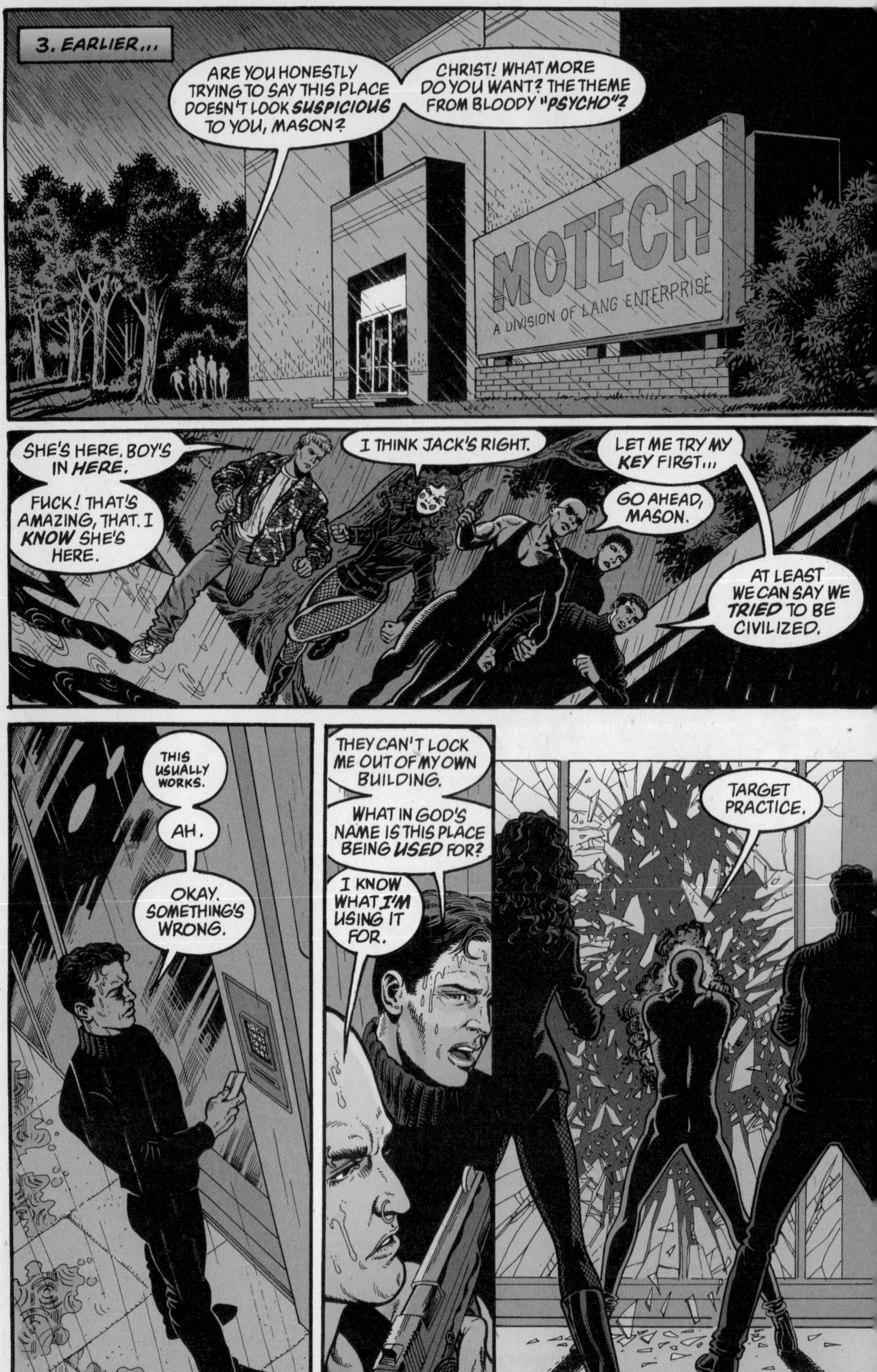
3. EARLIER...
ARE YOU HONESTLY TRYING TO SAY THIS PLACE DOESN'T LOOK SUSPICIOUS TO YOU, MASON?
CHRIST! WHAT MORE DO YOU WANT? THE THEME FROM BLOODY "PSYCHO"?
MOTECH
A DIVISION OF LANG ENTERPRISE
SHE'S HERE. BOY'S IN HERE.
FUCK! THAT'S AMAZING, THAT. I KNOW SHE'S HERE.
I THINK JACK'S RIGHT.
LET ME TRY MY KEY FIRST...
GO AHEAD, MASON.
AT LEAST WE CAN SAY WE TRIED TO BE CIVILIZED.
THIS USUALLY WORKS.
AH.
OKAY. SOMETHING'S WRONG.
THEY CAN'T LOCK ME OUT OF MY OWN BUILDING.
WHAT IN GOD'S NAME IS THIS PLACE BEING USED FOR?
I KNOW WHAT I'M USING IT FOR.
TARGET PRACTICE.

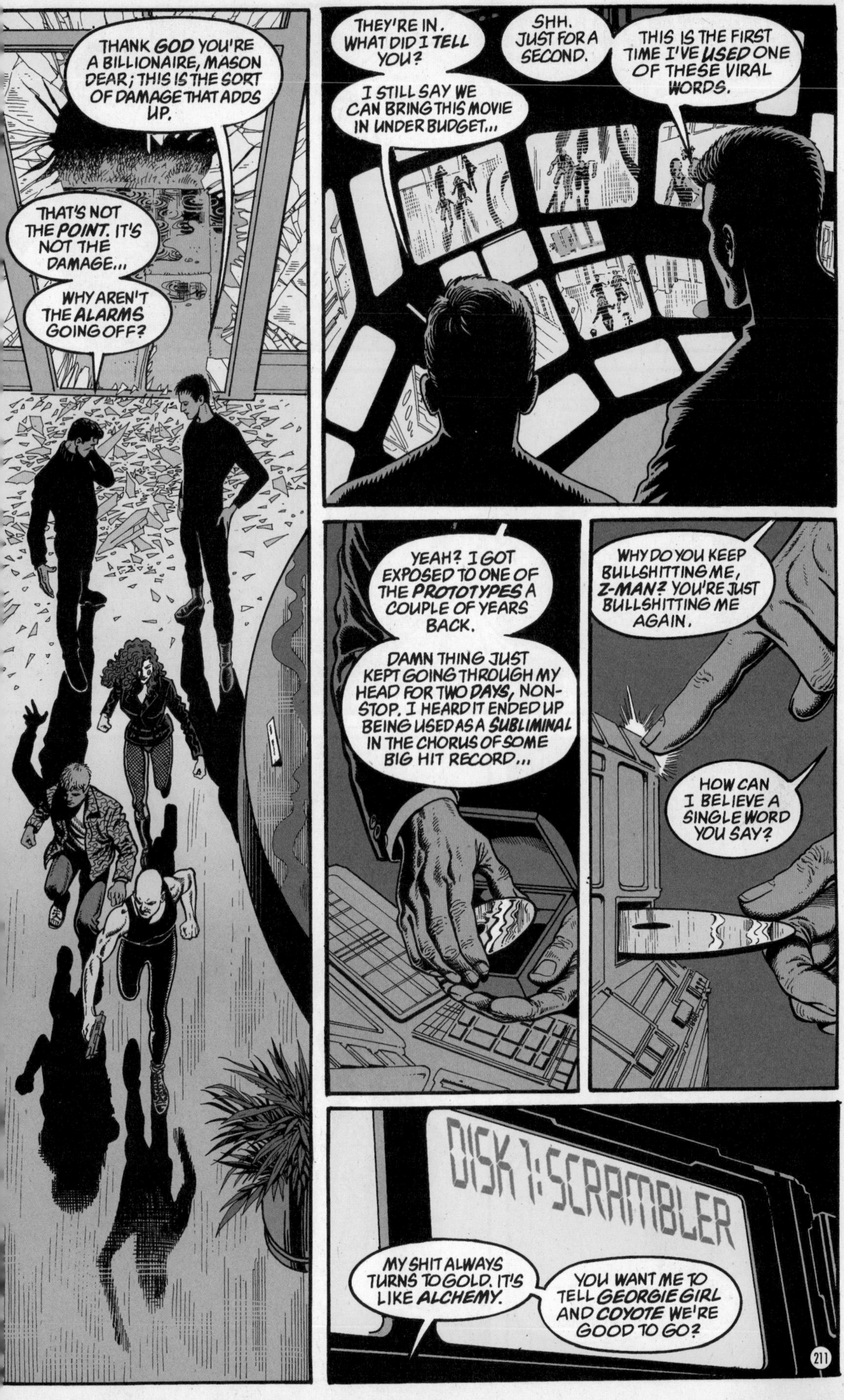
THANK GOD YOU'RE A BILLIONAIRE, MASON DEAR; THIS IS THE SORT OF DAMAGE THAT ADDS UP.
THAT'S NOT THE POINT. IT'S NOT THE DAMAGE...
WHY AREN'T THE ALARMS GOING OFF?
THEY'RE IN. WHAT DID I TELL YOU?
I STILL SAY WE CAN BRING THIS MOVIE IN UNDER BUDGET...
SHH. JUST FOR A SECOND.
THIS IS THE FIRST TIME I'VE USED ONE OF THESE VIRAL WORDS.
YEAH? I GOT EXPOSED TO ONE OF THE PROTOTYPES A COUPLE OF YEARS BACK.
DAMN THING JUST KEPT GOING THROUGH MY HEAD FOR TWO DAYS, NON-STOP. I HEARD IT ENDED UP BEING USED AS A SUBLIMINAL IN THE CHORUS OF SOME BIG HIT RECORD...
WHY DO YOU KEEP BULLSHITTING ME, Z-MAN? YOU'RE JUST BULLSHITTING ME AGAIN.
HOW CAN I BELIEVE A SINGLE WORD YOU SAY?
DISK 1: SCRAMBLER
MY SHIT ALWAYS TURNS TO GOLD. IT'S LIKE ALCHEMY.
YOU WANT ME TO TELL GEORGIE GIRL AND COYOTE WE'RE GOOD TO GO?

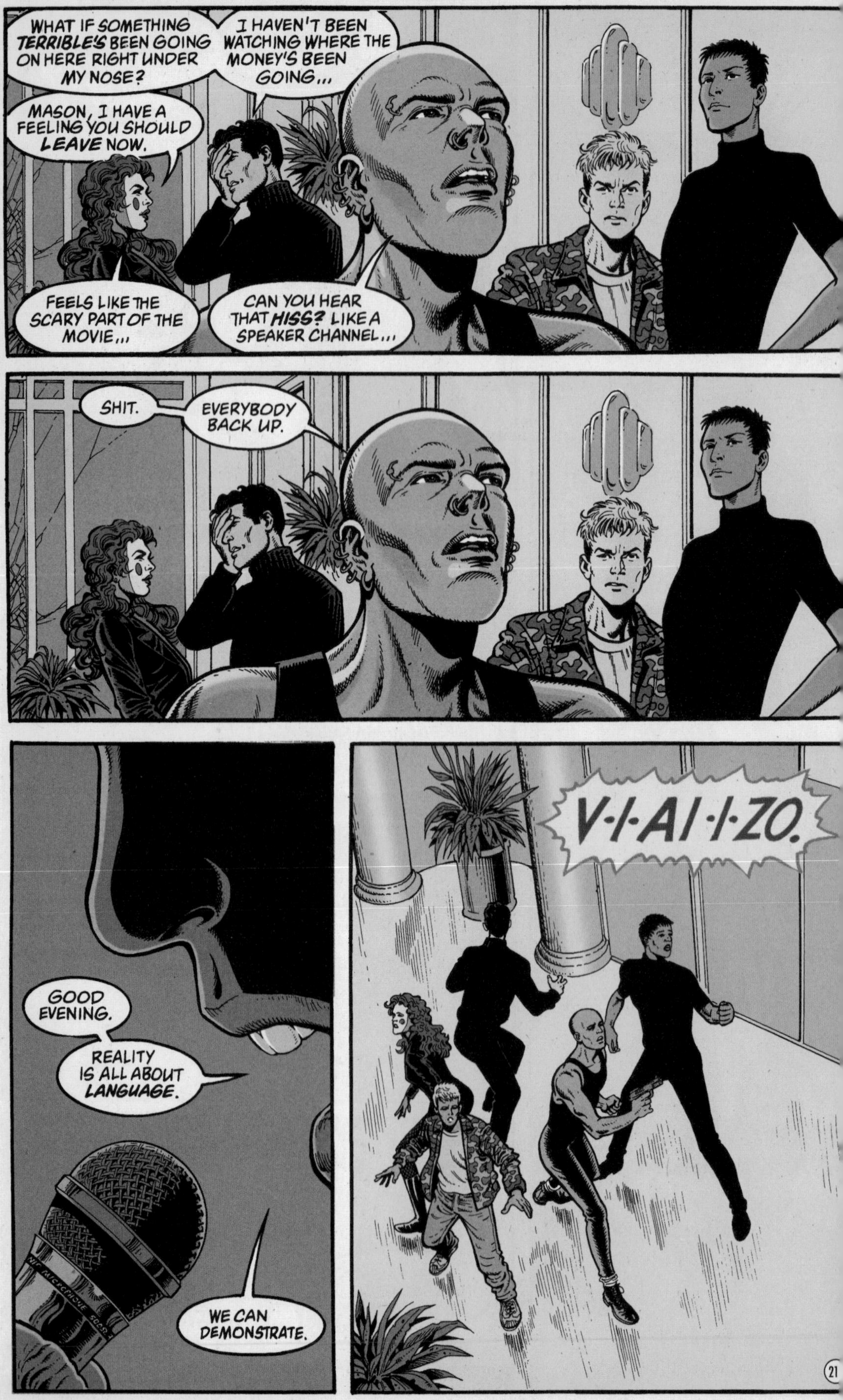
WHAT IF SOMETHING TERRIBLE'S BEEN GOING ON HERE RIGHT UNDER MY NOSE?
I HAVEN'T BEEN WATCHING WHERE THE MONEY'S BEEN GOING...
MASON, I HAVE A FEELING YOU SHOULD LEAVE NOW.
FEELS LIKE THE SCARY PART OF THE MOVIE...
CAN YOU HEAR THAT HISS? LIKE A SPEAKER CHANNEL...
SHIT.
EVERYBODY BACK UP.
GOOD EVENING.
REALITY IS ALL ABOUT LANGUAGE.
WE CAN DEMONSTRATE.
V-I-AI-I-ZO.

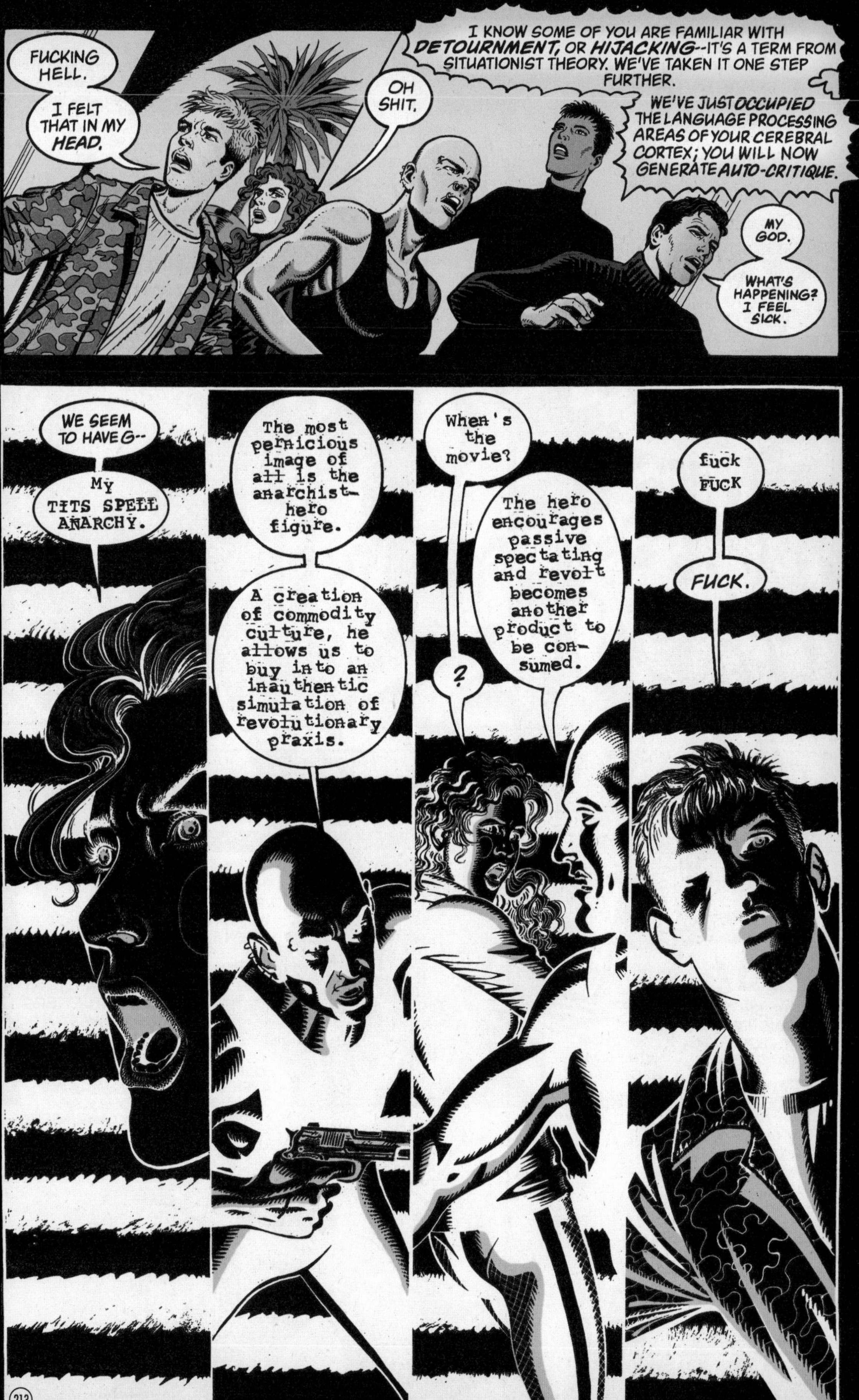

FUCKING HELL.
I FELT THAT IN MY HEAD.
OH SHIT.
I KNOW SOME OF YOU ARE FAMILIAR WITH DETOURNMENT, OR HIJACKING--IT'S A TERM FROM SITUATIONIST THEORY. WE'VE TAKEN IT ONE STEP FURTHER.
WE'VE JUST OCCUPIED THE LANGUAGE PROCESSING AREAS OF YOUR CEREBRAL CORTEX; YOU WILL NOW GENERATE AUTO-CRITIQUE.
MY GOD.
WHAT'S HAPPENING? I FEEL SICK.
WE SEEM TO HAVE G--
My TITS SPELL ANARCHY.
The most pernicious image of all is the anarchist-hero figure.
A creation of commodity culture, he allows us to buy into an inauthentic simulation of revolutionary praxis.
When's the movie?
?
The hero encourages passive spectating and revolt becomes another product to be con-sumed.
fuck FUCK
FUCK.

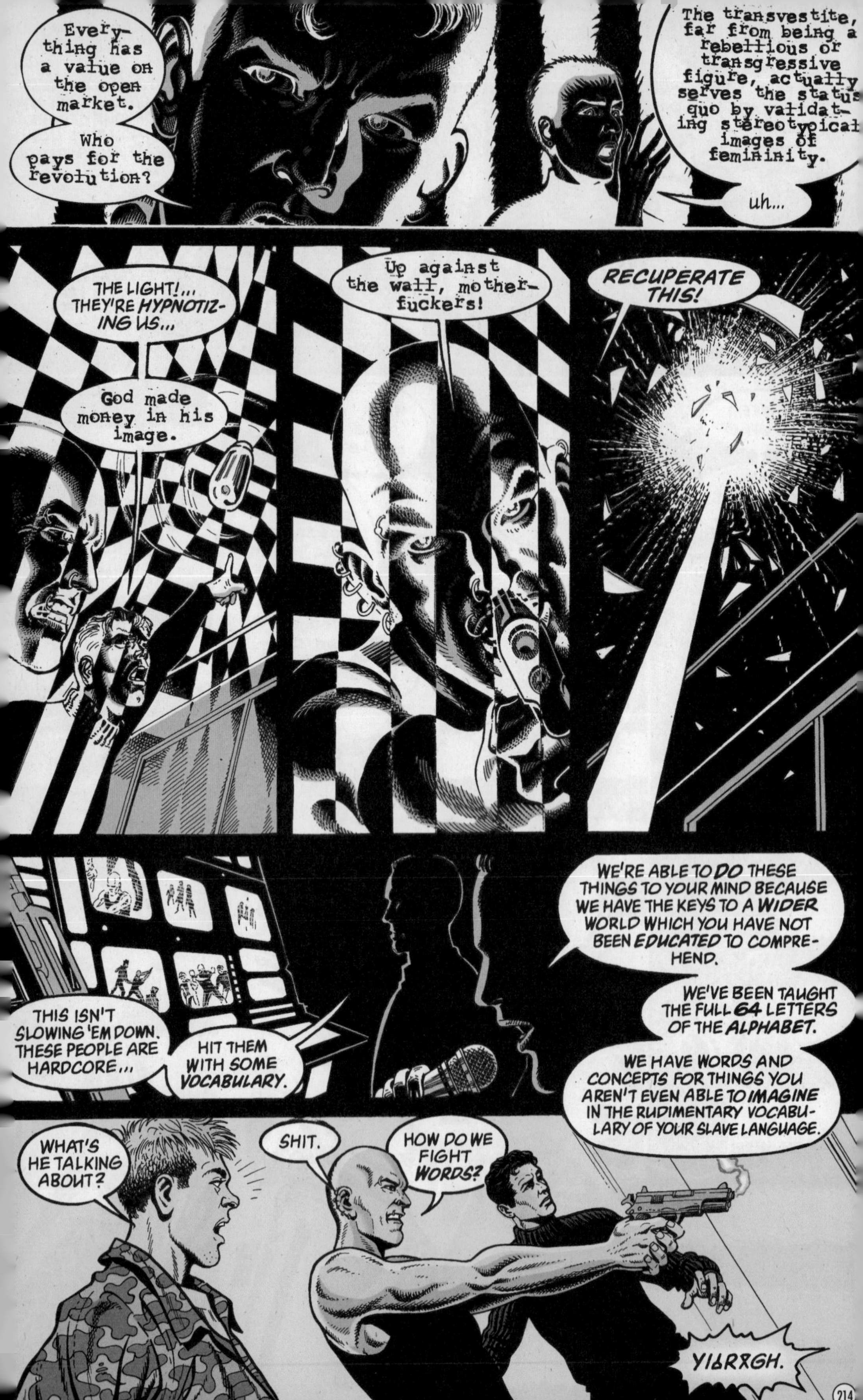

Everything has a value on the open market.
Who pays for the revolution?
The transvestite, far from being a rebellious or transgressive figure, actually serves the status quo by validating stereotypical images of femininity.
uh...
THE LIGHT!... THEY'RE HYPNOTIZING US...
God made money in his image.
Up against the wall, motherfuckers!
RECUPERATE THIS!
THIS ISN'T SLOWING 'EM DOWN. THESE PEOPLE ARE HARDCORE...
HIT THEM WITH SOME VOCABULARY.
WE'RE ABLE TO DO THESE THINGS TO YOUR MIND BECAUSE WE HAVE THE KEYS TO A WIDER WORLD WHICH YOU HAVE NOT BEEN EDUCATED TO COMPREHEND.
WE'VE BEEN TAUGHT THE FULL 64 LETTERS OF THE ALPHABET.
WE HAVE WORDS AND CONCEPTS FOR THINGS YOU AREN'T EVEN ABLE TO IMAGINE IN THE RUDIMENTARY VOCABULARY OF YOUR SLAVE LANGUAGE.
WHAT'S HE TALKING ABOUT?
SHIT.
HOW DO WE FIGHT WORDS?

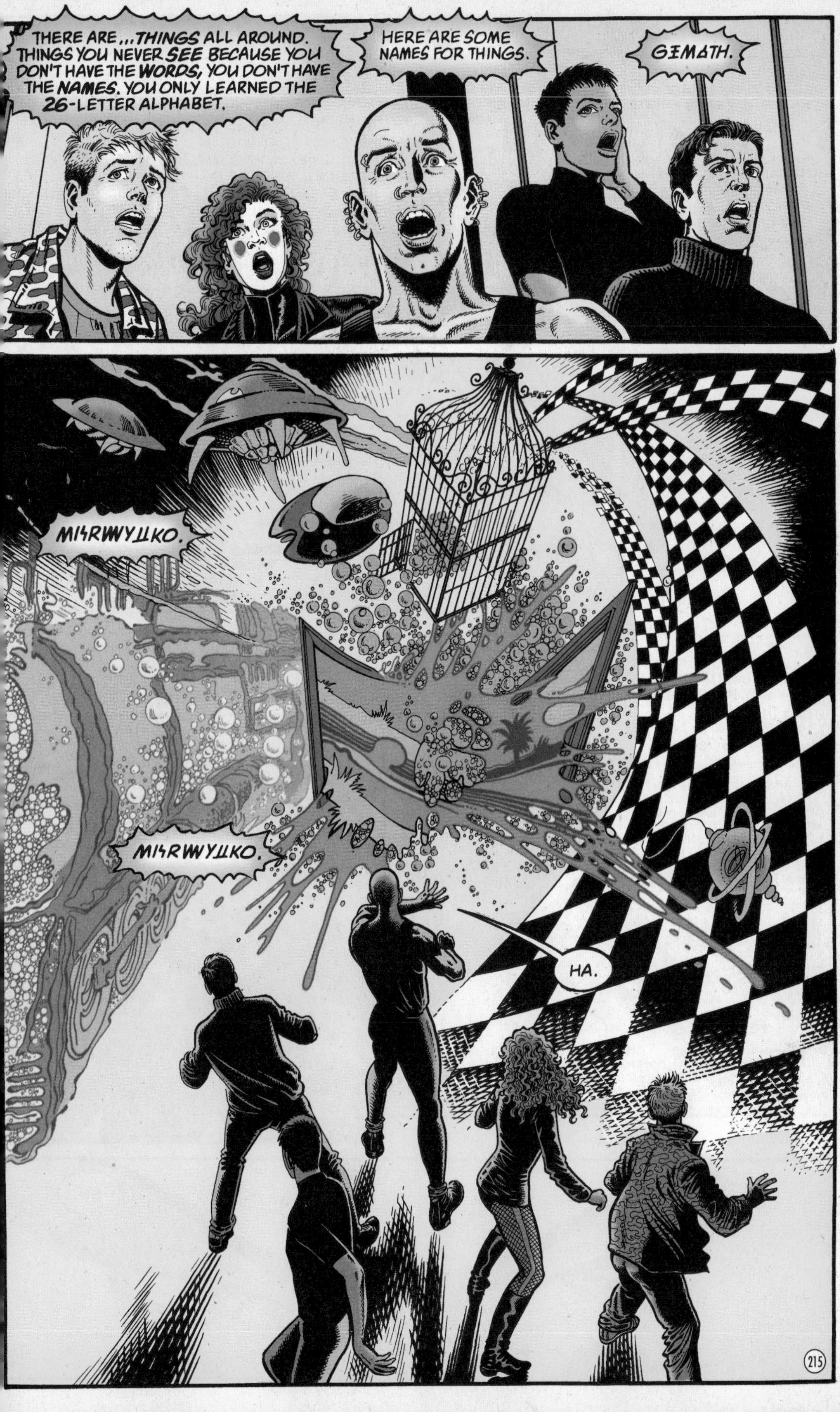
THERE ARE ... THINGS ALL AROUND. THINGS YOU NEVER SEE BECAUSE YOU DON'T HAVE THE WORDS, YOU DON'T HAVE THE NAMES. YOU ONLY LEARNED THE 26-LETTER ALPHABET.
HERE ARE SOME NAMES FOR THINGS.
GEMATH.
MISRWYLLKO.
MISRWYLLKO.
HA.

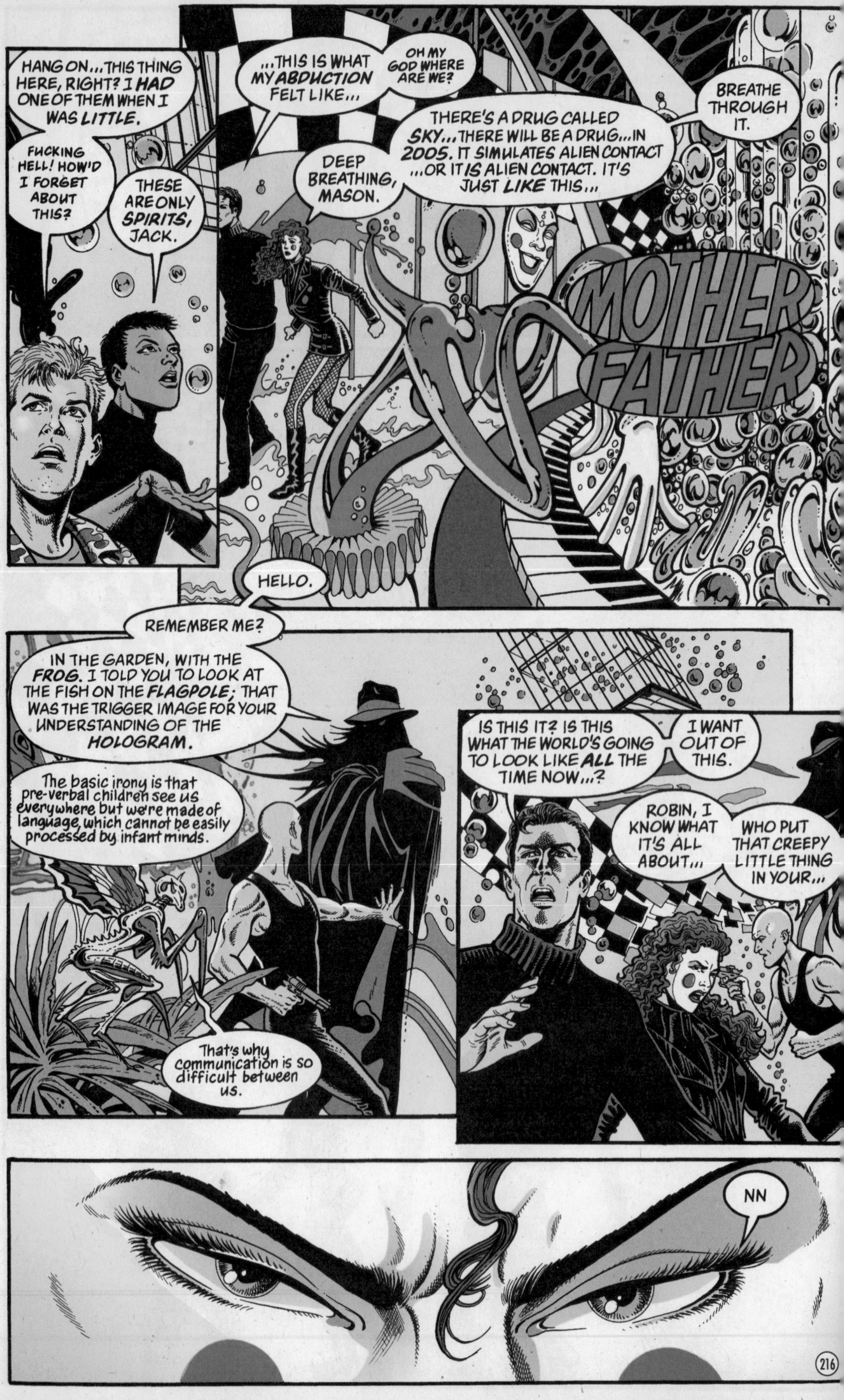

HANG ON... THIS THING HERE, RIGHT? I HAD ONE OF THEM WHEN I WAS LITTLE.
FUCKING HELL! HOW'D I FORGET ABOUT THIS?
THESE ARE ONLY SPIRITS, JACK.
...THIS IS WHAT MY ABDUCTION FELT LIKE...
OH MY GOD WHERE ARE WE?
DEEP BREATHING, MASON.
THERE'S A DRUG CALLED SKY... THERE WILL BE A DRUG... IN 2005. IT SIMULATES ALIEN CONTACT ...OR IT IS ALIEN CONTACT. IT'S JUST LIKE THIS...
BREATHE THROUGH IT.
MOTHER FATHER
HELLO.
REMEMBER ME?
IN THE GARDEN, WITH THE FROG. I TOLD YOU TO LOOK AT THE FISH ON THE FLAGPOLE; THAT WAS THE TRIGGER IMAGE FOR YOUR UNDERSTANDING OF THE HOLOGRAM.
The basic irony is that pre-verbal children see us everywhere but we're made of language, which cannot be easily processed by infant minds.
That's why communication is so difficult between us.
IS THIS IT? IS THIS WHAT THE WORLD'S GOING TO LOOK LIKE ALL THE TIME NOW...?
I WANT OUT OF THIS.
ROBIN, I KNOW WHAT IT'S ALL ABOUT...
WHO PUT THAT CREEPY LITTLE THING IN YOUR...
NN

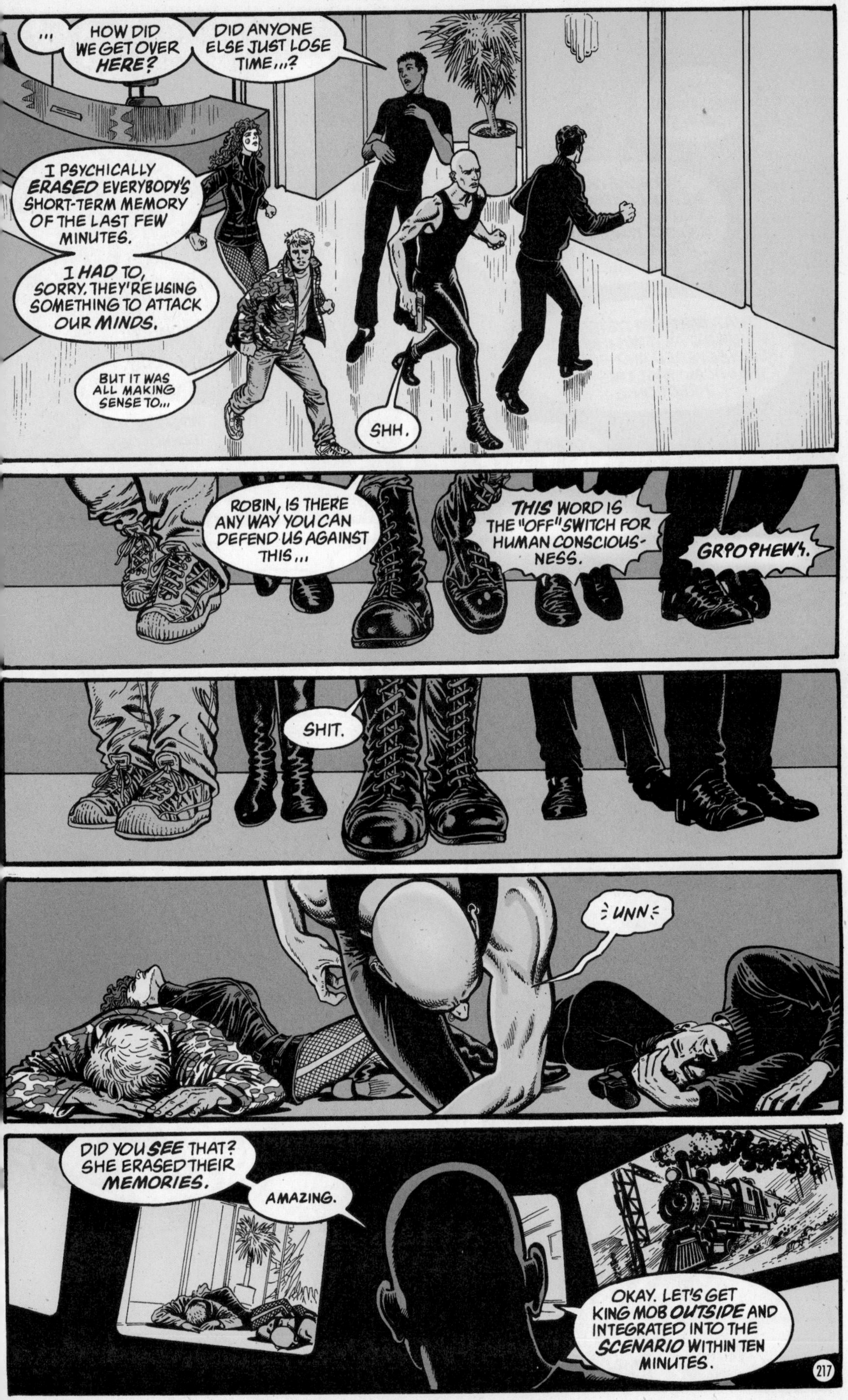
...
HOW DID WE GET OVER HERE?
DID ANYONE ELSE JUST LOSE TIME...?
I PSYCHICALLY ERASED EVERYBODY'S SHORT-TERM MEMORY OF THE LAST FEW MINUTES.
I HAD TO, SORRY. THEY'RE USING SOMETHING TO ATTACK OUR MINDS.
BUT IT WAS ALL MAKING SENSE TO...
SHH.
ROBIN, IS THERE ANY WAY YOU CAN DEFEND US AGAINST THIS...
THIS WORD IS THE "OFF" SWITCH FOR HUMAN CONSCIOUS-NESS.
SHIT.
UNN
DID YOU SEE THAT? SHE ERASED THEIR MEMORIES.
AMAZING.
OKAY. LET'S GET KING MOB OUTSIDE AND INTEGRATED INTO THE SCENARIO WITHIN TEN MINUTES.

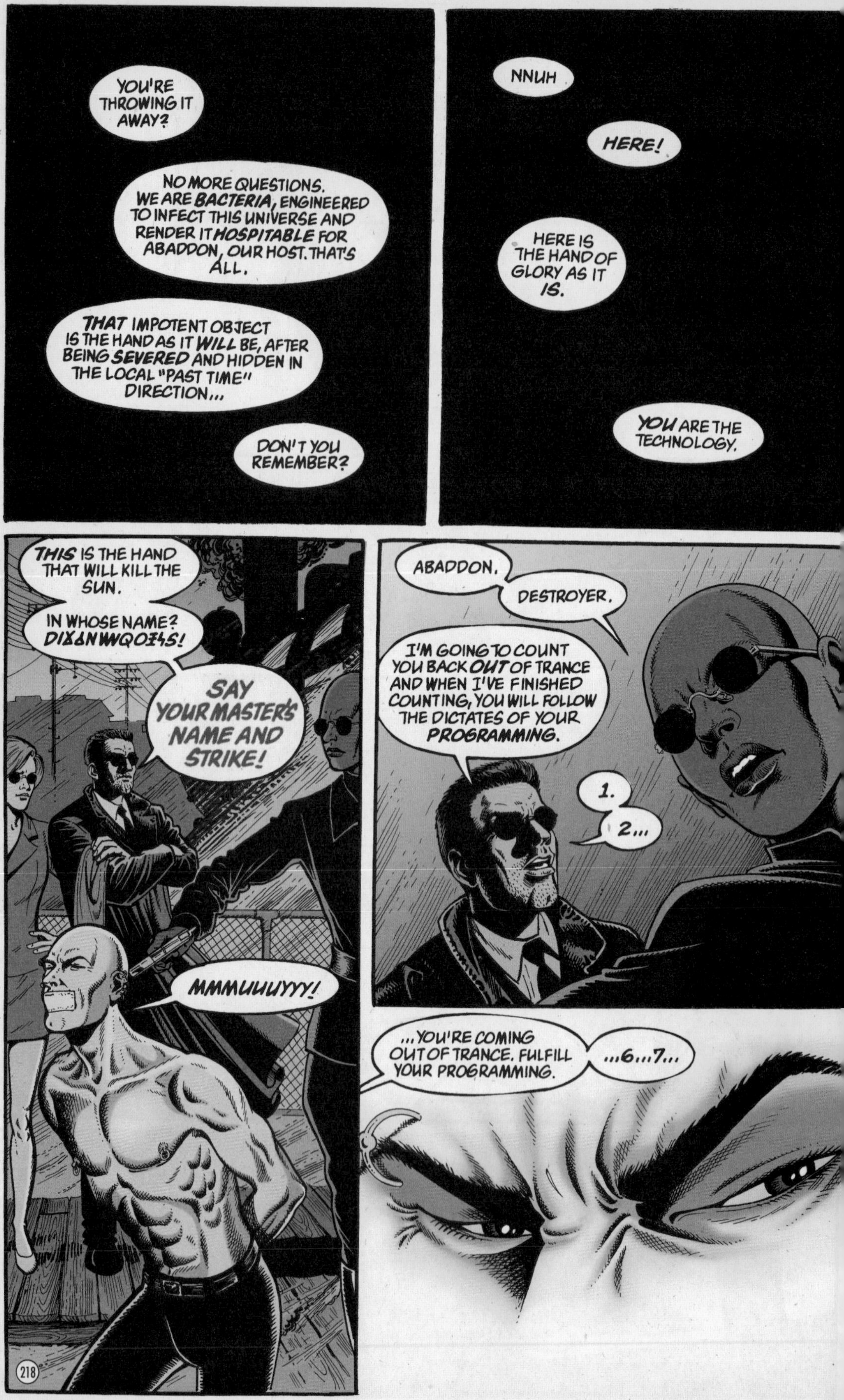
YOU'RE THROWING IT AWAY?
NO MORE QUESTIONS. WE ARE BACTERIA, ENGINEERED TO INFECT THIS UNIVERSE AND RENDER IT HOSPITABLE FOR ABADDON, OUR HOST. THAT'S ALL.
THAT IMPOTENT OBJECT IS THE HAND AS IT WILL BE, AFTER BEING SEVERED AND HIDDEN IN THE LOCAL "PAST TIME" DIRECTION...
DON'T YOU REMEMBER?
NNUH
HERE!
HERE IS THE HAND OF GLORY AS IT IS.
YOU ARE THE TECHNOLOGY.
THIS IS THE HAND THAT WILL KILL THE SUN.
IN WHOSE NAME?
SAY YOUR MASTER'S NAME AND STRIKE!
MMMUUUYYY!
ABADDON.
DESTROYER.
I'M GOING TO COUNT YOU BACK OUT OF TRANCE AND WHEN I'VE FINISHED COUNTING, YOU WILL FOLLOW THE DICTATES OF YOUR PROGRAMMING.
1.
2...
...YOU'RE COMING OUT OF TRANCE. FULFILL YOUR PROGRAMMING.
...6...7...

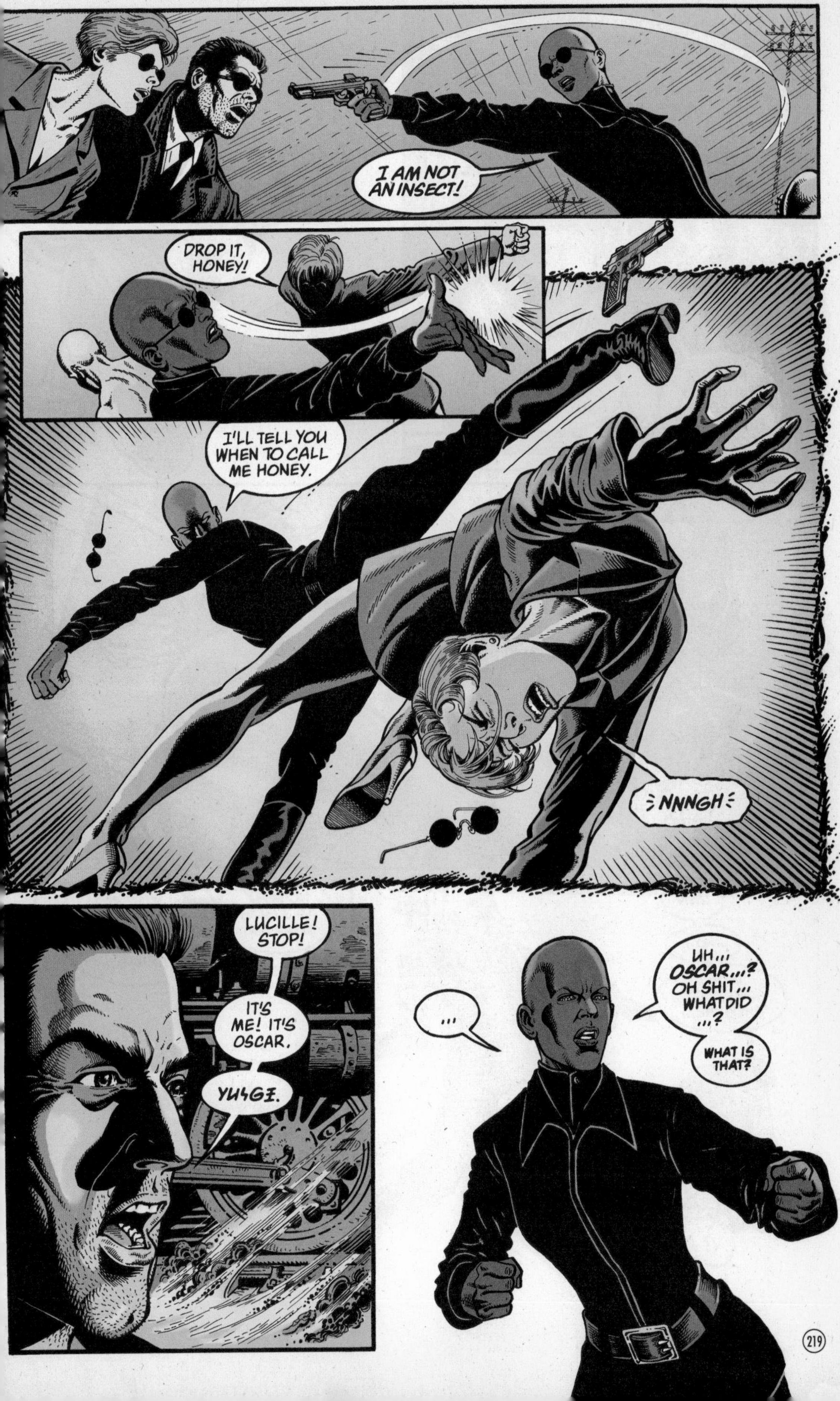
I AM NOT AN INSECT!
DROP IT, HONEY!
I'LL TELL YOU WHEN TO CALL ME HONEY.
NNNGH
LUCILLE! STOP!
IT'S ME! IT'S OSCAR.
YUGE.
...
UH... OSCAR...? OH SHIT... WHAT DID ...?
WHAT IS THAT?

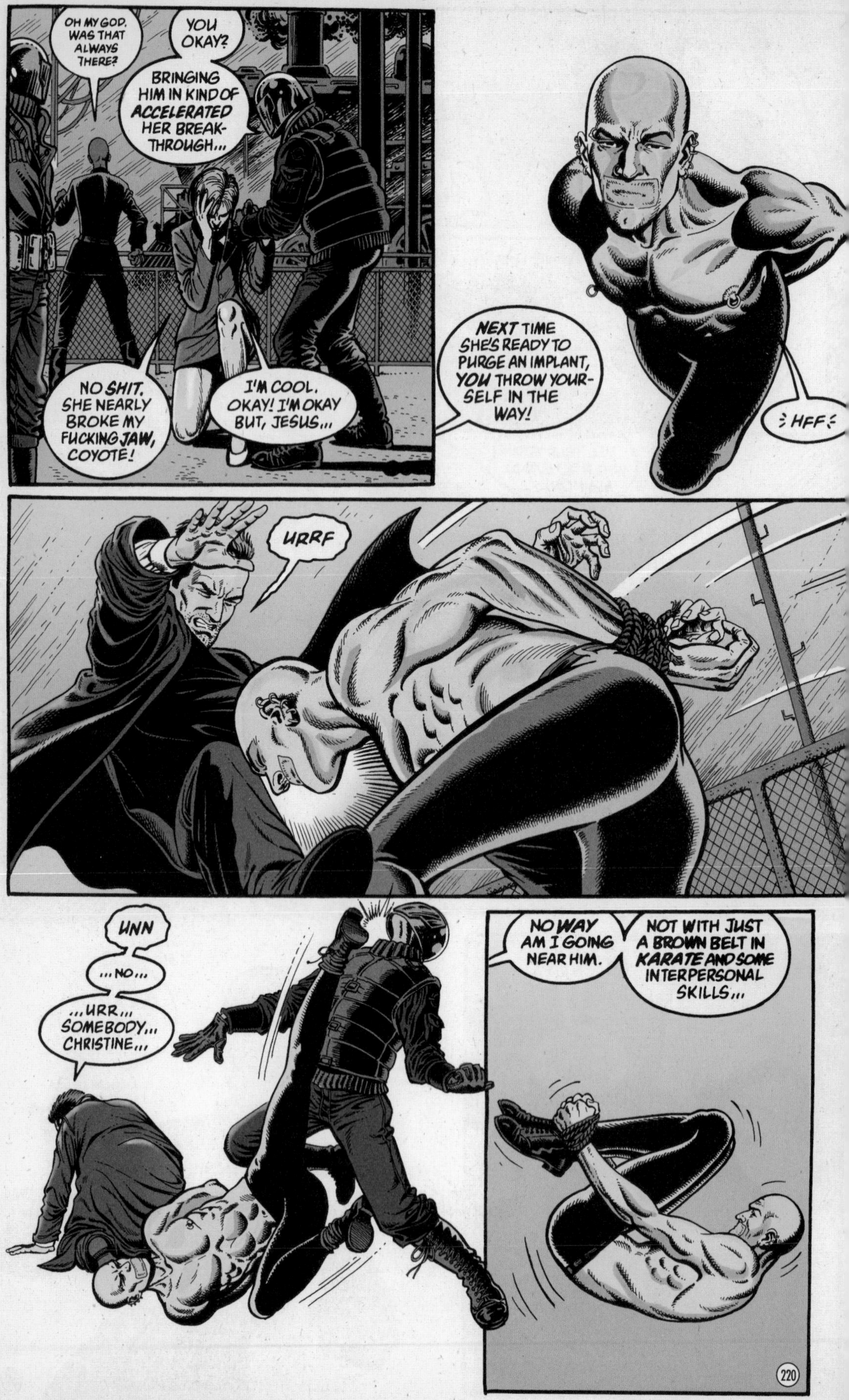
OH MY GOD. WAS THAT ALWAYS THERE?
YOU OKAY?
BRINGING HIM IN KIND OF ACCELERATED HER BREAK-THROUGH...
NO SHIT. SHE NEARLY BROKE MY FUCKING JAW, COYOTE!
I'M COOL. OKAY! I'M OKAY BUT, JESUS...
NEXT TIME SHE'S READY TO PURGE AN IMPLANT, YOU THROW YOUR-SELF IN THE WAY!
HFF
URRF
UNN
...NO...
...URR... SOMEBODY... CHRISTINE...
NO WAY AM I GOING NEAR HIM.
NOT WITH JUST A BROWN BELT IN KARATE AND SOME INTERPERSONAL SKILLS...

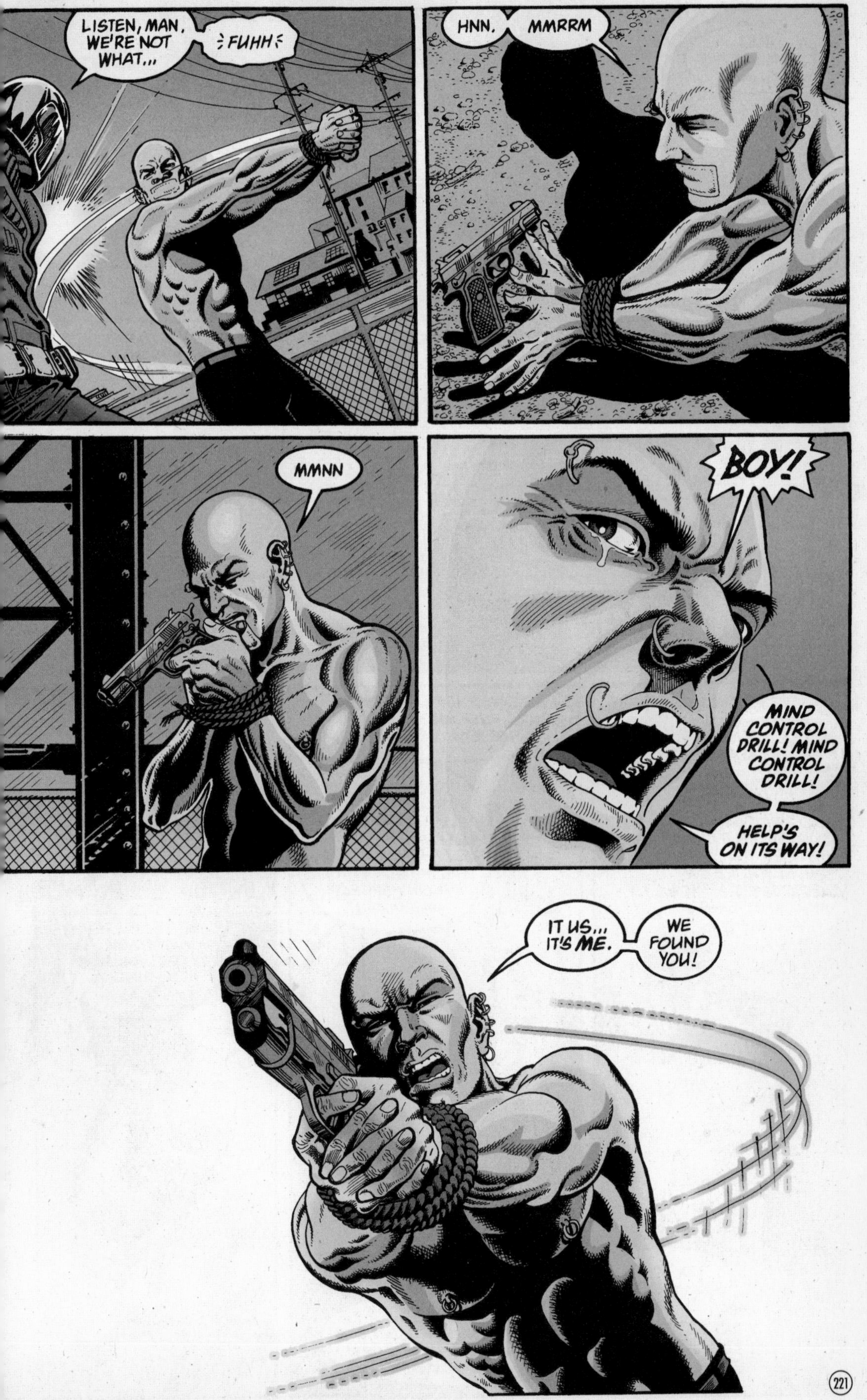
LISTEN, MAN. WE'RE NOT WHAT...
FUHH
HNN.
MMRRM
MMNN
BOY!
MIND CONTROL DRILL! MIND CONTROL DRILL!
HELP'S ON ITS WAY!
IT US... IT'S ME.
WE FOUND YOU!

AND I'VE GOT THE GUN!

KLIK

BAD NEWS FOR...

IT'S EMPTY.

KLIK KLIK

FORGET IT. IT'S A PROP.

WE'RE CELL 23.

YOU KNOW WHAT THAT MEANS, DON'T YOU?

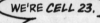

CELL 23.

NO... WAIT A MINUTE. SO WHAT? I'M SUDDENLY SUPPOSED TO HEAR "SMILE! YOU'RE ON CANDID CAMERA!" NOW AND EVERYTHING'S ALL RIGHT?

LOOK WHAT YOU DID TO HER!

WE SAVED HER LIFE. AND YOURS. FUCK KNOWS WHY. WE LIKE YOU, I GUESS.

KING MOB, RIGHT?

I USED TO WORK WITH LUCILLE IN THE POLICE DEPARTMENT. WE SPOKE ON THE TELEPHONE ONCE. I WAS THE GUY WITH THE PHONY SPEECH IMPEDIMENT.

SHE WAS ALL SET TO TAKE THE HAND OF GLORY STRAIGHT TO THE OTHER SIDE. THEY'D HAVE KILLED HER.

YOU'D HAVE DIED TRACKING HER DOWN. ONE OF OUR PSYCHICS SAW IT COMING.

THE IMPLANT'S COMING LOOSE NOW.

SHE'S GONNA NEED HER FRIENDS.

THIS IS FUCKED.

222

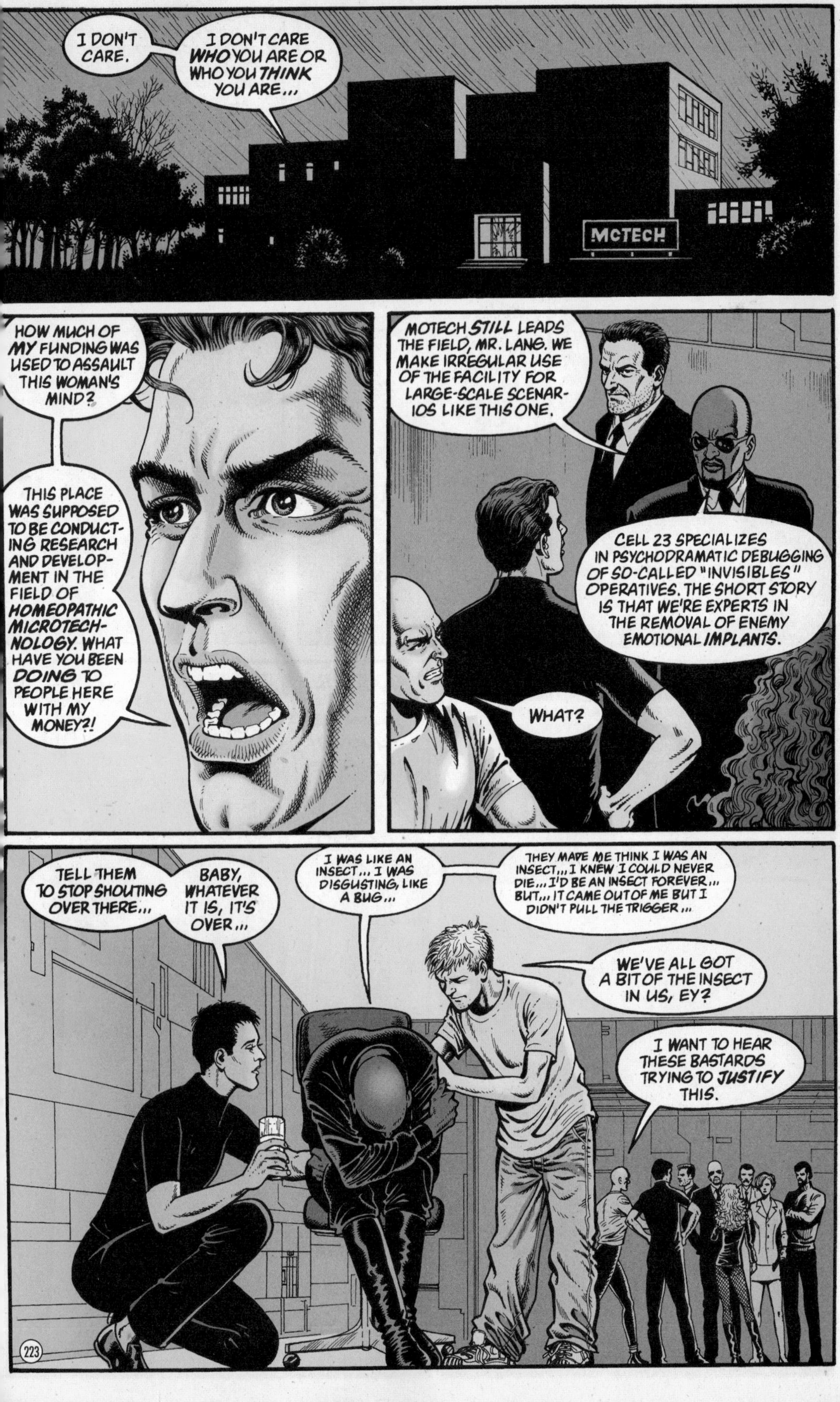

I DON'T CARE.
I DON'T CARE WHO YOU ARE OR WHO YOU THINK YOU ARE...
MCTECH
HOW MUCH OF MY FUNDING WAS USED TO ASSAULT THIS WOMAN'S MIND?
THIS PLACE WAS SUPPOSED TO BE CONDUCTING RESEARCH AND DEVELOPMENT IN THE FIELD OF HOMEOPATHIC MICROTECHNOLOGY. WHAT HAVE YOU BEEN DOING TO PEOPLE HERE WITH MY MONEY?!
MCTECH STILL LEADS THE FIELD, MR. LANG. WE MAKE IRREGULAR USE OF THE FACILITY FOR LARGE-SCALE SCENARIOS LIKE THIS ONE.
CELL 23 SPECIALIZES IN PSYCHODRAMATIC DEBUGGING OF SO-CALLED "INVISIBLES" OPERATIVES. THE SHORT STORY IS THAT WE'RE EXPERTS IN THE REMOVAL OF ENEMY EMOTIONAL IMPLANTS.
WHAT?
TELL THEM TO STOP SHOUTING OVER THERE...
BABY, WHATEVER IT IS, IT'S OVER...
I WAS LIKE AN INSECT... I WAS DISGUSTING, LIKE A BUG...
THEY MADE ME THINK I WAS AN INSECT... I KNEW I COULD NEVER DIE... I'D BE AN INSECT FOREVER... BUT... IT CAME OUT OF ME BUT I DIDN'T PULL THE TRIGGER...
WE'VE ALL GOT A BIT OF THE INSECT IN US, EY?
I WANT TO HEAR THESE BASTARDS TRYING TO JUSTIFY THIS.

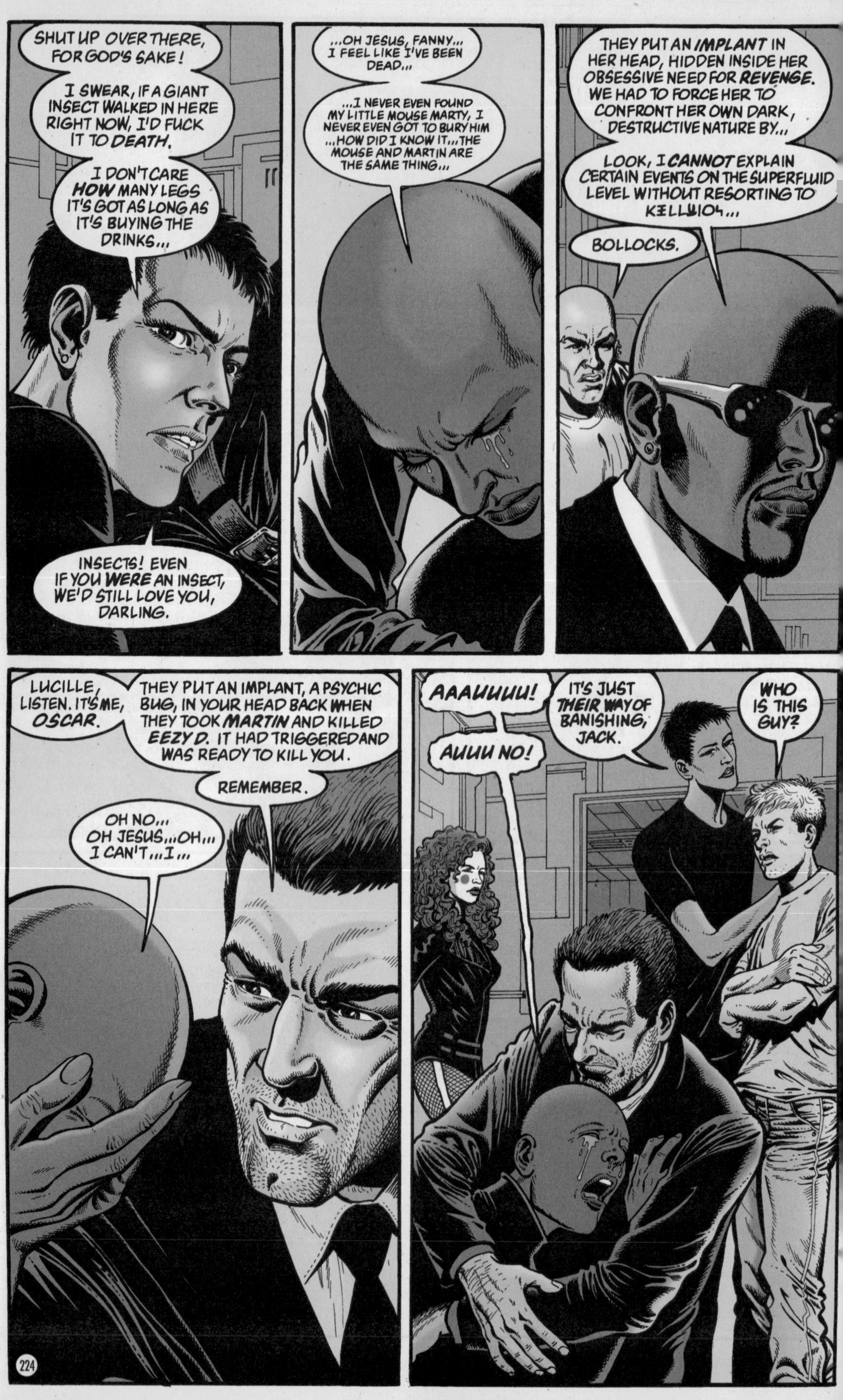
SHUT UP OVER THERE, FOR GOD'S SAKE!
I SWEAR, IF A GIANT INSECT WALKED IN HERE RIGHT NOW, I'D FUCK IT TO DEATH.
I DON'T CARE HOW MANY LEGS IT'S GOT AS LONG AS IT'S BUYING THE DRINKS...
INSECTS! EVEN IF YOU WERE AN INSECT, WE'D STILL LOVE YOU, DARLING.
...OH JESUS, FANNY... I FEEL LIKE I'VE BEEN DEAD...
...I NEVER EVEN FOUND MY LITTLE MOUSE MARTY, I NEVER EVEN GOT TO BURY HIM ...HOW DID I KNOW IT...THE MOUSE AND MARTIN ARE THE SAME THING...
THEY PUT AN IMPLANT IN HER HEAD, HIDDEN INSIDE HER OBSESSIVE NEED FOR REVENGE. WE HAD TO FORCE HER TO CONFRONT HER OWN DARK, DESTRUCTIVE NATURE BY...
LOOK, I CANNOT EXPLAIN CERTAIN EVENTS ON THE SUPERFLUID LEVEL WITHOUT RESORTING TO
BOLLOCKS.
LUCILLE, LISTEN. IT'S ME, OSCAR.
THEY PUT AN IMPLANT, A PSYCHIC BUG, IN YOUR HEAD BACK WHEN THEY TOOK MARTIN AND KILLED EEZY D. IT HAD TRIGGERED AND WAS READY TO KILL YOU.
REMEMBER.
OH NO... OH JESUS...OH... I CAN'T...I...
AAAUUUU!
AUUU NO!
IT'S JUST THEIR WAY OF BANISHING, JACK.
WHO IS THIS GUY?

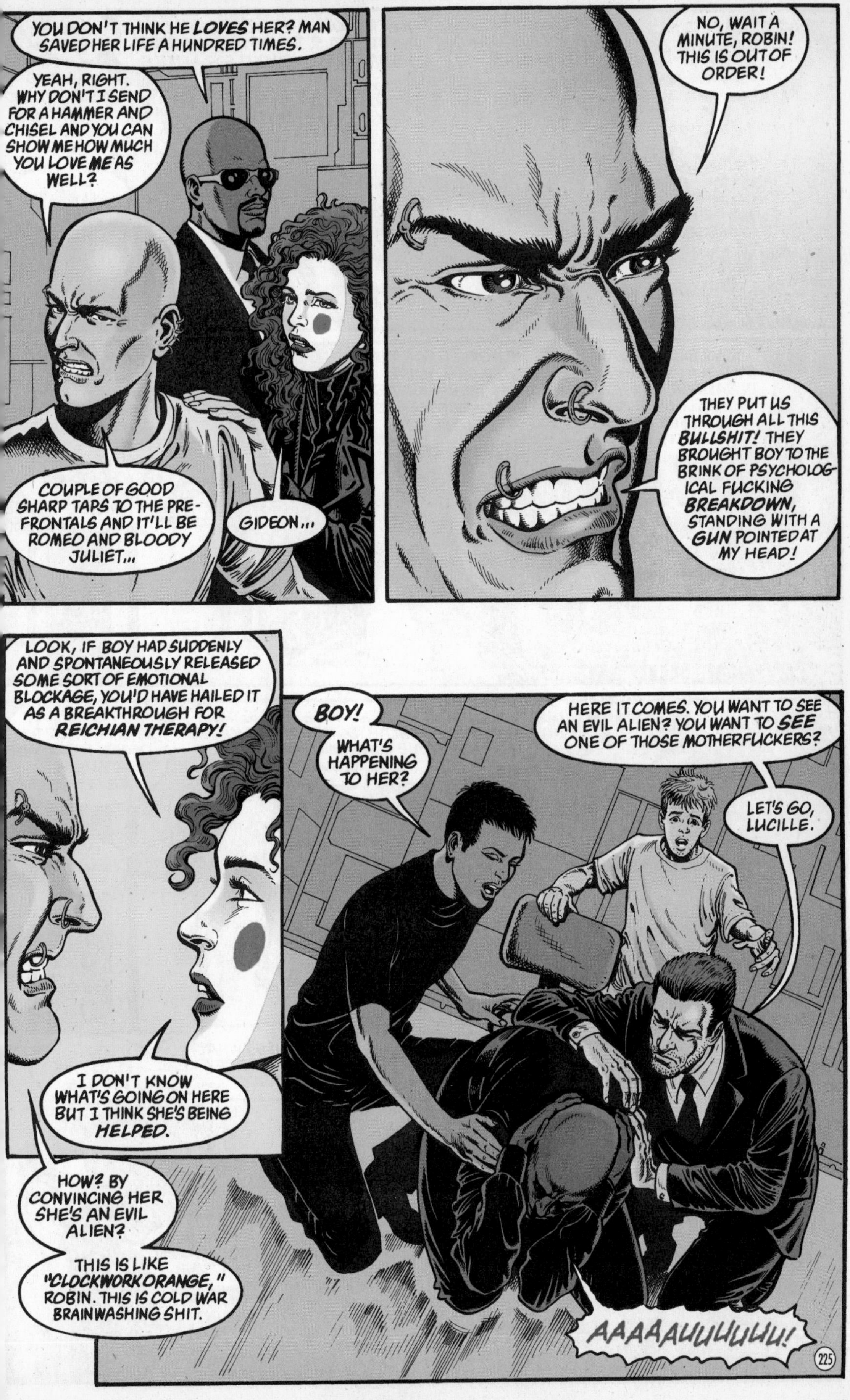
YOU DON'T THINK HE LOVES HER? MAN SAVED HER LIFE A HUNDRED TIMES.
YEAH, RIGHT. WHY DON'T I SEND FOR A HAMMER AND CHISEL AND YOU CAN SHOW ME HOW MUCH YOU LOVE ME AS WELL?
COUPLE OF GOOD SHARP TAPS TO THE PRE-FRONTALS AND IT'LL BE ROMEO AND BLOODY JULIET...
GIDEON...
NO, WAIT A MINUTE, ROBIN! THIS IS OUT OF ORDER!
THEY PUT US THROUGH ALL THIS BULLSHIT! THEY BROUGHT BOY TO THE BRINK OF PSYCHOLOG-ICAL FUCKING BREAKDOWN, STANDING WITH A GUN POINTED AT MY HEAD!
LOOK, IF BOY HAD SUDDENLY AND SPONTANEOUSLY RELEASED SOME SORT OF EMOTIONAL BLOCKAGE, YOU'D HAVE HAILED IT AS A BREAKTHROUGH FOR REICHIAN THERAPY!
I DON'T KNOW WHAT'S GOING ON HERE BUT I THINK SHE'S BEING HELPED.
HOW? BY CONVINCING HER SHE'S AN EVIL ALIEN?
THIS IS LIKE "CLOCKWORK ORANGE," ROBIN. THIS IS COLD WAR BRAINWASHING SHIT.
BOY! WHAT'S HAPPENING TO HER?
HERE IT COMES. YOU WANT TO SEE AN EVIL ALIEN? YOU WANT TO SEE ONE OF THOSE MOTHERFUCKERS?
LET'S GO, LUCILLE.
AAAAAUUUUUU!

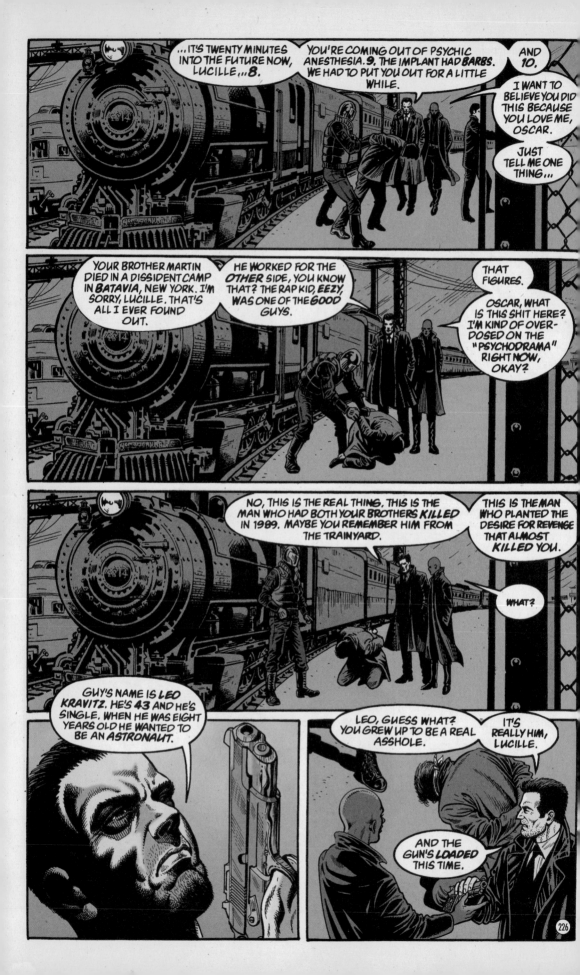

...IT'S TWENTY MINUTES INTO THE FUTURE NOW, LUCILLE,...8.

YOU'RE COMING OUT OF PSYCHIC ANESTHESIA. 9. THE IMPLANT HAD *BARBS.* WE HAD TO PUT YOU OUT FOR A LITTLE WHILE.

AND 10.

I WANT TO BELIEVE YOU DID THIS BECAUSE YOU LOVE ME, OSCAR.

JUST TELL ME ONE THING...

YOUR BROTHER MARTIN DIED IN A DISSIDENT CAMP IN *BATAVIA,* NEW YORK. I'M SORRY, LUCILLE. THAT'S ALL I EVER FOUND OUT.

HE WORKED FOR THE *OTHER* SIDE, YOU KNOW THAT? THE RAP KID, *EEZY,* WAS ONE OF THE *GOOD* GUYS.

THAT FIGURES.

OSCAR, WHAT IS THIS SHIT HERE? I'M KIND OF OVER-DOSED ON THE "PSYCHODRAMA" RIGHT NOW, OKAY?

NO, THIS IS THE REAL THING, THIS IS THE MAN WHO HAD BOTH YOUR BROTHERS *KILLED* IN 1989. MAYBE YOU REMEMBER HIM FROM THE TRAINYARD.

THIS IS THE MAN WHO PLANTED THE DESIRE FOR REVENGE THAT ALMOST *KILLED* YOU.

WHAT?

GUY'S NAME IS *LEO KRAVITZ.* HE'S 43 AND HE'S SINGLE. WHEN HE WAS EIGHT YEARS OLD HE WANTED TO BE AN *ASTRONAUT.*

LEO, GUESS WHAT? YOU GREW UP TO BE A REAL ASSHOLE.

IT'S REALLY HIM, LUCILLE.

AND THE GUN'S *LOADED* THIS TIME.

226

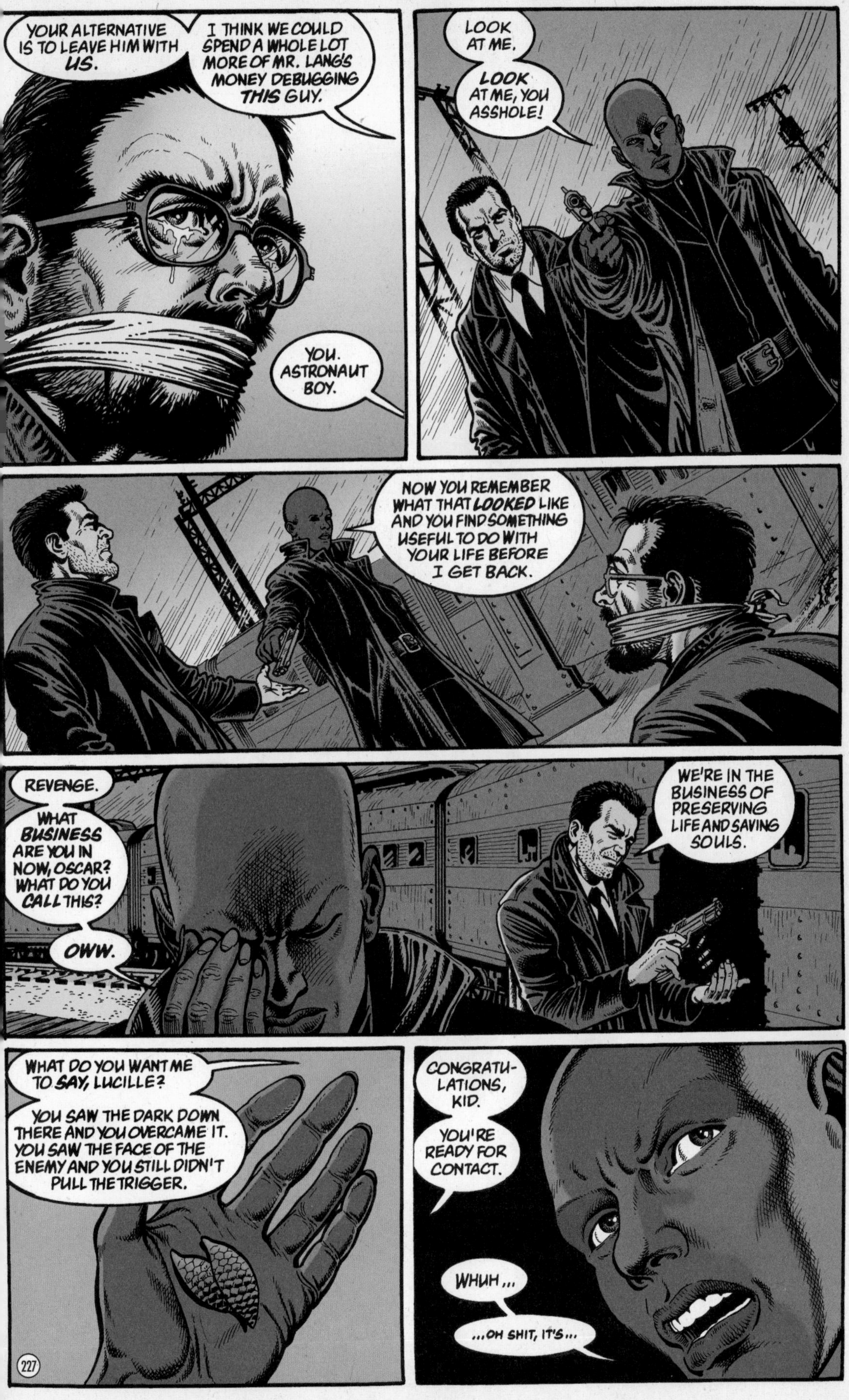
YOUR ALTERNATIVE IS TO LEAVE HIM WITH US.
I THINK WE COULD SPEND A WHOLE LOT MORE OF MR. LANG'S MONEY DEBUGGING THIS GUY.
YOU. ASTRONAUT BOY.
LOOK AT ME.
LOOK AT ME, YOU ASSHOLE!
NOW YOU REMEMBER WHAT THAT LOOKED LIKE AND YOU FIND SOMETHING USEFUL TO DO WITH YOUR LIFE BEFORE I GET BACK.
REVENGE.
WHAT BUSINESS ARE YOU IN NOW, OSCAR? WHAT DO YOU CALL THIS?
OWW.
WE'RE IN THE BUSINESS OF PRESERVING LIFE AND SAVING SOULS.
WHAT DO YOU WANT ME TO SAY, LUCILLE?
YOU SAW THE DARK DOWN THERE AND YOU OVERCAME IT. YOU SAW THE FACE OF THE ENEMY AND YOU STILL DIDN'T PULL THE TRIGGER.
CONGRATU-LATIONS, KID.
YOU'RE READY FOR CONTACT.
WHUH ...
...OH SHIT, IT'S...

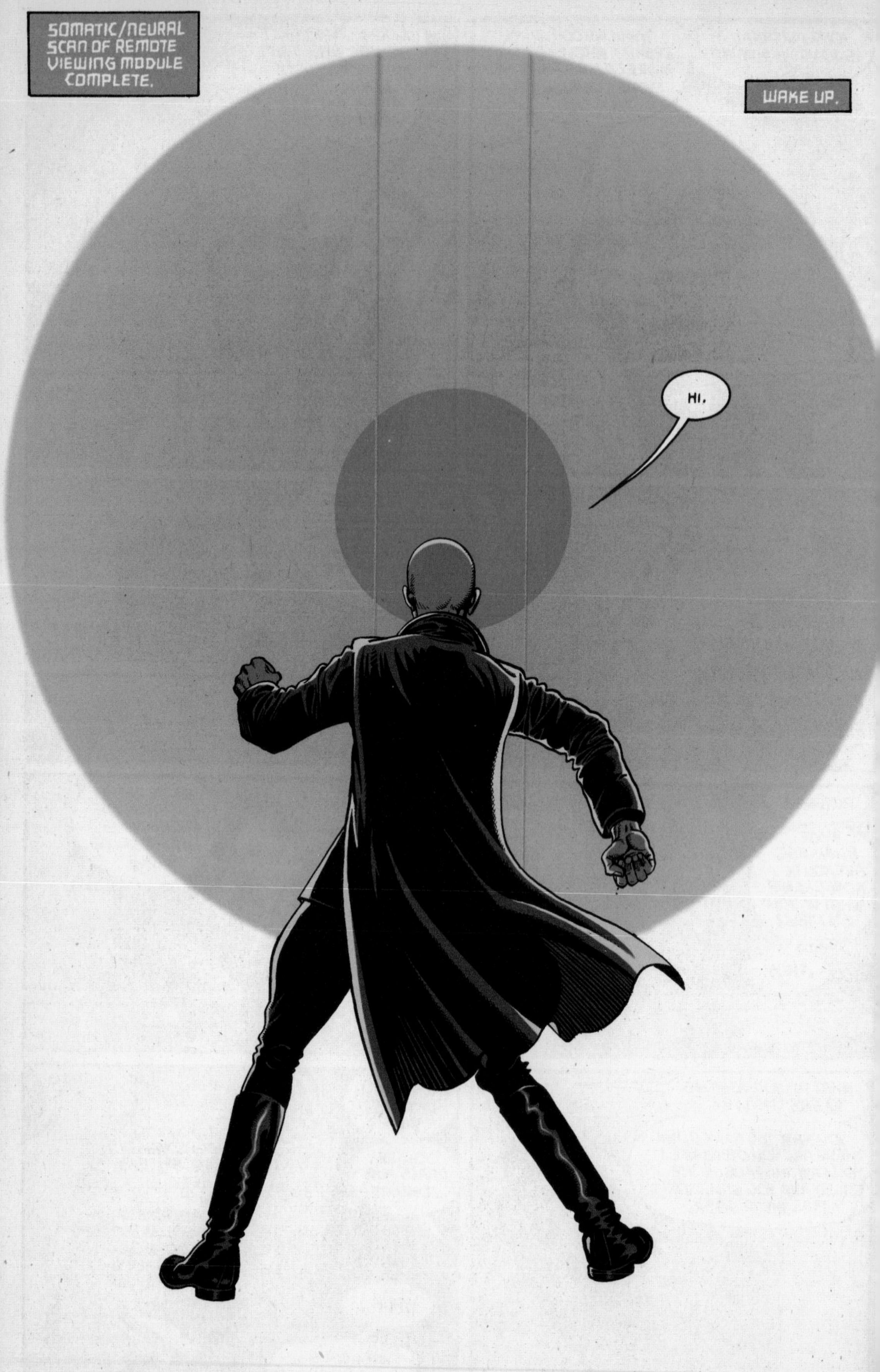
SOMATIC/NEURAL SCAN OF REMOTE VIEWING MODULE COMPLETE.
WAKE UP.
HI.

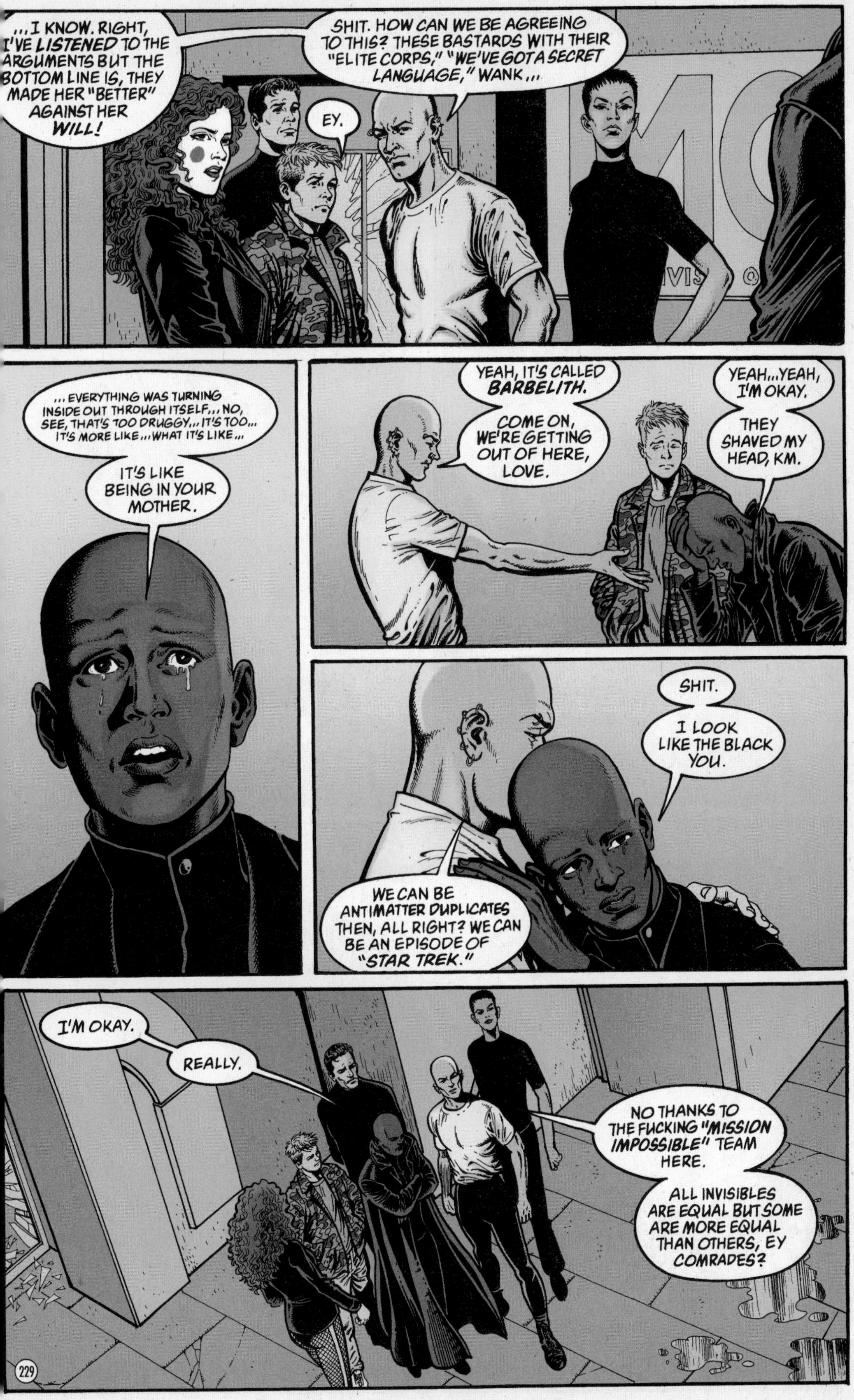
...I KNOW. RIGHT, I'VE LISTENED TO THE ARGUMENTS BUT THE BOTTOM LINE IS, THEY MADE HER "BETTER" AGAINST HER WILL!
SHIT. HOW CAN WE BE AGREEING TO THIS? THESE BASTARDS WITH THEIR "ELITE CORPS," "WE'VE GOT A SECRET LANGUAGE," WANK...
EY.
...EVERYTHING WAS TURNING INSIDE OUT THROUGH ITSELF... NO, SEE, THAT'S TOO DRUGGY... IT'S TOO... IT'S MORE LIKE... WHAT IT'S LIKE...
IT'S LIKE BEING IN YOUR MOTHER.
YEAH, IT'S CALLED BARBELITH.
COME ON, WE'RE GETTING OUT OF HERE, LOVE.
YEAH...YEAH, I'M OKAY.
THEY SHAVED MY HEAD, KM.
SHIT.
I LOOK LIKE THE BLACK YOU.
WE CAN BE ANTIMATTER DUPLICATES THEN, ALL RIGHT? WE CAN BE AN EPISODE OF "STAR TREK."
I'M OKAY.
REALLY.
NO THANKS TO THE FUCKING "MISSION IMPOSSIBLE" TEAM HERE.
ALL INVISIBLES ARE EQUAL BUT SOME ARE MORE EQUAL THAN OTHERS, EY COMRADES?

I UNDERSTAND YOUR RESERVATIONS BUT I'D STILL LIKE TO THANK YOU FOR YOUR PARTICIPATION AND FOR BEING HERE WITH LUCILLE.

WE'LL GET THE HAND OF GLORY BACK TO YOU AS SOON AS *TESTS* ARE COMPLETE.

TAKE CARE OF YOURSELF, LUCILLE.

I SHOULD... I DON'T KNOW... I FEEL LIKE I SHOULD CALL THE POLICE...

DON'T BE RIDICULOUS, MASON.

YOU'RE GOING TO NEED SOME SERIOUS REST, DARLING.

YEAH. NO, I FEEL... PRETTY AMAZING...

THAT'S LIKE WHAT I HAD. IT'S LIKE *E* BUT BETTER.

GROUP HUG IN THE VAN, ALL RIGHT?

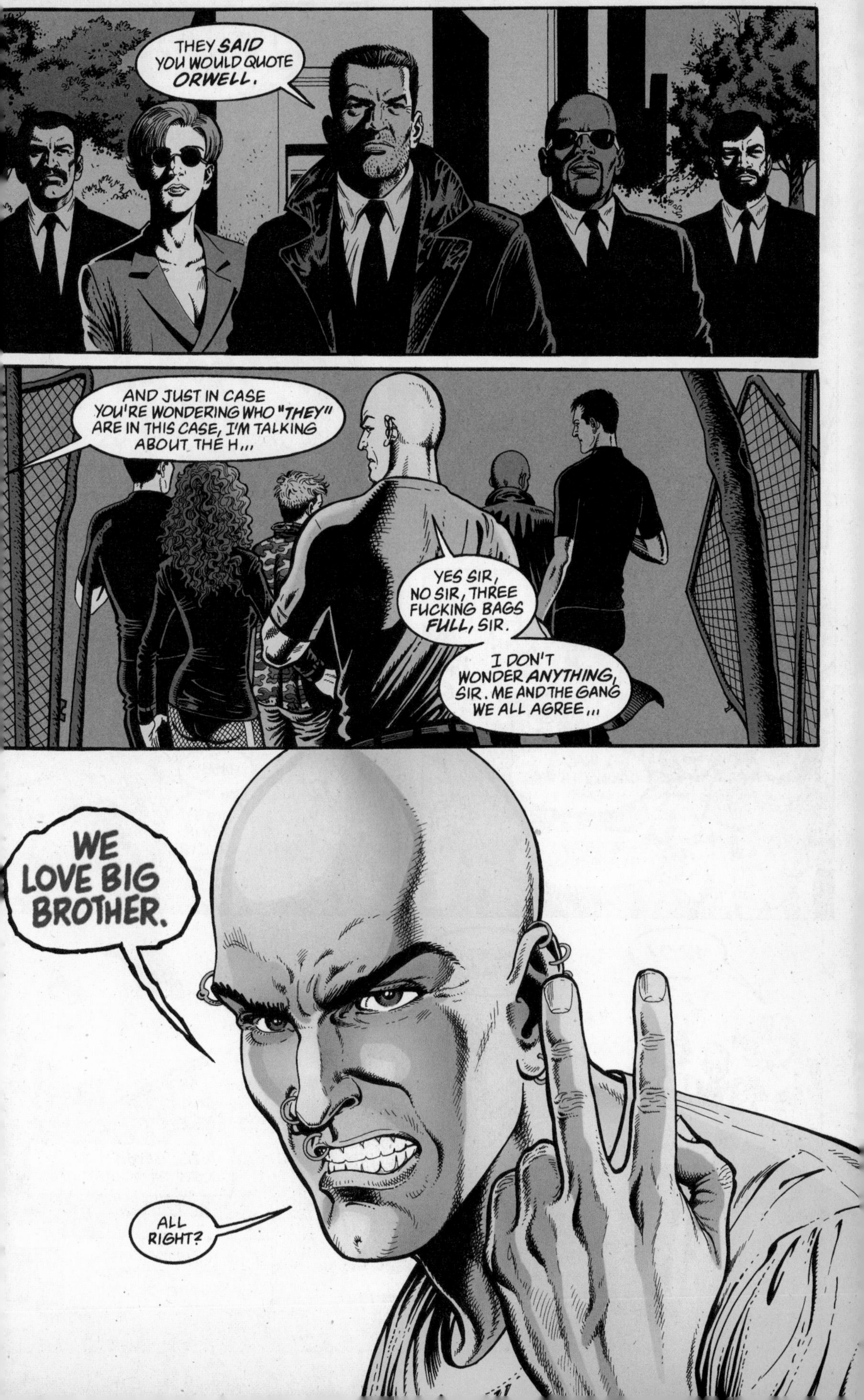
THEY SAID YOU WOULD QUOTE ORWELL.
AND JUST IN CASE YOU'RE WONDERING WHO "THEY" ARE IN THIS CASE, I'M TALKING ABOUT THE H...
YES SIR, NO SIR, THREE FUCKING BAGS FULL, SIR.
I DON'T WONDER ANYTHING, SIR. ME AND THE GANG WE ALL AGREE...
WE LOVE BIG BROTHER.
ALL RIGHT?

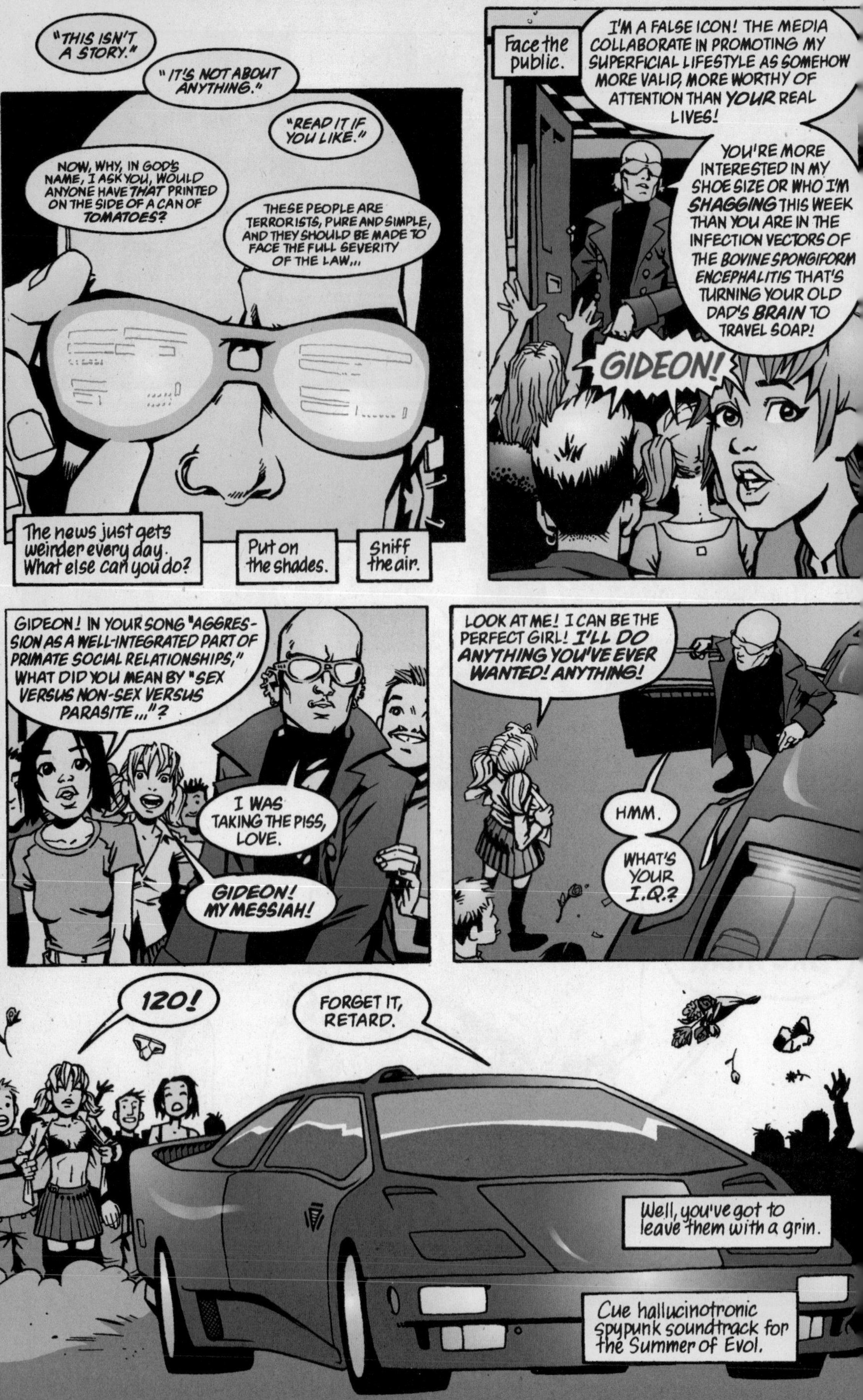
"THIS ISN'T A STORY."
"IT'S NOT ABOUT ANYTHING."
"READ IT IF YOU LIKE."
NOW, WHY, IN GOD'S NAME, I ASK YOU, WOULD ANYONE HAVE THAT PRINTED ON THE SIDE OF A CAN OF TOMATOES?
THESE PEOPLE ARE TERRORISTS, PURE AND SIMPLE, AND THEY SHOULD BE MADE TO FACE THE FULL SEVERITY OF THE LAW...
The news just gets weirder every day. What else can you do?
Put on the shades.
Sniff the air.
Face the public.
I'M A FALSE ICON! THE MEDIA COLLABORATE IN PROMOTING MY SUPERFICIAL LIFESTYLE AS SOMEHOW MORE VALID, MORE WORTHY OF ATTENTION THAN YOUR REAL LIVES!
YOU'RE MORE INTERESTED IN MY SHOE SIZE OR WHO I'M SHAGGING THIS WEEK THAN YOU ARE IN THE INFECTION VECTORS OF THE BOVINE SPONGIFORM ENCEPHALITIS THAT'S TURNING YOUR OLD DAD'S BRAIN TO TRAVEL SOAP!
GIDEON!
GIDEON! IN YOUR SONG "AGGRESSION AS A WELL-INTEGRATED PART OF PRIMATE SOCIAL RELATIONSHIPS," WHAT DID YOU MEAN BY "SEX VERSUS NON-SEX VERSUS PARASITE..."?
I WAS TAKING THE PISS, LOVE.
GIDEON! MY MESSIAH!
LOOK AT ME! I CAN BE THE PERFECT GIRL! I'LL DO ANYTHING YOU'VE EVER WANTED! ANYTHING!
HMM.
WHAT'S YOUR I.Q.?
120!
FORGET IT, RETARD.
Well, you've got to leave them with a grin.
Cue hallucinotronic spypunk soundtrack for the Summer of Evol.

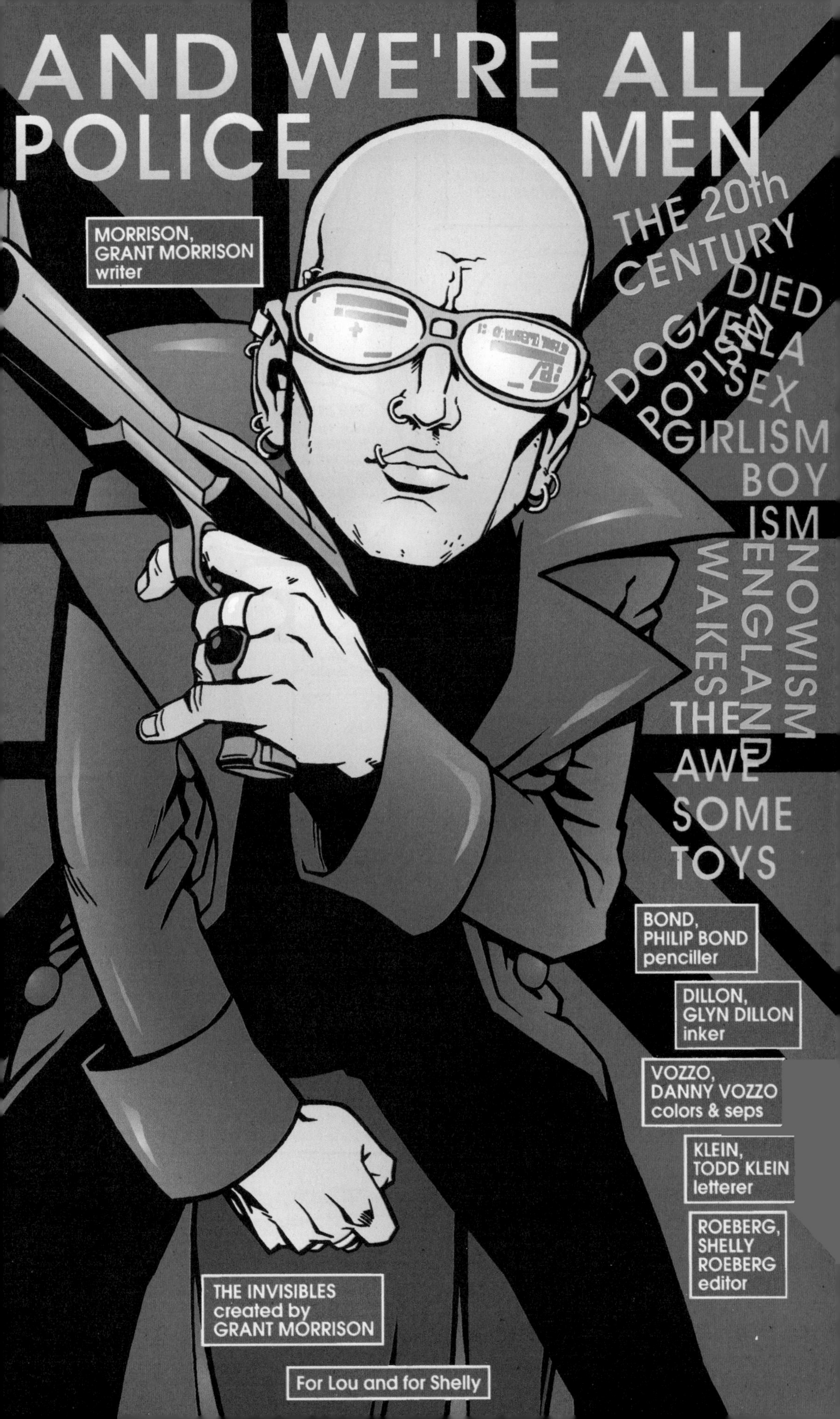
AND WE'RE ALL POLICE MEN
MORRISON, GRANT MORRISON writer
THE 20th CENTURY DIED
POPISM
SEX
GIRLISM
BOY
ISM
ENGLAND
WAKES
NOWISM
THE
AWE
SOME
TOYS
BOND, PHILIP BOND penciller
DILLON, GLYN DILLON inker
VOZZO, DANNY VOZZO colors & seps
KLEIN, TODD KLEIN letterer
ROEBERG, SHELLY ROEBERG editor
THE INVISIBLES created by GRANT MORRISON
For Lou and for Shelly

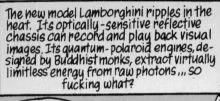

The new model Lamborghini ripples in the heat. Its optically-sensitive reflective chassis can record and play back visual images. Its quantum-polaroid engines, designed by Buddhist monks, extract virtually limitless energy from raw photons... so fucking what?

I LOVE THE CAR ADS. THEY MAKE ME FEEL LIKE I'M TRIPPING.

DON'T THINK FOR YOURSELVES! THINK FOR GOD! LET'S START MAKING THAT MOTHERFUCKER'S DECISIONS FOR HIM, HUH?...

THANKS FOR ... AH... THANKS, CHET, FOR THAT VERY UNUSUAL AND INDEED, MOVING LOOK AT TOMORROW'S WEATHER ...

PORNOPLASM TURN *ON*. MODEM THE FOLLOWING TO MY WORLD-WEB HOTEL PAGE.

THE UNDERLYING MOTIF OF HUMAN CIVILI-ZATION IS NO LONGER *SUFFERING* BUT PLAY.

THE CRUCIFIED GOD-IMAGE HAS BEEN REPLACED BY THE NEW AEON'S DOMINANT RELIGIOUS MOTIF -- A *CHILD* FUCKING ABOUT WITH THE BUILDING BLOCKS OF REALITY ITSELF, RESTLESSLY DE-STROYING TO CREATE.

It was the best the coul[e] of in a hurry; let's face Samaritans should hav[e] someone else to compo[se] message for their new "We're at a party!" answ[er] machine service.

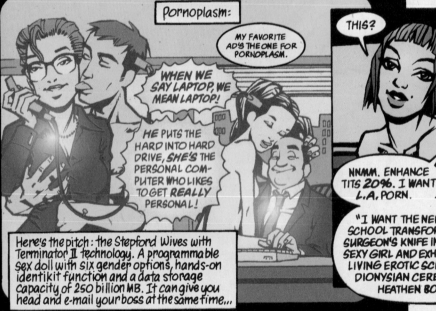

Pornoplasm:

MY FAVORITE AD'S THE ONE FOR PORNOPLASM.

WHEN WE SAY LAPTOP, WE MEAN LAPTOP!

HE PUTS THE HARD INTO HARD DRIVE, *SHE'S* THE PERSONAL COMPUTER WHO LIKES TO GET *REALLY* PERSONAL!

Here's the pitch: the Stepford Wives with Terminator II technology. A programmable sex doll with six gender options, hands-on identikit function and a data storage capacity of 250 billion MB. It can give you head and e-mail your boss at the same time...

THIS?

NNMM. ENHANCE TITS 20%. I WANT L.A. PORN.

"I WANT THE NERDIEST GUY IN SCHOOL TRANSFORMED BY A GIFTED SURGEON'S KNIFE INTO A BEAUTIFUL, SEXY GIRL AND EXHIBITED AS A LIVING EROTIC SCULPTURE AT DIONYSIAN CEREMONIES OF HEATHEN BONDAGE..."

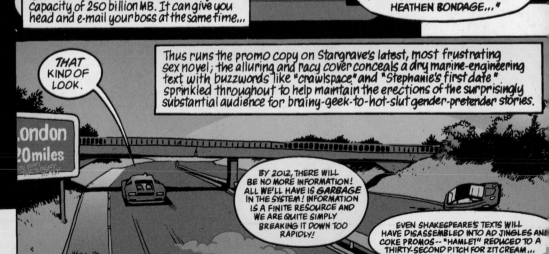

THAT KIND OF LOOK.

Thus runs the promo copy on Stargrave's latest, most frustrating sex novel; the alluring and racy cover conceals a dry marine-engineering text with buzzwords like "crawlspace" and "Stephanie's first date" sprinkled throughout to help maintain the erections of the surprisingly substantial audience for brainy-geek-to-hot-slut gender-pretender stories.

London 20 miles

BY 2012, THERE WILL BE NO MORE INFORMATION! ALL WE'LL HAVE IS *GARBAGE* IN THE SYSTEM! INFORMATION IS A FINITE RESOURCE AND WE ARE QUITE SIMPLY BREAKING IT DOWN TOO RAPIDLY!

EVEN SHAKESPEARE'S TEXTS WILL HAVE DISASSEMBLED INTO AD JINGLES AND COKE PROMOS -- "HAMLET" REDUCED TO A THIRTY-SECOND PITCH FOR ZIT CREAM ...

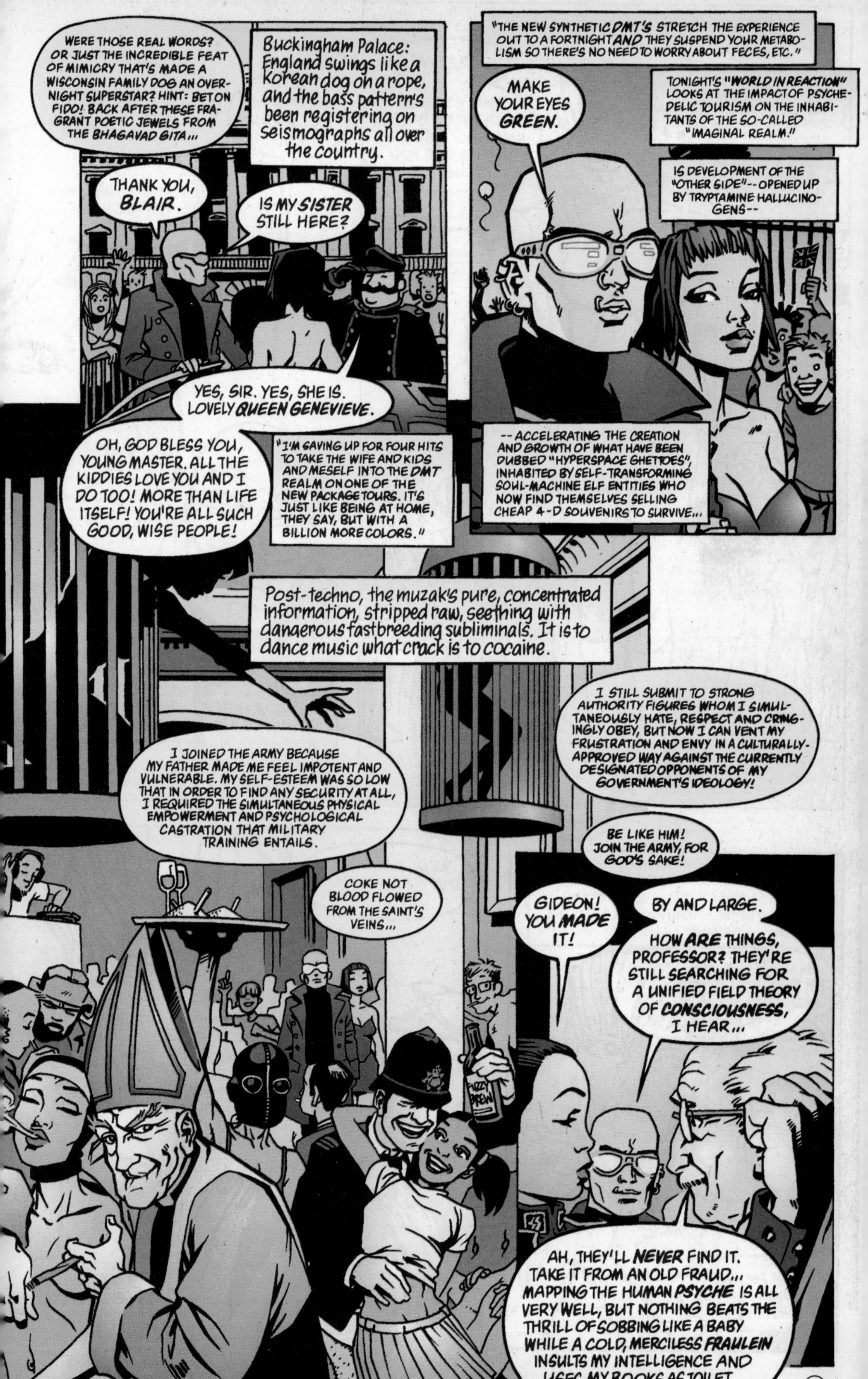
WERE THOSE REAL WORDS? OR JUST THE INCREDIBLE FEAT OF MIMICRY THAT'S MADE A WISCONSIN FAMILY DOG AN OVERNIGHT SUPERSTAR? HINT: BET ON FIDO! BACK AFTER THESE FRAGRANT POETIC JEWELS FROM THE BHAGAVAD GITA...
Buckingham Palace: England swings like a Korean dog on a rope, and the bass pattern's been registering on seismographs all over the country.
THANK YOU, BLAIR.
IS MY SISTER STILL HERE?
YES, SIR. YES, SHE IS. LOVELY QUEEN GENEVIEVE.
OH, GOD BLESS YOU, YOUNG MASTER. ALL THE KIDDIES LOVE YOU AND I DO TOO! MORE THAN LIFE ITSELF! YOU'RE ALL SUCH GOOD, WISE PEOPLE!
"I'M SAVING UP FOR FOUR HITS TO TAKE THE WIFE AND KIDS AND MESELF INTO THE DMT REALM ON ONE OF THE NEW PACKAGE TOURS. IT'S JUST LIKE BEING AT HOME, THEY SAY, BUT WITH A BILLION MORE COLORS."
"THE NEW SYNTHETIC DMT'S STRETCH THE EXPERIENCE OUT TO A FORTNIGHT AND THEY SUSPEND YOUR METABOLISM SO THERE'S NO NEED TO WORRY ABOUT FECES, ETC."
MAKE YOUR EYES GREEN.
TONIGHT'S "WORLD IN REACTION" LOOKS AT THE IMPACT OF PSYCHEDELIC TOURISM ON THE INHABITANTS OF THE SO-CALLED "IMAGINAL REALM."
IS DEVELOPMENT OF THE "OTHER SIDE"--OPENED UP BY TRYPTAMINE HALLUCINOGENS--
--ACCELERATING THE CREATION AND GROWTH OF WHAT HAVE BEEN DUBBED "HYPERSPACE GHETTOES", INHABITED BY SELF-TRANSFORMING SOUL-MACHINE ELF ENTITIES WHO NOW FIND THEMSELVES SELLING CHEAP 4-D SOUVENIRS TO SURVIVE...
Post-techno, the muzak's pure, concentrated information, stripped raw, seething with dangerous fastbreeding subliminals. It is to dance music what crack is to cocaine.
I STILL SUBMIT TO STRONG AUTHORITY FIGURES WHOM I SIMULTANEOUSLY HATE, RESPECT AND CRINGINGLY OBEY, BUT NOW I CAN VENT MY FRUSTRATION AND ENVY IN A CULTURALLY-APPROVED WAY AGAINST THE CURRENTLY DESIGNATED OPPONENTS OF MY GOVERNMENT'S IDEOLOGY!
I JOINED THE ARMY BECAUSE MY FATHER MADE ME FEEL IMPOTENT AND VULNERABLE. MY SELF-ESTEEM WAS SO LOW THAT IN ORDER TO FIND ANY SECURITY AT ALL, I REQUIRED THE SIMULTANEOUS PHYSICAL EMPOWERMENT AND PSYCHOLOGICAL CASTRATION THAT MILITARY TRAINING ENTAILS.
BE LIKE HIM! JOIN THE ARMY, FOR GOD'S SAKE!
COKE NOT BLOOD FLOWED FROM THE SAINT'S VEINS...
GIDEON! YOU MADE IT!
BY AND LARGE.
HOW ARE THINGS, PROFESSOR? THEY'RE STILL SEARCHING FOR A UNIFIED FIELD THEORY OF CONSCIOUSNESS, I HEAR...
FUZZY BREW
AH, THEY'LL NEVER FIND IT. TAKE IT FROM AN OLD FRAUD... MAPPING THE HUMAN PSYCHE IS ALL VERY WELL, BUT NOTHING BEATS THE THRILL OF SOBBING LIKE A BABY WHILE A COLD, MERCILESS FRAULEIN INSULTS MY INTELLIGENCE AND USES MY BOOKS AS TOILET PAPER...

...NEUROVISION SONG CONTEST WINNER, SZANDOR L-DOPA FROM NEO-BELGIQUE, PERFORMING HIS HIT "BEFORE THE WHEEL, WERE THERE REVOLUTIONS?" LATER, SZANDOR WILL BE TELLING US ALL ABOUT THE MAN HE KILLED WITH A DART, FAIR AND SQUARE.

GIDEON!

WHAT'S THE NEW LOOK? PUNK PANTO? ADAM AND HIS ANTS? WHAT HAVE YOU COME AS?

A GESTURE OF GOODWILL, SIS.

YOU DON'T LOOK MUCH LIKE ONE.

LISTEN, YOU'VE MADE IT JUST IN TIME FOR MY ANNOUNCEMENT. THE NEW AEON STARTS HERE!

YEAH, I HEARD A NEW BLACK HOLE'S APPEARED IN THE SKY...

Hexstasy's one of the new generation MDMA derivatives, with molecules designer-sculptured using one of the new 4-dimensional "witch-tech" processes.

The drug deprograms the entire musculature...

...it's like shapechanging. But you can always spot a Hexstasy user on the morning after -- they look like stroke patients.

AT LAST! I'M TRULY A WOMAN!

EVERY-BODY!

I'M HAVING A LOVELY LITTLE BABY!

WELL, ACTUALLY, I'VE HAD THE LITTLE DEVIL.

GAZE UPON MY WORKS, YE MIGHTY, AND DESPAIR!

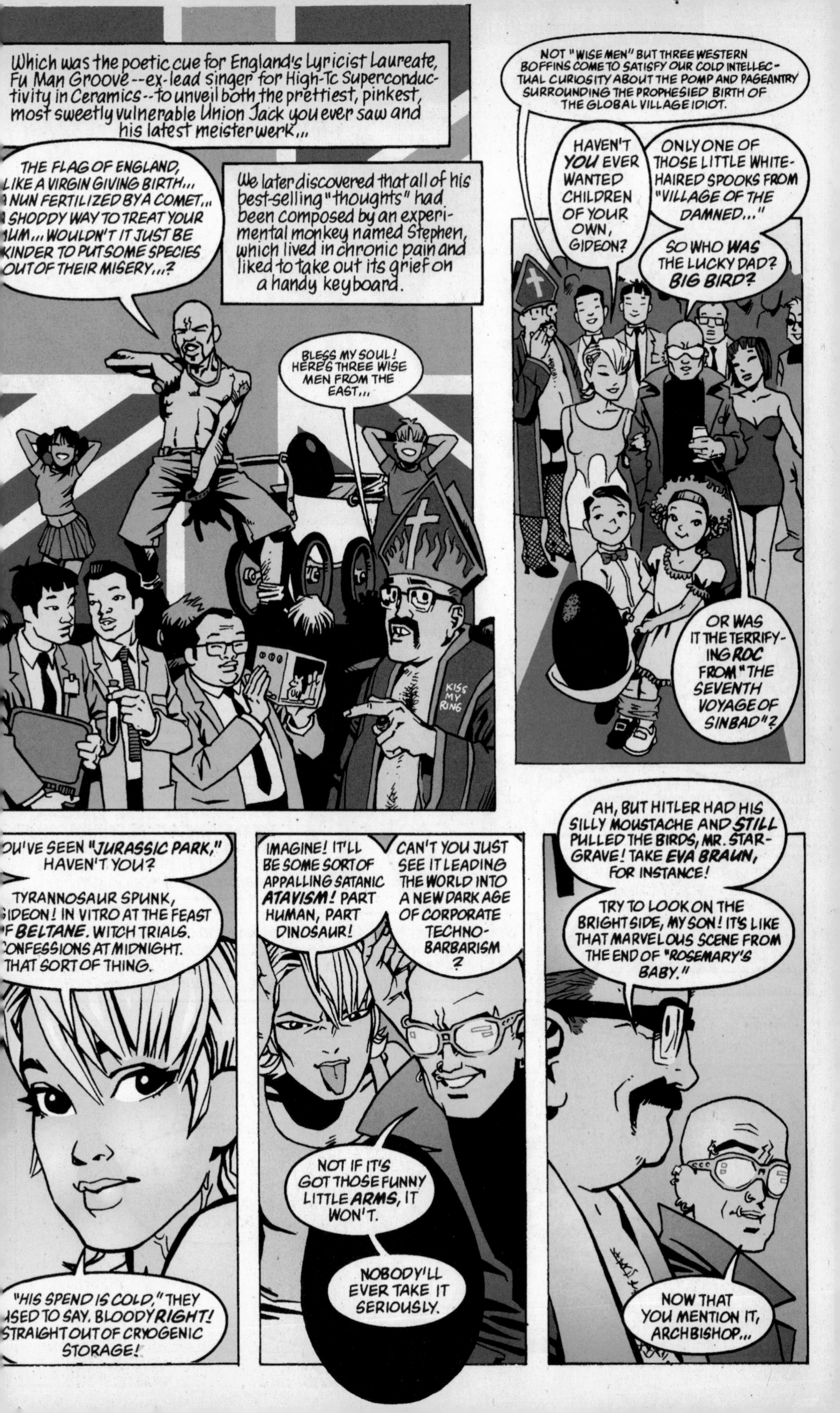
Which was the poetic cue for England's Lyricist Laureate, Fu Man Groove--ex-lead singer for High-Tc Superconductivity in Ceramics--to unveil both the prettiest, pinkest, most sweetly vulnerable Union Jack you ever saw and his latest meisterwerk...
THE FLAG OF ENGLAND, LIKE A VIRGIN GIVING BIRTH... NUN FERTILIZED BY A COMET... SHODDY WAY TO TREAT YOUR UM... WOULDN'T IT JUST BE KINDER TO PUT SOME SPECIES OUT OF THEIR MISERY...?
We later discovered that all of his best-selling "thoughts" had been composed by an experimental monkey named Stephen, which lived in chronic pain and liked to take out its grief on a handy keyboard.
BLESS MY SOUL! HERE'S THREE WISE MEN FROM THE EAST...
KISS MY RING
NOT "WISE MEN" BUT THREE WESTERN BOFFINS COME TO SATISFY OUR COLD INTELLECTUAL CURIOSITY ABOUT THE POMP AND PAGEANTRY SURROUNDING THE PROPHESIED BIRTH OF THE GLOBAL VILLAGE IDIOT.
HAVEN'T YOU EVER WANTED CHILDREN OF YOUR OWN, GIDEON?
ONLY ONE OF THOSE LITTLE WHITE-HAIRED SPOOKS FROM "VILLAGE OF THE DAMNED..."
SO WHO WAS THE LUCKY DAD? BIG BIRD?
OR WAS IT THE TERRIFYING ROC FROM "THE SEVENTH VOYAGE OF SINBAD"?
OU'VE SEEN "JURASSIC PARK," HAVEN'T YOU?
TYRANNOSAUR SPUNK, IDEON! IN VITRO AT THE FEAST F BELTANE. WITCH TRIALS. CONFESSIONS AT MIDNIGHT. THAT SORT OF THING.
"HIS SPEND IS COLD," THEY SED TO SAY. BLOODY RIGHT! STRAIGHT OUT OF CRYOGENIC STORAGE!
IMAGINE! IT'LL BE SOME SORT OF APPALLING SATANIC ATAVISM! PART HUMAN, PART DINOSAUR!
CAN'T YOU JUST SEE IT LEADING THE WORLD INTO A NEW DARK AGE OF CORPORATE TECHNO-BARBARISM?
NOT IF IT'S GOT THOSE FUNNY LITTLE ARMS, IT WON'T.
NOBODY'LL EVER TAKE IT SERIOUSLY.
AH, BUT HITLER HAD HIS SILLY MOUSTACHE AND STILL PULLED THE BIRDS, MR. STARGRAVE! TAKE EVA BRAUN, FOR INSTANCE!
TRY TO LOOK ON THE BRIGHT SIDE, MY SON! IT'S LIKE THAT MARVELOUS SCENE FROM THE END OF "ROSEMARY'S BABY."
NOW THAT YOU MENTION IT, ARCHBISHOP...

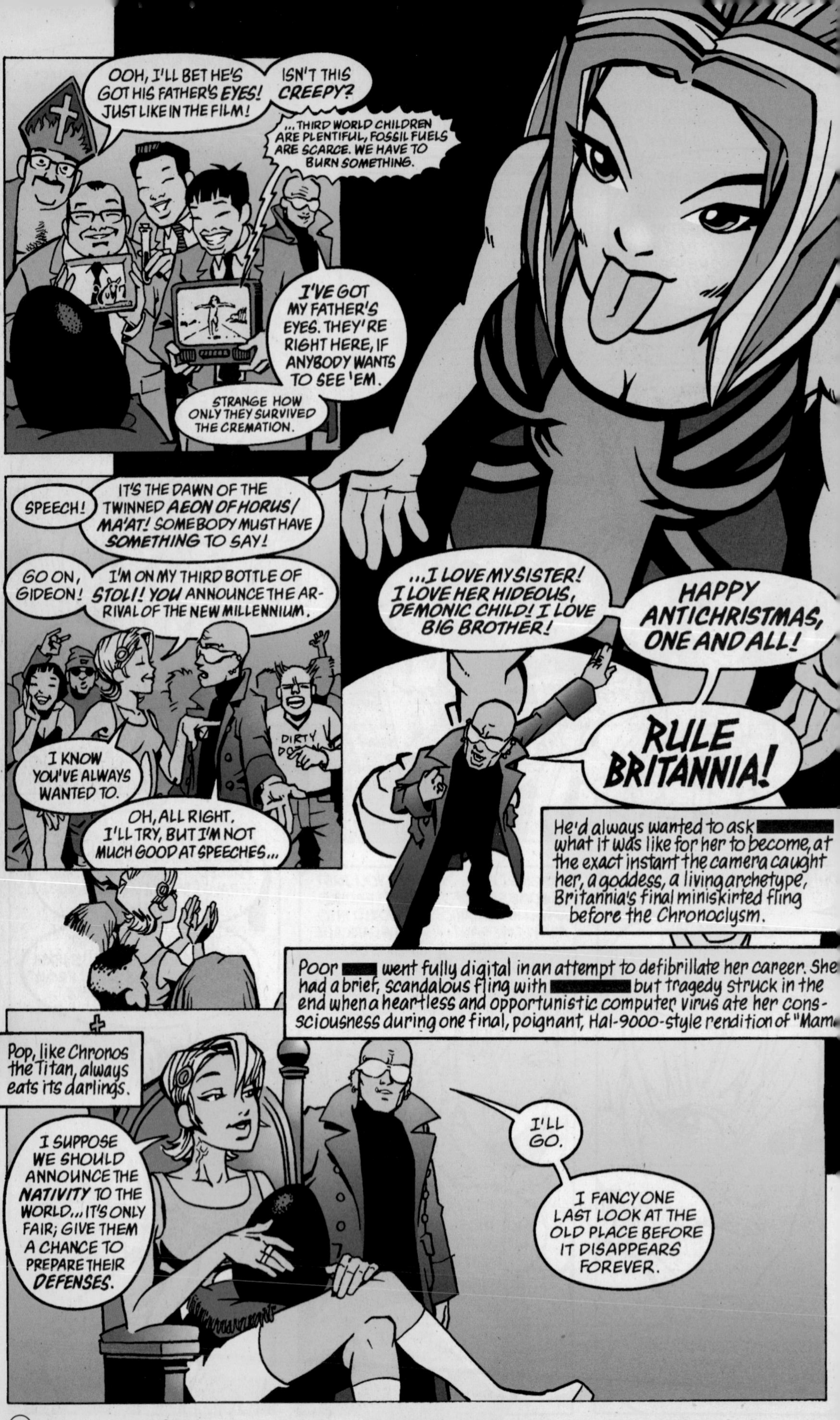
OOH, I'LL BET HE'S GOT HIS FATHER'S EYES! JUST LIKE IN THE FILM!
ISN'T THIS CREEPY?
...THIRD WORLD CHILDREN ARE PLENTIFUL, FOSSIL FUELS ARE SCARCE. WE HAVE TO BURN SOMETHING.
I'VE GOT MY FATHER'S EYES. THEY'RE RIGHT HERE, IF ANYBODY WANTS TO SEE 'EM.
STRANGE HOW ONLY THEY SURVIVED THE CREMATION.
SPEECH!
IT'S THE DAWN OF THE TWINNED AEON OF HORUS/MA'AT! SOMEBODY MUST HAVE SOMETHING TO SAY!
GO ON, GIDEON!
I'M ON MY THIRD BOTTLE OF STOLI! YOU ANNOUNCE THE ARRIVAL OF THE NEW MILLENNIUM.
I KNOW YOU'VE ALWAYS WANTED TO.
OH, ALL RIGHT. I'LL TRY, BUT I'M NOT MUCH GOOD AT SPEECHES...
...I LOVE MY SISTER! I LOVE HER HIDEOUS, DEMONIC CHILD! I LOVE BIG BROTHER!
HAPPY ANTICHRISTMAS, ONE AND ALL!
RULE BRITANNIA!
He'd always wanted to ask [redacted] what it was like for her to become, at the exact instant the camera caught her, a goddess, a living archetype, Britannia's final miniskirted fling before the Chronoclysm.
Poor [redacted] went fully digital in an attempt to defibrillate her career. She had a brief, scandalous fling with [redacted] but tragedy struck in the end when a heartless and opportunistic computer virus ate her consciousness during one final, poignant, Hal-9000-style rendition of "Mam
Pop, like Chronos the Titan, always eats its darlings.
I SUPPOSE WE SHOULD ANNOUNCE THE NATIVITY TO THE WORLD... IT'S ONLY FAIR; GIVE THEM A CHANCE TO PREPARE THEIR DEFENSES.
I'LL GO.
I FANCY ONE LAST LOOK AT THE OLD PLACE BEFORE IT DISAPPEARS FOREVER.

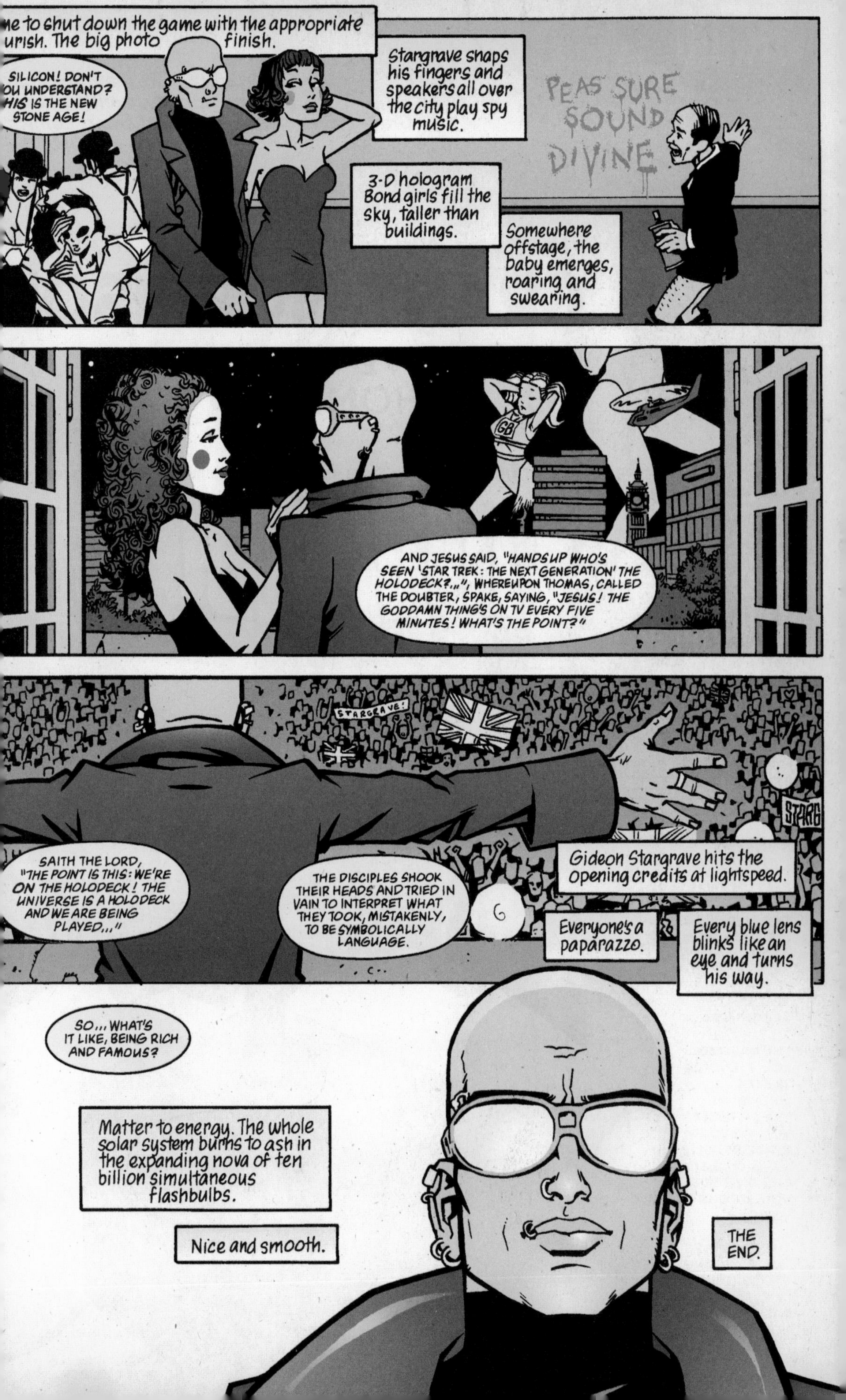
me to shut down the game with the appropriate urish. The big photo finish.
SILICON! DON'T OU UNDERSTAND? HIS IS THE NEW STONE AGE!
Stargrave snaps his fingers and speakers all over the city play spy music.
PEAS SURE SOUND DIVINE
3-D hologram Bond girls fill the sky, taller than buildings.
Somewhere offstage, the baby emerges, roaring and swearing.
GB
AND JESUS SAID, "HANDS UP WHO'S SEEN 'STAR TREK: THE NEXT GENERATION' THE HOLODECK?..", WHEREUPON THOMAS, CALLED THE DOUBTER, SPAKE, SAYING, "JESUS! THE GODDAMN THING'S ON TV EVERY FIVE MINUTES! WHAT'S THE POINT?"
STARGRAVE!
STARG
SAITH THE LORD, "THE POINT IS THIS: WE'RE ON THE HOLODECK! THE UNIVERSE IS A HOLODECK AND WE ARE BEING PLAYED..."
THE DISCIPLES SHOOK THEIR HEADS AND TRIED IN VAIN TO INTERPRET WHAT THEY TOOK, MISTAKENLY, TO BE SYMBOLICALLY LANGUAGE.
Gideon Stargrave hits the opening credits at lightspeed.
Everyone's a paparazzo.
Every blue lens blinks like an eye and turns his way.
SO... WHAT'S IT LIKE, BEING RICH AND FAMOUS?
Matter to energy. The whole solar system burns to ash in the expanding nova of ten billion simultaneous flashbulbs.
Nice and smooth.
THE END.

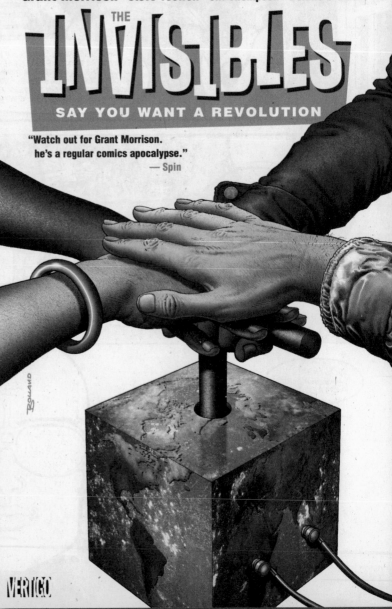